Gnosis on the Silk Road

Gnosis on the Silk Road

Gnostic Texts from Central Asia

TRANSLATED & PRESENTED BY

Hans-Joachim Klimkeit

HarperSanFrancisco

A Division of HarperCollins*Publishers*

For Bill and Beulah Jones,
spiritual parents, friends, and gurus,
with fond memories of boarding school at Darjeeling

Project of the Main Publication Program, UNESCO Integral Study of the
Silk Roads: Roads of Dialogue

The author is responsible for the choice and the presentation of the facts
contained in this book and for the opinions expressed therein, which are
not necessarily those of "The Integral Study of the Silk Roads: Roads of
Dialogue" Project and do not commit UNESCO.

UNESCO

The maps on pages xxi and xxii are adapted from maps prepared by the
Cartographic Institute, University of Queensland, Australia.

FIRST EDITION

Library of Congress Cataloging-in-Publication Data

Gnosis on the Silk Road : Gnostic texts from Central Asia / translated
    & presented by Hans-Joachim Klimkeit. — 1st ed.
    p. cm.
Translations from Iranian and Turkish.
Includes bibliographical references.
ISBN 0-06-064586-5 (alk. paper)
1. Manichaeism—Asia, Central. 2. Asia, Central—Religion.
I. Klimkeit, Hans-Joachim.
BT1410.G66 1993   90–56455
299!932'0958—dc20   CIP

93 94 95 96 RRD(H) 10 9 8 7 6 5 4 3 2 1

Contents

Abbreviations

AA	Acta Antiqua Academiae Scientiarum Hungaricae
AcOr	Acta Orientalia (Copenhagen)
ADAW	Abhandlungen der Deutschen Akademie der Wissen-schaften (Berlin), Klasse für Sprachen, Literatur und Kunst
AF	Asiatische Forschungen (Originally: Göttinger Asiatische Forschungen)
AO	Acta Orientalia (Budapest)
AoF	Altorientalische Forschungen
AOH	Acta Orientalia Academiae Scientiarum Hungaricae
AGWG	Abhandlungen der Gesellschaft der Wissenschaften zu Göttingen
APAW	Abhandlungen der (Königlich-) Preussischen Akademie der Wissenschaften (Berlin), Phil.-hist. Klasse
ARWAW	Abhandlungen der Rheinisch-Westfälischen Akademie der Wissenschaften (Düsseldorf)
AR	Arbeitsmaterialien zur Religionsgeschichte
B	Mary Boyce
BAIS	Bulletin de l'Académie Impériale des Sciences de St.-Petersbourg
BASP	Bulletin of the American Society of Papyrologists

BBB	W. B. Henning, *Ein manichäisches Bet- und Beichtbuch*
BHSD	F. Edgerton, *Buddhist Hybrid Sanskrit Grammar and Dictionary.* Vol. 2: *Dictionary.*
BSOAS	Bulletin of the School of Oriental and African Studies
BSOS	Bulletin of the School of Oriental Studies
BT	Berliner Turfantexte
BZRGG	Beihefte der Zeitschrift für Religions- und Geistes-geschichte
CAJ	Central Asiatic Journal
CMC	Codex Manichaicus Coloniensis. See Henrich Koenen and Koenen and Römer
CSCO	Corpus Scriptorum Christianorum Orientalium
DAWB	Deutsche Akademie der Wissenschaften zu Berlin
EPRO	Études Préliminaires aux Religions Orientales dans l'Empire Romain
FRLANT	Forschungen zur Religion und Literatur des Alten und Neuen Testaments
H	London Hymnscroll (Chinese Manichaean)
HO	*Handbuch der Orientalistik*, ed. B. Spuler
HR I	F. W. K. Müller, "Handschriften-Reste" I
HR II	F. W. K. Müller, *Handschriften-Reste* II
HSCP	Harvard Studies in Classical Philology
JA	Journal Asiatique
JAOS	Journal of the American Oriental Society
JRAS	Journal of the Royal Asiatic Society of Great Britain and Ireland
JSFO	Journal de la Société Finno-Ougrienne
JThS	Journal of Theological Studies
MAIS	Mémoires de l'Académie Impériale des Sciences de St.-Petersbourg
MHC	Mary Boyce, *The Manichaean Hymn-Cycles in Parthian*
MIO	Mitteilungen des Instituts für Orientforschung (Berlin)
Mir. Man.	See Andreas and Henning, "Mitteliranische Manichaica"
MSFO	Mémoires de la Société Finno-Ougrienne

MStI	See C. Salemann, *Manichäische Studien* I
MW	M. Monier-Williams, *A Sanskrit-English Dictionary*
NGWG	Nachrichten der Gesellschaft der Wissenschaften in Göttingen, Phil.-hist. Klasse
NKGWG	Nachrichten von der Königlichen Gesellschaft der Wissenschaften zu Göttingen
NT	New Testament
OLZ	Orientalistische Literaturzeitung
OT	Old Testament
PsB	C. R. C. Allberry, *A Manichaean Psalm-Book*
RAC	Reallexikon für Antike und Christentum
RHLR	Revue d'Histoire et de Littérature Religieuses
RHPR	Revue d'Histoire et de Philosophie Religieuses
RHR	Revue de l'Histoire des Religions
RM	Religionen der Menschheit
RWAW	Rheinisch-Westfälische Akademie der Wissenschaften (Düsseldorf)
RO	Rocznik Orientalistyczny
S	Werner Sundermann
SBE	Sacred Books of the East
SDAW	Sitzungsberichte der Deutschen Akademie der Wissenschaften zu Berlin, Klasse für Sprache, Literatur und Kunst
SH	Soothill and Hodous, *A Dictionary of Chinese Buddhist Terms*
SPAW	Sitzungsberichte der (Königlich-) Preussischen Akademie der Wissenschaften (Berlin), Phil.-hist. Klasse
StOR	Studies in Oriental Religions (Wiesbaden)
S-W	Sims-Williams
ThLZ	Theologische Literaturzeitung
TP	T'oung Pao
TPS	Transactions of the Philological Society
Tr	(Chinese Manichaean) Traité
TRE	Theologische Realenzyklopädie

TT	W. Bang and A. von Gabain, Türkische Turfan-Texte
Türk. Man. I–III	A. von Le Coq, *Türkische Manichaica aus Chotscho* I–III
Uigurica I	F. W. K. Müller, *Uigurica* [I]
Uigurica II	F. W. K. Müller, *Uigurica* II
UAJb	Ural-Altaische Jahrbücher (Wiesbaden)
UigWb	K. Röhrborn, *Uigurisches Wörterbuch*
UJb	Ungarische Jahrbücher
WL I	Waldschmidt and Lentz, *Die Stellung Jesu im Manichäismus*
WL II	Waldschmidt and Lentz, "Manichäische Dogmatik aus chinesischen und iranischen Texten."
WZKS	Wiener Zeitschrift für die Kunde Süd- und Ostasiens und Archiv für indische Philosophie
Z	Peter Zieme
ZAS	Zentralasiatische Studien
ZDMG	Zeitschrift der Deutschen Morgenländischen Gesellschaft
ZIEME, Diss.	P. Zieme, *Untersuchungen zur Schrift und Sprache der manichäisch-türkischen Turfantexte*
ZII	Zeitschrift für Indologie und Iranistik
ZMR	Zeitschrift für Missionskunde und Religionswissenschaft
ZNW	Zeitschrift für die neutestamentliche Wissenschaft und die Kunde der älteren Kirche
ZPE	Zeitschrift für Papyrologie und Epigraphik
ZRGG	Zeitschrift für Religions- und Geistesgeschichte

Note on Textual Signs

[ ]   Square brackets in the translation indicate a lacuna in the manu-
        script. Missing words or word parts have been supplied within the
        brackets where possible.

. . .   When a text with a lacuna cannot be reconstructed, or when it is so
        ill preserved that it has not been translated, this is indicated by three
        dots. Missing or illegible words are also indicated in this way. A
        fourth dot, if appropriate, may function as a period. The extent of a
        missing or ill-preserved portion of a text is not indicated when three
        dots are used.
            Three dots on a line by itself means that the whole line or verse
        is missing, or that the following portions cannot be translated or
        have not been translated here.

( )   Parentheses in the translation indicates words supplied by the trans-
        lator for the sake of greater clarity or to provide necessary informa-
        tion for the reader.

~   This sign denotes the correspondence between two terms, either in
        the sense that a term in one language corresponds to one in another
        language or in the sense that there is a theological correspondence
        between two terms, that is, a god and a virtue.

(?)   When the meaning of a term is unclear, a question mark is added.

*   An asterisk refers to a reconstructed word that is not or is only par-
        tially preserved in the original, or to a word whose meaning has been
        derived from similar words.

..."...   When words introducing a quotation and the beginning of the quota-
          tion itself are lacking, this is identified by two elipses.

  <   If a word in one language (e.g., Parthian) is derived from a similar
          work in another language (e.g., Sanskrit), this symbol is used.

  n   This is the numbering of a verse whose exact position in a canto, or
          hymn, is unknown. The following verses are numbered n + 1, n + 2,
          etc.

  +   A plus sign after a source number (e.g., M 98) indicates that the
          translation is based on a larger number of fragments than the one
          mentioned. These are indicated in the editions referred to.

(*sic*)   The word *sic* ("so, thus") in brackets calls the reader's attention to the
          fact that there is apparently a mistake in the text.

          In quoted material, the original textual signs are retained. Square
          brackets indicate additions to the quotation made for the sake of
          greater clarity. In quotations from German, words in parenthesis
          may be added to express an idea implied in the German text, though
          not made explicit there.

Foreword

The concept of Gnosticism as a world religion was launched when the Nag Hammadi Codices came to light a generation ago. That discovery did in fact help to free Gnosticism from the traditional stigma of being no better and no more than a Christian heresy, by providing documentation for non-Christian, especially Jewish Gnosticism. But the Gnosticism traditionally known through such heresiologists as Irenaeus, Hippolytus, and Epiphanius, and then through modern manuscript discoveries such as the Nag Hammadi texts, was primarily a movement in the Mediterranean world of late antiquity. Within the confines of the Roman Empire, once it had become Christian, this Gnosticism was soon stamped out, apart from occasional recurrences in the Balkans (the Bogomils) and France (the Cathari) early in the Middle Ages.

One of the most notorious brands of Gnosticism condemned throughout the Middle Ages went by the name of the "Manichees," whose most famous convert had been Augustine prior to his conversion to Christianity. Its founder Mani, born in the third century A.D. in what today is Iraq, developed out of the Jewish-Christian Elkesaite sect an intentionally syncretistic religion that quite programmatically sought to become a world religion—and succeeded to a remarkable degree.

The Manichaean religion spread rapidly, reaching not only as far West by the end of the fourth century as North Africa and Italy (Augustine), and to Egypt (where there survived from late antiquity seven Manichaean codices in Coptic translation and the Cologne Mani Codex in Greek), but ultimately as far East as China. Throughout our century, manuscript discoveries in this eastern expansion of Manichaeism, less known to a popular audience than such familiar items as the Dead Sea Scrolls, have nonetheless been of very basic significance to the scholarly community. Indeed it has become clear that there is a substantive continuity from the Qumran Scrolls and the Nag Hammadi Codices to the Manichaean texts of the East, where early Jewish and Christian apocryphal and gnostic traditions, including the Gospel of Thomas, continued to be cited and have even left their mark on Buddhism.

Manichaeism has not received the attention due a world religion, partly because it did not survive to be one of today's world religions, and partly because its expansion was throughout Central Asia, a world hardly known in the West. Under Zoroastrian persecution many Manichaeans fled from Persia to the Sogdians of Samarkand and along the silk caravan routes to the court of China. A kingdom with its center in Mongolia elevated Manichaeism to the state religion in the eighth and ninth centuries A.D. In the East it survived a millenium after its extinction from the West.

This "Religion of Light" has here been made available to us in readable form, through the carefully selected, introduced, translated, and annotated edition by Professor Klimkeit of the University of Bonn. It will no doubt become the standard work on this important religion from a much too neglected expanse of the world.

James M. Robinson

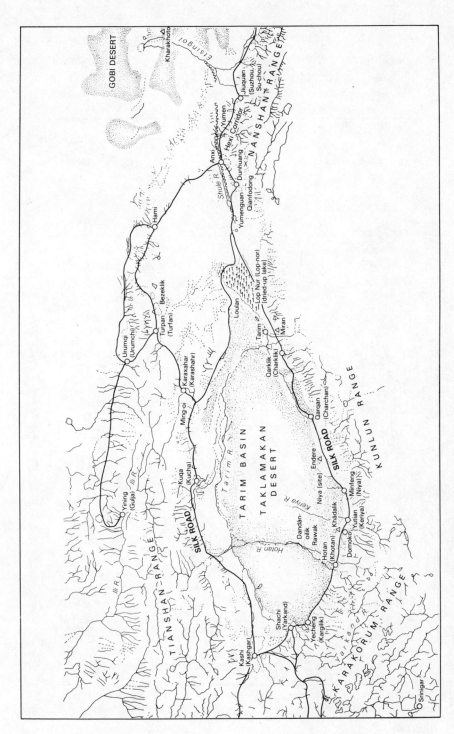

The Silk Road of Central Asia (East Turkestan). Courtesy of Kodansha Ltd.

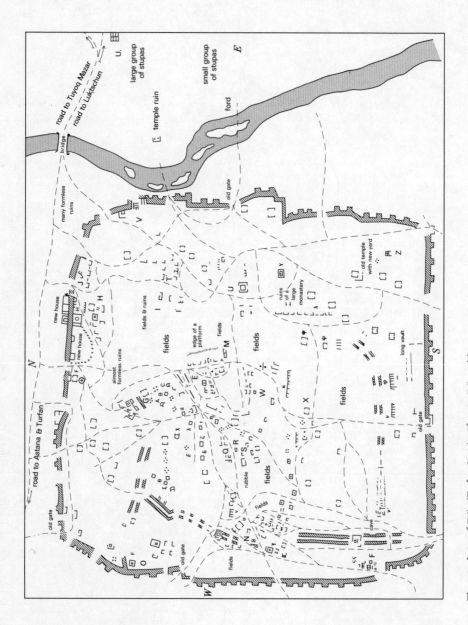

The ruined city of Kočo (Turfan Oasis). After A. Grünwedel.

Preface

The Gnostic or Manichaean texts presented here have so far hardly been known beyond a small circle of specialists. Within this circle, they have been known for a number of decades. They are, for the most part, based on the texts found by the German archaeological expeditions under the leadership of Albert Grünwedel and Albert von Le Coq to the ancient ruined towns on the northern fringe of the Taklamakan desert. In reference to the main site where important finds were made, they are called the "Turfan Expeditions," and the documents found there are the "Turfan texts." Four expeditions were undertaken between 1902 and 1914; they returned to Berlin with a great number of documents of Manichaean as well as Christian and Buddhist provenance. Their discovery aroused great interest in scholarly circles as well as in the general public, for such treasures, among them the first original documents of the Gnostic religion founded by Mani (216–276), were not expected to be found in such remote areas. Their importance can be compared to the Dead Sea scrolls and the Nag Hammadi documents discovered decades later. After the initial expedition, the German Emperor himself took great interest in the discoveries, and supported subsequent expeditions, which came to be known as the "Royal Prussian Turfan Expeditions." In a document preserved in the "Museum für Indische Kunst" in Berlin, addressed to "The Secret Civil Cabinet of His Majesty the German Emperor and King of Prussia" and dated Berlin, 18 January 1904, we hear that "His Majesty the Emperor and King has received with thanks and the most lively interest the report on the expedition to Turfan, undertaken in the interest of the Museum of Ethnology (Berlin). His Majesty also consents [to the request of A. Grünwedel] to express thanks, through diplomatic channels, in the name of the highest authority, to the Imperial Chinese Government for the assistance given to that undertaking. . . ."

Today, more than eighty years after their discovery, only about one-quarter of the Gnostic texts from Turfan has been published, so demanding is their philological analysis. Much of what remains is in very fragmentary condition; the work of piecing together fragments into larger texts continues, promising more valuable discoveries to come.

The first scholar to realize the significance of these documents was F. W. K. Müller, who was competent to scrutinize Oriental texts from Syriac to Chinese. He was among the first to decipher the hitherto unknown languages of Sogdian and Tocharian among the seventeen languages in which the documents were written, and he took a leading role in promoting the study of Middle Persian, Parthian, and Uighur (Old Turkish). As early as 1904, he published the first specimens of texts written in the Manichaean "Estrangelo script," a script derived from Syriac.[1] The Iranian texts, of which he translated a limited number, were then studied by F. C. Andreas and his student W. B. Henning, who went on to devote his scholarly career to the edition, translation, and elucidation of the Iranian Turfan texts. When Henning had to leave Germany in 1934, he settled in London, where the study of these documents flourished at the School of Oriental and African Studies. A distinguished scholar who was to continue his work was his student Mary Boyce, who was the first to edit and translate the important Parthian hymn cycles as well as other documents of the "Religion of Light." She was also the first to survey the vast material and to publish a catalog of the Iranian texts in Middle Persian and Parthian in so far as they were written in Manichaean script.[2] The number of texts and fragments covered in the catalog exceeds nine thousand. In the catalog, the texts are renumbered according to M-numbers (e. g., M 17). The old numbers (e. g., T II D 63) referred to the place where the documents had been found (e. g., T for Turfan), the expedition which found it (e. g., II for the "Second Prussian Turfan Expedition"), and the exact site of origin (e. g., D for Dakianus Shahri = Kocho). In some cases this old numbering has still been retained along with the new one, notably in the case of the Uighur texts, which, however, have also been given new consecutive U-numbers (e. g., U 121). The Sogdian fragments have also been renumbered consecutively, but here also, many important documents are known by their old numbers. The main corpus of documents is housed in the former Academy of Sciences of the GDR (today Department of Turfan Research), or in the "Stiftung Preussischer Kulturbesitz" in West Berlin. However, some texts are preserved in the "Museum für Indische Kunst," Berlin (West); they bear an IB number.

In 1975 Mary Boyce reedited the major portion of the Manichaean texts in Middle Persian and Parthian,[3] producing the first arrangement of the material according to central themes. She included texts edited by F. W. K. Müller, F. C. Andreas, and W. B. Henning in her *Reader in Manichaean Middle Persian and Parthian,* as well as documents published by W. Lentz, who together with the Sinologist E. Waldschmidt had published Iranian texts together with their Chinese parallels.[4]

Apart from the London school, which also produced the Danish scholar Jes P. Amussen, who was to make major contributions in the field,[5] mention must be made of the American scholar A. V. W. Jackson, who in his *Researches in Manichaeism with Special Reference to the Turfan Fragments*[6] presented a number of essays on the material published, making it known in the English speaking world at a relatively early time, in the thirties.

On the European continent, materials other than the Berlin texts were dealt with by scholars in Paris and St. Petersburg. Thus before World War I, É. Chavannes and P. Pelliot studied the Chinese Manichaean *Traité* from Dunhuang in the light of all sources available, including St. Augustine's anti-Manichaean writings,[7] and C. Salemann devoted himself to the Manichaean texts brought by Russian expeditions to St. Petersburg.[8]

Research on the Turkish Turfan texts in Germany was given a strong impetus by W. Bang and A. von Gabain. The 1970s heralded a new beginning of work which had been neglected after World War II. Important publications of Iranian and Turkish texts were made by W. Sundermann and P. Zieme, respectively. The two successfully continued the editorial work of W. Lentz and W. B. Henning, W. Bang, and A. von Gabain.[9]

Even before the unification of Germany I was privileged to be in close contact with Dr. Sundermann and Dr. Zieme, who aided in every conceivable way to prepare a new German translation of the Manichaean hymns and prayers from Turfan.[10] Furthermore, I was able to enlist the help of Dr. Jens P. Laut in reviewing Uighur texts of older publications which were in need of new translation. Both Iranian and Turkish studies had made considerable advances since the initial publication of many of these documents in the 1920s and 1930s. This English translation of Manichaean Turfan material is partly based on that work, but also includes important prose texts, some of which have been known for a longer period, and some recently edited by Sundermann and Zieme, as well as D. N. MacKenzie and M. Hutter.

A special word of thanks is due to Sharon Modayil, daughter of my teachers in India, Bill and Beulah Jones, to whom this work is dedicated. Her contribution in revising and correcting my English style goes far beyond the technical level. After many years of studying and teaching, thinking and writing in German, my appreciation for the English language, which her parents had instilled in me as a child and adolescent, was renewed once again by her contribution to the whole. She has been of special help to me in meeting the challenge of rendering poetry as poetry, trying to do justice to the material in form as well as content.

Thanks are also due to those at our Institute of Comparative Religion at Bonn University who were instrumental in procuring pertinent material, in checking quotations, and in writing the manuscript. In this respect my special thanks go to my secretary Liesel Werner, my assistant Dr. Wassilios Klein, and my students Claudia Seele, Carmen Holzer, and Holger Rennert.

Thanks and recognition are due to the Klopstock Foundation, Hamburg, and the Gerda Henkel Foundation, Düsseldorf, for supporting this venture by their grants for research. This work would not have developed beyond the nascent stage without their assistance, which allowed me to collect important materials on the subject and visit English language libraries for consultation. Mr. Doudou Diène of UNESCO'S Project "Silk Roads— Roads of Dialogue" has constantly encouraged me in the tedious task of translation, which took much more time than initially anticipated. The pertinent body of UNESCO accepted this work in the Main Publication Program of its Silk Roads Project at its Delhi meeting in 1991.

Finally I would like to express my appreciation to Harper San Francisco, particularly executive editor John V. Loudon and his team, for their interest in this work and most of all for their patience in anticipating the final draft of the material included here.

Hans-J. Klimkeit
Bonn, December 1992

Notes

1. F. W. K. Müller, "Handschriftenreste" I and II.
2. M. Boyce, *A Catalogue of the Iranian Manuscripts in Manichaean Script in the German Turfan Collection.*
3. M. Boyce, *A Reader in Manichaean Middle Persian and Parthian.*
4. E. Waldschmidt and W. Lentz, *Die Stellung Jesu im Manichäismus*; idem, *Manichäische Dogmatik.*
5. Cf. J. P. Asmussen, *X^uāstvānīft. Studies in Manichaeism.* (A study of the Manichaean confession for laymen); idem, *Manichaean Literature.*
6. New York 1932.
7. Chavannes and Pelliot, "Un traité manichéen retrouvé en Chine."
8. C. Salemann, "Ein Bruchstük manichäischen Schrifttums im Asiatischen Museum"; idem, "Manichäische Studien I"; idem, "Manichaica I–IV."
9. For the main works of Bang and von Gabain, Sundermann and Zieme, see Bibliography.
10. H.-J. Klimkeit, *Hymnen und Gebete der Religion des Lichts.*

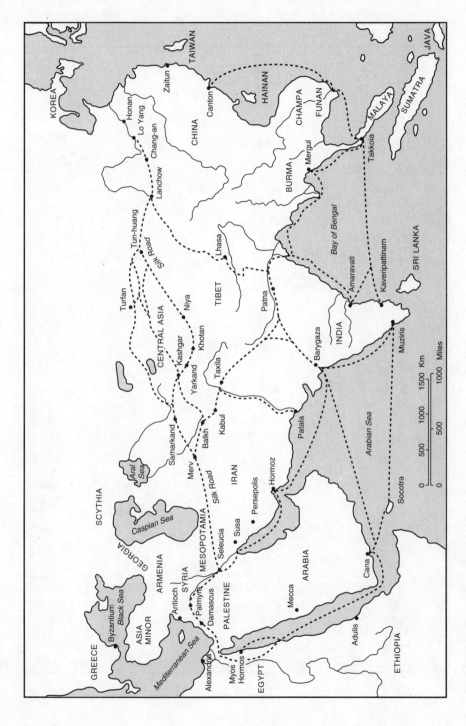

The Silk Road and other ancient trade routes in Asia.

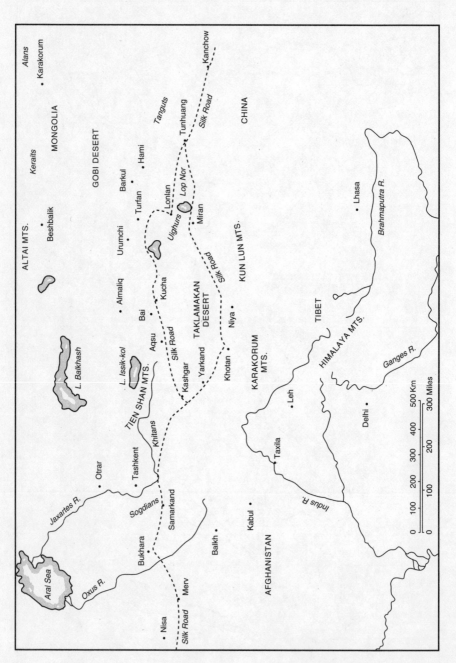

The Silk Road in Central Asia.

Mani and Manichaeism

The Founder Mani

> Mani's is the only gnostic system which became a broad historical force,
> and the religion based on it must in spite of its eventual downfall be ranked
> among the major religions of mankind. Mani indeed, alone among the
> gnostic system-builders, *intended* to found, not a select group of initiates,
> but a new universal religion; and so his doctrine, unlike the teaching of all
> other Gnostics with the exception of Marcion, has nothing esoteric about
> it. . . . Mani's work was not to penetrate the secret aspects of a given revela-
> tion and to establish a minority of higher initiation within an existing church
> but to supply a new revelation himself, a new body of Scripture, and lay the
> foundation for a new church that was meant to supersede any existing one
> and to be as ecumenical as ever the Catholic Church conceived itself to be.[1]

wrong

In his celebrated book *The Gnostic Religion,* Hans Jonas describes the
aims and the effect of the message proclaimed by Mani (216–276), whose
"novel attempt at an organized mass-religion concerned with the salvation
of mankind"[2] led to the establishment of a Church, after the early Catholic
model, that was to rival the Christian Church first in the West, then in the
East, in areas as far flung as Central Asia and China. While it was ousted
from the Roman Empire by the combined pressure of Church and state by
the sixth century, it continued to thrive in the East, notably in China, for
another thousand years. In Central Asia, where our material was found, it
was to overshadow the Syrian Church of Nestorian persuasion and to rival
Buddhism.

The ecumenical character of Mani's Church was grounded in his very
message. As Jonas points out,

1

In one respect Mani's "catholicity" went beyond the Christian model: whether for the sake of universal appeal or because of his own many-sided affinities, he made the doctrinal basis of his church as syncretistic as was compatible with the unity of the central gnostic idea. In principle he recognized the genuineness and provisional validity of the great earlier revelations; in practice, in the first attempt of this kind in recorded history, he deliberately fused Buddhist, Zoroastrian, and Christian elements with his own teaching, so that not only could he declare himself to be the fourth and concluding prophet in a historical series and his teaching the epitome and consummation of that of his predecessors, but his mission could in each of the three areas dominated by the respective religious traditions emphasize that aspect of the Manichaean synthesis which was familiar to the mind of the hearers.[3]

As Jonas further points out, Mani's method was syncretistic, but his system was not:[4] "It was on the contrary the most monumental single embodiment of the gnostic religious principle, for whose doctrinal and mythological representation the elements of older religions were consciously employed."[5] This was possible because Mani grew up in an area where the most varied religious traditions prevailed, the Sassanian Babylonia of the third century A.D. Here he was raised in a Jewish-Christian "Baptist" sect, the sect of the Elchasaites, as we know from the recently edited *Cologne Mani Codex*, a Greek text from fourth or fifth century Egypt.[6] From this document, which was apparently part of a Manichaean Church history, we learn that this community had specifically Jewish traditions, apparently going back as far as the Qumran community. Though rooted in that tradition, it regarded itself as a Christian community as far back as its founder Elchasaios, who must have preached his message around 100 A.D.[7] Gnostic tendencies may have already had an impact on the thinking of the community, as they influenced various groups in Mesopotamia, which was contiguous to Syria and Iran. In the Mesopotamia of that time, ancient Babylonian mythology, as well as the Jewish, Christian, and Iranian religions were in evidence. Furthermore, Babylonian ports were the gates to India and other areas farther east. Thus Mani became familiar with the teachings of the great founders of religions before him, namely Jesus, Zoroaster, and Buddha.

Mani left the Elchasaite community at age twenty-four, under the spiritual guidance of his heavenly "Twin," in order to found a religion and Church of his own. In the Coptic *Kephalaia* we learn that this "Twin," there referred to as "the Living Paraclete," came down and spoke to him. Mani reports,

> He revealed to me the hidden mystery that was hidden from the worlds and the generations: the mystery of the Depth and the Height: he revealed to me the mystery of the Light and the Darkness, the mystery of the conflict and

the great war which the Darkness stirred up. He revealed to me how the Light [turned back ? overcame ?] the Darkness by their intermingling and how [in consequence] was set up this world . . . ; he enlightened me on the mystery of the forming of Adam, the first man. He instructed me on the mystery of the Tree of Knowledge of which Adam ate, by which his eyes were made to see; the mystery of the Apostles who were sent out into the world to select the churches [i. e., to found the religions] . . . Thus was revealed to me by the Paraclete all that has been and that shall be, and all that the eye sees and the ear hears and the thought thinks. Through him I learned to know everything, I saw the All through him, and I became *one* body and *one* spirit [with him]. (*Kephalaia* 14,29–15,24).

After being called and instructed by "the Living Paraclete," Mani engaged in missionary activity, first in the Mesopotamian part of the newly established Persian kingdom of the Sassanians, who had ousted the previous Parthian power. (Mani was of royal Parthian descent.) As we learn from the Central Asian text M 2, he sent missionaries to the west as far as Alexandria, and to the east as far as the Kushan kingdom (in present day Afghanistan).

In 240 or 241 Mani sailed to India, to the Indus valley and adjacent areas in today's Beluchistan, and there converted a Buddhist king, the Tūrān Shāh. In India, he must have built up a community that did not exist for a longer period of time. In the *Kephalaia* (184,27) he says that he "moved the whole land of India." Yet he prophesies that certain forces there will rise up against him, because he was "too heavy for it (i. e., India)" (*Keph.* 185, 4ff.).

After the death of King Ardashīr I and the coronation of his successor Shāhpur I (reg. 241–272), Mani journeyed to the Sassanian capital and won the ear of the new ruler. As various religious traditions thrived in his wide realm—Zoroastrianism in the central parts, Buddhism in the east, and Judaism, Christianity, and various ethnic religions in the Mesopotamian west—he must have been attracted by the catholic, that is, all-encompassing spirit of the new religion. Though he did not convert to the new faith, he did allow Mani to preach the new message throughout his realm.

When Shāhpur died and Ohrmizd/Hormizd I (reg. 272–273) ascended the throne, Mani's privileges were renewed. Under Bahrām/Vahrām I (reg. 273–276), however, the representatives of the Zoroastrian Church under the leadership of Kartēr managed to influence the king to promote their ecclesiastical interests. A persecution of the Manichaean religion set in, and Mani was imprisoned; he died in chains in 276. Yet his spirit lived on, and in spite of all the tribulation his Church spread as far as the Atlantic and the Indian Ocean, even to the China Sea. Of course, the accounts of his life, composed by his community, are determined by its understanding of him as the final divine Messenger. Yet this material, when reviewed critically, can throw light on his historical life as well as his community's interpretation of it.[8]

Mani laid down his teaching in various books that were to gain canonical significance throughout his world-wide Church. Coptic, Iranian, Turkish, and Chinese Manichaean literature provide primary sources. The names of these Manichaean scriptures written by him are as follows: 1. Living Gospel, 2. Treasure of Life, 3. Treatise, 4. Book of Mysteries (Secrets), 5. Book of Giants, 6. Epistles, 7. Psalms and Prayers. All of these survive only in fragmentary form.

Of course, Mani's teaching was developed further after his death and elaborated and applied in various ways. Yet, the various sources reveal a remarkably unified system.

"The heart of Manichaeism," says Jonas, "was Mani's own speculative version of the gnostic myth of cosmic exile and salvation, and this version showed an amazing vitality: as an absolute principle stripped of most of the mythological detail with which Mani had embroidered it, it again and again reappeared in the sectarian history of medieval Christendom, where often 'heretical' was identical with 'neo-Manichaean.' Thus, . . . from the point of view of history of religions Manichaeism is the most important product of Gnosticism."[9]

The Manichaean Doctrine

BASIC CONCEPTS

Manichaean doctrine, as H. J. Polotsky points out, is a remarkably unified, symmetrical system in spite of the great diversity of sources from which it may be gleaned.[10] These include the ancient Mediterranean (notably Coptic) texts; the writings of the Church Fathers, which take a polemical stance; the (often more objective) works of Islamic historians; and the Iranian, Turkish, and Chinese documents from Central Asia. Primary and secondary sources from the West and East attest to the cohesiveness of this religious system, which was conceived of and inspired by one religious authority, namely Mani.

This system was, to be sure, developed further in various ways and was adapted to Christian terminology in the West, to Islam in the Abbasid realm, to Buddhism in Central Asia, and to Taoism in China. Yet a closer look at such adaptations reveals that they were often only of a superficial, linguistic nature, and did not really affect the basic concepts of the religion. They were linguistic adjustments made in accordance with the precept to combine "wisdom and skillful means." This principle, found in the *Cologne*

Mani Codex (e. g., 5,3), was also basic to Mahāyāna Buddhism and to the Eastern type of Manichaeism it influenced. The *Codex* makes it clear that this was a principle followed by Mani as well. Even in his *Šābuhragān,* an exposition of his doctrine written for the Sassanian ruler Šābuhr/Shāhpur I, Mani took great liberty in expressing his teaching in accordance with the concepts of Middle Persian Zoroastrianism. On the other hand, his disciples, like Mār Ammō, who was active in Parthian East Iran, remained more faithful to the original teaching of their master and to its terminology, which was originally Aramaic.[11] Yet even in this earliest period, there was an attempt to assimilate Buddhist concepts, for Buddhism was well entrenched in eastern Iranian areas.[12] In fact, we can observe Eastern Manichaeism adapting increasingly to Buddhism as we move from Parthian to Sogdian and then on to Turkish literature.[13] Finally, in Chinese texts from Tunhuang, the Western gateway to China, these texts remind one at first sight of Mahāyāna sūtras. On closer inspection, however, the Buddhist terms turn out to be mere husks around an unmistakably Manichaean kernel.[14]

Thus, even if the surface suggests an *interpretatio Buddhica,* a closer look at the apparently Buddhist terms reveals that they are but new labels for Manichaean concepts. Thus when the Chinese *Hymnscroll* (H) repeatedly speaks of man's "Buddha nature," it actually refers to the divine spark, the soul in man, which, in opposition to the Buddhist notion, is determined by a specific substance consubstantial with the World of Light. Furthermore, "the Buddhas," to whom reference is frequently made, are actually the Manichaean divine Messengers of Light. And even when a "Buddha" is called a specific Buddhist name like Vairocana (Lu-shê-na), a Manichaean divine being is meant, in this case "the Column of Glory." This also applies to the Bodhisattvas. Thus in the *Hymnscroll* (H 391), the Gods "Call" and "Answer" are referred to as Avalokiteśvara (Kuan-yin) and Mahāsthāmaprāpta (Shih-chih), the two Bodhisattvas seen flanking the central cultic figure of the Buddha in the art of the Silk Road. Even groups of Buddhas like "the five Buddhas," "the Buddhas of the ten directions," or "all the Buddhas," are interpreted in a Manichaean sense, the first group representing the five Sons of the First Man, and the other groups the sum of all Messengers of Light. There is notably a strong convergence between the Manichaean description of the Realm of Light and the Buddhist notion of *Sukhāvatī,* which are, after all, comparable concepts.[15]

In spite of all such adaptations, the basic concepts of Mani's system are preserved in Eastern, specifically Iranian and Central Asian, Manichaeism. It remains a basically dualistic system, grounded on the distinction between "the two principles" (Light and Darkness) and "the three times" (the primeval time of the separation of the two; the present time where they are mixed; and the future, eschatological time when their separation will be reinstated). In the Turkish confession for auditors, the $X^u\bar{a}stv\bar{a}n\bar{i}ft$ (I C), there is an attack on all attempts to relativize the dualism; it repudiates a primeval principle or deity (Zurvān) from which the two principles are derived. Salvation from evil is possible only "by the insight into dualism and by adhering to the rules of life derived from this knowledge."[16]

According to Mani's dualism, which is of the "Iranian," not the "Syrio-Egyptian" type,[17] evil is not derived from good, nor is it to be understood mythologically as the consequence of the fall of an angel or divine being to a lower state. Rather it stands in contrast to the good from the very beginning. From the outset God and Satan, Light and Darkness, Spirit and Matter (hylē), stand over against each other as two "natures," or "substances." But this is a matter not only of cosmological but also, eminently, of anthropological significance. Both natures also stand in opposition to each other within man, who hence becomes their battlefield. His physical nature and his psychological makeup—psychē being sublimated matter—are constantly engaged in a struggle against his soul (pneuma), the substance of which is divine Light. The present state of man is determined by the "mixture" (MP. gumēzišn) of the two principles, and the (associated) substances or natures. The aim of divine activity vis-à-vis the world and man is to recreate the original condition by "distilling," as it were, the Light from Matter (hylē) to which it is bound. It is man's task to assist the saving deities in bringing about this separation, which also implies the separation of good from evil and the vanquishing of evil on an ethical level. This is achieved by subduing the forces of evil, particularly the forces of the psychē in its negative aspects.

In order to help him in his task, the divine world sends man the Nous, which brings him the knowledge of his original home—and destination— namely, the World of Light. The Nous teaches man that his soul has been imprisoned by evil powers. The Nous can be perceived at work, bringing this crucial knowledge for man's salvation.

Having once been roused from the "sleep of forgetfulness" regarding his true divine nature, man can not only be saved himself, but can join the gods in seeking to save all souls, all "Light Elements" that are bound to the world of matter. At the time of death, the soul endowed with divine knowledge is granted final redemption, for it leaves behind a husk, "the garment of the body," in order to be clothed anew with a divine, heavenly garment, which is the sign of its perfection and redemption.

Mani's teaching about man, his original heavenly home, his subjugation to the forces of evil, and his future destiny are part of an all-encompassing cosmology, in which ethical and spiritual principles are associated with concepts of substance.[18] Here good and evil, the divine and the satanic are depicted as substances that originally stood in opposition to each other in duality, but then mixed in the course of events. This "mixture" led to suffering and woe. The grand cosmological drama projects into cosmic dimensions a specific insight into the nature of man, his divine origin, his present plight, and his potential for attaining salvation. Such mythological imagery used to express realities about man certainly contrasts with the intellectual and conceptual thinking developed by Greek philosophy and established in Western Christian thought, with its dogmatic considerations and credal assertions. The mythological imagery may have been one reason why Western Christendom was suspicious of this world view, but it recommended itself to peoples of the East where imagery and symbolism, rather than conceptual philosophy or theology, were persuasive.

Mani took up and developed Jewish and biblical imagery and symbolism, relating them to the symbolical and mythological languages of Persia in his *Šābuhragān,* thereby paving the way for a *translatio* of his message into the mythological (and symbolic) languages of the East. Thus he could be assured that his religion, incorporating the wisdom of all nations and religions, would prevail throughout the world. This notion is expressed in a parable, taken from Buddhism (*Udāna* V,5; *Cullavagga* IX,1), in which he likens his religion to the world ocean, into which all rivers, that is, other religious traditions flow. The Manichaean missionary can therefore legitimately employ the symbols, myths, and even concepts of other traditions.

For all the metaphysical and figurative character of his system, operating as it does with images and series of images (to which, to be sure, concepts and series of concepts correspond), Mani shrinks from describing the highest Godhead, the Father of Light, in images. Following a basic Gnostic tendency, he asserts that the Godhead becomes visible in the emanations issuing from Him. These are characterized by beauty and the perfectness of their forms. This is borne out by the hymns to the Father of Light and his emanations, often referred to as his "Sons" (cf. ch. I). In the Jewish thought of intertestamental times, much prominence was given to an angelology (teaching about angels) in which divine qualities and functions of God were hypostacized and a great number of intermediary beings were introduced to fill the space between God and the world. Basically, this also applies to Gnosticism with its concept of the "remote" or "alien" God.[19] In Mani's system, in contrast to the Gnostic Valentinian, the divine beings called into existence by the Father of Light, and thence from each other in successive steps and stages, become increasingly important in soteriological terms. Thus "the Living Spirit," who creates the cosmos, is more relevant for the process of redemption than the Great Builder, who "called him forth," and the Friend of Lights, from whom the Great Builder issued. And the so-called "Third Messenger" becomes effectively active through the beings he in turn has "called forth,"—the Nous and "Jesus the Splendor."

A key fact for the understanding of the Manichaean system is that the gods are grouped into triads, pentads, and dodecads (groups of twelve). They are related to and therefore are themselves expressions of certain virtues and ethical qualities. Thus they serve to express the whole ethical system inherent in Mani's teaching. In such relationships between gods and values, the principle of analogy prevails, which is more important for the self-understanding of man than abstract conceptualization. The forces in the world, and in man, are comprehended by being related to analogous entities, whereby the analogy between microcosm (man) and macrocosm (the world) plays an important role. Thus the five "limbs,"—qualities of the soul—are related to the five basic aspects of God, to the five areas in the Realm of Light, and to the five "Sons" of the First Man, who initially succumbed to the forces of Darkness. The First Man was eventually saved, but his sons were devoured by the dark forces. Now they yearn for redemption. Hence they have prototypical significance for the fate of every soul longing for salvation.

Other relationships also exist; for example, the five limbs of the soul are also related to the five classes of the Church hierarchy. Last but not least, there is a relationship between the earthly Mani and his representative in heaven, his *alter ego,* his divine "Twin" who guides and protects him. So also every devout person has his "Form of Light" in heaven, which finally appears to him, clearly visible, at the time of death. Thus the relationships between the things of the world and the things of the spirit, as revealed in Mani's teaching, serve as orientation and guidance for the devout in their earthly life.

THE SUBSTANCE OF THE MANICHAEAN MYTH

The Two Principles

As already pointed out, in Mani's teaching the Realm of Light was originally separated from and contrasted to the Realm of Darkness. In the Realm of Light, which consists of a "Light Earth" and a "Light Air (or Ether)," reigns the Father of Light, or the Father of Greatness (who is called Zurvān in Eastern texts, in accordance with the Zoroastrian conception). His nature is expressed in a series of terms. These are (in the translation of Middle Persian terms by M. Boyce) Reason, Mind, Intelligence, Thought, and Understanding.[20] (The exact meaning of the terms employed in various Central Asian languages differs somewhat, but we can use this series of English concepts as "canonical" for purposes of reference.) These, then, are intellectual attributes of the Supreme Deity. Figuratively, they are called his "limbs" or his "dwellings." The first term sums up all others, as is characteristic of Manichaean thinking:[21] The Father of Light is the origin and sum of all divine powers, or deities, that have issued from him.[22] Together with three other of his attributes, namely his Light, his Power, and his Wisdom, we have a quaternity, referred to by the term "the Fourfold Father of Greatness."[23]

Like courtiers surrounding a king, there are myriad, even countless "Aeons" and "Aeons of Aeons" surrounding the Father in the Realm of Light. Thus the infinite temporal expanse of the Realm is expressed.[24] Of the many Aeons, there are twelve closest to the Father, three in each direction. (This is probably a reflection of Iranian speculation about time, made up of four great Aeons, each consisting of three epochs, as we find in Zurvanite thought.)[25] The twelve Aeons are called "the Firstborn of the Father"; they are thus differentiated from other deities that he calls forth in the course of time. The Realm of Light is also inhabited by "the Great Spirit," who holds sway here along with the Father of Light. He is, as Polotsky points out, "a kind of *syzygos* ["Twin"] of the Father of Greatness, who actually represents . . . the preexistent form of the 'Mother of the Living.'"[26]

Corresponding to the five areas of the Realm of Light, represented by the five intellectual powers of the Father of Greatness—Reason, Mind, Intelligence, Thought, and Understanding—five areas, or "worlds"—sometimes identified as Dark Reason, Dark Mind, and so forth—comprise the Realm of Darkness. In another image, they are summarily referred to as "the five dark elements"—smoke, fire, wind, water, and darkness. From these elements spring five "trees of death." This dark pentad is also figuratively related to five types of animal-shaped demonic beings that inhabit the five dark "worlds"—bipeds, quadrupeds, flying creatures, swimming creatures, and crawling creatures. Their bestial urges, particularly lust and concupiscence, correspond to their animal forms. In every category there are male and female beings, who arouse sexual desire in each other. A "king" rules over every one of these dark "worlds"; he has faces corresponding to those of the beings he rules—the faces of a demon, a lion, an eagle, a fish, and a dragon. The King of the Dark Realm—Satan, who is at the head of all of them—combines the five hideous forms in his person. He personifies *hylē* (Matter) as a demonic, avaricious power, or "the thought of death" (*enthymēsis* of death, that is, the moribund manner of thinking, which is avarice or greed); he himself is thus "the superior instrument" (Polotsky) of that Dark Realm. In the Iranian (MP, Pth.) texts, he is called Ahriman; in the Sogdian and Turkish documents Šmnw/Šïmnu. As avarice and greed animate and inspire the beings in the Realm of Darkness, unceasing strife and conflict reign. It is a place of constant unrest and turmoil, uprising and revolt.

The events at the beginning of time which were so fateful for the present condition of the world and man are narrated by Mani in three cosmological acts. They correspond to three "creations."

The First Creation

In the beginning, the Realm of Darkness was completely separated from the Realm of Light. Once the Dark had beheld the Light, it wanted to partake of it. So the lower Realm gathered its dark powers to invade the world above. In order to forestall the attack, the Father of Light decided to go into battle "himself" (as we hear from Theodor Bar Khonai). However, he did so indirectly, by issuing forth from himself a divine power that assumed charge. He first "called forth" the Mother of the Living, who then evoked the deity "the First Man." (In the Iranian texts he is called Ohrmizd, in the Turkish Xormuzda.)

Equipped with five divine powers that appear either as his "sons" or his "arms"—that together constitute "the Living Soul" (or "the Living Self"), the sum of "the five elements of Light" (Ether, Wind, Light, Water, and Fire)—the First Man went into battle.[27] He offered himself up as a bait for the powers of Darkness, in order to satisfy their greed temporarily and destroy them in the long run. The forces of Darkness pounced on these "Elements of Light," tore them apart and devoured them. Through this ingestion, that fateful "mixture" of Light and Darkness that characterizes the present condition of the world was brought about. The demons later used the Light they had devoured to fashion man's soul as the divine and living element in him. The forces of Darkness, having once tasted and devoured the Light, were quite unwilling to relinquish it. It became like a drug without which they could no longer live, and therefore they would do everything in their power to retain it. This moved the World of Light to stage a second cosmological act.

The Second Creation

The sons of the First Man had been captured by the dark powers, and he himself had been vanquished. He lay unconscious in the depths. But now aid came to him. In order to help him, the Father of Light sent forth a series of emanations, each issuing from the previous one. First he sent forth from himself "the Friend of the Lights," from whom issued "the Great Builder." He in turn produced "The Living Spirit," who, like the First Man, had five sons. They were later instrumental in forming and holding up the cosmos. Their names are the King of Splendor, the King of Honor, the Adamas of Light, the King of Glory, and Atlas.

The Living Spirit sent a "Call" from the lowest boundary of the World of Light to the First Man lying in the depths. He heard this "Call" and responded with an "Answer." "Call" and "Answer"—primeval prototypes of every religious address and the response to it—were hypostacized and rose as gods to the Realm of Light. In Manichaean theology, the "Answer-God" (MP Padvāxtag) is counted as the sixth son of the First Man, whereas the "Call-God" (MP Xrōshtag) becomes the sixth son of the Living Spirit.

The First Man, having been roused from his unconscious state by the Call from the other world, was now in a position to receive salvation. The Living Spirit, together with his five sons and the Mother of Life (the Mother of the Living), descended to the depths to receive him and to lead him up to the World of Light. In explaining this part of the myth, Polotsky points out, "Although the First Man is actually identical in nature with the Elements of Light, [i. e.] his sons, . . . his fate is distinguished from theirs. He embodies the 'consciousness', the *nous*, that they have lost and that is now preserved in safety for the time being in the Realm of Light, in order to return to them later at an appropriate time."[28] The fate of the First Man thus highlights the basic potential of salvation in every soul, whose five "limbs" are of the same substance as the five sons of the First Man ("the Fivefold God," as he is called in Turkish).

In Central Asia, this classical account of the fate of the First Man is sometimes modified. The Manichaeans' self-image must have been affected by the fact that Manichaeism had been able to establish itself as a state religion among the Uighur Turks of the Mongolian Steppes when Bögü Khan embraced this faith and made it the official religion of his realm in 762/763, (which it remained until the destruction of the kingdom in 840); and also by the circumstance that in the Turkish state of Kocho (ca. 850–1250), for some time at least, Manichaeism had the status of an official religion. The Manichaeans had now become the exponents not of a persecuted religion, as in previous times, but of a triumphant faith. The Light of the Divine Realm was shining into the world, ennobling and dignifying it. Because of this new understanding of the condition of the world, the myth is sometimes modified so that the First Man does not succumb to the forces of Darkness, but rather vanquishes them. Various Turkish texts of this type have been preserved, and the motif can be found also in Parthian texts.[29] We can interpret this new worldview as an expression of a triumph over evil (that is, non-Manichaean) forces, of a positive reassessment of the body and the corporeal dimension of life, as well as of the part to be played by lay people, the "auditors." Thus our Central Asian texts can speak of "the perfect auditor" who is almost equal to the elect in his potential for gaining salvation in this life.[30] Such an ideal status may be conferred on the Manichaean king as "defender of the faith." Thus he is called "the son of Mani," one who is "clothed with the Great Nous" (*Nom Qutï kädilmiš*).[31]

Returning to the Manichaean myth in its classical form, we remind ourselves of the fate of the First Man, who was first vanquished by the demons, but was then awakened from his unconscious state by the Call from the other world. That Call and his Answer together form what the texts term "the thought of life" (*enthymēsis* of life, the life-promoting thinking). "The thought of life" is opposed, then, to "the thought of death" (*enthymēsis* of death) which is characteristic of the Realm of Darkness, and which is sometimes qualified as "Greed" (*Āz*), a prominent demoness in that Dark Realm. In each case, a thought promoting life or death respectively is signified. Polotsky points out that "the thought of life" seems to be "a kind of substitute for the lost *nous,* and at the same time a preparation for its future recovery . . . , the natural feeling of affiliation to the Realm of Light, and the capacity to answer the [otherworldly] 'Call' of the *nous.*"[32]

The task of the Living Spirit after resuscitating the First Man was to create the world as a mechanism for the liberation of the Light still captured— "devoured" in mythological language—by the forces of Darkness. That Light is referred to cumulatively as "the Living Soul" (or "the Living Self"). In contrast to other schools of Gnosticism, it is not an evil demiurge that creates the world, but rather a divine being. However, for the creation of the cosmos this being does use material of mixed substance, an amalgamation of good and evil, of Light and Darkness. In mythological imagery, this consists of the slain bodies of the powers of Darkness, the "archons" (or archontes) that have devoured the Light constituted by the sons of the First Man. Out of these, the Living Spirit fashioned eight earths (layers of the world) and ten heavens (skies) which were stacked one on top of the other. He fastened the archons who had not yet been slain to the firmament (the myth speaks of their "crucifixion"). The sons of the Living Spirit were commissioned with the task of carrying the earths, holding up the skies, and ruling the cosmos. From the pure elements of redeemed Light, the Living Spirit fashioned the Sun and the Moon; from the light particles still infested with *hylē* and hence not so pure he made the stars. Furthermore, he created three cosmic "wheels," of fire, water, and wind, which would serve in future to purify Light redeemed from the cosmos and send it up to its original place.

The Third Creation

After the creation of the world, the Father of Greatness called forth the Third Messenger, and charged him to extract and purify the Light still retained by the powers of Darkness and contained in their bodies. By taking advantage of the innate sexual lust of the archons, he made them relinquish the Light they had devoured and still retained. The Light is especially concentrated in their seed, or semen, if they are male, and to a lesser degree in the fruit of their wombs if they are female. The Third Messenger called forth a beautiful female deity, the Maiden of Light, who could also appear in the form of twelve maidens, and, according to some texts, twelve hand-some gods. According to other texts, the Third Messenger himself takes on this appearance. The twelve figures of the Maiden of Light are ultimately the twelve Dominions of Light, a series of attributes of the New Man (as opposed to the Old Man [cf. Rom. 6:5; Col. 3:8–10; Eph. 4:22–24], which we shall discuss presently). The Living Spirit entered the Sun, and the Maiden of Light the Moon. They showed their naked bodies to the archons. The male devils were attracted to the beautiful female figures, the female devils to the handsome gods, after whom they lusted. The archons spilled their seed, thus losing their light. The seed fell on "wet and dry ground," that is, water and earth. From the water into which it fell an ocean giant emerged, but was overcome by the Adamas of Light, the third son of the Living Spirit. From the seed that fell on the dry ground, five kinds of trees and plants sprang up. When the female archons, pregnant from unions in hell, saw the divine figures above them, they miscarried, and their aborted offspring, which contained less light than the demons' seed, fell to earth, where they devoured the fruits of the trees that had grown out of the seed of the male archons. Driven by sexual lust, they united with each other and brought forth the five kinds of living creatures, corresponding to the five species of demons. (Whereas men are included in the five kinds of living beings, the creation of Adam and Eve, and thus of mankind, is narrated at a later point). This somewhat tangled myth, known as the story of "the seduction of the archons" seeks to show how and why, in spite of the activity of the Living Spirit, the power of sexual greed remains alive in the world of the demons, and how they reproduce themselves.

In order to continue the work of liberating the Light imprisoned in *hylē* (that is, Matter, Darkness) the Third Messenger then called forth "the Column of Glory," "who is both a God, and a path by which the redeemed Light ascends to the sky. Its visible appearance is the Milky Way."[33] As a deity, the figure is referred to as "the Perfect Man." As a path for the saved Light particles, it allows them to ascend to the Sun and the Moon, which are referred to as "palaces," "chariots" or "ships of Light," that transport this Light to the World of Light beyond the cosmic spheres, or skies, more speci-fically to the New Paradise. This Paradise had been created by the Great Builder of the second creation at the command of the Living Spirit, to serve as a place of rest for the gods engaged in battle, and as a first haven for the Light Elements (saved souls). With the creation of the New Paradise, the original Realm of Light could remain untroubled by the turbulence and restlessness connected with the great cosmic battle. The ruler of the New Paradise is the First Man.

The Living Spirit now set the world into motion, which caused the pas-sage of day and night and of the various seasons. He did this by making the

Sun and the Moon rotate and assume their natural functions. Furthermore, they assumed their specific soteriological functions. The waxing of the moon denotes that the "ship of Light" is gradually being filled up with Light filtered out of the world. Just as gradually, the Moon passes on this liberated Light to the Sun, thus waning again. From the Sun, that Light finds its way to the New Paradise. Sun and Moon are later also assigned the task of serving as "thrones" for the most important redeeming deities of the three creations. In the Sun reside the Third Messenger, the Mother of Life, and the Living Spirit; in the Moon the Light Messenger Jesus, called "Jesus the Splendor," the Maiden of Light, and the First Man, who is also the Lord of the New Paradise. In the Sun and Moon two other groups of saving deities also reside, namely, the seven and the twelve "shiplords," who are invoked cumulatively but not named individually.[34]

The other gods of the third creation are "evoked," that is, called to Life by the Living Spirit. They are, in the order of their appearance, Jesus the Splendor, the Great Nous (MP/Pth. "Vahman"; Turk. "Nom Qutï") and the Just Judge (or Just Justice). The five "limbs" of the Great Nous are the five intellectual attributes that characterize the Father, the Realm of Light, and, indeed, every soul—reason (*nous*), mind, intelligence, thought, and understanding.

The Creation of Man

Alarmed by the activity of the Third Messenger, *hylē* was seized by fear and turmoil, for it was terrified at the prospect of losing all the Light it had appropriated. To check the divine process of salvation, it conceived a plan to create man, and to imprison within his body the Light it had seized as his soul. Through the process of reproduction—by constantly passing on the Light acquired through the seed to a new generation—the soul, being perpetually enthralled by the body, would remain in *hylē*'s power. *Hylē,* personified in the Demoness of Greed (*Āz*), or lust, caused two demon-animals that had fallen to the earth—the male demon Ašaqlon (Pth. Shaklōn) and the female demon Nemrael (Pth. Pēsūs)—to devour the issue of other animal-like demons, in order to ingest their light. Then, incited further by *Āz*, they mated and thus engendered man, who was made after the images of the Third Messenger and the Maiden of Light, which the demons had seen on high. Thus the first human pair, Adam (MP Gēhmurd) and Eve (MP Muhrdiyānag) were born, even though the texts say that they were "created" or "formed" according to those divine images; there is even a whole creation myth telling us how *Āz* actually created that first pair.[35] Both images, that of creation and that of procreation, are freely interchangeable, as is particularly evident in the hymns. In both cases the main point is the demonic origin of the body which is to serve as Āz's instrument, or in another image, her "garment," wherein she can clothe herself. Thus, in a Middle Persian text (M 98 and 99 and M 7980–84) she says to herself prior to the act of creation, "According to those two figures of the God Narisah [i. e., the Third Messenger], the female and the male figure,[36] which I have seen, I will form (*dēsān*) those two creatures so that they may become a garment and a husk for me."[37]

The Light that had been collected in the bodies of the demon-animals was passed on to Adam and Eve as their souls; at the same time greed, the lust for procreation, envy, hate, and other evil qualities were imprisoned in their bodies and charged with the task of guarding the soul of Light, so that it should remain covered with qualities alien to itself. It should thus remain oblivious of its divine origin. These negative aspects together form what is called the "dark" or "material soul."[38]

But this is only the dark background against which the qualities and virtues of the divine soul shine all the brighter. The hymns on the Living Soul (ch. III) give us an impression of its divine merits and surpassing excellence. Being "a thing of beauty,"[39] it is likened to gold covered by dust, or a pearl held in the clutches of a demon. The evil qualities covering or suppressing it will be shaken off, and it will be restored to its pristine beauty, purity, and integrity. It gains these, first and foremost, through an inward process, that of the integration of all its aspects or spiritual powers. These are represented by its five limbs, which have to be "gathered in," assimilated and integrated. In order to help assemble these scattered "limbs" and thus redeem the soul, Jesus is sent forth.

Jesus and the Nous

After the creation of man, "Jesus the Splendor"—an emanation of the Third Messenger, and as such a redeeming emissary from the Realm of Light—descended and brought Adam the saving knowledge (*gnosis*) of his origin and of the truth about himself. He made clear to Adam that his soul stemmed from the divine World of Light. Having forgotten its original home, overpowered by *hylē* and mixed with its substance, and having succumbed to the stupor it causes, the soul had sunk here into "the sleep of death." According to the Syrian writer Theodor bar Khonai (131, 4–7), Adam then raised a cry of woe, lamenting "the creator of my body, the one who has fettered my soul, and the rebels that have enslaved me." He decided to overcome lust and greed by continence. But Eve, whose body contained less Light than his, allowed herself to be seduced by a demon, whereupon she gave birth to Cain and Abel. Then, together with Adam, she engendered Seth. Thus by an act of procreation, the Light in his body, concentrated in his seed, remained fettered to *hylē*.

Yet the Realm of Light strives on to save the divine soul. Jesus, who brought Adam *gnosis,* remains an active savior up to the present, continuing to bring man redeeming knowledge.[40] Other redeeming deities emanate from him: the Maiden of Light and the Great Nous. The three are often grouped together to form a triad of redeeming gods that corresponds, within a frame of manifold analogies, to another triad consisting of the Third Messenger, the twelve Maidens (a specific representation of the Maiden of Light) and the Column of Glory. Speaking in terms of the cosmological myth, Jesus (the Light Messenger) resides in the Sun, whereas the Third Messenger lives in the Moon.[41]

Jesus also appears on the scene at the end of the world, as the Judge. This role of his is described in the *Šābuhragān,*[42] a Middle Persian work written by Mani for Šābuhr/Shāhpur I. In accordance with Iranian terminology, he is called "the God of the World of Wisdom" (Xradeshahryazd).[43] Besides Jesus the Splendor and Jesus as Judge, there is the figure of "Jesus the Messiah" or "Jesus of Nazareth," that is, the historical Jesus, who lived and died as a man. The Gnostic concept of a docetic savior, one who only appears to be human, is applied.[44] Jesus' suffering and death, however, are significant as exemplifications of the suffering of the "Living Self" fettered to *hylē*. This leads us to a further concept of Jesus in Manichaeism, that of "the suffering Jesus" (*Jesus patibilis* according to St. Augustine). This is "the name given in Western Manichaeism to the Living Self, i. e., the sum of the Light suffering in Matter, 'crucified' as Jesus was crucified on the cross."[45] Boyce points out that "the three concepts of Jesus are not always kept wholly distinct."[46] Mani, having grown up in a Judeo-Christian tradition, often refers to the historical Jesus as "the prophet Jesus." He regards him as his immediate forerunner and understands himself as an "Apostle of Jesus Christ," sent to continue and fulfill his work.

The Great Nous is closely connected with Jesus the Splendor in that he is an emanation, in the sense of a specific quality or function of Jesus.[47] The work of all great religious founders and apostles, including Zoroaster and the Buddha, is ultimately that of the Great Nous, who inspires them all, so that he is termed "the Father of all Apostles." The five sons of the First Man—Ether, Wind, Light, Water, and Fire—are "clothed" by his "limbs," which are the "limbs" of God, so that they appear as and assume the function of the "limbs" of the soul. The Nous enters into the minds of those that open themselves to him, and he is instrumental in eradicating the seeds of evil in man. In the Chinese *Traité,* a translation of the Parthian *Sermon on the Nous of Light,* this notion is expressed through a wealth of different images. A Turkish text (TM 296) even says of a Manichaean king that he is "clothed with the Great Nous (*Nom Qutï*)."[48] It is the Nous that awakens the individual soul from its sleep of forgetfulness and imparts to it the knowledge of its divine origin, which is what Jesus has done for Adam and for mankind. According to the *Traité,* there arise out of the limbs of the Nous five "gifts" that are actually five virtues issuing from his presence: love, faith, perfection, patience or forebearance, and wisdom. The soul that is endowed with these "gifts" represents New Man, as opposed to Old Man, who is still subject to sinfulness. This notion is inspired by Pauline doctrine, and is particularly well elaborated in the *Traité* (Tr. 1282b10ff.).[49]

As Jesus and the Nous are closely related, so too are Jesus and the First Man. The First Man, representing the saved *nous* of the soul, epitomizes the potential for the salvation of the soul. Jesus in turn bestows this capacity for salvation on the soul.[50] It is striking that in the Iranian texts, the second limb of the soul (MP/Pth. *manohmēd,* translated as "mind" by Boyce) assumes the role of the *nous,* which is the first limb of the soul in the Western tradition, where the *nous* represents the whole soul *pars pro toto.* In the Iranian hymns, Jesus is called the "New Aeon" or "New Dispensation" (lit., "New Realm," Pth. *šahr ī nōg*), or the "New Dominion" (Pth. *sahrδārīft nawāg*), while the First Man is called "the King of the New Aeon" in the Coptic *Homilies* (41,20). Jesus and the Nous are also associated with each other in that both reside in the Moon, together with the Maiden of Light.

Salvation and Damnation

Ultimate salvation implies the return of the captured Light to its original home, the Realm of Light. Two necessary prerequisites for the release of man's soul are redemptive knowledge about the soul's origin, and the observance of the ethical code that is derived from that knowledge. However, as an absolutely perfect life is not possible here, regular confession of sins is necessary.

Man must nevertheless strive to separate the "two natures" within himself, to allow the New Man and his virtues to prevail over the Old Man and his vices. Only one who can observe the commandments for the elect can hope for conditional salvation here and full salvation after death. The layman who is not willing to relinquish the worldly life but does obey the ten commandments for auditors can hope for rebirth in the ranks of the elect, from where he can gain redemption. Yet the Coptic as well as the Central Asian texts tell of the ideal of the "perfect auditor," who is counted among the blessed and receives complete salvation at the time of death. It is difficult to say to what extent there may have been a notion of redemption within the lifespan, as in Buddhism. Some passages of the *Kephalaia,* as well as the *Traité,* would suggest such a concept when they speak of the "signs" of the New Man as a "son of righteousness." But they hasten to add that sin and folly can always raise their heads (*Keph.* 96,24ff.; Tr. 1282b8ff.). Yet we have a Turkish text (T II D 173b,2) which, in quoting an apocryphal word of Jesus ("the Messiah-Buddha"), a word not preserved anywhere else, speaks of the differences between auditors: "And there are (also) perfect auditors. There *are* such; they are noble-minded. There *are* such; they are the men who love the (religious) Law."[51] In spite of this ideal of perfection however, everyone, be he an elect or an auditor, is summoned to make confessions regularly. Thus we have in Manichaean literature a number of confessional formulae, for the elect as well as auditors, which serve the purpose of expiating sins and allowing the New Man to vanquish the Old Man again and again.[52] It is the task of the Church, in whom the Nous dwells, to keep alive the consciousness of belonging to a heavenly realm, through preaching, teaching, and admonishing to confession. Those who unrelentingly close their minds to the "Call" of the Church, which *is* the "Call" from beyond, lose all hope of salvation; ultimately they will be shut into the huge, dark "lump" (*globus*) which will be bereft of all divine and redeeming powers and will be left to itself at the end of time.

But punishment and recompense can be meted out after death—or even in this life—not only at the end of time. Central Asian texts, partly inspired by Zoroastrianism and Buddhism, depict various vivid images to portray the fate of the condemned soul. If it is not acquitted in a post-mortal judgment, it is tormented by a wretched old demoness and left to suffer terrible punishment in Hell (cf. ch. XXIV texts 6–7). The concept of an individual judgment is old, found even in the earliest stratum of Manichaean dogma. We also read in Western (Coptic) sources about an impending judgment before the Great Judge, or the Justice of Truth. Whoever is acquitted in this judgment receives "the prize of victory"—the symbols of salvation: the diadem, wreath, and crown.[53] A classical idea is that the judgment opens up three ways, or paths: the way to "life"; the way to the state of "mixture," to a new rebirth in the world; and the way to death, to eternal damnation. Following a Zoroastrian image, the instrument of judgment can be a bridge which the soul has to cross. For the unrighteous, it becomes as narrow as a razor's edge, so that the convicted soul falls without fail into the depths below, into perdition. For the righteous, however, it widens, so that he can cross it easily. Thus it says in a Manichaean prayer, "May the bridge be wide. I would cross it without hesitation (lit., doubt)."[54] According to another Iranian image, also found in Zoroastrianism, the soul of the righteous, upon being severed from the body, sets out on a journey to its heavenly home. On the way it is met by its "Form of Light," or its "Second Self"

(Turk. *ikinti grīv*), its "personified righteousness."[55] Some texts also speak of the "garment of Light," the symbol of the soul's spiritual garb, or form, which can also appear as its *alter ego*. It is accompanied by three angels who give the soul the signs of its "victory," that is, the symbols referred to above.[56] Finally, the soul can unite with its divine *alter ego,* or clothe itself in the heavenly garment.[57] The *alter ego* represents the new existential condition for which the soul, hitherto clad in the body, had been yearning.[58]

Eschatology

According to Manichaean belief, the gods will continue their task of redeeming souls from the world until the end of time. Cosmologically, so much Light will be filtered out of the world that evil will prevail. Faith will decline, and bitterness and strife will be the order of the day. Then a great war will break out, during which Jesus will come again. He will rule as the "Great King," and will judge the quick and the dead, separating the sheep from the goats. The elect will then be transfigured into angels, whereas the auditors will sit at Jesus' right hand and obtain salvation. The sinners, however, will be directed to his left and sent off to damnation. In these eschatological conceptions, Mani takes up Biblical images, as we find them in Matthew 24 and 25:31–46 as well as in Mark 13 and Luke 21; but he also employs concepts found in early Christian apocalyptic literature, as in the *Apocalypse of Thomas.*[59]

According to Mani, the final dissolution of the world will take place when Jesus returns to the Realm of Light. All the divine powers supporting the cosmos, including the sons of the Living Spirit and the Column of Glory, will give up their functions and return to that Realm of Light. The structure of the world will cave in, and a great cosmic fire will destroy everything that remains. The Elements of Light in the world that can still be redeemed, inspired by the "thought of Life" (life-promoting thinking), will gather together and ascend to the New Paradise in the form of a God, that is, the "Last God" or the "Last Statue (or Image)." Now the New Paradise, which had been created to preserve tranquility in the original Realm of Light while the redeeming gods were fighting, will merge forever with that eternal Realm (cf. ch. II, text 8). *Hylē* (Matter, Darkness) will now once again be completely separated from the Abode of Light, and imprisoned in a large jail called "the grave." In another image, it is collected in a huge "lump" (Gr. *bōlos*, Lat. *globus*) which is sealed off from the Realm of Light by a huge stone. (Whether or not there was any divine Light left in this "lump" of perdition was apparently a matter of discussion among the Manichaeans. There were two schools of thought representing opposing views.) The beings of Light, however, will see the Father face to face and live eternally joyful in his presence.[60]

The Manichaeans, like the Zoroastrians, engaged in numerical speculations about the time when the final events were to take place. One calculation set it for the year 690 A.D.[61] There must have been great disappointment when the year elapsed without any such occurrence taking place.

ETHICS

The Manichaean Church was divided into the elect and auditors (laymen). Each group observed a different set of commandments and cultic practices.[62] As Polotsky explains, "The basic thought of Manichaean ethics in so far as it pertained to practical life . . . is basically expressed in negative terms in the demand to avoid everything that could harm the Light contained in men, and in the world."[63] To inflict pain or harm on the Light in any manner was sinful and to be avoided.[64] Thus most worldly activities, including agriculture, were forbidden for the elect. But since Light was dispersed throughout the world, and was present in every speck of dust, even the most pious could not avoid "injuring" it. This was especially true of auditors who followed any worldly profession. Consequently, in the Turkish confessional prayer for elect, the $X^u\bar{a}stv\bar{a}n\bar{\imath}ft$ (ch. XXV, text 1), the confessor asks for pardon for hurting "the Fivefold God," the sum of the Elements of Light in the world, who is "the beauty and the essence (lit., form), the self and the soul, the power and the light, the origin and the root of everything on earth." Since Light was contained in every plant, in every grain of wheat, even food could not be acquired without sin. Agriculture was made the task of the auditors. However, they were forgiven for such sin, since their work served the pious cause of sustaining the elect. The latter, however, were allowed to eat only vegetarian food, and the consumption of meat and alcohol was strictly forbidden. Their belief was that when they ate and digested food, the Light contained in it was ingested in the body and then passed on, through a process of spiritual transformation, in the form of prayer and meditation to the world beyond. This notion had prompted St. Augustine to ridicule the Manichaeans (*De natura boni* 45). Sexual activity in particular was strictly prohibited for the elect. Chastity was such a central commandment that it is circumscribed as "behavior in accordance with religion." The requirement of inner detachment from all types of lust or greed was based on the myth in which sexual lust led to the creation of man and his fall into his desperate state. And this state is perpetuated by the lustfulness associated with procreation. "Greed" in all its aspects is one of the main characteristics of the demons and is epitomized by the demoness of

Greed, *Āz*. The elect are repeatedly warned against the burning fire of greed and sexual lust. However, as the male elect were at times dependent on the female elect in worldly matters, particularly in having their food cooked, a Parthian text (M 4577) admonishes them to deal with women as a skilled craftsman deals with the fire, using it for his purposes, but not letting it burn him.[65]

In classical Manichaeism, the elect are charged to live in "blessed poverty," not bound by any worldly possessions. They are to wander about from place to place, preaching the word, carrying only enough food for a day and clothes for a year. In Central Asia, it became customary for the elect to live in monasteries, like the Buddhists; apparently there were also devout adherents of the "religion of Light" who followed that old ideal in their peregrinations. In the early Church histories we hear that Mār Addā, Mani's disciple to the West, specifically to Egypt, also built monasteries,[66] so the custom of living together in monastic centers was old and was not derived from, albeit later inspired by, Buddhist practice. As we know from an official charter of a Manichaean monastery in Turfan (Central Asia), such religious centers, like the Buddhist monasteries, grew rich and powerful in the course of time. They possessed wealthy estates and employed servants of various grades, on whom they imposed draconian penalties if they did not do their work as expected.[67] Another Turkish text (T II D 171), a colophon to "The Book of the Two Principles" (Mani's *Šābuhragān*), tells us that the scribe did his work of copying the text in a monastery protected by a strong Turkish tribe. It is referred to as "the residence of the Great Nous, the 'place of healing' of the Elements of Light, the dwelling place of the pure, bright, strong angels."[68]

The financial base for the elect, whether they wandered about or lived in religious centers, was formed by the donations of pious laymen, who like their Buddhist counterparts, would collect "merit" (Turk. *pwn* ~ Skr. *puṇya*) by providing the monks the material means for their sustenance. This was called "soul-service," for by the pious act of giving to "the Church," the layman was also serving his own soul. Time and again we read of the need to "give alms" to the elect and thereby engage in "soul-service."[69] As Polotsky puts it, "The relationship between the elect and the catechumens (i. e., the auditors) is determined by the fact that the former are the actual M[anichaeans], whereas the latter belong to the Manichaean Church by virtue of a necessary concession to the *hylic* conditions of human existence."[70]

In Central Asia, however, the position of the layman was an elevated one, which had to do with the increased value accorded to worldly matters, including the body. As pointed out previously, this is a consequence of the fact that the "Religion of Light" was, at least for some time, a victorious religion, established as a power within the world, not merely pointing to a world beyond. Here the Light of the other world was already shining into this world. Thus an invocation of the Manichaean king says that he is "worthy of both (kinds of) bliss, (of) both (kinds of) life, (of) both (kinds of) dominion, temporal and spiritual," (cf. ch. XXII, text 1). We can assume that the Mongolian teaching about the two "orders of life" (the political and the spiritual, each supporting the other), which was probably formulated at the court of Khubilai Khan (reg. 1260–1294), was inspired by such a Manichaean conception.[71] At any rate, the revaluation of the worldly and physical sphere at the time of Manichaean kingdom led to the easing and mitigation of the great tension between this world and the world beyond, with their respective claims and demands. Both the life of the community and of the individual were affected. We have from Turfan a worldly Manichaean love song, which would be quite inconceivable in classical Gnosticism (ch. XXIV, text 9). The old tension, then, gave way to a more composed, tranquil, and cheerful attitude, such as we often find in Mahāyāna Buddhism. At least this is what the many expressions of elation and victory at the prevalence of the faith found in the colophons to the Turkish texts would suggest.[72]

The concrete ethical commandments were summed up in a catalog of specific ethical values or ideals.[73] The five commandments for the elect were 1. truthfulness, 2. non-injury (nonviolence), 3. chastity ("behavior in accordance with religion"), 4. "purity of mouth," and 5. "blessed poverty." From St. Augustine (*De moribus Manichaeorum*, ch. 10) as well as from Iranian and Turkish sources, we know that there was also a more general summary of the commandments in "three seals" (*tria signacula*), the "seal" of the mouth, the hands, and the bosom. The term "seal" is derived from the notion that the senses are to be "sealed off" from the outside world, guarding the soul against the outward pleasures of the world, that is, against *hylē* and its charms.

For the catechumens (auditors) there were ten commandments which have not been preserved uniformly. The decalogue encompassed the prohibition against killing, lying, making false accusations, leading an unchaste life, stealing, and engaging in black magic. In the *X^uāstvānīft*, the commandments for the auditors are summed up in four groups: three of the mouth (pertaining to speech), three of the heart (pertaining to thought), three of the hands (pertaining to actions), and one "of the whole self." The list given in the *X^uāstvānīft*, however, is a number of examples of sinfulness rather than a set of sins to be avoided. According to aš-Šahrastānī (192,8), the Golden Rule was included in the commandments for auditors. Ibn an-Nadīm (64,12ff.) has left us a list which might be close to the original commandments.

Of great importance, however, is the fact that Manichaean ethics is not exhaustively expressed by prohibitions and regulations; it also encompassed positive values. These values are concretized and particularized in the analogies between the saving deities and their virtues. Thus the Four-fold Father is related to Love, Fear (of God), Faith, and Wisdom; these can be referred to as the four divine qualities, and called "the four bright seals." In fact, the whole system of gods, with its various series of deities, appears as a representation and illustration of such values or virtues. These values are traced in all their ramifications in the *Traité,* where the "tree of life," with its roots, branches, flowers, and fruits is contrasted with the "tree of death," and all these elements are interpreted religiously and ethically.[74] Here it becomes obvious that, in spite of all orientation toward the other world, ethical values are meant to have concrete meaning in life, to the extent that they display "signs" in the lives of men.

THE CULT

The cult's most important forms of expression were regular prayers, services, and fasts. Within this cultic setting the hymns had their place, their *Sitz im Leben* ("seat in life"). There were seven two-day fasts (*yimki*-fasts) every year, which had developed out of five two-day periods of commemoration of specific "martyrs" of the Church, including the first "martyr," the First Man. In the seven *yimki* days, to which an-Nadīm's *Fihrist* (64,5) also attests, specific deities and Church leaders were commemorated: 1. the First Man, 2. Mār Sīsin (Mani's successor), 3. Jesus, 4.–6. three "presbyters," and 7. Mani. Besides these days, which were also days of prayer, there was—as in Islam later on—a month of fasting.[75] This was probably the "Major Fast" (Turk. *uluγ bačaγ*), as opposed to the "Minor Fast" (*kičig bačaγ*), which referred to the two-day periods of fasting.[76] Part of a liturgy for such a "Minor Fast" is preserved (cf. ch. XXV, text 2).

Ritual prayer had its place within the days of fasting as well as in other cultic acts. According to the *Fihrist* (64,15ff.), four or seven daily prayers were prescribed (for elect and auditors respectively). Such prayers included hymns of praise to the Father of Light and the saving deities, including Jesus and Mani. Of course prayers also played a role in weekly services, along with hymns, scripture readings, sermons, and so on.[77] We hear little of freely formulated or spontaneous prayers, but of course there must have been some, as there are in every religion. On the whole, however, spiritual life took avail of and leaned on the traditional patterns of prayer that had developed over the course of centuries. The prayers and hymns collected in this volume were used in the Monday ritual (equivalent to the Christian Sunday service), in the ritual of weekly confessions, on the fast days mentioned, at the sacred meal of the elect, and on other religious festivals. Of these, the Bema festival was of special importance. It was celebrated in commemoration of Mani's death, on the thirtieth day of the month of fasting. The Western Manichaeans celebrated it in lieu of Easter.[78] We cannot rule out the possibility that it took the place of a high Buddhist festival in the East, since the Parthian Bema hymns speak of the Realm of Light, which Mani entered as *Nirvāṇa*.

In spite of the liturgical character of our texts, they do not by any means reflect only an ossified ritualism, even though they include various schematically formulated hymns and prayers. The majority of our documents are inspired by the living spring of a very authentic and original religiosity. No less an authority than W. B. Henning, who was to do so much to make these documents accessible philologically, noted, "Among the texts there are prose pieces (of literature) and especially hymns full of fervor and religious devotion, full of ardent desire for the salvation promised, the powerful words of which can touch our hearts even today. Maybe they stem from an earlier period. But it is they that give us the right to concern ourselves earnestly with Central Asian Manichaeism, unless we were to study these fragments only to fill a gap in our knowledge of Iranian languages."[79]

Notes

1. H. Jonas, *The Gnostic Religion: The Message of the Alien God and the Beginnings of Christianity.* 2d ed. (Boston, 1963), p. 206.
2. Jonas, *op. cit.*, p. 207.
3. Jonas, *ibid.*
4. Jonas, *ibid.*
5. Jonas, *op. cit.*, pp. 207f.
6. L. Koenen and C. Römer, *Der Kölner Mani-Kodex.* Opladen, 1988. Partial English translation in D. Cameron and A. J. Dewey, *The Cologne Mani Codex.*
7. Cf. R. Merkelbach, "Die Täufer, bei denen Mani aufwuchs," in Bryder, ed., *Manichaean Studies,* pp. 105–33.
8. For a critical evaluation of Manichaean, mainly Iranian, material on his life, compare W. Sundermann, "Studien zur kirchengeschichtlichen Literatur der iranischen Manichäer I–III," *AoF* 13 (1986), pp. 4–92, 239–317; 14 (1987), pp. 41–107.
9. Jonas, *op. cit.*, p. 208.
10. Polotsky, "Manichäismus," cols. 240–71, esp. col. 241.
11. Sundermann, "Prosaliteratur," p. 240.
12. Cf. Sims-Williams, "Indian Elements in Parthian and Sogdian," pp. 132ff.
13. Cf. Klimkeit, "Buddhistische Übernahmen," pp. 58ff.
14. Cf. H. Schmidt-Glintzer, "Das buddhistische Gewand des Manichäismus," pp. 76ff.; Bryder, *The Chinese Transformation of Manichaeism.*
15. Compare the description of the Realm of Light, as we find it in the Parthian hymn cycles (of which at least *Huyadagmān* I was probably composed by Mār Ammō), and the account of Amitābha's Western Paradise in the Greater and Smaller *Sukhāvativyūha.* Cf. F. M. Müller, *Buddhist Mahāyāna Texts.* 1891; repr. Delhi 1965 (SBE XLIX, Part II.).
16. Polotsky, "Manichäismus," col. 245.

17. Cf. Jonas, *Gnosis und spätantiker Geist* I. 3d ed., pp. 250f.
18. Cf. Polotsky, "Manichäismus," col. 245.
19. Cf. Jonas, *The Gnostic Religion.*
20. Boyce, *Reader,* p. 10.
21. Cf. Bryder, *The Chinese Transformation of Manichaeism,* pp. 124f.; 128ff.
22. Cf. Asmussen, *X^uāstvānīft,* p. 12. In this connection Asmussen speaks of "the Manichaean principle of identity."
23. For this term compare Asmussen, *X^uāstvānīft,* pp. 220f.
24. Polotsky points out that the temporal, eschatological concept "Aeon" is used by Mani in a spatial sense, which suggested itself by the corresponding Syrian term *'alma.'* Compare Polotsky, "Manichäische Studien," p. 260.
25. Cf. Widengren, *Die Religionen Irans,* pp. 283–95; Zaehner, *Zurvan,* pp. 96ff.
26. Polotsky, "Manichäismus," col. 249.
27. The Turkish texts speak of the God of Ether and others.
28. Polotsky, "Manichäismus," col. 253.
29. Cf. Türk. Man. I, 19–20 (text T I δ). A Pth. text reflecting such an image of the First Man is the cosmogonic hymn S 13 and S 9. Compare ch. II, text 6.
30. Cf. Türk. Man. III, 12 (text T II D 173b,2).
31. Cf. Klimkeit, "Manichaean Kingship," pp. 18–32.
32. Polotsky, "Manichäismus," col. 254.
33. Boyce, *Reader,* p. 6.
34. Correspondences can obtain, however, to the groups of seven and twelve deities and virtues.
35. *Mir. Man.* I, pp. 195–99.
36. Here the figure of the Maiden of Light appears as a female form of the Third Messenger.
37. Boyce, *Reader,* p. 71 (MP. text).
38. This is the *psychē* that is connected with the body.
39. Cf. Gershevitch, "Beauty as the Living Soul."
40. For Jesus in Manichaeism, compare Rose, *Die manichäische Christologie.* Wiesbaden, 1979, summarized in Rose, "Die manichäische Christologie."
41. Cf. Polotsky, "Manichäische Studien," p. 254.
42. Cf. MacKenzie, "Mani's *Šābuhragān* I, II."
43. Boyce points out, though, that this term could also refer to the Great Nous (Boyce, *Word-List,* s.v.), whose activity nevertheless is closely connected with that of Jesus.
44. For docetic christology, compare P. Weigand, *Der Doketismus im Urchristentum.* Dr. theol. thesis, Heidelberg, 1961; B. Blatz, *Studien zur gnostischen Erlösergestalt.* Dr. phil. thesis, Bonn, 1985.
45. Boyce, *Reader,* p. 10.
46. Boyce, *ibid.* Recently, P. Nagel, in a forthcoming article ("Wie gnostisch ist die Gnosis des Mani?") has underscored the fact that "Jesus the Messiah" is portrayed as a true person even in his suffering, and that Mani's conception of him is therefore not completely Gnostic.
47. C. Schmid and H.-J. Polotsky, *Mani-Fund,* p. 68.
48. Türk. Man. III, 36.
49. For the Manichaean teaching about the Old and the New Man, compare Klimkeit, "Die manichäische Lehre vom alten und vom neuen Menschen."
50. Polotsky, "Manichäismus," col. 258.
51. Türk. Man. III, 12.
52. We are reminded here of Luther's dictum which, employing Pauline terminology, says that the Old Man (in us) must be "drowned" anew every day.
53. Arnold-Döben, *Die Bildersprache des Manichäismus,* pp. 154f.
54. Zieme, *Texte,* p. 39.
55. Polotsky, "Manichäismus," col. 60. For this concept in Iranian religion, compare C. Colpe, "Daēnā, Lichtjungfrau, zweite Gestalt."

56. Cf. Arnold-Döben, *op. cit.*, pp. 149ff.

57. Cf. Arnold-Döben, *op. cit.*, pp. 151ff.

58. This image is vividly preserved in the "Hymn of the Pearl," in the Acts of Thomas, origi- nally a Syrian work of the third century (compare E. Hennecke and W. Schneemelcher, *New Testament Apocrypha* II, pp. 498–564). In Zoroastrian imagery, the soul of the unrighteous is met by a wretched old hag, symbol of its evil deeds. Compare Colpe, *op. cit.*, pp. 58ff.; compare also the imagery of the demoness referred to previously.

59. Cf. A. de Santos Otero, "Apocalypse of Thomas," in Hennecke and Schneemelcher, *op. cit.*, pp. 798–803. For a detailed study of Manichaean eschatology and apocalypticism, com- pare L. Koenen, "Manichaean Apocalypticism at the Crossroads of Iranian, Egyptian, Jewish and Christian Thought"; in addition M. Hutter, "Das Erlösungsgeschehen im iranisch-manichäischen Mythos," in K. M. Woschitz, M. Hutter and K. Prunner, *Das manichäische Urdrama des Lichts,* pp. 153–236.

60. For a succinct sketch of Manichaean eschatology compare Polotsky, "Manichäismus," col. 261f.

61. Cf. Haloun and Henning, "Compendium," pp. 201ff.

62. Cf. Sims-Williams, "Commandments."

63. Polotsky, "Manichäismus," col. 262.

64. This idea seems to have influenced Buddhism in Central Asia. In a Turkish Buddhist text from Turfan (T II D 200), exactly this idea is expressed. Compare Zieme, "Uigurische Steuerbefreiungsurkunden für buddhistische Klöster," *AoF* 8 (1981), p. 242, n. 6.

65. Sundermann, *Texte,* p. 61.

66. Cf. *Mir. Man.* II, p. 302. Compare also to this text (M 2) Sundermann, *Texte,* pp. 17f.

67. Cf. Zieme, "Ein uigurischer Text über die Wirtschaft manichäischer Klöster im uigurischen Reich," in *Researches in Altaic Languages.* Budapest, 1975, pp. 331–38.

68. Türk. Man. I, pp. 26f.

69. In a Turkish text (TM 512) which requires the laymen even to provide a house for the elect, the drastic consequences of failing to give alms are depicted in terms of punishment in hell. Türk. Man. III, pp. 28f.

70. Polotsky, "Manichäismus," col. 263.

71. Cf. K. Sagaster, *Die weiße Geschichte,* pp. 9–49.

72. Thus it says in the colophon to the "Book of the Two Principles" (*Iki yiltiz nom*), "It (this book) was recited with great joy and written down with deep love. . . ." Türk. Man. I, p. 25.

73. Cf. N. Sims-Williams, "Commandments."

74. Cf. Schmidt-Glintzer, *Chinesische Manichaica,* pp. 87ff., 94ff.; Arnold-Döben, "Die Sym- bolik des Baumes im Manichäismus," pp. 10ff.

75. For the Manichaean feasts and fasts compare Henning, "The Manichaean Fasts"; Asmus- sen, *Xᵘāstvānīft,* pp. 224ff.

76. Cf. Zieme, "Zu einigen Problemen des Manichäismus bei den Türken," p. 175.

77. Cf. Schmidt and Polotsky, *Mani-Fund,* pp. 31ff.; Sundermann, "Die Prosaliteratur der iranischen Manichäer."

78. For the Bema festival compare Alberry, "Das manichäische Bema-Fest," and Asmussen, *Xᵘāstvānīft,* pp. 227ff.

79. Henning, "Zum zentralasiatischen Manichäismus," p. 11.

Iranian Texts

CHAPTER ONE

Hymns to the Father of Light

The texts on the Father of Light and the Realm of Light in this chapter are hymns of praise. The poet addresses the Father of Greatness with laudatory invocations. With his spiritual eye, he envisions the whole glorious Realm of Light, with its radiant, perfect divine figures. Everything in that Realm is noble, wrought with wondrous power and perfection, especially the beings of Light, who are endowed with a perfect form. This form, for which the poet yearns, is the heavenly garb that replaces the earthly garment of the body when the soul sheds the "husk" (MP *niδāmag*) of its physical form upon death. Hence the garments which clothe the soul before and after death, in the earthly realm and the Realm of Light, are indicative of an existential situation. The yearning for the heavenly garb or form reflects the desire for an existence other than the earthly one. The perfect form (MP *čihrag*) and the noble shape (MP *pādgirb*) that the Father of Light bestows upon the beings in his Realm stand in marked contrast to the "loathsome body" of the soul on earth, as well as to the terrifying forms of the evil powers here, which express their absolutely loathsome and repulsive nature. The presence of these beings heightens the longing for a different state of existence, where all is fair of form.

The Father of Light Himself is not described anywhere. He is the source and origin of all divine beings endowed with perfect form; He is the Highest Being, encompassing all forms. Nevertheless it becomes clear in these hymns that He, too, has a radiant appearance and a shining beauty, which surpass those of everything that exists in the noble Realm. He is not seen directly, but He presents Himself through the divine forms He has created "by his word," that is, spiritually. These are "the Twelve Greatnesses" or "Twelve Aeons" that surround Him as His twelve "Sons," three in each direction. In addition, He has an entourage of resplendent gods and deities. In His presence, and in the Realm of Light, which encompasses an infinite number of "worlds" or "aeons," existence is perfect being and the fullness of life. Accordingly, the Divine Realm is described in mythological terms as pure, bright, beautiful, calm, and joyful. "Ambrosia" and "fragrance" are characteristics

of such an existence. When the poet invokes the Father as "the Primeval Ancestor,"
he expresses his own spiritual relationship with the beings of the Divine Realm, and
hence with the Divine Family, even though the feeling of great distance from it is
occasionally depicted in temporal and spatial terms. The poet can understand himself as belonging to "the Family of Light," for the five "limbs" of his soul correspond
to the five "limbs" of the Father, from whom he has issued. By singing the praises
of the Father of Light he anticipates the communion with Him and those that surround Him, "the community of the beings of Light."

1. Verses from Mani's Psalm "The Praise of the Great Ones" (Parthian)

These verses stem from one of the two long Psalms Mani wrote in Aramaic. Portions are preserved in Parthian translations. The Coptic *Psalm-Book* (*PsB* 47,140)
makes reference to these Psalms.

(Title):   [Praise] of the Great Ones

> . . . Praised and glorified are you, Father!
> —You are the Living One and the First One, the Original One, the
> Superior One, the Ruler of Light, the Zealous One among the holy
> beings and the Strong One.[1]
> You are the Father of all these fair forms (*karišn*), jewels, strong ones
> of Light and mighty ones[2] that have been called forth [from you];
> they gain strength from you, . . .

2. Verses from Mani's Psalm "The Praise of the Lesser Ones" (Parthian)

These verses stem from the second Psalm of Mani written originally in Aramaic.
The "Praise of the Lesser (lit., Small) Ones" (*Qšūdagān Afrīvān*) complements the
"Praise of the Great Ones" (*Vuzurgān Afrīvān*).[3]

> 1.   . . . Eternally shall we praise you, we and our kin, who are chosen, and
> the family (*nāf*), to which we belong, (that is) those that are of
> you.[4]
> 2.   Father, we would call upon you, we would lift up (our) eyes to you. Our
> souls (*gyānān*) sing before you, so that you may be merciful to us
> in your great mercy, so that you may send us the helper . . .
> [*some verses missing*]
> 3.   [Holy, Holy], to your twelve Worlds of Light.[5]
> Holy, Holy to the Worlds of Light that are appointed as jewels by your
> Greatness,[6]
> Holy to the Living Ether,[7] the bright storeroom of the wonderful
> worlds,
> Holy, Holy, Holy to the praised Earth,
> Holy to the bright appearance (*dīdan*) of the blessed inhabitants . . .
> [*some verses missing*]

4. Holy, Holy to your Greatness, you highest of all epiphanies,[8]
   And to (your) bright beauty which is immeasurable.
   Holy, Holy to you, [Father]!
   Holy, Holy, Holy, Holy to your praised reign!
   Holy, Holy, Holy, to you, Father!
   Holy to your chosen name!
   Holy, Holy, Holy to you, Father!
   Holy, Holy, Holy, . . .
   [*some verses missing*]
5. Holy, Holy, Holy to your great Thought (*andēšišn*)[9] from which every
   beneficial and zealous thought has arisen.
   Holy to your great Understanding (*parmānag*)[10] from which every bene-
   ficial and zealous understanding has arisen.
   Holy, Holy, Holy to you, Father!
   Holy to your great and praised Ether[11] that is above all ethers in the
   world.

3. *Verses from a Hymn on the Father of Light* (Parthian)

Here a portion of a hymn is preserved in which the Father of Light and the deities
surrounding him are invoked.

1. . . . He holds the twelve diadems of Light, and before Him stand twelve
   great ones,
   His own sons, like twelve bright forms (*čihrag*) of the Father of Light.[12]
2. Many gods, deities and jewels[13] have been created, called forth and set
   up as attendants of the Lord of Paradise. And beside them (there
   are) the twelve great firstborn kings and rulers.[14]
   [*some verses missing*]
3. . . . Strong One, Superior One among the gods, Lord of the great ones,
   most divine of gods! Praise to (that) God, oh Glory of Lights
   (*rošnān farrah*)![15] Exalted is the praised Realm of Light where you
   dwell, pure and bright, beautiful and calm, full of joy, peace and
   hope, life, ambrosia and fragrance . . .

4. *Verses from a Hymn on the Realm of Light* (Parthian)

These verses apparently stem from a hymn in honor of all gods in the Realm of
Light.

1. . . . Those worlds . . . (and) messengers (*freštagān*) that have come into
   being from Him, all with souls in one accord bring [praise] to that
   bright form (*dīdan*) and wonderful epiphany (*pādgirb*). So we, too,
   together with them and with all (others) shall worship with bended
   knee and shall pray for blessing . . .
   [*some verses missing*]

2. With the five thoughts (*panj parmānag*)[16] [we invoke] the Mother of the
    Righteous, the Father, the God Ohrmizd, together with the five
    Bright Ones,[17] the Friend of the Lights, the wonderful God of
    Brightness,[18] and the Living Spirit with (his) five sons, . . .[19]

5. Verses from a Hymn to the Father of Greatness (Parthian)

This text consists of the first seven verses of an abecedarian hymn. They are composed according to the letters of the Syriac alphabet, from which the scripts used
by the Manichaeans are derived. The initial verse is not related to any particular
letter. Since verses *alif* to *zain* are preserved, sixteen verses must have followed.

(-) You are worthy of praise, beneficent Father, primeval Ancestor!
     Blessed are you, beneficent God!

(') You, Lord, are the first *alif* and the last *tau*.[20]
     Through you yourself your pious wish has been fulfilled and
        accomplished.

(b) All gods and aeons, the deities of Light,
     And the righteous bring praise (to you), singing "holy" repeatedly.

(g) The spirits (*gyānān*), the plants and all . . . truly implore (you) for
        blessing
     And bring forth supplications with one voice.

(d) Grant us (our) pious wish, . . .
     They bear the form (*čihrag*)[21] that we have [given up] from afar.[22]

(h) Be merciful unto us in (your) mercy;
     Show us your form (*čihrag*), the noble epiphany (*pādgirb*), for which we
        yearn.

(v) Let your brightness shine upon us, sweet source and breath of life!
     Make us, (your) children, strong.[23]

(z) In vain the dark foe boasts, together with the bellicose, rebellious
        giants,
     In vain he wishes to cling to the Aeons.

     . . .

6. Verses from a Hymn on Paradise and the Father of Greatness (Parthian)

These are the last verses of an abecedarian hymn (*ain* to *tau* and a last verse on
n) in which the Paradise of Light, with its Radiant Earth and Radiant Air, is
described, and the Father of Greatness is invoked. Since the last verse prays for
blessing for Mani and his disciple Mār Zaku, the hymn does not belong to the earliest period.

1. . . . The immortal, fragrant Breeze (Air) (p) attends the gods together
       with the Earth and (its) trees. (c) The source of Light, the blessed
       plants, (k) the echoing, bright mountains of divine nature[24] (are

wonderful). (r) The house of the jewels (gods) is a place full of
blossoms, (š) with countless lands, houses and thrones . . .

2. (t) You are worthy of praise, highest King.
3. (n) Honor and praise to the Lord Mani of good name! Blessed, blessed
be, on this Great New Year's Day,[25] the Teacher Mār Zaku with the
whole Assembly of Light.[26]

Notes

1. These words in the third person were probably sung antiphonally.
2. All references to the gods in the Realm of Light.
3. For *qšūdagān* as "Lesser (lit., Small) Ones," compare Sundermann, "Der chinesische Traité Manichéen," p. 233, n. 1.
4. S sees in this phrase a two-fold emanation: one, gods that emanate from the Father, and two, men that emanate from the gods.
5. These are the twelve Aeons or Great Ones surrounding the Father.
6. Or, "who appointed fitting jewels in your Greatness" (S).
7. Literally, Air. In the Realm of Light there is a "Radiant Earth" (*terra ingenita*) and a "Radiant Air" (*aer ingenitus*).
8. Literally, appearances.
9. I.e., the fourth limb of the soul. In the gap above, probably the first three limbs were named: reason (Pth. *bām*), mind (Pth. *manohmēd*), and intelligence (Pth. *uš*).
10. This is the first limb of the soul.
11. Literally, Air.
12. These are the twelve Aeons that surround the Father. In Chinese Manichaean texts they are called "the twelve jewel kings of Light." The series consists of the five "Light Elements," the five "gifts" and the Gods Call and Response (Answer).
13. Another word for "gods."
14. Again a reference to the twelve Aeons.
15. A "glory" (*farrah*), usually a divine *alter ego,* is here ascribed to every being in the Realm of Light.
16. I.e., the five "limbs of the soul."
17. I.e., the five sons of the First Man.
18. I.e., the Great Builder.
19. This is a list of the twelve Light Dominions.
20. I.e., the first and the last letter of the Aramaic alphabet. Cf. Rev. 22:13.
21. Or, They have the nature. . . .
22. This is a reference to the divine form man has lost by being clothed in a body. In the Realm of Light, this bodily garment will be exchanged for a heavenly one, which represents the completeness of form.
23. Or, and make thy children strong.
24. The echo of the mountains is a reponse to the praise of God (S).
25. The celebration of the New Year's Day is originally Iranian. Compare Boyce, "On the Calendar of the Zoroastrian Feasts."
26. I.e., the Manichaean community, including the powers of the Realm of Light.

CHAPTER TWO

Hymns on Cosmogony and Eschatology

1. *Hymn on the Father of Greatness and His Creation* (Parthian)

Cosmogony, the account of the creation of the cosmos, and eschatology, the description of its final events, provide the setting for world events and the framework within which man can understand his own existence. The knowledge of the origin of the world and of man, and of their present state and future destiny, is part and parcel of the *gnosis* that leads to redemption. On the basis of such knowledge, man can understand his present condition as one that can be overcome by returning, ultimately, to a primal state of affiliation to and participation in a heavenly, perfect world. Man has lost his original, true being. This occurred at the beginning of time, when the five sons of the First Man, who ultimately *are* the limbs of his soul, succumbed to the power of dark forces. They rent apart the soul and greedily devoured it, finally banishing it into the earthly body. But everyone who has *gnosis* knows of his heavenly origin and has intimations of the beauty, peace, and joy of the transcendent World of Light from which he comes. At the same time, however, he becomes aware of the terror of the Realm of Darkness, whose driving forces are lust and avarice, and where wrath and strife prevail. There the horror of an existence remote from God manifests itself in the terrible, threatening demonic and bestial forms. Vivid and forceful images like poisonous springs, smoky fog, and burning fire describe this godless existence where the powers of evil hold sway. In the classical Manichaean understanding of the world, signified by the fate of the First Man in the myth, the soul is delivered into the hands of such powers. And yet, like the First Man, man can hope for salvation from the prison of such a woeful existence. As the First Man "saved his own Light" by responding to the "Call" from the other world, and ascended to the heights, so too can man be redeemed if he responds to the message, the Call, as it was and is brought by the Third Messenger, in the form of the Nous or Jesus. As the Third Messenger bound and vanquished many demons, according to the myth man can set his hope on his saving power. In the following hymns, the saving power of the Third Messenger (who appears as the Nous, or Jesus the Splendor) is—quite in contrast to classical Manichaean mythology—also ascribed to the First Man, who is said to have opened the way of salvation for all souls. The redeeming work thus ascribed to him will be fulfilled, the devout are convinced, when Jesus appears again on earth to usher in a renewal of the world. At that time the power of Darkness, especially as it affects the hearts of men, will be vanquished, and "the Dark thought," the source and origin of all sin, will be displaced while the Light is ultimately liberated.[1] The verses on the Triumph of Light (text 8) lend expression to this conviction.

Three verses of an abecedarian hymn about the Father of Greatness and the deities he created (or rather evoked) in the Realm of Light are preserved here. The text was preceded by four verses and followed by sixteen (with a final verse on *n*).

(h) [All the gods] and deities were evoked [and established] by Him;
       All rejoice in him and [give] him honor.
(v) The Land of Light . . . by its five pure thoughts;[2]
       It is fragrant with sweet-smelling breezes; it shines in all regions.
(z) Powers, gods and deities, jewels, joyful Aeons,
       Trees, springs and plants rejoice in Him every day.

2. Verses on the King of Darkness and Hell (Parthian)

Here are eight verses preserved from an abecedarian hymn. Three verses must have preceded our text, and six (with a final verse on *n*) must have followed it. Because of gaps in the text, eight other verses are missing.

(d) The hideous demon (*dēv*) . . . and the (ugly) form (*čihrag*);
(h) He scorches, he destroys, . . . and he terrifies,
(v) He flies on wings as of air. He swims with fins as in water. And he
       crawls like a being of Darkness.
(z) He is armed on his four limbs, to repel the children of fire, rushing
       upon him like the beings of Hell.[3]
(j) Poisonous springs gush forth from him, and he exhales [smoky] fog;[4]
       (his) [claws] and teeth[5] are [like] daggers.
       [*eight verses missing or damaged*]
(s) They (the beings of Hell) rot upon a couch of darkness; in lust and in
       pursuit of desire they give birth to each other and then destroy
       each other.
(') The bellicose Prince of Darkness has subjugated the five pits of death
       through great . . . terror and wrath,
(p) He has spurted forth streams of (deadly) poison and wickedness from
       the depth . . .

3. Verses about the Battle of the First Man (Parthian)

Here are the first five verses preserved from an abecedarian hymn on the First Man and his battle against Darkness. The lines in the manuscript preceding our text belong to a discourse mentioning Maitreya, the future Buddha. However, the title of that discourse is not preserved. Nine verses must have followed our text.

(') Out of pity . . .
     He (First Man) put on a body . . .
(b) The first garb of [the God] Ohrmizd;
     When he had clothed the enemy with (his) five sons,
(g) He surrendered (his) soul to the Darkness;
     He sacrificed his own soul;
     He scattered[6] (his limbs) for the sake of (his) sons.
(d) He bound the enemies, he brought (his) sons to life,
     And with gentleness he redeemed the Kingdom.[7]
(h) [Then] came the beneficent Father[8] [with his] brothers[9]
     And [saved] his own Light.[10]
          [*six verses missing or badly preserved*]
(k) [He who] had understanding and remembered everything,
     The first, the intermediate and the final things:
(l) (His) lips and tongue responded
     And he uttered great praises with . . . his mouth.
(m) He revealed the path of salvation and the road of purity
     [To all] souls who were in harmony with him.
(n) The worlds no longer wait (in vain) . . .
     For (their) coveted good . . .

4. *Verses from a Hymn on the Third Messenger and the Archons* (Parthian)

This is the second part of an abecedarian hymn describing the seduction of the Archons and the redemption of Light. Fifteen verses must have preceded our text.

(') He (the Third Messenger) takes the Light away from them (the
         demons) in many forms and fashions, by gentle means and harsh.
         He releases the captives from bondage.
(p) He purifies His own life and he exhorts them[11] to approach the visible
         form (*dīdan*) and to follow (its) appearance (*pādgirb*).
(c) Bright Sadvēs[12] shows her form (*čihrag*) to the Demon of Wrath.
         She seduces him with (her) own appearance, (and) he thinks it
         is real.[13]
(q) He sows (his seed),[14] . . . he groans[15] when he no longer sees her form.
         Light is born in the sphere of the world; she passes it on to the
         higher powers.
(r) Filth and dross flow from him[16] to the earth. They clothe themselves in
         manifold forms (*dīdan*) and are reborn in many fruits.
(š) The dark Demon of Wrath is ashamed, for in his confusion he had
         become naked. He[17] had not attained the heights,[18] and he had
         been robbed of whatever he had achieved.

(t)   He left the body an empty shell and descended in shame. He was
      clothed in the womb of the earths, from where he had risen in
      brutishness.
      [*final verse on* n *badly preserved*]

5. *Verses from a Hymn about the Captivity of Light* (Parthian)

The first seven verses of an abecedarian hymn on the Captivity of Light by the
powers of Darkness and the creation of man's body as its prison are preserved.
Eighteen verses (with a verse on *j* and final *n*) must have followed.

(')   Lo, that great Kingdom of Salvation [waits] on high,
      Ready for those who have *gnosis,* so that they may finally find peace
           there.
(b)   Sinful, dark Pēsūs[19] runs hither and thither brutishly,
      She gives no peace at all to the upper and the lower limbs (of Light);[20]
(g)   She seizes and binds the Light in the six great bodies,
      In earth, water and fire, wind, plants and animals.[21]
(d)   She fashions it into many forms; she molds it into many figures;
      She fetters it in a prison so that it may not ascend to the height.
(h)   She weaves (a net) around it on all sides, she piles it up; she sets a
           watchman over it.
      Greed and lust are made its fellow-captives.[22]
(v)   She mixes destructive air[23] into those six great bodies.
      She nurtures her own body but destroys their sons.
(z)   The powers of Light on high confuse all the demons of wrath,
      The sons of that Pēsūs,[24] who is in a higher place.[25]
      [*three further verses badly preserved*]

6. *Cosmogonical Hymn* (Persian with Parthian words)

This is a poetic rendering of the Manichaean creation myth, in the form of an
abecedarian hymn. Eight verses preceding our text are missing, in which the Realm
of Light and the Realm of Darkness were probably described. The preserved text
deals with the origin of the world and the creation and redemption of man.

1. (ḫ)   ... That king of the demons (*devān*) [was moved] towards the Light [by]
          envy.
   (t)   ... He wished ... to seize ... this ... mighty ... warlike one (the First
          Man).
   (y)   God, the [highest] of the gods, Zurvān, ... [was] convulsed in bat-
          tle ... with darkness, poison and [bur]ning.[26]
          [*four verses missing or badly preserved*]
2. (s)   Āz, (the Demoness of Greed), [that] evil mother of all demons, grew
          angry,[27] and she stirred up great turmoil to aid her own soul (*grīv*).

('for') And from the impurity of the demons and from the filth of the she-demons she fashioned the body and entered into it herself.

(p) Then she formed the good soul (*gyān*) from the five Light Elements, the armor of the Lord Ohrmizd, and bound it within the body.

(c) She (*Āz*) made him (the first person) as though blind and deaf, senseless and confused, so that he might not know his origin and his family.[28]

(q) She created the body as the prison, she fettered the miserable soul (*gyān*). (It cried out): "The captors, the demons, she-demons and all the she-devils, are cruel to me."[29]

(r) She fettered the soul firmly to the accursed body; she filled it with hate and sin, anger and vengeance.

3. (-) Then Ohrmizd, the Lord, had mercy upon the souls (*gyānān*). And he descended to the earth in the [form] of man.[30]

(š) He put to shame the evil (Demoness) *Āz;* he made visible to him (Adam) and clearly showed him all that had been and that was to be.

(t) In a flash he revealed to him that Ohrmizd, the Lord, had not himself created this fleshly body and had not fettered the soul.

4. (-) Resurrection[31] was the destiny of the discerning soul of (that) fortunate one (Adam). He believed in the message of Ohrmizd, the good Lord. He eagerly accepted all the commandments, ordinances and seals[32] of virtue,[33] like a mighty hero; he put off the mortal body and was redeemed eternally. He was lifted up to Paradise, to the Realm of the Blessed.

7. *Hymn about the Second Coming of Jesus* (Persian with Parthian words)

In this text, Jesus is asked about his Second Coming by a boy, an incarnation of the *"enthymēsis* of life." There follows a prophecy about the signs and time of his appearance. This is also an abecedarian hymn. The two last verses are missing.

1. (') Speak to me, Lord and Friend, and reveal to me, Son of the most Beloved,[34] the time of your coming, when you will appear at the end.

(b) Oh great Redeemer, my Teacher, speak of that time and its signs.

2. (g) The speakers, the righteous and chosen ones, who (must) live in the Realm of the Lie,[35]

(d) Do not accumulate herds and belongings. Therefore they are persecuted.

3. (h) Ha, this irate potentate! How long will he continue to rule?

(v) How long will the poor and the Family of Peace[36] be persecuted?

(z) Tell me what reward the wise and righteous ones that are (now) persecuted will have.

(ḥ) You of compassionate race, tell of the (coming) subjugation of the sinners that are (now) exalted.[37]

4. (ṭ) The strong and valiant Son of the Most Beloved told (lit., taught) me what I had asked him:

(y)   That time, the coming years and periods, will be different (from now),
      because of the ensuing battles.[38]

(k)   (For) they (the years) shall flow like water in the rivers.[39] (Now) that
      time is near at hand.

(r for l)   The covetous heretics that now rejoice
            Shall you (then) vanquish, you Wrathful One.

(m)   They will be persecuted, as they have persecuted,
      And they shall do penance for all their offences.

(n)   (Then) shall those who have wept be joyful,
      And those who now laugh weep.

(s)   He who is grieved and (belongs to) the Family of Peace
      Shall be rewarded with prosperity and protection.

('for')   Then this righteous religion (dēn)[40]
          Shall hold sway over (false) teachings and nations.

(p)   Then shall the springs of Living Water
      Open their mouths in praise.

5. (c)   Lament, give honor and praise, for the time is near,
         Of which (these are) the signs.

(x for q)   . . .[41] the annointed,
            The vīhidān (?) of the Ruler are called.

(r)   Persecution and suppression shall (then) be recompensed [by] eternal
      life.

8. *Verses on the Triumph of Light* (Parthian)

This is the second half of an abecedarian hymn on the conquest of darkness and
the Triumph of Light. Thirteen verses must have preceded our text. Of these, only
some are preserved, in bad condition.

(n)   . . . They will be joined together, the limbs,[42] . . . [to] the New Aeon
      (*šahr navāg*), the Land of Greatness.

(s)   They (the New Paradise[43] and the eternal Realm of Light) will be
      united into one, like a single rock and a single body, eternally,
      securely and for ever.

(')   The demon of Darkness will be buried together with his abyss within
      that new and noble building.[44]

(p)   They will make it (the New Paradise) just like (that) eternal Land of
      Light, with divine streams springing and sweet winds blowing
      through it.

(?)   For the nature (redeemed Light) . . . they will prepare thrones, [and]
      they will . . . in the New Aeons.

(q)   They will make and establish many splendid thrones for the Last
      Prince,[45] together with all the Fathers, the [prosperous] gods.

(r)   All the beings of Light, the righteous (elect) and the auditors, who have
      endured much suffering, will rejoice with the Father.[46]

(š)　They will be glad and rejoice, and they will reign over His foes and the rebels in the New Aeon.

(t)　For they have fought together with Him,[47] and they have overcome and vanquished that Dark One who had boasted (in vain).

Notes

1. For a fragment of a hymn on the eschatological events in which the Living Spirit plays a decisive role, compare Sundermann, "Some More Remarks on Mithra," pp. 487–89. Here it says, "And also that Dark *enthymesis* [i. e. "the thought of death," the moribund thought], the producer of every sin, [who, by way] of that [terrib]le (?) shape, produces her [ter]rible gang, . . . they will throw her into that furnace and prison, and into eternal bonds, which are made by the Light Architect [i. e. the Great Builder] in the rea[lm] of the [Light] Nou[s], i. e. the New Para[dise], the resting-place of the warlike powers. And *Mihr-yazd* [i. e. the Third Messenger] will bind her with those fast bonds."
2. I. e., its five spiritual realms corresponding to the five limbs of the soul.
3. Translation doubtful.
4. Cf. *Kephalaia* 78, 3–10.
5. After a reading suggested by S.
6. Or, loosened.
7. I. e., the Light scattered in Darkness.
8. I. e., First Man, or the Living Spirit.
9. I. e., the saving deities.
10. The verses *d* and *h* as well as the following verses anticipate the victory over the demons, ascribing it, as in other Central Asian texts, to the First Man.
11. I. e., the Archons fettered in the sky.
12. I. e., the Maiden of Light.
13. Being but her appearance, it is not real.
14. I. e., he lets his seed fall.
15. The groaning of the demons is heard on earth as thunder.
16. I. e., the Demon of Wrath.
17. I. e., the Dark Demon. He "represents in this verse the active spirit of Hyle, which now abandons the fettered Archontes to inhabit the earth." Boyce, "Sadwēs and Pēsūs," p. 912, n. 8.
18. Literally, what is higher.
19. The name of the female animal in the Realm of Darkness that gives birth to the first human pair.
20. I. e., the elements of Light.
21. I. e., "the four elements of Greek philosophy (fire, air, water, earth) with the addition of plants and animals." Boyce, *op. cit.*, p. 913, n. 4.
22. I. e., "the particles of Light were shut into the human body with evil desires." Boyce, *op. cit.,* 914, n. 3.
23. I. e., one of the five Dark Elements.
24. B points out that phrases like "Hyle and her sons" often occur in the Coptic Psalms (e. g., *PsB* 54, 17; 108, 24).
25. The meaning of his last verse is obscure.
26. Darkness, poison, and fire (burning) are three of the five dark elements. Poison represents dark water, the water of perdition. Usually, smoke, wind, darkness, and fire are named. Compare Henning, "Ein manichäischer kosmogonischer Hymnus," p. 216, n. 5.
27. Because the captured Light was being redeemed by the Living Spirit.
28. I. e., in the Realm of Light.
29. Here the first created person, Adam, is speaking.

30. This verse is inserted between *r* and *š*. A second descent of the First Man—in human form—contradicts classical Manichaean dogma, but is in accordance with his redeeming, demon-vanquishing role in some Central Asian texts. Here he assumes the function of the Third Messenger or Jesus.

31. Resurrection is here not meant in the concrete Christian or Zoroastrian sense. It is rather a symbol of the salvation of the soul.

32. The "seals" are the commandments.

33. Or, peacefulness (*xvāštīh*). Henning points out that this refers to the true religion. Henning, "Hymnus," p. 224.

34. I. e., Jesus as the Son of the Father of Light.

35. A Zoroastrian term. There, the "Realm of the Lie" is the Realm of the Devil. Here the world is meant.

36. The poor or miserable one is the person opposed to the (wicked) potentate; the "Family of Peace" denotes the Manichaean community (S).

37. I. e., that are honored by men (S).

38. According to Manichaean eschatology, conflicts and battles will multiply at the end of time, for most of the Light will have been filtered out of the world.

39. I. e., when they pass by quickly.

40. Or, the righteous of this religion (S).

41. Half a verse is missing here.

42. I. e., the dispersed particles of Light.

43. I. e., the Paradise created for the gods during their battle.

44. I. e., when that new building of which the previous verse speaks is established.

45. I. e., the Last God (*kā[v] ištomēn*), the "Last Giant."

46. I. e., the First Man, Lord of the New Paradise.

47. I. e., at the side of the First Man.

CHAPTER THREE

Hymns to the Living Soul

A great number of Iranian hymns invoke the Living Soul or Self, that is, the Light scattered in the world. The human soul, being a representative part of the Light, is itself addressed as such. A list of Parthian hymns contained in a hymnbook, of which only a part survives, contains fifty hymns of this kind.[1] Of course only a portion of them is preserved. Besides these, there was also a whole Middle Persian cycle, also concerned with the fettered Light, called "The Utterance of the Living Self"; of these texts, too, only a portion survive.[2]

The content of the hymns to the Living Soul is not homogenous. It is concerned with the nature of the Living Soul (MP *grīv zindag;* Pth. *grīv zīvandag*), which, as indicated, encompasses more than the individual soul. It refers to the Light that was bound by matter in primeval time. Hence these hymns refer to the cosmogonic myth about the First Man and his five sons, who ultimately constitute the five limbs of the soul. Its destiny, from its capture by *hylē* to its final liberation, is the theme of these texts.

1. Hymn on the birth and commission of the First Man as the archetype of the soul (Parthian)

This abecedarian hymn is a poetic rendering of the birth and commission of the First Man. His five sons, ultimately identical with him, constitute the Living Soul (lit., Living Self) with its five limbs. His victory over the Prince of Darkness, as it is presented here, clashes with classical Manichaean mythology and reflects a new, elated outlook on life and the world. In Central Asia, Manichaeism was in fact a victorious religion, at least for a certain period of time. Even though it is written in Parthian, the text could very well have been written in Central Asia.

The first sixteen verses of the hymn are preserved, with one verse, sung antiphonally, inserted between *beth* and *gimel*. The last sixteen verses are missing.

[Title]:   Hymn to the Living Soul

  1. (')   You have come with salvation (*drōd*), you Radiant Soul,[3]
         Salvation be yours, you are the Father's own.[4]

  2.(b)   The righteous God, the highest of the gods, the diadem and the eternal
           glory (*farrah*), . . .
         —Praise to you, Living Soul, holy, holy, Lord Mār Mani![5]

    (g)   The Blissful One of Lights[6] rejoiced and was glad when you (the First
         Man) were born in the Realm.

    (d)   The twelve sons and the Aeons of the Aeons in the Air[7] were (then)
         gladdened also.

    (h)   All the gods and inhabitants [of the Realm of Light], the mountains,
         trees and springs,

    (v)   The spacious and strong palaces and halls exulted at thy advent, Friend!

    (z)   When the lovely virgins and maidens that had sprung from the Nous[8]
         saw you,

    (h)   They all blessed you with one accord, you youth without blemish!

(x for k)   Voices came from the Air, melodious songs from the Radiant Earth.[9]
         They said to the Father of Light, "The battle-seeking one[10] who
         will bring peace is born."

  3. (l)   He who is supreme throughout eternity, the highest of the gods
         (the Father of Light), entrusted three tasks to you:

   (m)   Destroy death, vanquish the foe and hide all of the Paradise of Light
         from his eye.

  4. (n)   (Then) you paid homage and went out to [battle], you hid the entire
         Paradise of Light.

    (s)   (And) the tyrannical Prince (of Darkness) was bound [forever], and the
         ruthless dwelling of the dark powers was destroyed.

    (')   The Radiant Friend,[11] the First Man, remained there, until he had
         carried out the Father's will . . .

2. *Hymn to the Living Soul* (Parthian)

This is a complete, short-versed abecedarian hymn, which ascribes a number of
symbolical attributes to the divine Living Soul. As often is the case, one line of
responsive praise is inserted between the verses *beth* and *gimel*.

[Title]:   Hymn on the Living Soul

    (')   You are worthy of honor,

    (b)   Redeemed Light [-Soul]!
         —Salvation be yours, oh Soul (*grīv*),
         And may we[12] also receive salvation!—

    (g)   You are the soul (*gyān*) and (its) splendor (*bām*),

    (d)   You are benign, an epiphany (*dīdan*) and (its) radiance,

    (h)   You are friendly and righteous,

    (v)   You are sweet and ambrosial,

(z) You are beautiful and without blemish,

(j) You are wise and meditative,

(ḥ) You are fortunate (?) (and) a bringer of blessing,

(ṭ) You are diligent and kind,

(y) You are blessed (?) and radiant,

(x for k) Wise are you and noble,

(l) You are king and ruler of the earth,

(m) You are the Messiah and the judge,

(n) You are valiant and skillful,

(s) You are the guide and the helmsman,[13]

(?) You are a messenger (and) an interpreter,

(p) You bring order and safety,

(c) You are an eye and an epiphany (*pādgirb*),

(q) You are a creator[14] and a redeemed one,

(r) You are the Light which we (possess).

(š) You are joy . . .

(t) You, you are the great Soul (*grīv*),

(n) You are the first and the last.

    Praised and lauded are you with many blessings.

3. *Hymn on the Living Soul* (Parthian)

Here again we have a complete abecedarian hymn with short verses going from *alif* to *n*. The responsive verse is inserted between *d* and *h*.

[Title]: Hymn on the Living Soul

(') To you will I call,

(b) mighty God,

(g) Living Soul (*grīv*),

(d) gift of the Father!—Blessed, blessed [be] you, radiant Soul! Arrive at your homestead safe and sound!—

(h) Most fortunate Might,

(v) elect Greatness,

(z) mighty Power,

(j) judicious and wise!

(ḥ) All the bright gods

(ṭ) [have] . . . for your sake.

(y) The elect strive

(k) to exalt you.

(l) They tremble . . .

(m) in the midst of the world.

(h) . . . to you,

(s) son of Srōshav.[15]

(') The oppression,

(p) affliction and distress,

(c for š)   that you have borne,
(k for q)   who could endure them?
    (r)   Bringer of Light, merciful
    (š)   Lord, blessed,
    (t)   mighty and noble!
    (n)   Beneficent Mār Mani!
        We would ever praise his divine glory (*farrah*), which showed you, radiant soul, [the path] of salvation!

4. Hymn on the fate of the Living Soul (Parthian)

Here are the first four and one-half verses preserved from an abecedarian hymn about the Living Soul. The distinguishing characteristic of this hymn is that the initial letter of each verse is repeated within the stanza. This is, of course, lost in the translation. The inserted response comes after the first verse.

    (')   I hail from the Light and from the gods,
        (Yet) I have become (as) one banished, separated from them.[16]
        The foes assembled above me
        (And) took me to the realm of death.[17]
        —Blessed be he who rescues my soul from distress, so that it may be saved.—
    (b)   A god am I, born of the gods,
        A bright, radiant and shining,
        Beaming, fragrant and beautiful god.
        But now I have fallen into misery.
    (g)   Countless demons seized me,
        Loathsome ones captured me.
        My soul has been subjugated (by them),[18]
        I am torn to pieces and devoured.
    (d)   Demons, *yakshas*[19] and *peris*,[20]
        Black, hideous, stinking dragons
        That I could hardly repulse:
        I experienced much pain and death at their hands.
    (h)   They all roar and attack me,
        They pursue (me) and rise up against me,

        . . .

5. Hymn with an invocation of the Living Soul (Parthian)

This is an abecedarian hymn, complete but for two gaps. In all, five verses are missing. As Boyce points out, "It appears to be a liturgical fragment, with citations of lines from other hymns; but it is not always clear what is citation, what text."[21] In identifying citations, we mainly follow Henning.

    1. (')   . . . pious responses[22] to you, who do sing, chosen ones. You shall gain eternal life.

—Purify the radiant Soul, so that it may in turn redeem you!—

(b)   Intonate the wondrous hymn: "To salvation, peace and faith."

(g)   Sing joyfully[23] and sweetly (the hymn): "The light lute of the soul."[24]

(d)   Blow (the melody) from the joy-inspiring trumpet: "Lead the souls together for salvation."

(h)   At the sweet melody of their sound,[25] the sons of the gods come joyfully.

(v)   Say: "Holy, Holy," call: "Amen, Amen."

(z)   Let (the melody) sound: "The radiant wisdom," respond with holy speech.[26]

(j)   The living word of Truth liberates him who was bound.

(ḥ)   Praise as it behooves you, with one accord,[27] you who intone and you who respond.

(ṭ)   Brand into every limb the fear (of God), the commandments and the prohibitions.

[*over two verses badly preserved*]

2. (l)   ... who is the eye and the ear of the souls (*gyānēn*).

(m)   Invite the Son of God[28] as a guest to the divine meal,

(n)   Prepare the abode with care,[29] show the path to the Light.

(s)   Perfect all the limbs (of the Soul) in the five, the seven and the twelve:[30]

(')   These are the seven bright jewels,[31] which are themselves the living Aeons.

(p)   All words and all beings endowed with souls live through their power.

(c)   (They are) like a lamp in a house, shining into the darkness.

[*three verses badly preserved*]

3. (t)   You shall reach the palace,[32] you righteous elect and meritorious auditors.

(n)   Prepare the Soul for purification and keep this true mystery sacred.[33]

6. The so-called "Zarathustra-Fragment" (Parthian)

In this abecedarian hymn, the first ten verses of which are preserved, Zarathustra appears as a representative of the messengers sent to man to bring divine *gnosis*. He communicates with the Living Soul that is bound to the world and yearning for salvation. The text has nothing to do with the teaching of the historical Zarathustra. Rather, his figure is appropriated by the Manichaeans to put forward their own teachings.

(')   If you wish, I will teach you from the testimony of the ancient Fathers.[34]

(b)   When the savior, the righteous Zarathustra, spoke with his soul (*grīv*),[35] (he said):

(g)   "Deep is the drunken stupor in which you sleep;[36] awake and look at me.[37]

(d)   From the World of Peace, from which I have been sent for your sake: "Hail!"

(h) And it (the Living Soul), answered, "I, I am the tender, innocent son of
      Srōshāv.

(v) I am in the state of impurity,[38] and I endure suffering. Lead me out of
      the grasp of death."

(z) Zarathustra said, "Hail," and put to it the age-old question: "Are you my
      limb?"[39]

(j) "The power of the living and the salvation of the highest worlds come
      upon you, from your home.

(ḥ) Follow me, son of mildness,[40] and set the wreath of Light[41] upon your
      head,

(ṭ) You son of mighty ones that has become so poor that you must go beg-
      ging in every place . . ."[42]

7. *Hymn exhorting the soul to remembrance* (Parthian)

In this abecedarian hymn, the second part of which is preserved—the first thirteen
verses are lost—the self is addressed as part of the Living Soul. It is admonished
to listen to the divine word and to remember the primeval events.

(n) . . . all sins, the inner and the outer (ones), of thought, word and deed,
      what (is their) harmful consequence?

(s) Teach that pious and sinful thought are intertwined,[43] and distinguish
      between them.

(') Comprehend your being (and) the pure word, which is the master of the
      soul in the body,

(p) And thereby learn to see through the false word that leads to Hell, even
      the Hell of Darkness.

(c) Weigh, as with a judge's scales, those redeemed and those condemned
      by the word,

(q) Remember the (cycle of) rebirths and the torture of Hell, where souls
      are hurt and oppressed.

(r) Maintain the fervor of the soul (and) the treasure of the word, so that
      you may enter [the Paradise of Light].
      [*two verses badly preserved*]

(n) Restrain heart and mind from sinful rebellion, walk on the path of
      peace unto the home of Light.

8. *Hymn admonishing the soul to remembrance* (Parthian)

In these seven verses of an abecedarian hymn, the Living Self is addressed and
admonished to remember the deeds of the powers of Darkness. This is reminiscent
of confessional texts where the speaker confesses that he has not kept the primeval
events alive in his memory.

1. (') To you will I [speak], my captive soul (*grīv*). Remember your home . . .
         [*three verses missing*]

2. (x for h) Remember the devouring (monsters) that [captured] you and
           devoured you hungrily.
  (v)   Remember the many . . . dark [powers (?)] that led you into tumult and
           flung you into the deep.
  (z)   Remember the fierce primeval battle and the [many] wars that you
           fought with the [powers] of Darkness.
           [*four verses missing*]
3. (h)   Remember . . . , and you saw the saviors that came to you when you
           yearned for them.
  (l)   Remember . . .

9. *Verses from a Parthian hymn*

This is the last part of an abecedarian hymn (*samech* to *n*) with an additional final
verse. Every half-line begins with a new letter of the alphabet, but the sequence
of initial letters cannot be indicated in the translation.

> . . . Look up to the mighty, divine form (*pādgrib*) of the beloved
> Fathers.[44] The pious, the righteous believers, (and) the blissful auditors
> will attain (their) divine nature (*čihrag*).[45] The beneficent ones will reach
> the divine hall. This is (in store for) the blissful elect[46] (and) the meri-
> torious auditors, and this is the piety that is necessary [to save] the soul.

10. *Verses from a hymn on the First Man as prototype of the Living Soul* (Parthian)

This abecedarian hymn sings of the captivity and redemption of the First Man.
Besides the lacunae in the text, two verses are missing. They must have preceded
the preserved portion.

1. (g)   . . . [the son] of the primeval Fathers, the Prince, the Son of the
           King,[47]
  (d)   He surrendered his soul to the foes.[48]
  (h)   All Aeons and Dominions were in distress for his sake.
  (v)   (Then) he[49] prayed to the Mother of the Living, and she implored the
           Father of Greatness, (saying),
  (z)   "The fair son who does no harm, why has he been imprisoned among
           the demons?"
           [*four verses missing*]
(x for k) Xrōshtag . . . ". . . gather your limbs together!"[50]
  (h)   The eternally fair one went up in his radiant appearance (*čihrag*) to his
           borderland.
  (m)   The mother embraced and kissed him, (saying),
  (n)   "Go hastily to the Light, for your family yearns for you."
  (s)   Then heaven and earth were formed and ordered . . .[51]
           [*five verses missing*]

3. (š)   Be bliss[ful], righteous ones and auditors, limbs of Light.
   (t)   Be strong . . . May the worlds be blessed through this wealth and his
         cherished treasure.[52]
   (n)   Fix a new diadem upon (your) heads . . .

11. Verses from the hymn "The Discourse[53] of the Living Soul" (Parthian)

In this hymn, the Living Soul speaks about what it has experienced at the hands
of men, and then about its salvation. It interprets the sacred water and sacred fire
of the Zoroastrian cult in a Gnostic sense.

1.   You buy me as slaves from thieves,
     And you fear me and implore me as (you do) lords.
2.   You choose me from the world as pupils (to be among) the righteous,
     And you show me reverence as (you do) to masters.
3.   You beat me and torture me like foes,
     And you redeem and revive me like friends.
4.   However, my Fathers (the Light Gods) have power and might,
     To offer you thanks in many ways,
5.   And to give you eternal joy
     As reward for one day of fasting,
6.   And to send you your apportioned share, through me.
     They (the Fathers) will send the gods before you,[54]
7.   (And they will send you) the reward as your portion
     For the hardship and distress that you bear and endure for my sake.
         [*some verses missing*]
8.   I am the fire that Zarathustra kindled.
     And he bade the righteous to kindle me.[55]
9.   From the seven consecrated, sweet-smelling fires
     Bring to me, the Fire, purified fuel.
10. (Come and) bring clean firewood
     And soft, sweet-smelling incense.
11. Kindle me with knowledge,
     And pour on me pure libations (*zōhr*).[56]
12. I am the water which (is) fit
     That you should give me the water-offering (*ab-zōhr*), so that I may
         become strong (*zōrmad*).[57]
         [*several verses missing or badly preserved*]
14. And he (Jesus) shall free my body from pain,
     And from a despised being he shall make me into one worthy of honor.
15. And he will wash away from me the filth and great sinfulness,
     And he will bathe me and make me shine.
16. And he is my great mediator,
     And my protection and my true refuge.
17. (He is) the guide who leads me away from all sins,
     And the redeemer . . .

18. He is the [savior] who leads me out of woe,

 . . .

12. *Hymn to the Living Soul* (Parthian)

This is the first of a series of hymns to the Living Soul. The others have not been preserved. The text has no alphabetical arrangement. It stresses the importance of "gathering together" the limbs of the soul as a prerequisite for salvation.

1. You, oh Soul, would we praise, our bright Life!
   You would we praise, Jesus Messiah!
   Merciful savior,[58] look upon us!
   Worthy are you of honor, redeemed Soul of Light!
   Salvation to you, and may we also receive salvation!
   Worthy are you of the Soul of Light, bright shining limb (of Light).[59]
2. You have salvation, bright Soul of the gods that shines in the darkness.
   You sons of Truth, praise the Soul, the valiant god eager for battle.[60]
   This fettered Soul has arrived, gathered in . . .
3. . . . from heaven and from the depths of the earth,
   And from all creation.
   Meritorious and blessed is the auditor who gathers the Soul together,
   And blissful is the elect who purifies it.
4. This redeemed Soul has come,
   It has come to this Church of Righteousness.
   Praise it forever, you elect,
   So that it may wondrously purify me
   And lead me to life.
5. Blessed are you, oh Soul, (you) with the divine form (*pādgirb*)!
   Blessed are you, oh Soul, weapon and battlement of the gods,
   Blessed are you, radiant Soul,
   Splendor and glory of the . . . Worlds of Light!
   Blessed are you, divine radiant Soul,
   Weapon and might, soul and body, gift of the Father of Light!

13. *Verses from a hymn to the Living Soul* (Persian with Parthian words)

The extant verses (*hau* to *teth*) are from an abecedarian hymn to the Living Soul (*grīv zīndag*). Four verses must have preceded our text, fourteen must have followed it.

(h) For this the bright Apostles of Light were killed,
   And for this the priests mourn.
(v) It itself keeps all lands broken (?),[61]
   And itself shines by the Sun and the Moon into the world.
(z) It is the weapon and the lance of the god Ohrmizd which wounded the
   foe,
   And he (the foe) is destroyed from the root.

(h for ḥ)   All we awakened ones stand (prepared),
            So that it is saved through us daily.
   (t̲)   Strong it is . . .

14. Lamentations of the Living Soul (Parthian)

As Henning has shown,[62] this text has the form of a *qaṣīde*, an Arabic or Persian
poem which continuously repeats the same rhyme. One of the earliest Persian
poems of this type, it was probably written before the tenth century, in Manichaean
script. Apparently the text was first written in Arabic script. It appears to be an
elegy, put into the mouth of a buried dead person. He laments the evil times and
the triumph of evil powers, and especially the fact that he has been deserted by
his comrades. The text is full of Islamic concepts and images, probably used as
camouflage in times of persecution by Muslims. Henning points out that "the
adherents of Islam were justified in being on their guard against the crypto-
Manichaean *zindīqs,* who conceal their true thoughts behind an impenetrable
hedge of familiar phrases."[63]

The text probably stems from Islamic West Turkestan, where the religion of the
Arabic prophet established itself in the eighth century. It is a remarkable instance
of Manichaean adaptation of Islamic terminology. The person buried and left alone
represents the Living Soul, isolated in an alien world where it is subjected to malice
and neglect.

   1.   . . . sated with water and juicy.
   2.   Pitiable [is the being] that cannot reply.[64]
        [With the help of] the *dhulfaqār*[65] of reason, begin your speech [with
            lamentation]!
   3.   I cry for help against this age, [against the tyranny] of men.
        I cry for help against this age, the age of quarrel and strife.
   4.   . . . and pearls . . . Aaron . . .
   5.   [Whenever] the wind of virtue brings the wine [of truth] before me,
        The *simum*[66] of [passion mingles with the deluding] venom.
   6.   Ever [since] . . . I was a horseman, I recognized for sure. . . thy bridle
            (?), four unsaddled horses.[67]
   7.   [They laid] me forcibly into an ark,[68] like Noah,
        That (ark) that [is] . . . grounded helplessly [in the] shallows.
   8.   They threw me violently into a pit,[69] like Joseph,
        That pit from which I shall arise (only) at the time of the (last)
            judgment.
   9.   [When they] lay [me] down to sleep under the plank . . . ,
        They strew camphor and myrrh-leaves [upon] me.
   10. They joined . . . [no] companion to me,
        They gave me not . . .
   11. [The mourners] have returned grieving from my grave,
        I (am) left alone under the earth. . . .

12. (They have) turned their backs upon [me], upon the man who has been
    sent on his way,
    . . . over the gilded crest of the tomb [brambles are already growing].

13. Once, perhaps, or twice they will [think of me],—that is all.
    . . .

Notes

1. Müller, "Hofstaat," pp. 27ff.
2. Sundermann, "Der Gōwišn ī Grīw Zīndag-Zyklus."
3. Literally, "Soul of Light" (*grīv rōšn*). A similar invocation in the Coptic *Psalm-Book* is, "Thou didst come in peace" (*PsB* 20, 20).
4. These are the typical introductory words to many hymns to the Living Soul. The actual hymn begins with verse *b*.
5. The invocation is often inserted at the beginning of such hymns. It is probably a response sung by the congregation.
6. I. e., the Father of Light.
7. I. e., the *aer ingenitus* in the Realm of Light.
8. Either the general sense as Nous (*manohmēd*), or as second "limb of the soul," and hence of God.
9. Literally, the Earth of Light.
10. Literally, the one eager to fight. This term (*razmyōz*) is often used in reference to the redeeming gods.
11. Literally, "the Light Friend," not to be confused with "the Friend of the Lights," the Second Messenger.
12. The plural refers to a number of responsive singers.
13. I. e., guide on land and navigator on waters.
14. Or, a mighty one (*kirdagār*).
15. I. e., the Father of Greatness.
16. I. e., the gods.
17. Literally, of the dead.
18. Henning translates, "made docile."
19. Demons in Buddhism.
20. She-demons.
21. Boyce, *Reader,* p. 107.
22. In the sense of antiphones.
23. Or, sincerely (*vxišmid*).
24. Henning, taking *pandūrag* to mean "signpost, guide," translates, "Sing beautifully and joyfully, 'The bright guide of the soul!'"
25. Possibly referring back to the trumpet sound (B).
26. Boyce suggests as a possible translation, "Let sound the 'light Wisdom,' make the pure response." Boyce, *Reader,* p. 107, n. 1.
27. Literally, of one voice.
28. I. e., the Living Self or Living Soul, "whose physical redemption is furthered at each of the ceremonial meals of the Elect." Boyce, *Reader,* p. 107, n. 2.
29. Henning translates, "Decorate the lovely lodge for invitation" (*Mir. Man.* III, p. 871).
30. These are the sacred numbers of the Manichaeans.
31. It is not clear what is meant. The five Light Elements are sometimes called "the life of the worlds" (*Mir. Man.* III, p. 871). Possibly the seven bright jewels are these plus Call and Answer.
32. Literally, the hall (*talavār*), symbol of the Realm of Light.

33. Or, keep this mystery truly holy (S).
34. I. e., the divine messengers of old.
35. I. e., his own Self, which is ultimately identical with the Living Soul he is addressing.
36. For the image of sleep and the drunken stupor in Manichaeism compare V. Arnold-Döben, *Die Bildersprache des Manichäismus,* pp. 120ff, 125ff.
37. I. e., the Father of Greatness.
38. Literally, mixture.
39. I. e., a member of the world of Light.
40. I. e., son of the First Man.
41. For the image of the wreath or crown of Light compare Arnold-Döben, *op.cit.,* p. 149ff.
42. Probably an allusion to the parable of the Lost Son (Luke 15).
43. I. e., teach that both forms of thought are mixed (B).
44. I. e., the gods.
45. Or, divine form, symbol of salvation. The fact that even the auditors will attain salvation contradicts *Kephalaia,* p. 234f., although the Coptic as well as the Central Asian texts do know of the "perfect hearer" who can be redeemed without having to first become an elect.
46. Literally, just one (*ardāv*).
47. I. e., the First Man.
48. Grammatically, one could also translate, "Through him (i. e., the First Man) he (i. e., the Father of Greatness) gave. . ." compare Boyce, *Reader,* p. 111.
49. I. e., the First Man.
50. I. e., words of the God Call to the First Man.
51. Or, completed, made perfect.
52. I. e., of Light.
53. Or, Utterance (*gōvišn*) of.
54. I. e., "to reward the good done by man to the Self," that is, the Living Soul. Boyce, *Reader,* p. 112, n. 6–7.
55. B remarks that "in this and the following verses the Living Self [i. e., Living Soul], as the sum of scattered Light, is represented as the holy Fire and pure Water of Zoroastrian worship." Boyce, *Reader,* p. 112, n. 8. The word we translate as "kindle" literally means "build up."
56. The three offerings to the fire in Zoroastrianism are clean, dry wood, incense, and *zōhr,* the fat of a sacrifical animal, here a libation. Compare Boyce, *Reader,* p. 113, n. 10–11. Compare also Boyce, "*Ātaš-zōhr* and *Āb-zōhr,*" p. 100–110.
57. Translation according to B, who remarks, "the Self now speaks as Water, and in this context *zōhr* is the libation of milk mixed with herbs . . . which is made to the water for its strengthening and purification. . . . The pun on *zōhr* and *zōrmand* [strong] is found also in Pahlavi books." Boyce, *Reader,* p. 113, n. 12, compare Boyce, *art. cit.,* pp. 111–18.
58. Literally, life-giver (*anjīwag*).
59. In the sense of personal soul, as a part of the universal Soul of Light.
60. Literally, battle-seeking (*razmyōz*).
61. B: "perhaps because it has 'poisoned' the Dark Powers, who can never more be content lacking it." Boyce, *Reader,* p. 114, n. 2.
62. Henning, "Persian Poetical Manuscripts," pp. 89ff.
63. Henning, *ibid.,* p. 100.
64. I. e., to the angels that examine it in the grave.
65. The sword of the Prophet Mohammed which he bequeathed to Ali.
66. I. e., the hot desert wind, called "the poisonous wind," that whirls up sand and sweeps it along.
67. Maybe a reference to the horses that bring the coffin to the grave.
68. I. e., the coffin.
69. I. e., the grave.

CHAPTER FOUR

Hymns to the Third Messenger

In the third creation, or cosmological act, the Father of Greatness sends out the Third Messenger (*tertius legatus*) to redeem the elements of Light still imprisoned in matter. In Iranian Manichaeism, he is identified with the divine Zoroastrian messenger Nairyōsangha and is called Narisah (Persian) or Narisaf (Parthian). In the hymns, he is equated with Mithra, elements of whom he assimilates. The Sogdian tradition follows the Parthian by calling the Third Messenger either the God Narisaf (*nr'ysβ yzδ*) or the God Miši (*miši βaγi* = Mithra). In Middle Persian, there are a number of names for the Third Messenger—for example, "God of the Aeon of Light" (*Rōshnshahr yazd*), a name also known in Parthian, or the "God Zēnārēs" (*Zēnārēs baγ*).

In the following texts, praise is given to the Third Messenger as an individual entity, independent of the emanations through which he affects the world. Thus he has an individual profile in the piety of the community.

1. Verses from a hymn to the Third Messenger (Parthian)

Here are fourteen verses preserved from an abecedarian hymn to the Third Messenger. One short verse, an antiphon, is inserted between *alif* and *beth*. As the title shows, the text stems from a collection of hymns to the God Narisaf, the Third Messenger.

[Title]: Hymn to the God Narisaf

1. (') Oh just and kind God, providential deity,
        Be my help and stay always.
        You are blessed, illuminating Sun God, great Light!

   (b) You are the radiance and the splendor of the seven climes of the
        world.[1]
        Your Light shines[2] in every land and region.

55

  (g) Your spiritual course is quicker than thought,[3]
     Swifter than the wind moves, and more rapid than night (comes) at
      twilight.
  (d) Your appearance is bright, and splendid your white banner,
     Lofty is your beautiful banner which all the redeemed follow.
2. (h) The seven climes of the world have been arranged in East, West, North
      and South,
     According to the course of the Judge.[4]
  (v) The twelve gates up in heaven are opened,
     Three in each direction, each with its two wings.
  (z) The zone[5] is divided exactly into twelve regions and lands, (with) their
      respective borders and boundaries,
     According to the course of the illuminator (the Sun).
  (j) The wise helmsman passes on high through the six thresholds,[6]
     He lets light shine upon the earth through those twelve gates,
  (ḥ) Three hundred and sixty "houses" with gates (are) on one side,
     Three hundred and sixty "houses" with gates (are) on the other side.
  (ṭ) In those thirty rotations[7] those palaces are arranged separately,
     The twelve hours[8] as well as straight and crooked (?) paths.
  (y) The creations (*karišn*)[9] are manifested individually: the boundaries,
      [borders], lands and thresholds,
     The doors, rotations, hours[10] and houses.
3. (k) When the illuminator first shone, his course was in the North,[11]
     For the First Man had also come into battle from there.
  (l) In the realm of the world where he himself resides there are six
      hours.[12]
     Three after and three before (the culmination), so that the day is
      twofold there.
  (m) . . . he always runs from North to East,
     From East to South, (and) from South to West.
  (n) He runs swiftly and fervently . . .

2. *Verses from a hymn to the Third Messenger* (Parthian)

In this abecedarian hymn, verses *lamed* to final *n* are preserved. In addition, there
is a second final verse. Eleven verses must have preceded our text.

1. (l) The joy of earthly things, the pleasure of the (sensual) forms and the
      things of the world
  (m) Are like sweet food in which poison is mixed.
  (n) It (the food) holds the soul in its (the demons') net.[13]
2. (s) The beings that have been deceived by the (false) religions are
      frightened;
  (') They cannot find a way out . . . and they do not perceive wisdom.
  (p) Like a blind man, they go to ruin.[14]
  (c) Their nature has been changed to eternal bondage and destruction.[15]

(k for q)   They fall into eternal hells from which they find no way out;

    (r)   Within (in those hells) there is neither peace nor salvation.

  3. (š)   (But) for us, (ye) elect and auditors, joy is prepared:

    (t)   The palace, the throne and the wreath in all eternity.[16]

    (n)   Even the auditors will be immortal.[17]

    4.   Be merciful, beneficent God, to me, the grateful . . . , the lowest (of your) sons, the believer.

        I pray day and night, lead my soul to the eternal paradise!

3. *Hymn to the Third Messenger* (Parthian)

This is a complete hymn to the Third Messenger.

  1. (')   I will bring praise to your Light,

    (b)   Second Great One, God Narisaf,

    (g)   Beautiful form (*dīdan*), radiance (*bām*),

    (d)   Judge and observer[18] of all . . .

    (h)   Light with a thousand eyes[19] . . .

    (v)   Where you set is extinction, and Light [is where you arise].[20]

(j for z)   [With you lives the Mother] of the Righteous,

    (ḥ)   With you abides also the Living Spirit;

    (ṭ)   (With you are) the mighty Fathers that gather pearls,

    (y)   The twin lights, the two great lamps.[21]

(x for k)   It is a house[22] of peace where the gods abide,

    (l)   They move the world and radiate light.

    (m)   Full of joy are the divine abodes,

    (n)   The noble ships, the ferries that are created by the word.

  2. (s)   The mighty powers, the giants eager for battle,

    (')   Withdraw Light from all creatures.

    (p)   In two bright forms they seduce the demons of wrath.[23]

    (c)   As (in) open joy of heart

(k for q)   They come and go independently and in wondrous power.

    (r)   The chariots of Light are the gate[24] to the Kingdom,

    (š)   Joyful are the melodies that sound from them.

  3. (t)   You will I praise, God Narisaf,

    (n)   Honor first to you and to (your) whole Greatness;

        In your mercy redeem even me, (your) child.

4. *Hymn to the Third Messenger as Sun God* (Parthian)

This is a complete abecedarian hymn with an antiphonal line inserted between *alif* and *beth*. The verses *k* and *c* are missing. The hymn reflects a time of triumph for the Manichaean religion.

  1. (')   May the radiant[25] God of the Realm of Light be blessed with great blessing!

—You are my beloved, God of the Realm of Light! Merciful God,
 redeem me !—

(b) (Your) banner, (your) standard and (your) radiance became visible from
 the twelve gates (of heaven).

(g) Splendid is your form, magnificent are your deeds.

(h) You radiate brightly all splendor into the whole world.

(v) From heaven the gates are opened, the splendor shines out radiantly.

(z) You are born in wondrous power,
 And you have gone forth as a helper for the Father of men.[26]

(j) The sons of the depths of the earth take the Light from heaven,

(ḥ) All of your holy wish has been fulfilled;
 The liberated are freed and the convicted condemned.

(ṭ) The sons of the Darkness have been conquered upon earth;
 The sons of the Day, who have awakened, praise you.

(y) You bring into motion heaven and earth . . .
 [*eight verses missing*]

2. (q) You have mercy upon . . . ,
 The lost yearn for [you], (since) you (give) salvation.

(r) (Like) jewels[27] (are) the treasures that you collect,
 Your sons whom you lead upwards.

(š) You are the Sovereign who gives as a gift
 The diadem, the banner and the white standard.[28]

(t) You, even you are the merciful Sovereign;
 Show mercy and grace even unto me.

(n) I will proclaim your glory for ever;
 Redeem me, for I am weak.

5. Verses from a Parthian Hymn

Here are some verses preserved from the beginning and end of an abecedarian
hymn. There is a verse inserted between *beth* and *gimel*. The hymn was apparently
sung on a festive day, maybe the birthday of Mani, who is referred to as the "Son
of God." The "new book" of which verse *g* speaks may be Mani's *Living Gospel*.

1. (') Blessed be this day above (all) days; the day on which the Son of God
 descended to earth,

(p for b) On this day of the assembly of angels.[29]

(g) A new book, spiritual and noble, to us

(d) Was given . . .
 [*sixteen verses missing*]

2. (t) Strive, you auditors,

(n) Add piety to piety, ever anew,
 That you, too, may come to the resting place of the gods and may be
 joyful in the New Paradise.[30]
 [Patron]:[31] Kulmaγ[āyd]an

6. *Verses from a Parthian Hymn*

This is a complete short abecedarian hymn in which almost every word starts with a new letter. Boyce speaks of "highly artificial compositions."[32] The text can hardly be translated in its original order.

> Blessed be the shepherd, the judge, the good ruler, the leader, the powerful one, life!—Blessed be the eternal Dominion—[33] (Blessed be) the fortunate, divine Lord of the strong, the abiding king of the valiant chieftains (gods).
> We pay homage to the throne of the righteous Lord of the holy messengers and mighty spirits.
> We bend our knees to your glory, we pray to (you), God Narisaf, Ruler of Light!

7. *Verses from a Parthian Hymn*

Few more than ten verses of this abecedarian hymn have been preserved. Six verses must have preceded our text and five must have followed it. Longer verses of three lines alternate with shorter ones of one line each.

(j for z) ... Lead me, [Father], to my own family!
(h) [Fortunate] is every man who in purity and truth
(t) Recognizes your skill, manliness and wondrous power, oh God!
(k) To fulfill completely, oh God, your counsels and your commandments,
(y) I shall strive and wait (on you). I am ardent, by day and night.
(l) Earthly pleasures and things of the world, which Greed (*Āz*) has avidly and cunningly prepared,
(m) Have I given up according to your counsel.
(n) Hear, oh God, my supplication, and do not hesitate to accept my veneration and prayer.
(s) Lead me out of this poisonous deep!
(') This is the way, this is the mystery, this is the great commandment and the gate of salvation.[34]
(p) Fulfill in me, (oh) God, your will. May your glory protect me and always foster patience, zeal and fear (of God) in me.
(c) My eye and ear ...

8. *Verses fom a Parthian Hymn*

Here are some verses preserved from a conventional hymn to the Third Messenger.

[Title]: [Hymn] to the God Narisaf
1. Praise the great Light,
   Bring praise with one accord!

We would bring praise to his glory,
We would become (of) one spirit (with him).
We would truly adore this Father, the beneficent Father,
The desire of souls, (their) power and zeal.

2. We would praise and venerate that Great One, the blessed Father,
The beauty of Light, in which there is no flaw,[35]
The lovely, sweet form that is full of joy.
It is the Lord who [illuminates?] all regions . . .
And who causes bright life to shine over all.

9. Verses from a Parthian Hymn

Here are six verses preserved from an abecedarian hymn. Eight verses are missing between *lamed* and *šin*, and eight verses must have preceded our text. The first verses preserved refer to the myth of the seduction of the archons. They are bound to the sky and look longingly at the Third Messenger.

1. (t̲) The darkness and the dross that they[36] ejected you[37] decant into the world.

    (y) The *yakshas*[38] and demons were put to shame, but the Light was freed from bondage.

2. (x for k) You are Lord, Ruler and King of this world of seven climes and the Powers.

    (l) You convulse the world and all creations for the sake of the clan,[39] that they may be redeemed.
    [*eight verses missing*]

3. (š) They[40] go to the Heaven of Light where the gods abide and are at peace.

    (t) They receive their (true) nature (*čihrag*),[41] the original splendor of the radiant palace, and are joyful.

    (n) They put on the resplendent garment, and they live in Paradise eternally.
    [Patron]: Rōzshād

10. Verses from a Middle Persian hymn

The first two verses of a Middle Persian hymn on the Third Messenger are preserved here. He is identified with the Sun.

(') The dawn and the morning have come, the bright Light from the East.

(b) The wondrous Wise One has appeared, the Ruler-God Narisah.

Notes

1. According to Zoroastrian cosmology, the world consists of seven climes, or regions (*kišfar*).
2. In another manuscript, M 480, it says, "May your Light shine. . . ."

3. In a Sogdian text, Mār Addā says he has the "good thought" which is swifter than the wind. Compare ch. XXI, text 3.

4. Boyce points out that it is the Iranian Mithra rather than the Manichaean Third Messenger who appears as Judge and on whose course the Sun follows its path. Boyce, *Reader*, p. 115, n. 2.

5. The zone (*zōnos*) is probably the zodiac with its twelve regions (S).

6. Literally, runs in the six thresholds (*āstānag*). *Āstānag* can also mean double-month, which would only be a transposition into temporal categories.

7. I. e., days.

8. *Čaman* means hour, but since the usage is metaphorical, it can also mean something like "path" (S).

9. Either, 1. creation, thing created, or 2. fair form, beautiful shape.

10. Or, "racecourses" (S).

11. The North is the direction in which the Paradise of Light lies.

12. I. e., double-hours. At the midpoint (culmination of the sun), the day of light is divided into two halves.

13. Asmussen translates, "Hold back your soul from their trap!" Asmussen, *Manichaean Literature*, p. 139.

14. Translation according to S.

15. I. e., their divine nature has adapted itself to the foreign nature of the demons and has been assimilated to matter, and they are no more "of the same nature" (*hāmčihrag*) as the gods. Compare Boyce, *Reader*, p. 116, n. 2.

16. For these symbols, compare Arnold-Döben, *Die Bildersprache des Manichäismus*, pp. 149ff.

17. The Central Asian texts repeatedly stress that auditors can attain salvation. Compare Asmussen and Böhlig, *Gnosis III*, p. 40.

18. Literally, witness.

19. B observes, "In these lines, with the god as 'judge and witness,' and with the epithet '1000-eyed,' the concept of the Iranian Mithra overlays that of the Manichaean Third Messenger." Boyce, *Reader*, p. 117, n. 1.

20. S suggests this translation. Compare Sundermann, *Texte*, p. 175.

21. Asmussen translates, "the light leaders of the two great lamps," that is, Sun and Moon. Asmussen, *Manichaean Literature*, p. 140. The Third Messenger actually resides in the Sun. As both heavenly bodies are related to him, he assumes aspects of the cosmic Jesus. Compare Rose, *Die manichäische Christologie*, pp. 161f.

22. Or, source (*xān*).

23. I. e., the gods emanating from the Third Messenger seduce the demons in male or female forms, appearing to the male demons as females, and vice versa. Hence this is a reference to the myth about the "seduction of the archons." Compare Augustine, *De natura boni*, p. 44.

24. For the image of the gate or door, compare Arnold-Döben, *Die Bildersprache des Manichäismus*, pp. 139ff; Sundermann, *Texte*, p. 48; Klimkeit, "Das Tor als Symbol im Manichäismus."

25. Literally, bright-faced.

26. I. e., the First Man.

27. Usually a term for gods, here for souls.

28. The signs of victory, or salvation, that the soul receives after death are usually the garment of light, the diadem, and the wreath or crown. Compare Arnold-Döben, *Die Bildersprache des Manichäismus*, pp. 149ff.

29. Or, apostles.

30. Or, the New Aeons.

31. The names at the end of the hymns could refer to authors or writers of the verses. Probably, however, they indicate the donor or patron who gave money to have the hymn copied. Compare Sundermann, *Texte*, p. 80, n. 5; *idem*, "Iranian Manichaean Turfan Texts," pp. 73f.

32. Boyce, *Reader*, p. 119.

33. Inserted, to be sung antiphonally.
34. In the Middle Persian text M 5794, Mani's religion is designated "the gate of salvation" (*dar ī uzēnišn*). Boyce, *Reader,* p. 30, n. 3.
35. Literally, shame (*nang*).
36. I. e., the demons of Darkness.
37. I. e., the Third Messenger.
38. A class of demons in Buddhism.
39. Literally, the relatives, the kin, that is, the Family of Light.
40. I. e., the saved.
41. Or, form.

CHAPTER FIVE

Hymns to Jesus the Splendor

A number of hymns are addressed not to the historical Jesus, called "Jesus the Messiah," but to the Light Messenger Jesus, referred to as "Jesus the Splendor." He is a being of Light sent out by the Father to bring *gnosis,* and hence salvation, to Adam and to all men. As Boyce points out, "He is thus the saviour of mankind, and very closely linked with the Great Nous."[1]

1. Verses from Mani's Psalm "We Would Fulfill" (Sogdian)

This hymn, originally written in Aramaic, was known in a Parthian and a Sogdian translation in Central Asia. The beginning, translated here, is preserved only in Sogdian. The continuation, preserved in Parthian, is found in the ensuing text.

[Title]: Hymn in Praise of Jesus, the King: "We Would Fulfill"

1. With mouths full (of praise) we would bless (thee),
   Praise and honor to the great Moon of Light,[2]
   To the life-giver, the dear son of the god Zurvān,
   To the merciful Lord of the whole world!
   You we do invoke with a loud voice,
   May your light enter our minds;
   Your power is gathered in our limbs.[3]
2. You have come with salvation,
   You have come with salvation,
   You have come with salvation,
   Light of the whole world!
3. You have come with salvation, our whole Self,
   You have come with salvation, Light in our minds,[4]
   You have come with salvation, beneficent God
   Who are kindlier than all (other) gods.

2. Verses from Mani's Psalm "We Would Fulfill" (Parthian)

This is a continuation of the verses above.

1. You have come with salvation, great life-giver of all life-givers.
   You have come with salvation, Third Great One,[5] who are the mediator between us and the Father.
   You have come with salvation, redeemer of our souls from the midst of the dead.
   You have come with salvation, our upper eye,[6] and our ear with which we hear.
   You have come with salvation, our primeval right hand and our breath of life.
   You have come with salvation, our unified[7] nous (bām) and our true mind (manohmēd).
   You have come with salvation, our whole intelligence (uš), our ardent thought (andēšišn) and our understanding (parmānag) free of grief.
   [some verses missing]
2. You have come with salvation, our great door[8] and ship of our souls.
   You have come with salvation, our new dominion and our exalted flock,[9] beloved Son.
   You have come with salvation, our beneficent Father and our true hope.
   You have come like a father, our beneficent physician.
   You have arisen like a mother, (and) you are helpful like a brother.[10]
   You have been sent out like a son,
   You have served like a servant.
   Come quickly, beneficent Father, put our souls in order . . .

3. Verses to Jesus from Mani's Psalm "Praise of the Great Ones" (Parthian)

This hymn was originally written in Aramaic by Mani.

1. Praised, living, vigilant and immortal are you, oh (beautiful) form, Lord Jesus the Splendor, best loved of all the beings of Light, Ruler, Messiah!
   Give to us, Lord, of your good gifts, for you are the beginning of all good gifts . . .
   You are the physician . . .
   You are, Lord, the redeemer, the savior, . . .
   [a number of lines missing]
2. Praised, living, vigilant and immortal are you, Oh (blessed) sign,[11]
   Spirit and (beautiful) form, Lord Jesus the Splendor!
   [Most] noble of the beings of Light,
   . . . loving and beneficent one,
   Ardent, bright and glorious one!
   You are our God . . .
   Ruler, God, . . . Life-giver!

4. *Verses from a hymn of Mani's to Jesus* (Persian)

This Middle Persian hymn, consisting mainly of invocations to Jesus, was also originally composed in Aramaic by Mani. The poetic parallelism, typical of Semitic verse structure, is discernible in verses 4 and 5. The recurring phrase "Welcome" can also be rendered as "Come to save." As Boyce remarks, "Some of the imagery (physician, Son etc.) shows the blending of the conceptions of Jesus the Splendour and Jesus the Messiah."[12]

[Title]: Praise of Jesus the life-giver
1. . . . all in one mind.
   And we would stretch out our hands in invocation,
   And we would lift up our eyes to your (beautiful) figure,
   And we would open our mouths to call upon you,
   And we would prepare our tongues to praise (you);
   We would call upon you, who are the fullness of life,
   And we would praise you, Jesus the Splendor, the New Dispensation.[13]
2. You, even you are the just [God], the [noble] physician,
   The dearest son, the most blessed [soul].
   Welcome, liberated sovereign!
   Come to help, good spirit, messenger of peace,
   Helper of the meek and victor over the aggressors!
   Welcome, new sovereign!
   Welcome, redeemer of the imprisoned
   And physician to the wounded!
   Welcome, you who do awaken the sleepers,
   Who do rouse those that slumber,
   Who do cause the dead to rise!
   Welcome, mighty God and sanctifying Voice![14]
   Welcome, true Logos, great lamp and bountiful Light!
   Welcome, new ruler and new day!
   Welcome, foundation of the worlds and (sacred) meal of many!
   Welcome, gift of the good, blessing of the gentle,
   Who is venerated by those that sanctify!
   Welcome, loving Father, munificent benefactor
   Of those that take refuge in you!
   Welcome, (our) Father, who are our mighty refuge,
   In whom we firmly trust!
   [*six lines missing or badly preserved*]
3. Have mercy upon us and show us (your) love,
   (Oh) beneficent one who (are) all love!
   And reckon us not among the evildoers!
   Save those that have taken refuge in you,
   And be merciful to us.
4. Oh most beloved and loving one,
   We have seen you, the New Dispensation,[15]

And we have yearned for you who (are) all love.
Joyfully have we seen you, loving Lord,
And your name do we acknowledge, *Mam-sin*.[16]
Separate us from the company of sinners
And distance us from the aggressors.
Lord, we are your own, have mercy upon us!
Come quickly, hasten to vanquish the sinners,
For they are haughty and have said,
"We are who we are, and no one is like us."
Be mighty and vanquish the aggressors!
   [*three lines badly preserved*]

5.   [We praise] your name which is truly praiseworthy,
And (your) noble greatness which is pure joy.
Praise be to your name, Father,
And honor to your greatness!
Be it so for ever and ever!

5. *Verses from a hymn to Jesus* (Persian)

As in other similar hymns to Jesus, we have here an introductory verse, followed
by a list of predications. The hymn probably also contained a prayer for help and
concluding verses of praise.

1.   We would fill our eyes with praise
And would open our mouths to invoke (you).
We would bring to you . . . honor and greatness,
To you, Jesus the Splendor, liberated ruler and New Dispensation.

2.   You are, you are the garment of blessing.
You are the dearest brother.
Come for salvation, who are complete salvation.
Come for beneficence, who are complete beneficence.
Come to bring love, who are complete love.
Come as physician, who are complete healing.
Come to bring peace, who are complete peace.
Come as victor, who are complete victory.
Come as lord, who are complete lordship.
Come for redemption, who are complete soul-service.

3.   Welcome, new lord and new physician.
Welcome, new redeemer and new redeemed one.
Welcome, new God, noble lustre and great light.
Welcome, (oh) day that is complete joy.
Welcome, (oh) year that brings a good harvest.
Welcome, original one and primeval first-born one.
Welcome, good mediator . . . who (mediates) between us and the
   Father.

6. *Verses from a hymn to Jesus* (Parthian)

Nine verses from an abecedarian hymn to Jesus are preserved here. Eight verses must have preceded our text and five must have followed it.

(t) Oh, mighty Father, who are worthy of the praise of all tongues,[17]

(y) Oh, Son of the gods, who gives life to many,

(x for k) Oh, great Caller who awakes this my soul from sleep,

(l) Oh, bright lamp that illuminates my heart and my eye,

(m) Oh, perfect seal of my hand, my mouth and my thoughts,[18]

(h) Oh, bearer of the spear,[19] my wisdom and my sign of victory,

(s) Oh, good sword which I [hurl] into the [den?] of the wild lion,

(f for p) Oh, my loving, equanimous thought (*parmānag*) . . .

(c) Oh, . . . of the eyes, . . . my understanding (*izvārišn*) . . .

7. *The hymn "Primeval Voice"* (Parthian in phonetical Chinese transcription; Parthian, Sogdian and Turkish parallels).

This text, consisting of twenty-two invocations, is partially preserved in Parthian and Sogdian (referred to here as list A). Another Parthian fragment (here called list B) contains the numbers 8–18.[20] They are indicated by "B." Furthermore, this text is also preserved in another Parthian fragment, written in Sogdian script.[21] The Turkish text "Pelliot Chinois 3049" also enumerates these twenty-two terms, though in a wider context. The twenty-two qualities or virtues invoked here probably represent epitheta or aspects of Jesus the Splendor. As twenty-two is the number of letters in the Aramaic alphabet, this number represents wholeness. This is also indicated by the last phrase, "This is the wholeness of the revelation[22] (of Jesus)." In the lists preserved in various languages, the terms differ somewhat. Here we translate the Parthian/Sogdian terms, taking the Turkish ones into account where there is a substantial discrepancy.

[Chinese]: The first voice; praising Jesus; (it) creates a meaning that is very mysterious; it should follow the Parthian (language or phonetics).[23]

[Parthian/Sogdian]:

1. Primeval Voice
2. Primeval Word
3. Primeval Messenger (of Joy) [Turkish: He who lets joy be heard]
4. Primeval Epiphany [Gr. *epiphanaios*]
5. Primeval Wisdom
6. Primeval *Wonder [Turkish: Truth]
7. Primeval Love
8. Primeval *Faith
9. Primeval Fulfillment [B: Primeval Perfection]
10. Primeval Pleasantness[24] [Turkish: Sweetness; B: Primeval Sweet Taste]
11. Primeval Patience

12. Primeval Meekness
13. Primeval Equanimity
14. Primeval Righteousness [Turkish: Sinlessness]
15. Primeval *Kindness[25]
16. Primeval Gift
17. Primeval Attainment
18. Primeval Blessing
19. Primeval Praise
20. Primeval *Chosen Grove [Turkish: Chosen Acquisition]
21. Primeval *Garment of Light
22. Primeval Light [Chinese]: This is the wholeness of the revelation (of Jesus).

Notes

1. Boyce, *Reader,* p. 122.
2. I. e., Jesus the Splendor.
3. Since the light in the body is consubstantial with the light of the gods.
4. Hence Jesus the Splendor is the illuminator.
5. I. e., Jesus the Splendor, who in H 15b is called "the third interpreter."
6. I. e., eye that looks up?
7. In the sense of "gathered together, integrated."
8. Compare John 10:7ff. For the image of the door in Manichaeism compare Arnold-Döben, *Die Bildersprache des Manichäismus,* pp. 139ff.
9. As B remarks, "Such paradoxes, though most usual in hymns to the Living Self, are proper for any of the gods, who seek to redeem their own 'Self.'" Boyce, *Reader,* p. 122, n. 2.
10. Or, "Thou hast been helped like a brother" (S).
11. I. e., of the world of Light.
12. Boyce, *Reader,* p. 123.
13. Literally, New Kingdom, or New Aeon (*šahr ī nōg*).
14. Jesus is here identified with the God Call (*Xrōštag*).
15. Literally, New Kingdom.
16. *M'm-syn,* may be an unutterable "taboo-name" for Messiah (S).
17. Literally, mouths.
18. For the three seals, see Introduction.
19. Literally, "spear-bearing youth," as one who bears arms in battle (S).
20. S very kindly made his reading and German translation of these terms in M 2402 available to me.
21. Y. Yoshida, ed., in *Bulletin of the Society for Near Eastern Studies in Japan* 28,2 (1985), pp. 54–57 (in Japanese). Compare also his notes on the transcription of Iranian words in Chinese, in *Studies on the Inner Asian Languages* II. Kobe City University of Foreign Studies, 1986, pp. 1–15 (in Japanese).
22. Literally, form.
23. So in the translation of Morano. Schmidt-Glintzer, *Chinesische Manichaica,* p. 33, translates, "Primal invocations praising Jesus, the mysterious one, who judges righteously. According to and dependent on the Pahlavi (i. e., Parthian)."
24. Also, Sweetness.
25. This is borne out by M 2402.

CHAPTER SIX

Hymns and Liturgical Texts about Jesus the Messiah

A number of Manichaean texts from Central Asia call to mind the suffering and death of the historical Jesus of Nazareth, usually called "Jesus the Messiah." Some of these texts, entitled "Crucifixion Hymns," were translated from Aramaic. In their accounts of Jesus' suffering, they depended not on a single gospel, but on Syrian "gospel harmonies," that is, accounts harmonizing the events in various gospels. At least two such gospel harmonies were used by the Manichaeans, one being Tatian's *Diatessaron,* a harmony of the four canonical gospels, which was also used in the Syrian Christian Church up to the fifth century. The other gospel harmony made use of canonical as well as apocryphal gospels, including such texts as the *Gospel of Peter* and the *Gospel of Nicodemus.*

In one of our documents (text 5), called "The Proclamation of the Crucifixion," Mani's suffering and death and those of Jesus are in apposition, indicating an attempt to show that they were parallel events. For the Eastern Manichaeans, the Christian term crucifixion and the Buddhist term *Parinirvāṇa* (that is, death and entry into the highest Nirvāṇa) were freely interchangeable. Thus we find texts entitled "Proclamation of the Parinirvāṇa," or "Proclamation of the Crucifixion," both titles being also interchangeable.[1]

The suffering and death of Jesus were not important to the Manichaeans as real events (in spite of their docetic conceptions they could regard them as having taken place in reality).[2] Rather, they were important as images of the suffering of the "Living Soul," dispersed throughout the world and bound to *hylē* (matter), yearning to be liberated. But even then the hymns can refer to Jesus of Nazareth as "the Son of God" or "the Son of Greatness." Apparently the image of the transcendent savior, coming from the World of Light and termed "Jesus the Splendor," influenced the understanding of the historical Jesus, even though the two were clearly distinguished dogmatically.

In keeping with the spiritual interpretation of Jesus' suffering and death, his resurrection was also interpreted as a spiritual, not a physical event. When the Christian term *resurrection* is used here, it refers to the liberation of Jesus' soul from the body and its return to the Realm of Light. In this sense, too, Mani's death could be paralleled to that of Jesus.

1. Verses from a Crucifixion Hymn (Parthian)

These are a few verses from one of the "Crucifixion Hymns," which are sometimes also called "Parinirvāṇa Hymns." They speak of Jesus' death, using the Parthian Indic loanword *parniβrād*, "to go into Parinirvāṇa." Of course the term has come to mean "to die" in general; however, the Buddhist connotation is very clear.

The verse structure of this hymn is no longer discernible, since it is the Parthian translation of an Aramaic hymn. Our text is based on a Syrian gospel harmony drawing upon apocryphal gospels. The beginning of the fragment reflects the *Gospel of Peter*.[3] The text has a homiletical character. One of the sources of our text was Tatian's *Diatessaron*, "the other (others?), the origin of which is unknown, combines contents of canonical and apocryphal gospels and freely remodels material transmitted by them."[4] In these texts, as in other portions of Manichaean literature, anti-Jewish tendencies are apparent. The Manichaeans were prone to ascribe the guilt for Jesus' death on the cross to the Jews, stressing that Pilate was guiltless. This is a trait found even as early as the *Gospel of Peter*, which was probably written in Syria in the second century A.D. and showed marked Gnostic tendencies.

[Title]:   Crucifixion Hymn

1.   "[In] truth, he is the Son of God."[5]
     And Pilate said, "Lo, I have no part in (shedding) the blood of this
     Son of God."
     The captains and soldiers received this order from Pilate, "Keep
     this secret well.[6] And the Jews themselves are responsible."[7]
     But it shows[8] that on Sunday, at the break of dawn, Mary,
     Salome and Mary (Magdalene) came with many other women.
     And they brought sweet-smelling spices toward the grave . . .
          [*some verses missing*]
3.   . . . see the wonder.[9] According to the testimony, the two angels said[10] to
     Mary, Salome and Arsenoe:[11] "Seek not the Living One among the dead
     [Luke 24:6f.]. Go in haste to Galilee and inform Simon . . . and the others
     [Mark 16:7] . . ."[12] [What did the women do?]
4.   They turned to the grave. And they came [and found it open, and they saw
     two] angels, [who said to them], "The Lord [Jesus has] disappeared from
     the grave, and [we] do not [know] where he has been taken." And [the
     angels], both of them, came near . . .
5.   ". . . and send word to Simon and [John and James and the] other [disciples
     of the Lord] that the Lord [has risen]. [And he on the] right side said,

"[Stand up and] do [not] come here, do not seek Jesus here [among the dead]."

. . . [13]

2. *Verses from another Crucifixion Hymn* (Parthian)

The content of this text makes it clear that this hymn was composed during the time of the teacher Mār Zaku, who died around 300 A.D. Thus this hymn belongs to the earliest Parthian hymns translated, probably from the Aramaic.

1. . . . Because [of Satan] the elect were chosen by Jesus.[14] He (Satan) wanted to break through the fiery waves, to burn the whole world with fire. The noble ruler (Jesus) changed his garment[15] and appeared before Satan in his power. Then heaven and earth trembled, and Sammaēl[16] plunged into the deep. The true interpreter (Jesus) was filled with pity because of the Light which the foe had devoured. He had raised it (the Light) up from the deep pit of death to that place of zeal[17] from which it had descended.
2. Honor to you, Son of Greatness (Jesus), who has liberated your righteous ones. Protect, now, too, the Teacher Mār Zaku, the great keeper of your radiant herd.

3. *Further verses from the above Crucifixion Hymn* (Parthian)

This is a continuation of the above text.[18] That this hymn was translated from Aramaic or Syrian is confirmed by the mechanical transposition of the day of Jesus' death from the Syrian to the Iranian calendar. The Parthian "Parinirvāṇa Hymns," that speak of Mani's death and entry into the Realm of Light as his entry into Parinirvāṇa, were composed according to the pattern of hymns like this one.

1. Awake, brethren, you chosen ones, on this day of the salvation of souls,[19] the fourteenth (day) of the month of Mihr, on which Jesus, the Son of God, entered Parinirvāṇa!
2. Harken, all you faithful: When the time for the perfection of the Son of Man had come, all the demons knew it.[20] And the lord of the sinful doctrine . . . covered himself in deceit. And the demons took counsel with each other. The twelve thrones above were disturbed.[21] Poison flowed down on the lower creation, upon the sons, and the chalice of death was prepared for him (Jesus). The Jews, the servants of the most high God,[22] conceived of a deception . . . They conspired against the Son of Man. They devised evil; in deception they brought forth false witnesses. Accursed Satan, who had always troubled the apostles, molested the herd of Christ. He turned the treacherous (?) Iscariot into a steed,[23] when the Most Beloved (Jesus) trusted the disciples. He (Judas) indicated him to the night-watchman (?) by [a kiss] on his hand.[24] He delivered the Son of God to the foes. He betrayed Truth. For the sake of a reward that the Jews gave, he offered up his own lord and teacher.[25]

4. *Further verses from the above Crucifixion Hymn* (Parthian)

In this fragment, Jesus is questioned by the High Priest Caiphas. The text takes as its point of departure John 18:21, but then it deviates from that passage, showing a tendency to ascribe guilt to the Jews,[26] as in the *Gospel of Peter.*

> Jesus answered the Jews well, "Ask those that are my disciples what the teaching is that I have taught, and what the deeds are that I have done to them."
> Caiphas, the High Priest, and all the Jews clothed themselves in malice and wrath. And they grievously tortured Jesus, the beloved, with torments of deadly pain . . . But, gentle like the God Ohrmizd, . . .

5. *Fragment of a Manichaean version of the account of Jesus' suffering* (Parthian)

Under the title "Proclamation of the Crucifixion," the suffering of Jesus is depicted in Manichaean terms, and the (cumulative) suffering of other "apostles" is also mentioned. Jesus' passion, at the focal point of the text, is not dealt with chronologically, as this is a liturgical rather than a historical text. The text shows some relation to the passion story in Tatian's *Diatessaron,*[27] the Syrian gospel harmony that was composed in the second part of the second century. The text shows that Jesus was addressed as "Father" by Mani.[28] Furthermore, it makes clear that all kinds of suffering for the sake of the faith could be referred to as "crucifixion."[29]

> [Title]:   The proclamation of the Crucifixion
>
> . . . and he lost consciousness and died.
>   [*two lines free*]
> Thus was the Parinirvāṇa of our Lord, as it is written. And no one should esteem it to be more glorious.[30]
>   [*up to six lines missing*]
> Redeem (us) from all these things that have come upon us. It shows[31] that when—as we all know—Jesus Christ, our Lord, was crucified, they seized him like a sinner. And they clothed (him) in a robe and [gave] him a stick in [his hand]. And they venerated him . . . and said, ". . . King, our Christ!"[32] And then they led him to the cross.
>   [*eight lines badly preserved or missing*]
> . . . [There are] also others [who] have [left the world (?)] through crucifixion. There [are] many [who have been] killed by the sword . . .
>   [*up to three lines missing*]
> And there are some that went into distant lands, and, having arrived there, were killed. And every one of these apostles was known [throughout the world], for it has been reported [to us] how they suffered and by what sort of a crucifixion they left the world. And they also had disciples, some that were thrown to wild beasts, others that were chased from land to land. And they were like aliens and *enemies in the entire world, and

everywhere they were said to be deceived and corrupted. And many are the temptations (that they) [faced] and that they bore . . .

[*two lines badly preserved*]

. . . [as] also our beneficent Father, . . . our living . . . , so the Jews desired to remove him from the world, as it shows: on the morning, the teachers, priests, scribes [and] the religious heads held deliberations, taking counsel with each other, in order to [kill] him. And they sought false witnesses, but their testimonies did not agree. And then they brought forth two others, and they said, "This man says, 'I am able to destroy this temple [that] is made with hands, and to build another that is not made with hands in three days.'" And their testimony, too, [did not agree].

[And the High] Priest demanded, "By the living God, I admonish you to take an oath, telling me whether you are the Christ, the Son of God, the Blessed One."[33]

Jesus said to him, "At first you yourself said that I am he . . ."

[*up to six lines missing*]

". . . But from now on you will see the Son of Man sitting on the right hand of the Divine Power, when he comes from heaven in a chariot."[34]

6. *Jesus' trial before Pilate* (Parthian)

These are verses about Jesus' trial before Pilate (cf. Jn. 18:33–36; Lk. 23:7) and his humiliation by Herod and the Roman soldiers (cf. Mk. 14:65; 15:17–19; Jn. 19:2–3). Though the canonical gospels mention the scene before Herod (Lk. 23:8–12), they describe in greater detail Jesus ridiculed as King of the Jews before Pilate or Caiphas (Mt. 27; Mk. 15; Jn. 14). Here these scenes are connected to Herod.[35] We can thus discern the tendency, also found in the *Gospel of Peter* and the *Acts of Pilate,* to exonerate Pilate from the responsibility for Jesus' suffering and death.

1. He [remained?] holy (and) without [grief] when he was brought in and led to the great ruler. And Pilate asked [him], "[Are you] in truth [king] in the house of Jacob and among the children of Israel?"
   The righteous interpreter (Jesus) answered Pilate, "My kingdom is not of this world."

2. Then, at the urging of the Jews, he bound him and [sent] him to king Herod.[36]
   [*some verses missing*]

3. . . . [Silently] he stood there. And king Herod . . . clothed (him) with a garment and put [a crown of thorns] on his head. They came to pay homage, they covered his head, they hit (him) on the chin and mouth with a cane, they spat into his eyes and said, "Prophesy for us, Lord Messiah!"

4. Then the Romans (the soldiers) came and fell down (before him) three times. For he constantly turned his beautiful countenance to them and (let them hear his) voice, in his great miraculous power.[37]

7. The crucifixion of Jesus (Parthian)

This fragment is from a text with the caption "The Proclamation of the Parinirvāṇa is completed." In the first part of the text, Mani's suffering—and probably his death—is related. Then follows an account of the suffering and death of Jesus, to which Mani's last experiences are compared. The account of Jesus' trial before Pilate is followed by the account of his crucifixion. Here again, as in the *Gospel of Peter*, the *Gospel of Nicodemus*, and the *Acts of Pilate*, there is a tendency to exonerate Pilate from any responsibility for Jesus' death and to put the blame on the Jews.[38] The short text preserved follows that fragmentary passage.

> He (Pilate) crucified him with the evildoers. Then Pilate wrote an inscription[39] on parchment (?)[40] in Greek and Latin and hung it up on the cross. And he wrote, "This is Jesus of Nazareth, king of the Jews. Whoever reads this should know that no fault was found in him."

Notes

1. Cf. Sundermann, *Texte,* pp. 76ff. and 80f.
2. Cf. Nagel, "Wie gnostisch ist die Gnosis des Mani?" (forthcoming).
3. Cf. C. Maurer, "The Gospel of Peter," in Hennecke and Schneemelcher, eds., *New Testament Apocrypha* I, 1st ed., pp. 179–87.
4. Sundermann, "Evangelientexte," p. 399.
5. According to the *Gospel of Peter,* the men "of the centurion's company" say to Pilate, after seeing the miracles following the crucifixion, "In truth he was the Son of God." Maurer, *op. cit.,* p. 186.
6. Thus according to Sundermann, *Texte,* p. 151, s.v. *'ndrzyw.*
7. Literally, "should give requital." Emphasis on the guilt of the Jews. In the *Gospel of Peter,* it is at the command of Herod that Jesus is crucified, but the Jews as a whole are held responsible. After describing the crucifixion and the heavenly signs it brings forth, it says, "Then the Jews and the elders and the priests, perceiving what great evil they had done to themselves, began to lament and to say, 'Woe on our sins, the judgment and the end of Jerusalem is drawn nigh.'" Maurer, *op. cit.,* p. 185.
8. Maybe, as in Pahlavi literature, the text to which the author is referring. Or is this a reference to Mani's Illustrated Gospel (*Ārdahang*)?
9. Or, the wondrous (miraculous) power (*varž*).
10. Literally, inquired of them (*pursēnd*).
11. Arsenoe is also mentioned in the Coptic *Psalm-Book* (192,24 and 194,22).
12. There follow the *recto* and *verso* side of the fragment M 2753, as S kindly informs me.
13. S points out to me that the resurrection account itself is not closer to the *Gospel of Peter* than to the canonical gospels.
14. Translation according to a suggestion of Sundermann. B translates, "For the sake of the Ancestor (i.e., the Father of Greatness) the Elect (i.e., the disciples) were chosen by Jesus." Boyce, *Reader,* p. 127, n. 1.
15. I.e., he clothed himself with a body.
16. I.e., the Devil. The name is otherwise not attested to in Manichaean literature.
17. I.e., the Realm of Light, or the New Paradise, where the gods reside, ever ready for battle.
18. For the reconstruction of the part on the suffering of Jesus in this crucifixion hymn (M 104), compare Sundermann, "Evangelientexte," pp. 394ff.
19. Or, spiritual salvation (*gyānēn bōxtagīft*). Translation suggested by S.
20. Translation suggested by S.

21. I. e., the thrones in Heaven, the thrones of the "watchers." Compare Flügel, *Mani,* pp. 86ff.
22. Apparently an ironical description of the Jews. Compare Dn. 3:32; Acts 16:17.
23. In the sense of a servant obeying his commands.
24. Translated according to Sundermann, *Parabeltexte,* p. 115, s.v. *'dyšyg.*
25. Translated according to a suggestion of S.
26. Cf. Sundermann, "Evangelientexte," p. 398.
27. Cf. Sundermann, *ibid.*
28. Sundermann, *Texte,* p. 76, n. 1.
29. Hence Mani's death could be referred to as his "crucifixion."
30. Meaning not clear.
31. I. e., probably the text to which the author is referring.
32. Sundermann points out that the expression "our Christ" or "our Messiah" does not appear in the canonical gospels. Boyce, *Reader,* p. 130.
33. This expression goes back to the Old Testament, but can also be found in Mark 14:61.
34. Jesus' coming to earth in a chariot is not in accordance with the biblical tradition which talks about his coming "in the clouds of heaven." (Compare Mt. 26:64 and Mk. 14:62.) Apparently the Manichaean image of Jesus riding in the chariot of the moon is taken here and connected with the eschatological event. Compare Sundermann, *op. cit.,* p. 78, n. 9.
35. Cf. Sundermann, "Evangelientexte," p. 396.
36. Translated according to Sundermann, "Altgriechische Typenbegriffe," pp. 27ff.
37. Translation suggested by S.
38. Cf. Sundermann, *Texte,* p. 79.
39. Literally, seal (*muhr*).
40. S reads *'b(r)hyyg,* "on, of parchment (?)" contrasting with MacKenzie who amended the word to **br'yyg'w,* "Hebrew." Compare Boyce, *Reader,* p. 131, n. 1, and Sundermann, *op. cit.,* p. 81, n. 6.

CHAPTER SEVEN

Texts on the Twelve Dominions of Light

Eastern Manichaeism took up the notions of Mani's teachings and developed them further, unfolding a system of concepts based on the principle of holy numbers. Groups of three, five, and twelve concepts were especially significant. There is a basic duodecimal systematization of gods and related virtues. The series of virtues is called the "Twelve Dominions" (*šahrdārīft* or *šahryārī*). The complete list is preserved in Parthian, and the Turkish and Chinese terms are also known.[1] Contrasting with the "Twelve Dominions of Light" are the "Twelve Dominions of Darkness," a series of twelve evil qualities or vices. The Iranian names are known only in Parthian.[2] As Boyce points out, "The Light Dominions may be compared in some respects with the Zoroastrian Ameša Spentas [Bounteous Immortals]. They are qualities to be possessed by the virtuous or 'New Man,' and they are also personified deities."[3]

The numerical categories referred to are basic to Eastern Manichaean thinking, and they are also to be found in the Chinese Manichaean texts, the Chinese *London Hymnscroll* and the so-called *Traité,* which was translated from a Parthian original, the *Sermon on the Nous of Light*. Portions of the Parthian original are preserved. On the basis of the Turkish and Chinese material, we can discern the following correspondences among the Twelve Dominions of Light:

1. Father of Light   ~ dominion
2. The Mother of Life   ~ wisdom
3. The First Man (Ohrmizd)   ~ "victory," salvation
4. The five sons of the First Man   ~ contentment, joy
5. The Friend of the Light   ~ zeal
6. The Great Builder   ~ truth

7. The Living Spirit	~ faith
8. The Third Messenger	~ patience
9. The Column of Glory	~ righteousness
10. Jesus the Splendor	~ kindness
11. The Maiden of Light	~ harmony, mildness
12. Vahman, the Great Nous	~ Light

There are, of course, no deities or specific evil powers related to the Twelve Dominions of Darkness.

1. *The Twelve Dominions of Light* (Sogdian and Parthian)

This is a text on the New Man, in contrast to the Old Man, a concept taken from Pauline theology (I. Col. 3:10; Eph. 4:24). The Twelve Dominions of Light, the names of which are indicated in Parthian, belong to aspects of the New Man. The whole text presents itself as an exposition. The ensuing portion, explaining the "images" of the Old Man, is not preserved here.

[Sogdian]:   (Here) begins (the chapter on) the Old and the New Man

1. The number of "images" of the New Man are these, the five Elements (of Light), (namely) ether, wind, light, water, fire.
   The substance and the essence (lit., self) of the soul are: life, power, light, beauty, fragrance.
   The pure limbs of the soul are reason (*nous*), mind, intelligence, thought, understanding.
   The five gifts of the "Glory of Religion"[4] are love, faith, perfection, patience, wisdom.
   Together with the five gifts and (the Gods) "Call" and "Answer" they (the five limbs) are (all related to) purification.[5]
   The creation of the "Glory of Religion" is the Word of Light, which is itself [Parthian] the body of the Word.[6]
   [Parthian] The Twelve Dominions (of Light) are dominion, wisdom, salvation, contentment, zeal, truth, faith, purity, righteousness, kindness, harmony, Light.
   [Sogdian]: The four divine qualities[7] are love, fear (of God), the "Glory of Religion" and its wisdom in the assembly.[8] The New Man is in the midst (thereof).
   This disposition of the New Man is the creation of the "Glory of Religion" (the Great Nous).
2. Second: The twelve limbs of the soul residing in the world[9] are these: life, power, light, beauty and fragrance, the five commandments (for the elect), (namely): truthfulness, nonviolence, behavior in accordance with religion (i. e., chastity), purity of mouth, blessed poverty, (furthermore) vigilance

and zeal. This is the "Glory of Religion" of the soul residing in the world, which has the Word as its body.

Scribe:—

3. This (is) the revelation of the Old Man: . . .

2. *The Twelve Dark Dominions* (Parthian)

These are the aspects of the Old Man. Their enumeration is intimated in the above Sogdian text (M 14), but the fragment breaks off at this place. The twelve aspects in this Parthian text do not correspond to the Twelve Light Dominions.

> The Twelve Dark Dominions are 1. evil knowledge, 2. greed, 3. ostentatiousness, 4. restlessness, 5. wrath, 6. defilement, 7. destruction, 8. annihilation, 9. death, 10. fraud, 11. tumult, 12. darkness.

3. *Hymn in honor of the hierarchy and the Dominions of Light* (Parthian)

In this hymn, which is preserved only partially, the Light Dominions are invoked and compared to certain deities. According to Henning, the text contains "a comparison between the hierarchy on earth and in heaven, with the inclusion of the Dominions: the head [i. e., of the community] is compared with the Father of Light, the teacher with the Mother of the Living."[10]

1. By a good omen and a good . . . , may he institute for the whole sacred community and may he establish (for it) the sacred meal of the Radiant Friend (Jesus); and (may he) adorn you, praised head,[11] who stand as a sign of the gods of Light, and (may he shine) over the whole community of the chosen ones of Light.[12]

2. First: Dominion, you exalted God. You are like Zurvān, the crowned rulership . . .

    [three lines badly preserved]

    . . . who through . . . and love takes care of all the gods and Elements of Light.[13] And they receive his gifts from him, which are piety, light, beauty and fragrance, (furthermore) beautiful singing and creating the Word by the spirit; and they become glad and joyful eternally. So you care for us, loving and merciful Father. You illuminate the elect and the hearers and [bestow upon them] . . . the wisdom of the gods.

3. Second: Wisdom, you good teacher, our merciful Mother; in wisdom you are like the Mother of the Living, the most beloved of all gods, from whom all pious teachings issued forth. Thus you (the teacher) are also a living mother, who bears children by word-created wisdom. And you nurture them with spiritual milk and lead them to the maturity of godliness.

4. Third: Victory . . .

4. *Hymn in honor of the Dominions of Light* (Persian)

This hymn is constructed in a manner similar to the last one, except that the virtues, to which certain Dominions are related, are named at the beginning of each verse.

1. Third: Victory (salvation), [our] Father, God Ohrmizd. You, oh Lord, will I praise! You are the great one eager for battle, [of the same] nature in all battles, conqueror of foes and liberator of friends.
2. Fourth: Contentment, the five Elements of Light. You, oh Lord, we praise!
   [*two verses missing*][14]
3. Seventh: [Faith], Mihryazd (the Living Spirit) . . . , who separates the living from the dead, men of Light from men of Darkness, and the redeemed from the condemned.
4. Eighth: Patience, God Narisah (the Third Messenger). You, oh Lord, will I bless, for you have [come] from the World of Light.
   [*three verses badly preserved or missing*][15]
5. Twelfth: Light,[16] bright Vahman.
   You, oh Lord, will I bless . . .

5. *Hymn in honor of the Dominions of Light* (Persian)

In this hymn, which is similar to the previous ones, the virtues are named first, and the deities they represent are named at the end, after their qualities have been invoked.

[Title]:   On the Twelve Dominions

1. Ninth: Righteousness, the sower of goodness. You are a living tree, a firm column,[17] with which you put the living powers of the Vahmans in order,[18] with righteousness and generosity. And you proclaim them with great righteousness in the lower community and the upper community.[19]
2. Tenth: Thankfulness, you good redeemer, resurrector of dead souls.[20] You fulfill the wishes of the three immortal ones,[21] and you give understanding and beneficence to the children of the faith, whose limbs (members) you have vitalized with thankfulness. And you caused Jesus the Splendor to be honored.
3. Eleventh: Goodness,[22] which is the living spirit,[23] the wisdom of the Father and the splendor of all the gods. You are the revelation of the life of the World of Light, and the first of those revelations,[24] that are full of wondrous power and wisdom. And you caused the spirit of Zurvān to be strengthened.
4. Twelfth: Light.[25] You are Light from the World of Lights. Those that are illuminated by you [are] (themselves) signs of Light. (You are) yourself the praised spirit in the hearts of the blessed. And you freed them from the slavery of (being in the state of) confusion (mixture of good and evil). And you praised the radiant Vahman, the ruler of the Church.
5. We revere with great beneficence the whole community of the elect . . .

Notes

1. Cf. Klimkeit and Schmidt-Glintzer, "Die türkischen Parallelen zum chinesisch-mani-chäischen Traktat," pp. 108ff.
2. Cf. Klimkeit and Schmidt-Glintzer, *op. cit.,* p. 114.
3. Boyce, *Reader,* p. 132.
4. The "Glory of Religion" (Sogd. δnyy frnyy ~ Pth. *dēn farrah*) corresponds to Turkish Nom Qutï, which is the Great Nous (Vahman).
5. Apparently the five limbs of the soul, the five gifts, and the Gods Call and Answer are meant cumulatively. In the Chinese *London Hymnscroll* (H) and the Chinese *Traité* (Tr) they constitute, cosmologically, "the twelve jewel kings of brightness," which are here related to purification.
6. Thus according to a suggestion of S who takes *sxvn tnb'r* to mean "having the Word as (its) body."
7. Literally, kinds of godliness (godliness in the plural): βγy'q.
8. Thus according to WL II, pp. 70f. [547f.]. Henning translates, "the wisdom belonging to (i. e., of) the assembly (*Versammlung*)." BBB, s.v. 'njmnyq.
9. Thus according to Henning for *myn'dyy rw'n*. WL II, *op. cit.,* translate "the spiritual soul." With Sims-Williams, one could speak of "the sojourning soul" (Sims-Williams, "The Manichaean Commandments," p. 574).
10. Henning, "Zum zentralasiatischen Manichäismus," p. 10.
11. I. e., head of the Manichaean community.
12. I. e., the community of the elect.
13. I. e., the *amahrāspandān,* the five Elements of Light bound in matter. The term also refers to the elect and beings of Light.
14. Here probably diligence and truth were invoked and related to the Second Messenger (the Living Spirit) and the Great Builder.
15. The virtues named here were righteousness, thankfulness, and kindness. They are related to the Third Messenger, Jesus the Splendor, and the Column of Glory.
16. Light (*rōšnīh*) in an abstract sense, in contrast to Light (*rōšn*) as a substance or quality.
17. Reference to the Column of Glory (Ninth Dominion).
18. It is unusual to have Vahman named in the plural. This is probably a reference to the functions or forces of Vahman in individual believers.
19. I. e., in the community on earth and in the Paradise of Light (?). S thinks that it might be a reference to the Western Church, with its center in the "lower land" of Mesopotamia, and the Eastern Church of the "upper land," the Iranian plateau and the area east thereof.
20. I. e., Jesus the Splendor, who symbolizes and is related to the head of the Church.
21. I. e., Jesus, the Maiden of Light, and the Great Nous.
22. This virtue is associated with the Maiden of Light.
23. Living spirit (*wāxš zīhrēn*) in general terms, not in the sense of the deity "the Living Spirit."
24. Again, Jesus, the Maiden of Light, and the Great Nous are meant.
25. Again, Light (*rōšnīh*) in an abstract sense.

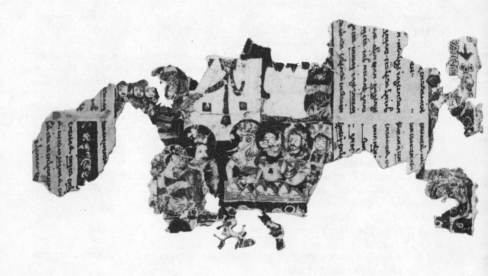

On this fragment inscribed in Middle Persian, the Hindu deities Ganesha, Vishnu (as boar), Brahma, and Shiva appear. Above, a Manichaean bishop stretches out his hand to a king in suit of arms, who accepts the Manichaean faith. Staatliche Museen—Preussischer Kulturbesitz, Museum für Indische Kunst, Berlin.

CHAPTER EIGHT

Hymns to Mani and Individual Church Leaders

In the course of Manichaean Church history, Mani was deified more and more. According to Mani's own self-image, he was an "Apostle of Jesus Christ," and it is likely that he understood himself as "*the* Apostle of Light," the final Apostle in a succession of divine messengers sent out by the Father of Light to teach and redeem men on earth. Mani's followers were quick to celebrate him not only as "the Lord of the Church," but as "the great Redeemer" and "Savior of souls" stemming from "the race of the gods." The qualities characteristic of the gods, and of Jesus the Splendor, were soon ascribed to Mani. Like Jesus, he was called "the Physician," "the Illuminator of hearts," "the true Resurrector of the dead," and "the collector of souls"; he was conceived of as a savior *par excellence*. Mani's historical appearance in the world was hailed with the same phrases as Jesus' advent; his return to earth, just like Jesus', was anticipated eschatologically. It was also celebrated at every Bema festival, when his image was placed on the Bema throne and he was honored, if not indeed venerated, with divine status. In the Bema hymns, he is addressed as a god, as a (beautiful) "form that was created by the Word" (of the Father of Light) (text 3), as the divine Word that has assumed visible, incarnate form. Hence the *Cologne Mani Codex,* which narrates his biography, bears the title "On the Genesis of His Body," indicating that Mani was an eternal divine being. In the hymns, there is often reference to his divine "Twin," his *alter ego* in heaven, who inspired, guided, and led him while he was on earth.

The so-called "Parinirvāṇa-Hymns" are of special importance. They recall Mani's death and entry into the Realm of Light, which is called "the highest Nirvāṇa" (Parinirvāṇa) here. These Parthian hymns, which contain a number of Buddhist loanwords, describe the sorrow and distress that befell Mani's community when he departed. The expectation of his return, and the yearning for that return is expressed in these hymns by referring to the number of years that have elapsed since his departure. Thus these hymns are at the same time commemorative and anticipatory.

The hymns to other Church leaders are clearly commemorative. Thus the memory of Mār Zaku, who had inspired his followers and whose light had shone into the world beyond, remained sacred to the Church.

1. Hymn in praise of Mani (Persian)

A portion of an abecedarian hymn to Mani is preserved here. Its construction is similar to that of the hymns to Jesus in chapter V, text 2. There is first an invocation of the Messenger of Light. Fourteen verses are missing after the verse on *gimel*, which is only partly preserved. These verses probably contained further invocations of Mani in his various functions as Savior.

1.   You have come with salvation,[1] oh Savior[2] of (our) souls, Lord
      Mani, Apostle of Light!

   (ʼ) You have come with salvation, oh Redeemer of (our) souls!

  (b) You have come with salvation, oh great Savior!

  (g) You have come with salvation, oh great Shepherd . . . !
        [fourteen verses missing]

  (c) [You have come with salvation], oh bright [gatherer] (of souls)!

  (q) You have come with salvation, oh mighty and strong One!

  (r) You have come with salvation, most Beloved of the Lights![3]

  (š) You have come with salvation, oh Lord of the Church!

  (t) You have come with salvation, oh beautiful trunk![4]

  (n) You have come with salvation, oh [Name] . . .

2. (d) [You have come with] salvation, oh [dearest] and most Beloved One!
      Hail to your Twin and to your Glory (*farrah*),[5] that have come forth
      with you!

  (h) [You have] come with salvation, oh Twin of the gods!
      Hail to the bright [gods] of whom you are born!
        [seven verses missing]

 (m) You have come with salvation, oh Messenger of Joy!
      Salvation to the auditors that hear your message!

  (n) You have come with salvation, oh (Savior of) beautiful and most
      beloved name!
      Hail to the blessed that honor you!

2. Hymn in praise of Mani (Persian)

Here six verses from an abecedarian hymn to Mani are preserved. Our text must have been preceded by eleven verses and followed by at least one.

(r for l) Lo, he comes, the illuminator of hearts, the King of the beings of Light,
      who himself illuminates the Darkness!

  (m) Lo, he comes, who is the true Resurrector of the dead, who cures
      illness . . .

(n) Lo, he comes, the valiant, benign and blessed helmsman, who himself steers the ship across the ocean.[6]
     [*five verses missing*]

(r) Lo, he comes, the wise King of the Lights, who distributes good gifts!

(s) Lo, he comes, who puts our foes to shame, who destroys and annihilates them.

(t) You, our Father, Lord Mani, are worthy of praise and blessing! From the gods and Elements of Light . . .

3. *Hymn in praise of Mani* (Parthian)

Here we have the opening verses (*alif* to *p*) of a highly condensed abecedarian hymn to Mani. Each half-line begins with a new letter of the Syrian alphabet. An antiphonal verse is inserted between *d* and *h*. Six half-lines are missing at the end.

The fact that Mani is here invoked as the "eighth firstborn one," connected with the eighth "Dominion of Light," shows that he is placed in a dodecadic series of gods.

1. (') We bless you, Father, (b) bright God, (g) for whom the souls yearn, (d) (beautiful) form[7] and hope (of all)!—Blessed, blessed are you, oh God who issues good commands!

    (h) We believe in you, (v) oh form[8] that was created by the Word!

2. (z) Oh, patient force, (j) vital wisdom, (h) *eighth Firstborn,[9] (t) powerful understanding,[10] Lord God, Mār Mani, our loving Lord, (k) who, out of mercy, (l) took on a worldly form and (g) gave men (n) a visible sign.

3. (s) Living Word, (') complete Commandment, (p) on us [is] put[11]. . .

4. *Commemorative hymn for Mani* (Parthian)

This is an abecedarian hymn from the cycle of Parinirvāṇa-hymns. It is apparently based on a prose text. It was composed 110 years after Mani's death, in 387 A.D. In spite of the early date, Indian Buddhist loanwords appear in it. The verses from *kap* to *tau* with a final verse on *n* are preserved. Hence ten verses must have preceded our text.

[Title]: Parinirvāṇa-hymn

1. (k) . . . For he left . . . the land of Egypt.[12]

    (l) The one that is eternally mighty (Mani) stood in prayer. He made supplication to the Father in praise, (saying): "I have levelled the earth and scattered the seed and brought before you the fruit full of life."

    (m) "I have built a palace and a very peaceful[13] abode for your Nous (*manohmēd*). And I have sown the chosen Spirit[14] in the garden, the green park, and I have laid before you a beautiful wreath."

    (n) "I have made bright trees fruitful, and I have showed the way to the sons on high. I have completely fulfilled your divine commandment; for its sake was I sent into this world."

(s) "Receive me now in the peace of salvation, so that I may no longer see the forms of the foes and hear their mighty voice. Give me now the wreath of great victory."

2. (') The righteous God[15] heard the prayer, and he sent the angels and the great gifts,[16] (saying): "Give instruction to the chosen community, and then ascend to the abode of eternal Peace."

3. (p) On the fourth of the month of Sharevar,[17] on Monday, at the eleventh hour, when he stood in prayer, he cast off the base garment of the body.

(c) (Then), shining, like a flash of lightning, he ascended. The chariot shone brighter than the light of the Sun, and the angels answered, saying, "Hail" to the righteous God.

(q) The house of the heavens burst (out) and fell down, the earth trembled, a mighty voice was heard and men who saw these signs were perplexed and fell on their faces.

(r) It was an hour of grief and a day of sorrow when the Messenger of Light entered Parinirvāṇa. He left behind him the leaders that tend the community, and he bade farewell to the whole great flock.

4. (š) The noble Lord fulfilled the promise which he gave us (when he said): "For your sake I will wait above in the water chariot;[18] I will send you help at all times."

(t) Lo, already 110 years have now passed, since you, (oh) God, ascended to the assembly of Peace. Now the time has come that you should raise up the righteous and should establish your throne on high.

(n) Bravely and patiently will we wait, the true shepherds, the faithful elect and the auditors. We will keep in mind the commandment of the gods . . .

5. *Commemorative hymn for Mani* (Parthian)

This composition also belonged to the cycle of Parinirvāṇa-hymns and was therefore probably written in memory of Mani. Eleven verses must have preceded our text; a final verse on *n* would have followed it.

[Title]: Parinirvāṇa-hymn

(l) The eternally First One, the redeemed One, received great honor from the Father and the radiant Mother and all (his) merciful brothers.

(m) The radiant First Man, bountiful in help, with his five sons . . .
[*three verses badly preserved or missing*]

(f for p) The glory of your greatness, who can express and proclaim it? Teach your Truth[19] fully: the deeds of Light and of Darkness.
[*four verses badly preserved or missing*]

(š) . . . creation,[20] area of rebirth,[21] for everybody needs it.[22] *Strive (all) you for a quick Renewal of the world (*frašegird*).[23] Hear this, you that would be redeemed!

(t) For all the Buddhas,[24] the former wise Fathers, have said that of creation[25] . . .

6. *Commemorative hymn for Mani* (Parthian)

This text is written on the same fragment as the preceding one. Only the first verse of the abecedarian hymn and the beginning of the second one have been preserved. It was written fifty-five years after Mani's death, in 332. Thus it is one of the earliest preserved lyrical texts of the Eastern Manichaean Church.

(') In the year 55 after the Parinirvāṇa of the Apostle, Mār Mani, when he was raised up into the chariot of the Moon and found peace with the Father, the God Ohrmizd. We would bless the redeemer Mār Mani.

(b) The great saint wept[26] . . .

7. *Commemorative hymn for Mār Zaku* (Parthian)

Mār Zaku, one of the first generation of Mani's disciples, accompanied the master at his last public appearance at Ctesiphone. We know him as the recipient of a letter from Mani. This hymn in Mār Zaku's memory must have been written shortly after he died (ca. 300 A.D.). It is one of the outstanding examples of Parthian poetry. In spite of its early date, it contains Indian Buddhist loanwords. The hymn is abecedarian, with the verse on *s* to the Father of Light being antiphonal. The text is from the document M 6, the opening words are restored from M 1.

1. (') Oh great Teacher, Mār Zaku, . . . Shepherd!
   (b) Oh great Lamp that was so suddenly extinguished!
        Our eyes were darkened, made faint and weak.
   (g) Oh battle-seeking Hero who left (his) army behind;
        Terror seized the troop, the army was thrown into confusion.
   (d) Oh great Tree whose height was felled!
        The birds started to quiver; their nest had been destroyed.
   (h) Oh great Sun that sank below the earth!
        Our eyes saw only darkness, for the light was veiled.
   (v) Oh zealous Caravan leader who left his caravan behind
        In deserts, wastes, mountains and gorges!
   (z) Oh Heart and Soul that have departed from us!
        We need your skill, your reason and your glory.
2. (j) Oh living Sea that has dried up!
        The course of the rivers is obstructed and they no longer flow.
   (h) Oh green Mountain on which sheep graze!
        The milk for the lambs runs dry, the sheep bleat pitifully.
   (t) Oh mighty Father, for whom many sons mourn,
        All the children that have been orphaned.
   (y) Oh Lord who was spared no pains, who endured want!
        You cared for the well-being of the house of God in every way.
(x for k) Oh great Spring, whose source is stopped up!
        Sweet nourishment is held back from our mouths.

(l) Oh bright Lamp whose radiant light shone into another world!
      Darkness befell us.

3. (m) Oh Mār Zaku, Shepherd, blessed Teacher!
         Our power is now[27] separated from you.

(n) No longer do we look into your bright eyes;
      No longer do we hear your sweet words.

(s) Oh God Sroshāv[28] with the sweet name, bright Lord!
      None is like to you among all the gods.[29]

(') We sigh and weep bitterly, we are grieved,
      We constantly remember your love.

(p) You were exalted[30] in all the lands,
      The kings and the great ones honored you.

(c) Lovely and kind (was your) nature, mild (was) your speech
      That never succumbed to bitter wrath.

4. (q) Oh great, strong Giant who displayed great patience!
         You tolerated everyone, you were renowned.

(r) Oh righteous Father, meek and merciful,
      Magnanimous and generous, compassionate and kind,

(š) You brought joy to the oppressed; many souls
      Did you save from misery, guiding them home.

(t) Strong, good, powerful One who has attained a throne
      Like all the Apostles, Buddhas and Gods,

(n) First to you will I pay homage, I (your) meanest son
      Who was left behind as a homeless orphan by you, Father.

[Additional note]:   Come, let us write a letter to the beneficent King of Light.
We will request him: Forgive us our sins!

8. *Opening lines of three hymns to Shād Ohrmizd* (Persian and Parthian)

The first verses of three hymns in honor of Shād Ohrmizd, the founder of the Eastern Dēnāvarīya branch of Manichaeism, have been preserved. The hymns could
not have been written before the seventh century. Here many epithets which were
usually ascribed to Jesus and Mani have been attributed to the great Church leader.

1. I bless you, Oh Lord, God Shād Ohrmizd, Savior (*bōzāgar*)!
     You have awakened us anew from the dead,[31] oh Life-giver (*anjīwag*)!

2. I honor Shād Ohrmizd, Giver of Life (*zīndakkar*)[32] to our souls!
     It is fitting to give you praise and new blessing, most beloved one.

3. I honor Shād Ohrmizd, the Son of the Most beloved, of Mani, the Lord,
     Ruler of the community.[33]

9. *Lines in honor of Vahman-Xvarxshēd* (Persian and Parthian)

This is the beginning of an abecedarian hymn to a teacher, Vahman-Xvarxshēd,
who was head of the Province East, or Eastern Patriarchate. He is referred to as
the author of the Parthian hymn cycle *Huyadagmān* in one manuscript thereof.[34]

Since he bears the title "Head of the Four-Tuγr Country" (*Cahār Tuγristān*)—the area comprising Bišbaliq, Kocho, Karashahr, and other places on the northern Silk Route—he probably resided at Kocho, the main seat of spiritual power from the time of the Manichaean Uighur Empire (762–840) to the time of the Uighur state of Kocho (ca. 850–1250). The teacher in question, as well as the bishop mentioned beside him, probably lived in the beginning of the eleventh century, as indicated by the reconstructed name of the king at the end of the text. Boyce remarks, "The elegant setting out of the text, with each verse preceded by the appropriate letter of the alphabet, written separately, is unusual."[35] In this abecedarian hymn, ten verses (with a verse on *j*) preceded the preserved text, and nine verses followed it. The title of the page is "Hymns for the leaders," so that various hymns of this type were united in the book from which it came.

(k)   . . . the pure righteous ones (the elect);
(r for l)   the guidance and leadership of our blessed lord,
(m)   Mār Vahman-Xvarxshēd, by name, Teacher of the Province "East,"[36]
(n)   Famous (religious) Head of the Four-Tuγr Country,[37]
(s)   And of Mār Bārist Xvarshēd, the good bishop.
(c)   (At the time of the) lordship and rule of the praised and blessed (king):
        (Ay) tängridä qut [bulmiš qut] ornanmiš [alpin ardämin il tutmiš alp arslan].

Notes

1. Or, well-being (*drōd*).
2. Literally, life-giver (*zīndakkar*).
3. Or, of the beings of the Light (*rōšnān*).
4. *Tanvār* is the trunk (of a tree), or a body. On the image of the tree, compare Arnold-Döben, *Die Bildersprache des Manichäismus*, pp. 7–44.
5. Probably the "form of Light" (*Lichtgestalt*).
6. The ocean is an image of the world.
7. *Dīdan* can also mean "appearance, epiphany, thing seen."
8. Again *dīdan* is used.
9. As the eighth divine manifestation, Mani is related to the Sun, the eighth "Light Dominion." In the *Cologne Mani Codex,* Mani is also named in the eighth place after the Third Messenger. Compare Henrichs and Koenen, "Vorbericht," p. 183. Boyce, in following Schaeder, suggests that "as the 'eighth First-born' Mani is hailed as the last of the great cosmogonic deities, the preceding seven presumably being the Friend of the Lights, the Great Builder, and the Living Spirit (second creation) and the Third Messenger, the Maiden of Light, Jesus and the Nous (third creation)." Boyce, *Reader,* p. 143, n. 2.
10. As the fifth limb of the soul (*parmānag*).
11. In the sense of, we are clothed in. . . .
12. Egypt is a metaphor for the material world. The word for Egypt, *mičrēm,* is given in the Hebrew form.
13. Or, very joyful (*huārām*).
14. I. e., the divine Word.
15. I. e., the Father of Greatness.
16. These gifts are virtues.
17. I. e., the sixth month of the Zoroastrian calendar.

18. I. e., the Moon. It can either be understood as a chariot of water, or a ship ploughing through water. According to St. Augustine (*De haeresibus,* p. 46), the Moon is made of wind and water. Here it is also called a *navis vitiatium aqua bona.* Compare Baur, *Religionssystem,* p. 226; Sundermann, *Parabeltexte,* p. 64, n. 17.

19. Or, Righteousness (*rāštīft*).

20. Or, creature (*dām*).

21. Literally, zone in the cycle of rebirths.

22. Literally, corpse of the body. Every body requires Light substance to live, or it is a corpse.

23. I. e., the final consummation and Renewal of the world. The term is Zoroastrian.

24. In the sense of "Messengers."

25. Or, of the creatures . . .

26. In the Coptic *Homilies* (54,29; 56,19), we also hear that Mani wept during his last prayer.

27. Translation suggested by S for *'v's* (instead of *'v'hs*).

28. I. e., the Father of Light.

29. This appellation of the Father of Light is inserted, to be sung antiphonally.

30. Literally, enthroned (*padγāhīg*).

31. Literally, You are our new Raiser of the dead (*muhrdāhēz*).

32. Or, Savior, Redeemer.

33. Or, Church (*dēn*).

34. Compare Sundermann, *The Manichaean Hymn Cycles,* p. 9. For Mār Xvarshēd, compare also Sundermann, "Iranian Manichaean Turfan Texts," pp. 67ff., where this fragment has been recently republished. For new material on this teacher, see I. Colditz, "Hymnen an *Šād Ohrmezd.*"

35. Boyce, *Reader,* p. 141.

36. This is probably the title assumed after the conversion of the Uighurs to Manichaeism in 762/763.

37. This seems to be the original, more modest title of the Teacher. The name of the king, reconstructed by Sundermann, refers to a very popular Uighur ruler of Kocho whose dates of reign are given as 1007–1019 by Zieme and Sundermann (cf. Sundermann, *op. cit.,* p. 68; see also introduction to chapter XXII.) The title of the king means "Alp Arslan ('the brave lion'), who received his charisma (*qut*) from the Moon God (i. e., Jesus), who is embellished by divine favor and who has held (together) the kingdom by valor and virtue."

CHAPTER NINE

Hymns for the Church Hierarchy and Church Dignitaries

Although these hymns are very schematic in form and content, they give us an insight into the role and function of various office-bearers of the Manichaean Church. A number of hymns invoke blessings on the hierarchy and the auditors—lay members of the community—others are written for particular teachers and leaders. Some of them are composed for specific functions, for example, the enthronement of bishops. They would be used on any occasions of this kind.

The significance of these hymns arises from the fact that the Manichaean Church understood itself as a community of the "elect" or "chosen ones" *(vizīdagān)*. The "Elect Church" or the "Church of the Elect" is the community of "the righteous ones" *(ardāvān)*. It constitutes "the Universal Church" which will arise in triumph over the trials of the Great War at the end of days.

The Church is led and inspired by Vahman, the Great Nous, who is called "the Charisma of the Church" *(Nom Quti)* in Turkish. He is present in the Church and its members, and his spirit rests especially upon its bishops and leaders. Hence he is evoked during their enthronement. Of course other deities are also called upon in these hymns and their blessings are solicited, notably Jesus and the deified Mani; however, Vahman figures most prominently, since he is "the King of the whole Church" (Turk. *qamaγ nom iligi*).

The Manichaean Church, then, is the place where Vahman is active and where the message of Mani is handed down to coming generations. At its head stands an "Apostle" or "Messenger" (MP *frēstag*) who takes the place of Mani on Earth. He is called "the Head of the Apostles" or "the leader of the Church" *(dēn sarār)*. The Manichaean hierarchy was organized according to the principle of holy numbers, as we already know from St. Augustine *(De haeresibus* 4). In the first rank were twelve "Apostles" or "Teachers" *(magistri,* MP *hammōzagān)*, "the Head of the Apostles" was the *princeps* and highest dignitary. The teachers were the heads of various Church provinces; the Central Asian Manichaeans belonged to the Eastern Church Province. The second rank was that of the bishops *(episcopi,* MP *ispasagān)* of which there were seventy-two, six in each Church province. Next in rank were the 360 presbyters (*presbyteri,* MP *mahistagān*) or "houselords" (*mansārārān*), five under each bishop. The male and female elect (*electi* and *electae,* MP *vizidagān* ("chosen ones") or *ardāvān* ("righteous ones")) belonged to the fourth rank and constituted the main body of the Church. They could have specific functions and act as "preachers" (MP *xrōhvān*), scribes (MP *dibirān*), lectors, precentors, and so on. The laymen, the male and female auditors (*auditores, auditrices,* MP *niγōšāgān, niγōsāgčānān*), who supported the elect and their leaders financially, constituted the fifth rank.

The hymns of this section are directed either to the hierarchy as a whole or to teachers, bishops, and other Church leaders; they also pray for blessing for the whole community.

1. *Hymn for the hierarchy and the community* (Persian)

The first verses, probably an intercession for the Apostles and Church leaders, are missing from this hymn. In the portion preserved, the blessing of the gods is invoked for the Church members by rank, beginning with the head of the Church. Finally, the auditors are remembered. The heavenly powers are also asked to guard the monasteries and sanctuaries of the Manichaean Church.

1. May they (the gods) protect . . . the community and the monasteries in every land and region, wherever they (the elect) go.
2. May [blessing ever come] anew upon you, teacher [of good name], who have seated yourself on the throne of the prophets.[1] . . . You are the head and the leader, a worthy heir to the throne,[2] a . . . of the Messengers, a merciful Father, our loving [Mother]. You encourage us with love and lead us into joy and to the life of the blessed. You are the lord (of the Church) and the blessed ruler. You render all good deeds to the children who desire you. Now flourish in glory, health and victory, growth and help (?), brightness and beauty, through the founder (lit., ancestor) of our freedom (Mani), for ever.
3. The seventy-two bishops of Truth, the teachers of the path of virtue: May their glory and joy also increase! And may their fame spread with praise to all communities and to every diocese.
4. The 360 ardent presbyters who raise the children of the gods, the sons of Mani, the Lord: May they delight and be joyful in the constant increase of beneficence and joy.
5. The wise teachers who teach and reveal the mysteries of wisdom, the fluteplayers of [valiant] Vahman [who play melodies] according to the time of the First Call,[3] . . .
6. . . . the good scribes, the sons of the gods, the strong men, the messengers of the spirit; the pure virgins who execute and fulfill the will of the redeemer: [May they attain] invulnerability . . .
7. All the pure elect, the lambs from on high, the white-feathered doves that mourn, lament and are grieved over the highest soul (*grīv*) that is the son

of Jesus the Friend,[4] and who sing praise to the Holy Spirit: (May they be blessed).

8. Blessed be the sisters, the holy virgins, the brides of the Bridegroom of Light (Jesus).[5] May the right hand of salvation adorn them,[6] and may they enter into the Realm of the Living.

9. The pious auditors of the living Word, who are the walls[7] of the Holy Church: May they attain fortune and blessing increasingly and may they become perfect by the commandment of the Redeemer.

10. The monasteries and dwelling places of the gods, the cottages and huts in which bright Vahman fulfills the wish for godliness; the strong gods, the powerful messengers, the mighty twins, the glories, the spirits, the sons of the right hand that have entered (there, that is, into the monasteries): May they come to salvation. Salvation and blessing upon this blessed garden of fragrant flowers . . .[8]

11. Blessed be God, Light, Power and Wisdom,[9] so that they themselves may continually increase salvation and peace for the whole holy Church and (that they may lead us) to blessedness and perfection.

2. *Hymn for the Church hierarchy* (Persian)

This text is similar to text 1 of this chapter. It seems to stem from a time of persecution, as verses 1, 2, and 11 would indicate.

[Title]:   Praise of the teachers[10]

1. [. . . the teachers] . . . who have received salvation as well as much woe from you(?).
   —Blessings upon this holy meal of the blessed,[11] of those who weep and wail and mourn, upon this [community][12] that is being persecuted.—

2. Salvation to the good messengers who bring peace to the oppressed Church!

3. May the head of the Church be blessed with the blessing of the Father, of the Son and of the Holy Spirit.

4. And we honor with praises the great teachers who support and sustain the valiant Vahman, the ruler of the holy Church.

5. Furthermore, may the seventy-two bishops who tend the well-cultivated garden (the Church) be praised.

6. May salvation and peace, life and happiness [come] upon all presbyters, those who guard the treasure of the praised Mother.[13]

7. And may the preachers of the secret mysteries be given new power by Vahman, the Redeemer.

8. Peace and joy upon the good scribes who write the living words of the gods!

9. Blessing upon the righteous ones (the elect), the green trees that bear fruit . . . eternally.

10. Praise to the blessed sisters who wait for the handsome bridegroom.[14]

11. . . . Peace, life and salvation . . . upon the pious auditors who gather together the community of the oppressed.

[*seven verses badly preserved*]

12. May we gain glory (*farrah*) and victory and live eternally in health of body and salvation of soul.
     Scribe:—

3. *Hymn in honor of a leader of the Church* (Persian)

Here the last three verses of a hymn in honor of the leader of the Manichaean Church are preserved. The page bears the title, "Hymns to the Leaders," indicating that praises of other leaders must have preceded our text.

1. May new blessing come from God Zurvān, and may the great beings of Light of the whole holy Church bestow new joy upon the blessed leader and the whole community of the elect.
2. May new blessing come from the God who is the highest of (all) gods; may new trust be placed in you, leader of praised name, by the power of the Mighty One.
3. May fortune (*farrah*) come from Zurvān, the King, and may peace and new salvation be granted to you by the God Zēnārēs (the Third Messenger), Lord of exalted name, shining as the Sun, radiant Ruler of the elect.

4. *Hymn in honor of a teacher of the Church* (Persian)

Some verses of a hymn in honor of a teacher are preserved here. They are written on the back of the above hymn.

1. May [blessing] come from the three who are to come,[15] the redeemers of our souls. Brothers, messengers and spirits, bless this teacher of exalted name whom Vahman has sent us.
2. May new blessing come from God Zurvān and salvation (*drōd*) from the gods and messengers, as a good omen, to the teacher of exalted name who came for salvation, as one who brings Light to (our) hearts.
3. Adoration, blessing and honor to God, Light, Power and Wisdom, because we have seen, Lord, your perfection and renewed encouragement, Lord, redeemer [of our souls] . . .

5. *Hymns for the enthronement of bishops* (Persian)

These verses were sung at the enthronement of bishops. Instructions for the execution of the ceremony and the use of specific melodies are included.

[Title]: Hymns for the bishops

1. . . . May the messengers continually give you peace through renewed peace and joy.
     Come before the teacher of blessed name.[16]

2. *To the melody: "Vahman has pardoned"*
    New fortune (*farrah*) has come, and a new diadem and a bright garment[17] (have been given) by Vahman and the teacher-God to you, Lord. Take it in love. Be joyful and flourish. Come in joy before the good Lord (the teacher).

3. *Presentation of the bishop to the teacher. Melody: "Most strong God"*
    A new omen has come: abundance and an [auspicious sign] have been sent by the gods, deities and messengers . . .
    > [*one or two lines missing*]

4. . . . a new bishop, a good son of Vahman. Be happy and blissful and flourish as a good omen, so that the leader may receive ever new support. Bless, confer gifts upon and gather your "Light Form" (the Living Self), so that it may flourish in blessedness and live eternally.

5. *Melody: "New Peace and Trust"*[18]
    A new omen of joy has come as an auspicious sign to the teacher of Truth: a new bishop of exalted name. Be blissful, Lord, together with the children of the Church (*dēn*). And may the angels and spirits watch over you. [Live] in peace!

6. *Hymn for the installation of a teacher* (Persian)

This is a hymn invoking blessings on the leader of the Church.

1. . . . Leader of the Mazdā-worshipping religion.[19] (Praise to) you, new teacher of the East and leader of those of the good religion.[20] For, in the race of rulers, you are born under a happy star. The three [who are to come]: Jesus, the Maiden (of Light) and Vahman . . .
    > [*some verses missing*]

2. . . . the rulers: May they honor you, may they accept your commandments, may they obey your teaching. May every knee bow before you in honor and respect.

3. May the angels give you victory over all your foes. May the spirits, . . . the beloved . . .

7. *Hymns for the Church hierarchy* (Persian)

These hymns are from a badly preserved double-sheet invoking blessings on the Church and its leader. Occasionally there is an indication of the type of melody to be employed. In verse 9, a prince is referred to as entering the spiritual orders. From the text M 897 we know that he was a Turk with the name Ögürtmiš ("The one who has been delighted").

1. . . . And we bless this holy meal, the victory of the pious and the bane of the unworthy.[21]

2. And we praise you, blessed[22] leader, our loving patron, our head and our
    good captain, (our) merciful Father and our loving Mother.
    [*some lines missing*]

3. All the elect, the mighty and the prominent ones, the blessed children of
    the Holy Spirit: (may they) live and flourish in twofold bliss, illustrious in
    body and redeemed in soul![23] Be it so eternally! Amen, Amen!

4. . . . Lord of the triumphant ones[24] who has set the twelve diadems of
    Light on his shining helmet. May new fortune and new bliss, new bene-
    ficence and new joy come from this whole Realm of Light, the Blessed
    Land.
    [*some lines missing*]

5. May love, redemption and divinity, wisdom, insight and knowledge of the
    Father, of the Son and of the Holy Spirit come from the Messenger of
    Light (*frēstagrōšn*), and from Jesus, the Maiden (of Light) and Vahman.
    May peace, salvation and protection come from the bright messengers and
    be given . . .
    [*some lines missing*]

6. . . . striving according to the custom of the prophets.[25] May you finally
    receive the gift of the mighty!
    [Be it so forever!]
    [*some lines missing*]

7. May new well-being (*drōd*) come from Zurvān, the King. May peace and
    joy be prepared for you anew, (oh) Lord, blessed teacher.
    [*some lines missing*]

8. . . . and flourish in joy; be joyful and blissful eternally!

9. *(In a) melody of its own*
    May new fortune, new bliss, new joy and new beneficence come from God
    Zurvān. May your new appearance (heavenly form) be prepared for you,
    triumphant prince, ruler's son; (may it be) beautiful and bright, full of
    love . . .
    [*some lines missing*]

10. Then may you finally[26] receive the helmet, wreath and diadem[27] from
    God Ohrmizd, the Father in the Paradise of Light. Be joyful there, flourish
    and exult in joy eternally.

11. *This according to (the melody of) ṯyṯyṯnv'*[28]
    May glory come continually from the gods; may bliss, happiness and new
    well-being always be prepared (for you) . . .
    [*some verses missing*]

12. *(In a) melody of its own*
    May new well-being and new blessing come from Zurvān, the King of the
    beings of Light. May new power and new aid come from the strength of
    the mighty ones (the gods); may blessing and praise from Vahman,[29] the
    King, be bestowed anew on the Church (*dēn*) . . .

8. *From a hymn for the community* (Persian)

Here the end of a hymn is preserved that invokes blessing on the community again.

1. ... and (he) should exalt the words of the bright Vahmans ... in all purity to the dwellings of immortality. And they will send love, fear (of God) and faith to us, the pure elect and the pious auditors. May it be so for ever and ever!

9. *From two hymns in praise of the angels* (Persian)

The angels (*frēstagān*) praised in these hymns are heavenly messengers, protective powers or "supernatural spiritual powers" (S).

1. The bright angels, the mighty twins, the strong gods and the praised Elements of Light (*mahrāspandān*), the strong friends, the good protectors, the guardians of the flock and the chosen of the gods: May they be lauded and praised before Jesus.
   [*some lines missing*]
2. ... May they (the faithful) be firm in this holy faith (*dēn*), and may they (the angels) protect them (the faithful), guard them and care for them. And may they (the angels) ward off, scatter, drive and chase away all foes of Truth and opponents of Goodness with the shelter of Light and the strong shield and the trusty battle-ready[30] lance, and may they also overcome all storms and burning fires. The eye [of the envious one] and the heart of the accursed Ahriman ...
   [*some lines missing*]
3. ... Be it so [eternally].
   [End of the first hymn.
   Beginning of the second hymn]
4. The bright gods, the praised Elements of Light, the soul-gathering angels, those that receive the Living Self: May they themselves accept from us this hymn, as well as prayer and praise and good works, the fruit and aid of the bright Vahmans. And may power and strength and kind protection come from Him (Vahman) for the whole Church (*dēn*). More and more [may there come] upon us, the elect and the auditors, ...

Notes

1. The prophets (*padištān*) are literally also "stations" in the process of divine revelation.
2. Literally, thronekeeper (*gāhdār*).
3. I. e., the Call sent out to the First Man who was imprisoned by the demons. The preachers (*xrōhvān*), "those who shout out the call," likewise call men to arise from the sleep of nescience.

4. The son of Jesus the Friend is the "Living Soul," imprisoned in matter, the *Jesus patibilis* of the Western Church (S).
5. This term for Jesus is derived from biblical usage. Compare Mt. 9:15, 25:1–13; Jn. 3:29.
6. I. e., may they receive salvation.
7. In the sense of "protectors."
8. For the garden motif in Manichaeism, compare Nagel, *Die Thomaspsalmen,* pp. 122–36.
9. I. e., the divine tetrad invoked by the Manichaeans.
10. Waldschmidt and Lentz point out, "This is a praise of the hierarchy of which only the first rank is referred to eliptically in the title, the *magistri."* WL II, p. 115.
11. Literally, those that have been pardoned (*avezaxtān*).
12. I. e., the community of the elect that partakes of the holy meal.
13. I. e., the Mother of the Living. Her treasure is Wisdom.
14. Probably a reference to the wise virgins of Mt. 25:1–13.
15. I. e., Jesus, the Maiden of Light and the Great Nous (Vahman).
16. I. e., the new bishop is to appear before the teacher.
17. These are probably the emblems of the bishop.
18. There were apparently various hymns to be sung to this melody. Compare *Mir. Man.* II, p. 330, n. 1.
19. As B notes, the term is "a name for Zoroastrianism, adopted presumably for Manichaeism as (hypothetically) the true form of the more ancient faith." Boyce, *Reader,* p. 149, n. 1.
20. This is also a term used by Zoroastrians for their own religion.
21. Cf. 1. Cor. 11:27 and 29.
22. Literally, being of good omen.
23. The emphasis on bodily as well as spiritual well-being is noteworthy since the body is despised in Gnosticism.
24. I. e., the Father of Light.
25. Here again, the prophets are "stations" (*padištān*) on the path of successive revelation.
26. I. e., after death.
27. These are the signs of victory that the soul receives upon entering the Realm of Light. Compare Arnold-Döben, *Die Bildersprache des Manichäismus,* pp. 149ff.
28. S: probably *nv'* = *nv'g,* "melody"; *tytyt,* a name?
29. In this verse, there is a reference to the Fourfold Father: God (Zurvān), Light (beings of Light), Power (strength of the mighty ones), and Wisdom (Vahman).
30. Literally, battle-seeking (*razmyōz*). This word usually describes the saving gods.

CHAPTER TEN

Verses from the Parthian Hymn Cycles

Two long Parthian hymn cycles have been preserved. They are ascribed to Mani's disciple Mār Ammō. The Turfan text M 2 tells us that he was active as a missionary in Parthian East Iran (cf. ch. XVII, texts 1.2). He went up into the area of the Oxus river and into the Kushan kingdom, a great part of which had been incorporated into the Sassanian Empire by then, that is, in the middle of the third century A.D. These areas, contiguous with Gandhara (Northwestern India), were partly Buddhist. Thus the question arises as to whether the early Mahāyāna texts about the "Western Paradise" of the Buddha Amitābha/Amitāyus (the Buddha of Light and Life) which was called *Sukhāvatī* ("The Realm of Bliss") were inspired by Manichaean depictions of the Realm of Light, or vice versa. The major Buddhist text of this category, the "Greater *Sukhāvatīvyūha*," was translated into Chinese in 252 A.D. Mār Ammō would have been active in the Kushan kingdom, and hence the Indo-Iranian border area, in the decade prior to this time. In his descriptions of the Realm of Light, he would have drawn on earlier West Asian, especially Gnostic and Christian, apocryphal material. An index of Parthian hymns which is preserved on a double-sheet from Turfan (M 1) attests to the Manichaeans' extensive repertoire of hymns on the Realm of Light (cf. ch. XV). It seems possible that Gnostic ideas on the Realm of Light and the Father of Light, as they emerge in such hymns as these, inspired the Buddhist conception of the "Western Paradise" *Sukhāvatī*. Mani himself had been in Northwestern India (the Indus Valley, Baluchistan, and maybe even Gandhara) in 241/242 A.D. on his first major missionary trip; this fact would suggest that there were already Gnostic and Christian groups in that area, for Manichaeans tended to address themselves to these circles first.

The text M 2 states specifically that Mār Ammō was sent to the Parthian East (and the Kushan kingdom) because he knew the Parthian language and script. It was in this language, then, that he composed these hymns.

The first of the hymn cycles (*Huyadagmān*),[1] the beginning of which is ascribed to Mār Ammō (the rest were composed by Mār Xvarxshēd-Vahman) corresponds to the opening words of the first hymn: "How fortunate we were." Similarly, the second hymn cycle, *Angād Rōšnān,* is named after the introductory words, "Bountiful Friend of the beings of Light" (*angād rōšnān fryānag*).

The hymn cycles were divided into cantos, called "members," or "sections." We have a number of verses from eight cantos of each cycle. The cycles, reflecting the Gnostic understanding of man, start by depicting the plight of the soul separated from its native home, the Realm of Light, which is described in detail in both introductions. The soul, imprisoned in matter, fettered to the body and tormented by evil powers, is an alien in the world. It is subjected to overpowering forces, completely at their mercy. This state is expressed in language rich in imagery. The recurring motifs include the stormy sea and turbulent waters through which a ship has to pass, and the terror aroused by fierce wild animals and destructive demons. Trapped in such dire circumstances, man yearns for a Savior. In the sixth canto of each hymn cycle, a Savior finally appears and promises redemption to the enslaved soul, thereby dispelling its fears and banishing its woes. Once saved, the soul can visualize itself as a pearl snatched away from demonic powers, or a lost treasure which has been found, or a being of Light destined to find its rest among the gods in the Abode of Light.[2]

In this translation, we have frequently followed Mary Boyce's virtually unsurpassable rendering.[3] Sundermann has made important new suggestions with regard to reading and translation, on the basis of the original manuscripts.[4]

1. Verses from the hymn cycle Huyadagmān

This hymn cycle originally contained four hundred verses. The first canto is preserved in its entirety in the Chinese *London Hymnscroll.* This text was first translated into English by Tsui Chi, and later, partially, by A. Waley; it was rendered into German by Schmidt-Glintzer, with Bryder making important observations on the text.[5] Boyce points out about the Chinese version, "In this the Parthian verses of two lines are rendered by Chinese ones of four, of which the second and fourth rhyme. Sometimes the sense of the original appears to have been altered slightly for the sake of the rhyme."[6] Furthermore, the Chinese text is strongly colored by Buddhist terminology,[7] which is completely absent in the Parthian. Turkish fragments on the Realm of Light, published by Henning,[8] belong to this hymn; however, the ones edited and published by Zieme do not.[9] They were apparently part of another text.

I. *(Here) begins (the hymn) Huyadagmān*[10]
First Canto

1. How fortunate we were to receive and accept your teaching, through
   you (with your help)!
   Beneficent Sovereign, have mercy upon us!
2. The Envoy [of the Father] heals (our) spirits (*gyānān*);
   He gives joy [to all], and he removes everyone's sorrows.

[*three verses missing or badly preserved*]

6. [All] the monasteries (in the Realm of Light) [are magnificent], and the
    dwelling places [of those that live there] . . .
    For they (the inhabitants) rejoice in the Light and know no pain.

7. All who enter there stay for ever,
    [Neither] pain nor want [ever] afflict them.
    [*eleven verses missing or badly preserved*]

18. [The clothes that they wear] have [not] been fashioned by hands,
    [They are ever clean and bright, and] there are not ants (?) in them.
    [*three verses missing or badly preserved*]

22. Their verdant garlands never fade;
    They are brightly woven in countless colors.

23. Their bodies never droop and are never heavy,
    None of (their) limbs is ever paralyzed.

24. Their souls never succumb to heavy sleep,
    Deceptive dreams and delusions [are unknown to them].

25. [There is no forget]fulness in [their thoughts] . . . ,
    [They see . . . all that is] hidden (?).
    [*two verses missing or badly preserved*]

28. There is no hunger or anguish [in that land],
    (There is) no thirst . . .

29. A [wondrous] fragrance emanates from [the waters] of all its lakes;
    [Floods and] drowning are [unknown to them].
    [*two verses missing*]

32. Their gait is quicker than lightning,
    There is no sickness in their bodies.

33. (None of) the (host of Dark) Powers are active . . . in them;
    (There) are no attacks (on them), nor are there any battles.

34. There is no fear or terror in those places,
    And there is no destruction in those lands.
    [*three verses missing or badly preserved*]

38. Fragrance arises from [all the gardens] . . .
    [Stones and thorns are] never [found] among [them].

39. [The whole land] shines . . .
    . . . is revealed (?) amid them . . .
    [*eight verses missing*]

48. [All who] ascend to their (the gods') land, and who have knowledge
    (*gnosis*),
    [Will praise] His lauded and beneficent form.

49. Of those among them none has [dark shadows],
    [All the bodies] and visible things in that land (are) [radiant].

50. Their dominion . . .
    The expanse of that [land is boundless].

51. Precious are they, [with bodies that are free from injury],
    Feebleness and [old age do not touch their limbs].
    [*seven verses missing or badly preserved*]

59. They are joyful, (uttering) wonderful praises,
    They laud the exalted and beneficent (Lord).
60. [Everything is filled] with joy and sweet delightful song,
    From all the monasteries . . .
61. They praise one another . . .
    They [all] dwell [in well-being] eternally.[11]
        [*two verses missing*]
64. [The monasteries are all splendid].
    Fear is unknown there, . . . peace . . .
        [*two verses missing or badly preserved*]
66a. [No frightful sound] exists [in their] land,
    And the searing wind does not blow there.[12]
67. Their dwelling place is free from blackness and smoky fog,
    And there is no darkness therein.
68. [Their eternal life is] all full of light;
    [They dwell together in] mutual esteem and happiness.
69. [They rejoice] in gladness and [inhale sweet perfumes];
    There is no limit to the [hours] of their life.
70. [Birth and death] do not exist [in] their land,
    Nor the union in the bed of passion.
71. The oppression of destruction and the fruit of passion
    Are unknown in that pure place.
        [*seven verses missing*]
    (*End of the first canto*)

The Turkish version of Huyadagmān *I, 66–70*[13]

66. The barking of dogs, the call of birds, and great herds
    Which cause disturbances and trouble are not heard in that land.
66a. There is no terrifying sound among them;
    The burning hot wind does not blow (there).
67. [Of] darkness and fog . . .
    There is none within the pure dwellings.
68. Full of Light is their "Living Soul" (lit., "Living Self"),
    They love each other in gladness and purity continually and are so
        beautiful (?).
69. They rejoice in gladness, they are fed on fragrance,
    Their "Living Souls" have no numbered days (that is, are not limited).
70. No ["Living] Soul" [among] them [dies] . . .[14]
    . . .
    (*End of the first canto*)

II. (*This canto deals with the punishment of sinners*)

III. (*This canto, again, is about the Realm of Light*)

IV. (This canto is in too fragmentary a condition for identification)

IV. A

1. Who will redeem me from all the pits and prisons,
   Where terrible lusts[15] are contained?
2. Who will carry me over the flood of the tossing sea,
   The zone (*zōnos*)[16] of conflict where there is no calm?
3. Who will save me from the jaws of all the beasts
   That terrify (?) and destroy each other mercilessly?
4. Who will lead me beyond the walls and take me over the moats,
   Which ravaging demons fill with fear and trembling?
5. Who will lead me beyond the rebirths, and free me from (them) all,
   And from the waves where there is no rest?
6. I weep for (my) soul, saying: May I be saved from this,
   And from the terror of the beasts devouring each other!
7. The bodies of men and of birds in the air,
   Of fish in the sea, (of) four-footed creatures and of (all kinds of)
   insects,[17]
8. Who will carry me beyond these and save me from (them) all,
   So that I should not turn and fall into the doom of their hells,[18]
9. So that I should not pass through defilement in them,
   Nor return in rebirth (to the places) where all kinds of plants[19] . . .
10. Who will save me from being sucked up by the heights,
    (And) from being swallowed by the depths which are pure hell and
    distress?
    [*eighteen verses missing or badly preserved*]

IV. B

1. They will collapse on the whole frame (of the earth),
   And all the (Dark) Powers shall perish in agony and perdition.[20]
2. Wickedness will overtake all its inhabitants,
   And the perdition of hell where there is no mercy.[21]
3. Who will save me and carry me over all of these,
   So that I should not be devoured in those depths of hell?[22]

V.[23] *[Sogdian title]: Who [will offer to save]* . . .

1. Who will offer to save me from the pit of destruction,
   And from the dark valley where all is harshness,
2. Where all is anguish and the stab of death?
   There is no helper and friend there.
3. Never ever is there any safety there.

(It is) all full of darkness and fume-filled fog.

4. (It is) full of wrath, and there is no pity (?) there.
    All who enter there are pierced by wounds.

5. (It is) dry from drought, and parched by hot winds.
    Not one golden drop (of water)[24] is ever (found) there.

6. Who will save me from this, and from all the stabs,
    And transport me far away from all the distress of hell?
        [*two verses missing*]

9. Not one of all the lusts, nor the comfort of wealth
    Will help them in that hellish place.
        [*one verse badly preserved*]

11. Not one of all (their) idols, altars or images
    Can save them from that hell.[25]
        [*seven verses missing or badly preserved*]

19. Who will carry me far away, so [that] I may not fall (?) into them;
    And that I may not tumble and fall down into every bitter hell?

20. [No one who enters] there can find a way out . . .
    To them the stench . . .
    (End of the first part of the fifth canto)

V. A

1. They shriek [aloud], all those who . . .
    [Neither demons] nor the Devil give them any peace.

2. They shriek and implore the righteous Judge . . .
    He does not answer to help them.
        [*eight verses missing*]

11. They are forever hungering inside, within that hell . . .
    (That) devouring deep, where hope [is unknown].

12. It is a desert place, where there [is] no water;
    All who enter there are pierced by its torment.
    (End of this part of the fifth canto)

V. B (*Description of the Realm of Light, preserved only fragmentarily*)

V. C [*Sogdian title*]: *Who will deign to save*[26]

1. Their fragrant garlands are holy and immortal;
    Their bodies are full of pure living drops.

2. They all praise one another with one accord;
    They bless (each other) with living blessings, and [so] are blessed for
        evermore.

3. In my mind I remembered; and I wept [aloud] in [misery], (saying):
    Who [will save] me from all terror and fear?

4. Who will take me up to that happy Realm,
   So that I shall find joy, as all (its) inhabitants have?
   (Here) ends the fifth canto: Who will deign to save . . .

VI.[27]

VI. A
[two verses fragmentarily preserved]

3. I shall save you from every [battle ?] of the rebellious Powers
   Who have afflicted [you] with fear.
4. [I shall release you] from all attack (?) and turbulence,
   [And shall free you from ?] the torment of death.
   [three verses missing or badly preserved]
8. [I shall put an end ?] to the arousal of all the (forces of) destruction,
   And to every sickness which has threatened you with death.
9. I will overthrow all the [foes ?] before you
   And hurl down . . .

VI. B
[twenty verses missing or badly preserved]
21. You shall [not] fall (?) into . . .
    Where all is fire, distress and injury.
22. I shall [free] you from the hands of the guardians of hell,
    [Who have no] mercy on (your) spirit (*gyān*) and soul (*grīv*).
    [two verses badly preserved]

VI. C

1. I shall eagerly take (you) up and (we shall) soar upon (my) wings,[28]
   High above all the (dark) Powers and rebellious Princes.
2. I shall carry (you) into the primeval peace of that Land,
   And I shall show (you) the Fathers, *my own divine [being].[29]
3. You shall rejoice in gladness, in the place of praise;
   You shall be free of grief and . . . shall forget all hardships.[30]
4. You shall put on a radiant garment and gird on Light;
   And I shall set upon your head the diadem of sovereignty.[31]
   [five verses missing or badly preserved]
10. With a spiritual invocation the high and vast fortress
    [Was built] on that [edifice][32] of the noble [Emperor].[33]
11. A palace is the dominion of the primeval Firstborn,[34]
    For in it he clothes himself with gladness and ties on the diadem of
       sovereignty.[35]

12. And he ties the diadem on all his friends,
    And clothes their bodies with the garment of joy.

13. And all the believers and the pious elect
    He clothes in praise and ties the diadem on them.

14. They reign now in gladness, even as (once they were) fettered for the
        sake of the (mere) name,[36]
    And underwent torture at the hands of (their) foes.
        [*five verses missing or badly preserved*]

20. [The return from] the . . . depth was won in victory,
    [For] the enemies are subdued and the Height is ahead.

21. [Blessed is] the day when He will reveal His (beautiful) form,
    [The] beneficent Father, the Lord of the Aeons of Light.

22. [He will reveal his radiant shape] and brilliant, glorious form
    [To all the gods] who shall dwell there.

VII.
    [*eight verses missing or badly preserved*]

 9. For to Him the chosen and all the beneficent will go out,
    And all who have known the mystery and understood the faith.

10. The Savior of my soul revealed these things to me,
    . . . mighty . . . through this . . . greatness,[37]

11. [On that day] of departing he came to me with mercy,
    [And saved me] from every torment and prison.
        [*seven verses missing or badly preserved*]

19. All who affright (you) will fall down in (your) presence;
    That mighty splendor will overcome their forms.[38]

20. Truly you shall pass through their (the demons') border,
    And shall not be held at (their) watchposts.
    You shall be saved from (all) anguish . . .

21. You shall not fall into Hell . . .
    There shall be no gladness . . .

22. [You shall be locked] no longer within the foul body . . .
    [You shall no more endure] that [burden] of illness.
        [*last verses fragmentarily preserved*]

VIII.

 1. [He] said to me: Whatever loathsomeness you have endured with them,
    For (that) you shall receive praise and the diadem of joy.

 2. I shall take you up and show (you your) own origin,
    You shall rejoice there and [dwell] in gladness [evermore].
        [*eight verses missing or badly preserved*]

11. [He ?] promised me eternal perfection,

And the recompense (?) for my pious suffering (for the sake of
   religion).
12.   And even as I (had) firmly believed and been patient in righteousness,
   [So he gave] me victory over all the (Dark) Powers.
      [*last verse fragmentarily preserved*]

VIII. A

1.   But you shall pass in safety through every [gate ?],
   You shall reign in gladness and in freedom [for evermore].
2.   You shall enter into that land [of bliss ?],
   And shall rejoice in the gladness of that [Realm ?].
3.   You shall abide in tranquility . . .
   And anguish [shall nevermore overtake you].
   (Here) ends *Huyadagmān*. . . . together (?) four hundred
      (?) . . . [strophes].

1.1 VERSES FROM THE SOGDIAN VERSION OF HUYADAGMĀN

This version differs somewhat from the Parthian original in formulation and
sequence of verses.

I.[39]

1.   [It is] fortunate [for us] that through you
   [We] took to heart your holy word.
   Beneficent *Sovereign, have mercy [upon us]!
2.   You are [the envoy] from [God the Father ?] . . . ;
   You [reveal] every hidden secret [to them],
   And you remove their sorrow.
3.   You reveal every hidden secret;
   You un[veil] the two powers[40]
   [That] are hidden in the world.
4.   One is the Light *Paradise, without borders and [limits],
   In light without darkness;
   . . . dwelling place.

II.[41]

n.   [*fragmentarily preserved*]
n + 1.   In all eternity they will have no comforter.
   With this . . . is a cessation . . .

n + 2.   And this is the second [death ?][42] which is . . . ,
         Swallowing its own . . . ,
         Who is not and [will never be].

n + 3.   [*fragmentarily preserved*]
         (Here ends the second canto of *Huyadagmān*).

   III.[43]

   IV.[44]

   V.

Several portions of the cantos V–VI are preserved in various Sogdian texts, namely
texts A, B, and C.[45] They have another sequence of verses.[46]

   Text A[47]

   1.   [Who will] offer to save [me] from all the [pits of destruction ?]
        It was as if some should fall down . . . (and) be oppressed (?) . . .

   2.   Who will take me far away from them (the foes),
        So that I may not be suppressed down (?) under them?

   3.   For whoever falls therein can find no way out,
        Nor will anyone help him.

   4.   All this destruction and oppression (?),
        Who will deliver me from them, and from the eternal trap,

   5.   And from all the boun[daries] whence my soul . . .
        And my mind was exceedingly . . . from all the dwell[ings]?

   6.   Who will raise me up to the world of love,
        Which is completely full of bliss, and where there is no sorrow?

   7.   For all who are there rejoice in eternal bliss,
        And (they) have a royal diadem on their heads.

   8.   And all praise the Father with one accord,
        The Head of the hidden Light (and) Ruler of the exalted World.

   Text B[48]

        (*recto*)
   1.   [*fragmentarily preserved*]
   2.   And it is clothed all around in fierce wrath,
        And the blaze, the flame and the merciless fire prevail unchecked.

   3.   Those that dwell there are ruthless demons;
        On that whole path there is no gladness.

   4.   [*fragmentarily preserved*]
        (*verso*)

5. [*fragmentarily preserved*]
6. The noise of the *cracking *ice, and the . . . *roar of the waters,
    And the gnashing and *gulping of the devouring wind is heard therein.
7. (Those) who lament and moan at their lot in that (place)
    Complain with burning voices and broken spirits.
8. (They) who lament [in every] quarter,
        . . .

Text C[49]

1. And I remembered [in my] mind and wept in [my misery],
    (Saying), "Who [will save] me from my [fear] and terror?"
2. "Who will lift me up to that happy world,
    [So that I] may be joyful together with all those dwelling (there)?"
    (Here) ends the fifth canto: Who will deign to save

(From Text C)[50]

1. [*badly preserved*]
2. There is no [unwholesome ?] food in (that) [Paradise],
    Nor any food and drink that would choke.
3. A fragrant garland is their pure immortality,
    And with living, purified drops their bodies are filled.
4. And (they) all with one accord praise one another,
    (They) bless (each other) with living blessings; they become
    eternally blessed.

VI.

Two manuscripts contain verses from this canto, namely, Text C. In view of this text, S points out that it "is likely to belong to H [*Huyadagmān*] VI too, although it cannot be identified with any of the existing parts of the Parthian text."[51]

Text C[52]

1. And while I thus wept and shed tears on the ground,
    I heard the voice of the beneficent King.

Text D[53]

    (*recto*)
2. . . . Fear not,
    For I shall redeem you from that great distress.
3. I am the redeeming god, and the root and ground of [your] soul,
    Who are born [from me] and made visible [from] the beginning [of
        your] life till now.

4. [You] are the garment of my own body,
    And I am your [heart], and the strength of your limbs.

5. You are my [weapon], I have fought with you . . . ,
        (*verso*)

6. . . . the demons and the rulers of [Hell];
    And . . . the world is built with all . . .

7. You are the *substance of the whole *building,[54]
    And I am your splendor and . . . , the lord of your beauty.[55]

8. Through you I made visible the battle against every sin,[56]
    And you yourself did become light in great strength.

9. I am your strength and your immortal (?) . . . mind,[57]
    . . . and your . . . diadem . . .

2. Verses from the hymn cycle Angad Rōšnān

This hymn cycle was probably composed in the middle of the third century A.D.,
again by Mani's disciple Mār Ammō. It must have been as long as *Huyadagmān,*
which contains four hundred verses. The description of the events in the last days
in VII and VII.A are once more reminiscent of apocryphal apocalyptic literature,
especially of the *Apocalypse of Thomas,* which is known to have been used by the
Manichaeans. Furthermore, there is a reference to the *Shepherd of Hermas (Pastor
Hermae),* a work written in Rome in the second century. Even though this book
is apocalyptic more in form than in content, it does contain apocalyptic material,
which is interpreted ethically. Fragments of a Manichaean version of the *Shepherd
of Hermas* have been found in Turfan.[58]

I. (Here) begins (the hymn) Angad Rōšnān.

1. Bountiful Friend of the beings of Light! In mercy
    Grant me [strength, and] help me with every gift!

2. Equip [my soul], oh Lord! Answer me!
    [Help me] in the midst of the foe!

3. Let all the ravages of the deceitful body pass from me,
    (The body) that tortures me with pain.

4. You are the Friend, praised and beneficent!
    Free me . . .
        [*six verses missing or badly preserved*]

11. My soul weeps within (me),
    And cries out [at each] distress and stab.

12. The hour of life and this carnal form
    Are finished for me. What exiting days![59]

13. It (my soul) was tossed and churned as a sea with waves,
    Pain was heaped on pain, with which they ravaged my soul.

14. On all sides anguish afflicted (me);
    A fire was kindled, and the fog (was full) of smoke (?).

15. The wellsprings of darkness had all been opened.
    The [giant] fishes transfixed me with fear.[60]
16. [My] soul was dismayed at the sight of their forms,
    For they were visible in all their dreadfulness;
17. For all were hideous and horrifying to [behold].
    The human form is not to be found among their bodies.[61]
18. (Seeing) all the demons, the banished Princes,
    I was transfixed with fear and dismayed and anguished.
19. Their fury gathered, like a sea of fire;
    The soothing waves rose up to engulf me.[62]
        [*two verses badly preserved*]
22. For in every region stormy *winds gathered,
    And rain and the fume of all the vapors,
23. Lightning and thunder and banked clouds (?) of hail,
    The crash and roar of all the waves of the sea.
24. The ship rises up, lifted on the crest of the wave,
    And glides down into the trough, to be hidden within.
25. With all the *beams . . .
    And on every side water [pours ?] in.
26. All the clamps were loosened . . .
    The iron rivets were wrenched out . . .
27. Each deck[63] [was covered] by the storm,
    The masts were broken (?) in the turmoil.
28. The rudders (?) fell into the sea,
    [Fear gripped] those on board.
29. The helmsmen and all the pilots
    Wept bitterly and wailed aloud.
30. There was terror and destruction [before] the break of day,
    . . . [were] consumed and perished.
        [*twenty-eight verses missing or badly preserved*][64]

I. A

1. All the bands, links and nails of the prison[65]
   Have been weakened (?) by repeated redemptions.[66]
2. All the comets quivered, and the stars were whirled about,
   And every planet went awry in its course.
3. The earth shook, the foundation beneath [me],
   And the height of the heavens tumbled down above (?).
4. All the rivers, the veins of my body,[67]
   Are dried up at (their) source in every way.
       [*two verses missing or badly preserved*]
7. All my limbs fall apart,[68]
   Once they are broken, they get prepared for (the next) existence.[69]
8. The reckoning of (my) days and months is ended;
   Evil befell the course of the zodiac's wheel.

[*two verses missing*]

11. [The ankles] of my feet and the joints of my toes,
    Each link of the life of my soul was loosed.[70]

12. Each joint of (my) hands and of (my) fingers,
    Each was loosened and its seal taken off.

13. And all the gristly parts—their strength grew feeble;
    Each one of my limbs became cold.

14. My knees were fettered by fear,
    And strength was drawn out from each leg.
    [*one verse badly preserved*]

I. B

1. [*fragmentarily preserved*]

2. And the faculty [of thought] (*andēšišn*)[71] of my heart that [saw]
   all the . . .[72]
   Was shaken by it all, and hid itself inside the soul (*grīv*).

3. And my whole intelligence (*uš*)[73] could no longer plan at all any
   longer;
   [I was disabled] in my understanding (*parmānag*),[74] and in my own
   [mind (*manohmēd*)].[75]
   [*eight verses missing or badly preserved*]

12. And [when I saw] the Dark, the strength of my limbs[76] was broken;
    And my soul moaned at all its forms.[77]

13. I was afraid (?); in all my limbs [there was] suffering,
    My spirit (*gyān*) (was) tortured.
    [*one verse badly preserved*]

II.-V. [*Preserved only fragmentarily*][78]

VI.

1. After I had said these words, (my) soul trembling,
   I beheld the Savior shining before me.

2. I beheld the sight of all the helmsmen[79]
   Who had descended with him to equip my soul.

3. I lifted up my eyes in that direction,
   And saw that all deaths had been hidden by the Envoy.

4. All affliction had been removed far from me,
   And grievous illness, and the anguish of their distress;

5. The sight of them was hidden, their darkness had fled away.
   All (was of a divine) nature (*čihrag*), and beyond compare.

6. Light [shone forth], refreshing and lovely
   [And] blissful,[80] pervading all my mind.

7. In joy unbounded he spoke to me,
   Raising my soul up from deep affliction.

8. To me he said, Come, oh spirit (*gyān*)! Fear not!
   I am your Mind (*manohmēd*),[81] your glad tidings of hope.

9. And you are my body, the [martial] garment,
   That had been oppressed by the Powers (of Darkness) . . .[82]

10. I am your Light, radiant (and) primeval,
    Your Great Mind[83] and consummate hope.
       [*ten verses missing or badly preserved*]

21. You are my word,[84] and my panoply of war,[85]
    [Which saved me] decisively [in the fight] [from] all sinners.

22. I am your exalted [standard], your primeval sign,. . .
       [*nine verses missing or badly preserved*]

32. I shall release you from every *dungeon,
    Bearing you away far from all wounds and afflictions.

33. I shall lead you out of this torture . . .
    You shall no [more] be fearful at every encounter.
       [*eight verses missing or badly preserved*]

42. Beloved! Oh beauty of my bright nature (*čihrag*)!
    I shall lead you out of these and from these lowly prisons (?).

43. I shall save you from all perdition,
    And free you for ever [from] all wounds.

44. With perfect Light, [shall I cleanse] you,
    Of all the filth and corrosion through which you have passed.[86]

45. I shall rescue (you) from all the waves of the sea,
    And from its depth into which the floods flung you,[87]
       [*three verses badly preserved*]

49. I shall set you free from every sickness,[88]
    And from every distress which made you weep.

50. I shall not willingly leave you any longer in the hands of the sinner;
    For you are my own, in truth, for ever.

51. You are the buried treasure, the greatest of my wealth,
    The pearl which (is) the beauty of all the gods.[89]

52. And I am the righteousness sown in your limbs,
    And (within) the frame of (your) soul—the gladness of your mind
       (*manohmēd*).

53. You are my beloved, the love in my limbs;[90]
    And the heroic mind, the essence (*čihrag*) of my limbs.

54. And I am the light of your whole form,[91]
    The soul above and the base of life.

55. In the beginning from the holiness of my limbs did you descend
    Into the dark places, and did become their light.

56. Because of you a diadem was bound onto all (our) foes,[92]
    It became manifest and held sway during the hours of tyranny.

57. For your sake there was battle and turbulence
    In all the heavens and the bridges of the earths.

58. For your sake . . .
    Did all the (Dark) Powers run [and speed away].

60. For your sake . . .
    Was taken away the diadem . . .[93]

61. For your sake did the Apostles shine forth and become visible,
    They who reveal the Light above, and uncover the root of
        Darkness.

62. For your sake did the gods go forth and appear,
    They struck down Death and slew Darkness.[94]

63. You are the exalted trophy,
    The sign of Light that puts the Darkness to flight.

64. And I have come forth to save you from the sinner,
    To make (you) whole and rid you of pain,
    And to bring gladness to your heart.

65. All you have desired of me shall I bestow upon you.
    I shall make your place new within the lofty Kingdom.

66. I shall set open before you the gates in all the heavens,[95]
    And shall make your path smooth, free from terror and vexation.

67. With might shall I take you, and enfold (you) with love,
    And lead (you) unto (your) home, the blessed Abode.[96]

68. For ever shall I show you the noble Father;[97]
    I shall lead you in, into (His) presence, (clad) in pure raiment.

69. I shall show you the Mother of the beings of Light,
    For ever shall you rejoice in lauded happiness.

70. I shall reveal to you the virtuous brethren,
    . . . who are filled with happiness.

71. You shall [dwell] joyfully among them all for ever,
    Beside all the jewels[98] and the venerable gods.

72. Fear and death shall never overtake (you more),
    Neither shall destruction, distress or wretchedness.

73. Peace shall be yours in the place of salvation,
    In the company of all the gods and those who dwell in Peace.
    (*End of the sixth canto*)

VII.

1. Come, oh spirit! Fear no more!
   Death has fallen, and sickness has fled away.

2. The time of troubled days has ended,
   Its terror has departed amid clouds of fire.

3. Come, spirit, step forth!
   Let there be no desire for the house of affliction,[99]

4. Which is mere destruction and the anguish of death,[100]
   Truly you were cast out of your native abode.

5. And all the pangs you have suffered in Hell at the outset
   You have undergone for (the sake of) this (joy).

6. Come yet nearer, in gladness, without regret;
   Lie not content in the dwelling of death.

7. Turn not back, nor regard the (ugly) forms[101] of the bodies,
   Which lie (there)[102] in wretchedness, they (and) their followers.
8. See, they return (to earth) with every rebirth,
   Through every agony and every choking (?) prison.[103]
9. See, they are reborn among all (kinds of) creatures,
   And their voice is heard in burning sighs.
10. Come yet nearer, and do not dote on this worldly beauty
    That perishes in all (its) variety.
11. It falls and melts as snow in the sunshine,
    (For) no fair form survives.
12. It withers and fades as a dying flower,
    Whose grace is destroyed, and it wilts in the sun.
13. Yet come, you spirit, and be not fond
    Of the passing of the hours or the fleeting days.
14. Turn not back to every outward show (*dīdan*).
    Sensual desire (is) death, and leads to destruction.
15. Hence, spirit, come! . . .
    I shall lead (you) to the height, [to your native abode.]
16. I shall show (you your) *home,[104]
    The hope you have yearned for . . .
17. Remember, oh spirit! Look on this *anguish
    That (you have) borne through the fury of all (your) enemies.
18. Behold the world[105] and the prison of creation;
    For all desires will be destroyed quickly.
19. Terror, fire and destruction
    Will overcome all those who dwell therein.
20. The height will be shattered with all (its) dwellings;
    All the heavens will fall down into the deep.
21. The trap of destruction will swiftly close
    Upon those boasting deceivers there.
22. The whole dominion, with the brilliance of all the stars,
    Ruin will come upon them, and the pangs of their iniquity.
23. All the princes and the border rebels
    (Will suffer) in wretchedness within the blazing fire for ever.
24. Every desire and every bright appearance (*dīdan*)
    Will dissolve (?) . . .
25. All of life, from every seed and [stem]
    Will be destroyed swiftly and brought to ruin.
26. [All] of the lusts, gilded with all (their) charm,
    . . . fire will be heaped upon them.
27. . . . each mansion . . . which has been established—
    (Each) will be broken open, and will fall down upon them.
    [*three verses fragmentarily preserved*]
31. [In] the troubled deeps where all is chaos
    They will receive (their) deserts in endless distress.
    [*three verses fragmentarily preserved*]

35. The parts of the dead souls will be [fettered]
    In the tomb of Death where all is darkness,[106]
36. And (where) all (is) the woe of darkness . . .
    Truly they will be clad in distress . . .[107]

VII. A Seventh canto of Angad Rōšnān

1. They (the sinful) will become the bricks (which are) faulty and
       broken,
   Which are not fit to go up to the keepers of the Building.[108]
2. They will fall into the deep and be devoured by death
   They will clothe themselves in darkness, agony and fire.
3. They will nevermore find anyone to pity them
   None will open for them the gate of hell.
4. They will be grieved with sorrow amid all the quakings;
   They will groan and shriek in bondage for ever.
5. There is none who will *hear and have mercy upon them,
   For the sake of . . . destruction.
       [five verses missing or badly preserved]
11. Be of good cheer on this day of departing,
    [For] (your) sickness is ended, and all your rigors.
12. And you shall go forth out of this deceiver[109]
    Which has made you weak through distress and the agony of death.
13. You were held back within the abyss, where all is turmoil;
    You were captured (?) in every place.[110]
14. You were suspended in all the rebirths;
    You have suffered injury in all the cities.
       [last three verses badly preserved]

VIII. Eighth canto of Angad Rōšnān

1. The course of death (?)[111] has been diverted (?)[112] from me,
   Which dragged me down stumbling during many a battle.
2. My soul is saved from all the sins
   Which [led] (me) with anguish every day.
3. The dark image is taken away from me,
   Which imprisoned me in (its) snare.
4. I am clothed with a bright garment of Light,[113]
   Every kind of [dirt?] is taken from me.
5. I have passed beyond the pain and anguish of their bodies[114]
   All guilt has been (far) removed from [me].
6. I am equipped and aided by the Savior of my spirit,
   Through the . . . power, which was never constrained.
       [four verses missing or badly preserved]
11. Those who are of the same nature[115] as the demons
    Will pass again through all the prisons[116] and the cycle of death.

12. I saw that it (the abandoned body) became dark, and there was no
    Light in it;
    Hideous in appearance and overpowering in form.
13. The Savior said to me: Spirit, behold the husk (*niδāmag*)[117]
    That you have abandoned in the deep, in terror [and] destruction!
14. Truly it was a deceptive partner for you,
    A distressful prison in every hell.
15. Truly it was a harsh death for you,
    Which [severed] your soul from life for ever.
16. Truly it was a path of stumbling for you,
    [Which] was nothing but dreadful deeds, and much sickness.[118]
    [last verse only fragmentarily preserved]

Notes

1. This reading of the word seems more probable, in view of MacKenzie's "Two Sogdian *HWYDGM'N* Fragments," than the older reading *Huwīdagmān*.
2. For this typically Gnostic imagery, compare Arnold-Döben, *Die Bildersprache des Mani-chäismus*, pp. 45ff.; *Die Bildersprache der Gnosis*, pp. 215ff.
3. Compare also the superb introduction to these hymns in Boyce, *Hymn-Cycles*, pp. 1–23.
4. Sundermann, *The Manichaean Hymn Cycles Huyadagmān and Angad Rōšnān in Parthian and Sogdian*, London, 1990. Dr. Sundermann was so kind as to make available to me his new readings and translations even before the publication of that book.
5. In the Chinese *London Hymnscroll*, verses 262–338, is a rendering of the first canto of *Huyadagmān*. It bears the title, "In Praise of the World of Light. Containing seventy-eight Odes, each of which is in four lines. By Wei Mo [= Mār Ammō], the Mu-she [Teacher]" (Tsui Chi's translation). This text was translated in: Tsui Chi, "Mo Ni Chiao Hsia Pu Tsan," pp. 199–208; A. Waley, translation indicated in Boyce, *Hymn-Cycles*, pp. 68–77 (notes); Schmidt-Glintzer, *Chinesische Manichaica*, pp. 44–52. Compare also Bryder, *The Chinese Transformation of Manichaeism*, pp. 63–74.
6. Boyce, *Hymn-Cycles*, p. 67, n. 1.
7. Cf. Bryder, *op. cit.*; Schmidt-Glintzer, "Das buddhistische Gewand des Manichäismus."
8. Henning, "A Fragment."
9. Zieme, *Texte*, pp. 31f. and 46f.
10. In the Pth. text M 233 (ed. and trans. Sundermann, *Hymn Cycles*, p. 14) it says, "(Here) begins (lit.: Begun [is]) *Huyadagmān*. Mār *Xwaršxēd-Wahman, the Bishop, reveals it and makes it manifest. . . ." Parts of hymns in honor of this church leader are known. Compare Boyce, *Reader*, p. 141 (text ck); Colditz, "Hymnen an Šād Ohrmezd." S believes that this bishop completed the *Huyadagmān* cycle, at least the first canto of which is ascribed to Mār Ammō.
11. The fragment no. 6386 of the Otani collection, Kyoto, (Pth. text in Sogdian Script) reads, ". . . melody, when they [praise] one another. They [dwell] in spiritual [well-being] eternally." Compare Sundermann, *Hymn Cycles*, p. 22.
12. The verses 66a–70 are translated after the rendering of Sims-Williams, who in his publication of the Pth. text T M 406a in late Sogdian (Uighur) script, containing the verses 66a–67 and 70–71, gives the full text from 66a (partially preserved) to 71. Sims-Williams, "A New Fragment from *Huyadagmān*," pp. 323–24 (with following commentary). To verse 66a S-W notes, "This verse was omitted by mistake from the otherwise complete Chinese version. The beginning of the verse survives only in the Turkish fragment [TM 278: Türk. Man. III,45] . . ." Compare also Sundermann, *Hymn Cycles*, p. 22.

13. These verses are translated from the Turkish fragment of *Huyadagmān* I (mentioned previously). Compare Henning, "A fragment of the Manichaean Hymn-Cycles in Turkish," pp. 122–24. Henning also gives the translation of the more verbose Chinese version. I am thankful to Dr. J. P. Laut for making suggestions for improving the reading and translation.

14. The Chinese reads, "All the Saints are void of birth and death,/And the killing devil of Impermanence will not attack and hurt them. . . ." Henning, *op. cit.*, p. 124.

15. Literally, "lusts that are not pleasing" (B).

16. The *zōnē*, that is, the zodiac, is meant in cosmological terms (S).

17. These are the forms of living beings in which one can be reborn, according to Manichaean belief.

18. I. e., the animal types of existence.

19. This is a reference to a possible rebirth among plants, which, according to the Manichaean view, also contain divine Light, that is, have souls. The meaning of the last sentence remains unclear.

20. An image often found in Christian and Zoroastrian apocalyptic literature. Compare *The Apocalypse of Thomas*.

21. Again, an image common in apocalyptic texts, especially apocryphal ones.

22. Literally, in the distress of these hell-deeps (B).

23. Another order of the verses V and V.A and others is suggested by the Sogdian texts edited by MacKenzie, "Two Sogdian *HWYDGM'N* Fragments."

24. "Probably a reference to the best kind of Persian water, the *water called golden,* which no one was allowed to drink, on pain of death, except the Persian king and his eldest son." Boyce, *Hymn-Cycles,* p. 87, n. 2.

25. This is a motif to be found in the apocryphal *Apocalypse of Thomas.* Compare Hennecke and Schneemelcher, *The New Testament Apocrypha* II, p. 801 (art. by A. de Santos Otero).

26. Compare the Sogdian text in 1.1. We here render the Parthian text.

27. One verse from VI preserved in Sogdian. Compare 1.1.

28. Compare *Psalm-Book* 188,21f.: "Take me up upon thy wings, o eagle, fly with me to the skies./ Set my white robe upon me: take me in as a gift to my Father."

29. B amends *[sad] f.*

30. That is, the soul had formerly forgotten the Realm of Light as its place of origin. For the symbolism of forgetfulness, compare Jonas, *The Gnostic Religion,* pp. 68ff.

31. For the symbols of the garment, the diadem, and so on, compare Arnold-Döben, *Die Bildersprache des Manichäismus,* pp. 149ff.; *Die Bildersprache der Gnosis,* pp. 124ff.

32. That is, the structure in which the Dark Powers are imprisoned. This usually refers to eschatological events (as in *Mir. Man.* I, p. 185), and it is interesting that in Parthian and Central Asian Manichaeism the demons can be seen as already having been vanquished. This is in accordance with the present interpretation of eschatological imagery in the *Shepherd of Hermas,* used by Manichaeans in Iran and Central Asia. Compare also the *Apocalypse of Thomas,* referred to previously. For the eschatological motif of the structure, or building, compare Arnold-Döben, *Die Bildersprache der Gnosis,* pp. 107f.

33. The Paradise of the First Man. In a text published by Henning (*Mir. Man.* I, pp. 184f.), it says, "And above that new structure (i. e., wherein the demons are captured), make the New Paradise, so that it may be a place (of rest) for Ohrmizd (the First Man) and the gods . . . and (also) for us . . ."

34. I. e., the First Man.

35. This and the following verses after B.

36. I. e., as Manichaeans.

37. Reference to a god, maybe the Great Nous, or the Third Messenger.

38. S. suggests the reading *u hw b'm syzdyft* . . . in line (*b*).

39. The verses 1–4 follow the editing and translation of the Sogdian text So 14.470 (T II K) by Sundermann, *Hymn Cycles,* p. 23 (text 36.1). (verses 1 and 3 are written in red, verses 2 and 4 in black).

40. Light and Darkness.

41. The following verses are rendered after Sundermann's edition and translation of the text So 14.610 (2) (T II K 178). Sundermann, *Hymn Cycles,* p. 25 (text 36.6). The last four verses have been only partially preserved.

42. The "second death" is mentioned in *Kephalaia* I, p. 104, 6–10. "It denotes the fate of the irredeemable souls who will remain separated from the World of Light for ever and will be locked up in the *bōlos* of darkness in the end." Sundermann, *Hymn Cycles,* p. 25, n. 27.

43. Only the first verse has been preserved fragmentarily in text So 14.610 (2) (T II K 178). Compare Sundermann, *Hymn Cycles,* p. 25.

44. Nothing preserved.

45. Compare Sundermann, *Hymn Cycles,* pp. 25f.; D. N. MacKenzie, "Two Sogdian *HWYDGM'N* Fragments." The texts referred to are *text A*: So. 14.445 (= T II D 170). Sundermann's text 36.7; *text B*: So. 14.557 and various fragments (Sundermann's text 36.8); *text C*: So. 14.651 (= T II K 178), Sundermann's text 36.9. In II–VI (Sogdian) also *text D* is used: So. 14.610 (T II K 178), Sundermann's text 36.10.

46. MacKenzie remarks, "Although the text presents a number of linguistic problems, it is patent that the second and third Sogdian verses . . . correspond to verses V 19 and 20 of the Parthian original (*MHC* 88f.), and the fifth verses . . . almost certainly to Vb (*MHC* 92). As only one verse, the fourth, separates these, it becomes clear that the tentative placing of the sequence numbered *V a 1,2 . . . 11,12 here (*MHC* 41f.) cannot be maintained. Although the theme changes here, from hell to heaven, *V a may belong to later part of the fifth canto." MacKenzie, *op. cit.,* p. 426.

47. Translation after MacKenzie.

48. Translation after Sundermann.

49. Translation after MacKenzie.

50. Translation after MacKenzie.

51. Sundermann, *Hymn Cycles,* p. 27. Text D follows text C immediately. Cf. n. 46.

52. Translation after Henning in Boyce, *Hymn-Cycles,* p. 95.

53. Translation after Sundermann.

54. The divine Light, of which the soul is part, is the "substance" of the structure of the cosmos.

55. Literally, "niceness" (S) for *xwych-'kh.* For this word, compare Sundermann, *Hymn Cycles,* p. 28, n. 50. For the concept of the soul's beauty, compare I. Gershevitch, "Beauty as the Living Soul in Iranian Manichaeism."

56. The battle of the pious individual against sin reflects the cosmic battle of Good against Evil. The translation of this verse is Sundermann's.

57. It is not clear whether the word "immortal" (*nvšy,* partly legible) really qualifies "mind" (*m'nprm't'k = m'n*).

58. Compare Müller, "Eine Hermas-Stelle in manichäischer Version"; Cirillo, "'Pastor Hermas' and 'Revelatio manichaica.'"

59. Translation suggested by S.

60. Compare *Psalm-Book* 70,3–5: "The sea and its waves thou hast destroyed by thy faith (?); the beasts that are in it, . . . thou hast overpowered (?) them . . ." Compare also *Hymn-scroll,* 19.

61. For the terrible forms of the powers of Evil and their significance, compare Klimkeit, "Das Gestaltprinzip."

62. Compare *Mir. Man.* iii,k 1–2: "He (Jesus) wanted to have the fiery waves break asunder, so that everything would be roasted in fire." Compare also *Psalm-Book* 54,13–15: "I am in the midst of my enemies, the beasts surrounding me; the burden which I bear is of the powers and principalities. They burned (?) in their wrath, they rose up against me. . . ."

63. Or, banner (*drafš*). Thus B.

64. Traces too scanty for identification.

65. The prison is a metaphor for the body and the world.

66. Or, by much anguish, if we read *'njvgyft* for *'njyvgft.*

67. Here it becomes obvious that there is a correspondence between the body and the world, between macrocosm and microcosm.
68. The limbs here probably refer to the limbs of the soul.
69. I. e., through rebirth (B).
70. Translation suggested by S.
71. The fourth limb of the soul.
72. Only *cy* (.) preserved.
73. The third limb of the soul.
74. The fifth limb of the soul.
75. The second limb of the soul; in the first or the fourth verse there would have been a reference to "my reason" (*bām*), the first limb of the soul.
76. Limbs of the soul.
77. Literally, all its kinds (*gōnag*).
78. In III.C,13 it says, "Who shall take off from me this [carnal?] body, and clothe [me] in a new body . . . ?"
79. I. e., gods in the Moon.
80. Compare *Psalm-Book* 38,30: "Let us set before us gladness which is the sign of God, but let us kill grief, which is the sign of the Darkness."
81. Here, in the saving function of the Nous (S).
82. Translation suggested by S; Boyce translates, "Thou art the . . . garment of my body, which brought dismay to the Powers (of Darkness). . . ." B refers to *Psalm-Book* 116,26f.: "I am the love of the Father, being the robe clothing thee."
83. I. e., the Great Nous.
84. Compare the Turfan fragment M 7 II Ri (Hymn to the Living Soul), ch. III, text 7, v. ('): "Understand your nature, the pure word, which is a leader for the soul in the body." Compare Bornkamm, *Mythos und Legende*, pp. 13f.
85. Compare S 9 (R II 30), v. (*p*): "Then she (the demoness *Āz*) fashioned the good soul (*gyān*) from the five Light Elements, the armory of Ohrmizd [the First Man], the Lord, and imprisoned it in the body." Compare ch. II, text 6, v. (*p*).
86. Compare M 551: "I am washed of dirt and much stench." (*HR* II, p. 67; *MStI.*, p. 29).
87. Literally, "wherein thou hast gone through these drownings" (B).
88. Compare *Psalm-Book* 153,3: "Because of thy strong protection, lo, my diseases passed far from me."
89. For the image of the treasure and the pearl, compare Arnold-Döben, *Die Bildersprache des Manichäismus*, pp. 45ff.; *Die Bildersprache der Gnosis*, pp. 215ff. It is clear that the Manichaeans were well acquainted with the Gnostic "Hymn of the Pearl" in the apocryphal *Acts of Thomas*.
90. Cf. *Psalm-Book* 116,26, n. 63.
91. Compare *Psalm-Book* 152,19f.: "Many are the labours that I suffered while I was in this dark house. Thou therefore, my true Light, enlighten me within."
92. That is, the Dark Powers were invested with Light when they devoured the "sons" of the First Man after his descent to their world. These are essentially the limbs of the soul.
93. I. e., the Light was taken away from the demons by the Third Messenger.
94. I. e., the redeeming gods and messengers appeared in the world to liberate the souls of Light from Darkness, that is, Death.
95. For the image of the gate, compare Arnold-Döben, *Die Bildersprache des Manichäismus*, pp. 139–41, *Die Bildersprache der Gnosis*, pp. 111ff.; Klimkeit, "Das Tor als Symbol im Manichäismus."
96. The New Paradise (B).
97. The First Man (B).
98. A term for deities.
99. Compare *Psalm-Book* 70,29–30: "Henceforth thou hast no cares, for thou hast left the house of care behind, even the body of death, and hast cast it down before the face of its enemies."

100. Compare *Psalm-Book* 87, 3–5: "[I] strip myself of the body of destruction, the habitation [of] the powers of death (?) and ascend on high to thy Aeons from which I was once separated."

101. For the principle of form in Manichaeism compare Klimkeit, "Das Gestaltprinzip im Manichäismus."

102. On the earth (B).

103. The various forms of possible rebirths are regarded as "prisons."

104. *Pdys[t]* amended to *pdyšt*.

105. Probably in the sense of, Look down on the world.

106. That is, those souls that have not found the way to salvation will be doomed eternally. The *Apocalypse of Thomas* says of the sixth day (of the seven days of the Judgment), "Then all men will flee into the tombs and hide themselves from before the righteous angels, and say, 'Oh that the earth would open and swallow us.'" A. de Santos Otero, "Apocalypse of Thomas," in Hennecke and Schneemelcher, eds., *New Testament Apocrypha* II, 1st. ed., (pp. 798–803), cf. p. 801.

107. The events at the end of the world, described also in Mani's *Šābuhragān* (compare ch. XIX, text 2), are reminiscent of the descriptions in apocryphal apocalyptic literature known to the Manichaeans. Compare A. de Santos Otero, *art. cit.*; Koenen, "Manichaean Apocalypticism."

108. If indeed *h(y)štyg*, "brick," not *h(v)štyg*, "strong (one)," is to be read. According to Boyce, *Hymn-Cycles*, p. 165, n. 5, Henning sees here a reference to the *Shepherd of Hermas (Pastor Hermae)*, comparing it with its Manichaean version, found in Turfan (fragment M 87a, ed. Müller, "Eine Hermas-Stelle," p. 2; cf. *MStI.*, p. 34). Here it says (l. 17–21), "And all stones that have come in (i. e., have been brought in) through the door are layed down in the foundation, and those that have not come in through the door were destroyed, and they took them back to the place from where they had been brought." There follows an "explanation" (*vizārišn*), the part referring to this passage not being preserved in the Turfan fragment. In the Latin (Vulgata) version of *Pastor Hermae*, six young men who build a tower are mentioned. Here it says, "Did you see the stones . . . that came into the structure of the tower by the gate laid down (there), whereas those that did not come in (i. e., through the door) were put back in their original place?" Compare Müller, *op. cit.* For the tower and its symbolism (as referring to the Church) Compare P. Vielhauer, "Apocalyptic in Early Christianity," in Hennecke and Schneemelcher, *op. cit.*, p. 631: An old lady, (herself the Church), shows the shepherd, after his long prayer and fasting, "six young men building an enormous tower, raised upon the waters, using white stones which were being brought by thousands of men . . . ; she explains the building of the tower as an allegory of the Church." Compare also P. Vielhauer, *Geschichte der urchristlichen Literatur.* Berlin and New York 1975, pp. 513–23 ("Der Hirt des Hermas").

109. The body (B).

110. In the course of infinitely many rebirths. The idea often recurs in Uighur Buddhist literature from Central Asia. Thus in the *Maitrisimit* (Hami Version) it says, "[Since] ancient times the children of men, being reborn in this *saṃsāra*, dying and changing their forms, suffer pain and woe." Geng Shimin and H.-J. Klimkeit, *Das Zusammentreffen mit Maitreya*, Pt. I. Wiesbaden 1988, p. 125. Compare also p. 295f.

111. Reading *cmg [m]rmyn*.

112. *Pdyzb'd*, from *pdy(y)z-*, "chase away, drive off"?

113. For the image of the garment of Light, compare Arnold-Döben, *Die Bildersprache des Manichäismus*, pp. 149ff.; *Die Bildersprache der Gnosis*, pp. 124ff.

114. Cf. I, 3b.

115. Or, of the same form (*hāmčihrag*); H: "homophoric"; Puech: "consubstantial." Compare Boyce, *Hymn-Cycles*, p. 171, n. 2.

116. Reincarnations.

117. In the Turfan fragment M 2 a (cf. ch. XIII, text 4, v. 2) it says in the "Funerary Hymns," "Set up (or: Set [into the world]) am I, in this divine form, deprived of my (heavenly)

apparel (*niδāmag*)." In Gnosticism, the self, or soul (Gr. *pneuma,* not *psychē*) needs to be clothed, either in a corporeal garment ("husk"), the body, or in a heavenly garment, for otherwise it would be "naked." The *Corpus Hermeticum* 7,1–3, says, "Search for the leader, who will lead you to the gates of knowledge, to the place where bright Light shines . . . But first you must rend the garment that you wear (i. e., the body) . . ." (Quoted after Bultmann, *Das Urchristentum.* Hamburg, 1962, p. 159). P. Vielhauer has pointed out the close relationship between the *Shepherd of Hermas* and Hermetic litera-ture. Compare Vielhauer, *op. cit.,* pp. 518ff. The analysis of the *Shepherd of Hermas* in *all* its versions—including the Ethiopian version, as well as the works pointed to by Viel-hauer in this connection, namely Hermetic literature, *Poimandres,* the Christian *Sibyl-lines,* and even Boethius' *Consolation of Philosophy*—is bound to throw light in a significant way on Mahāyāna works that originated not only in Central Asia, where Manichaeans long had a leading role, but also in Gandhara and the Kushan Realm, where Mār Ammō was successfully active as a Manichaean missionary in the third century.

118. This is again reminiscent of the *Corpus Hermeticum,* from which we have quoted previ-ously. Compare Bultmann, *op. cit.,* p. 159 and pp. 239–40, and his elucidation of Gnosti-cism, pp. 152–62 (inspired by Jonas). Compare also the imagery—not only of the garment—in the "Hymn of the Pearl" in the *Acts of Thomas.* Jonas compares it with the imagery of the *Odes of Solomon.* Jonas, *Gnosis und spätantiker Geist* I, 3d ed., pp. 327f. For the *Odes of Solomon* compare M. Lattke, *Die Oden Salomos,* Vol. I–II (including Ia).

CHAPTER ELEVEN

Miscellaneous Verse Texts

This chapter encompasses verse texts in which various redeeming gods are invoked and praised. A hymn from one of Mani's hymn cycles (text 1) probably lauds Jesus the Splendor as the Redeemer. Mani invokes him to assist him in the spreading of the new faith. He regards his own mission in the world as a battle against the forces of Darkness, and hence his activity is related to that of the redeeming gods which are described as "battle-seeking" (razmyōz).

Of special importance is a dialogue (text 2) between the soul, depicted as a boy, and a redeeming figure who is most probably Jesus the Splendor. The boy yearns for redemption, but Jesus, pointing to previous Messengers of Light and their beneficence, urges him to be patient and strengthens him in his struggle against the powers of Darkness.

Texts 4 and 6 reflect the conflict with other religions, specifically Judaism, Christianity, Zurvanism, and "idolatry." These texts belong to the Iranian tradition and show that in Iranian lands Manichaeism vehemently criticized other faiths, in spite of its tendency to adopt alien religious notions. Who the "idolaters" may be, we do not know. Such criticism is probably directed against Babylonian and Hellenistic cults in Mesopotamia and Iran. The Buddhists are not mentioned specifically anywhere, even if a critique of the cult of the Buddha image might be implied. Rather, there seems to have been a tolerant attitude toward Buddhists in Central Asia, even though a warning against tendencies toward the excessive adoption of foreign ideas is sometimes discerned.

In spite of their criticism of idolatry, the Manichaeans did honor, if not venerate the image of Mani, as we can infer from texts pertaining to the Bema festival. Mani was depicted in iconic form in Central Asia and China, and one such image survives even to this day.[1]

Text 7 gives us an insight into the cultic observances on the holy Monday, the sabbath of the Manichaeans. It was a day of confession and prayer, as our document bears out. The fact that the Manichaean community regarded itself as part of an extensive "Community of Light," encompassing gods, messengers, and angels as well, is documented by text 8. An invocation of the gods in the Moon (text 9) is probably part of a general invocation of all protective deities. Text 10, finally, is part of a large hymn, the main content of which is unknown.

1. *Verses from a hymn cycle by Mani* (Persian)

These are verses of a psalm, originally written in Aramaic, and probably stemming from Mani. There are a Middle Persian and a Parthian translation; here we have rendered the Persian version into English. Boyce observes, "It is not certain which of the redeeming gods is invoked, but it seems probable that it is Jesus the Splendour."[2]

 1. Welcome,[3] my great stature,
     Welcome, my bright form,
     Welcome, my shining appearance!
 2. . . .
     Welcome, my [powerful] word,
     From which I let others drink eternal life!
     . . .
 3. . . .
     Welcome, my nourishing meal,
     With which I satisfy the hunger of my friends!
     Welcome, my chalice of salvation,
     With which I delight the loved ones!
     Welcome, my strong shield and my trusty sword of speech and
         hearing,[4]
     And my well-prepared armor, which is all alertness.[5]
     Welcome, comrade and companion[6] in all battles!
     . . .

2. *Dialogue between the soul and the redeemer* (Parthian)

This is a dialogue in the form of a hymn between a "boy," representing the soul yearning for salvation, and the Redeemer. They speak the verses of the hymn alternately. The hymn is an abecedarian one, arranged so that the letters beginning the verses are arranged backwards, starting with the last letter of the Syrian alphabet. The first three and the last three verses are missing. One verse is inserted between *zain* and *waw*. The hymn was probably sung antiphonally. The boy is, as Henning comments, "the soul's personified will for salvation, i.e., about the same as the *'enthymēsis* of Life.'"[7] The Redeemer is most probably Jesus the Splendor, but as Boyce points out, there is an attempt in verse *heth* to relate him to the historical Jesus, Jesus the Messiah.[8]

 (p) [Jesus]: . . . the garment of the beings of Light. [For] out of stupefaction
      the four quarters of the world were plunged into turmoil. But you, beloved
      one, endure here (in the world) for the sake of the souls,[9] so that (their)
      salvation may be attained[10] through you.

(f for ') [Boy]: The love and the service that you, oh God, have always shown to me are fully manifest. But I suffered this one time when you ascended and left me behind like an orphan.

(s) [Jesus]: Remember, oh Boy, how the chief of the battle-seeking ones,[11] the Father, the God Ohrmizd, left his sons behind in the depths when he ascended from the Dark for the sake of great gain.

(n) [Boy]: Hear my supplication, you most beloved of beloved names! If you do not free me (from the world) this time, send many gods so that I may gain victory over the evildoers.

(m) [Jesus]: I have instructed the Great Nous to send you messengers when . . . had come. Be patient, like the burdened beings of Light[12] are.

(l) [Boy]: The world and (its) children were alarmed. For my sake Zarathustra descended into the realm of Persia. He revealed the Truth and he chose my "limbs"[13] from among the beings of Light of the seven regions.[14]

(k) [Jesus]: When Satan saw that he had descended, he sent out the demons. Before the gods were able to return the attack, they had hurt you, oh beloved one, and wisdom was distorted.[15]

(y) [Boy]: My suffering ceased at the time when I was . . . by Buddha Shākya-muni. He opened the door of salvation[16] for the fortunate souls among the Indians which he freed.

(p for t) [Jesus]: Because of the (skillful) means and wisdom[17] that you received from the Buddha, Dībat,[18] the great Virgin, envies you. When he (Bud-dha) entered into Nirvāṇa, he commanded you: "Await Maitreya[19] here."

(h) [Boy]: Then Jesus had mercy for a second time.[20] He sent the four pure winds[21] to help me. He bound the three winds,[22] he destroyed Jerusalem with the steeds[23] of the demons of wrath.

(j) [Jesus]: The cup of poison and death . . . was poured out over you by Iscariot, together with the sons of Israel. And much further sorrow . . .
   [three lines illegible]

(z) [Boy]: . . . [The number] of the prophets is small, and the numbers of the two armies attacking me are countless.[24]

(v) [Jesus]: Your great battle (is) like (that of) the God Ohrmizd, and your col-lection of treasures[25] is like that of the Chariots of Light.[26] You can also redeem the Living Self that is (trapped) in flesh and wood[27] from Āz (the demon of Greed).

(h) [Boy]: All three gods[28] protect this child, and they sent me Mār Mani as the savior who leads me out of this servitude, in which I served the foes in fear against my will.

(d) [Jesus]: I gave you freedom, my comrade . . .

3. *Verses from an abecedarian hymn* (Persian)

Only a few verses of this abecedarian hymn, which is rich in imagery, have been preserved. Unfortunately the meaning of the imagery mostly remains obscure because of the fragmentary nature of our text. Six or seven verses at the end are missing.

    (') Blessing, praise and honor to the Lord, . . . the holy Name, . . .
             [eight verses missing]

    (j) . . . of [frag]rance.

(x for k) The bright Sun and the shining Full Moon,

(r for l) They gleam and glitter from the trunk of this tree.

    (m) The lustrous birds strut about there in joy,

    (n) Doves and peacocks of all [colors] exult there.

    (s) They sing and call . . .

    (') They praise . . . the body which he . . .

4. *Verses from an abecedarian hymn* (Persian)

This hymn is a *memento mori*. It refers to the futility of earthly joys in view of the Day of Judgment. Eleven verses preceded our text; five or six followed it.

(r for l) . . . the corrupt heresies and (false) teachers,

    (m) Mantle, garment, monochrome and multicolored damask,

    (n) The coquetry of women and the songs of joy,

    (s) The truly lovely appearance of orchards and gardens,

  ('for') Presents, gifts and promises:
          —they can not help on the day of distress.

    (p) The image of the Father, of the Maiden of Light,[29]

(h for c) This alone can help on the day [of distress].

5. *Verses from a hymn on salvation* (Parthian)

Only a short portion from a hymn on the joys of salvation is preserved.

    1. . . . drunkenness . . . it[30] moves (on) the paths (?) . . . ; In separation
          (from the body) it lays down . . . illness, old age and eternal death.

    2. It attains salvation, fearless confidence, health and youth.

6. *Verses from two polemical hymns* (Persian)

Only the last two of a collection of polemical hymns are translated here. The first of these is directed against idolaters, the second against Zurvanists, Jews, and Christians.

[Title]: Homilies of the congregation of Abursām[31]

First Hymn

    (š) The lands are confused by the idols that misled (them),
          By the images on walls, (made of) wood and stone.[32]

    (t) They fear deception,[33] they bow down before it and honor it.
          They have abandoned the Father in Heaven and pray to deception.

Second Hymn

[*the first four verses are omitted*]

(h)   And they who venerate the burning fire, do they not know that their end will therefore be by fire?

(v)   And they say that Ohrmizd and Ahriman are brothers, and because of these words they come to ruin.[34]

(z)   They display their deceit and contempt for Ohrmizd (when they say) that the demon Māhmī taught him how to fill the world with light.[35]

(h)   They kill the creatures of Ohrmizd and Ahriman and cut them into pieces;
      They have been foes to both their families.
      [*two verses omitted*]

(x for k)   They (the Christians) call the son of Mary, the son of Adonai,[36] the seventh one.[37] If he (Adonai) is the Lord of all, why did he crucify his own son?[38]

(r for l)   It is just that the infidels go to Hell for they themselves are the cause of sin and the ruin of evildoers (?).

(m)   That which they (the Jews) did is like (the deed) of the God of Marcion,
      Who led him who was not his own; and they seized him and killed him.[39]
      [*seven verses omitted*]

(š)   In the end, on that last day, they will be put to shame,
      all they who worship the idols, and they will go to their ruin.
      [*last verse missing*]

7. *Verses from a Monday hymn* (Parthian)

This is an abecedarian hymn sung at the holy Monday ceremony. One verse preceded our text, and eight or nine must have followed it. The Monday hymns were particularly concerned with moral striving, the confession of sins, prayer, and praise.

(')   . . .

(b)   Devout and beneficent brethren,
      Chosen elect and noble sons!

(g)   Souls of light, noble community of the elect,
      Pillars of love and children of brightness!

(d)   Preserve (your) zeal for God's commandment,
      So that you may become flawless, perfect and great.

(h)   Keep all the members prepared
      For the praise of the peace of the community.

(v)   You are the chosen and the elect from among the many,
      One of a thousand and two of ten thousand.[40]

(z) You are the children of the higher wisdom,
    The Firstborn of the perfect Day.[41]

(h) . . .

(t) The Light shines, immortal love,
    He gives seed to his own laborer.[42]

(y) Strive zealously on this Monday,
    The blessed day of sinlessness.

(k) Every one of you who confesses
    Should praise and pray.

(l) Supplicate and pray before one another,
    Forgive (each other's) sins, put away (your) misdeeds.

(m) Lead the guest of Light, the imprisoned Man,[43]
    In peace to tranquility.

(n) Ponder attentively the strict commandment,
    And consider (this) deep wisdom.[44]

8. Verses from an abecedarian hymn (Persian)

Here an almost complete abecedarian hymn has been preserved. It invokes blessings on the gods, the angels, and the Manichaean community.

1. (') Much blessing and praise to the Messengers of Greatness. May they
       bring peace to the Religion of the East[45] in every land and in
       (every) province . . .

2. (g) Wakeful shepherd, Kaftinus,[46] Leader,

   (d) Valiant, loving Jacob Nariman,[47]

   (h) Community of valiant Light Elements[48] that have been pardoned,

   (v) Strong community of chosen ones and congregation of peace,

   (z) May your power increase through the Father, the God Zurvān;

   (h) It (that power) is always praised by the whole Greatness (the commu-
       nity of gods).

   (t) Accept strength from the gods on high

   (y) And godliness and praise from the powers of Greatness.

3. (x for k) May the Lord Jesus, the chief of the Messengers,
       Delight you in (his) brightness, you strong ones!

4. (m) May the Lord Mani, the Son of Greatness,
       Strengthen you benefactors with wisdom.

5. (s) May many[49] praises and blessings of the living ones (gods)
       Descend from the whole community of gods upon us happy ones!

   (p) He answers my call and helps me,
       As (he), (endowed) with great power, did in the beginning.

   (q) He establishes weal and peace in all lands,

   (r) He grants peace to the beneficent ones and puts the demons to shame.

   (š) He increases the joy of the leaders of peace

   (t) (And) quickly gladdens all the pious ones.

9. *Invocation of the gods in the Moon* (Parthian)

This text contains praises to various redeeming gods. It is an abecedarian hymn where the initial letters of the verses start with the last letter of the Syrian alphabet and go backward. In verse *t/s* Jesus is invoked, in verse *n* probably the First Man, in verse *m* the Maiden of Light and in verse *l* the soul-gathering angels and the seven "shiplords." Thus this is an invocation of the gods in the Moon. This was probably supplemented by invocations of other gods, including those in the Sun. Six verses preceded our text, and eleven or twelve followed it.

(')   Eternal praise from the whole community that has been pardoned.

(t for s)   Chief of the messengers, Lord, Friend, Jesus, Savior, Ruler of the holy religion,—(you are) eternally holy!

(n)   The first of those that go out, . . . who dispel the dark foes, beloved of the Lights,—(you are) eternally (holy)!

(m)   Merciful Mother, Maiden of Light, soul of the God Zurvān, head of all wisdom, who has [enlightened] all the gods,—(you are) eternally holy!

(l)   Soul-gathering angels, seven [shiplords], . . .

10. *Verses on the Euphrates* (Persian)

Here three verses of an abecedarian hymn describing the mighty river in Mani's homeland are preserved.

(h for z)   That Euphrates, the king of rivers; from its bed are born . . .

(h)   It nourishes all trees with its radiance.

(t)   It flows swiftly and waters all the lands.

Notes

1. See Bryder, ". . . Where the faint traces of Manichaeism disappear."
2. Boyce, *Reader,* p. 169.
3. Literally, Hail to thee; in Pth., Hail upon thee.
4. As B points out, in accordance with Henning, "The simile is a twofold one, with chiastic placing of its parts, since active speech is compared with the aggressive sword, and passive hearing with the defensive shield." Boyce, *Reader,* p. 169, n. 3.
5. As Henning points out, there is a wordplay here between *zēn,* "armor, arms," and the derivative of Av. *zaēnah,* "wakefulness." Compare Boyce, *Reader,* p. 164, n. 3.
6. In the sense of "fellow traveller."
7. *Mir. Man.* III, p. 878, n. 4. For the image of the boy, compare Arnold-Döben, *Die Bildersprache des Manichäismus,* pp. 112ff.
8. Boyce, *Reader,* p. 175.
9. The Elements of Light dispersed in the world.
10. Literally, created.
11. The First Man.
12. The suffering Elements of Light in the world.
13. Elements of Light.

14. According to Iranian cosmology, the world consists of seven regions. Compare Boyce, *Textual Sources for the Study of Zoroastrianism*, p. 17.

15. That is, Zarathustra's teaching was corrupted.

16. For the image of the door, compare Arnold-Döben, *Die Bildersprache des Manichäismus*, pp. 139ff.; Klimkeit, "Das Tor als Symbol."

17. The duality of skillful means (Skr. *upāyakauṣalya*) and wisdom (Skr. *prajñā*) is basic to Mahāyāna Buddhism.

18. Dībat = Dilbat, the planet Venus, which for Mani was a power of Darkness. Compare *Mir. Man.* III, p. 880, n. 3.

19. The future Buddha, often identified by Manichaeans with the coming Mani.

20. B observes, "The hymn-writer appears to be linking the coming of Jesus the God to Adam with the appearance of the prophet Jesus in Israel." Boyce, *Reader*, p. 172, n. 10.

21. Probably the four Gospels. The Chinese Manichaean Hymn (H 138c) speaks of "The clean and pure Winds of Emancipation" (Tsui Chi, "Mo Ni Chiao Hsia Pu Tsan," p. 188), or "The Four Pure Winds of Salvation" (Schmidt-Glintzer, *Chinesische Manichaica*, p. 28).

22. The scriptures of the Jews: Thora, Writings, and Prophets (?).

23. The word *bāragān* either means "steeds" or "walls" (of the city).

24. It is unclear what the *two* armies stand for.

25. The "collection of treasures" is the gathering of redeemed Light. Compare *Psalm-Book* 202. For the images of the treasure and the merchandise, compare Arnold-Döben, *Die Bildersprache des Manichäismus*, pp. 61ff.

26. The Chariots of Light are Sun and Moon, the ferries transporting redeemed souls to the Realm of Light.

27. In living beings and in plants.

28. Either Zarathustra, Buddha, and Jesus (thus Böhlig, *Gnosis* III, p. 344, n. 96) or, according to B, "the three redeeming gods who, together with the Father of Greatness and the Shape of Light [Form of Light], make up the five Fathers: namely, the Third Messenger, Jesus the Splendour and the Nous." Boyce, *Reader*, p. 172, n. 14. compare Schmidt and Polotsky, *Mani-Fund*, p. 74.

29. The "Form of Light" that appears to the redeemed soul at death. Compare Schmidt and Polotsky, *Mani-Fund*, p. 72; Asmussen and Böhlig, *Gnosis* III, pp. 215f.

30. Either the soul, or the "Form of Light" as guide of the soul (thus S).

31. Abursām is the name of a person who was converted by Mani together with a woman called Xēbra. Compare Sundermann, *Texte*, pp. 119 and 148f., s.v. 'bvrs'm.

32. Thus according to S.

33. Deception (*wiftagīh*) is the tenth of the Twelve Dark Dominions. Deception and falsehood ("lie") are common characterizations of idolatry. Compare *Mir. Man.* II, pp. 311f.

34. Here it is clear that those attacked are the Zurvanists, for whom Ohrmizd and Ahriman were twin spirits, sons of the Time God Zurvān.

35. B, in accordance with Henning (*Zoroaster*, 50–51), points out, "According to the Armenian writer Eznik, in Zurvanite myth Ohrmazd created the world but did not realise how to illumine it, till the demon Māhmī prompted him to create the sun (thus betraying his own master, Ahriman)." Boyce, *Reader*, p. 175, n. 5.

36. Jewish name for God.

37. Probably meaning Jesus as seventh in a series of messengers. The notion could be Judeo-Christian.

38. This apparently follows Marcionitic criticism of Christianity. Compare Boyce, *Reader*, p. 175, n. 9; the detailed study of A. von Harnack, *Marcion. Das Evangelium vom fremden Gott.* 2d ed., repr. Darmstadt, 1960.

39. Translation according to S.

40. Compare *The Gospel of Thomas* (v. 23) from Nag Hammadi: "Jesus said, 'I shall choose you, one out of a thousand, and two out of ten thousand . . .'" J. M. Robinson, ed., *The Nag Hammadi Library in English*. 3d ed., p. 129. (Transl. T. O. Lambdin). S points out to me that this phrase recurs repeatedly in apocryphal literature. B. Blatz points to other parallel passages in apocryphal Christian literature. Compare Blatz, "The Coptic Gospel of

Thomas," in W. Schneemelcher, ed., *New Testament Apokrypha I,* 2d ed., pp. 121 and 130, n. 30.

41. For the first and second Light Day, compare Klimkeit and Schmidt-Glintzer, "Die türkischen Parallelen," pp. 106ff.

42. S interprets this sentence as meaning, The laborers of the Light are to disseminate the seed of love.

43. The soul.

44. Of Mani's message.

45. I. e., Manichaeism, which now had its stronghold in the East.

46. Name of an angel.

47. Nariman, Old Iranian Nairyō-manah, "he with manly mind." For this characterization of the angel Jacob compare Böhlig, "Jakob als Engel."

48. This refers first to the elements of Light dispersed in matter and then to the members of the community.

49. Literally, a number of.

CHAPTER TWELVE

A Book of Prayer and Confession

This *Book of Prayer and Confession* was used in divine services. It consists of two parts: a liturgy for the Bema festival, at which Mani's death was commemorated and his return to earth anticipated; and confessional texts for the elect, probably used on Monday, the day of confession. The first part is written in Middle Persian and Parthian, the second mainly in Sogdian, with portions and quotations in Persian and Parthian.

1. *Bema liturgy* (Persian and Parthian)

This part of the book contains the final portion of Mani's "Letter of the Seal," which he wrote to his community from prison prior to his death. It was read annually at the Bema festival, hence it was part of the Bema liturgy. Then follow three Bema hymns in which Mani is lauded and identified with the future Buddha, Maitreya. These hymns also contain invocations of the gods. Then come hymns in praise of the Third Messenger, the Column of Glory, and Jesus. We can surmise that the Maiden of Light and the Great Nous were invoked in the following lacunae. The next portion is comprised of hymns in praise of the "messengers," as the Church leaders are called. Here the dignitaries of the Manichaean Church are called to mind in hierarchical succession. This hymn ends with prayers for the whole community, including the auditors. The second hymn in praise of the messengers is preserved only in part. In the following Bema hymn, the whole "Community of Light," from the redeeming gods to the lowest laymen, is remembered again. The feeling of unity with superhuman powers is well expressed in the term "the whole flock of Light." A second Bema hymn has not been preserved, nor is the beginning of a third one, but its final portion shows that the members of the Church did actually conceive of themselves as belonging to a Family of Light with Mani at its head. He is also the main point of reference in the final "hymns of the joyful."

I. The Letter of the Seal

[Persian]: . . . and from Ammō, my [most beloved] son, and from all the very dear children who are with (me). To all shepherds, teachers and bishops and all the elect [and auditors, to the brothers] and sisters, great and small ones, the pious, perfect and righteous ones,[1] and to all of you who have received this good message from me and who have been happy[2] with this teaching and these pious deeds that I have taught (you), and who are firm in the faith and free of doubt. To everyone personally.

[Sogdian]: (Here) ends the Letter of the Seal.

II. (Here) begin the Bema [hymns]

1. [Persian]: You would we praise, Mani, oh Lord! You would we praise, Mani, oh Lord, king of the holy Church, wisest of the [great] Apostles!

2. We would praise your name, God, Lord Mani! [Parthian]: Make me joyful, [Persian] loving resurrector of the dead! Give us power and might so that we may become perfect according to your commandment, oh God!

3. We would praise the God Mani, the Lord! We honor your great, bright glory (*farrah*), we bow down before the Holy Spirit, together with the glories and mighty messengers.[3]

4. [Parthian]: Master Maitreya, Maitrāgar Maitr Čaitr,[4] God Christ, Mānī'ū, Mānī'ī, Mānī'ā-Xaios,[5] Savior, God Mār Mani!

5. [Persian/Parthian]: Mani has come from Paradise, rejoice, brothers! A bright day has come to us, the sons of the right hand.

6. From Paradise the gate was opened and we were overcome with joy: the Lord Maitreya has come; Mār Mani, the Lord, (has come) for a new Bema!

7. The gods opened the gate of prosperous[6] Paradise. The wreath, crown and diadem[7] [have been given] to us . . .

   [*a few pages missing*]

8. [Parthian]: . . . preserve my body and redeem my soul; grant to me my pious wish, the eternal Paradise of Light.

9. [Persian]: You would we laud, Jesus! You would we praise, Mani! Brightly illuminated was the day, brightly illuminated was the day, oh Lord Mani of noble name!

10. You would we praise, bright king, son of kings, Mani, oh Lord! Mani, oh Lord, bright king, you are worthy of praise!

11. You would we praise, Lord Mani, (and also) Jesus, the Maiden (of Light) and Vahman, and the beautiful Bema, and the messengers!

12. To you do I call, oh Lord; answer me, Lord! Mār Mani, Oh Lord! [Parthian]: Forgive my sins, oh Lord!

13. Buddha Maitreya has come, Mār Mani, the Apostle: he brought "victory"[8] from the righteous God (the Father of Light). I would honor you, oh God! Grant remission of my sins, redeem my soul, lead me up to the New Paradise!

14. Maitreya . . .

[*several pages missing*]

III. Praise of Narisah-yazd (the Third Messenger)

. . . and the blissful ancestors who are themselves the bright chariots (the Third Messenger and Jesus), the valiant hunters and the keen helmsmen, the praised messengers, the great organizers and the mighty powers, the spirits that have been created by the word, the blissful rulers, the bright appearances, the best of gods, the great redeemers, the valiant helpers, the liberators who bring joy, the keen fighters, the strong warriors who have overcome death and have vanquished the foes, who have risen up victorious and are (now) in peace: May they always be blessed with the blessing of the bright aeons, and always be praised by a benevolent keeper of the entire Church, and be its living food. (May there also be blessing) especially on this place and this blessed community . . .

[*several pages missing*]

IV. [Praise of] Srōsh-Ahrāy (the Column of Glory)[9]

1–4.   . . .

5.   [Parthian]: . . . to all of us, the righteous believers and the meritorious auditors. May it be so eternally!

6.   Blessing and praise to this strong power, the bright and beneficent God, the Perfect Man, who is the abode and the garment for all souls, the way and the path for all beings of Light, and for the redeemed souls. May he be blessed so that his splendor, full of life, may shine upon the chosen Church, so that he may give us peace, well-being and hope in all the lands. May he protect us, bringing us wonderful joy. May he accept from all of us this pure prayer, this living melody and (this) divine song. So be it eternally!

[Persian]: (Here) end the Srōsh-Ahrāy (hymns), (all together) six.

V. (Here) begins (the praise) of Jesus the Savior.[10]

1.   Praise to holy wisdom: Jesus the Splendor, the Maiden of Light and the great Vahman, (these) valiant redeemers who raise the holy Church from the dead. Blessing to these great physicians, the healers of the highest Self, so that they may also enhance our peace and well-being, joy and piety, redemption and the victory of the valiant and mighty ones. May they make us worthy of the great glory (*farrah*) and of the eternal diadem. So be it for ever and ever!

[Patron or Scribe]: Kirbakkarzāδαγ.

2.   Blessing and praise to Jesus the Savior, the New Aeon, the one who truly raises men from the dead, who is himself the life-giving mother of those who have died on account of the wounds and the gall of greed and sensual desire, who is the physician for those who have lost their senses because

of weakness of the body. He himself became sight for the blind, hearing for the dumb, . . .

[*several pages missing*]

VI. [Praise] of the Messengers

1.   . . . the seventy-two bishops, the 360 presbyters, all the pure and holy elect that are perfect in (keeping) the five commandments and the three seals: May they be remembered as a pious deed.[11]

The great Glory (*farrah*) and the Spirit of the whole Eastern Church who is the guard and protector of this flock and righteous community of gods (elect): May they be remembered as a pious deed.[12]

Mār Nāzaγyazd,[13] the Teacher at the head of the Eastern Church Province: May he be remembered as a pious deed.

And all bishops, presbyters, prayer leaders,[14] wise preachers, valiant scribes, singers of melodious hymns, and all pure and holy brothers: May they be remembered as a pious deed.

The pure and holy sisters, together with their convents and nunneries: May they be remembered as a pious deed.

And all auditors, brothers and sisters, in the East and the West, in the North and the South, who confess God, Light, Power and Wisdom: May they be remembered as a pious deed.

May the praise, acclaim, intercession, prayer and supplication of us all ascend in purity and forgiveness and be accepted by our kind fathers and venerable ancestors.

May they send us power and aid, sal[vation] and [victory], health and [invulnerability], joy and piety, peace and trust, goodness (?) and protection, righteous zeal and the pursuit of perfection, and the remission of sins, the true light of salvation.

May (all this) remain with the whole holy Church, especially in this place and in (this) blessed congregation; (may they remain) with me and you, most beloved brothers, pure and holy sisters and pious auditors, so that they may be protected by the hands of the bright angels and powerful (heavenly) twins.

Be it so eternally, in a living [and holy] name.

2.   [Parthian]: We laud and praise the bright messengers . . .

[*one page missing*]

. . . the presbyters, the prayer leaders, the preachers, the scribes, the pure, righteous ones (the elect), brothers and sisters, at all places, wherever they are dispersed,[15] with their flocks, communities and monasteries. May they be protected and led together by the right hand of the Holy Spirit, the friend.

And also the faithful auditors, brothers and sisters, the friends and sons of salvation, in all areas, lands and regions, wherever they are dispersed, those who believe in God, Light Power and Wisdom: May they be remembered as a good deed.

May the worship and praise, prayer and petition, supplication and invocation of us all ascend and be accepted by the gods and deities, so that they may send us strength and zeal, so that we may become perfect and perfected in love, in spirit and in body.

May the Living Self (*grīv zīvandag*) attain salvation. May those giving alms become sinless and may we all gain salvation.

[Persian]: May it be so forever and ever, in a living and holy name.

(Here) end the hymns in praise of the messengers, all together two in number.

VII. (Here) begin the hymns in praise of the Bema[16]

1. We bend our knees in deep veneration, we worship and praise the mighty God, the praised King and Lord of the Worlds of Light, worthy of honor, according to whose wish and will you (Mani), our exalted God, did come to us.

    We worship Jesus, the Lord, the Son of Greatness, who has sent you, blessed one, to us.

    We worship the exalted Maiden (of Light), the bright Twin,[17] who was your comrade and companion in every battle.

    We worship the great Vahman whom you have planted in the hearts of the pious.

    We worship your great Glory (*farrah*), our Father, Apostle of Light, oh Mani, oh Lord!

    We worship this wonderful Bema and the bright seat on which you did seat yourself.

    We worship the shining diadem that you did place upon your head.

    We worship this wondrous apperance and this beautiful image.[18]

    We worship the gods and messengers that came with you.

    We honor the whole community of elect and your blessed representative,[19] oh Lord.

    We honor the great teachers.

    We honor the mighty bishops.

    We honor the wise presbyters.

    We honor the virtuous scribes.

    We honor the singers of the melodious hymns.

    We honor the pure righteous ones (the elect).

    We honor the holy virgins.

    We honor and praise the whole Flock of Light which you yourself chose in the spirit of Truth.

    Of your Glory, oh Lord, and of the glory of all of these, I would request, as a grace for all my (soul's) limbs, that remembrance may come into my heart, thought into my mind, consciousness into my nous, . . .

    [*at least two pages missing or badly preserved*]

2. ...

3. ... Light, whereby you have appeared in the world of the tyrants and
have assembled your family members.

(Here) end the hymns of the bright Bema, all together three.

VIII. (Here) begin the hymns of the joyful.[20]

1. You did rise and shine like the Sun, blessed image, Leader of Truth, who
are like the God Zurvān in appearance. On this day of joy our love would
shine from our hearts to you. Come in good health! May the messengers
give you peace!

2. May this Leader who has come to a great day of joy be blessed (in view
of) a new good omen.

May the gods give you peace, may the angels protect you and may Vahman
lead you anew to eternal life.

3. *Melody: Come forth to a new good omen*:

Come forth to a new good omen, and to an auspicious sign and to days of
unceasing joy, to this community of gods and messengers. From all provinces (of the Church) and from many lands, the glories and spirits and
bright gods have assembled joyfully on this day, in order to greet you lov-
ingly, Lord, Leader of exalted name, and to protect you, Lord, Leader of
exalted name, from all foes and destroyers of the Church. With great joy
will we worship you, and at your glory (*farroxīh*) will we rejoice.

[Patron or Scribe]: Istāyīaδaγ

4. *(To be sung) with pančīxazān melody*[21]

Come, light-bringing Sun, shining full Moon; come wise Lord, strong and
full of insight. Receive blessing ever anew from Vahman, the King. Rejoice
and be glad in unceasing joy!

5. *(This hymn is to be sung) according to (the melody): Mani, the Lord has come.*
The light-bringing Sun has come, it shone brilliantly in the skies. Its light
shines in all lands and provinces. It is meet for us, brethren, to bow down
before it, so that it may give us joy and eternal life.

6. *(This hymn is to be sung) according to (the melody): You are the strong God.*
The Savior (*drōdegar*) who brings salvation (*drōd*) to the whole Church has
come. Increase the salvation of the flock, of the congregation and the community of elect. May salvation come to you from the strong, the highest
God. May salvation give you Light, Power and Wisdom. You shall be
praised and blessed by the holy Church. May the messengers, the glories
and the spirits give you peace. Live in joy, be glad and blessed in new
peace. Illumine the children by the Living Spirit (*vāxs i zīhrēn*).

[Patron or Scribe]: Bay Aryamān

7. *(This hymn is to be sung) to the Sogdian tune.*

A new light-bringing Sun has come, a new Apostle, a Teacher for the Eastern Province. He has brought new joy, new hope and new, vital encouragement to the whole Holy Church. The messengers and glories are joyful

on your account, blessed Leader, Teacher of exalted name. Live in health and new peace . . .

2. *Confessional text for the elect* (Sogdian with Persian and Parthian citations)

This text was introduced by a discussion of the five commandments for the elect. Only the titles of the second commandment ("nonviolence") and third commandment ("behavior in accordance with religion") have been preserved. The fourth commandment ("purity of mouth") and the fifth commandment ("blessed poverty") are not expressly mentioned.

I. [The Commandment: Truthfulness][22]

. . .

II. A. The Commandment: Nonviolence

[Sogdian]: . . . as He (Mani) teaches in the Scripture: [Persian]: "Whoever wishes to come to that World of Peace should from now on gather together (the limbs of) his soul, like the gods of Paradise."
[Sogdian]: And every time I injure and afflict the five elements, the captured Light [that] is in the dry and wet earth.

1. If (I should have allowed) the weight of my body, the cruel [self (body)] to beat or hurt (that Light) while walking or riding, ascending or descending, (walking) quickly or slowly; or by digging or shovelling, building or constructing a wall in the dry, cracked, injured, oppressed and trodden earth, by going into the waters, walking on mud, snow, rainwater or dew, by treading, breaking or cutting, injuring or tearing the five (types of) plants or the five (types of) fleshly beings, be they wet or dry; if I myself should have done this or if I should have caused [someone] else to do this;

2. if for my sake human beings were beaten or imprisoned, or if they had to endure humiliation or insults; if I should have inflicted injury on four-footed animals while ascending or descending, or by beating or spurring them on; if I should have planned to harm wild animals, birds, creatures in the water or reptiles creeping on the ground, and should have harmed their life;[23]

3. furthermore, if I should have . . .[24] opened my mouth (to eat it), thinking it to be a fig (or) a medicine; if I should have haughtily taken pleasure in battle between armies, or the death and destruction of sinners, or even in the misfortune of another person;

4. if I should have been lazy in the art of writing, disliking it or neglecting it, holding a brush, a slate (?), a piece of silk or paper in my hands and doing much harm and damage thereby;

5. if I should have spilled a little bit of water from a water jug so that it was wasted;—(then) for all this (I pray for) pardon.[25]

II. B.

The second part [of the commandment nonviolence] pertains to the "religious spirit" (δynyy frn)[26] of living human beings and to the living Vahmans who abide in the righteous ones (the elect).

1. If I should have injured them in the lust of passion, if I should have neglected to strengthen them . . . ,
2. if on account of my unthoughtfulness a brother, living with me, should ever have suffered mental discord, if words were spoken in the community (of brethren) that incited a companion to strife, and if many people (were thereby made) to suffer perdition of their souls and spiritual diminution: as He teaches [Persian]: "Who sees himself (only) outwardly, not inwardly, causes the diminution of himself and others,"
    [Sogdian]: (Then) for (all) this (I pray for) pardon.

III. [The Commandment]: Behavior in accordance with religion.[27]

. . . I am especially sinful and guilty (regarding) the commandment: Behavior in accordance with religion. This *yaksha,*[28] the evildoing foe,[29] who turning hither and thither, [constantly] persecutes [me] and who is mixed into this body, its spiritual and physical limbs, and is clad with them, has implanted his artfulness in all plants, and in fleshly bodies; he seeks everywhere for that which would incite his greed and his lusts;

1. if, on a spring morning, I should have touched but [a few] . . . of the blossoms or sprouts of the trees, . . . the seed-grain . . . of the roses, or . . . ,[30] (wanting) to plant or to sow fruit-yielding (plants or seeds) in the earth and (to give) the necessary water to the cultivated land at the right time, (but) behaving in great impurity (lit., lewdness) in gardens and estates;
2. if I should have touched snow, rain or dew;
3. if I should have trod on the womb of the earth where something sprouted or grew up, so that harm (lit., mixture) was caused by me; and furthermore,
4. if [I should have] . . . in impure, base [intentions] . . .
    [*one page and thirteen lines missing*]
    . . . in these manifold lusts, . . . the passions brought with them spiritual and physical diminution, impurity [and] harm . . .
    [*fourteen lines missing or badly preserved*]
    . . . if . . . mixed in with food . . . and intoxicating drinks should have entered my stomach . . .
    [*at least one page missing*]

IV. Commandment

. . . [Persian]: ". . . He should be merciful to his own soul, and he should weep and lament, pray and make supplication and ask for the forgiveness of (his) sins."
[Sogdian]: Likewise,

1. if I should have thrust . . . into the injuring limbs of the body . . . ,

2. if I should not have made a complete confession because of indifference, forgetfulness, evilmindedness, weakness, or because it seemed demeaning (to do so) to me, or out of fear of (being put to) shame, or out of fear of rebukes or reproof;
3. if (my) superiors should have asked (me) something, and I then did not confess in truthfulness, (but) concealed (something), being constrained by the passions of sin; then for all this (I pray for) pardon.

V. The five gifts[31]

I have also sinned . . . [against] the five gifts that are held to be the heart (lit., soul) of religion:

1. if I did not allow them (the five gifts) to abide in my five (spiritual) limbs,[32] in *nous,* thought, mind, intelligence and understanding, (then I am sinful). In the first place, love, which nurtures all good deeds, as He teaches: [Persian]: "Where love is slight, there all deeds are incomplete";[33]
2. [Sogdian]: if I should have lacked love, if hate should have taken its place, and if disbelief should have taken the place of faith, imperfection the place of perfection, violence the place of patience, folly the place of wisdom, and if I should have not warded off from me[34] the fivefold devilish passions,[35] so that they brought about my regression in various ways;
3. if the Holy Spirit should have been grieved by me;[36] in (all) this I am a sinner worthy of the death penalty.

VI. The "closing of the five gates"

I was also less than perfect in the closing (lit., collection, integration) of the five gates (senses).[37] As He teaches in the scriptures: [Persian]: "What good is a righteous one who says, 'I have power in my limbs', if he brings about ruin with the eye, ear and other senses?" [Sogdian]: Thus if (I have left) the eye open to seeing, the ear to hearing, the nose to smelling and the hand to touching and feeling unseemly things, (I am guilty). For the (demon of) Greed ($\bar{A}z$) that has formed this body[38] and is wrapped up in it constantly provokes contention through these five "gates." (Through them), it brings the internal demons together with the external ones, in the course of which a small part (of the soul) is destroyed day by day. If I should (thus) have left my "gates" open and should have (so) aroused the passion of the mental demons and should have provoked them so that I was deprived of the treasure of the Living Self,[39] then for all this (I pray for) pardon.

VII. Prayers and [hymns]

I have also been sinful with respect to the seven prayers, the seven hymns, the seven confessions and the seven "services."[40] If I should have a restless, unreliable, unruly, fearsome, weak, indifferent or badly inclined body

and if I should have neglected the prayers and hymns out of ill will, or with the purpose of harming someone, or because of sleepiness, or misfortune, either in the morning or in the evening, at night or in the day, on a journey or in the city, in illness or pain, and if I should furthermore have done [wrong] with respect to the thirty [days of fasting] . . . ,[41]
[then for all this (I pray for) pardon.]

[*one page missing*]

VIII. *Zeal*

. . .[42] If I was . . . [not] watch[ful] . . . and if the passions should have caused harm, then I pray for [pardon]!
[*more than three lines badly preserved*]
. . . if, because of my weakness or ill will, I should have neglected . . . ; if one day I should [have] sent (someone) out of [the house] (at night) without a lamp, (acting) in folly and with injurious scorn, out of confusion or absentmindedness, . . .
Every day a small portion of the Living Self is [lost] to the body, like water, . . .
[*three lines destroyed*]
[then for all this (I pray for) pardon!]

IX. *The four Monday prayers*

Also with respect to the [Monday] ritual I do not observe the four [commandments] and the four prohibitions with (correct) zeal, as it is commanded by God. For if I [should have neglected]

1. (to make) confession with my whole heart and my whole soul;
2. (to say) the prayers (and sing) the hymns with a pure heart;
3. to direct my thoughts to the sermon;
4. to engage in asking for and granting change of mind and pardon, as He teaches: [Persian]: "At all times you should assemble for the confession and pardon of sins; ask each other (for forgiveness) and grant each other (forgiveness): whoever does not grant (remission) will not receive remission (of his sins);"
5. [Sogdian]: If on my part I should have neglected the ordained Monday ritual;

then, my God, for all this (I pray) for pardon.

X. *The divine table*

Furthermore, in receiving the daily gifts from the divine table, I did not sit down with a thankful heart, thinking of God, the Buddha,[43] and men. I also do not call to mind the primeval battle, (as I should). And also I do not ponder the question: In whose sign do I stand now? What is that which is eaten? What kinds of demons are they that are usually eaten?[44] Whose flesh and blood is it (that is eaten)?[45] What kind of a debt, what kind of an entrusted gift is it that I receive? Furthermore, why was I not (reborn) in the class of pigs, dogs or *yakshas*[46]. . . ?

Notes

1. Auditors, elect, and members of the hierarchy (S).
2. Or, content (*hunsand*).
3. Or, angels (*frēstagān*).
4. Probably only a magical variation of the name of Maitreya, with whom Mani is here identified. Compare *BBB*, p. 19, n. 1.
5. Again the magical variation of a name. It is noteworthy that Mānī'ā-Xaios corresponds to the Greek form of the name: *Manichaios*.
6. Or, well-cared for (*ābād*).
7. For these symbols of redemption, compare Arnold-Döben, *Die Bildersprache des Manichäismus*, pp. 149ff.
8. The word *paryōžān* ("victory") is "used of the symbol of victory given to the saved soul." Boyce, *Word-List*, s.v. Here it is probably used in the sense that he displayed his victory (i.e., redemption) to the Father of Light.
9. The colophon shows that in the missing part above there were four hymns to the Column of Glory. Preserved here is the end of such a hymn and a complete hymn to that god.
10. Preserved here is a complete hymn to Jesus and the beginning of a second one.
11. May their remembrance be considered a pious deed.
12. The glories and spirits, protective deities, are usually invoked in the plural, together with the angels.
13. This name is Sogdian.
14. Literally, leaders of the blessing (*āfrīnsārān*). Henning translates, "prayer (hymn)-leaders." (Cf. *BBB*, p. 24).
15. Translation according to a suggestion by S.
16. These Bema hymns are actually hymns to Mani, and thus they are called "Hymns in Praise of the Apostle" (*āfurišn frēstag*). Our text originally contained three such hymns. The first has been preserved almost completely, as has the last part of the third one.
17. The Twin and the Maiden of Light are perhaps named together because they both appear at the time of death (S). For Mani's Twin, compare Henrichs and Koenen, "Ein griechischer Mani-Codex," pp. 161–89.
18. The hymn is apparently inspired by the image of Mani.
19. The present leader of the Manichaean Church, called Mani's "After-Self" (*pasāgrīv*). The word we here render as "honor" is the same as that for "worship" (*nambarēm*).
20. The seven short hymns preserved here celebrate Mani's coming at the Bema and express the joy of his community in the wake of his appearance. The last hymn at least seems to be devoted to the appointment or installment of a new Church leader.
21. Melody with five strong notes or cadences.
22. For the Manichaean commandments, compare Sims-Williams, "The Manichaean Commandments."
23. In the Buddhist confessional texts in Uighur, the confessor also accuses himself of having injured all kinds of life.
24. The meaning of some of these words has not yet been established.
25. Literally, (I pray for) absolution (*krmšvhn*).
26. Literally, "Glory of Religion."
27. This commandment implies chastity.
28. A Buddhist type of demon, here an incarnation of the evil principle that has entered man.

29. The Devil.
30. Various words are unclear here.
31. The five gifts are enumerated in verse 1.
32. We give the terms of these five limbs of the soul according to the Sogdian. Compare *BBB*, p. 37. The classical rendering of the Persian/Parthian (according to Boyce, *Reader*, p. 10) is reason, mind, intelligence, thought, and understanding.
33. Cf. 1 Cor. 13: 1–3.
34. Literally, from my soul (γγγν).
35. I. e., the vices just enumerated.
36. Compare the sins against the Holy Spirit in Mark 3:29 and Luke 12:10.
37. The closing (literally collection) of the gates of the five senses was apparently an act of meditation, referred to in various texts.
38. Cf. *Mir. Man.* I, pp. 193ff.
39. The divine Light in man.
40. We know from an-Nadīm that Mani instituted seven prayers for the elect. Compare Asmussen and Böhlig, *Gnosis* III, p. 190. The other heptads are unknown.
41. For the month of fasting, compare Henning, "The Manichaean Fasts," pp. 146ff.; Asmussen and Böhlig, *op. cit.*, p. 42.
42. Here is the final portion of a Persian quotation, probably from one of Mani's scriptures.
43. Or, the God Buddha, that is, Mani.
44. Or, What kinds of demons are they that eat . . . (S). Henning translates as above. He is of the opinion that in this sentence reference is made to Non-Manichaeans eating meat. *BBB*, p. 88.
45. The Light substance in the food partaken of is called "Jesus' flesh and blood" in the *Cologne Mani Codex*. Compare Henrichs and Koenen, "Ein griechischer Mani-Codex," pp. 147f., 150f.
46. According to the Manichaean view, these beings are of especially low status. Compare *BBB*, p. 41, n. 2.

CHAPTER THIRTEEN

Diverse Liturgical Texts

Just like their brethren in the West, where Coptic psalms attest to the richness of liturgical material, the Eastern Manichaeans possessed a wealth of psalms and hymns for special occasions in the life of the Church. These were ordered according to their content, and also according to their place in the ecclesiastical year. Thus they throw light on various Church celebrations. The most important of these occasions was undoubtedly the Bema festival, which celebrated Mani's death and ascent into the Realm of Light, as well as his anticipated return to earth. In the ceremony, as we learn from Coptic texts, a picture or image of Mani was placed and venerated on an altar with five steps. Whereas a number of Bema psalms are preserved in Coptic (cf. *Psalm-Book* 1–47), only two Bema liturgies from Central Asian finds have hitherto been published. A hymn preserved in Chinese belongs to the annual cycle. It was sung at the conclusion of the Ten Day Fast (H 339–46). The "body-and-soul rite" was probably also celebrated periodically.

The weekly and daily cultic acts were important as well. Among the former was the Monday ceremony, when the elect and the auditors, in their respective ways, asked for the remission of sins. The Monday hymns were sung on such occasions. Among the daily cultic acts of the elect was the sacred meal. It was introduced and concluded with hymns, some of which are extant in Chinese. We also have a group of hymns in Sogdian which were to be sung after the meal. Auditors could apparently join in the singing of these hymns, and they could listen to the sermon following the meal. Evening hymns also belonged to the daily liturgy. They were sung after the precatory prayers and at sunset (H 339, 347, 356, 380, 387).

The major "rites of passage" must also have been accompanied by the singing of hymns. Among these, hymns used at funerary ceremonies were of special significance.

Beside hymns, readings from sacred scriptures were also common. This is indicated by the index of a liturgical book (text 10). This text reflects the flowering of the Manichaean religion. This was the time when every category of Manichaean literature was assiduously copied and distributed.

1. Prooemium and Beginning of Mani's "Living Gospel" (Sogdian and Persian)

Here the opening words of Mani's *Gospel* have been preserved. They are prefaced by a doxological introduction which was probably part of a hymn for the Bema festival. The first sentence of the *prooemium* is preserved completely in Sogdian in the manuscript M 172.[1] Mani's *Gospel,* starting in our text with part 2, consisted of twenty-two chapters, beginning consecutively with the letters of the Syrian alphabet.[2] Here we have the beginning of the chapter on *aliph* ("arab"). A Greek version of the opening lines is quoted in the *Cologne Mani Codex.*[3]

[Page title]:   The Gospel *arab* is taught
1. The most beloved son, the Savior Jesus, the head of all these gifts, who is a refuge for the holy and a blessing (?) for the wise is exalted. May he be praised! The Maiden of Light, the chief of all wisdom is exalted. May she be praised! The Holy Religion (*dēn yōjdahr*), by the power of the Father, by the blessing of the Mother and by the wisdom of the Son, is exalted. May it be praised! Well-being (*drōd*) and blessing to the sons of goodness (*drōdī*) and to the speakers and hearers of the true Word! Praise and honor to the Father and the Son and the Holy Spirit and to the holy recollection![4] He (Mani) teaches the word of the Living Gospel for Eye and Ear,[5] and he preaches the fruit of righteousness.
2. I, Mani, the Apostle of Jesus the Friend, by the will of the Father, the true God, of Him, by whom I have become . . . Everything that is and everything that was and will be is by His power. The blessed ones will receive this message, the wise ones will understand it, the strong ones will take on the wisdom of the wise[6] . . .

2. Liturgical hymns (Parthian)

This is a longer fragment of a liturgy which contains the titles, that is, first lines, of various hymns. Every group of hymns commences with an introductory formula and is concluded by a colophon. The first heading, "hymns to the soul," refers to a specific category of hymnody. Unfortunately, none of the hymns of this group has been preserved completely. Whereas Reitzenstein saw in each hymn of this category "an abbreviated mass for the dead,"[7] Boyce correctly points out, "In Manichaeism the release of the individual soul through death symbolises, and is part of, the general release of Light from the world. It is impossible, therefore, to be sure that M 4 [this text] was designed for a funeral service rather than for, say, some general festival of redemption."[8]

Along with the hymns of the soul, there are "hymns of death," which must have had their place in the funeral service. They correspond to the funerary hymns in the Coptic *Psalm-Book* (pp. 49ff.). Maybe the "body-and-soul hymn," which was part of a "body-and-soul rite" (cf. text 7 in this chapter) also belonged to this category, although it might also have been part of an annual ceremony.

Then there are hymns about the end of the world and its renewal (*frašegird),* which form a category of their own. These hymns are followed by a hymn on Mani that reveals Semitic verse structure and therefore could be the translation of an Aramaic original. The chapter is concluded by a hymn whose title refers to the hymn cycle *Angād Rōšnān.*

1. [(Here) begin] the hymns to the soul.
   . . . Worthy are you of salvation,[9]
   To you, oh soul of Light, will I give much counsel, so that you may attain redemption.
   Come, oh souls, to this ship of Light!
   My most beloved soul, (who is) happy[10] and noble, where have you gone? Return![11]
   Awake, dear soul, from the sleep of drunkenness into which you have fallen!
   Look upon the foes, (see) how they prepare death all around you!
   Reach (your) home, the (heavenly) earth created by the Word, where you were in the beginning.
   The distressed soul cries out loudly because of wicked greed, deceptive delusion and the devouring blaze of fire.[12]
   An angel from Paradise has come, a herald from the Kingdom.
   (Here) end the beautiful hymns to the soul.
2. (Here) begin the funerary hymns.
   Set (into the world) am I, this divine form, deprived of my (heavenly) apparel.[13]
   And I saw the redeemer, as he spoke to me in loving kindness.
   Hope (then) came to me when I was constantly oppressed.
   The marvel was illumined for me,
   My mind became joyful.
   How quickly, how hastily has come the end of my life (?).
   Free me from terrible distress on this day of death!
   Come, my redeemer, accompanied by praise, saving God,
   Lord Mani, (together) with the three sons of gods.[14]
   Remember, kind God, this believing soul of your own child, an auditor, who follows you.[15]
   Beneficent God, think of me, my thoughts are fixed upon the final day.
   Come, oh God, look upon me, my helper at this time (of death)!
   (Here) end the funerary hymns.
3. (Here) begins the hymn on body-and-soul.
   Sweet place of rest, (oh) garden!
   May you be a sweet place of rest for me.
   Return (to me), remain in me.
   May we be of one accord through your beneficence.
   (Here) ends the hymn on body and soul.

4. (Here) begins the hymn on the end of the world.
   The message of heaven[16] and the earth's answer,[17]
   Hear, oh world, the words of the Lord!
   We would invoke the gods that they may save us
        from this evil age of tyranny, (full) of strife and unbelief.[18]
   Oh, angels and twins,[19] save us from all distress.
   That time (the end) has come,
   Just as the redeemer (Mani) has written.[20]
   (Here) ends the hymn on the end of the world.

5. (Here) begins the *mvqr'nyg* hymn.[21]
   A thankful pupil am I (Mani).[22]
   I have come from the land of Babylon.
   I have come from the land of Babylon and I am posted at the door of
        Truth.[23]
   I am a young pupil, come forth from the land of Babylon.
   I have come forth from the land of Babylon so that I might shout a call
        into the world.
   I make supplication to you, oh gods, all (you) gods, forgive my sins
        through righteousness!
   (Here) ends the *mvqr'nyg* hymn.

6. Here begins the hymn of *Angād Rōšnān*.[24]
   Bountiful Friend of the beings of Light! In mercy
   Grant me strength, and help me with every gift!
   . . .

3. Fragment of a confessional prayer for the elect (Sogdian)

This text, which is preserved only fragmentarily, deals with the five commandments.[25]

1. [The first commandment: Truthfulness]
   . . .

2. [The second commandment: Nonviolence]
   . . . [if by me their] divine light (*frn*)[26] has been injured; daily a small portion is lost on the way. For all this I say: Forgive me!

3. The third commandment: Behavior in accordance with religion,[27]
   with its two parts. I cannot remain virtuous . . .
   First: (I do not fret at) the cutting off or planting of trees (or even whole)
   groves of trees. I do not consider the affliction of the sprouts of trees or
   even the holy Light Elements[28] on a spring morning. We (all) strive to
   plant and to sow a garden or a piece of land with (our) bodies.
   Second: The male and female bodies . . .

4. Fragments of a confessional prayer for the elect (Sogdian)

This text deals with sins of thought, word, and deed. The first fragment pertains
to sins of thought and starts enumerating sins of word. The second recalls the

difficult path to becoming one of the elect. This is probably the introduction to a confessional prayer. The translation is based on Henning.

1. . . . For the *dēnāvar* (the elect).

    . . . I am [not] . . . , as is my duty and obligation, according to God's commandment. First of all, I am sinful because of the incorrect moribund thought,[29] which is the root of the following:[30] If I should have thought greedy, unruly, shameless or bad thoughts against the admonitions of the three supervisors; if I should have been stimulated by the power of greed, inflamed by evil lust, consumed by the devouring fire (of greed); if the passions should have been roused by vengefulness, vexation, anger, fury or hate, by these sinful, evil thoughts, both spiritually and physically, then I ask for forgiveness for all this. And again, with respect to all kinds of unseemly, impure, harmful, provocative, heated or incorrect words . . .

2. . . . As I have been born in this terrible, phantasmic house, this castle of death, this poisonous form, the body made of bone,[31] as I received a human form and appearance in the house of an auditor, . . . he made (me) worthy . . . From then on, I received this godly quality as a *dēnāvar* (elect) from the "Glory of Religion" (δynyfrny)[32] and from the superior ones, the gods being witness, by a great oath and through a difficult (process of) admission.[33] . . .

5. *Lamentation about the fate of the soul* (Sogdian)

Here a person speaks to his own soul, which is part of the light substance diffused into the world, lamenting the fact that it has lost its heavenly home and is now subject to the forces of evil. (Translation after Henning.)

1. Who has transformed you into so many different forms?[34] And who has
        cast you into male and female bodies, putting you to shame?
    Oh god of Light, dear soul! Who took away the Light from your eye?
    . . . And then you did writhe (in pain);
    And you are afflicted ever anew, and you yourself are not aware of it.
    Oh god of Light, dear soul!
    . . .

2. Exposition
    . . .
    And who led you from your wonderful divine land into banishment, and
        who fettered you?
    And who jailed you in this dark prison, this incarceration, this place
        with no refuge, which constitutes this body of flesh?
    Oh god of Light, dear soul!
    Who trapped you in this satanic creation, that oozes sweet poison, and
        why (did he do so)?
    And who gave you over as a slave to the Devil who nourishes himself in
        this body in which a great snake (greed) resides?

And who has made you a servant of his dark, shameless,
    unquenchable, vile fire?
Oh god of Light, dear soul!
Who has sundered you from eternal life?
    . . .

6. *Bema liturgy* (Persian, Parthian, and Sogdian)

This text is a liturgical passage used for the celebration of the Bema festival. On
this occasion, the community commemorated Mani's death and entry into the
World of Light, and anticipated his return to earth. In Eastern Manichaeism, the
returning Mani is frequently invoked as Maitreya, the coming Buddha. In this text,
as often, the Sogdian portions contain instructions for the officiating priests.

[Parthian]: From Paradise Mani, the Lord, would come. When you come,
oh Lord, release us from the cycle of rebirths.[35]—You come, oh Mani,
redeem me, Master Maitreya.
[Persian/Sogdian]: Two times.
[Sogdian]: And later. [Parthian]: To you would we call, Lord of fair name,
Lord Mani! You, (oh) Bringer of Light, would we praise aloud!
[Sogdian]: And when the names of the souls are mentioned, and the hymn
is ended, make a small pause. And then take . . . from the *Gospel* and show
honor to the Apostle and the righteous ones.[36] Then begins the confes-
sion. When it has ended, these three hymns should be sung: [Parthian]
"Mār Mani, wonderful majesty (*farrah*), beautiful appearance (*dīdan*)";
"To you, Father, do I supplicate, forgive my sins,"—"Gracious Mār Mani,
oh God, answer us!"[37]
[Persian/Sogdian]: Two times.
[Persian]: Oh Mani, Savior of fair name, save me, oh save, and forgive my
sins.
[Sogdian]: And when the words of the "Letter of the Seal"[38] have faded
away, intone this hymn before the Apostle:[39] [Parthian] My Father of
Light, the Lord Mani, ascended to Paradise.
[Sogdian]: And after the meal these three hymns are to be sung:
[Parthian]: "Master of fair name, God Mār Mani!" "Oh Lord, you go away,
lead me up to Paradise" . . .

7. *Liturgy for the celebration of the body-and-soul rite* (Sogdian with Persian and Parthian citations)

The body-and-soul rite, which is rather obscure to us, was apparently part of a
ceremony for which this text was intended. It shows us that in Central Asia, Buddhist elements and even the recitation of Buddhist stories had entered the cult.
Such stories were undoubtedly interpreted as parables in a Manichaean fashion.

[Sogdian]: ". . . the five assemblies of the five Buddhas of Mahāyāna."[40] It will be well to indicate how much of it is to be recited. Then the noon prayer should be said, (together with the singing of) the Apostle hymn, (beginning with) [Persian]: "Come, blessedness."

[Sogdian]: Then the body-and-soul rite takes place.[41] First of all the preacher should preach a sermon on body and soul. When the day draws to a close, a parable should be recited, (for example) "The Prince with the *Čandā* . . . son."[42]

[Sogdian]: Then (the hymn cycle) "Body (and) Soul" should be sung. This is to be followed by some exegesis. When you have gone through this order (of worship), sit down at the table, . . . recite the dinner prayer. It consists of the following three hymns: [Parthian]: "Oh soul of Light, great Light-Self!" [Persian]: Two times. [Parthian]: "Lord Mani, forgive my sins." "Redeem, Lord Mani, my soul.". . .

8. *Homily on the correct preparations for the sacred meal* (Sogdian)

This text throws light on the correct preparations for the sacred meal. In the meal, the holy Light Elements are contained in the sacred food; they will be transported to the Realm of Light through prayer and meditation. (Translation after Henning.)

> . . . and receive it (the sacred meal) like (?) gold, transmit it correctly (lit., in right measure) and completely to its owner (the Father of Light) so that you may not be subjected to evil. Guard it with care, preserve it with great steadfastness, so that it may not be soiled by dry or wet blood,[43] just as it, in turn, makes you glad and joyful. And all of you together, keep it from being . . . by jealousy and hatefulness . . . Remember (your) fault on the day of . . . , when by greed it was . . .
>
> Begin [to ponder]: One's body, with whose sign is it decorated or covered? In whose service does it stand? And what is it that you eat? For everyone who partakes of the meal and is not worthy of it loses the fruit of his great efforts and is shut out of the Paradise of Light.[44] (But) the chosen righteous ones and the auditors who believe realize the greatness of the Living Soul and will be joyful in the Paradise of Light, in eternal life . . .[45]
>
> [Dear brother], cleanse yourself and hear the good [message?] from me. It is a duty and an obligation for those who know to stand in the Church under this sign and to serve . . .

9. *Homily on confession* (Sogdian)

This is, according to Henning, a fragment of a doctrinal or homiletical treatise on confession, especially on the significance of forgiveness and on the effect of a ban on absolution.[46]

> And you, dear brother, know that it is very difficult to find the "perfect auditor." For in the Church sins are forgiven but once, (namely) at this

(sacred) meal, when he (the penitent) turns away from his dire offences and renounces the tenfold sins and the former evil deeds; then he acquires absolution and forgiveness this time. And should later some violation (temptation?) occur, then it is his duty to disregard the body for the sake of the soul and not to break the commandment. But should he be guilty of such an unusual evil deed by which he does not disregard the body for the soul's sake and should he break the commandment, then . . . the breech (of commandment) applies to . . . the old as well as the new [deeds?]

    [*five lines badly preserved*]

And the ban on absolution is levied by the Church with such serious consequences that, should an elect or an auditor be banned from absolution, henceforth neither the elect nor the auditor can have communion with the person involved, neither at the divine service, nor in fasting, nor in the distribution (of the sacred meal?).[47] And whatever good deeds he does, they will all be separated (from him) in the zodiacal sky.[48] Yes, even his former good deeds are separated from his soul. Furthermore, he is driven away from the monasteries of the righteous (the elect) and from the convent of brethren . . .

10. *From the index to a liturgical book* (Persian with Parthian forms)

In this index the titles of forty-five Manichaean "homilies" or "discourses" (*gōviš-nān*), which have not been preserved, are recorded. This shows how popular such texts were. In particular, the book contained homilies for the *yamagān* or *yimki* days, days of fasting and prayer, when the Church commemorated the early martyrs.[49] There were five such two-day *yamagān* periods in the Manichaean year. Boyce points out, "Each fast appears to have been devoted to the memory of a martyr for whom intercession was made: the first to the First Man (the first and greatest of martyrs); the second to Mar Sisin, Mani's successor; and the fifth and last to Mani himself. The dedication of the third and fourth fasts is not very certain, but according to the present fragment, the third is devoted to Jesus, and the fourth embraces the whole community (*ardāvīft*)."[50]

1. These *yamag*-day homilies of Light (lit., the Lights) are completed. And there are (here), all in all (?), forty-five homilies about divinity.
2. The Evangel *arab* is taught.[51]
   The Evangel *tau* is taught.[52]
   The Evangel of the twenty-two wondrous things.[53]
   (The homily) for [the *yimki*] of Ohrmizd.[54]
3. On the homily about the twelve words.[55]
   (The homily) for [the *yimki*] of the Lord Sisin.[56]
4. About the crucifixion of the Lord Sisin.
5. About the twenty-two battles of . . . The coming of Jesus the Savior.[57]

6. About the kindly utterance of Jesus.[58]
7. About the homily of the [Apostle] Paul.
8. About the homily on the city of Qennešrē.[59]

Notes

1. See Henrichs and Koenen, "Ein griechischer Mani-Codex," p. 197.
2. Cf. Puech, "Gnostic Gospels and Related Documents," in Hennecke and Schneemelcher, *New Testament Apocrypha* II, pp. 350ff.
3. In the Greek *CMC* the opening sentences are these:
   "I, Mani, an apostle of Jesus Christ through the will of God, the Father of Truth, from whom I also was born, who lives and abides forever, existing before all and also abiding after all. All things which are and will be subsist through his power. For from this very one I was begotten; and I am from his will. From him all that is true was revealed to me; and I am from [his] truth. [The truth of ages which he revealed] I have seen, and (that) truth I have disclosed to my fellow travellers; peace I have announced to the children of peace, hope I have proclaimed to the immortal race. The Elect I have chosen and a path to the height I have shown to those who ascend according to this truth. Hope I have proclaimed and this revelation I have revealed. This immortal Gospel I have written, including in it these eminent mysteries and disclosing in it the greatest works, the greatest and most august forms of the most eminently powerful works. These things which [he revealed], I have shown [to those who live from] the truest vision, which I have beheld, and the most glorious revelation revealed to me." R. Cameron and A. J. Dewey, trans., *The Cologne Mani Codex,* p. 53.
4. The word *mādayān* can also mean "book, writing," in which case the term would refer to Mani's Gospel. The holy recollection would be that of the Manichaean myth as well as that of the death of Mani and his successors. Compare Henrichs and Koenen, "Ein griechischer Mani-Codex," p. 198, n. 258. The trinity mentioned probably represents the Father of Greatness, Jesus the Splendor, and the Holy or Great Spirit (B).
5. B remarks, "Mani's Evangel is probably called that of Eye and Ear because it contained exhortations for guarding the senses." Boyce, *Reader,* p. 33, n. Maybe one could also think of Mani's *Ārdahang,* the illustration of his Gospel, in this connection, as Henrichs and Koenen suggest ("Ein griechischer Mani-Codex," p. 198, n. 259).
6. This last sentence does not belong to Mani's Gospel. Compare Henrichs and Koenen, "Der Kölner Mani-Kodex . . . Edition der Seiten 1–72," p. 67.
7. Reitzenstein, *Das iranische Erlösungsmysterium,* p. 11.
8. Boyce, *Reader,* p. 160.
9. The soul is addressed here.
10. Or, well-intentioned.
11. B: "The image of the 'absent' soul is probably similar to that of a soul 'asleep.' . . . Both represent the soul which has abandoned its task of conscious striving." Boyce, *Reader,* p. 160, n. 4.
12. The fire of greed.
13. Literally, separated from my covering or sheath (*niδāmag*).
14. The Manichaean conception is that the soul in ascending to the Realm of Light after death is greeted by a god of Light (Jesus), or the "Form of Light," together with three angels. Compare Arnold-Döben, *Die Bildersprache des Manichäismus,* pp. 149f.
15. Follows thy word.
16. The "Call" that comes from on high.

17. In commenting on this, S writes to the translator, "I think it is important for the understanding of this hymn that the myth of 'Call and Answer' is reenacted in the cosmogonic events."

18. Apparently a reference to the evil times before the Second Coming of Jesus. See MacKenzie, "Mani's Šābuhragān" I, II. Compare also Ch. XIX, text 1. "The 'words of the Lord' are perhaps those of Jesus at his Second Coming." Boyce, *Reader*, p. 161, n. 17.

19. The twin (*yamag*) is the heavenly *alter ego* of a person.

20. The Manichaeans expected the end of the world, apparently on account of indications in Mani's writings, in 690 A.D.

21. This is a hitherto unexplained word. Compare Henning, *Sogdica*, p. 7; Klíma, *Mani*, pp. 338 and 358f.

22. For Mani as student or pupil, compare Lidzbarski, "Ein manichäisches Gedicht," p. 504.

23. Or, door of righteousness (*rāštīft*). S points out that the image of the door here presupposes the notion of Babylon as the "door of God." Compare Lidzbarski, "Ein manichäisches Gedicht," p. 503.

24. Cf. ch. X, text 2.

25. Cf. Sims-Williams, "The Manichaean Commandments." Translation after Henning.

26. Literally, glory.

27. Chastity in the widest sense of the word.

28. Sogd. *mrδ'spndẕyy* = Pth. *(a)mahrāspandān*, the five Light Elements also present in plants and trees.

29. That is, the "*enthymēsis* of death" which is sometimes used in apposition to greed, or the demon of Greed.

30. Literally, which is the basis for all the following steps. Compare Asmussen and Böhlig, *Gnosis* III, pp. 197 and 335, n. 36.

31. Cf. Gershevitch, *Grammar*, § 1053.

32. The Nous.

33. Hence the godly character of being elected is bestowed upon the adept by the Great Nous, and ritually by the higher religious authorities.

34. For the principle of form in Manichaeism, compare Klimkeit, "Gestalt, Ungestalt, Gestaltwandel."

35. Literally, From birth-death (*zādmurd*); this is a general reference to human existence.

36. S infers that this presupposes that an image of Mani is venerated together with the elect surrounding it.

37. In fact, only two hymn titles are given here, with an invocation of Mani.

38. Mani's last letter to his community from prison.

39. Apparently before his image.

40. Apparently this is a specific text used in the liturgy. In a Chinese Manichaean hymn (H 129a, 244a, 247c) the five light elements (fire, water, light, wind, air) are termed "the five classes of (or fivefold) Light Buddhas," or "the Five Great Buddhas of Light," or "the five Light-Buddhas." Cf. Tsui Chi, "Mo Ni Chiao Pu Tsan," pp. 187 and 197.

41. Apparently the hymn on body-and-soul belongs to this rite.

42. Henning suggests supplying Candā[la] = Skr. *caṇḍāla*, and notes, "As a caṇḍāla is an outcaste . . . , the theme of the story, certainly stemming from India, would be the bridging of caste differences." (*BBB*, p. 99, n. d 9). A *caṇḍāla* is, however, also a hangman. This may be a reference to a Manichaean version of the *Mūgapakka Jātaka*, which deals with a prince and a number of hangmen. There is a Tocharian version of the story from Central Asia. Compare E. Sieg, *Übersetzungen aus dem Tocharischen* II, pp. 17ff. The Pāli version of this Jātaka (Jātaka no. 538, vol. VI, pp. 1ff.) differs from the Tocharian version.

43. In a Turkish text (TM 168R) we hear of a commandment to the elect not to eat dry blood (Türk. Man. III, p. 39). The same would have been true of "wet blood."

44. As in 1. Cor. 11:27 and 29, there is a warning here not to partake of the sacred meal in an unworthy state.

45. It is noteworthy that salvation is also promised to "believing auditors" here.

46. *BBB*, p. 48f.

47. Literally, nor in the gift, that is, with respect to the gift.
48. Henning interprets this as meaning that his good deeds that ascend to heaven together with his (other) pious deeds, praises, and so on are held back by the powers of Darkness when they pass through the zodiacal sky. *BBB,* p. 50, n. 1.
49. Cf. Sundermann, "Überreste manichäischer Yimki-Homilien," p. 309.
50. Boyce, *Reader,* p. 186. Compare Henning, "The Manichaean Fasts." Henning explains why the five *yamag(ān)* days appear as "the seven *yimki*" in Turkish (p. 148). For the Zoroastrian festivals after which the *yimki* days are modelled, compare Boyce, "Iranian Festivals," pp. 792ff.
51. This is the first chapter (numbered *aliph = arab*) of Mani's *Living Gospel.*
52. This is the last chapter in Mani's *Gospel.*
53. Mani's *Living Gospel* had twenty-two chapters, in accordance with the twenty-two letters of the Syrian alphabet. B observes, "Mani's *Evangel* stands first, before the texts concerned with the individual *yamagānīg* days." Boyce, *Reader,* p. 186, n. 2.
54. The first of the *yimki* or *yamagān* days.
55. It is not clear which twelve words are meant.
56. Mani's successor in the leadership of the community.
57. Literally, life-giver (*zīndakkar*).
58. Or, "about the worship of Jesus" (B).
59. The name means "eagle's nest." This is a city on the Euphrates where a famous Christian monastery, called Bar Aftōnyā, was erected in the sixth century.

An illuminated manuscript fragment reveals part of a hymn and the name of a Manichaean king who ruled in the 11th century. Staatliche Museen—Preussischer Kulturbesitz, Museum für Indische Kunst, Berlin.

CHAPTER FOURTEEN

Prayers, Invocations, and Incantations

This chapter contains various prayers: blessings for the ruler and his court, invocations of angels and divine beings, and magical incantations.

The texts concerned with rulership throw an interesting light on the Manichaean institution of divine kingship at a time when "the Religion of Light" had established itself as a political power in Central Asia. These documents, like the Iranian and Turkish colophons (ch. XXII; ch. XXXII), show how Manichaean kingship was "legitimized" by reference to divine powers. The virtues and duties expected of kings were derived from and related to the attributes of the Heavenly Ruler, the Father of Light. These texts, which are supplemented by the Turkish texts on divine kingship, refer to the kings of the Manichaean Uighur realm in the Mongolian Steppes (762–840) and in the small Turkish state of Kocho in the Turfan basin (850–1250). Our documents make it quite clear that it was the king's duty to defend, uphold, and support the faith; his role was that of a *defensor fidei*. The fact that the kings of Kocho increasingly leaned toward Buddhism is certainly one of the main reasons for the gradual demise of Manichaeism, which, however, still may have been flourishing to a certain degree in Mongol times (thirteenth/fourteenth century).

The invocations of angels and heavenly beings are primarily late Persian texts which contain Parthian forms and were probably written by Sogdians in the sacred language of the Eastern Church. At times the constructions indicate that the language was no longer spoken and had become something like ecclesiastical Latin in the West during the Middle Ages. In the invocations and prayers we often come across set formulae which are employed repeatedly. Hence some of these texts are marked by a certain shallowness and ossification, which would explain the often reiterated hope for a renewal and rejuvenation of the Church.

The magical texts and amulets throw light on the folk religion of Eastern Manichaeism. They have much in common with corresponding texts of other religions.

At the same time, however, they show how many Jewish and Gnostic conceptions about demons, angels, and so on remained alive in Central Asia, where they were associated with corresponding Buddhist concepts.

1. *Prayer for an Uighur king* (Persian)

This is a prayer invoking divine blessing on an Uighur king. Though he cannot be identified, we can say that he was a Manichaean ruler of the Kingdom of Kocho (ca. 850–1250 A.D.)

1.   . . . May they (the gods) always preserve the King[1] of the East, *our divine Khan,*[2] together with the Family of Light.[3]
     May you, (oh King), live in health and happiness, in peace and good fortune. May you live forever, you who are created by the Word of God,[4] glorious, strong, valiant and mighty one, (oh you) first one and (you) leader of heroes, battle-seeking one, brave one!
2.   May Jacob the great angel[5] and the mighty glories and spirits[6] bless you, ruler, renowned king, crowned one!
3.   *Divine Khan, Kül,*[7] *wise Khan:*[8] May new well-being increase . . . [furthermore peace] and new fortune. May a good omen and new victory . . . come . . . May the gods, deities and angels become your protectors and guardians. May they ever grant you peace. May your throne be established. Dwell in unceasing joy for many years, ever happy . . .

2. *Fragment from a description of a royal ceremony* (Persian)

This fragment, retrieved from Kara-Khoja by Sir Aurel Stein, was first published by Lentz.[9] Despite its brevity, it gives a glimpse of a royal ceremony, perhaps on New Year's Day. It may be this ceremony that is depicted in the miniature painting on the reverse side of the text. Various personages are named, in order of rank, the first probably being the king himself, then the princes, fourth the "great ones," and fifth the nobles. We hear that wine and butter were presented to the guests attending the ceremony.

> . . . [fourth] the great ones of honor and rank; and fifth those who have honor and nobility. And he (the king) had the entrance hall and . . . [decorated ?], where he himself, together with the distressed (the auditors ?) and the messengers (the elect), stand up and where wine and butter are brought and given to all the guests . . .

3. *Invocations of heavenly beings* (Persian)

The verses of this text are short invocations of angelic and divine powers. The hymn was probably composed during a time of persecution, hence the repeated expression of hope and renewal.

[Title]:   Invocation of the angels[10]

1.   Come,[11] you shall live together with the mighty angels.
     Guard[12] and protect the holy Church,
     And cut off the heads of the adversaries,
     The foes of peace.

2.   May Raphael, Michael, Gabriel (and) Sarael,[13]
     Together with all the most powerful angels,
     Increase peace and faith
     For the whole Church of the Eastern Province.

3.   Blessing upon the mighty angels!
     May (these) powerful ones, (these) humble ones, be praised,
     So that they may protect "the sons of the right hand"[14]
     From the spiritual (demonic) and temporal (fleshly) powers.

4.   I bless the God Mani, the Lord,
     I venerate your great, bright glory (*farrah*),
     I pray to (?) the Holy Spirit,
     Together with the glories and strong angels.[15]

5.   Praise to the almighty angels! May they protect
     [The religion of the gods],
     And may they overcome
     Those attacking righteousness.

6.   The angel full of wisdom[16], the loving deity,
     Beautiful (?) in appearance, the strong God,
     He of noble name, King Frēdōn,[17] and the valiant Jacob,[18]
     May they protect the Church, and us, (their) children!

7.   May blessing and praise from all of us
     Be accepted by the three Lords,[19]
     So that they may send us power and strength
     On this day and at (this) time of joy.

8.   May blessing come from the gods on high
     And new help from the power of the mighty;
     (May it come) upon the land and its ruler,
     So that their faith in the holy religion may increase.

9.   Invocation of Bar Sīmūs:[20]
     I venerate Bar Sīmūs and Jacob
     And praise Bar . . .
     So that they may increase . . .
     [With] joy ever anew . . . for this whole community.
     Mihr Yazd,[21] (our) Father, Redeemer and Benefactor,
     Together with the valiant Frēdōn and all the angels.
     May they protect and care for the holy Church
     And its blessed head, the Lord of good name.

10. (Oh) Sun that brings Light, God Zēnārēs,[22]
     Together with the Mother of the Living,
     Mihr Yazd, together with the angels, the five and the twelve,[23]
     May they all be praised by the holy Church!

11. May new blessing, new victory, come from God Zurvān
     Upon the glories and angels (and) the spirits of this world,
     So that it (the world) may accept the holy religion.
     May He (Zurvān) be guardian, friend and protector within and
          without.[24]

12. I invoke the powerful angels, the mighty ones,
     Raphael, Michael, Gabriel, Sarael,
     So that they may protect us from all misfortune
     And deliver us from evil Ahriman.

13. I venerate the Lord (bay) Jacob the angel,
     Together with the glories, powers and valiant spirits,
     That they may protect us with (their) mighty power
     And may lead us within and without.

14. I joyously venerate the mighty power,
     Jacob the angel, the leader of the angels;
     Receive from the whole holy Church
     Blessing ever anew, and mighty praise!

15. May peace and new salvation come from God Zurvān,
     You glories and spirits! May blessing and new joy
     From the gods and the angels be prepared for you!
     May you lead us on this way to salvation!

16. May new power come from Jacob the angel,
     New joy from all the angels!
     May this land receive new aid,
     May they (the angels) lead it to peace ever new.

17. Come, you glories, spirits and powers,
     Grasp the right hand . . .

4. Invocation of heavenly powers (Persian)

This text, preserved only fragmentarily, is written on a double-sheet. It is similar
in content to the preceding text.

1. . . . Jacob the angel, the Lord Bar Sīmūs, Kaftinus the mighty one,
    Raphael, Gabriel, Michael, Sarael, Narses, Nastikus . . .[25]
        [some lines missing]

2. . . . you (divine powers) shall not forget (our) invocation, nor the voice of
    our grief, for we are of the righteous and not of the [evildoers].
        [some verses missing]

3. . . . behold and judge this holy Church,[26] the bride of the King.[27] Is not
    the hallowed right hand of the redeemer to be clasped rather than a reli-
    gion that . . . ?
        [some verses missing]

4. . . . the sorrow and the prayer of the Church; and its afflicted voice, hear
    you (all) and be its protectors . . . !

5. *Invocation of the saving deities and of Mani* (Persian and Parthian)

This is a rather formalized prayer, probably from a late period. The New Moon is Jesus the Splendor.

1. Oh, New Moon that rose from the New Paradise!
    —And a new joy came to the whole Church.
2. Oh Jesus of fair name, the first of the gods!
    —You are the New Moon, oh God, and you are the noble Father!
    Oh Full Moon, Jesus, Lord of fair name!
    Oh Full Moon, Jesus, Lord of fair name!
    Oh light of hearts, honor (to you)!
    Oh light of hearts, honor (to you)!
3. Oh Jesus, Maiden (of Light) and Vahman (Great Nous)!
    Oh God of Splendor,[28] we would praise the God Narisaf-yazad![29]
    Oh Mār Mani, you would we praise!
4. Oh new Full Moon and Spring, . . . Oh Lord Mani!
    We would praise the angels, the gods, . . .
    The New Sun, . . . the [God] Zēnārēs.[30]
        [*some lines missing*]
5. May the new Full Moon shine upon the Church!
    Hail to you, oh Lord!
6. Come bringing salvation, oh Lord!
    Truly, . . . merciful Lord Mani, oh God!
    Redeem me, oh God!
    Redeem me, [oh God]!
7. A new day has come, and new joy!
    A new day has dawned; may new joy come!
    Oh (sacred) meal that sustains the living,[31] full of joy!
8. Holy! (Holy! Holy!) Jesus, forgive my sins!
    God Mār Mani, redeem my soul!
    Holy! (Holy! Holy!), God, Light, look upon me!
    Power, Wisdom, God, save me![32]
9. And I heard the message of my Lord,
    And the voice of the sermon . . . ,
    . . . [that] awakens me.

6. *Prayer for a Church leader and invocation of gods* (Persian with some Parthian words)

The title of this double-sheet indicates that this is a prayer for "a new Church leader." The term used for "Church leader" is, interestingly enough, *famšiy*,[33] a Chinese loanword originally denoting a Buddhist spiritual leader.

1. Highest God, immortal Lord, (you) kings,[34] (you) two enthroned luminaries,[35] strong and mighty Srōshahrāy,[36] redeemer of souls, Lord Mani,

you three divinely created rulers: [1.] eternally loving redeemer[37] Jesus, [2.] beautiful, noble Maiden of Light, [3.] highest of those that come, bright Vahman: these almighty gods, endowed with wondrous power, these strong deities, may they bestow powerful new blessing, cheerfulness and new joy upon us . . . (and furthermore) happiness and new salvation!

2. . . . May you[38] always live in happiness and remain unharmed. May the angels protect you and the spirits give you peace. May you be healthy in body and redeemed in soul.[39] May you live long, for many years, together with those entrusted to you, with the family[40] and the friends. May the gods give you power. Fulfill every divine word righteously. May you zealously do spiritual works, and seek divine wisdom and godly gifts.
And we would fulfill the commandments of the Lord, the instructions of the savior and (his) perfect orders,[41] completely and perfectly.
May you finally receive the gift of the blessed and the joy of immortal [Paradise], together with the gods and deities and all [wise ones] . . .

7. Prayer for a Church leader (Persian)

This is a badly preserved Middle Persian prose text containing a liturgical prayer. There is no indication of a late date. As the name of the person for whom the prayer is said is indicated by "N. N." (*avāhmān*), this is a prayer formula applicable to different Church leaders in similar situations.

1. . . . with all wisdom and the attitude[42] of truthfulness, with the five good commandments of virtue, and with the three seals,[43] with the five great garments[44] and with vigilance and zeal[45] . . .
    [*some lines badly preserved or missing*]
2. . . . [46] by exhorting the auditors to piety, so that I may become perfect through love, in spirit and body, and that through your power, oh Lord, I may vanquish the three she-devils who deceive my soul,[47] and those who subjugate . . .
    [*some lines badly preserved or missing*]
3. . . . not the rich with (their) [wealth] . . . ; nor the [poor] who are without knowledge of the gods; nor the idolaters who serve images, (who serve) the God of Deceit; nor the false heretics . . .
    [*some lines badly preserved or missing*]
4. . . . May they become worthy, in soul and [body], of . . . [the gift] of all the mighty ones, . . . day by day, . . . And (you gods), give the feast and the reward of the good to the fortunate and lauded N. N., the Lord, the great and venerable Ruler.

8. Prayer to Mani as Maitreya (Parthian)

In the few lines of this late prayer, Mani is invoked as Maitreya, "united essentially with the dual divinity of Jesus—the Maiden of Light" (B).

... Great Maitreya,[48] noble Messenger of the gods, interpreter of the religion,[49] ... Jesus—Maiden of Light, Mār Mani, Jesus—Maiden of Light—Mār Mani, have [mercy] upon me, oh merciful Bringer of Light! Redeem my soul from this cycle of rebirth,[50] redeem my soul from [this] cycle of rebirths ...

9. Spell for fever (Parthian)

In this spell for fever, essentially an element of folk religion, the names of gods and angels are used in a magical way to ward off illness. Comparable Aramaic and Greek spells exist.[51]

[Title]: Spell for fever and the spirit [of fever?]

1. It is called Idra[52]. It has three forms and wings like a griffin. It settles in the [bone] and in the skull of men. It is called the [Great] Fever. It is bewitched by water [and] ... of copper and ashes. Bewitch it thus ...

2. ... May this fever of N. N., the son of N. N., leave (the body) and [be vanquished] by the name of the Lord Jesus the Friend (Yišō Aryāmān), in the name of his Father, the Highest, in the name of the Holy Spirit, in the name of the Best Spirit,[53] in the name of holy El,[54] in the name of Baubo,[55] in the name of the exorcisms that Michael, Rafael and Gabriel have bound,[56] in the name of ... (and of) the glutton, [in the name of] ... Sabaoth,[57] ...[58]

3. ... Frēdōn[59] shall subjugate ... all. There are three forms [in] me and a belly of fire. In my hands I hold a sharp and lethal hatchet, and I am protected all around with a whetted sword and a [dagger] of pure andamant; I have with me the whip of speech and of the hearing of the angels ... The seven daggers of hard steel that I have [grasped] with my hand ...

4. ... all the ... of the house, all secret spirits of the house, and all evil spirits of the house, all the wrathful "robbers" of the house: I shall smite them and their subjugated, oppressed slaves, so that they will not take up arms and stand (against me). I shall [take away] their light and add it to my own brightness. I shall take away their strength and add it to my own [strength] ...

10. Amulet (Parthian)

The incantation in the first part of this Parthian amulet inscription calls upon Jesus, Mani, and various angels of the Jewish tradition. They were probably known in the Elchasaite community in which Mani grew up. Several of these names can be found in Aramaic magical texts.

The second part of the amulet text contains an ill-preserved catalogue of *yakshas*, that is, Buddhist demons. It draws on a type of Buddhist literature, written between the fourth and the sixth century, represented foremost by the *Mahāmāyūrī* ("The Great Peacock Formula") and the *Candragarbha-Sūtra*. These texts belong to the category of "the five *rakshās*," a group of magical texts used for defensive purposes.[60] In them, series of demons and deities are invoked in order to strengthen protective spells (*dhāraṇīs*).

Our text, stemming perhaps from Balkh and dated by Henning to the sixth century, refers to various regions in Northwest India, as well as to *Činestan* (China), whatever that term may have designated. The correlation between certain geographical areas and particular *yakshas*, their sons, the food they eat, and so on, as we find it here, is also characteristic of the Buddhist texts mentioned. Of the twenty-four original paragraphs of our *yaksha* catalog, only five are preserved. Here we find the names of four *yakshas*.

With respect to our text, Boyce points out, "It is possibly the product of the church founded by Mar Ammō at Balkh, where there must have been close contacts with the Buddhists."[61]

1.   ... In your[62] name, by your will, at your command, and through your power, Lord Jesus Christ. In the name of Mār Mani, the Savior, the Apostle of the gods, and in the name of your [chosen], praised and blessed spirit who destroys all the demons and powers of Darkness. In the name of Michael, Sarael, Rafael and Gabriel, ... of Kaftinus and the angel Bar Sīmūs,[63] ... in the name of An-el, Dad-el, Abar-el, Nisad-el and Raf-el,[64] [who will smite] all you demons, *yakshas*, *peris* (she-devils), *drūjs*, *rākshasas*,[65] idols of Darkness, and spirits of evil. All you sons of [Darkness] and of night, of fear and terror, of pain and sickness, of ... [and] old age: [go] away from the strong power and the word,[66] ... away from this man who wears it.[67] Flee,[68] ... vanish, take flight, go away ... to a place far away ...

2.   ...

The fifth hour of the day: a *yaksha* by name of Viśvapāṇi[69] rules it. He occupies Purushapura.[70] He has twenty thousand sons. Their food is of salt.

The sixth hour of the day: a *yaksha* by name of Kucchatra (?)[71] rules it. He occupies ... He has twenty-five thousand sons. Their food is of ...

The seventh hour of the day: a *yaksha* by name of Nārāyaṇa (?)[72] rules it. He occupies China. He has eighty thousand sons. Their food is of fruit.

The eighth hour of the day: a *yaksha* by name of Naragān (?)[73] rules it. He occupies Dzartabuhr.[74] He has ... thousand sons. Their food is of milk ...

Notes

1. Literally, the Lord of the throne.
2. These words are in Turkish.
3. Literally, the Family of the Lights (*tohm ī rōšnān*). This refers to either the Manichaean community or the royal family (B).
4. Created spiritually, not materially. As B remarks, the term is perhaps employed mechanically in this late text. In the following, attributes of the redeeming gods are ascribed to the king.

5. For this expression, compare Böhlig, "Jakob als Engel."
6. The glories and spirits are the powers of the Realm of Light.
7. Name of the king. The name is common to many Turkish Khans, so we have no means of identifying this king.
8. Title in Turkish. The wise Khan is an ideal praised as far back as in the old Turkish inscriptions of the eighth century.
9. W. Lentz, "Note on the Fragment of a Manichaean Parchment," in M.A. Stein, *Innermost Asia* III. Repr. Delhi 1981, Appendix P. I am indebted to Sundermann for his transcription of the text, made at the British Museum, and his German translation.
10. As in Judaism, the angels constitute "the upper family," complementing "the lower family" of the righteous on earth.
11. It is not clear who is addressed here. It could be the living ruler.
12. *Nihumm* also means "conceal" (S).
13. We encounter the names of these four archangels as early as in the Qumran texts (e. g., 1 QM IX, 10ff.), as well as in Enochic literature and other OT apocrypha. Compare Rohland, *Der Erzengel Michael*, pp. 14ff.; Milik, *The Books of Enoch*, pp. 30 and 435 s.v. Michael.
14. This is an expression for "the righteous," that is, the Manichaeans.
15. The expression "glories and angels" refers cumulatively to the protective powers of the Realm of Light.
16. This translation for *rāymast* is suggested by S, who sees this and the following phrases as referring to Frēdōn.
17. King Frēdōn is the hero Thraētaona in the Avesta. He is invoked by Zoroastrians in times of illness. In Iran, he was regarded as the chief of divine physicians. In Western Manichaeism, he is known by the name "Aphrellon" (e. g., in Codex Brucianus). Compare Böhlig, "Jakob als Engel," pp. 9ff.
18. For the angel Jacob in Gnosticism and Manichaeism, compare Böhlig, *op. cit.*, pp. 9f.
19. Mani, Frēdōn, and the angel Jacob. Compare Böhlig, *op. cit.*, p. 9.
20. Apparently an angel. It is not clear whether this is the angel Balsamos of the *Cologne Mani Codex* or not. For Balsamos, compare J. Michl, "Engel V (Engelnamen)," in *RAC* V, p. 208. Angelic powers with the name "Bar . . ." (e. g., Bar Salminu) are invoked in Aramaic amulets. Compare J. Naveh and S. Shaked, *Amulets and Magic Bowls*, p. 41.
21. The Living Spirit in Middle Persian.
22. The Third Messenger.
23. For the five and the twelve angels residing in the ships of the Sun and the Moon as "shiplords," compare WL II, pp. 505f.
24. In Turkish Manichaean and Buddhist texts we often find the expression "the Religion within and the Realm without," which would refer to the spiritual and political dimensions of life. However, in Chinese Manichaean texts, especially in the *Hymnscroll*, the terms refer to "the inner and outer nature" (of man).
25. All names of angels.
26. Or, religion (*dēn*).
27. The Church as bride of the King, the Redeemer, is an image found in Rev. 21:9 and 22:17.
28. The God of Splendor (*bām-yazd*) is the Great Builder (the second God of the second creation).
29. The Third Messenger.
30. Also the Third Messenger.
31. This sentence is a reference to the sacred meal of the elect.
32. Here we have an invocation of the Fourfold Father.
33. *Fmšyy = Chin. fapshi, fa-shih* (B).
34. The gods are meant.
35. Literally, throne-possessing luminaries, that is, the Sun and the Moon, and the gods connected with them, the Third Messenger and Jesus.
36. The Column of Glory.
37. Literally, vivifier (*zīndakkar*).

38. The newly installed Church leader is now addressed.
39. The reference to body *and* soul is quite characteristic of Central Asian texts.
40. The Manichaean community regards itself as a family (*tōxmagān*).
41. Literally, gifts (*dāšin*). This is a reference to the commandments implied in the "gifts."
42. Thus for *brahm,* literally, form, appearance.
43. For the five commandments and three seals, compare Introduction.
44. Probably the following five virtues are meant: love, faith, favor, patience, wisdom.
45. In the Sogdian fragment M 14 (WL II, pp. 70f., 113), vigilance and zeal are listed right after the five commandments.
46. The missing words would be something like, "May I fulfill thy commandments."
47. These three she-devils are otherwise unknown.
48. Mani is meant.
49. Often Jesus is called "the interpreter."
50. Literally, birth-death (*zādmūrd*).
51. For ancient Jewish amulets and magical texts, compare J. Naveh and S. Shaked, *Amulets and Magic Bowls.* For Greek magical texts, compare H. D. Betz, ed., *The Greek Magical Papyri in Translation, Including the Demotic Spells.* Vol. I: *Texts.* Chicago and London, 1986; R. Merkelbach and M. Totti, eds., *Abrasax. Ausgewählte Papyri religiösen und magischen Inhalts.* Bd. I: *Gebete.* Opladen, 1990. (ARWAW, Sonderreihe: Papyrologica Coloniensia, Vol. XVII.1).
52. Name of the spell or of the spirit causing the fever. The word is not Persian.
53. Or, of the first thought (*handēšišn naxustēn*), as B suggests. The First Man is meant (S).
54. A Jewish name for God. For the name El in magic texts, compare Navel and Shaked, *Amulets and Magic Bowls,* p. 36.
55. Name of an angel? The word is written *bvbvv* = Baubo according to Boyce (*Word-List,* s.v. *bwbww*).
56. Translation suggested by B in Boyce, *Reader,* p. 187. For the idea of "binding" in magical texts, compare Naveh and Shaked, *Amulets,* p. 76.
57. Jewish name for God. For this name in Aramaic magical texts, compare Naveh and Shaked, *Amulets,* p. 36.
58. Here we find the words "fetter of Light."
59. For Frēdōn, cf. n. 29.
60. Cf. BHSD 449a, s.v. *rakṣā.*
61. Boyce, *Reader,* p. 188.
62. The "your" could refer to Jesus, or the Father of Greatness, probably invoked in missing lines (B).
63. These are names of angels of the Judaic tradition, where such angelic powers could be grouped together in various classes. The best known of these is the class of the four archangels: Michael, Gabriel, Raphael, and Uriel or Sari'el.
64. Names of Jewish angels. Various names of this type with the ending -el are to be found in Aramaic incantations. Compare Naveh and Shaked, *Amulets,* pp. 37, 41f., 51, 61, 69, 76, 91, 225.
65. *Yaksha*s and *rakshasa*s are specific classes of Buddhist demons; *peri*s and *druj*s are Iranian demons.
66. From the presence of this amulet (B).
67. The amulet.
68. Or, be destroyed.
69. In Northern Buddhism, Viśvapāṇi is not a *yaksha,* but a "Dhyāni-Bodhisattva." He is related to the Dhyāni-Buddha of the North, Amoghasiddhi. Yet, as Henning remarks, "As his colleague *Vajrapāṇi* appears frequently as a *yaksha,* . . . there is no reason why Viś-vapāṇi should not play such a homely role too." Henning, "Magical Texts," p. 52.
70. Pth. Puškavur (*pvskvr*), the present Peshawar. According to the *Candragarbha-Sūtra,* Maṇipuṣpa is the *yaksha* of Purushapura.

71. Or, Kukṣetra? Pth. *qvčtr*.
72. Pth. *naragān*. According to the *Candragarbha-Sūtra*, Pāñcika is the *yaksha* of "China." Compare Henning, "Magical Texts," p. 56.
73. According to Henning, the name is the same as in the seventh hour: Naragān.
74. An unidentified place name. In the *Mahāmāyūrī*, there is a place called Jaṭāpura between Kashmir and "China." Henning, *op. cit.*, p. 57.

CHAPTER FIFTEEN

An Index of Parthian Hymns

This index of Parthian hymns contains a relatively great number of first words of various hymns.[1] Of these, four groups are enumerated, namely:

I.   Parinirvāṇa Hymns (13 of 20 titles preserved)

II.   Hymns of Supplication (77 titles)

III. Hymns of Praise (68 titles)

IV. Hymns of a category the name of which is not preserved.

We have tentatively called these last "Hymns of Praise II" (55 titles). Thus we have here the titles or first words of 213 hymns. Yet this is only a part of what the index originally contained. A double-sheet on which these titles are written is preserved. The titles are neatly set out in Manichaean script, with the chapter headings, indicated at the end of each chapter, written in red.

    Our double-sheet (M 1) belonged to a book containing two other texts which are also translated in this volume. The first but earlier fragment is a double-sheet containing the colophon to the hymnbook. The second but older text (originally numbered T II D 135) invokes blessings on King Bögü Khan (Chin. Mou-yü, reigned 759–780) who adopted Manichaeism as the state religion of the Uighur Turks in 762/763. He assumed a Manichaean title in 764. Both double-sheets came from different places in the original book. The second was probably preceded by a painting of the Manichaean Turkish court, as Müller surmised.[2] It would thus have been comparable to a similar painting on the first sheet.[3]

    Though the hymns mentioned here are not preserved, their titles are revealing. We are made aware of the great wealth of hymnodic literature possessed by the Manichaeans in Central Asia. These hymns must have been composed in different languages, as the names mentioned in the blessings suggest: There are twenty-five Iranian (Persian/Parthian/Sogdian) names, four Indian names, and twelve Chinese names. These are just the men's names. In addition, there are names of four Turkish royal ladies, names of fourteen Iranian ladies, one Indian and one Chinese lady's name. Most of these names can be translated, as they have a religious meaning like "Jesus' Power," or "Jesus' Grace." Of course, the Indian names mainly have a Buddhist significance (Mahāyāna, Gotama, and so on).[4]

I. [Parinirvāṇa Hymns]
. . .

8.   To the place of peace . . .
9.   To the rest and . . . (of) the gods
10.   Thus I perceived the fragrance . . .
11.   Prince of Light, Lord Mani
12.   Come, I will write a letter
13.   In the year one hundred (and) . . .
14.   In the year fifty and . . .
15.   Ascended to Paradise is my Father
16.   Oh Shepherd, Light that has departed
17.   Oh great Teacher, Lord Zaku
18.   Assemble, oh beings, to this . . .
19.   Come, you beings, see . . .
20.   Our Father, the beneficent God

Parinirvāṇa [Hymns], 20 (in number)

II. [Hymns of Supplication]

1.   Remember, Beneficent One, (oh) Friend
2.   You would I praise, (oh) God, Lord Mani
3.   You would I praise and entreat[5]
4.   You would I praise, desirable Light
5.   You, (oh) God, would I entreat, (oh) Light
6.   You, (oh) God, would I entreat, who for me . . .
7.   You, (oh) God, would I entreat, redeem me
8.   You, (oh) God, would I entreat; to you . . .
9.   You, (oh) God, will I praise
10.   To you, (oh) God, (be) praise
11.   You, (oh) Beneficent One, would [we] bless always
12.   You, (oh) Messiah, would I entreat
13.   To you, good Lord, all days
14.   You, (oh) Merciful One, would we entreat
15.   To you, foremost of men
16.   You would I bless, (oh) God, Lord Mani
17.   You will I worship, (oh) God
18.   For you do I yearn, (oh) Father
19.   You do I await, (oh) God, Bene[ficent One]

20. I will praise the Lord Mani
21. Grant me the wish
22. Look upon me, (oh) Master
23. Ten commandments for the auditors
24. To you will I call
25. Oh! To you, oh God, I call
26. Oh God, merciful Lord Mani
27. Oh Father of Light, would that for us
28. Oh Father of blessing
29. Oh beneficent and desired [Lord]
30. (Have) mercy upon us, (oh) Light
31. Merciful and compassionate one
32. Great mercy and compassion
33. Come, hearken, (you) beings
34. Come, let us seek salvation
35. Come! Hark, you God!
36. Come! Hark, (you) auditors!
37. Come, you auditors, hark!
38. Come, you beings, to the Ship of Light!
39. The Light of sweet name has come
40. Delightful abode, original home[6]
41. Peace, sweet abode of Paradise
42. All the days and months have passed
43. Have mercy upon me, (oh) Loving One
44. (Oh) Messenger, who from the Father
45. Increase power in me
46. Save us, (oh) gods!
47. Help me, (oh) God, Lord [Mani]!
48. The Superior One[7] are you, the Friend
49. The Kingdom has come, and *yamag*[8]
50. Peace has come from Heaven[9]
51. (Lo), hope has come to us!
52. After so much time at the gate
53. After . . . so many battles
54. Of you we desire, (oh) Father, Lord [Mani]
55. I have departed
56. In God's name will I go
57. May not . . .
58. Be zealous, (oh) my soul!
59. There, my soul, remember
60. We would bless the angels and gods
61. Blessed is this auspicious day
62. Blessing and praise
63. Turn to me and redeem me
64. Turn to me, (oh) God, Lord Mani
65. Come, (you) elect, [from] all four [quarters]

66. Come, (you) elect, [sons] of Truth
67. Come, (you) angels and spirits
68. Worthy are you of great praise
69. May it be so,[10] (oh) great power
70. Brethren, as many as there are
71. Oh Self (that is) of noble[11] form and beauteous appearance
72. Behold my worship, [hear] my song
73. The valiant, the humble (and) the strong
74. Worship and praise, you . . .
75. Worthy are you of praise
76. Arise, brethren, and praise
77. Look upon our bended knee, oh God

[Hymns] of Supplication, 77 (in number)

III. [Hymns of Praise I]

1. Blessed are you, (oh) blessed day
2. Blessed are you, (oh) light-bringing Master
3. Blessed are you, (oh) great day
4. Blessed are you, (oh) day of goodness[12]
5. Blessed are you, (oh) day of redeemed Light
6. Blessed be this day
7. Blessed be this our . . .
8. Blessed be this day
9. Blessed be this day
10. Blessed is this longed-for day
11. Blessed is this great day
12. Blessed day, this day when . . .
13. Blessed the hour of this day
14. Blessed (is) this day of salvation
15. Blessed (is) this day, on the first . . .
16. Blessed day, goodness of the elect
17. We would bless the highest of the gods
18. Blessing (be) on you, (oh) blessed day
19. We would bless and praise
20. We would bless the King
21. Bless, (oh) righteous and chosen one
22. Blessed[13] is this wished-for day
23. Blessed fast day, the highest of days
24. Blessed day, blessed be . . .
25. Merciful one that came, (oh) Light
26. Mercy would we receive from you
27. Seek mercy and compassion
28. Have mercy upon me, (oh) gods
29. Have mercy, (oh) gods

30. Have mercy on me, (oh) great God
31. Have mercy, (oh) my loving savior
32. To you, (oh) God, would we make supplication on this [day]
33. To you would we pray, (oh) Beneficent One
34. Praise (be) to thy name
35. To you would we sing, you would we entreat
36. You would we praise, (oh) compassionate God
37. To God the Messiah may there be much blessing
38. Assemble, (oh) chosen ones, righteous ones
39. Assemble, (oh) brethren, chosen ones
40. Come, assemble, you chosen ones
41. Assemble, (you) auditors, members (of the community)
42. Come, (oh you) brethren, the *agreement
43. Instruction came to those assembled
44. An invitation came from the most divine of the gods
45. Have pity on me, (oh) great God
46. The assembly of believers, one with another
47. Brethren, believers, beings of Light
48. Come, (oh you) believers, let us bless
49. He has shown[14] me your wisdom
50. Instruction and commands
51. Higher is this chosen day
52. Oh commandment, our . . .
53. Oh, the most divine of the gods
54. Oh light-bringing God, Lord Mani!
55. Bountiful King, fortunate and happy
56. We brethren would remember
57. May there be salvation, peace and joy
58. Light-bringing God, Lord Mani
59. Blessed and exalted day
60. (This) day, this Monday
61. The blessed day of joy has come
62. The blessed day has come to us
63. The light-bringing day has come
64. The light-bringing . . . has come to us
65. Hear my word, beautiful . . .
66. Hear our prayer, you day
67. Honor to you, blessed day
68. Oh dearest of the beings of Light!

[Hymns] of Praise: 68 (in number)

IV. [Hymns of Praise II]

1. Arise, (you) worthy ones
2. Of the bright Self we believe

3. Upon you, (oh) bright Self
4. We would . . . upon the bright Self
5. Have pity,[15] you . . .
6. Have pity, brethren
7. (Oh) you Self, may there be . . .
8. You have come with salvation, you Spirit
9. You have come with salvation, Spirit of the gods
10. You have come with salvation, you Spirit
11. You have come with salvation, you Spirit of Light
12. This fettered spirit has come
13. This redeemed spirit has come
14. Blessed are you, noble[16] Spirit
15. Blessed are you, great primeval Spirit
16. Blessed are you, (oh) Spirit of Light
17. Blessed are you, (oh) Spirit of Light
18. Blessed are you, (oh) [redeemed?] Spirit
19. Blessed are you, (oh) Spirit of [Light]
20. Blessed be the souls
21. Bless, all (you) believers
22. Bless, brethren, this . . .
23. Blessing and praise[17]
24. We would bless and praise
25. We would bless you, Spirit of Light
26. We would bless the spirit of the gods
27. (Lo) brethren, see this . . .
28. Come, brethren, have pity on . . .
29. (Oh ye) assembled brethren
30. Oh children of Light, (you) righteous ones
31. Oh noble, excellent seed grain
32. Oh beneficent spirit, reveal . . .
33. Oh noble, redeemed soul
34. (You) believers and beneficent ones
35. Come, (oh) brethren, let us find
36. Come, let us sing a hymn (of praise)
37. Come, chosen ones, righteous ones
38. Come, chosen ones, [sons] of Truth
39. Come, sons of wisdom, to the Father's . . .
40. Come, let us praise the Spirit of Light
41. You who are worthy of praise
42. We would bless you, loving Spirit
43. To you, Spirit of Light, that (has) five [limbs?]
44. You, Spirit of Light, would we adore
45. You would we praise, (oh) spirit
46. Praise to you, (oh) spirit
47. To you would I speak, (oh) my captive soul
48. You would we praise, (oh) Jesus, Messiah

49. You would we praise, (oh) blessed Spirit
50. To you would we pray,[18] (oh) virtuous[19] God
51. I am the living spirit
52. It is I who taught the Buddhas
53. I am the blessed spirit
54. I will make supplication to you, (oh) God, redeem [me]
55. Noble, flawless, radiant One

. . .

Notes

1. I am very thankful to Werner Sundermann for corrections and modifications of my translation of this chapter.
2. Müller, "Doppelblatt," p. 6.
3. Müller, "Hofstaat," p. 207.
4. Müller, "Doppelblatt," pp. 32–36.
5. Only the letters *'xš///* are preserved. If we supply *'xš[vz]*, this would be "desirous." Other possibilities are, *'xš'd*, "distressed"; *'xš'dyh*, "suffering"; *'xšd* and *'xšdg*, "merciful"; but hardly *'x'št*, "raised up."
6. The word *padišt*, "place, home" is used "of Paradise as the home of the spirit." Boyce, *Word-List*, p. 69, s.v. *pdyšt*.
7. Literally, the higher or upper one (*abardar*).
8. *Yamag* is either the Twin, "used as title of the head of the Manichaean church, and also of divinities"; or the "holy day in honour of a head of the Church." Boyce, *Word-List*, p. 102, s.v. *ymg*.
9. Or, from the Aeon (*šahr*).
10. This corresponds to the Biblical "Amen."
11. Or, free (*āzād*).
12. Or, piety, charity (*qārbag = qirbag*).
13. Literally, merciful (*axšaδāg*).
14. Or, explained, taught (*aβδēs-*).
15. Or, forgive (*abaxšāh-*).
16. Or free (*āzād*).
17. Literally, hymn (singing) (*bāšāh*).
18. Or, make supplication (*nigāy-*).
19. Or, valiant (*hunarāvend*).

CHAPTER SIXTEEN

Parables

While freely adopting the myths and legends of the peoples they addressed, the Manichaeans apparently collected a great number of stories and narratives that they used as parables, explaining the content in terms of their own theology. Such parables were referred to as *āzend/āzind* in Middle Persian. The texts normally distinguish between the story itself and its subsequent interpretation, which is added as an epimythion (final explanation). A story can, however, also be introduced by a promythion, a religious message, which it then illustrates. The great wealth of such narrative materials, which served didactic purposes (the purpose of illustrating the message), shows that "skillful means" in the transmission of the word played just as big a role here as it did in Buddhism. As the Manichaean Church had an ecumenical character, it was familiar with narrative materials from the most diverse parts of the world. Thus we find the Central Asian texts reflecting a knowledge of the Greek fables of Aesop, Jewish accounts connected with Enochic literature, Mesopotamian and Iranian mythology and folklore, Indian fables of the *Pañcatantra* and *Kathāsaritsāgara* cycles, Buddhist *Jātakas* and *Avadānas* (stories about Buddha's former lives), as well as Central Asian folklore. In fact, the Manichaeans turned out to be great transmitters of such literary materials from West to East and from East to West. As Asmussen points out, "They (i. e., Mani and his missionaries) combined the useful with the pleasant by narrating appropriate parables and good stories; and they had a great repertoire, for as representatives of the only really universal and perfect religion they thought they could use all the Christian, Zoroastrian and Buddhist material they found to be useful. Thus, with their specific goal in mind, they became mediators in the literary exchange between East and West."[1]

Thus, Greek and even Jewish materials were found among the Manichaean manuscripts from Central Asia, in Iranian and Turkish translations. Conversely, the Manichaeans were probably among the first to transmit to the West the Buddha legend, that is, the legend of the young prince who leaves his palace in search

177

of enlightenment, after encounters with an ill man, an old man, and a dead man. By various successive stages (Sogdian, Persian, Arabic, Armenian, Georgian, Hebrew, Latin, Italian) this story became known as the "Barlaam and Josaphat legend" in the Western world and found its way into the literatures of various European peoples, including even the Danes.[2]

Many a parable lived on as a story or legend long after Manichaeism itself had ceased to exist. This is true of both Iranian and Turkish Manichaean parables, of which only portions have been preserved. Particularly in Islamic lore, such stories have remained alive, and we find them, or motifs from them, in places as unexpected as modern collections of Kurdish or Kashmiri folktales.[3]

Of the various partially preserved parables in Sogdian that are edited and translated by Henning, we quote only the first. The others are, on the whole, too fragmentary.[4] There are probably further fragments of parables in the as yet unpublished texts in the various Central Asian collections. Sims-Williams has made us aware of Manichaean parables in the Sogdian texts of St. Petersburg; at least one of these stories has its parallels in South Indian and Singhalese versions of the story, "which enable one to reconstruct the plot of the incomplete Sogdian tale."[5] This becomes plausible if we consider that there might have been Manichaeans in South India.[6] Other Sogdian tales from St. Petersburg are more complete, again showing close agreement with modern South Indian versions.[7] In certain cases, as in our text 11, and in other instances, "where the stories are provided with a historical or legendary framework, the genre of tales and parables merges into that of church history."[8]

Needless to say, the Manichaeans were also acquainted with the New Testament parables, but these are referred to thematically rather than quoted verbatim.[9]

1. *Parable about the world-ocean* (Sogdian)

This is the first of two stories preserved in a Sogdian Book of Parables[10]. At least one other parable must have preceded this one. The concluding line is preserved and would indicate that it dealt with a judge. It reads, "(Here) ends the parable of the judge and. . . ."

Our parable likens Mani's religion to the world-ocean into which all rivers—that is, previous religions with their wisdom and their insight—flow. The text contains a number of words of Indian origin, for example, *rtny*, "jewel" (Skr. *ratna*) and *sm'try*, "world-ocean" (Skr. *samudra*). Although such words are of general Sogdian usage, the text itself is, as Sundermann has shown, of Buddhist inspiration, since a number of comparable Buddhist texts exist.[11] Even in early Buddhist passages (*Udāna* V, 5; *Cullavagga* IX, 1, 4), Buddha compares his doctrine with the ocean which has only one taste, the taste of salvation. In the Coptic *Kephalaia* the ocean is on the whole not so pure and perfect that it could be compared to Mani's teaching. It contains the sediment of dark water, fire, and darkness which in primal times were swept from the firmaments to the "spheres" of the world, and into cosmic ditches connected with the ocean. Hence the salty and bitter taste of ocean water. An ocean giant arises out of the dark substances (*Kephalaia*, pp. 113f.). The giant can assume a positive aspect, for, by moving the waters and causing the tide, he cleanses the ocean. The image of rivers flowing into the ocean, however, had already been used in the Coptic texts to demonstrate the relationship between the former religions and Mani's teaching. In *Kephalaia,* chapter 154, Mani compares the books of the former religions, whose wisdom is incorporated into his teaching, with water "that will be added to (another) water, and they become many waters."[12] This is reminiscent of the Persian text M 5794 where Mani claims supremacy for his own faith.[13]

According to the fragmentary colophon (not translated here), this parable as well as the next one were written down by a scribe by the name of Navēmāx ("New Moon," a Sogdian name), who had heard them from a certain Tataɣur (a Turkish name). The many mistakes in the Sogdian text would suggest that the scribe was, however, a Turkish Uighur. The book was probably written in the decades after 840 when the Uighurs, coming from the Mongolian Steppes, settled in the oasis towns of the northern Tarim Basin and established a partly Manichaean state in Turfan.

(Here) begins the story about the Religion and the world-ocean.
[And] now hear [the story about the Religion and the world-ocean]. The Religion [is similar to] the world-ocean which is [different from the other] waters in ten points.

One point is that it is mightier, greater and stronger [than] other waters. It is infinite, and none of the living beings [know] or comprehend it, and [they cannot] understand it.

Second: [No one knows] its other [shore].

Third: It changes the taste of other [waters] . . . [and of the precipitation?] that falls into it, but it itself does not change because of its . . . , and (within itself) it is not different at all.

Fourth: [It absorbs the bodies that] fall [into it] and . . . it does not reject [anything]. [But the world-ocean] never seems fuller, for it does not increase (?) [at all, and] it remains [still?] and tranquil.

Fifth: It is [clear?] and pure and undefiled, [and] it does not absorb impurity [and] defilement; it refuses to accept these [and it hurls them back] onto the shore immediately.

[Sixth:] . . . then . . . [arises] there in the midst of the light of fire.[14] . . .

[Seventh]: In the world-ocean and on its bare (?) [shore?] the great bipeds and otherwise fashioned men and [other?] living beings and wild animals appear. They are born as strong giants . . .

[Eighth]: In the world-ocean, [priceless and varied pearls and] jewels are [born, which are not born in (any other) deep place (in the earth)].

Ninth: The strong demon of the world-ocean [lifts up] (the water) and the whole world-ocean trembles.[15]

Tenth: When the waters of the world [fall] into the world-ocean, they all roar and come thundering down; but when they are about to enter there, their [roaring] and thundering [cease].

And the wonderful Religion of the Apostle [is similar] to the world-ocean [in ten ways].

[First]: It is wise (full of wisdom), and no one knows nor can estimate its wisdom . . . , nor the quantity and [number] of its sermons and explanations; and no one can comprehend it. The former religions are similar to the small waters which arise in [different places] . . . [But] the religion of the Apostles which [is similar] to the great world-ocean can be [seen] in the whole world and in every place. And it is ripe to be presented in [the darkness] in a most open manner and to be proclaimed in all languages. And [one can] find the explanation and systematization (?) of all wisdom in it.

Second: The other shore that no one [knows] is the fragrant, wonderful Paradise that the living beings [on earth], apart from the elect and the [auditors], do not perceive and will never comprehend.

Third: The [waters] of the world-ocean have one taste, and the other waters have different tastes and appearances, but its own taste does not change. That is [the] deep wisdom of the Law and the commandments of the Religion, and the sweet, wonderful words that are preached. The fine parables and (their) explanations [and] interpretations, the rich and wholly pure [practice] of (its) mode of life, the noble exercise of its good customs, the humble . . . change of mind which the Religion shows (suggests) to [men], teaching and instructing (them). . . . But it itself has not been instructed by anyone in anything.

Fourth: The world-ocean absorbs the bodies . . . and does not reject anyone. These are the mighty [spirits?] and men; and [whoever] of these comes to the Church of the Apostle is absorbed [by the Church], for it does not reject anyone. Rather, according to the order of its Law and commandments, it gives them their [places]. And as many as approach it [repeatedly], in order to enter it, (all) of them have their places either amongst the auditors or the elect. And they all do their works according to their rank, their zeal and their strength. And [the Religion] does not make . . . and honor . . . , and out of love it does not shout out loud. And however many of these people may be mighty, nothing takes it by surprise, nor does it rejoice, for it remains placid and tranquil at all times. [Thus] it is like the world-ocean.

Fifth: The Religion of the Apostle [is] without stain, (being) clean and pure and holy; and it immediately refuses to retain those men who are confused and immoral and [have] filthy thoughts, men who are like corpses, excrements and diverse (forms of) pollution. It tosses them back onto the shore.

Sixth: When an elect one sees another elect one face to face, or an auditor sees (another) auditor, then the pure, loving gaze gives rise to great joy among them. And [so] great blessing comes upon them, and like light it appears in the faces of the light gods and becomes visible.

Seventh: The many great, strong bipeds and otherwise fashioned wonderful beings and animals [that are born] in the world-ocean are (like) the elect that behave quite differently from the world. And [they] bear the burden and the heavy load of the Law and endure great pain and suffering. And they always accept personally, what no man in the whole world would bear or take upon himself.

Eighth: In the world-ocean, . . . varied priceless pearls and beautiful, miraculous jewels are born which are not born in (any) deep [place] (in the earth). Never can this be comprehended and never can it be seen. This reflects the difference between the two places, the good and the evil one, and the self-realization of the soul which is not born in a learned place.[16] It (that wisdom) can never be attained except in [the Religion] and in the Law and in the commandments of the Apostle.

Ninth: The strong one[17] and the demon[18] of the world-ocean that shakes the whole world-ocean when it rises (in the tide) is the Nous of the Religion, which is in the [whole] Church, shaking the bodies (of men). It (the Nous) seizes (them) mightily and draws out [the light] (they have accumulated), this being the daily work (of the men) of the Religion. (That light) ascends daily from the whole body of the elect to the light [chariots] (the Sun and the Moon); and the gods in command of these chariots draw it up [and] constantly send it on to the world of Paradise.

Tenth: All roaring and thundering waters that flow into the ocean, that then become still and stop roaring, are the adherents of (other) religions and men of worldly wisdom [and] eloquent men who remain (mere) creators of words, believing themselves to be wise. But when they come to the door of the Religion of the Apostle, they all become silent and their (own) words silence them. And now they do [not] exalt themselves (any more), and henceforth they do not dare to make any more speeches [and] dare not say anything.

(Here) ends the story about the Religion and the world-ocean.

2. *Parable about the two snakes* (Sogdian)

This is the second story preserved in the Sogdian Book of Parables. It is a parable about two snakes who appear as two brothers. Apparently the old motif of a pair of snakes, commonly found in folklore, is taken up here and given a Manichaean interpretation, even though snakes are repulsive animals to the Manichaeans (cf. *Kephalaia*, p. 288), as they are to Zoroastrians. Here their bodies are compared to the bodies of men. Unredeemed man (the Old Man) loses his soul, which is represented by a jewel in the head of the snake, by being bound to the body. Redeemed man (the New Man) can give up his body for the sake of his soul.

(Here) begins the story about (the snakes) "Heavy-to-carry" and "Light-to-carry."

Furthermore it was heard that there were once [two snakes], and the first snake was called "Heavy-to-carry." Their bodies were equally large, and their tails were very long. Being of one [mind], they loved [each other] so much that one could not bear [to be separated] from [the other]. And lo, they went along a path together. After they had traversed much land, one snake glided into a depression. And the other snake proceeded along the way. On one side of the path there was a very high mountain, and on the other side a [very deep] body of water. And on the path, a trapper had set up a [snare] and a pitfall. Inside it was full of (burning) coals, and all (kinds of) fiery apparitions rose from it into the air. The trapper [was hiding] nearby. And when the snake came to that place, it was pleased and amazed [at the] fiery [apparitions in the air]. But it was not possible [for it] to avoid the pitfall, for, alas, it [had to] go ahead along this path and there was no way back. And lo, it paused (?), and then darted ahead, thinking, "I want to jump over the pitfall with my whole body." But, because the pitfall was very wide and the snake's body was long and very thin (?) in the middle, [and] its tail was very long, it could not cross the pitfall. (Its) head came across, but the tail remained behind, and the middle of the body remained lying across the pit, and the snake could not pull it over to its neck. So it burned there and died. And the trapper came quickly, [stretched out] his hand toward the [pit], cut open the head neatly, took the stone, and went away very happy.

The second snake came along and found its [companion] dead, its head mutilated. [It cried] out from the depths of its soul, "[Alas!] You were very dear to me." And it wept and lamented bitterly, wailed pitifully and [said], "O wonderful brother, how have you died without your brother [and] in shame?" When it had stopped lamenting, it thought to itself, "My [brother] died because he had not thought of a [remedy] for the body. If I, too, do not find a remedy for the body, I will also have to [die]. [And] it considered (the matter) carefully. And the snake said, "Because he was a male, [he could not bear] the separation from his dear tail; he could not endure corruption and suffering in his body. [But] there is really no other way out. If I endure separation from (my) dear tail and endure a little pain in my body [for the sake of] my soul, then I will be able to jump over the pitfall." Then it [returned] to the depression [and] found the abandoned fire of a shepherd. And it burned off as much of its tail as could be harmful [to its body]. And, when it had become smaller, the tailless body jumped very lightly and crossed (the pitfall) safely. [Of these] two snakes, one is the person who loves the body, for whom bearing . . . is troublesome, (but)

who is unconcerned (about the soul). And his . . . is long. The second
snake is the person for whom the soul is dearer (than the body). There
is very little poison in him and his (attachment) to the world is very weak,
and the fetters binding his soul (?) are very thin. And the pitfall, the high
mountain and the deep body of water are the three trenches.[19] [The trap-
per] is Ahriman, and the stone is the soul. Ultimately the [Old Man],[20]
being without good works, is the one who cannot jump over the [three]
ditches with the tail of the body.[21] But the [chosen New] Man has
[purged] the three poisons[22] from the body and has borne in his body the
agony (caused by observing) the Law, and he can endure separation [from]
(his) dear wife and children and from riches, and on the Final Day (his)
soul [will] arise [from the body] and will attain the peace of Paradise . . .

3. *Parable about the good and the bad crops* (Parthian)

In this parable, as explained by Colditz,[23] a farmer sows good seed on his land and
reaps a bountiful harvest. Thereafter, thistles and weeds grow in his field, along
with grain-bearing crops. Then someone pours poison on the plants bearing grain.
One day some blind men and some sighted men come along the way beside the
field. The men who can see and discern take only some good grain. The blind ones,
however, take the poisoned grain, without avoiding the thorns and heedless of the
others' warnings in their convinction that the field still bears only good crops.

   Although the explanation is not preserved, it seems obvious that the parable
pertains to the right attitude of believers to nonbelievers, the adherents of other
religions, from which many elements were adopted. These, our parable says, have
to be examined critically. The first farmer represents the former "Messengers,"
Jesus, Zarathustra, and Buddha. They brought good seed to men in the past; it
grew and was harvested. But their truths were distorted and mingled with false
teachings (thorns and weeds) in the course of time. Then the Devil poisoned the
crops in order to prevent men from gaining insight. The passersby on the way are
Manichaeans, some seeing, others blind regarding the true state of affairs. Those
endowed with vision can distinguish between what is good and bad in other teachings. They take only what is useful. The blind men, however, take what is useless
and harmful, considering the other religions to be as true and good as they were
originally. They do not heed the warnings of their brethren. But for them there are
founts at the far end of the field, whose water can cleanse their eyes. As Colditz
suggests, this probably reflects a dispute within the Manichaean community
between those who were all too willing to accept other beliefs and those who called
for critical discrimination.

[Title]:   The speech [on the unbelievers]

> . . . They are [similar] to a land that came into the hands of [a] farmer, and
> he scattered much seed on it and gathered much grain from that land (?),
> and filled the (grain) in a vessel.[24] And (then) many *weeds and thorny
> scubs grew on that land. And then another one came and poured poison

over them. And they also grew and bore [fruit], and far and wide that [crop?] and . . . were spoiled by the [poisonous] crop . . . And when it grew on [the land], each one of the sowers [let] his (part of the crops stand). And that land lay [neglected] above (?) the way. And seeing as well as blind men walked on that way, back and forth, and they heard that a certain farmer had sowed on that land. And when the seeing men passed by that way, they gathered and [ate] of the grain. And when (some) of the blind men passed that way and heard [that] a certain farmer had sowed seed on that land, then they took and ate of the poisonous crop. And when the seeing men noticed them, and said, "Do not eat (that which is) between the thorns there, and do not eat of the [poisonous] crop," then . . . the blind men were *insistent . . . , (saying), 'A [farmer] has sowed good seed on his land, and [you] say that one should not eat of that crop!'"

And then at the boundary of that field there were many deep wells and fountains, and when [those] men [turned away?] from that land, then (the water) was [soothing] for their eyes . . .[25]

4. Parable about threshing wheat (Parthian)

This parable starts with an instruction of Mani which might have been the promythion, the introductory explanation of the parable. He talks about the "two principles" (dō bun) or two natures, constituting man and the world, and especially about the evil principle and its effect. He explains how the Devil harms the souls of those he has ensnared, imprisoning them in the cycle of rebirths.

The parable itself is contained in the short second paragraph, and it is clarified again in the epimythion, the explication at the end. It interprets the image of the farmer separating wheat from chaff with the help of the wind and a flail. The mixture symbolizes the amalgamation of the two natures: the bright spiritual nature and the dark material nature. With respect to man, these natures are eventually separated from each other in the course of manifold rebirths. The farmers are, in Mani's words, "my children," that is, the elect. They do their work with the help of the wind ("the true Word," the Word which is preached) and the flail (the righteous deed). When the hearers hear their words and do righteous deeds, they become aware of the state of convolution in which they exist. In the first part, the hearers were probably exhorted not to become unbelievers and thus slaves of the Devil who leads them into the deep.

[Title]:   The sermon about the unbelievers

> . . . Then the beneficent Father (Mani) himself spoke thus in love [and] *joy to that disciple and to all believers, "You, too . . . every one, . . . like my . . . that this . . . which to men . . . about the two principles and [the two kinds?] . . . every one of them mixed (?) . . . descends into the depth and [is] the evildoer and the foe. [And] those that must descend into the depth [are] Ahriman's slaves and *prisoners, . . . and [that] Ahriman is the ruthless ruler (?) and the cruel Prince. And those souls that are his own are those which he harms, and he seizes (?) them, [and] he seduces (their)

beauty [through] *attachment (to the world) and throws [them] into the cruel (cycle of) rebirths and into Hell."

"And these two kinds (of natures) are mingled with each other in the course of rebirths, like [wheat] and *chaff that are [mixed] with each other. [Then] the farmers separate those [things] from one another with the mighty power of the wind and the flail, and . . . lay [them] . . . and . . . bring (them) . . ."

"Thus this [man] is also similar to that wheat, [and] my children are similar to the farmers . . . My mind [and my true] Word are similar to the wind, [and] the just Law is similar to the flail. And when the elect preach my Word, then those that come (?) to Paradise . . . become manifest . . ."

5. *Parable about free men, debtors, and slaves* (Parthian)

This story is from the same collection of parables as the previous one. Here the fates of those that have been liberated from the world—that is, from worldly passions—are contrasted with those that have not. The latter are likened to debtors and servants. The three categories of men—free men, debtors, and slaves—are explained in the next text. Since we hear of slaves imprisoned forever, this could be a text from the Māsiya tradition, the sect that claimed that not all souls or particles of light will be saved.[26]

> . . . Then he seizes them [and] says, "First pay those debts [which you] owe in this land, and then go wherever you want to."
>
> But those that are free and have no debts in that land go confidently and [fearlessly] past that watch-(post), and that evildoer can do nothing to them. [In] that land where they have gone, where the evildoer has no dominion . . . , they rest . . . And they go . . . (and) they serve until . . .[27] [those] that have been their helpers also go with them and save themselves.
>
> But those that are his slaves, then willy-nilly serve that lord. And when that evildoing Prince (the Prince of Darkness) realizes, "My slaves have fled," they are fettered even more tightly with *ropes around their limbs (?) and chains, and he leads them into the dark prison where they nevermore [find] a door or an escape . . .
>
> Thus know now[28] . . . this (cycle of) rebirths . . . the evildoing Prince . . .

6. *Explanation of the parable about free men, debtors, and slaves* (Parthian)

This text is closely connected to the previous story. It is an epimythion, a concluding explanation, in the form of an utterance by Mani himself. The word "debt" refers to a tribute that has to be paid to Ahriman by being reborn in the cycle of births, whereby the soul is bound ever anew to matter. According to our text, men belong to three categories, reflecting, as Colditz points out, the three main social groups in Sassanian Iran: the nobles (originally exempt from tax); the working people, farmers, craftsmen, and merchants (who had to pay taxes); and the slaves. They represent, in this Manichaean interpretation, the elect, the auditors, and "the children of this world." These three classes correspond also to the Western Gnostic distinction between the *pneumatikoi,* the *psychikoi,* and the *hylikoi,* those that are condemned without hope of redemption.[29] Those free from debt, then, are "the chosen ones," the elect, who can free their souls from the world and its entanglements by *gnosis.* They are not bound to further rebirths and when they die and leave the world, they can pass the watchposts and enter the Realm of Light. The debtors are the auditors, the Manichaean laymen. Basically, they can leave the land of the evil Prince of Darkness (that is, they can be redeemed from the material world) but first they must pay the debts that they owe Ahriman by being reborn in the world. Still, they can strive for perfection by fullfilling the commandments and doing good deeds. The slaves, finally, are the unbelievers who do not observe the Manichaean religion. They will never be redeemed unless they emulate the slaves who flee successfully, those who depart from false teachings and turn to the Manichaean religion. Our text probably also contained exhortations to the auditors, telling them how they could speed up their salvation.

> . . . Old age, harm (?) and illness . . . and many other kinds of sins . . . And the watchpost [where they are] seized is the body of men. The free ones are those that hear the (Mani's) word; believe, accept and truly keep my religion; and do not relinquish my commandment up to the day when they depart from the body. The Realm where they go and [where] Ahriman has no power [is] Paradise; *Nirvāṇa* and peace [prevail there?], and [not] even one sinner [is to be found there?]. The slaves [are] those [who] . . . do not . . . They torture and [do?] harm . . . [The debtors] are those who [hear] the true word of [the Beneficent One, Mani] and [yearn for it]. They cannot [completely] condemn and remove their own sin, but at the same time they do find pleasure in the true word and the righteous deed, and they become helpers (of the elect). And there are debtors, some with many debts and some with few. Those with many debts are like this: . . . when the true word [is preached?], . . . and they [have] not heard (it) in time . . .

7. *Parable about the poor man and the king* (Parthian)

The previous four texts came from one manuscript, a collection of parables. The following story is from another book, but it also mentions the three classes of men. First, there are the elect. Second, there are the auditors, who have as yet to fulfill their religious duties. They can be redeemed, but only at a later point, when they have gone through the cycle of rebirths and are finally reborn in a state worthy of an elect. Third, there are those outside the Manichaean Church who have no hope of redemption, either because they have been deceived by their "churches" or because they themselves are "liars," that is, evildoers. As Colditz points out, the parable is an exhortation to auditors to listen to the call of the Church and fulfill the commandments.[30] Maybe the text also contained an implied exhortation to the contemporary Manichaean communitiy of the elect to follow the example of Mani's and his disciples' religious fervor and purity.[31]

After the intermediary Sogdian title there follows a second parable. It is about a man of humble origin who wins the favor of the king by praising him and giving him a present which he made himself.[32] He probably receives a rich reward, we may surmise. A recurrent motif in such parables is a lowly man being praised by the king and elevated to the rank of a noble, an image of an auditor giving alms to the elect and then being granted absolution and the hope of salvation. Thus, in our parable, the king probably raises the poor man to the rank of a noble and accepts him into his entourage. This would be an image of the perfection an auditor could attain if he engaged in wholehearted praise of the King of Light and observed the religious commandments for the elect. Colditz declares, "The admittance of the simple man into the suite of the king symbolizes his admittance into the Realm of Light as a perfect auditor together with the chosen ones, and his redemption from further reincarnations. This parable would then deal not with the hearer [i. e., auditor] as such, but with the perfect hearer who strives for sinlessness and is characterized by the special giving of alms."[33]

> ... And the *summons [is] the wisdom of the gods. All men who went together with that merchant are the souls that have been saved together with the Apostle, and they that followed are those that fulfill the commandment of the gods now, and ascend thereafter to the Light. And those [that] did not accompany [him] are (those of the) deceived churches and (of) the liars. [Sogdian]: (Name of scribe). [Sogdian]: To be preached on Jaidan Monday.[34]
>
> [Parthian]: Furthermore it is said: There was a man of lowly descent, and he loved the king very much. And he made (fashioned) [a present?]. Then he went and learned from the wise men how to bless and praise the king. And when the king went forth from the palace in glory, that man immediately went and stood near the stairway, and he began to praise the king with a loud voice, together with the nobles. And when the king saw how the man blessed and praised him with a cheerful face and good words, the king joyously approached the steps. And he turned [to the chief accountant of the court?] who came and stood there [at his service]. Then the king ...

8. *Parable about the seduced youth* (Persian)

This parable is concerned with the demonic power in man, the internal dark fire that perpetuates the sway of the body by devouring the light contained in plants and food that have been eaten. The demonic power is referred to as "devouring" and "greedy." Since the body is regarded as a prison for the bright soul, the five limbs of the soul or Elements of Light are consumed by this fire of greed.[35] The body with its divine spark of light is here symbolized by a building in which a youth (*rahīg*) is imprisoned. The captured youth represents the soul. The king who has him captured is Ahriman, and his daughter, who desires to marry the youth, is Greed (*Āz*), the embodiment of avaricious Matter.[36] The aspect of the boy being made unconscious with an intoxicating drink after being tricked into coming down from his tree (a symbol of the Realm of Light) is quite compatible with Manichaean teaching. The bull that frees the boy from his impregnable prison is, as Sundermann suggests, probably the "Form of Light" (*Lichtgestalt*), an emanation of the Light Nous. According to *Kephalaia* 36, 9ff., the elect and catechumens (auditors) meet and adopt this "Form of Light" when they forsake the world; it "reveals itself to everyone who departs from his body."[37] The interpretation of various minor aspects of the parable as set forth in the epimython (the concluding explication) is unfortunately lost, since the text has been preserved only fragmentarily. Thus we do not know who the old woman who tricks the boy into descending from his tree is; she may be the personification of the Realm of Darkness. The bull's breaking a horn while destroying the prison and liberating the boy also remains uninterpreted. As Sunderman suggests, the parable probably started with the description of the king's daughter, lovesick and yearning for the wonderful youth. In order to cure her, the king sends out his men to capture the youth.[38]

> . . . "If you bring that youth, then [give] me to him as (his) wife."
> The king sent out (his) horses and men three times, (commanding them), "Go and bring the boy."
> They went and stood around the tree, (and) they said, "The king is calling (you)."
> [The youth said], ". . . not."
> . . . (many) times the man, . . . he did . . . (and) killed (them).
> The king said, "What should I do? (My) horses and men have been destroyed, my daughter is near death."
> Then there was an old woman. She said, "Another . . ."
> The king said, "How will you lead (him) here?"
> Then she took wine and a lamb. She went and sat down under the tree; she bound the legs of the lamb together (and tried to) kill it (by cutting its) [tail].
> The youth said, "Cut its neck."
> But she (still cut) its tail to kill it. Then she said to the youth, "Come and show me how."
> Then the youth descended from the tree, (thinking), "I will show her how." The woman gave him (some) wine. As soon as he drank it, he fell unconscious. Then she put (him) onto a donkey (and) [brought] (him) to the king. He gave (him) to the girl. In the . . . he made three doors, [two of them] of copper and lead. [For] the inner (door) he (assembled and) put together immeasurable amounts of iron (and) lead (and) made a door (from them). When the youth regained consciousness, he played his flutes.[39] The bull heard it, (and) it came and broke open the doors. Then it approached the third door. It broke it by force, and one of its horns broke. It went and abducted the boy and seduced him. It said to the boy, "According to . . ."

The ruler is Ahriman ... The old woman ... The three flutes are [the five] commandments for the elect.[40] The three doors are fire, sensual lust [and avarice] ...

9. *Parable about the oblivious envoy and the peacock* (Persian)

The editor of the text explains that this parable is concerned with the fate of the soul separated from its divine home.[41] As in the "Hymn of the Pearl," where the son of the King of Kings leaves his father's palace as a royal envoy to fetch a precious pearl from Egypt, which symbolizes the world,[42] so here an envoy is sent to India. In the "Hymn of the Pearl," the pearl, clutched by a dragon, represents the soul that must be redeemed from demonic powers. The envoy, upon clothing himself like the Egyptians (that is, adopting the garment of the body) and eating their food, forgets his divine mission. It is only when a call in the form of a letter from his father's realm is sent out to him that he becomes aware of his divine origin. Thus his power is renewed, and he is able to secure the pearl.

This parable must have been similar in structure to the "Hymn of the Pearl." India, like Egypt, could be seen as an image of the world. As the figures in the "Hymn of the Pearl" can be interpreted on various levels—the envoy representing either the First Man, or Mani, or the soul of the individual—so it is in our story. Here too the envoy could be the First Man, or Mani, or any soul. The envoy forgets his mission and has to be reminded of it by a herald representing the divine Call. It is Mani's heavenly Twin, or the "Form of Light" of the believer.[43] The soul is here represented by the image of the peacock, the symbol of beauty and immortality. It is entrusted to the envoy who brings it back home, that is, brings it into the Realm of Light.

> Again he[44] said, "There was a ruler who had [sent] his *envoy to India. Then he sent a command to India, "... let (him?) go away (?)" The *envoy did not keep (the commandment) [in mind?]. He bought (believed in) words of no [avail?].[45] A herald ... came to the land ... peacock ... was not.
>
> He said to the *envoy, "The peacock is very heavy (?) for me (?). Now you watch (it). I trust you." The *envoy took it. He brought it home. He obeyed the commandment regarding the bird.
>
> After a long time the *envoy ...

10. *Parable about the lowly born rich man* (Persian)

As the editor of this text explains,[46] a king sends out messengers to a lowly born but apparently wealthy man to announce his visit. The man gives a banquet for the king and his entourage, and then he liberally bestows presents upon them, including houses and property, after the king has presented him with garments and ornaments. The following main part of the narration is well preserved. The king and his courtiers enjoy the banquet. When the sun sets, the host forgets to light the lamps, so arousing the suspicion of the king and the nobles. But when the man's servants light a thousand lamps to illuminate the house, it becomes clear that the man had no bad intentions. The king rebukes him a little, gives him a present and leaves in friendship.

Much of the explanation is preserved, and what is missing can be convincingly adduced. The king, according to Sundermann, represents the Nous, active in the Manichaean Church. His gifts include the holy scriptures. The messengers he sends out are the Apostles. The wealthy man of lowly birth represents the auditors who have worldly goods that they should give liberally to the Church and the elect. In contrast to the "perfect auditor," in whom there is no fault, the rich man of lowly birth symbolizes the auditor with good intentions but who grows slack in his religious duties and in wisdom. Yet in spite of this negligence, thanks to the grace of the saving Nous, he can count on his good works as a basis for his future salvation.[47]

> . . . (He) was (?) wealthy . . . The nobles . . . and also all . . . received a gift of . . . clothes with many ornaments.
>
> They went, enjoyed a banquet (and) received presents. They were happy. When the sun set, the man, in his contentment, did not light his lamps immediately. The king became suspicious. His intimate friends said, "This man has prepared an excellent banquet (and) has given (us) gifts, but he has not lit his lamps. Does he intend to commit a crime?"
>
> The man heard them, became afraid (and) fell unconscious. Then the servants of that man set up a thousand lamps before the king. The king realized that the man was innocent (and) had acted out of forgetfulness, not with an evil purpose. The king reproached the man a little; then he gave (him) a present (and) dismissed (him) in friendship (and) kindness.
>
> The interpretation: The lowly born man represents the auditors, the king is . . . , the messengers of the king (?) . . .
>
> The messenger [is the] Apostle . . . of the gods; . . . garden, vineyard, house, shade: these are the alms. The auditors give them to the Church (and) build monasteries. The intimate friends of the king are the elect. The clothes (and) ornaments that he made are the illustrated book and the scripture[48] (of the sacred teaching). The lamp is wisdom.[49] The (lamp) that is not lit immediately is that of the auditors. From time to time they become slack and forgetful in their works. (They) are (then) called to account (for their negligence). They gain victory (salvation) thereupon and are redeemed. The servants who light the lamps and become helpers of that man are the meritorious deeds that help the auditors. Just as the auditors of this parable, (who), if possible, honor the Church in love with (their whole) hearts, (as) they become the friends of the gods (the elect), gain victory by the help of the "Glory of Religion" (the Great Nous),[50] . . .

11. Parable of the (female) auditor Xēbra (Persian)

This short fragment of a parable was part of a historical account of the death of a relative, probably the son, of a female auditor named Xēbra. With the help of a short parable, Mani makes clear to her how futile it is to mourn. The parable talks of a foolish woman who believes she must make the same wedding preparations for her daughter as another woman for her son.[51] It is not quite clear how this illustrates the foolishness of weeping over the death of a loved one, which was the usual custom in the Orient (cf. *Psalm-Book* 62, 25; 65, 13–17; 75, 19–20 and passim). In Manichaean texts the exhortation not to weep on the death of a believer is found repeatedly, as death marks the end of a struggle and opens up the way to final salvation.

[Title]:   On the parable[52] of the (female) auditor Xēbra

> . . . Then that woman, the mother of a girl that is a bride, thinks, "This woman has a son and has prepared all of this, and I also have a daughter. Everything that this woman began to [prepare] . . . in the same manner as that [woman] . . ."

> ". . . to me (?) who up to now did not know that if I mourn about the bodily son, I kill the spiritual (son). But from now I will no (longer) weep and kill him." And she asked him (Mani) for forgiveness for her sin and for compassion. Then they blessed the Lord (Mani) greatly, and then . . . he went away [from] there . . .[53]

12. Parable of the treasure in the corpse (Parthian)

Though the main outline of this parable is clear, its interpretation remains a matter of conjecture, since the epimythion is not preserved. A man is induced by another to exhume a corpse and carry it away. But he is unable to remove it from his back because it sticks to his body. At home his wife frees him from the burden, and it is then found to be full of treasures. The treasures probably symbolize the soul, or the divine Living Soul, hidden within the body, which is often referred to as a corpse.

> . . . When it [was] dark . . . [in order to lift up] the [treasure]. And . . . [they agreed?], "[You] take the corpse [out]."

> . . . He did not want to at all . . . Reluctantly he put the corpse on (his) back and brought it . . . And however much he tried to remove it, he could not loosen the corpse from (his) back. At night [he went] back to his [house and] ordered his wife, "Quickly, cut this corpse off my [back]." And after great torment the man [was freed] . . . , and (the corpse) [was] full of treasures and pearls . . .

> The man did not return . . . And as often as his wife said to him, "Now we have a great fortune . . . ," (he) did not want to . . . at all . . . And then outside . . . "How many times [have I told?] you . . . and you did not hear . . . ; we are . . . content and in [harmony] . . ."

And the interpretation is this: . . .

13. *Parable of the monk and the girl* (Parthian)

This parable, as explained by the editor of the text,[54] probably warns against the selfish use of alms by the elect, dramatically illustrating the drastic consequences of such greed. In the Chinese *Traité,* such a warning is also given.[55]

"... I want to place the alms therein (in the vessel)."

Then [the woman?] gave [him a girl], and the monk [placed] that [girl in it]. And he went away. And that woman [was visited by?] ... [a] ... hunter. He had caught a wolf [and] brought [it] to ... He wanted to put (it) in the vessel.[56] [When he opened] it, he saw the girl, (and she) was very beautiful. Immediately he [asked the woman?], "What is in the vessel?" And [she answered], "A monk put his alms into it." At once [the hunter] took the girl out and put the wolf in ...

At night time, the monk came, (thinking), "I want to take the [girl] ... out." When he [put] his hand into the vessel, ... [the wolf] came out and [ate up] the [monk].

This [parable] deals [with the] sinners who, being constantly (?) [seized by?] ... think this ... [But] they go to dark Hell. Just [as that monk] looked [for the girl] and found [the wolf] ...

14. *Homily about the perfect auditor, with a parable* (Persian)

We have here a typical example of Manichaean homiletical literature. It expounds the deeds and characteristics of the "perfect auditor" who equals the elect in the possibility of gaining salvation. One of the characteristics of the perfect auditor is the constant willingness to offer even that which is most dear to him to the elect. This is illustrated by the parable of the lowly born man who gives his beloved daughter to the king. Unfortunately, the epimythion, which could have explained certain aspects of the story, is lost.

... (They, the perfect auditors) [become benefactors of] (their) own souls. One point is that they will walk with the [chosen ones] and (that they) restrain their hands [from] mistreating and injuring [any] light.[57] By this one good deed they become helpers of their own souls. And a second (point) is that they approach the sign and the form[58] of the bright Vahman (the Great Nous), who has entered into the holy Church, so (that they) may honor him, praise him and pay him homage. And they know he is, and they testify to his greatness and glory. [And] a third (point) is that at the sign of peace (?) they enter into the circle of the peace-loving ones, that they stay away from the precincts and boundaries of the foes and are separated from those false ones who find no pleasure in the sign [of peace] ... (to) this Living Race[59] that is [peace-loving?], and they are contented. And fourth, they have ... and gather together their souls (the limbs of their souls),[60] and they know that . . . at the judgment . . . they [will] respond.[61] And they . . . . . . the holy Church . . . , and they are born (anew) with vital calls [and] united *nous* and with words full of light.[62] And by the alms they themselves (have given), they incorporate themselves into[63] the holy Church, and they have the same share as the elect (with respect to salvation).[64]

And an auditor who brings those alms to the elect is similar to a lowly born man to whom a fine daughter is born. She is very appealing, friendly and noble-minded. And that lowly born man nurtures[65] the beauty of that girl, for she is very [beautiful]. And [he adorns?] that beautiful daughter and brings her before the king, and the king [finds] favor with the girl, [and] he himself takes [her] to be his wife. And according to [the providence of the gods?] she bears him a son . . . The son that the daughter of that [lowly] born [man bears] . . .

15. *Parables about auditors* (Parthian)

Here again we have a homiletical text about auditors. First we learn of the auditor who avails the possibility of gaining absolution from sin by confession. Then follows a description of the auditors who strive to fulfill the commandments for the elect, that is, who strive for sinlessness. A badly preserved portion follows and then two parables are narrated "that serve to illustrate the perfect auditor's attitude to sin."[66] The last part, again badly preserved, must have contained the epimythion of the stories related.[67] We can infer that the perfect auditor, though not sinless, thinks constantly of his sin, as a man with an itching sore is constantly reminded of his malady, or a conscientious debtor is constantly aware of his debt.

> . . . And like the highway robber [who] killed [those] sons, so you [all] who stretch out your hand against the earth . . . and harm it in every (manner) . . . And with your whole body you trample and injure the earth . . . And you *martyr and ill-treat this Living [Soul][68] from which you were [born]. And it cries out and laments constantly because of your hands (that mistreat it).[69] You auditors who stand there (laden) with so much sin and guilt, you need absolution [and] grace once and for all for your many sins. Therefore ask the elect day after day for conventions (?) and absolution [so that] they . . . may bring [grace] upon you.[70]
> [*eight lines badly preserved*]
> They (the perfect auditors) are like [a man who is] . . . healthy in his whole body and [free from pain?], and who has no pain or illness of any kind. Yet he scratches himself a little at some [limb], and he stands up *restlessly [and] turns to it (that limb) again and again, and wonders when [this] sore will be healed, so that his whole body will be well and free from pain.
> And again, they are comparable to a rich man who . . . is not used to borrowing anything from anyone. And the necessity for something arises,

and he borrows a drachm [from] someone else. Thereafter, he constantly thinks, "When will I pay back the drachm to my [creditor] according to . . ."
Similar to that . . .

16. *Parable about the farmer* (Parthian)

This parable is about a farmer who sows, reaps, harvests the crop, and then returns to his home. It probably illustrates Jesus' mission on earth. After fulfilling his divine task, he returns to his heavenly home. The Gospel quotations at the end of the preserved text, which refers to Jesus, would indicate that no other divine messenger is meant, even though Mani's mission is often paralleled to that of Jesus.

> . . . He gathers in that wheat, and he takes (it) to the vessel[71] from which it had come. And he goes to his house from which he had come, for he has accomplished the task for which he had come, and (because) he has reaped and gathered in what he had come for, and because that which is stored in his vessel . . .
>
> ". . . We want to receive . . . favor and accompany him safely on even paths." And this testimony that he has spoken is true.[72]
>
> Furthermore he said, "Take heed that no one leads you astray, for many shall come in my name, saying, 'We are Jesus' [disciples?], and his time [has come]." And many [will deceive them].[73]

17. *Parable of the pearl-borer* (Sogdian)

This parable is preserved in two Sogdian manuscripts (TM 418 = So. 18.300, in Sogdian script = S; and M 135, in Manichaean script = M). The versions represent two recensions of the same story. Although the accounts of the story hardly differ except in some orthographical points, there is a greater divergence in their allegorical explanations. Since the second manuscript (M 135) continues with a *kephalaion,* a (probably spurious) teaching of Mani to his disciples, the parable there must have formed part of such a discourse.

As Henning remarks, this text, like the other Sogdian tales preserved, undoubtedly translated from Middle Persian or Parthian, is written in good Sogdian, "partly because the Manichaeans were better translators than their Christian and Buddhist compatriots, partly because it was easier to translate from Middle Persian and Parthian, languages closely related to Sogdian, than from Syriac or Chinese."[74] The translation following is by Henning.[75]

The story is known from Burzōi's preface to *Kalīla wa Dimna,*[76] and hence is probably Persian, and not Indian by origin. Unlike Burzōi's version, the Sogdian narrator told it in the form of a lawsuit. In Burzōi's version it says (according to Nöldeke's rendering),

> A merchant had many precious gems. In order to have them bored, he hired a man for a hundred pieces of gold per day, and he went with him to his domicile.

When he (the hired man) sat down, a lute happened to be there, and the worker looked at it. When the merchant asked him if he knew how to play the lute, he answered, "Yes, very well." For he was really skilled in this art. He (the merchant) said, "Then take it." He (the hired man) thus took it and played beautiful melodies in a correct manner for the merchant the whole day long, leaving the box with gems open and beating the time with his hand and swaying his head to it, with great joy. In the evening, the worker said to him (the merchant), "Have my wages given to me." When the other one said, "Have you done anything to earn wages?" he answered, "You hired me, and I did what you told me to do." Thus he urged him, until he received the hundred pieces of gold without any deduction, while the gems remained unbored."[77]

... There was a quarrel, it could not be settled. So on the next day they went before a judge for a trial. The owner (of the pearls) spoke thus, "My lord, I hired this man for one day, at a hundred gold dēnārs, that he should bore my pearls. He has not bored any pearls, but now demands his wages from me."

The workman, in rebuttal, addressed the judge thus: "My lord, when this gentleman saw me beside the bazaar, he asked me, 'Hey, what work can you do?' I replied, 'Sir, whatever work you may order me (to do), I can do it all.' When he had taken me to his house, he ordered me to play the lute. Until nightfall I played on the lute at the owner's bidding."

The judge pronounced this verdict, "You hired this man to do work (for you), so why did you not order him to bore the pearls? Why did you bid him play on the lute instead? The man's wages will have to be paid in full. If again there should be any pearls to be bored, give him another hundred gold dēnāres, and he shall then bore your pearls on another day."

Thus under contraint, the owner of the pearls paid the hundred gold dēnāres, his pearls remained unbored, left for another day, and he himself was filled with shame and contrition.

(M) The wise give this allegorical explanation: That man who understood all arts and crafts represents [the body]...

(S) The pearl-borer is the body. The hundred [gold] dēnāres represent a life of a hundred years. The owner of the pearls is the soul, and the boring (?) of the pearls represents piety.

(*Kephalaion*)

(M) That one is a righteous *dēndār* [elect], who saves many people from Hell, and sets them on the way to Paradise. And now I command you, Hearers [auditors], that so long as there is strength in your bodies, you should strive for the salvation of your souls. Keep my instructions and [my words] in mind, that Straight Path and True Mold which I have shown to you, namely, the Sacred Religion. Strive through that Mold so that you will join me in eternal life.

Thereupon all the Hearers became very joyful and happy on account of the divine words and priceless instructions which they had heard from the Apostle, the Lord Mār Mani. They paid exquisite homage, and received . . .

[Subtitle]:   To divide the day into three parts

And again the Apostle, the Lord Mār Mani spoke thus: The wise and soul-loving person (the auditor) should divide the day into three parts. The first part (should be devoted) to the service of the kings and lords so that they will be well content, that their majesty not be infringed, and that they do not start quarreling and scheming. The second to the pursuit of worldly affairs, to tilling and sowing, to allotments and legacies, to buying and selling, so that the house be maintained, the wife and children not be in distress, and that kinsmen, friends, and well wishers can be served . . .[78]

Notes

1. Asmussen, "Der Manichäismus als Vermittler literarischen Gutes," p. 8.
2. Compare, for the story of this transmission, D. M. Lang, *The Wisdom of Balahvar*. London, 1957, pp. 11–65; Asmussen, *op. cit.*, pp. 14ff.; W. C. Smith, *Toward a World Theology*. Philadelphia, 1981, pp. 7–11.
3. Thus, as Henning already pointed out, the parable of the pearl-borer (text 17), preserved in two Sogdian manuscripts (TM 418 and M 135), is to be found in Burzōi's preface to the *Kalīla wa Dimna*. Compare Henning, "Sogdian Tales," pp. 465–68. The parable of the prince and the three magical utensils, preserved in Turkish (cf. ch. XXVI, text 4), survives in Kurdish and Kashmiri tales. Compare MacKenzie, *Kurdish Dialect Studies* II. London, 1962, pp. 59 and 127; J. H. Knowles, *Folk-Tales of Kashmir*. London, 1893, p. 86.
4. Henning, *op. cit.* Henning has been able to trace the continued existence of these tales in various instances. Compare also Asmussen, *op. cit.*
5. Sims-Williams, "The Sogdian Fragments of Leningrad [I]," *BSOAS* 44 (1988), p. 237. Most of the remaining MP and Pth. material of the German Turfan collection has been published by Sundermann, *Parabeltexte,* and his student Colditz, "Bruchstücke manichäisch-parthischer Parabelsammlungen." For the St. Petersburg texts, compare Sims-Williams, *art. cit.*, pp. 231–40; *idem,* "The Sogdian fragments of Leningrad II: Mani at the court of Shahanshah." Here Sims-Williams has been able to join a number of fragments to a continuous story, with the beginning of a second one.
6. Cf. H. H. Figulla, "Manichäer in Indien."
7. Sims-Williams, *art. cit.* [I], p. 237.
8. Sims-Williams, *art. cit.* [I], p. 238.
9. Colditz, *op. cit.,* p. 274.
10. Edited in Sundermann, *Soghdisches Parabelbuch,* pp. 19–28.
11. Sundermann, "Eine buddhistische Allegorie in manichäischer Überlieferung," pp. 148–206. Sundermann refers to chapter 32 of the Chinese *Da ban nie pan jing (Mahāparinirvāna-Sūtra,* translated by Dharmakṣema [or Dharmarakṣa according to Nanjio, no. 113]) and the various texts referred to in Shinkyo Mochizuki, *Bukkyo daijiten* ("The Great Encyclopaedia of Buddhism"), vol. IV, p. 3210.
12. Schmidt and Polotsky, *Mani-Fund,* pp. 41f.
13. Cf. ch. XVII, text 4.2.
14. May be an explanation for marine phosphorescence.

15. Probably a reference to the tide. *Kephalaia,* pp. 113ff. speaks of an "oceanic giant," probably meant here. He arises from the demonic substances that are poured into the sea from the spheres of the world, but within the cosmic order the giant gains a positive aspect, for he makes the waters quiver, thereby purifying them (S).

16. This implies that worldly learning stands in opposition to the wisdom of the Religion which is represented by the ocean (S).

17. The ocean giant referred to above.

18. Personification of the demonic substance referred to above.

19. In the Manichaean image of the world, corresponding to the image of man and explicated in the cosmogony, the three ditches were made at the time of the creation of the world by the Living Spirit. They contain dark water, darkness itself, and dark fire, from which the heavens and the earths had been purified. Compare *Kephalaia,* pp. 106, 116 and 118 (S).

20. As opposed to the New Man. This image is taken from Paul. Compare Col. 3:9f; Eph. 2:15 and 4:24.

21. The concept that the soul of the deceased has to first pass over the (three) ditches before it can reach the World of Light is expressed in the Parthian hymns: "Who will lead me beyond the walls and take me over the moats, which ravaging demons fill with fear and trembling?" (*Huyadagmān,* Canto IV a, v. 4).

22. The three poisons in the body correspond to those in the three "ditches" of the cosmos. Literally, (he) *swept out the three poisons.

23. Colditz, "Bruchstücke," p. 282f.

24. Henning gives the meaning of *qndvg* as "a big earthern vessel to keep grain in." Henning, "List," p. 184.

25. Probably a reference to the healing power of the correct, orthodox teaching.

26. Colditz, "Parabelsammlungen," p. 291; cf. Flügel, *Mani,* p. 90.

27. The editor suggests a reconstruction as such: "They serve until [they have paid their debts. And when they leave the land without debts, then those] that have been their helpers also go with them. . . ." Colditz, *op.cit.,* p. 292.

28. This was the beginning of the explanation.

29. Colditz, "Parabelsammlungen," p. 296. Cf. Puech, "Begriff der Erlösung," p. 170.

30. Colditz, "Parabelsammlungen," p. 303.

31. *Ibid.*

32. Cf. Sundermann, "Commendatio pauperum," p. 182f.

33. Colditz, *op. cit.,* p. 303f.

34. The Jaidan is the Bema feast, the highest festival of the Manichaeans, commemorating the death and ascension of Mani. Jaidan Monday is the most important day of this festival.

35. Compare Henning, "Giants," p. 71f. According to *Kephalaia* 172, 13f., its seat is in the stomach.

36. Cf. the Chinese *Traité,* ed. Chavannes and Pelliot, pp. 528–30; Schmidt-Glinzer, *Chinesische Manichaica,* p. 79.

37. Cf. Schmidt and Polotsky, *Mani-Fund,* p. 72f.

38. Cf. Sundermann, *op. cit.,* pp. 83f.

39. For the image of the boy playing the flute, compare Arnold-Döben, *Die Bildersprache des Manichäismus,* p. 112–15.

40. One would think that the text refers to the three "seals" summing up the commandments for the elect. But the word used here for the commandments (*andarz*) is distinct from that for "seals" (*muhr*).

41. Sundermann, *Parabeltexte,* p. 84.

42. Cf. Bornkamm, "The Acts of Thomas," in Hennecke and Schneemelcher, *New Testament Apocrypha* II, pp. 425–531.

43. Sundermann, *ibid.* Cf. Henrichs and Koenen, "Mani-Codex," pp. 171ff.

44. Probably Mani.

45. Probably a reference to the acceptance of false faiths.

46. Sundermann, *Parabeltexte,* p. 87.

47. Sundermann, *ibid.*
48. The scripture probably refers to Mani's *Gospel*, the illustrated book to the illustration of the *Gospel*, the *Ārdahang*.
49. For the image of the lamp, frequently recurring in Coptic Manichaean literature (cf. *Psalm-Book* 23, 8–9; 52, 23–24; 173, 16–18) and sometimes referring to Jesus' parable of the ten virgins (Mt. 25: 1–13), compare Arnold-Döben, *Die Bildersprache des Manichäismus*, pp. 81ff.; *Die Bildersprache der Gnosis*, pp. 114f.
50. The Great Nous, as a saving spirit, is present and active especially in the Manichaean Church.
51. Cf. Sundermann, *Parabeltexte*, p. 89.
52. Or, parables.
53. The story of the healing of Xēbra is related in the Parthian text M 177 V. Compare Sundermann, *Texte*, p. 118f.
54. Cf. Sunderman, *Parabeltexte*, p. 91.
55. Cf. Schmidt-Glintzer, *Chinesische Manichaica*, pp. 78ff.
56. The word *qndvg (qndwg)* is used here again. Compare n. 24.
57. They as auditors observe the second commandment for the elect, "nonviolence" (cf. Introduction, and *BBB*, pp. 14f.), referred to as "not killing" in the Coptic *Psalm-Book*, p. 33, 19–20.
58. The "sign and form" of Vahman, the Great Nous, refers to the elect and saints of the Church. According to the Coptic texts (e. g., *Kephalaia* 89,22f.; 201, 8–10; *Psalm-Book* 153, 20f.), the Nous clads himself with their "images," thus residing in their bodies (*Kephalaia* 95,2ff.); compare Sundermann, *Parabeltexte*, p. 102.
59. The family of Manichaean believers.
60. The "gathering in" of the limbs of the soul has its sociological counterpart in the "collection" of the souls of the faithful by the Nous, that is, their religious revival. Compare Sundermann, *Parabeltexte*, p. 103, n. 8.
61. This is a reference to the final judgment of the world by Jesus, from which only the elect are exempt. Compare Puech, *Manichéisme*, p. 84 and n. 351 there.
62. By the work of the Nous of Light, they become New Men and thus similar to the elect. Compare Sundermann, *Parabeltexte*, p. 103, n. 10 for references.
63. Literally, they mix themselves with. Compare Sundermann, *Parabeltexte*, p. 103, n. 11.
64. Such perfect auditors are, of course, the exception. Usually the auditor could only hope to be reborn in a state in which he could become an elect, and as such he would gain salvation directly. However, the category of the perfect auditor does exist, as both the Coptic and the Central Asian texts emphasize. Compare Sundermann, *Parabeltexte*, p. 103, n. 12.
65. Or, is desirous of. Compare Sundermann, *Parabeltexte*, p. 104, n. 12.
66. Sundermann, *Parabeltexte*, p. 104.
67. *Ibid.*
68. The light imprisoned in matter.
69. The idea that earth and water contain divine light capable of feeling pain is found in many Manichaean texts including the *Cologne Mani-Codex* (*CMC*). Compare Henrichs and Koenen, "Mani-Codex," pp. 150ff.; Koenen and Römer, *Der Kölner Mani-Kodex*, pp. 68f. Compare also Sundermann, *Parabeltexte*, p. 105, n. 3.
70. This does not mean that daily penitence was necessary for auditors. But they did have to confess their sins every Monday, as well as on the Bema day.
71. Vessel to store provisions (*qndvg*).
72. Apparently a Gospel quotation. It is reminiscent of John 5:32; 19:35; 24:24; cf. also III John 12.
73. A Gospel quotation. The first part corresponds to Luke 21:8, the second to Matthew 24:5. The text is very similar to the formulation in the Arabic version of Tatian's *Diatessaron* (Gospel Harmony). Compare E. Preuschen, trans., *Tatian's Diatessaron*. Ed. A. Pott, p. 194. Sundermann surmises that the slight changes in comparison to the *Diatessaron* reflect Manichaean polemics against various Christian communities. Sundermann, *Parabeltexte*, p. 108, n. 3.

74. Henning, "Sogdian Tales," p. 465.

75. Henning, "Sogdian Tales," pp. 468–69.

76. Henning points out, "It is noteworthy that of the two Pañchatantra-Kalīla wa Dimna stories that so far have been traced in Sogdian, the one [i. e., this one] occurs in K.-W. D. but not in the Pañchatantra, the other only in the Pañchatantra." Henning, "Sogdian Tales," p. 466. cf. *Kalīla wa Dimna* 28–29, ed. de Sacy. Beirut, 1896, p. 91 (reference in Henning, *op. cit.*).

77. Nöldeke, *Burzōes Einleitung zu dem Buch Kalīla wa Dimna*. Strassburg, 1912, p. 19.

78. The third part of the day was to be devoted to the care of the elect, the Manichaean monks.

CHAPTER SEVENTEEN

Historical Texts

1. Mani's missionary activity

A number of Middle Persian, Parthian, and Sogdian texts tell us about Mani's missionary activity, which commenced when he was twenty-four years old. He left the Elchasaite community at the calling of his heavenly "Twin" (MP *narjamīg*) to establish a church of his own. The *Cologne Mani Codex* (*CMC*) tells us of his first journeys to various areas in the western Sassanian Empire. However, the following portion of the text, which covers Mani's missions to the East—the eastern Sassanian Empire and India, including the Indo-Iranian border lands of Tūrān and Makrān—has not been preserved. At this point, the Central Asian texts shed further light on Mani's missionary activity, including his dispatching disciples to the West, to the Roman Empire, and to the East, to Parthia and the Oxus region. These texts were probably parts of early church histories, written in diverse Iranian dialects. They were, of course, written with specific intentions, namely, to show that the advent of the "Messenger of Light" and his missionaries had led to the successful establishment of Manichaean communities throughout the Sassanian Empire as well as in bordering areas to the West and to the East. Legendary healings, visions, and levitations figure prominently in these texts. Nevertheless a critical analysis of the material, as made by Sundermann,[1] does reveal a certain historical kernel beneath the husk of standardized legendary motifs.[2] Mani and his followers often addressed the nobility, princes and kings, high-ranking ladies and queens. Thus, at least in Iran, it was the upper stratum of society that the Manichaeans sought to win.

Mani himself travelled extensively, first in the western part of the Sassanian kingdom, in Mesopotamia, and the adjacent plateau to the North, as we learn from the *CMC* and from Coptic texts. His first major missionary journey led him to India, to the Indus Valley and the area of today's Baluchistan. His trip to India is mentioned in the *CMC* (144,1 and 149,9). It was here that he converted the Tūrān Shāh, the Buddhist king of Tūrān, as the Turfan texts testify.

The land of Tūrān had a prominent position in Iranian, especially Zoroastrian, eschatology and apocalypticism. In apocalyptic texts like the *Pahlavi Rivāyat* accompanying the *Dādestān ī dēnīg,* Tūrān is the place where the future paradise is to be established. And in the Persian national epic *Shāhnāme,* accounts of Tūrān and the mythical Behisht-Gang far beyond the seas are mingled inextricably.[3] The Tūrān referred to there, however, is usually the home of the "Turanians," who lived to the north of the Iranians and engaged in battle with them repeatedly. To what extent the apocalyptic motif of Tūrān (often referred to as lying in the East) colored our report is not yet clear.

After the accession of Shāhpuhr (Šābuhr) I to the throne, probably in 241 A.D., Mani travelled to the seat of government at Seleukia-Ctesiphon and won the attention of the new ruler.[4] Although the "King of Kings" was not converted, he evidently did take an interest in the new religion with its synthesis of the various religious traditions represented in his kingdom. During the time of Shāhpuhr's successor, Ōhrmizd I (reg. 272–273), Mani was able on the whole to continue his missionary activity unhampered. However, under Bahrām (Vahrām) I (reg. 273–276), the leaders of the Zoroastrian Church under the Great *Mōbad* Kardēr (Kirdēr) gained the upper hand in influencing the monarch. Oppression and persecution of the Manichaeans set in, in the wake of which Mani was thrown into prison, where he died in 267.

1.1 MANI SENDS A MISSION TO THE ROMAN EMPIRE

These texts are about the early Manichaean missions to the West, that is, the eastern Roman Empire. It becomes obvious here, as in texts translated further on, that the early Manichaeans' Church histories were written in the three Iranian languages they used, namely, Middle Persian, Parthian, and Sogdian.

Text A (Persian)

[Title]: The coming of the Apostle into the lands

... They (Addā and Pattēg) went to Rome (the Roman Empire). They observed (literally, saw) many disputes among the religions.[5] Many elect and auditors were chosen. Pattēg[6] was there for a year. Thereafter he returned to the Apostle. Then the Lord (Mani) sent three scribes, the *Gospel*[7] and two other scriptures to Addā,[8] and he gave him the commandment, "Do not take them (the scriptures) further away, but remain there like a merchant who accumulates his treasures."[9]

Addā strove greatly in these areas; he founded many monasteries and chose many elect and auditors.[10] He wrote scriptures and used wisdom as his weapon. He rose up against the (foreign) religions and thrived in every respect. He subjugated the religions, and he came up to Alexandria. He chose Nafshā[11] for the (new) religion. Many conversions were made and many miracles wrought in these lands. The religion of the Apostle flourished in the Roman Empire.

Text B (Parthian)

... And when the Apostle was in Veh-Ardaxshīr,[12] [he sent] Pattēg, the teacher, and Addā, the bishop, [and] Mani, the scribe,[13] to Rome (the Roman Empire). And [he gave them] four commandments ... [And Addā founded] many monasteries. [And he chose many lords (?) (for the Church)]. [And he wrote ...] and scriptures of Light. And he employed (?) [wisdom] to answer the (other) religions. In many [ways] he formed and fashioned it [to be a weapon] against [all the] religions. And he [routed (?)] all the doctrines and put them to shame, [as] one [with] mighty arms ...

Text C (Sogdian)

[Mani said], ". . . in the western [regions] . . . on this earth a blessed [place?] has been prepared for it (the new religion?), so that this good deed (message?) may be received in glory. And be very learned and well versed in it (the message), and wise and proficient in languages in every place, wherever you go. And if you do as I have commanded you, then the Church will now spread in these places through your teaching, and your pains and labors will be blessed. And so I com[mand] you: first, take of nothing more (than you need); you should [rather remain in] poverty and [blessedness],[14] which is the foundation of all bliss." And second, he spoke of association with women and [gave] exhaustive instructions (concerning this matter). Third, he said, "[Do not] extend (?) [your stay] at one place, but rather . . ." [Fourth], ". . . the community of the elect, . . . the others . . ." [Fifth] . . .

When the Apostle had [given] (these) com[mandments], he gave them the *Treasure of the Living*,[15] together with [other] books.

And Pattēg, the teacher, one of the twelve, Addā, the bishop, and Mani, the abbot, went forth with other brethren and reached the western places. And they had many doctrinal disputes . . . with the adherents of (other) religions and with the Roman . . . And they selected many elect and many [auditors] in these places. And Pattēg, [the teacher], was in the Roman Empire for a year, but in the second [year] he returned and came to Sūristān[16] to the Apostle.

And Mār Addā[17] wrote a letter to the Lord (saying), "The commandment . . ."

1.2 MANI SENDS MĀR AMMŌ TO THE EAST

Text A (Persian)

And when the Apostle of Light was in the provincial capital of Holvān,[18] he let the teacher Mār Ammō come, who knew the Parthian script and language and was familiar with . . . He sent him to Abarshahr[19] together with Prince Ardabān[20] and some brethren who could write well, as well as an illuminator. He said, "Blessed be this religion. May it flourish through teachers, hearers and soul-service."[21]

When they came to the watchpost of Kushan,[22] lo, there appeared the spirit of the border of the East (*xvārāsān*)[23] in the form of a girl. And she asked me, Ammō, "What do you want? Where have you come from?"

I said, "I am a believer (*dēnāvar*), a disciple of the Apostle Mani."

The spirit said, "I will not accept you. Return to where you have come from!" Then it disappeared before me.

Thereafter I, Ammō, stood in prayer to the sun for two days of fasting.[24] Then the Apostle appeared to me and said, "Do not be faint-hearted. Recite (the chapter) 'The Collecting of the Gates'[25] from *The Treasure of the Living*."

Then, on the following day, the spirit appeared again and said to me, "Why did you not return to your country?"

I said, "I have come from afar because of the religion."

The spirit said, "What is the religion you bring?"

I said, "We do not eat meat nor drink wine. We (also) keep away from [women]."

It said, "In my kingdom there are many like you."[26]

I recited (the chapter) "The Collecting of the Gates" from *The Treasure of the Living*. Then it (the spirit) paid respect to me and said, "You are a pure righteous one (*ardāv*). From now on I shall no more call you 'possessor of religion' (*dēndār*) but 'true bringer of religion' (*dēnāvar ī rāst*),[27] for you surpass all others."

Then I said, "What is your name?"

It said, "My name is Bagard,[28] I am the border guard of the East. If I receive you, the door to all the East will be open to you."

Then the spirit Bagard taught me "The Collecting of the Five Gates" with the help of parables:[29]

1a. The gate of the eyes, which is deceived by empty appearances, is like (this): (There is) a man who sees a mirage in the desert: a city, trees, water (and) many other things. That demon (who causes the mirage) deceives (him) and kills (him).

1b. Second, it is like a fortress which the enemies attack, whose entrance they have not found. Then they prepare a banquet, (singing) many songs and melodies. Those who are in the fortress desire to see the sight. The enemies ascend from the rear and occupy the fortress.

2a. The gate of the ears is like (this): (There was)[30] a certain man who was going along a safe road with many treasures. Then two thieves stood at (his) ear. He was deceived by sweet speech (their words). He was led to a distant place and was killed by them, and his treasures were taken away.

2b. (Furthermore it is) like (this): A beautiful girl was held captive in a fortress, and (there was) a deceiving man at the foot of the fortress wall who sang a sweet melody, until that girl died of sorrow (yearning).

3. The gate of the nose, perceiving fragrance, is like (this): (There was) an elephant on a hill above the king's garden. He was attracted by (lit., became desirous of) the fragrance of the flowers, and (so) one night he fell down the hill and died.

4. The gate of [the mouth] (is like this): . . .

5. . . .[31]

Text B (Parthian)

[Title]:   [How the Messenger of Light] gave four commandments

. . . [And when the Apostle was] in [the city] of Holvān, [he called] Mār Ammō, [the Teacher] . . .

. . . recite before [it] (the spirit Bagard) "The Collec[ting] of the Five Gates" [from *The Treasure of the Living*].

Then on the next day that spirit [appeared]. And it [said to me], "Why [have you not returned to] your [country]?"

[I said, "I have come] from [a faraway place for the sake of the religion.]"

[Then] that spirit said, ["What kind of a religion is it that you bring?"] . . .

Text C (Sogdian)

[Title]:   [How Mani] sent [Mār Ammō] to Abarshahr
[Subtitle]:   (Here) begins the sermon on Mār Ammō. He sent him to Abarshahr
[Second subtitle in the text]:   How Mār Ammō [reached] the border guard of Kushan

And when the Apostle of Light, the Lord Mār Mani, stayed in the region of Holvān, he called Mār Ammō, the teacher, who knew the Parthian language and script and who was acquainted with lords and ladies and with many nobles in those places. And he sent him together with Prince Ardabān to [Abarshahr]. And afterwards [he] also sent yet other [scribes and illuminators with] the scriptures. [He said], "Go forth, dear son, to the [different] places, for the [blessing] is such that in these [places?] (this) [religion] . . . shall be received and shall be proclaimed by teachers and bishops and preachers. Go afar, and many auditors shall dedicate themselves in those [places] as workers and helpers, and many gifts and alms will be dedicated in those places. [And] your glory and praise shall always be [excellent?] in those places. [And] constantly . . . preserve your love . . . over against this great divine matter[32] which is itself the . . . Father (the Great Nous) who has his place in this community of elect. And may your writing [and speaking (?) be accompanied by (?)] thanksgiving and prayer. And always keep your mind on spiritual things. For whenever the Buddhas (the divine Messengers) who raise men from death[33] descended to the world, and when they sent their disciples [to] ... and to preach in different places, [they kept the message?] in their minds and hearts ...

And [in] Abarshahr and Merv ... they made ... plentiful [gain] for the sake of ... the Church. And many lords and rulers ... and noblemen, queens and ladies, princes and princesses, did he (Ammō) sanctify for the Church, and he instructed them thoroughly about the Buddhahood (the prophethood) of the Apostle of Light. And he completely obeyed and fulfilled the orders and the commandments that [Mani had given] him ...

Text D
Fragment about Mār Ammō's mission in Varučān (Parthian)

This fragment from a church history tells us about Mār Ammō's mission after he left the Kushan territory. He went to Varuč or Varučān (here written Varuzān), which probably lay southwest of Balkh, in the Indo-Iranian border area. This Varuč, later known as Gharč or Gharčistān, is not to be confused with the Varuč in Western Iran (in present-day Georgia) that is mentioned as one of Shāpur's kingdoms in his inscription on the *Ka'aba-yi Zardušt*.[34] The church history from which this fragment stems probably narrated the conversion of Havzā, the ruler of Varučān. It is supplemented by a Turkish fragment[35] that suggests that a miracle performed by Mani, or Mār Ammō, or some other disciple preceded the conversion. King Havzā probably became a prominent member of the Manichaean community, since he is referred to there as "the beloved son of the Great Nous." Our text also has to do with events that preceded the actual conversion. As Sundermann, the editor, explains, "Some person, probably the king himself, is deemed worthy of a vision of the Apostle of Light which makes the greatest impression upon him. The king now inquires about Mani and his teaching and hears so much that is good and valuable that he eventually becomes a follower or at least promotor of Mani's."[36]

... [When he saw] the figure of the Apostle, he ... and fell down before (him) [and became uncon]scious. The people were [amazed]. Thereupon ... [implored] ... , "To us ... Jesus ... We shall ..."

... They vanquished the (false) teachings of the (other) religions (which were conquered) through their own evil (lit., sin). [Then] Havzā, the Varuzān-[Shāh, said], "What kind of ... [is] this ... ?"

And they said, "[This] is ..."

1.3 MANI'S CONVERSION OF THE TŪRĀN SHĀH (PARTHIAN)

This text deals with the conversion of the ruler of Tūrān, a small Buddhist kingdom in what is today Baluchistan, west of the Indus Valley. Mani visited it on his trip to India in 241/242.[37] Here too a miracle precedes the actual conversion. Mani levitates into the air, to converse with an *ardāv*, "a righteous man," as Boyce interprets the term.[38] Whereas Sundermann had originally thought this to be the spirit of a dead person, he later pointed out, with respect to Boyce's interpretation, "This alternative solution has won much ground by the traditions of the *Cologne Mani*

Codex about prophets of old who received their visions in regions ranging from the top of a mountain to the 'heavenly hall of the throne.' The fact that one of the prophets, Enoch, is expressly called 'a righteous one'. . . would suggest the possibility that the text published here speaks of a prophet who has already experienced visionary levitations to higher 'spheres', of which he speaks as 'his sphere.'"[39]

Text A (Parthian)

. . . [so that] I may bring [you to] a . . . righteous one (*ardāv*). He (Mani) went to a . . .[40] where a righteous one was. And [he][41] brought news [to the righteous one].

The righteous one said, . . .

The Apostle led the righteous one into the air, and he said, "What is higher?" The righteous one said, "My sphere." The Apostle said, "And [what] is (even) greater [than that]?" He said, "The earth that bears everything." Furthermore he (Mani) said, "What is even higher than these (things on earth)?" The righteous one said, "Heaven (?) . . ." . . ."What is even greater?" He said, "The Sun and the Moon." "And what is even brighter?" He said, "The wisdom of the B[uddha]." Then the Devout One (*dēnāβar*) (Mani) [said] to the Tūrān Shāh, "Even so shall you do [as] . . . you are . . ." [Then the Tūrān Shāh] said to the Apostle, ". . . all . . ."

Then the Lord Mani taught the Tūrān Shāh much [insight] and wisdom. And [he showed him] Paradise and Hell, the [puri]fication of the [worlds], Sun [and Moon, soul and] body, the apostles that had come into the lands, righteous ones and sinners and the work of the elect and [the audi]tors.

Then, when the Tūrān [Shāh and] the nobles heard this word, they became glad, accepted the faith and became benign towards the Apostle and the religion.

And furthermore, [when] the Tūrān Shāh was [in] . . . , he (?) redeemed him.

Then the brethren paid their homage to the Beneficent One, and the Apostle told the Tūrān Shāh a parable: "There was a man and he had seven sons. When the hour of [death] came (for him), he called his sons . . . Seven . . . original . . . and . . . stick . . . bound. He said, 'Break [all of them] together'. None of them [could] do so. Then he loosened [the string (around the seven sicks)] . . ."[42]

Text B (Parthian)

The story of the conversion of the Tūrān Shāh related previously has been pieced together from various Parthian fragments. Apart from the consecutive account, as translated above, there are also other fragments which give a somewhat different, or fuller, picture of the event. They are edited by Boyce in her *Reader,* after an earlier edition of Sundermann's.[43] This second text goes beyond the first one, as it is a continuation thereof.

And when the Tūrān-Shāh saw that the Beneficent One (*kirbakkar*) had risen, then he stood on his knees from afar and entreated him, speaking to the Beneficent One and saying, "Do not come here before me." But (yet) the Beneficent One came there. He (the king) (then) stood up and went forward and kissed him. Then he said to the Beneficent One, "You are the Buddha and we are sinful men. It is not fitting that you should come to us. We shall attain so much merit (*pun* < *Skr. puṇya*) and . . . salvation as (the number of) steps by which we approach you . . . And we shall have so much lack of merit (*apun* < Skr. *apuṇya*) and sin[44] as (the number of) steps by which you approach us."

Then the Beneficent One blessed him and said, "May you be blessed, for as you are now fortunate and honored among men, so will you be fortunate and pleasing in the eyes of the gods on the last day of the soul (on the Judgment Day).[45] And you will be eternally immortal among the gods and the beneficent righteous ones."

Then . . . he took his hand . . .[46]

2. Healings and conversions by Mani and his disciples

As the preceding texts show, Mani's mission, and that of his disciples, was marked by healings and other miracles, as reported in church histories and hagiographical accounts. They essentially took their cue from the biblical accounts of Jesus' miracles, thus endeavoring to show that the new mission was a continuation and fulfillment of that of Jesus and his disciples. However, as opposed to Jesus' activity, which was directed primarily toward the poor and needy, Mani's mission was to kings and rulers and men of authority and influence.

2.1 HEALING MIRACLES

In the texts A and B we hear of the healing of a girl named Nafshā.[47] When she has been restored to health by Mani, who evidently makes a miraculous appearance on the scene in response to Mār Addā's prayer, her sister, Queen Tadī, the wife of the "Roman Emperor," also turns to Mani. Mani then goes on to give religious instruction. In our text C it is Mani's disciple Gabryab who performs a healing miracle in the Christian community at Revān, after invoking Jesus, to whose healings he makes special reference.

Text A (Parthian)

[And] I (Mani) stepped before the [king] and said, "Hail . . . from the gods . . ." The king said, "From where are you?" I said, "I am a physician from the land of Bab[ylon]"[48] . . .[49] She came [forward]; her whole body . . . was restored. [In] great joy she said to me, "From where are you, my God and my redeemer?" . . .

Text B (Sogdian)

Nafshā herself cried to Jesus, "[Lend] me [aid], beneficent God, because . . . among the adherents of (other) religions . . ."

[And the Lord Mani], the Apostle, descended in the presence of all,
including Nafshā, and he laid his hand on her, and immediately Nafshā
was healed, and she was completely free from pain. All the people were
amazed at the miracle. Then many people accepted the faith anew. And
also Queen Tadī, the sister of Nafshā, the wife of the Emperor, appeared
before Mār Addā with great . . . and received the Truth . . . from him . . .

And in the night, the voice . . . , as it was said (?) to them . . . [They?]
stood there completely amazed, . . . idol temples, walls . . . so that there
may be an exit (?). At once, . . . , and the door was sealed with the seal
of the Emperor. And . . . there was no house anywhere round about.

And immediately Mār Addā stood there in prayer and supplication and
said to the Apostle, "I would like to have an explanation for these tidings."

And immediately the Apostle manifested himself and came and gave
him knowledge that there are twelve grades of men, [none] of which talk
with the others . . . [The Apostle said], ". . . And go . . . [to the] Emperor
and [give] him the secret . . . , and may none be disobedient, following
his own desires and wishes. Then their labor and burden will not go
unrewarded."

Finally he gave them all the commandments (concerning) morals and
propriety, (furthermore) laws and rules, (admonitions concerning) right
behavior and deportment. (He did so) comprehensively and in summary
form with the help of numbers: five commandments [in] ten parts, three
seals in six parts, five [garments (?) in] ten parts, vigilance and zeal, twelve
dominions in thirty-two parts, . . . seven hymns . . . and five expositions,
. . . [one] by one, in seven prohibitions and . . . [seven] prayers of confession, . . .[50] And therefore they are called devout auditors, and they have
a part in the Church, and the commandment is manifest to them. And
those who are auditors and who remain entangled (?) with earthly things
are saplings (?) and children with (of) divinity. And their food is spiritual
milk.[51] To them the commandment and the precepts [are] manifest in the
Church, because they are themselves [in the Church] and . . . the Living
Soul . . . the Holy Spirit, which is [in] . . . they serve . . .

Text C (Sogdian)

". . . [If I can] heal the girl [from her illness by] the grace of the gods, then
I would [request] this of you: Turn away from the Christian religion [and]
accept the religion of the Lord Mār Mani."

Then he (Gabryab) turned around and spoke to the Christians, "Christ
was a wonder-working Lord. He healed the blind as well as the lame and
crippled (?) from their infirmities. Similarly he raised the dead to life.

And usually the son has the appearance (?) of the father, and the disciple is similar to the teacher. If you are, now, indeed truly disciples of Christ and resemble Christ, step forth, all of you, and heal this girl from her illness, as Jesus said to his disciples, 'On whom you lay your hand, on him will I bring better health through the hand of God.'[52] If you do not do so, then I will heal the girl from her illness by [the hand] of God, and [then you Christians] should go out of the kingdom of Revān."[53]

The Christians said, "We shall not be able to [cure] her, rather you cure [the girl]."

Then Gabryab, with his [disciples?], stood [in prayer and praise on] the fourteenth day of the month, and around the evening, when Jesus (the moon) rose, Gabryab continued to praise Jesus and said, "You are a true God and a vivifier of souls; help me this time, beneficent Lord! Bring better health to this girl through my hand, so that your divinity may become manifest before all the people, and that (it may become clear) that we are the ones who are truly obedient to your commandments."[54]

Thereupon he asked for oil and water, and he blessed her in [the name of] the Father, the Son and the Holy Spirit, and he commanded her to apply the oil and to pour (?) the water over it. And immediately, on the spot, the girl was healed from this unclean illness. And Gabryab and his assistants remained with the girl the whole night.

[Title of new page]:   The Sermon of Gabryab

They sang and gave . . . praise in manifold ways, until the morning [came] and the sun rose. And he (Gabryab) remained in benediction before the glorious, great [Sun God].[55] And with a loud voice he said, "You are the light eye [of] the whole world and are the great ford and gate of all souls that have departed (from this world). Unworthy and unhappy are the dark beings who do not believe in you and who have averted their eyes and their gaze from you. [Help] me, great God of Light, and through our hand bring help and restoration to this girl, so that she may receive the benefit,[56] and also the patient souls for whom salvation has been prepared; become for them the new door and the land of salvation."

Then he asked for oil and water and blessed her. And he ordered (them) to write thereon (?), and at the same time he ordered (her) to partake of it (?). And immediately, on the spot, the girl was [healed] from the illness, [and was] completely free of infirmity, and she stood there, [healthy] in body, just as if she . . . had not been [ill] (at all).

And Gabryab received the . . . king [of] Revān and his wife, [the mother] of the girl, and also the girl herself into the community of auditors (by anointing them with) consecrated oil. [And he] commanded (them), "From now on, serve no more . . . the heretics [and] idols and demons."

Coming from the castle, Gabryab entered the city to great praise and honor. And he chose many people to be elect,[57] and there were many who converted from their heresies.

When Gabryab went away from there, to preach in another region, the Christians' month of fasting had come.[58] And the day when they preach about Christ's being raised to the cross was approaching.[59] And the Christians pressed the ruler of Revān, requesting him to come to church on this day. And the king of Revān agreed. When Gabryab heard this, he immediately came to that place for a second time. And the king of Revān, having come forth, ...[60]

2.2 MANI AT RĒV-ARDAXSHIHR (PERSIAN)

The first part of this text (*recto*) is a homily about the Church, or the religion (*dēn*). As the editor, Sundermann, points out, it starts by extolling Mani's acts of salvation, and it continues by referring to historical events concerning Mani's second visit to Rēv-Ardaxshihr.[61]

[Title]: (Here) begins the teach[ing] (*vifrās*) concerning the Church.
About the Church

... the Beneficent One (Mani) who brought to us the primeval extension of the right hand,[62] and the power of our souls. And the redeemer heals us from the attack of *Āz* (the demon of Greed) ...

... When our father (Mani) came (back) from India and arrived at the city of Rēv-Ardaxshihr,[63] he sent the Presbyter Pattēg[64] together with brother Hanni[65] to India, to Dēb.[66] And at that time he said, "This my community of elect is so blessed that in every land ..."

... from the Baptists[67] he collected the gifts. But it was not what he thought.

And when the Beneficent One was in the city of Rēv-Ardaxshihr for a second time, a nobleman from Abarshar, Daryāv by name,[68] came before him; he himself was with two other brethren, Valāsh[69] and Xusrō[70]. ...

2.3 ON THE CONVERSION OF THE RULER OF MESENE (PARTHIAN)

This fragment tells us of the conversion of the ruler of Mesene (Pth. Mēšūn), Mihr Shāh, who was the brother of Shāpuhr (Šābuhr) I. Boyce observes, "This event must have taken place before A.C. 262, because at that date one of Šabuhr's sons was ruling Mesene."[71]

[Title]: Mihr-Shāh, the Lord of Mesene

Furthermore, Shāpuhr, the King of Kings, had a brother, the Lord of Mesene, and his name was Mihr-Shāh. He was a bitter enemy of the Apostle. He had a garden, very fine and wonderfully spacious, the like of which no other man had ever possessed. Then the Apostle knew that the time of (his) redemption had come. And he arose and went before the Mihr-Shāh who was in his garden, greatly enjoying his feast.

... Then he (the king) said to the Apostle, "In the paradise of which you speak, is there a garden such as mine?"

Thereupon the Apostle realized that he had an unbelieving heart (lit., skeptical thoughts). In wondrous power (*varž*) he showed him the Paradise of Light with all gods, deities and the immortal Air of Life,[72] and a garden with all kinds (of things) and other desirable sights there. Then he (the Mihr-Shāh) fell down, unconscious, (lying there) for three hours. And he kept what he had seen in his heart.

Then the Apostle put his hand on his head, and he regained consciousness. When he had stood up, he fell down at the feet of the Apostle and clasped his right hand. And the Apostle said . . .

2.4 AN INCIDENT IN MANI'S TRAVELS (PARTHIAN)

This conversion story is again preceded by a miracle performed by Mani. He brings to life the son of a lady auditor named Xēbrā, whereupon she and her husband Abursām turn to him and his religion.

About the language of the text, Boyce observes, "There are awkwardnesses in syntax and construction in this passage which suggest a clumsy translation."[73]

He[74] said to Xēbrā, "Know that Dārāvpuhr has found salvation, and that I have seen an auspicious sign."

And in those days the Beneficent One (Mani) came there. And they did the soul-service for him.[75] At the time of the meal, when the Beneficent One said a prayer for the youth, he made obeisance three times. The sons asked him, "Tell us why you made obeisance."

He (Mani) said, "I made obeisance to Jesus, the Father and Lord, so that my wish, which I expressed before him, and the prayer that you have said, may indeed be accepted by him . . ."

"And lo, angels brought Dārāv's soul and set it before me, when it was arrayed in the customary dress of kings."

When Abursām and Xēbrā heard this, they went and fell down at the feet of the Beneficent One, saying, "We believe in thee, Lord, . . ."

3. *Texts on Mani's last journey, suffering, and death*

A number of documents, preserved only fragmentarily, report on Mani's last journey to the court of Bahrām I, who had summoned him to his residential city of Gundaishābuhr. We hear of his hostile reception, his imprisonment, his suffering, and his death in prison, which parallel Jesus' suffering and death. These texts supplement the information about Mani's suffering and death at the hands of the king and representatives of the Zoroastrian Church, headed by the "high priest" (*mōbad*) Kartēr, as we find it in the Coptic *Homilies*.

3.1 TEXTS ON MANI'S LAST JOURNEY

Text A (Parthian)

This fragment tells us of Mani's last journey. Having been summoned by King Bahrām I, Mani went to his court, following the ancient highway from Ctesiphon to Khuzistan. On the way he paid a last visit to his community at Gaukhai in the district of Bēth-Derāyē. He was accompanied by Bāt, probably a vassal of Bah-rām's, whose adherence to Mani's teaching apparently annoyed the King.[76] The passage is apparently taken from a report of Pattēg, a disciple of Mani. In the Coptic report on Mani's last journey (*Homilies* 44, 10ff.) we hear that Mani had wanted to go to the Kushan Kingdom, probably to visit his communities there (or perhaps to evade persecution) but the king forbade him to do so. Thereupon he went to Ctesiphon, and from there onward, hinting at his pending death. Here too, "Baat" (the Bāt of our text) accompanied him to "Belapat" that is, Bēth-Lāpat, (Bēlābād).

> [Furthermore Pattēg] said, "At that time when the Beneficent One departed from the city of Ctesiphon and (when) he was with King Bāt[77] . . ."
> [*a number of lines missing*]
> ". . . then when (he was) in Gaukhai, in (the district of) Derāyē . . ."

Text B (Parthian)

Here Pattēg narrates, "as in a prediction,"[78] what Mani's fate was at the royal city of Gundaishābuhr, also known by the Semitic name of Bēth-Lāpat.

> Furthermore Pattēg saw another sign and said, "I see the Beneficent One has arisen and for several days [has travelled along] the Tigris."
> [*a number of lines missing*]
> ". . . Majestically he enters and leaves the wide gate of the palace."[79]
> Thereupon Kardēr, the *mōbād* (high priest), plotted (evil against him, together) with his friends who served before the King, and (they) . . . (with) jealousy and cunning. . . "[80]

3.2 MANI'S LAST AUDIENCE WITH KING BAHRĀM I (PERSIAN)

"The text represents part of an account of Mani's last audience with Bahrām I, given by one of his companions, Nuhzādag (Bar Nūḥ), an interpreter. Of Mani's two other companions, one appears in the Coptic texts as Koustaios, a disciple to whom Mani addressed a letter that has survived. Abzaxyā has been identified as one of Mani's missionaries to Karkuk [where Christians were converted]."[81] The text is apparently taken from an autobiography of his interpreter Nuhzādag. We have another detailed report on Mani's last meeting with Bahrām I in the Coptic *Homi-lies* (45, 25–50, 6), which ends with Mani being fettered.

> Mani . . . came (to the audience of Bahrām I), after he [had summoned] me, Nuhzādag, the interpreter, Kushtai . . . and Abzaxyā the Persian, (and) we had been brought together by him. And the king was at (his) meal and he had not yet washed his hands.[82] The courtiers entered and said, "Mani has come and is standing at the door." And the king sent the Lord the message, "Wait a moment until I can come to you myself."

Then the Lord again sat down at one side of the guard (and waited there) until the king had finished his meal, and putting one hand around the Shāka queen[83] and the other around Kardēr, the son of Ardabān,[84] he came to the Lord. And his first words to the Lord were, "You are not welcome!"

Then the Lord answered, "Why? What wrong have I done?" The king said, "I have sworn an oath not to let you come to this land." And in anger he spoke thus to the Lord, "Ah, what need of you, since you neither go fighting nor hunting.[85] But perhaps you are needed for this doctoring?[86] And you do not do even that."[87]

Then the Lord answered, "I have done you no harm. (Rather), I have always done good to you and your family. And many and numerous are your servants from whom I have [cast out] male and female demons. And many are those whom I have freed from various kinds of fever and ague. And many are those who died, and I [revived] them . . ."

3.3 MANI'S LAST HOURS IN PRISON (PERSIAN)

This text is from an account of Mani's last hours in prison at Gundaishābuhr. "The opening sentences . . . are evidently the reported words of the prophet."[88] A longer account of these events is preserved in the Coptic *Homilies,* 50ff.

"... Through hymns, ... sermons and purification let each one support (?) the religion. And do not grow slack in enduring the labors of the Lord, so that you all find your reward and good recompense and eternal life on high."

Then he ordered the "Letter of the Seal,"[89] (his) final [letter, to be written?] . . .

[*a number of lines missing*]

He sent instruction to the whole Church (*dēn*) through the hand of Mār Ammō, the Teacher. And all his children, the righteous (the elect) and the auditors, honored the Lord, the Beneficent One. And he, the Lord of Light, bade farewell to all, and they went forth from him weeping. But Uzzi,[90] the Teacher, and the two righteous ones stayed [with him] . . .

3.4 MANI'S DEATH (PARTHIAN)

This Parthian fragment on Mani's death rests on the same authority as the preceding text, the account given by Uzzi. It is, however, "more poetically written."[91] A detailed albeit fragmentarily preserved report on these events is to be found in the Coptic *Homilies* (50ff.). None of these primary sources alludes to the events related by later Islamic authorities like an-Nadīm, who claims that Bahrām, "after executing him, gibbeted two halves of his body, one at a certain gateway and the other at a different gate of the city."[92] Traditions about his head being hung over the city gate and about his skin being stuffed with straw and hung up in public are apparently late.[93] In Manichaean circles, Mani's death was later conceived of as being analogous to the death of Jesus, and hence a "crucifixion."[94] The blame for it was put on the Zoroastrians under Kardēr,[95] just as the Jews were blamed for Jesus' death. Of course, in Manichaean parlance, the term "crucifixion" has a symbolic connotation, referring to suffering and death as exemplified by that of Jesus.

> Just as a sovereign who takes off his armor and his garment (worn in battle)[96] and puts on another royal garment, so did the Messenger of Light put off the warlike garment of (his) body; and he sat down in the Ship of Light (the Sun) and received the divine garment, the diadem of Light and the beautiful garland.[97] And in great joy he flew up, together with the bright gods[98] that accompanied him on the right and the left, to the sound of harps and songs of joy, in divine miraculous power, like a swift (bolt of) lightning and a bright, quick apparition,[99] to the Column of Glory, the path of Light, and the chariot of the Moon,[100] the meeting-place of the gods. And he stayed there with God Ohrmizd, the Father.
>
> He left behind the whole flock of the righteous (the Manichaean community), orphaned and sad, for "the master of the house" (*kadexvadāy*) had entered Parinirvāṇa (had died).[101]
>
> [*a number of lines missing*]
>
> And (it was) under the ascendency of the star[102] . . . , on the fourth day of the month of Shahrevar,[103] on the day of Shahrevar, Monday, at the eleventh hour, in the province of Khuzistān and in the city of Bēth-Lāpat, when this Father of Light, full of power, was taken up to his own Home of Light.
>
> After the Parinirvāṇa of the Apostle, Uzzi, the Teacher, gave this testimony to the whole Church with regard to what he had seen among the soldiery (*ispēr*),[104] for on that Saturday night he, Uzzi, had been left there with the Apostle of Light. And he communicated many pious injunctions from the Apostle to the whole Church community.
>
> After the Parinirvāṇa of the Apostle of Light, his *Gospel,* his *Ārdahang* (pictorial illustration of the Gospel), his garment and his staff[105] [were taken to?] the province . . . Sisin[106] . . .

4. Texts on Mani's self-image and his mission

A few documents give us an insight into Mani's self-image. He referred to himself as "the Apostle of Jesus Christ," but he also saw himself as the founder of a new, all-encompassing religion which would spread throughout the world and last to the end of time. His religion did last for well over a thousand years—the last faint traces were discernible in South China in the sixteenth century—and spread throughout the known Oikumene, finding adherents from North Africa and Spain to the Mongolian Steppes and China. Mani was convinced that in all his deeds his Heavenly Twin was guiding him and furthering his cause. This was his heavenly *alter ego* with whom he would unite upon returning to the Realm of Light.

4.1 TEXT CONCERNING MANI'S HEAVENLY TWIN (PERSIAN)

In this fragment, part of an autobiographical passage by the founder of the Manichaen religion, we hear of Mani's Heavenly Twin (MP *narjamīg*) who brought him enlightenment, and led and consoled him in his mission. The concept of such a Heavenly Twin is pre-Manichaean and is common to many Gnostic groups.[107] It probably evolved out of the ancient Jewish concept of the guardian angel, as well as the ancient Iranian concept of the *daēnā,* the heavenly being that represents one's own conscience and comes to meet one upon death.[108] Mani tells us in the Coptic *Kephalaia* (15,22–24) that his Twin revealed everything to him and had become "one body and one spirit" with him.[109]

> And now, too, he himself goes with me, and he himself holds and protects me, and through his strength I fight with *Āz* (the demon of Greed) and Ahriman (the Hostile Spirit, the Devil). And I teach men wisdom and knowledge and I redeem them from *Āz* and Ahriman. And [I teach] this matter of the gods, and wisdom and knowledge concerning the gathering of souls, which I received from the Twin . . .
>
> Through the Twin . . . I stepped before my family, and I was seized by the counsel of the gods,[110] and I began to speak and to teach that which the Twin had taught me. And when they heard it, they were amazed. Like a wise man who finds the seed of a good and fruitful tree in uncultivated earth, and plows (it), . . . and then [sows the seed] in the well-cultivated and prepared soil . . .[111]

4.2 THE UNIVERSALITY OF MANI'S RELIGION (PERSIAN)

This fragment is apparently from one of Mani's own writings. A similar passage is found in the Coptic *Kephalaia* (7,6ff.). The Islamic writer al-Bīrūnī also cites another such passage from the *Šābuhragān.*[112] These texts show that Mani recognized a number of "prophets," including Buddha, Zarathustra, and Jesus, as his forerunners.

> The religion (*dēn*) which I have chosen is greater and better than the other religions of the ancients in ten ways: First, the religions of the ancients were (spread) in one land and one language. But my religion is such that it will be manifest in all lands and in all languages and will be taught in distant lands. Second, the older religions were (in order) as long as there were holy leaders in them . . . , but when the leaders were raised up (died), their religions became confused, and they (the adherents) became slack in (observing the) precepts and in works . . . But my religion, by virtue of its living scriptures, (its) teachers, bishops, elect and auditors,[113] and by its wisdom and deeds will endure to the end. Third, those souls of the ancients who did not complete (good) works in their own religion will come to my religion, and for them it will truly become the door of salvation (*dar ī uzēnišn*).[114] Fourth, this revelation of the two

principles and my living scriptures, my wisdom and my knowledge, are more encompassing and better than those of the former religions. Fifth, as all scriptures, (all) wisdom and (all) parables of the former religions [have been added] to my religion . . .[115]

Notes

1. Sundermann, "Studien zur kirchengeschichtlichen Literatur der iranischen Manichäer," I–III.
2. Sundermann, "Studien" I, pp. 40ff.
3. Compare Boyce, "On the antiquity of Zoroastrian apocalyptic," pp. 64ff.
4. L. Koenen and C. Roemer, *Der Kölner Mani-Kodex*, pp. 102ff.; *Kephalaia* 184f.
5. Boyce translates, "much strife of doctrines between religions." Boyce, *Reader,* p. 39, n. 1.
6. Pattēg (Gr. Pattikios, Lat. Paticius) was the name of Mani's father, from whom this disciple of his is possibly to be distinguished.
7. Mani's *Living Gospel.*
8. Addā is the missionary sent west, to the Eastern Roman Empire.
9. Thus we differ from Henning, who translates "who opens his treasures."
10. For the question of Manichaean monasteries in Egypt, compare L. Koenen, "Manichäische Mission und Klöster in Ägypten."
11. Nafshā was the wife of the Roman "Emperor," Septimius Odaenathus, that is, "Queen" Zenobia, the Tadmōr/Tadamōr of the lost Coptic Manichaean texts. Compare Schmidt and Polotsky, *Mani-Fund,* p. 28. Septimius was actually a general who won a victory over Shāpur I in 260/261 A.D. In one Turfan text we hear that his wife Nafshā was cured of an illness by Mār Addā (text 2.1.A). Sundermann is of the opinion that, should this legend have a historical core, the conversion of Nafshā must have taken place at a later period, between 260/261 and 267, when Odaenathus was killed. Compare Sundermann, *Texte,* pp. 41ff.
12. This is part of Seleukia-Ctesiphon, the winter capital of the Sassanian kings, lying on the western bank of the Tigris.
13. According to a Sogdian text (cf. text 1.1.C), the scribe Mani was the abbot of a monastery.
14. These are two basic virtues of the elect, sometimes cumulatively referred to as "blessed poverty."
15. Or, *The Treasure of Life,* one of Mani's writings.
16. A part of Mesopotamia, the area around Seleucia-Ctesiphon.
17. Mār Addā is known as the author of various Manichaean books.
18. Capital of the ancient province of the same name. The city lay on the highway from Madāïn to Hammadān (B).
19. Abarshahr, "The Upper Lands," encompassed the northern provinces of the Sassanian (Persian) Empire.
20. This was "evidently a member of the fallen house of the Arsacids [i. e., Parthians], and as such kinsman of Mani's, and as such a man who spoke Parthian." Boyce, *Reader,* p. 40.
21. Alms-giving.
22. As Boyce points out, "The Western part of the land of the Kushans was at this time (c. A.C. 265–270) a dependency of the Sasanian state." Boyce, *op.cit.*
23. Here Xvārāsān refers to "the East" in a general sense, not to the province of Chorasan specifically.
24. Boyce points out that "the Manichaeans turned by day in prayer towards the sun, as do the Zoroastrians." Boyce, *Reader,* p. 48.
25. The "Collecting of the Gates" apparently refers to the closing of the senses against temptation.

26. This probably refers to the Buddhists, or ascetic Hindus, or Jains, living in the Kushan lands.

27. Here the eastern Dēnāvāriya school of Manichaeism, which was actually founded by Mār Shad Ohrmizd around 600 A.D., is pseudohistorically traced back to Mār Ammō, the great missionary to the East, who lived in the third century.

28. On the name Baɣard/Bagārd/Bagard compare Bailey, *Zoroastrian Problems,* pp. 67ff.; Henning, "Waručan-Šāh," p. 87, n. 14.

29. As Boyce points out, the following parables "are told in condensed form, like notes for preaching." Boyce, *Reader,* p. 41.

30. There is a change of tense here.

31. The last parable must have dealt with the sense of touch.

32. Literally, "godliness" (Sogd. βγ-y'kh), which is a mark of the elect, but also a characteristic of the "seals of light" (S).

33. Spiritual death.

34. Cf. Boyce, *Reader,* p. 34.

35. Turkish text in Zieme, *Texte,* pp. 50f.

36. Sundermann, *Texte,* p. 34.

37. For Mani's trip to India, compare Sundermann, "Mani, India, and the Manichaean Religion," pp. 11–18.

38. For *ardāv* as "just, right, righteous," compare Boyce, *Word-List,* s.v. 'rd'v.

39. Sundermann, *Texte,* p. 20.

40. As S points out, possible emendations of the missing word would be "to a home," "to a place," or "to a grave." But this could also be the name of the place where "the righteous one" was. Sundermann, *Texte,* p. 21, n. 3.

41. Or, [they].

42. Compare Sundermann's new edition and translation of this story in R. Merkelbach, "Manichaica (10). Eine Fabel Manis," pp. 93–94. A small fragment of a Turkish Turfan text could belong to this story. Compare Zieme, "Ein Turfanfragment einer türkischen Erzählung," pp. 367–68. This is, as Merkelbach has shown, originally an Aesopic fable in which a father on his death bed admonishes his sons to unity, likening them to arrows that can easily be broken separately, but not when they are bound together.

43. Boyce, *Reader,* pp. 34–37 (text e), after Sundermann, "Zur frühen missionarischen Wirksamkeit Manis," pp. 102–105; 371–76.

44. It is interesting to note how Manichaean and Buddhist concepts of sin, and the awareness of it, are closely connected here.

45. This utterance can be taken as a religious "legitimization" of Manichaean kingship in Central Asia.

46. This is a reference to the myth, in which the Living Spirit stretches out his hand to the First Man to save him.

47. For the person of Nafshā, compare n. 11.

48. Mani, as the redeemer, is frequently referred to as a "physician," and his teaching, the *gnosis* he brought, as a medicament of life.

49. The healing of the girl Nafshā must have been reported here.

50. Not all of these categories are known to us. This portion is translated after Sims-Williams, "The Manichaean Commandments," p. 574.

51. Compare the Pauline reference to spiritual milk in I Cor. 3:2 and Hebr. 5:12. Compare also I Peter 2:2. In the Middle Persian text IB 4974, it says about the teacher, "You who by the word bear children, [through] wisdom created by God, and who raises them with spiritual milk" (cf. ch. VII, text 3).

52. This statement of Jesus' is apocryphal and otherwise unknown. It is reminiscent of Mark 16:18.

53. A small kingdom in Armenia.

54. Here it becomes clear that the Manichaeans presented themselves as the true followers of Jesus and the true Christians.

55. The "Third Messenger" who in cosmological terms resides in the Sun. In hymns, he merges with Jesus (as Light Messenger).
56. Health and salvation.
57. Literally, chose many people for the state of being elect, for righteousness (*'rt'vy'kh*).
58. There was actually no Christian month of fasting. But starting in the fourth century, there was a so-called "Easter fast" of forty days. Compare Sundermann, *Texte,* p. 49, n. 19.
59. Good Friday.
60. The account of the king's conversion probably follows.
61. It was at Rēv-Ardaxshihr, a port of Mesopotamia, that Mani met some "Baptists" (*abšodagān*), among whom he had grown up, as we learn in this text. Compare Sundermann, *Texte,* p. 55.
62. The "extension of the right hand" is the sign of salvation. Compare Sundermann, *Texte,* p. 55.
63. For further information on this port city, compare Sundermann, "Zur frühen missionarischen Wirksamkeit Manis," p. 82, n. 27.
64. Sundermann opines that this presbyter was Mani's father Pattēg *(Pattikios).* Compare Sundermann, *Texte,* pp. 56f., n. 4.
65. Hanni is an abbreviated form of (Syrian) Yōhanni (John). He could be the Yāhhya whom an-Nadīm mentions as the recipient of two letters of Mani's. Compare Sundermann, *Texte,* p. 93.
66. Dēb was a port and important commercial city at the mouth of the Indus. It was also known as Dēbuhl.
67. The Baptists are probably the Judeo-Christian Elchasaites among whom Mani grew up. Compare A. Henrichs, "Mani and the Babylonian Baptists"; R. Merkelbach, "Die Täufer, bei denen Mani aufwuchs."
68. This is probably the person mentioned in text 2.4, whose soul is brought by angels before Mani.
69. Valāsh is otherwise not mentioned in previously published texts.
70. Xusrō was probably a Parthian. It seems that he is the one mentioned in Parthian letters by an *Archegos* (Leader of the Community), perhaps Sisinnius, to Mār Ammō.
71. Boyce, *Reader,* p. 38.
72. "The uncreated Air of Paradise" (B).
73. Boyce, *Reader,* p. 38.
74. Speaker unidentified.
75. That is, brought him alms.
76. Cf. Boyce, *Reader,* p. 43.
77. In the Coptic *Homilies* (45, 9f.), king Bāt also accompanies him to *Bēth-Lāpat.*
78. Boyce, *Reader,* p. 43.
79. "He passes under and through the gate" (B).
80. In the Coptic *Homilies* (45, 11ff.), the "Magi," together with Kirdēr (Kardel), plot against him.
81. Boyce, *Reader,* p. 44.
82. Had not finished his meal.
83. Boyce, after Henning, points out that "the position of King of the Sakas (prince-governor of Sakistān/Seistān) was held by one of the king's own family. Under Vahrām it was given to his grandson, later Vahrām III; and it is probably his wife who appears here." Boyce, *Reader,* p. 44.
84. Boyce points out that "this nobleman, to be distinguished from Kirdēr the priest, appears in the inscription of Vahrām's father Šābuhr I on the *Ka'aba-yi Zardušt.* . . ." Boyce, *Reader,* p. 45.
85. These are, as Boyce remarks, "the occupations proper to an aristocrat, which Mani was by birth." Boyce, *Reader,* p. 45.
86. Henning comments, "The use of . . . the demonstrative pronoun gives the phrase a perceptibly contemptuous note. The king, who apparently was not very broadminded, does

not seem to have been in sympathy with his father's efforts at raising the medical standards in his lands." Henning, "Mani's Last Journeys," p. 981.

87. It is said that Mani failed to cure one of the relatives of the king.

88. Boyce, *Reader,* p. 46.

89. The Letter of the Seal was written by Mani, or at his command, in his final hour. It was directed to his community, and subsequently read out annually at the Bema service, in communities as far apart as Egypt and China. Compare *BBB,* p. 18f. and our ch. XII, text 1.

90. The name Uzzi is Jewish. Uzzi was allowed to remain with Mani up to his death. Boyce, *Reader,* p. 46.

91. Boyce, *Reader,* p. 47.

92. Cf. Dodge, *Fihrist* II, p. 794.

93. Cf. Klíma, *Manis Zeit und Leben,* pp. 364f.

94. This development can clearly be noted in the Coptic *Homilies* (60, 2f): "This is the memorandum of the day of his crucifixion at the time when he went out [of the world]." Compare also 75, 30f.: "Then, after they had crucified our [Father, he fulfilled] the mystery of his Apostleship . . . of Jesus." A whole chapter in the *Homilies* is entitled "[The narrative] of the crucifixion of the *Sotēr,* the [true] Apostle." (85, 32f.).

95. For example, *Homilies* 75, 5ff.: "[The evil ones] . . . and those who crucified him, have gone out . . . ." Compare also 81, 10ff.: "But he (i. e., King Bahrām) [and] the whole [community of] magi [were responsible for?] the crucifixion of our Lord."

96. Mani's earthly mission is depicted here as a battle against the forces of evil.

97. For these signs of salvation ("victory"), compare Arnold-Döben, *Die Bildersprache des Manichäismus,* pp. 155ff.

98. Or, gods of Light (*baɣān rōšnān*).

99. A shooting star.

100. For the images of Sun and Moon, compare Arnold-Döben, *Die Bildersprache des Manichäismus,* pp. 155ff.

101. Boyce remarks, "The use of this denominative verb [i. e., **parniβrad*] formed secondarily from *parniβrān* < Skt. *parinirvāṇa,* suggests a later date for the text than that of Mani's martyrdom." Boyce, *Reader,* p. 47.

102. Or, constellation, sign of the zodiac (*axtar*).

103. Boyce remarks, "Mani died on Monday, the 4th day of Addaru, according to the Babylonian calendar: and this date was mechanically rendered into the calendars of the various Man[ichaean] communities. Šahrewar corresponds with Addaru in 274/277." Boyce, *Reader,* p. 47, n. 3.

104. Boyce points out, "*ispēr* is probably a loanword from Greek . . . , and may be used here deliberately to echo the Gospel account of Christ's death [Mark 15:16; Matth. 28:27], where too the Greek word is used in the *Peshitta* (H)." Boyce, *Reader,* p. 48, n. 4.

105. *Dast *avestām,* "hand support," that is, staff (S).

106. Mani's successor after an interim period of five years. He is known in Latin as Sisinnius.

107. Compare, for instance, Hennecke and Schneemelcher, *New Testament Apocrypha* II, p. 441.

108. To be sure, the *dāēnā* is regarded as feminine, whereas *narjamīg* means "male twin." Yet notions concerning the *dāēnā* have apparently had an impact on this concept of the Twin. For the *dāēnā,* compare C. Colpe, "*Dāēnā,* Lichtjungfrau, zweite Gestalt." In Gnosticism, the Heavenly Twin can assume the form of a heavenly gown, and the duality of Twin and Self can appear in the image of Call and Answer. Compare Arnold-Döben, *Die Bildersprache der Gnosis,* pp. 77ff. and 124ff. The Islamic author an-Nadīm was still very much aware of the significance of the Twin (or Companion) for Mani's self-image. He describes the figure in question as "the angel bringing [Mani] the revelation." Dodge, *Fihrist* II, p. 774.

109. More recent investigations of the concept of the Twin in Manichaeism are Henrichs and Koenen, "Ein griechischer Mani-Codex," pp. 161–89; W. Fauth, "Syzygos und Eikon."

110. Was divinely inspired.
111. Sowing the seed is an image for spreading the word.
112. E. Sachau, ed., *The Chronology of Ancient Nations,* p. 207. Compare Adam, *Texte,* pp. 5–8.
113. These are the ranks of the Manichaean Church. Mani, and later his successors, have the first rank in this hierarchy.
114. Literally, "the door of redemption (i. e., from the cycle of rebirths)."
115. This is illustrated in the parable about the world-ocean. Compare ch. XVI, text 1.

CHAPTER EIGHTEEN

Prose Texts on Cosmogony and Cosmology

In this chapter only the major texts on the primeval events and the making of the world by the Living Spirit are translated. A number of important but fragmentary texts, edited by Sundermann, are omitted.[1] The events concerning the battle of the First Man and his rescue (text 1), are treated as in the poetic documents on the subject (ch. II). Texts 2.1 and 2.2 give a detailed account of the fashioning of the cosmos. Of course, it does not always correspond to other accounts on the subject. Henning rightly remarked, "On whatever subject Mani was writing or talking, he was always lavish with details. Unfortunately he frequently failed to notice that the details he produced on the spur of the moment did not square with his teachings of the day before. His picture of the world is a case in point."[2] To clarify his cosmological views, though, Mani did publish a volume of drawings, or paintings, called the *Ertenk* in Persian, or *Ārdahang* in Parthian (*Eikōn* in the Coptic Manichaica). In the Chinese "Compendium of Doctrines and Styles of the Teachings of Mani, the Buddha of Light," it is defined as "the drawing of the two great principles." We can suppose that the main contents of his message on cosmogony and eschatology were illustrated here. The book of drawings, which is unfortunately lost, "would no doubt have helped us to understand many puzzling points," as Henning points out;[3] "nevertheless, one cannot help wishing Mani had made himself a little wax model of the world and kept it by his side and looked at it from time to time when talking on such enthralling subjects as the Eight Earths, the Exterior Hells, the Three Wheels, the Seven Great Columns, the posture of Atlas, the Giant of the Sea, the Veins of Connection, the Column of Glory, etc., etc."[4]

We can imagine what Mani intended from the descriptions of such elements in texts 2.1 and 2.2; another image is introduced in a Sogdian cosmogony (text 3): the Oriental bazaar, with its "rows," "streets," "sides" of a street, "shops," and "stalls." Unfortunately, however, not even the few fragmentary remains of the commentary to Mani's picturebook clarify how these different images were integrated.[5]

1. *The First Man's battle with the demons* (Parthian)

This short text, in which there is unfortunately a long gap, sketches the First Man's battle with the powers of Darkness, and his subsequent rescue. The major part of his prayer to the Mother of the Living is missing, as is her intercession in his behalf to the Father of Greatness.

[Title]   The battle of the God Ohrmizd

> The Prayer of the Mother of the Righteous Ones
>
> . . . And when the wind demons understood that . . . , they all attacked him in the land of the winds[6] like a fierce troop of soldiers. Then the God Ohrmizd prayed to his Mother,[7] and his Mother prayed to the Righteous God (the Father of Greatness), (saying), "Send helpers to my son, for he has fulfilled your will, and is being oppressed . . ."
>
> [*a long gap*]
>
> . . . The God [Call] descended swiftly.[8] He scattered the army of demons and he said, "Hail from the Father and from the whole Realm (of Light)." And he (the God Call) said, "Gather (together) your limbs (of the soul), for the Savior has come." And God Ohrmizd was glad at the good news that brought (him) happiness, and he created the God "Answer." And the two ascended . . . the Mother of the Righteous, the God "Answer". . .

2. *Cosmogonic Texts*

The first account of cosmogony presented here (text 2.1) is taken from the Middle Persian Turfan texts M 98 I and M 99 I, while the second account (text 2.2) is preserved on a number of sheets from another manuscript, M 7980–84. The texts were first published by Henning[9] and then by Boyce, with copious notes.[10] A new edition, with German translation, has been published by Hutter.[11] The English translation given here is based on this edition, which corrects Henning's first edition and German translation in various points. Hutter discusses at length the relationship between the two sets of texts. It becomes clear, as Boyce had already surmised, that they are not from the same book of Mani's, who as we saw apparently wrote various cosmogonic accounts that were not always consistent. Yet the passages preserved "fit well together."[12] As Henning remarked,

> As a good missionary and teacher Mani knew the value of repetition. With endless pains he had elaborated a story of the world, which was to explain all phenomena, of nature and the mind, that came within reach of his knowledge. Its comprehensiveness made it so complicated that it required—and still requires—a strong effort to remember all its details. All the greater was the need to force it, by ceaseless repetition, into the minds of those who were ready to listen to the new prophet. No doubt every one of his books and longer epistles opened with this story, which may have been the sole subject of several of them.[13]

And he adds, "Each form of the story has points that are peculiar to it and absent from all others."[14]

Our chief sources of Manichaean cosmogony and cosmology, then, are the two sets of texts mentioned here. In addition, there are the Sogdian accounts on Manuscript M 178 (text 3), which is no exception to the textual situation referred to previously. Some fragments preserved in Turkic (compare ch. XXVIII) also belong in this literary category. The most important secondary sources for Manichaean cosmology are St. Augustine's references to and quotations from Mani's *Epistula fundamenti;*[15] the Manichaean book quoted and summarized by Theodor bar Khonai;[16] the information to be gleaned from various anti-Manichaean writers like St. Ephrem;[17] and the references in an-Nadīm and aš-Šahrastānī.[18] The cosmogonic and cosmological hymns from Central Asia, which are a major source of our information on the topic, have already been presented (cf. ch. II). Finally, there should be a reference to the Coptic material, which has recently been summed up concisely by M. Heuser.[19]

One of the major issues in contemporary Manichaean studies is the relationship between primary sources on cosmology and Mani's *Šābuhragān,* the treatise he wrote in Middle Persian for Shāhpur I. A substantial portion of that text is preserved in the original, but since it mainly deals with eschatological matters, it is clear that other canonical scriptures must also have included a cosmogony similar to those preserved, albeit not completely identical with them.[20] Hutter would identify the texts 2.1 (M 98/99I) and 2.2 (M 7980–84) as parts of the *Šābuhragān.*[21] Furthermore, there is the question of the relationship between the *Šābuhragān,* a text only known in Asia Major but widely disseminated there,[22] and the fragments from the *Book of Giants* and Enochic literature in general, which also include cosmogonic and eschatological portions.[23] Since some of this material can be traced back to Jewish, even Qumranic tradition, as it was passed on to Mani through the Elchasaite community, it must be seen in the light of the Jewish tradition.[24] However, this does not justify an overemphasis on this tradition at the cost of the Iranian, particularly the Zurvanite influence on Mani,[25] as is evident from the *Šābuhragān.* Furthermore, the influence of the New Testament—especially of Paul, with his distinction between the Old and the New Man, the Old and the New Aeon, and so on—cannot be overlooked. It becomes increasingly clear that Mani interprets older material, both Jewish and Iranian, on the basis of his understanding of the New Testament, particularly Matthew 25 and Paul.

Of course Mani's interpretation of man and the world is strictly dualistic. To accentuate the radical difference between the body and its psychic makeup on the one hand and the soul on the other he conceives of a creation myth which cannot but make us shudder. Yet the pitch dark colors with which man's body and *psyche* are depicted only serve to heighten the divine character of the soul (*gyān*) imprisoned in the body.

2.1 FROM MANI'S ACCOUNT OF THE MAKING OF THE WORLD (PERSIAN)

> [And they[26]. . .] fixed the seven planets (to the firmament) and hung up the two dragons[27] and bound them fast (there). And they hung them up

on that lowest firmament, and in order to make them rotate unceasingly upon the Call, they appointed two angels, one male and one female.

And then they led it[28] up to the border (of the Realm of Ahriman) and (then) on to the Realm of Light. And of wind and light, water and fire, which had been purified from the mixture (of good and evil, soul and matter) he formed and created two chariots of Light. (First he made the chariot) of the Sun, (composed) of fire and light, (with) five walls, (namely), of ether, air, light, water and fire, with twelve gates, five houses, three thrones and five angels who collect souls in the wall of fire. Furthermore (he made the chariot of) the Moon god, of wind and water, with five walls, (namely), of ether, air, light, fire and water, with fourteen gates, five houses, three thrones, and five angels who collect souls in the wall of water. And they clothed themselves in . . . Then Mihryazd (the Living Spirit) (put on, of) the same[29] purified light, three garments, (namely), of wind, water and fire, and descended to the Earth of Darkness. And in order to create that great structure, the New Paradise, over it, he filled the five ditches of death and levelled (them). And he built four layers over the Earth of Darkness to correspond with the firmaments above, (layers) of hot wind, darkness, fire and water, (building them) one over the other. (Thus) he constructed them in layers. And he protected (the layers) with a wall, (starting) from the Earth of Light (and going) South, East and West, and he joined them back to the Earth of Light. And he made another great earth and placed it upon these layers. Then he appointed the God of Thought (*Parmānagēnyazd)*[30] to be the "lord of the house" (*mānbed*).

And over this earth (he erected) three pillars and five arches,[31] within another wall facing the East, South and West, with three regions (within them). The first (arch) spanned the (space) from the end of the wall in the West to the western pillar; the second (arch spanned the space) from the western pillar to the southern pillar, and the third from the southern pillar to the eastern pillar, the fourth from the eastern pillar to the end of the wall in the East, and the fifth great one (arch) from the eastern to the western pillar. And (he created) a great and sturdy earth with twelve portals, corresponding to the portals in the firmament(s).

And all around the same earth, he made four walls and three ditches. And he imprisoned the demons (*dēvs*) in those three inner ditches. Then he placed the lowest firmament on the head of Mānbed (Atlas, the "God of Thought"), and (he put) seven square pillars in his hand, in order to bind the zodiac to them. And he placed this great earth on the pillars and arches, and he put the two walls on the shoulders of Mānbed. Then he fastened [vaults] above the uppermost wall towards the East, South and West and towards the North in (above) the Earth of Light. And above this great *māzman* earth,[32] on this side of the ditches, he made two other mixed earths with portals, all (kinds of) channels and subterranean canals, which serve to lift up great volumes of wind, water and fire. Right around this earth he erected (lit., fastened) a wall with four portals. And in the four regions (the directions) he set up four angels that hold the lowest firmament(s) corresponding to and clad like the upper ones.[33]

2.2 THE CREATION OF THE COSMOS (PERSIAN)

Text A

[Title]: The discourse on that which is material

... and not to Hell, where they will also find no respite, until they are destroyed. And when Mihryazd (the Living Spirit) had made and ordered those four layers, the prison of the demons, and the four earths with (their) columns, structures, portals, walls, ditches, halls, channels in the cavities of the earth, hills, valleys, springs, rivers and oceans, and the ten firmaments with (their) regions, thrones, districts, houses, villages, tribes, lands, borders, border guards and portals, thresholds, rotations, double hours, walls and a zodiac with fixed stars and rotating stars, and the two chariots of the Sun and the Moon with houses, thrones, portals and the heads of the doorkeepers as well as jailers (lit., lords of the prison: *bannbed*), lords of the border guard (*pāhrbed*), lords of the house (*mānbed*), lords of the villages (*vīsbed*), lords of the tribes (*zandbed*), lords of the lands (*dahibed*) and all kinds of things in the cosmos, then the Messenger God (Mizdagtāzyazd, the God Call) and the God who brings news (Azdegaryazd, the God Answer), with which Mihryazd (the Living Spirit) and (the Goddess with the) Female Form (Srīgarkirb, the Mother of Life), the Mother of the God Ohrmizd, ... [were ... led up], and they stood before the Lord of the Land (Dahibed, the Keeper of Splendor)[34] who stands above the firmaments and holds these (five) gods (the five sons of the First Man, Ohrmizd).[35]

And Mihryazd (the Living Spirit) and the Goddess of Creation in Female Form (Mother of Life) were lifted up to Paradise. And together with the God Ohrmizd (First Man) and the most Beloved of the Lights[36] and the Creator God of the New World[37] they approached the Lord of Paradise, greeting him. Then they bowed down deeply and venerated him, saying, "We worship you, Lord, for we are created by your wondrous power and by (your) word of blessing. Through us you have fettered *Āz* (the demon of Greed), Ahriman, the demons (*dēvs*) and the she-devils (*peris*)."

Text B

... Order [it] (the Living Spirit) to go and look at that prison of the demons and to ascribe to Sun and Moon their cyclical courses and to (himself) become a redeemer and a savior for that radiance and beauty of the gods,[38] which from the beginning have been beaten by *Āz*, Ahriman, the demons and the she-devils, and which they even now keep subjugated, as well as for those who are held captive in the (different regions) of the world and of heaven, undergoing suffering, so that it (the Living Spirit) may prepare a way and a path to the Highest for (the divine) wind, water and fire.

Here ends the discourse on that which is material.

Text C

[Title]:   The discourse on the God Narisah (the Third Messenger)

Thereafter the Lord of Paradise created three gods by his own wondrous power and (by his) word of blessing: (the God) Rōshnshahr ("the God of the World of Light," the Third Messenger) and (the God) Xradeshahr ("the God of the World of Wisdom," that is, Jesus as Judge), for lifting up (the redeemed light), so that the God Rōshnshahr should become lord and ruler over heaven and earth, as the Lord (the Father of Light) is ruler over Paradise and holds all the light, and that he should hold the light of the cosmos, and that he should bring forth (lit., make apparent) the day and the night (by putting the Sun and Moon into motion).

And the God Xradeshahr [should] . . . that radiance and beauty [of the gods] . . .

[*a large gap*]

. . . Plants, flowers (and) herbs, both those without seed as well as every other type of vegetation, were sown and grew. And into them *Āz* mixed her own self. And out of that portion which had fallen into the ocean there rose up a hideous, thieving and terrible monster demon (*mazan*). And it tumbled out of the ocean, and began to sin in the world.

Then Mihryazd sent out from among the five gods of his own creation (his five sons) the god with four faces (lit., four forms) (the Adamas of Light)[39] who stretched out the monster demon (the *mazan* monster) in the northern region from East to West across the whole northern area, stamped his foot (on it) and subjugated (it).[40] And he stood on it, so that it could not sin in the world (any more). And this god became the "lord of the village" (Vīsbed)[41] over the cosmos with all its earths and heavens, (becoming lord) over the North and the East, the South and the West, so that he might protect the world. And like that lustful and lewd (seed or offspring), *Āz* fell down from heaven to earth, on that which is dry and that which is wet. And it was (there) together with all kinds of vegetation (mixed itself into it) and with the (other) monster demons of its own nature.

Then the demons and she-devils, the demons of wrath, the monster demons and archdemons that were female, two-footed, four-footed, winged, poisonous and reptile-formed, all that were pregnant from the beginning in Hell and that were thereupon[42] fastened to the eleven firmaments and had seen that radiance and beauty of the God Rōshnshar and become desirous of him, losing their senses, (they) all aborted the fruit of their own loins. And (the aborted offspring) fell down to earth, and they began to crawl (all) over the earth. They devoured the fruits from the trees and grew bigger, more monstrous and more like archdemons. And from the fruits of the trees (which they had devoured) that *Āz* (which had entered the fruits, etc.) overcame them. And they were aroused by sensual lust and mated with each other.

Then the God Rōshnshahr commanded the creator God of the New World (the Great Builder), "Go and build the New Construction beyond the cosmos of heavens and earths, (beyond) the five Hells, up to the southern region, (but) more towards (here) than there, over the Hell of Darkness, (so that) it stretches from the eastern to the western region, in accordance with (the original) Paradise. And in the middle of this structure make an impregnable prison for *Āz* and Ahriman, the demons and the she-devils. And (only) when that radiance and beauty of the gods (the light substance trapped by the dark powers) which Ahriman and the demons have devoured, which (is dispersed) in the cosmos and which writhes (in pain) as it suffers (at the hands of) the demons and she-devils, (only when) that is purified and lifted up to the Highest and when the Renewal of the world (*frašegīrd*) takes place, then *Āz* and Ahriman, the demons and the she-devils will be bound in that prison unceasingly for ever.

And above the New Construction erect the New Paradise, (so that) Ohrmizd and these (saving) gods—which *Āz* and Ahriman, the demons and the she-devils have seized and bound because of their wondrous power and light—(so that they), and we, too, [may have] a throne and . . .

[*nineteen lines missing*]

". . . By wisdom and knowledge concerning the (future) macrocosmos (?) create ether. And after ether create wind, and after wind, light, and after light, water, and after water, fire." And (hearing this) he (Ohrmizd) clothed himself with them (the five divine elements) and took fire into his hands. And he attacked Ahriman and the demons, struck them and subjugated them, . . .[43]

Text D

. . . [He (Ohrmizd) will purify] (the) wind (and) [light]. And he will appoint . . . and will purify water (and) fire. And they will always be together, being of one mind and of the same power. And the elements have that original radiance and beauty (of the gods) in their power. And they fulfilled the will of the God Ohrmizd . . .

Thereafter, when the God Rōshnshahr has set up that God Who Bears the World (Atlas)[44] at the center of the cosmos and has installed these (other) gods (the other sons of the Living Spirit), then he and the Goddess in Female Form (the Mother of Life) and the God Ohrmizd [appear?] in (their) own (beautiful) forms and [appearances] . . .[45]

Text E

[Title]:   The discourse on the position (of the Sun) and on (the length) of days

... These gods and the God Rahniguh[46] take their positions in the chariots of the Sun and the Moon, so that they may ... [redeem] the splendor and beauty of the gods which *Āz*, the demons and the she-devils, the male and female (powers of Darkness) had chewed and swallowed in the beginning and (which) they have seized even now, and also that (radiance and beauty) which [they will] chew and [devour] from wind, water and fire until the Renewal (of the world).

[*gap*]

... when Ohrmizd and Ahriman fought with each other. And thereafter he (the God Rahniguh) leads that radiance and beauty (of the gods) along the paths of Sun and Moon and (finally) takes them, by the care and protection of the gods, upward from the cosmos of heaven and earth. And [he leads them] to [Paradise] ...

[*gap*]

... (it) becomes day. And then, when the fifteenth of the month is there, at (the time of) Full Moon, the God Ohrmizd takes the light as well as the content (lit., increment) of the Moon (which is brought about) by the god of his own appearance (by the accumulation of saved light particles) and orders it. And from the Full Moon, the sixteenth (day) in the month, up to (the day of) the invisible moon (New Moon), the twenty[ninth in the month] ...

[*gap*]

[When] ... [the Sun?] and the New Moon are together, the God Ohrmizd arises ... from the chariot of the Moon and goes to the chariot of the Sun. And these gods which the God Ohrmizd [leads] from the Full Moon to the New Moon, day to day ...

... one month is counted as (consisting of) thirty days and includes New Moon, Full Moon and invisible Moon (New Moon again), and (thus) it appears. And that *Āz*, and Ahriman, darkness and gloom, evil-smelling hot wind and the poison of death, the wrathful burning and the poison of the demons, ...

[*gap*]

In that (threshold)[47] are the month Ābān (April/May),[48] corresponding to the burning, dark she-demons, similar to burning hot winds, and the constellation Taurus. And he releases that burning from them and lets it descend. And the trees ...

[*gap*]

... (when) the day is completed in the thirty rotations of this second "threshold," then there follows and appears (again) the month Ābān; the day (now) has eleven hours and the night thirteen. And then the whole world is as bright as the Sun, and (it) is open to the radiance of the Sun.

Then the Sun also ascends from the second threshold to the first threshold, which is higher, larger and wider than the others. And then thirty days of the month of Ādur are brought about by those thirty rotations and 360 double-hours of just this first threshold, where the month of Ādur has its time (lit., place). And in that (threshold) there are, in the month of Ādur, accordingly the burning dark she-demons, which are like hot winds, and the constellation Gemini. And he frees this heat to descend. Then plants and fruits begin to ripen. And in the thirty days of the month of Ādur, further 360 *visānag*,[49] which together make up an hour, are taken away from the night—daily twelve *visānag*— and they are added to those days. And (then) the day has twelve hours, and the night has twelve hours, and they are both equal. And thereafter the cosmos experiences summer and noon, (that is) *rapih*,[50] just as when the sun existed in the beginning.[51]

And then he divides the year into twelve months,[52] in accordance with the twelve zodiacal signs, (and) into Spring and Summer, Fall and Winter, and he calls them into being (successively). Then the trees become green, and herbs and grass (grow) and fruits and plants ripen and animals bring forth their young.

And when the sun is in the uppermost firmament in this latitude of the cosmos—as it is month after month in the zodiacal signs Aries, Taurus, Gemini, Cancer and Leo—then, in accordance with the five constellations, those five days are added to those five months, one day per constellation and month, which are now counted as Panz-Gāh in Iran.[53] And also in An-Iran (An-Ēran)[54] ten days are added in correspondence with these five constellations, (there being) two days per constellation.[55]

And in the same manner the constellation Virgo gains a day each month, (that is) that (month) when cold starts being released from it (the constellation) and starts to descend. Then the trees wither, it is considered Fall and the evening of the cosmos sets in.

And in the same manner the constellation Pisces gains a day every month, (that is) that month when heat starts being released from it (the constellation), and starts to descend. Then the trees become green, it is considered Spring and the morning of the cosmos dawns.

These, then, are the five days which are now reckoned as Panz-Gāh in Iran, and the twelve days in An-Iran. For because of the rotation of the sun, the summer [lasts] from the month of Mihr (March/April) to the month of Vahman (July/August), (which is) five months, in this latitude of the cosmos . . .[56]

[*at least one page missing*]

Text F

[Title]: The discourse on the decrease of day and night

. . . And he[57] will first draw it (the light that is to be saved) up from the cosmos, (away from?) Ahriman and the demons, and will lead it up to Sun and Moon, and will (then) usher it into Paradise, (to) its own family. Then the Renewal of the world will take place. And the demons will be destroyed, and the Sun and Moon and the gods will find rest and peace.

And in the beginning, too, when these gods had divided the regions and borders by the rotations (of the Sun and the Moon), and by their waxing and waning, and when they had (thus) made day and night apparent, bringing months and years (also) into being, and had retrieved the Light from the cosmos, leading it up, at that time *Āz* [was] . . . , (that *Āz*), whose progeny are beaten, who had fallen down from the firmament and had clothed themselves in trees and plants, and which, with the help of trees and plants, had clothed themselves in those abortive fetuses of the monster demons and archdemons. These (abortions) had fallen down from the firmament after they (the demons) had seen him (Narisah), and the glory of the God Narisah (the Third Messenger) had [appeared] to them . . .[58] And furthermore she saw the care[59] of the Sun and the Moon (in saving the Elements of Light) and she also saw that the radiance and beauty of the gods (the Light Elements), which she had seized, were being purified again and again (were being extracted from the world) by the gods, who led the Sun and the Moon; it (the light) was being led out (of *Āz*'s fangs) and out of the (old) cosmos, and being taken to the chariots (of the Sun and the Moon) and (finally) being led into Paradise.[60]

(Here ends) the discourse on day and night.[61]

Text G

[Title]: The discourse on Gēhmurd (i. e., Adam) and Murdiyānag (i. e., Eve)

Then that *Āz* who had been deceived was filled with great wrath; she desired to advance (in her cause) and thought, "I will make[62] these two creatures (the first human beings), a male and the female one, in accordance with the two forms of the God Narisah, the male and the female (form), that I saw (in the sky),[63] so that they may be a garment and a covering for me. And I would be appointed over them . . . , and these two beings shall not be taken away from me by them (the gods?), and I shall not inflict want and suffering (upon them)."

Then *Āz* clothed herself in (the substance of) all those offspring of the demons that had fallen down from the firmament to earth, (i. e.) those male and female archdemons that were like lions, greedy and wrathful, sinful and thieving. And it made of these a covering and a garment (for herself); (covering herself with) these she was avid. And just as *Āz* herself, from the very beginning, had taught lasciviousness and mating to the demons and she-devils, the demons of wrath, monster demons and archdemons in that Hell of Darkness, her own habitation, so she continued to teach lasciviousness and mating to the other male and female monster demons and archdemons that had fallen from the firmament to earth. (Her aim was) that they be excited and unite with intertwined bodies and bring forth dragon offspring which she (*Āz*) would take away, devour and then form from them the two (first human) beings, male and female.

Then those male and female monster demons and archdemons taught all (the others) lasciviousness and mating. And with intertwined bodies they united and brought forth offspring and raised them. Then they gave their own offspring to those two lustful lionlike archdemons, the male and the female, which form the garment of *Āz*. *Āz* devoured the offspring, and those two monster demons, the male and the female one, were excited and were impelled to mate. And they united with intertwined bodies, and from that union (lit., mixture), and from the children of those monster demons as well as of the archdemons, which she had devoured, she fashioned and formed, by her own lust, a body in male (human) form, with bones, nerves, flesh, arteries and skin. And she (*Āz*) fettered that radiance and beauty of the gods (the Light Elements) there (as the soul).

And the radiance and beauty of the gods which (was originally) in fruits and buds, and which was mixed with the offspring of the monster demons,[64] was fettered within that body (*tan*) as the soul (*gyān*). And into it (the body) she also sowed desire and lust, covetousness and (the urge to) mate, enmity and slander, envy and sinfulness, wrath and impurity, *darkening (of the mind) and unconsciousness, hostility to religion and doubt (regarding the faith), (the urge) to steal and to lie, to rob and to do evil deeds, obstinacy and falsehood, vengefulness and conceit (?), anxiety and grief, sorrow and pain, poverty and want, illness and the infirmity of old age, offensiveness[65] and thievishness (?). And she (*Āz*) gave to her creature as many languages and tongues as the issue of the monster demons had, from which her body was fashioned, so that it might speak and understand the different languages.[66]

And (it was) in accordance with (the image of) the male offspring (evocation) of the gods (the Third Messenger), whom she had seen in the chariot (of the Sun and the Moon) that she fashioned and formed that (creature, man).[67] But she (*Āz*) associated with him (man) from above, from the firmament, by origin and connection, the monster demons and the archdemons as well as the constellations and planets,[68] so that (by their design) wrath, greed and sinfulness should come (lit., rain) down on him from the monster demons and constellations (above), and that these should fill his mind. Thus he should become even more demonic, greedy and lustful. And when the male creature (man) was born, they called him "the first human being," namely Gēhmurd.[69]

Then those two lion-shaped archdemons, the male and the female, again devoured some of the offspring of their companions, and lascivousness and (the urge to) mate filled them. And they united with bodies intertwined. And that (demon) *Āz* that had filled them with the offspring of the monster demons which they had devoured, now formed and fashioned, in the same manner, another, a female body, with bones, nerves, flesh, arteries and skin.

[*The fashioning of the first woman, Murdiyānag, is now described in similar terms as the creation of Gēhmurd.*]

And (it was) in accordance with (the image of) the offspring (evocation) of the gods in female form (the Maiden of Light), whom she had seen in the chariot, that she also fashioned and formed that (woman).

And she (*Āz*) (also) associated with her, from the firmament, by origin and relationship, the constellations and planets above, so that over her (too) should come (lit., rain), from the archdemons and constellations, wrath, lasciviousness and sinfulness. Thus she (*Āz*) ensured that (such a) spirit should fill her (the first woman), (so that) she would become (even more) thievish and sinful, lascivious and covetous, and (so that) she (the woman) would deceive this man by lust. (Then) men would be born in the world of these two creatures (the first couple), and they, too, would become covetous and lascivious, wrathful, vengeful and ruthless, and they would injure water and fire, trees and plants. (They) would honor *Āz* and Greed, would fulfill the will of the demons and would (finally) go to Hell.

When that female creature was born, they called her "the female one of the glories," (namely), Murdiyānag. And when those two creatures, male and female, were born in the world, and had been raised and grew up, then *Āz*, the demons and the archdemons were full of joy. The leader of the archdemons (*Āz*) organized an assembly of the monster demons and archdemons. And she (then) said to those two people, "I have created earth and heaven, Sun and Moon, water and fire, trees and plants, wild and tame animals, for your sake, so that you will delight in them and be glad, and will (then) do my will."

And she (*Āz*) assigned a terrible dragon, whose nature was of the monster demons, to watch over the two children (the first human couple), and (she said), "He (the dragon) should guard them and not allow anyone to take them away from us."—For these monster demons and archdemons are very afraid of the gods.—"May no one come upon us and strike or bind us (to take them away); for these two children (of ours) have been formed and fashioned after the form and shape of the gods."

When the first human being (Gēhmurd) and "the female one of the glories" (Murdiyānag), the first male and female persons, began living on earth, then Greed awoke in them, and wrath filled them. And they started to clog up springs, to injure trees and plants, to be raging on earth and become greedy. They had no fear of the gods. And they did not see these five Elements (of Light dispersed in the world), on account of which the world is ordered, and (even now) they torture (them) unrelentingly.

Text H

[Title]:   The discourse on the soul (*gyān*) and the body (*nasāh*)

... This its (the fetus's) soul (*gyān*) (gradually) grows in life, power, light, fragrance and beauty, and at the (due) time (the child) is born. And when it (the human being) is born, it is also nourished in body and soul by these abortions of the demons and by that (matter) which is mixed with (the essence of) the gods; (thus) it grows and reaches maturity. It becomes a garment for *Āz* and a cover for sensual lust. And it injures and tortures water, fire, trees, and (other) creatures, its own family. It makes *Āz* and Lust glad, for it fulfills their wishes and instructions. But it makes neither water nor fire nor trees nor (their) creatures happy. For it becomes their enemy and tormenter. And it does not perceive (the truth), for *Āz* keeps it ignorant and evil in spirit (*duzravān*). And up to that hour and that constellation in which the child is born, it is not afflicted by (its) bigger companions. Up to this point (birth) the child lives and exists (unharmed); but then (after birth) it is afflicted by vengeance and sorrow. Then the child dies. (But if) it is reared (grows), it suffers (punishment as) expiation for its own deeds. All people that are born in the world, both male and female, are created by *Āz*.

From water, plants and foods of every kind which come to *Āz* (as greed) through man and are eaten by her, from (all this), by deception, *Āz* fashions and forms the child.[70] If that water and (those) plants remained in (different) places on mountains and in steppes and were not brought to men and (hence) to *Āz* (as food), then men would not be born from them. But when they are brought to men, *Āz* fashions and forms from them, by her deceptiveness, (the body of) the child. (It is) just like an architect who wants to build a palace and who uses his knowledge (first) to divide the palace into individual buildings (with their) gates, (plans it), and (then) builds it (completely). (Or it is) like a tailor who uses his knowledge to make a gown from different materials, or like a painter, who uses his skill to paint a picture with different colors. Now if those building materials for the palace and the materials for the gown and the colors for the picture which these craftsmen put together by their skill . . . were to remain unassembled, then no palace, gown, or picture would be created. . . . But when the craftsmen, with great care, combine those different building materials, cloths and colors, then (one can see how) they build, sew or paint the palace, the gown or the picture . . .

Thus also *Āz*, whose children are smitten, and who (herself) formed and fashioned (them), [nourishes herself] with the offspring of the demons and the mixture of the gods (with *hylē*), which are mixed into water and plants . . .[71]

3. *The Living Spirit and the Mother of Life create the World* (Sogdian)

This Sogdian text, the last page from a cosmogonic passage, uses the image of the Oriental bazaar to describe the world created by the gods for the purpose of extracting the Light from the "mixture" with *hylē*, matter, to which it has succumbed. Translation follows Henning.

[The Father of Light orders the Living Spirit and the Mother of Life to create[72] the world]: ". . . and clean them (the Elements of Light) of the poison of Ahriman and (thus) purify them; and then raise them to Paradise."

Thereupon at once the Lord of the Seven Climes (the Living Spirit) and the Mother of the Righteous Ones began to plan how to arrange this world. They began to fashion it. First they made five rugs, on which they seated the Keeper of Splendor (the first son of the Living Spirit). Under them they formed ten firmaments and set up one magic twelve-faceted lens. There they seated a Son of God as watcher, so that in all the ten firmaments the demons could do no harm. Furthermore he (sic) evoked forty angels, who hold up the ten firmaments.

In each firmament they fashioned twelve gates; they constructed another four gates in each of the four directions, there where those angels stand. The thickness of the ten firmaments is ten myriad parsangs; again, (the thickness) of the air (between them) is one myriad parsang.

For each of the twelve gates in each of the firmaments they constructed six thresholds, to each thresholds thirty bazaars, in each bazaar twelve rows, [in each row two sides].[73] On one side they made 180 stalls, on the other side (another) 180. In every stall they fettered and caged *yakshas* and demons, the males and the females separately.[74]

Thereupon the Maker of All (Vishparkar, the Living Spirit) called the Lord of the firmaments. They[75] seated him on a throne in the seventh heaven[76] and made him the lord and king over all the ten firmaments.

Then, below the firmaments, they fashioned a revolving wheel and (sic) zodiac. Within the zodiac they fettered those of the demons of Darkness that were the most iniquitous, vicious, and rebellious. They made the twelve constellations and the seven planets rulers over the whole Mixed World, and set them in opposition to each other.[77]

From all the demons that had been imprisoned in the zodiac they weaved, warp and woof, the roots, veins and links.[78] In the lowest firmament they bored a hole[79] and suspended the zodiac from it. Two Sons of God (sons of the Living Spirit) were placed by them (there) as watchers, so as to . . . the Superior Wheel continually.[80]

Notes

1. Cf. Sundermann, *Mittelpersische und parthische kosmogonische und Parabeltexte der Manichäer*, pp. 9–80 (cosmogonic texts).
2. Henning, "A Sogdian Fragment of the Manichaean Cosmogony," p. 310.
3. Henning, *op. cit.*, pp. 310f.
4. Henning, *op. cit.*, p. 311.
5. Cf. Henning, *ibid.*
6. The First Man had advanced to the area of the dark winds, into the middle of the Realm of Darkness (Henning).
7. For the prayer of the First Man, compare Schaeder, *Studien*, p. 343, n. 31.
8. It is the Living Spirit that calls the First Man, and it is his call, descending to him as fast as a streak of lightning, that is personified as the God Call (*Xrōshtag*).
9. *Mir. Man.* I, pp. 177–203.
10. Boyce, *Reader*, pp. 60–76 (text y).

11. M. Hutter, *Manis kosmogonische* Šābuhragān-*Texte*.
12. Boyce, *Reader*, p. 60.
13. Henning, "A Sogdian Fragment," p. 306.
14. Henning, *ibid*.
15. Cf. E. Feldmann, *Die "Epistula Fundamenti" der nordafrikanischen Manichäer*.
16. Cf. Asmussen and Böhlig, *Gnosis III*, pp. 103–8.
17. Cf. E. Beck, *Ephräms Polemik gegen Mani und die Manichäer*, ch. II–IV. Cf. also Asmussen and Böhlig, *op. cit.*, pp. 123–44.
18. Dodge, *Fihrist* II, pp. 773–88. Cf. also Asmussen and Böhlig, *op. cit.*, pp. 144–56.
19. M. Heuser, *Der manichäische Mythos nach den koptischen Quellen*. Phil. Diss. Bonn, 1992. An English translation of this book is being prepared by M. Franzmann.
20. Cf. Hutter, Šābuhragān-*Texte*, pp. 124–35.
21. Hutter, *op. cit.*, pp. 130–34.
22. Cf. Hutter, *op. cit.*, pp. 140–47.
23. Cf. Hutter, *op. cit.* pp. 135–39.
24. Cf. Reeves, *Jewish Lore in Manichaean Cosmogony*.
25. Cf. Hutter, "Das Erlösungsgeschehen im manichäisch-iranischen Mythos."
26. The Living Spirit and the Mother of Life.
27. That is, the lunar nodules.
28. That is, the rescued light.
29. This is a reference to something missing in the previous portion.
30. Atlas, the fifth son of the Living Spirit.
31. Cf. Sundermann, *Parabeltexte*, p. 56, n. 4.
32. This is the fifth or sixth earth. Compare Sundermann, *Parabeltexte*, p. 38, n. 3.
33. For a commentary on this section, compare Hutter, Šābuhragān-*Texte*, pp. 17–23.
34. This is the first son of the Living Spirit.
35. These are, in effect, the five Elements of Light (MP *amahrāspandān*).
36. The first deity of the second creation.
37. The Great Builder who builds the New Paradise as a place of rest for the gods engaged in the struggle.
38. The term "splendor and beauty of the gods" refers to the divine light spread out in the world.
39. The fourth son of the Living Spirit, called Taskirbyazd in Persian texts.
40. Compare the description of their subjugation in the Iranian text M 292 II (Sundermann, *Parabeltexte*, pp. 48f.)
41. The terms "lord of the house," "lord of the village," "lord of the tribe," "lord of the land" and "lord of the watchposts" are descriptions of the God Mithra in the Avesta, and are here personified by Mani as the five sons of the Living Spirit. Compare Hutter, *op. cit.*, pp. 130f.
42. Upon the Living Spirit's vanquishing them.
43. It is noteworthy that Ohrmizd, the First Man, clothed in the elements (his sons), vanquishes the powers of Darkness in this text. In most other texts he himself is vanquished by them. The idea appears again in Turkish cosmological texts. Compare ch. XXVIII, text 4.
44. The fifth son of the Living Spirit.
45. For a commentary on this portion, compare Hutter, *op. cit.*, pp. 49–55.
46. This may be the Column of Glory.
47. Within that calendric span.
48. On the Iranian calendar, compare Boyce, *Reader*, p. 68; also Boyce, "On the Calendar of Zoroastrian Feasts"; *idem*, "Iranian Festivals."
49. This is a unit of ten seconds.
50. This is a Zoroastrian term (Pahl. *rabih*), meaning "noon, midday."
51. This refers to the conjecture that before the struggle between Light and Darkness the sun stood still and there was always summer and noon (Hutter).
52. When the sun stood still before being set into motion by the Living Spirit, it was always day, or noon. Now that it rotates, the days and months and seasons are brought about.

53. Boyce points out that "the Zoroastrian calendar had consisted of 12 months of 30 days each, but at the beginning of the Sasanian period this was modified by the addition of 5 extra days, set after the 12th month and called officially the *Gah* (< *Gāthā*) days. . . . The explanation offered here for the existence of these 5 days is evidently prompted by the observation that the time of the sun's course across the sky is longer in spring and summer than in winter and autumn." Boyce, *Reader,* p. 70.

54. Probably Babylon and its neighbors are meant by An-Iran (An-Ēran) here. Compare Boyce, *ibid.*

55. Cf. Boyce, *ibid.*

56. For a commentary on the preceding text, compare Hutter, *op. cit.,* pp. 78–80.

57. A savior figure, probably the Third Messenger or Jesus.

58. This is a reference to the story about the seduction of the archons.

59. The word is in the plural.

60. This is a very free translation.

61. For a commentary on this portion, compare Hutter, *op. cit.,* pp. 78–80.

62. Literally, form, fashion (MP *dēsān*).

63. According to the myth ("Seduction of the Archons"), the Third Messenger (Narisah) showed himself to the male demons as a beautiful young girl, but to the female demons as a handsome youth.

64. Because they had devoured the fruits and buds, and with them the divine light they contain.

65. Literally, offensive smell, stench.

66. Here it is clear that the great variety of languages is regarded as something demonic.

67. Man is made in the image of a divine being, the Third Messenger, and has a divine soul, but his body and mind are filled with demonic thoughts, urges, and powers.

68. They are regarded as negative demonic forces.

69. The creation of the first male human being (Adam in Coptic texts) and of the first woman (Eve) merges the processes of procreation and fashioning.

70. Partaking of food is due to greed (*Āz*) in man, and actually feeds *Āz* (as the demon of Greed) who thereby misleads man to devour the light in the food, and thus constantly hurt his own divine nature.

71. Interpreting this peculiar sentence in a wider perspective, Hutter explains, "From such passages one can deduct that the aim of this institution is that man should discern the fraud and deception of *Āz* . . . and should act accordingly. In spite of the fact that man is smitten by *Āz*, he should not belong to the 'smitten children' of *Āz*, but become a 'New Man.'" Hutter, *op. cit.,* p. 115.

72. Or rather, to "arrange" or "fashion." As Henning points out, "The Manichaeans, strictly speaking, used the word *create* only of the process by which a divinity produces another divine being, of lower rank, by emanating it out of its own substance." Henning, "A Sogdian Fragment," p. 317, n. 1.

73. It seems that a whole line was omitted here by the scribe (Henning).

74. Hence steps are taken to prevent further procreation by the Powers of Darkness (Henning).

75. The Living Spirit and the Mother of Life.

76. The seventh firmament is the seventh counting from below. Compare *Kephalaia* 170,23ff. Here the King of Honor (the second son of the Living Spirit) resides and rules the lower seven firmaments. The upper three are within the realm of the Keeper of Splendor. However, we do note confusions in order.

77. Compare *Kephalaia* 167,14–15: "The twelve *zodia* which are attached to the *sphaira* as well as the five stars that rotate on them, they are all by nature archons (i. e., evil powers). They are all enemies and foes of one another." The text goes on to explain that the Living Spirit, "the great craftsmen who has fashioned all worlds," put them into opposition to one another.

78. On the roots, veins, links, compare Henning, "A Sogdian Fragment," p. 313, n. 8.

79. The North Pole. "The roots, etc., of the zodiac are passed through this hole and attached to the Superior Wheel, which lies before the *Rex honoris* [the King of Honor] in the seventh firmament." Henning, "A Sogdian Fragment," p. 313, n. 9.

80. In the text M 98 R 3–6 it says (in Henning's translation), "And they (i. e., the Living Spirit and the Mother of Life) suspended it (i. e., the zodiac) from the lowest firmament and, to make it turn ceaselessly at call, they set over it two angels, a male and a female." (Henning, *op. cit.*, pp. 313ff., n. 10). As Henning shows, in comparison with that document, "the description of the firmaments is complete in our text, except for two or three words" (Henning, *ibid.*).

CHAPTER NINETEEN

Prose Texts on Eschatology

As the previous chapter made clear, cosmogonic and eschatological texts were often closely related. Eschatological events lead to a clear separation between the principle of Light and the principle of Darkness as they had existed in the beginning. This final separation is not brought about without pain and suffering, epitomized by the "Great Fire" at the end of time that burns up the old cosmos to usher in the New Aeon. The Great Fire is a symbol of the purification that is necessary before the eschatological age can be ushered in. Another basic symbol of that great transition is the judgment of the quick and the dead in a final tribunal, headed by Xradeshahryazd, the "God of the World of Wisdom," who is no other than Jesus at his second coming. The scene is depicted in detail in the *Šābuhragān,* the Middle Persian work Mani wrote for Shāhpur I, and a substantial portion of this text has been preserved.[1] Here Mani's use of Matthew 24 and 25 as the basis of his eschatology is evident, though he uses Persian names and terms and shifts the emphasis of the biblical account to suit his own teaching. Thus it is not those who have fed and clothed and given shelter to the poor who find acceptance in the eyes of the Judge, but those who have done this to the "righteous ones," the Manichaean elect. This narrowing down of the biblical message in the interest of the Manichaean Church must certainly be an outcome of Mani's interpretation of the New Testament. Yet in spite of the limited perspective of this view, the resonance of this message in Asia Major almost exceeded that of the Nestorian Church.

First, we render here the *Šābuhragān,* which was widely disseminated in Persian and Central Asian lands, in Middle Persian, Uighur, and even Chinese, perhaps also in the Sogdian language. Second, we bring excerpts from the *Book of Giants,* its eschatological portions, which seem closely connected with the *Šābuhragān* and were widely known in Central and East Asia, as shown by over twelve texts (consisting of various fragments) written in different languages. From the *Book of Giants,* we have selected here a few portions pertaining to the Great Fire.

241

Third, we give here a Sogdian eschatological fragment (M 178) that describes the New Aeon awaiting the righteous one, after he endures the suffering and pain of the end of time.

1. Eschatological portions of the Šābuhragān (Persian)

The various manuscript pages that have been preserved bear intermediate titles that do not always mark the beginning of a new chapter, but are rather page head-lines indicating a shift to a new theme. Our translation is based on MacKenzie's edition and translation as well as on Hutter's new German translation and annotation of the text. This text is, then, eschatological in content, and it seems that its words and images had a far-reaching effect on people in Central Asia, even beyond the Manichaean Church, leaving its mark both on secular literature[2] as well as on Buddhist thought and imagery.[3]

[Title A]:   [The two principles of] the *Šābuhragān*

> . . . And they (the false prophets) say, "We are the ones who obey the instructions of the gods, [and you should go] along this path of ours." Most men [are] deceived and walk according to their (the false prophets') will (to do) evil deeds. And the righteous one (*dēnāvar*) who does not believe in his [own] religion will also follow suit. And at that time, when this is the state of affairs in the world, a great sign will appear on the earth, in heaven, on the Sun and the Moon (and) in the constellations and the stars. Then that god Xradeshahr (the God of the World of Wisdom, that is, Jesus as Judge), he who first [gave] that male creation, the original first human being (Adam), wisdom and knowledge, and (who) afterwards from time to time and from [age] to age sent wisdom and knowledge to man[kind]—in that last [age], just before the Renewal (of the world)—that god Xradeshahr, together [with]

[Title B]:   On the coming of the Son of Man

> [all] the gods (*yazdān*) and righteous ones (*dēnāvarān*) . . . will then stand [up] within the heavens, and a great call will resound and will be heard in the whole world. And those gods who, in the cosmos of heavens and earths, are lords of the house, lords of the village, lords of the tribe, lords of the land, lords of the watchposts (border guards) and vanquishers of demons will (all) bless Xradeshahr. And the men who are rulers in the world will quickly go to him and pay homage (to him) and accept his commands. And lustful, wicked and tyrannous men will repent. Then [Xrad]eshahr will [send] messengers to the [East] and West. They will go and [lead] the righteous ones together with their helpers, as well as the [wicked] ones, together with their accomplices, [before] Xradeshahr, and they will pay him homage.
>
> And the righteous ones will say to him, "[(Our) God and] our Lord, if it please you, we shall tell you something about what (these) sinners [have

done] to us." And God Xradeshahr will answer them, "Look upon me and rejoice. But whoever may have harmed you, I shall bring him to justice for your sake, and I will demand (his) * conviction.[4] But everything which you wish to tell me, I already know."

Then he blesses them and quiets their hearts and sets them on the right hand, and they will be in bliss [in the company of] the gods. And he separates the evildoers from the righteous ones, and sets them up on the left hand, and accuses them and says, "You shall not have a complete resurrection,[5] nor shall you become wholly bright, for [that] sin that you have committed and that suffering caused by deceit which you have brought about, that you [have done] to the Son of Man . . ."

[Title C]:   On the judgment and the separation

[And to the helpers] of the righteous ones who stand on his right hand he says,[6] "Welcome you who are blessed by the Father of Greatness, for I was hungry and thirsty, [and] you gave (me) food and nourishment. I was naked and you clothed me. I was ill and you took care of me. I was bound and you released me. I was a captive and you set me free. I was an alien and a wanderer and you took me into your houses." [Then] those helpers of the righteous ones will deeply venerate him and will say to him, "Lord, you are God and immortal, and *Āz* and Lust do not overcome you. You have neither hunger nor thirst, and [pain] and harm do not afflict you. When [was it that] we did this service for you?" And Xradeshahr will say to them, "That which you did [to] the righteous ones, that [service] you did to me. And I shall give you Paradise as a reward." He will [give] them great joy.

Then he speaks thus to the [evil]doers who stand on his left hand, "You evildoers, you were materialistic[7] and greedy, evil in your actions and intent on gaining material goods. I charge you, for I was hungry and thirsty, and you did not give (me) food or nourishment. I was naked and you did not clothe me. I was ill and you did not take care of me. I was a captive and an alien and you did not receive me into your houses." And the evildoers will say to him, "Our God and Lord, when was it that you [were] so distressed and we did not redeem you?" And Xradeshahr will say to them, "What the righteous ones have said (about you), by that you have sinned against me, and therefore I bring a charge against you."

[Title D]:   The two great principles of the *Šābuhragān*

"You are sinners, for you [were] deceitful friends of the righteous ones. And you have distressed (them) and shown them no mercy. And toward the gods (too) you are sinful and guilty." Then he appoints angels over those evildoers, and they seize them and cast them into Hell.

And when Xradeshahr sets the world in order, then months and years will come to an end, and weakness will befall *Āz* and Lust. And Pain and Sorrow, . . . and Hunger and Torment will tremble,[8] [and] will not (be able to) sin (any more). Wind, water and fire [will] be given free reign in the world, and mild rains will fall. And [trees], grass, fruits and plants will grow . . . And [in] the world there will be . . . and contentment. And mankind will listen to the religion. And all . . . benevolent and soul-loving. . . love . . . will shine. And when they pass by a graveyard or a cemetery, they [will] see [them]. [Then] they will remember their own kith and kin who have passed away, and they will say, "Alas for those who have died at the time of sin and were lost! But who can raise up their heads from the place of rest and show them this joy in which we now find ourselves?"

(Here) ends (the chapter on) "The coming of the Life-giver."

(Here) begins (the chapter on) "The ascension of X[radeshahr]."
. . . Xradeshahr . . . earth . . . mankind . . . and will himself [rise] up to . . . his own place. [And wind], water and fire . . . [will he raise] up [from the earth] in joy . . . . wind, water and [fire will cease]

[Title E = D]: The two great principles of the *Šābuhragān*

running. Then it will be the time of the Renewal of the cosmos of earth and heaven. And from the cosmos they will cause [the dead] to rise, and the righteous ones will ascend to [Paradise]. And the animals and trees and winged birds and water creatures and reptiles of the earth will disappear from the earth and go [to Hell].

[Then] wind, water and fire will be removed from that lowest earth, on which that House-Lord (Atlas) and the Wind-Raising God (the King of Glory) are standing. And that New World and the prison of the demons, which the New World–Creating God (the Great Builder) has erected will be fastened [to Paradise] and made fast . . . Then [will] Ohr[mizd], the Moon God, . . . the sheath (*niyām*) of the cosmos . . .

And when that radiance and beauty of [the gods] rises up, then [darkness] will enclose the cosmos of earths and heavens and will cover the whole world from the highest heaven to the lowest earth. And the sheath and arrangement of it (the cosmos, the old world) will become slack.

Then Mihryazd (the Living Spirit) will [descend] from the chariot of the Sun to the cosmos and a call will resound. And the gods who, in the different heavens, are lord of the house, lord of the village, lord of the tribe, lord of the land, lord of the border guard (the five sons of the Living Spirit) and vanquishers (of demons), and who hold the world in order [and] vanquish *Āz* and Ahriman, the demons (*dēvs*), she-devils (*peris*), demons of wrath (*xēšmān)*, monster demons (*mazanān*) and archdemons (*ašveštar*) . . .

[Title F]: On the collapse of the cosmos

Then that House-Lord God who stands on the lowest earth and holds the earths in order (Atlas)[9] (and) that Wind-Raising God who (is) with him (and) who raises up wind, water and fire (the King of Glory) and the Village-Lord God who stands on this earth and who keeps that gigantic dragon subdued in the northern clime (the Adamas of Light), together with (their) helpers, will all (proceed) to Paradise. Then the earths will all collapse, one upon the other, down onto those four (lower) layers, the prison of the demons.

[And the God] in Female Form, [the Mother] of God Ohrmizd, will appear from the chariot of the Sun and look upon the heavens. And that Lord of the Land, who stands above all heavens and holds the hands of those [five] gods (the five Elements of Light) . . . and that [other] god who [stands] . . . south . . . (the Keeper of Splendor and the King of Honor), together with those five gods who (at) first, with their own radiance and beauty had been seized by *Āz* and Ahriman, [and the male and] female demons . . . Paradise . . . . and those five gods who [at first? far from?] Paradise and the gods, had been struck down by *Āz* and Ahriman and the male and female demons, they too in Paradise will again become as whole and like (as they were at) their first creation (by) the God Ohrmizd, when they had not yet been struck down by *Āz* and the demons. And that World-Bearing [God] who keeps the earths and heavens (well) ordered (Atlas) leads them up to [Para]dise. Then the ten heavens and the one revolving circle of the zodiac with climes, thrones, houses and villages, tribes and lands, regions [and borders], guards and gates, months, days and [double hours], and the four (lower) layers (or earths), the prison [of the demons], and the (upper) earths with . . . thrones (?) and climes, mountains and valleys and excavated canals, and Hell, with *Āz* and Lust, Ahriman and the male and [female] demons, [witches, demons of wrath], monster demons and archdemons, [when they are all] assembled and [imprisoned] therein, (then) they (the earths) will all collapse.

[Title G]:   *On the fierceness of the Great Fire*

And (the context of) those three [poi]sonous dark ditches and the conflagration which have been made around the cosmos will be poured over them. And that raging conflagration which (was there to) surround and protect the cosmos on all sides will go on burning in the North and East, South and West, and (in the) height and depth, [breadth?] and length (of the cosmos). [And] the cosmos of earths and heavens will burn in that conflagration like wax in a fire.

And *Āz* and [Lust], Ahriman and the demons, the demons of wrath, the monster [demons and arch]demons and . . . will suffer for [1],486 years, will be tormented and writhe in distress. And the power and energy of that splendor and beauty of the gods, which have remained in the cosmos of earths and heavens and had been struck down and left back, vanquished by *Āz* and the demons, will now issue from that conflagration, becoming pure and ascending to the Sun and the Moon. And they will become divine (or gods) in the form of Ohrmizd. And together with the Sun and the Moon they will ascend to Paradise. And the God Ohrmizd from the northern region, [the God] Rōshnshahr (the Third Messenger) from the East, and the New World–[Creating] God (the Great Builder) from the South, Mihryazd (the Living Spirit) from the western region, their (respective) abodes, together with their (entourage) and hel[pers], will stand on that structure of the New Paradise, around that conflagration, and will look into it. And those [right]eous ones, [also], who [are] in Paradise, will sit [on] (their) thrones of Light.

[Title H]:   *On the souls [of the] evildoers.*

Then they will come into the presence of the gods and stand [around] that conflagration. [And the evildoers] in the conflagration [will be tormented] and writhe in agony. But the conflagration will not harm the righteous, just as now, too, this fire, namely the Sun and the Moon, does not harm (them). And when the evildoers are tormented and writhe in that conflagration, then they will look up and recognize the righteous ones and will beseechingly say to them, "May your good fortune befall us. Give us a lifeline into our hands to pull us [up], and save us from this burning. We did not think that it would befall us so [severely?] and harshly; but if we had known, we [would] have believed what was told to us. And [we] would have accepted the religion and . . . , and we would have subdued $\bar{A}z$ [and Greed]; to you we have been . . . helpers. And . . . suffering . . ."

[And the righteous ones] will say, "Do not prate, you evildoers, [for] we remember that in the [world] you were greedy and lustful and oppressive . . . . And you [did not] consider the soul (*ruvān*), and [to us you have been] hostile. You have pursued and persecuted us from land to land, and you did not believe [that] we are the ones who fulfill the wishes of the gods. And you did not consider (this), "Misfortune may befall us [and] hold us . . . ." But if you had [accepted] the wisdom and knowledge of the gods from us, and had been soul-loving (*ruvān-friyīh*) and had gone on the path of the gods and had been (our) travelling companions and helpers, then your bodies would not have [brought forth] $\bar{A}z$ and Lust. And [you would not have] kept company with robbers, thieves and . . .[10]

[Title I]:   *The two principles of the* Šābuhragān

Then (your) souls would not have come [to eternal] misfortune. [Now] do not beseech us, [and do not] prate and complain . . . that we have come into the presence of the gods. We have not come for (the sake of) you evildoers, but we have come . . . for (the sake of) those who were well-disposed toward the righteous ones in that [old] world. Because of you [evil]doers they did not see that it was necessary for them to join the religion and to do and accept (good) deeds, to cast off $\bar{A}z$ and Lust and to be travelling companions of the righteous ones, [and] to be completely happy. And therefore they have come to (this) grave misfortune, and . . . in [this] conflagration they are tormented and writhe and suffer distress. Now we fill . . . $\bar{A}z$ and Lust . . . and . . . we . . . with you . . .

And he (the half-righteous one) will not be bound in the eternal prison together with Ahriman [and] the demons. But you (may) rejoice at this misfortune, for it has come upon you from $\bar{A}z$ and Lust and your own actions! And how should we save you from this torment, when this (is) a judgment according to the justice [of the gods?].

And [then] every soul which shall be born in a body with *Āz* and Lust, that bears *Āz* and Lust and does not cast them off, and becomes unrestrained and greedy and keeps to (?) the [creatures] of Ahriman, shall be bound with Ahriman [and] the demons in the [eternal] prison. And he who shall do the will of the gods [and] be a travelling companion and helper of the righteous ones, [and he] too, who is well-disposed to them . . . shall be . . . with the gods [in] Paradise. . . . the evildoers in the grievous burning, and they will repent and be destressed.

[Title J]: *The two principles of the* Šābuhragān

And [those other] souls which bear *Āz* and Lust in the body and which—as long as earth and [heaven] stand—shall not accept the wisdom and the knowledge of soul-gathering and do [not enter] into the [religious] community, but have also not become [evil]doers, they that go into [statue-labor (rebirth) and] into war (are reborn on earth) and (further) fulfill the will of *Āz* and [Lust], and serve the evildoers, but also bestow [on the righteous ones] good and pleasant things, . . . shall not be . . .

2. *Fragments of eschatological texts from the Book of Giants* (Persian)

As already noted, about a dozen fragments of the Manichaean *Book of Giants,* written in Middle Persian, Sogdian, and Uighur, were found in Turfan. It is clear that this book of Mani's was based on an ancient Jewish *Book of Giants,* originally written in Aramaic. Remnants of it were found in cave 4 of Qumran. The connections between the Jewish *Book of Giants,* which belonged to Jewish Enochic literature, and the corresponding Turfan fragments were first noticed by Henning,[11] then discussed by J. T. Milik[12] and recently reviewed and further analyzed by J. C. Reeves.[13]

Of the many fragments (A–T, including Coptic texts) dealt with by Henning, and augmented by Sundermann ("Leningrad fragments"), we present here only columns D–F of Henning's text F.[14]

(col. D) . . . sinners . . . is visible, where out of this fire your soul (*grīv*) will be prepared (for the transfer) to eternal ruin (?). And as for you, sinful, misbegotten sons of the Wrathful Self (*grīv xēšmēn*), confounders of the true words of that Holy One, hinderers of the actions of Good Deed, aggressors upon Piety . . .

(col. E) . . . and on brilliant wings they (the righteous ones) shall fly and soar further beyond and above that Fire, and shall gaze into its depth and height. And those righteous ones that will stand around it, outside and above, they shall have power over the Great Fire, and over everything in it . . .

(col. F) . . . they are purer and stronger [than the] Great Fire of Ruin that sets the worlds ablaze.[15] They shall stand around it, outside, and

above, and splendor shall shine over them. Further beyond and above it
they shall fly (?) after those souls that may try to escape from the Fire . . .

3. On the World of Light as the destiny of the righteous ones (Sogdian)

This text is a description of the World of Light, as it existed originally, and as it
awaits those who have undergone suffering for the sake of the gods of Light. According to the Coptic Manichaean *Psalm-Book* (9,12–16), "The Kingdom of Light . . . consisted [and hence will consist] of five Greatnesses, and they are [1] the Father and
[2] the twelve Aeons and [3] the Aeons of Aeons, [4] the Living Air, [5] the Land
of Light, the Great Spirit breathing in them, nourishing them with his Light."

In our Sogdian text, only the description of the third, fourth and fifth Greatness
is preserved. There follows a description of the life of those who have been led,
by the gods of Light, into this realm of the New World.[16]

. . . .

The third: the blessed Places (= Aeons), countless and innumerable,
wherein dwell the Light gods, angels, elements, and powers in great bliss
and joy.

The fourth: the Pure Air in the Light Paradise, wondrous, beautiful to
behold, immeasureable in its goodness for them (the Light gods and others). By supernatural power it shall, on its own, bring into being the gods'
marvelous dress and garment, throne, diadem, and fragrant wreath, ornaments and finery of all kinds.

The fifth: the Light Earth, *self-existent, eternal, miraculous; in
*height it is beyond *reach (?), its *depth cannot be perceived. No enemy
and no attacker walk this Earth: its divine pavement is of the substance
of diamond (*vajra*) that never shakes. All good things are born from it:
beautiful, graceful hills covered completely with flowers, grown to perfection; green fruit-bearing trees whose fruits never *drop, never rot, and
never have worms; springs flowing with ambrosia that fill all of Paradise,
its groves and plains; countless mansions and palaces, thrones and
*benches that exist in perpetuity for ever and ever.

Thus is Paradise ordered, in these Five Greatnesses. They (that dwell
there) are serene in quietude and know no fear. They live in the Light,
free from darkness; in eternal life, free from death; in health without
sickness; in joy free of sorrow; in charity without hatred; in the company
of friends, without separation; in a shape that is not destroyed; in a divine body where there is no decay; on ambrosial food without limits,
where they endure no toil or hardship. Their appearance is beautiful,
their power strong, their wealth bountiful; of poverty they know not even
the name. Rather, they are well equipped, beautiful, and adorned; no
harm comes to their bodies. Their garment of joy is finery that never gets
soiled, of seventy myriad kinds, set with jewels. Their places are never
destroyed . . .

Notes

1. D. N. MacKenzie, "Mani's *Šābuhragān*" I, II; Hutter, *Šābuhragān-Texte,* pp. 116–23.
2. In the Old Turkish inscriptions (seventh/eighth century) of the Mongolian Steppes, there is a passage reminiscent of our text. Thus one Turkish Khan assures us that he has clothed and fed and provided for his people. Here it says, "I brought the people to life who were going to perish, and nourished them. I furnished the naked people with clothes and I made the poor people rich and the few people numerous." Quoted from T. Tekin, *A Grammar of Orkhon Turkic.* Bloomington and The Hague, 1968; p. 268; Turkic text p. 235 (Köl Tigin inscription, E 29). A similar passage, partially preserved, is found in the Bilgä Kagan inscription (E 24). Tekin, *op. cit.,* p. 275. These phrases seem to have become standardized. Of course the possible influence of the Psalms on these oldest Turkic documents in an area as remote as the Mongolian Steppes must be taken into account, since both Nestorians and Manichaeans (mainly Sogdians) lived among the Turks. Compare especially Ps. 105 and 106, which seem to be echoed in the *Geschichtstheologie* (theology of history) of these first documents of the Turks. This is clearly evidenced by the fact that Nestorian and other crosses at times embellish the inscriptional stones. Compare J. G. Granö, "Archäologische Beobachtungen von meinen Reisen in den nördlichen Grenzgebieten Chinas in den Jahren 1906 und 1907," plates II and III, figs. 5 and 9.
3. The influence of the *Šābuhragān,* with its visions of Judgment, of Hell and of Heaven, and hence of Mt. 24 and 25, on old Turkic Buddhist literature is becoming increasingly clear in the most ancient stratum of that literature, written in the so-called ñ-dialect. See the forthcoming study by Geng Shimin, H.-J. Klimkeit and J. P. Laut, *Eine buddhistische Apokalypse. Die Höllen- und Himmelskapitel der alttürkischen Maitrisimit.*
4. Thus Hutter, *op. cit.,* p. 118. MacKenzie, "Mani's *Šābuhragān*" I, p. 507, translates, "I shall . . . seek *account (from him)."
5. Thus Hutter, *ibid.*; MacKenzie, *ibid.,* has, "May you not arise whole . . ."
6. The following passage is based on Mt. 25:31–46. For the Manichaean nuances compare Hutter, "Mt. 25:31–46 in der Deutung Manis," pp. 279–83.
7. Literally, subject to that which is material (*tančay*). Compare Boyce, *Word-List,* s.v. *tncyy*: "grieving for the body, concerned with material things (?)."
8. As Hutter points out, the negative powers are personified here. Hutter, *op. cit.,* p. 119, n. 11.
9. Here and in the following the sons of the Living Spirit are referred to.
10. Thus according to MacKenzie, *op. cit.,* p. 519. Hutter translates, "And thieves, robbers and . . . would [not] have believed (you)." Hutter, *op. cit.,* p. 122.
11. Cf. Henning, "The Book of Giants"; cf. also Sundermann, "Ein weiteres Fragment aus Manis Gigantenbuch."
12. J. T. Milik, "Turfan et Qumran. Livres des géants juif et manichéen"; *idem, The Books of Enoch. Aramaic Fragments of Qumran Cave 4.*
13. J. E. Reeves, *Jewish Lore in Manichaean Cosmogony. Studies in the* Book of Giants *Traditions.*
14. Henning, *op. cit.,* p. 68f.; cf. Boyce, *Reader,* pp. 82f. (text aa).
15. It is also an old Iranian notion that the pure cannot be harmed by the fire of the tribulation.
16. Translation after Henning.

Fragment of an illuminated Manichaean manuscript. Staatliche Museen—Preussischer Kulturbesitz, Museum für Indische Kunst, Berlin.

Texts on the Soul and Salvation

1. On knowledge as the prerequisite for salvation (Persian)

The theme of this text is central to Manichaeism. The involved style would suggest that the passage is from one of Mani's works (B).

> ... The wise and those who judge astutely are capable of discerning the unbounded, timeless and unmixed (undefiled) goodness of Paradise in the limited, temporal and mixed goodness of the world.[1] And likewise, on account of the finite and limited evil which may be experienced in the world, they can see the unbounded and unlimited evil of Hell. If limited and temporal goodness and evil as well as the mingling (of good and evil) were not seen in the world, then no one's mind would entertain the thought of staying far from evil and coming to goodness.[2]
>
> When the soul (gyān) (of man) does not have (lit., see) the knowledge it has acquired through ten thousand births, ...
>
> [a number of lines missing]
>
> ... (and if it does not see) the advantage which arises from recognizing timeless, eternal and unmixed goodness, then it needs a guide who will show it the way to redemption from evil and (the blessed state of) the soul, to eternal unmingled and unceasing goodness.
>
> May no one say, "If knowledge can come to man only through these portals which I have described above, then all those in whom these portals (of perception of the Light) are healthy should be similar and equal in knowledge."[3] My answer would be, "I have shown in many places in this book that the amount of knowledge the soul (of man) has determines its mixture in mortality (?)"[4] ...

2. On body and soul (Persian)

This passage is evidently also from one of Mani's writings (B). One of its interesting aspects is its echoing of the Pauline trichotomy of body (Gr. *sōma;* MP *tan*), bodily soul (Gr. *psychē;* MP *mēnōg*) and spirit or divine soul (Gr. *pneuma;* MP *gyān*). In Paul, the classical Greek term for "soul" (*psychē*) is understood as being bound up with the body of unredeemed man;[5] here, the classical Zoroastrian term for spirit (*mēnōg*) is related to the body (*tan*) and hence distinguished from the divine, imperishable soul (*gyān*). This new interpretation of *mēnōg* is noteworthy; it corresponds to Paul's revolutionary understanding of *psychē,* the immortal soul of the Greeks. Paul's view of man is, like Mani's, quite in accordance with Gnostic anthropological trichotomy. Of course the distinction between *mēnōg* and *gyān* is not always maintained in Iranian translations of Mani's writings, or in later Manichaean literature in Iranian languages.

> . . . From that which I have written above, it is clear to the discerning that (the spirit of the body) is of the same nature as the body. Now if these two, that which is corporeal (*tanīgirdīh*) and that which is psychic *(mēnōgīh),* are both dark, ignorant, harmful and by their nature one, and that they (together) constitute the being and nature of the body, then the question is: What is the substance and nature of the (divine) soul (*gyān*) itself? As the nature and substance of the (divine) soul have been described in many places in this book, this insight is not false, (namely,) that the (divine) soul is of different substance (*judēgōhr*) from the body, and is so mixed and bound up with the (corporeal) spirit of the body (*menōgīh i tan*), with wrath and greed and sensuality (?) in the body, as . . .[6]
> [*some lines missing*]
> Except when the substance is the same, the mixture and fusion and amalgamation (of two different things) cannot be such as in the case of pure silver. Because it is one, the mixture, fusion and amalgamation (of silver with silver) remains pure. But when the silver is mixed with copper or with any other (metal), then that amalgamation becomes evident, as for instance in the case of a copper *drachmē* or a *sitōg* (a small counterfeit coin). And just as silver (is mixed with copper), thus the soul [is amalgamated with] the power and corporeality of the body, (i. e., bound up in) bones, flesh, skin, blood, breath, . . . and filth, by the fetter of the spirit of the body (*mēnōgīh i tan*), . . .

3. *On the limbs of the soul* (Sogdian)

This text on the limbs of the soul describes the soul as ultimately invisible and intangible, and hence free from worldly bondage. In this description, reference is made to a saying taken from I Corinthians 2:9, which was frequently quoted in early Christian literature.[7] In the Coptic *Gospel of Thomas,* logion 17, it reads, "Jesus said, I shall give you what no eye has seen and what no ear has heard and what has never occurred to the human mind"; compare also the *Acts of Thomas,* 36: "But we speak about the world above . . . about things which eye has not seen nor ear heard, neither have they entered into the heart of sinful men, which God has prepared for those who love him."[8] In *Kephalaia* 15,19–24 Mani stresses that the Paraclete has revealed everything to him, adding, "All that the eye sees and the ear hears and that thought thinks and . . . , all (this) I have perceived through him." The logion, in different variations, was widely known in the East. It was often quoted in Islamic *hadith* literature (there, of course, with reference to Mohammed)[9] but also in two other instances in hitherto published Turfan texts. Thus in the Parthian fragment M 789 as well as in the Parthian text M 551 it says, in the same words, "I shall give you what the carnal eye has not seen, what the ears have not heard, and what has not been grasped by the hand."[10] It is not clear from which Manichaean scripture this saying (which does not mention the carnal tongue) derives. It could, perhaps, belong to the introduction of Mani's *Living Gospel,* which is called "The Living Gospel for Eye and Ear."[11]

The text translated here is part of a Sogdian mission history on the activity of Mār Addā.[12]

> [They asked], "What is the steed that is swifter than the wind?"
>
> Mār Addā answered them, "I have good thoughts and a [quick] mind, the [course?] of which is swifter [than the wind]. And I have [wisdom?], the luster of which is [brighter] than the sun. And I have provisions . . . , the taste of which is [sweeter] than honey."
>
> And the viziers (?) asked Mār Addā, "What shape does the soul have, oh Lord?"
>
> And Mār Addā answered, "The soul is similar to the body (in) that (it) has five limbs, (namely,) a head, two arms and two feet. The soul [is] exactly like that. [Life] is considered to be the first limb of the soul, power its second limb, light its [third] limb, beauty its fourth limb and fragrance its fifth limb. And its form and appearance are an image [of the body], just as [Jesus] said, "It cannot be seen with eyes of flesh, and the fleshly ear does not hear it; it cannot be touched by the hand of flesh, and it cannot be described completely by the [fleshly] tongue."

4. On the three days and the final victory of Light (Persian)

This text summarizes the occurrences of the "three days," or three major periods in world history, which is actually salvation history.[13] The "two dark nights" between the three days are not mentioned. The text, comparable to the contents of the Coptic *Kephalaia,* thus represents a type of didactic literature also known to Iranian and Central Asian Manichaeans.[14] The text ends with a note reminiscent of the hymns about Paradise and the Father of Light, and the ultimate triumph of Light (ch. I).

> [Title]: He teaches about the three great days
>
> And concerning the three days he teaches this: The first day is when God Ohrmizd [comes] with his sons for the battle. And its consummation [is the time] when God [Mihr], the Second One,[15] draws [him up], and when God Ohrmizd has ascended for a second [time].

[*a gap of unknown length*]

[The consummation] of the second day [is] the time when the Father of Greatness draws up the firmament. And the beginning of the third day is from that time, when all the battle-seeking ones (gods) go to the Father's place of refuge and are eternally joyful. And they have then forgotten all the harm and sorrow that they have experienced at the hands of Ahriman, the evildoer . . .

5. *The Final Salvation of the Light* (Parthian)

This is a text on final salvation, that is, on the return to the Realm of Light, after the Great Fire at the end of the world has burned itself out. As Boyce notes, the first part of the text "is concerned with one of the most difficult points of Man[ichaean] dogma, namely that there is a portion of Light which cannot be saved, but which is to be imprisoned with Darkness eternally. Both content and style suggest that the author is Mani. . . . The Parthian version must therefore be a translation."[16] After Mani's death, that dogma seems to have been debated hotly.

[Title]:   He teaches the supplication and prayer of all aeons

And the battle-seeking gods then lead and guide their own aeons and (that which is) of the same nature (as they are), (that) which they have called and established on the Great Earth;[17] (they call these aeons) again by divine command (or: spiritually) to the New Aeon (the New Paradise), and they set (them) down there,[18] as nomads who, going from one place to another with their tents, horses and herds, load up their tents and (then) unload them again. (There is left back) alone that Light which is so mingled with Darkness that it cannot be separated from it and that is not of the same nature with it (the Light) . . .

Furthermore, the five lights (the fettered Elements of Light, the limbs of the soul) which had made supplication to the First Man in the battle (saying), "Do not leave us to the limbs of Darkness, but send us power and a helper," and to whom God Ohrmizd (the First Man) had promised, "I will not leave you among the powers of Darkness," (prayed to him); (and he gave power), which was not of that (dark) power which inspired it (the unredeemed Light) to think, "The original mixture with Darkness brings me harm and oppression so harshly that I cannot be freed and separated from Darkness."[19] Rather, (he gave) that (saving) power of Light which (caused it to) know, "My being mixed (with Darkness) is such that I can (only) be purified and redeemed by the help of the God Ohrmizd and his brothers (the gods of the second and third creation)."

And they (the divine Elements of Light) prayed not because they did not believe (lit., think) that the God Ohrmizd would not help them if they did not pray, but rather because prayer was [a joy] for them. And (this) hope (or, support) and promise increased their power, as in the case of fighters whose power is increased when their friends strengthen (lit., clad) their voices and hearts by (their) zeal (in cheering them on).

But the gods will not be sad on account of that little light (left over) that will remain mixed with Darkness and cannot be separated (from it). For it is not for them to sorrow. Rather, on account of (their) peace and joy, which is a basic characteristic of theirs, they are of happy disposition, also because they have (already) vanquished and overcome Ahriman and his enmity. They are joyous, and wear within the garment of joy . . . , while outwardly they take on an armed, warlike appearance. And, having fettered him (Ahriman) in a prison of forgetfulness and having themselves become lords over it, their mind is happy, joyous and blissful, for there is no one left who could harm them.

And when the battle-seeking ones (the gods) have rested for a while in the New Aeon (the New Paradise), and when even that small part of the Earth of Light and its mountains (from which material was taken for the creation of the New Aeon) is restored, and when the "Last God" (the last portion of Light to be saved) stands there redeemed, with full power in his limbs, and when the gods of battle, together with the five Light Elements have recovered from their wounds, then all the "jewels,"[20] the "messengers" and the battle-seeking gods will stand before the Lord of Paradise in prayer and praise (literally, supplication). (These are) 1. first the God Ohrmizd, together with "the Last God," 2. the Mother of the Righteous, 3. the Friend of the Lights, 4. God Narisaf (the Third Messenger), 5. God Bām (the Great Builder), 6. the Living Spirit, 7. Jesus the Splendor, 8. the Maiden of Light, and 9. the Great Nous.[21]

These fathers of Light with their gods, messengers and aeons (then) raise their voices in prayer, all in one accord, with one (utterance of) praise, with one voice, with one speech and with one desire, and they (then) bring praise to the Great Jewel Sroshāv (the Father of Light), the Primeval One, the Righteous God, the Highest of Gods, and they say, "You are the Father of Light, existing since primeval times, since eternity; there is no destruction of your dominion. And that evildoer who boasted falsely and fought with your greatness is imprisoned and shut into a mighty grave from which he can never escape. And the (old) earth, the abode of the foes, the house (of Darkness), is thrown into confusion (?) and levelled. And over it we (the gods of Light) have erected the bright foundation of the New Aeon.[22]

Now you (the Father of Light) have no more foes and rivals; rather, eternal victory is yours. Come now, and have mercy upon us. Reveal to us your bright countenance, and your most lovely appearance, (to us) who yearn to turn to it, so that we may become happy and joyful. For we have long desired ardently (to behold you)."

Notes

1. They recognize that Paradise is, and that it already can be experienced, to a certain degree, in the world. Of course the same is true of Hell, as the next sentence shows.
2. Translation after Boyce, *Reader,* p. 88., n. 4.

3. Translation suggested by S.
4. Boyce observes that this sentence plainly implies "that the greatest possible spiritual knowledge of the true nature of existence can be obtained from Manichaeism, and hence the greatest hope of salvation." Boyce, *Reader,* p. 89, n. 8.
5. Compare I Cor. 15:44: "It is sown a physical body (*sōma psychikon*), it is raised a spiritual body (*sōma pneumatikon*)." That the Pauline trichotomy of body, soul of the body (*psychē*), and spirit (*pneuma*) also determines Manichaean thinking becomes clear in *Kephalaia* 269,17–31.
6. Body and soul are not "of one substance" (*evgōhr*) (or one nature). As Boyce explains in view of the following portion, "their union cannot therefore be compared with a mixture such as the blending of two portions of pure silver, whose result can only be pure silver, but rather with a blending of different substances, such as an alloy of silver and copper." Boyce, *ibid.,* p. 90, n. 4.
7. Compare Hennecke and Schneemelcher, eds., *NT Apocrypha.* Vol. I, 1st ed., London, 1963, p. 300. For quotations in early Church history compare Hennecke and Schnee-melcher, eds., *ibid.,* and Schneemelcher, ed., *NT Apocrypha.* Vol. II, London, 1965, pp. 144, 320, 463 and 752; P. Prigent, "Ce que l'oeil n'a pas vu, I Cor. 2,9" in *Theologische Zeitschrift* 14 (1958), pp. 416–29. The origin of the word is being discussed widely, as my colleague in New Testament studies at Bonn, Professor H. Merklein, kindly informs me.
8. Quoted after J. M. Robinson, ed., *The Nag Hammadi Library in English.* 3d ed., Leiden, 1988, p. 128, and Hennecke and Schneemelcher, eds., *NT Apocrypha.* vol. II, 1st ed., London, 1965, p. 463.
9. Cf. W. A. Graham, *Divine Word and Prophetic Word in Early Islam.* The Hague and Paris 1977, pp. 17ff.
10. HR II, 67f.
11. Cf. ch. XIII, text 1.
12. For the MP and Pth. parallels, compare ch. XVII.
13. For the Manichaean teaching on the "three days" and "two nights," compare Klimkeit and Schmidt-Glintzer, "Türkische Parallelen zum chinesisch-manichäischen Traktat."
14. Cf. Sundermann, "Iranische Kephalaiatexte."
15. Here the Living Spirit, the main god of the Second Creation.
16. Boyce, *Reader,* p. 84.
17. It is not clear what is meant by the "Great Earth" here. "Possibly there was an earth attached to the New Paradise, where beings of light dwelt temporarily before passing to the Paradise itself." Boyce, *Reader,* p. 84, n. 1.
18. Translated freely after Boyce, *ibid.* The term "of the same nature" (*hāmčihrag*) refers to "that part of the Living Self which was not liable to corruption, and will therefore be redeemed." Boyce, *ibid.*
19. Translation after Boyce, *ibid.*
20. Gods, but also redeemed divine souls.
21. This enumeration differs somewhat from the usual list of gods.
22. This is the New Paradise that will ultimately be connected with the eternal World of Light.

CHAPTER TWENTY-ONE

Letters and Admonitions

As we know from an-Nadīm's *Fihrist,* Mani and his successors wrote a great number of epistles, many of which are listed there.[1] Of these only a few can be identified.[2] First and foremost, there is the famous "Letter of the Seal," which Mani
wrote to his community from prison, just prior to his death. It was read out to the
congregation on special occasions like the Bema festival. In his letters, Mani apparently followed a Pauline practice wherein exhortations and admonitions to the community were frequently put in epistle form. It is clear that some of the letters which
were ascribed to Mani are spurious (for example, text 2). Besides these "didactic
letters"—which also included Mani's *Šābuhragān,* his epistle to the Sassanian king
Shāhpur I (translated in ch. XIX)—there are some authentic letters that give us
an insight into the life of the community. To some extent, their form corresponds
to other letters from the Silk Road, where communication was often in written form
(compare the Turkish letters in chapter XXXII).

In addition to the letters, there are a number of admonitions and series of commandments, which have been collected in this chapter. These include the five commandments for the elect and the ten commandments for auditors. Then there are
a number of precepts for auditors and the elect.

Finally, examples of postscripts have been appended.[3] Unfortunately, little has
been preserved of such material, which is more personal in nature.

1. Quotations from the letters of Mani

The letters of Mani belonged to the canonical scriptures of the Manichaeans. They
are referred to and quoted in Coptic, Iranian, Turkish, and Chinese texts. Some of
the original letters were found in Coptic in Egypt, but their fate, following the turbulence of World War II, is unclear. We therefore have to rely on citations, which
are found in the following texts.

1.1 QUOTATIONS FROM MANI'S LETTERS (PERSIAN)

As Boyce describes it, this text "consists of brief citations from various of Mani's *Letters,* and also from other works of the prophet."[4] The text is unfortunately badly preserved. We give Sundermann's hitherto unpublished translation.

> (*recto*)
> "Do not bear witness, nor swear an oath time and again, nor make others swear."
>
> And in the *Epistle to (?) the Presbyters*[5] he says, "Do not speak in an irritated and confused manner, and let not a word of destruction go forth from your mouth, for it is of the word of destruction that a bloody demoness is born."
>
> And in the *Epistle to Ḥatā*[6] he says, "Be obedient, and in the speech of your mouth [do not be] dissolute (?), but rather recite, by day and night, the L[aw], and praise . . . , and lament for what the Redeemer [suffered (?)]."
>
> And in the *Gospel* and in the [*Treasure of the*] *Living* he says, "On earth and [in heaven (?)] . . ."
>
> (*verso*)
> . . . a[nd] (in?) patient . . . (and?) loving . . . soothe one [another] and build each other up (again), and (dispel) each other's sorrows, and be dear to one another in kindness and always r[un] (?) with these secrets and edify each other. And . . . be of my appearance and nature, [and one will be] and one will not. Perhaps you may do that . . . body . . . [it is] not fitting . . . brethren, . . . all of you helpers. And to the worthy . . . but to the best of my ability and . . . I shall be a helper to all of you. And I [do not] say: "This is mine [or: my] and this [is] a[nother one's own (or: task?)] . . ."

1.2. FURTHER QUOTATIONS FROM MANI'S LETTERS (PERSIAN)

According to Müller, who first published this material, this text is also from Mani's letters. The last part is a quotation from an *Epistle of Mēšun,* that is, Mesene at the mouth of the Tigris.[7] The king of Mesene was converted to Mani's religion (cf. ch. XVII, text 2.3).

> In the *Epistle of Mešun* about the two bodies he says, "We and you remember and desire (to go) to (our) own place. This wisdom that you have received in one spirit, remain (in it) fittingly. With clothes for one year . . . and food for one day . . ."
>
> [*a gap of unknown length*]
> . . . He led five people from among the worldly ones, and he said to them, "May there be no anger (among you)." To the auditors he said, "May no one dishearten you that you remain in the world.[8] For you are friends of the friends (the elect), you are auditors [who] by fasting . . ."

2. *Apocryphal letter from Mani to Mār Ammō* (Parthian)

This document presents itself as a letter to Mār Ammō, Mani's disciple who was sent to East Iran. "The text," says Boyce, "appears to be a pious fabrication of Dēnāwar [East Manichaean] origin. It is written as a letter from Mani to [Mār] Ammō, and there is a suspicious insistence in it on those names; but the number of Buddhist-Indian loanwords points to a date later than the third century for its composition."[9] It would appear that the Central Asian Dēnāvarīya branch of Manichaeism, which evolved around 600, was especially receptive to Buddhist influence[10] and sought to legitimize that openness with this purported letter from Mani.

[Title:]   The sweet teaching of the sinless (*nāgān*)[11]

... And if someone strikes you, do not strike him back. And if someone hates you, do not hate him in return. And if someone envies you, do not envy him for your part. And if someone is angry with you, speak kindly with him always. And do not do yourself what you detest in another person. Rather, one should endure insults and other abuses from one's superiors, from one's equals and from one's subordinates; nobody can make the patient *dēnāvar* (devout one) waver even slightly. It is like someone throwing flowers at an elephant: the flowers could not harm (lit., smash) the elephant. Or (it is) like raindrops falling upon a stone: the raindrops could not melt the stone. Likewise, insults and abuses should not cause a patient *dēnāvar* to waver even slightly.[12]

There are times when the *dēnāvar* should hold himself as high as Mount Sumeru.[13] And there are times when the *dēnāvar* should appear as a pupil, and there are times when he should appear as a teacher or a servant or a lord.[14]

Likewise, in this sinful time, the pure *dēnāvar* should sit down in pious meditation (*andēšišn*) and should turn away from sin and develop what is good ...

   [*a number of lines illegible*]

And I, Mār Mani, am this sinless one (*nāg*)[15] who is the writer,[16] and you, Mār Ammō, are the addressee.[17] And he whose name is Ākundag is Ahriman (the Devil).[18] I have spoken these words so that everyone will pay heed to them[19] and listen to them attentively. [For everyone] who hears and believes them and keeps them in mind and serves through pious deeds shall find salvation from this cycle of rebirths,[20] and shall be saved from his sins. For I, Mār Mani, and you, Mār Ammō, and all those people of old as well as all those fortunate ones that are reborn in this time, and likewise those that shall be reborn in the future, shall be saved from this cycle of rebirth through this behavior and (this) humility. For in this cycle of rebirths (this life) there is nothing good except for the merit accumulated by men of understanding and their pious deeds.[21] Those who follow me, Mār Mani, and put their hope in God Ohrmizd and want the pure and righteous elect to be their leaders, they are the ones that are saved and find salvation from this cycle of rebirths and attain eternal redemption.

Here ends the sweet teaching about the sinless.

3. *Letter from a church dignitary to Mār Ammō* (Parthian)

This is a letter from a high church dignitary, probably Sisin (Sisinnius), to Mār Ammō. According to Boyce "there seems to be no reason to doubt that this letter is what it purports to be."[22]

> ... And do not put off the good you can do now, for time is passing swiftly.
>
> And you should know this: I do not believe that the love and respect for you which now exist in Merv[23] could be any greater[24] even if you had been here in Merv in person. And you should know this: when I came up to Merv, I found all the brothers and sisters to be devout. And to dear brother Zurvāndād[25] I am very, very grateful because he in his goodness has watched over all the brothers. And I have now despatched him to Zamb,[26] and sent him to dear Mār Ammō, and to (the province of) Chorasan. He has taken (*The Book of*) *the Giants* and the *Ārdahang* with him. I have made another (copy of *The Book of*) *the Giants* and the *Ārdahang* in Merv. Furthermore you should know this: when I came, I found brother Rāshtēn[27] to be just as I would wish. And as for his devotion and zeal, he was just as Mār Mani would desire.
>
> [*seventeen lines badly preserved*]
>
> And I have written [these words] to you, because I know that you are pleased with the goodness in me. Quickly (?) they begin to glorify God and Mār Mani.[28] As long as I and you live, I will appoint bishops and teachers as watchmen in every city and province of the Upper Countries (Abarshahr) so that your name may be (honored) and that this religion of Mār Mani's may find leaders and advocates everywhere.
>
> [And] lo, I have sent the beloved brother Khusrō to you ...
>
> [*twelve lines badly preserved or missing*]
>
> ... and that you may be very glad. And you should act so that you labor for the auditors as much as you can, so that when I send brothers to you they may be received befittingly.
>
> As for Friyādar, you should know that since the time he came he has stayed close to me and has (remained in) love and faith. He will now come to you. (As for) you, you should receive him in joy and should care for him as if he were your own son, so that I also may be thankful to you.
>
> And lo, I have sent (another) beloved son of Mār Mani to you; he comes with love to you. You, for your part, should (also) receive him as your own son; instruct him well in the art of writing, and in wisdom. Teach them (both) like your own sons and do not regard them as arrogant rivals;[29] rather, remember that no pupil comes from home (already) instructed (full of insight), but rather he gains instruction day by day. There are pupils

who are of good heart and kind to their teacher; they follow him and honor his name and continually do what is pleasing to him. But there are also other pupils who are not, and are obstinate . . . It is necessary to be patient with all in like manner. You, however, should not turn away from anybody, but should . . . in faith to all who stretch out their hands to you[30] . . .

4. Sogdian letters from Turfan

The Sogdian letters preserved here give us a unique insight into the life of the Manichaean community.[31] They are especially interesting because they shed light on the relationship between the local community at Turfan and those brethren from Mesopotamia, here called "Syrians," that had settled in the Turfan area. That relationship was not free of tension, for the newcomers had a more liberal way of life than their Central Asian coreligionists. Therefore these texts, though short and fragmentary, are of great importance.

The opening portion of the first letter is too fragmentary to be translated. It speaks of a "blessed" (in the sense of "late") *Pγγv'n* (perhaps a title) Teacher (*mvj'k*), and about the followers of Mihr and Miklās (Arab. Miqlaṣ). These were two leaders of rival schools, or "denominations," as Henning realized as early as 1936.[32] He points to Ibn an-Nadīm's *Fihrist,* where we learn that in Mesopotamia a group of Manichaeans split off under the religious leader Mihr, who was in office ca. 710–740. This group was first led by one Zādhormuzd, then by Miklās.[33] The schism lasted till about 880. In our text, the first group is called Mihriyānd (Arab. al-Mirīyaḥ), the second Miklāsīktē (Arab. al-Miqlāsīyaḥ). As Henning pointed out, "The reason that emerges for the schism seems to be the more worldly oriented tendencies of Mihr and his group, which caused strong opposition on the part of the orthodox party."[34] Indeed an-Nadīm tells us, "Miqlāṣ differed with the community about matters of religion, among which were social relationships."[35]

With respect to the dates of these letters, Henning points out, "We can assume that those who disrupted the peace [i. e., the newcomers], against whom such bitter complaints are lodged in the Sogdian letters, belonged to the followers of Mihr. Thus we have an approximate date for the letters. They must have been written before 840 and after 763, the year of the introduction of Manichaeism in the Uighur Kingdom."[36]

4.1 FIRST LETTER[37]

. . . As regards (the fulfillment of) the law (in general), [they are weak] in (observing) the commandments . . . Firstly: [They sin] against the commandment to be truthful . . .

[*a gap of unknown length*]

. . . (Our) nun (electa) saw that their [nun] cut [a garment] and sewed it. Then again, our nun [saw] that [their] nun pressed . . . Furthermore, the virgin (?) [daughters] of Āzād-duxt . . . saw that their nun took a pickax and dug up the earth. Neither do they hesitate to crush medicinal

plants and strike blocks of wood.[38] Furthermore, our nuns also saw how
their nun let blood (caused someone to bleed to acquire the blood) and
washed . . . with water. And (when our) nun reprimanded them, they
answered, "Water in wells is dead, therefore it is allowed." And they also
crush medicinal plants themselves and kindle the fire themselves.[39] And
they see no fault or sin in this matter.

And furthermore, with respect to the commandment about "behavior
in accordance with religion" (chastity), (their observation thereof) is loose
and shameless.[40] For their leader, who is Mihr-Pādār,[41] was ill; he had a
malady affecting the lower part of his body. A hired girl (servant) entered
into his place and later came out. And when she came out, we were all
suspicious, and the monks (the elect) made inquiries. The hired girl servant said to Yazd Aryāmān, Drist-Rōshn, Mihr-Vahman and Vahman-
Shāh, "Two times did I extract blood behind the door, and I shall do so
once again."[42]

Then one of her servants started a quarrel with (our) nun. And Mihr-
Pādār, their leader, seized that servant by the arm and took her away from
the quarrel . . .

4.2 SECOND LETTER[43]

. . . Gavryav[44] . . . said: "It is altogether in accordance with the religious
law." And, oh lord, [in order . . . to prevent that] their own soul suffers
such a dire fate [as a result of their laxity], it is necessary to add that . . . ;
they come up (here) and mix with us, and if they stay for several years,
[they will] . . . It will be . . . according to . . . of the present superiors. And
this . . . unlawful and inappropriate order will be brought to the notice of
the present superiors . . . Those who were their (the Syrians') *spies will
finally take the place of our superiors, . . . and they will injure those direly
beset, and will cause great trouble for (our) superiors, and they will wash
[their hands] in [blood] . . .

At that time, . . . oh lord, you yourself were [bishop?]; the customs and
the manner of these base, vile Syrians are like this: They are experienced
and versed in schisms [and] quarrels, for the spirit of schism reigns supreme here. And . . . their word is very perditious. Therefore please
observe closely [whether] those that came here first have brought about
profit and gain (or not).[45] For the (Syrian) Teacher Māhdād has slan-
dered (our) Teacher Mihrān, strong in faith (?), just as Gavryav [has come
to prevail over?] (our) elect and (our) Teacher Nvānzādag, and the (Syrian)
Teacher Saxtōe and the (Syrian) bishop Ktvn' [have come to prevail
over?] . . . ; . . . the base Farraxān, who *seeks destruction, . . .

5. Five commandments for the elect (Sogdian)

As we know from the *Fihrist* of an-Nadīm, there were five commandments for
the elect. There it says, "He who would enter the religion must examine his soul.

If he finds that he can (5) subdue greed and covetousness, (4) refrain from eating meats, drinking wine (3) as well as from marriage, (2) and if he can avoid causing injury to water, fire, trees and earth, then let him enter the religion (become an Electus) . . . If, however, he loves the religion, but is unable to subdue greed and covetousness, then let him seize upon guarding the religion and the Elect (become a hearer or auditor), so that there may be an offsetting of his unworthy actions. . . ."[46]

With respect to this text, Sims-Williams points out, "In my view, this passage makes reference to the last four of the five commandments (in reverse order). As the context indicates, this list of prohibitions summarizes those obligations of the Elect which go beyond those incumbent upon Hearers. The first commandment is omitted, because 'truth' (that is, both 'truthfulness' and 'orthodoxy') is as much a duty of the Hearers as of the Elect."[47]

The five commandments for the elect are known from a number of Central Asian (Parthian, Sogdian, Turkish) as well as Chinese Manichaean sources.[48] In the Turkish *Great Hymn to Mani* (ch. XXIII, text 1), they are summed up as follows: 1. the commandment to be without sin (truthfulness); 2. the commandment [not to commit] filthy, evil deeds; 3. the commandment that the body must be pure; 4. the commandment that the mouth be pure; 5. the commandment to be blessed (and) poor.[49] In the Coptic *Psalm-Book* (161,21–22) it says, "[Five are the] commandments which God gave to the five [ranks], which he appointed to his Church." In another passage (33, 18–23) these are enumerated as follows: 1. the commandment that we tell no lie; 2. the commandment that we do not kill; 3. the commandment that we eat no flesh; 4. the commandment that we keep ourselves pure; and 5. the commandment of blessed poverty.[50]

The commandments in our text tally with these other lists.[51]

> Finally, he gave them all the commandments, (teaching them about) morals and propriety, laws and rules, (correct) behavior and deportment (?), fully and thoroughly according to numbers: five commandments in [ten] parts,[52] three seals[53] in six parts, five [garments (?)[54] in] ten parts, vigilance and zeal[55]. . .
>
> The twelve limbs of the sojourning soul are these: life, power, light, beauty, and fragrance.[56] The five commandments (are) truth, nonviolence, chastity, purity of mouth, (and) blessed poverty, (furthermore) vigilance and zeal.

6. *Ten commandments for auditors* (Persian)

As opposed to the five commandments for the elect, the ten commandments for auditors are not enumerated in full at any point in the original manuscripts preserved. There are references to them in Parthian, Sogdian, Turkish, and Chinese texts, but here, too, not all of them are cited.[57] In the Turkish $X^u\bar{a}stv\bar{a}n\bar{i}ft$ (VI A) "ten kinds of sins" are mentioned and even enumerated, but these are examples of sinfulness rather than commandments as such.[58] However, the *Fihrist* of an-Nadīm does preserve a complete list:

"The Ten Commandments: (1) renunciation of the worship of idols; (2) renunciation of lying; (3) renunciation of greed; (4) renunciation of killing; (5) renunciation of fornication (6) renunciation of theft; (7) (renunciation of) the teaching of pretences;[59] (8) and (of) sorcery; (9) and (of) holding two opinions, that is, doubt concerning the religion; (10) and of sickness and negligence in work."[60]

In the Turkish $X^u\bar{a}stv\bar{a}n\bar{\imath}ft$ (IX A) the ten commandments are summed up in a manner reminiscent of Augustine's "three seals" (*tria signacula*, scil. *oris, manuum et sinus*), which are frequently mentioned in the Central Asian texts. It speaks of the commandments as composed of "three with the mouth, three with the mind, three with the head, (and) one with the whole being."

1. . . . They shall [not] kill. [And] they [shall] also take pity on the animals that are [their] food. They may [not kill] them as infidels do.[61] But they may eat the dead flesh of any animal, wherever they may have obtained it, whether it has died (naturally), or whether it has been killed; they may eat it however they may have procured it, whether by purchase, or at a feast (?), or as a gift. That much is sufficient for them. This is the first commandment for auditors.

2. And the second commandment is that they should not be liars, nor [be] unjust to one another . . . And the auditor shall love his fellow-auditor like his own brother and relative. For they (the auditors) are children of the Living Family (the Manichaean community) and the World of Light.

3. And the third commandment is that they shall not slander anyone, nor bear false witness against anyone concerning what they have not seen, nor falsely swear an oath concerning any matter, [nor] . . . falsehood . . .

7. *Precepts for auditors* (Persian)

This is a homiletical fragment emphasizing the necessity of being concerned as much with the soul as with worldly things (B).

As he (the auditor) pursues (the enemy), takes revenge and defends the land (as a soldier) and does farm work and makes payments and enjoys meat and wine and has a wife and children and builds a house and has property and is concerned about the body and pays taxes to the kingdom and steals and harms (others) and acts tyranically and pitilessly, even so does it behoove him to ask about wisdom and knowledge concerning the gods and think about the soul (*ruvān*) . . .

[*a number of lines defective or missing*]

He should give up lewdness and fornication and evil thoughts, evil words and evil deeds and keep his hand from robbery and harm and mercilessness, and always keep away from earth, water, and fire, trees and plants,[62] as well as wild and tame animals; and he should not beat them. For they, too, continue to live by that Light and goodness of the gods . . .[63]

8. *Further precepts for auditors* (Persian)

This text describes the ideal relationship between the auditors and the elect. The style would suggest that it is probably from one of Mani's own works (B).

> . . . Through soul-service (giving alms) and through friendship they (the auditors) are united with them (the elect); and they strive wholeheartedly for the sake of their friendship. And they love them as if they were their relatives. And they are united with them through these two signs, through the sign of love and through the sign of fear . . . And they hold them in honor like someone who honors his lord and ruler. And they fear transgressing their commands, and (they fear) not to believe in these hidden things (pertaining to revelation) and (these) greatnesses (the gods), and they listen to what they hear from them at all times. In the same way, they also fear and avoid evil deeds and greediness. And by wisdom they are truly and intimately united with them.
>
> In commands and deeds, however, they are still inferior (to the elect), for they are still involved in worldly activity and are subject to desire and greed and sensual pleasure, both as males and as females . . . .
>
> [*some lines missing*]
>
> And because the auditors are inferior to the righteous (the elect), they will continue to be bound to (the cycle of) transmigration until they are liberated from these evil wanderings in places that are fitting for them, for they have not renounced the world, nor sin, as completely as the righteous have. For the righteous have renounced the whole world and its covetousness, and they have become perfect in their single-minded desire for godliness.
>
> (But) by being devoted to those two signs, they are of one mind and in harmony (with the elect), in the signs of love and fear.
>
> Therefore, because they have forsaken all covetousness and all rebirths and (all) distress and all suffering and destruction, and are undefiled, they are redeemed and pass on (to the other world), and are received and accepted in that great and blessed Kingdom and in that Light.[64]

9. *On giving alms* (Parthian)

This text is from the final portion of what was apparently a homily, for the first line of the preserved page reads, "Completed (is) the discourse on the lives." It is not quite clear what exactly this refers to; maybe different forms of possible rebirth are meant. We can say with certainty, however, that in the preserved fragment the admonition to give alms is connected with the fate of the soul. Hence such donations were referred to as "soul-service" (Pth. *ruvānagān*), for they have an effect on the soul of the giver. Henning points out about the opening portion of our text,

> not even the greatest gifts or sacrifices extinguish sins against the "Living Soul" (i. e., the divine substance scattered in the world). Actions are followed by retribution, which is governed by a mechanical law of cause and effect. Yet Mani

found himself compelled to allow several exceptions: joining the Manichaean church cancelled all previous sins (merely suspended them in case of relapse); and up to four-fifths of the minor sins committed by laymen could be forgiven in return for faithful service.... In chapter 115 of the *Kephalaia* Mani even concedes the effectiveness of prayers for the souls of the dead, provided they are accompanied by generous gifts to the church.[65]

Various ideas in this passage are reminiscent of Buddhism, including the depiction of the torments of Hell.[66] In Manichaeism, donations to the clergy were just as important as in Buddhism. The greatest emphasis is laid on the pure intention of the giver, and in this case also of the recipient. "The amount of *pvnv'r* [alms-food], our text tells us, is of no true importance: what matters is the purity of the recipient."[67] Of course this also applies to the donor. Buddhist texts from Turfan also stress that any gift (to the Buddha), even one as small as a "mustard seed" (used for the erection of a *stupa* in this case) brings merit.[68] Translation is adopted from Henning.

> . . .[69]
>
> And the man[70] who is in the Dēnāvariyya[71] should know how the service that he performs for the pure *Dēnāvars*[72] ultimately [accrues?] to the soul; and should understand the fruits that are born out of the gifts: then, even if his whole house were of gold and pearls and he gave it (to the Church) for the sake of the soul, he would not necessarily receive forgiveness. And [if it were] so that he would [bake] the flesh that is on his body into bread and would [cut] it with his own hand and give it to the *Dēnāvars,* . . . he should know . . . what . . .
>
> [*half a column missing*]
>
> . . . [he who] would take alms-food (*pūnvār*) as (much as) a big mountain and could redeem it, should eat it: he himself will be saved, he will also save him who gave him the alms food, and it[73] will reach the home of the gods unharmed. And he who would take alms-food as much as a single *grain of mustard but could not redeem it, then . . . better for him . . . fire . . .
>
> [*two thirds of a column missing*]
>
> . . . who will find his seed-grain multiplied a thousand times.
>
> And the man who breaks faith with the Buddha and Apostle and leaves the Church and violates the commandments will be led, in great shame and fear, before the Just Judge, and he [cannot] turn [aside]. To him [the Judge will say:] "You are . . . the word . . ."
>
> [*two thirds of a column missing*]
>
> . . . to eat his body . . . And time and again they cut off his ears, and time and again they hack his tongue (?) into *slices, and in the same manner they cut off all his limbs. And time and again they pour molten copper into his mouth and give him glowing hot iron to eat and drive iron nails into his ears—who can fully describe the wicked, horrible distress and suffering which that unfortunate unbeliever who soils[74] the pure religion

must undergo? Fortunate is the man that can fully keep . . . the pure religion and the commandments . . . because not . . . not ever . . . he does *punya*[75] . . .

10. On the evils of eating meat and drinking wine (Persian)

This text is addressed to the elect who were prohibited from eating meat and drinking alcoholic beverages. It is reminiscent of similar Buddhist texts found in Central Asia,[76] though this prohibition is an old Manichaean one.

. . .

Third: He (who drinks wine) becomes stupid. Fourth: His soul becomes unclean. Fifth: His sensual lust increases. Sixth: He becomes a liar. Seventh: He scandalizes many people. Eighth: (His) soul-work (alms) is impure (?). Ninth: The poor receive no alms (from him). Tenth: By cooking (a meal), sin arises. In the eleventh place: Reason wanes. In the twelfth place: He becomes murderous.

And there are nine kinds (of killing): 1. killing by oneself, 2. desiring (to kill), 3. inciting (others to kill), 4. eating (meat), 5. giving (meat to others) to eat, 6. teaching . . . 7. selling (meat), 8. buying (meat), 9. . . .

Nine kinds of harm and sin arise from wine and drinking: 1. losing the senses, 2. falling ill, 3. becoming depressive (?), 4. becoming violent in speech, 5. becoming fearful by falling down (intoxicated), 6. [becoming liable to] punishment, 7. . . . , 8. becoming shameless, 9. . . .

Notes

1. Cf. Dodge, *Fihrist* II, pp. 799f.
2. For these epistles, cf. Flügel, *Mani,* pp. 370–85.
3. For further postscripts, compare ch. XXXII.
4. Boyce, *Reader,* p. 184, n. to text do.
5. This Epistle of Mani's is mentioned by an-Nadīm. Cf. ch. XXXII.
6. An-Nadim mentions a Letter "of Ḥaṭṭā" by Mani. Compare Dodge, *Fihrist* II, p. 801. According to Boyce, *Word List,* s.v. *ht',* Hatā is a Semitic place name. However, see Dodge, *op. cit.,* p. 801, n. 314 on Ḥaṭṭā.
7. HR II, pp. 32f.
8. Boyce explains this as meaning that they, the auditors, should "remain in secular life, rather than adopting the strictly religious life of the Elect." Boyce, *Reader,* p. 185, n. 2.
9. Boyce, *Reader,* p. 50.
10. Cf. Klimkeit, "Buddhistische Übernahmen."
11. Title reconstructed from the last line of the text. "The meaning of the last word is doubtful. The editors [F. C. Andreas and W. B. Henning] took it to be from Skt. *an-āgas* 'sinless.' Schaeder . . . suggested that it might rather be derived from Skt. *nāga* 'elephant, great saint.'" [*nāga* is primarily "snake," or "serpent, demon": *MW* 532c]. Boyce, *Reader,* p. 50. Schaeder thinks that this text is a Manichaean copy of a Buddhist *Jātaka* [story of Buddha's former birth]. Schaeder, *Der Manichäismus,* p. 96.
12. This idea is often expressed in Buddhist texts. It implies the ideal of (Skr.) *upekṣā* (Pali *upekkhā*), "equanimity, patience." Cf. *BHSD* 147 b.
13. The central mountain of the world in Buddhist cosmology.

14. Literally, "when he (appears as) a servant and when he (appears as) a lord."

15. With Henning and Boyce we take *nāg* here to mean "sinless one," not connecting it with Skr. *nāga*.

16. Literally, "having the hither name" (*ēdar nām*).

17. Literally, "having the yonder name" (*abdar nām*).

18. Ākundag is the name of a demon. He appears in Pahlavi as Kund Dēv or Kundag Drūj. Compare *Mir. Man.* III, p. 856, n. 3.

19. Henning translates, with doubt, "may read (?) them." Here we follow Asmussen, *Manichaean Literature,* p. 58.

20. Literally, "birth-death" (*zādmurd*), *saṃsāra* in the Buddhist sense.

21. This is a typical Buddhist idea which is echoed repeatedly in Buddhist texts from Central Asia.

22. Boyce, *Reader,* p. 48.

23. Merv, present Mary in Turkmenistan, was a center of Manichaean and Nestorian Christian missionary activity directed eastwards. The remains of a Buddhist monastery and *stūpa* have also been found here.

24. In spite of your absence. Thus Asmussen, *Manichaean Literature,* p. 23.

25. Zurvāndād, "Created by Zurvān," is "a well-attested name in Sasanian Persia." Boyce, *Reader,* p. 49.

26. "Zamb, later Zamm, is modern Karkhī on the left bank of the Oxus, about 100 miles above Āmul, which itself lies approximately 120 miles to the north-east of Marv [i. e., Merv] . . . The name Zamb means 'shore.'" Boyce, *Reader,* p. 49.

27. This is probably the Rāshtēn to whom, together with Pērōz (prince-governor of Chorasan/Xvarāsān), Mani addressed a letter. Compare *Mir. Man.* III, p. 858, n. 5.

28. Translation according to Boyce, who explains, "i. e., the many converts, swiftly made, do honour to God and Mani?" Boyce, *Reader,* p. 49, n. 4.

29. Thus according to Boyce. Asmussen translates, "And do not mind, (even) if they ask inconsiderate questions." Asmussen, *op. cit.,* pp. 23f.

30. This idea is also expressed in Buddhist texts.

31. For a discussion of the fragments from this group of texts which have not been translated here, compare Sundermann, "Probleme der Interpretation manichäisch-soghdischer Briefe," p. 289, n. 1.

32. Henning, "Neue Materialien zur Geschichte des Manichäismus," pp. 16ff.

33. Cf. Dodge, *Fihrist* II, pp. 793f.

34. Henning, "Neue Materialien," p. 17.

35. Dodge, *op. cit.,* p. 793.

36. Henning, *op. cit.,* pp. 17f.

37. Translation after Sundermann and Sims-Williams.

38. Since the Manichaeans believed that these substances contain divine light, it was prohibited for monks (*electi*) and nuns (*electae*) to "injure" them in any manner.

39. Literally, "they lay the fire," probably in the sense of "ignite the fire." Sims-Williams points out that "this may have been regarded as an improper activity for electi, since it could cause pain for the fuel." Sims-Williams, in Sundermann, *op cit.,* p. 308, n. 24.

40. Translation suggested by Sims-Williams.

41. The name means "Protector of friendship" or "Protector of the Treaty." If Mihr is taken to be Mithra, it can mean "Servant of Mithra" or "Enduring in Mithra." If Mihr is taken as a specifically Manichaean name, it refers to a saving deity, either the Living Spirit (after MP) or the Third Messenger as Sun God (after Pth.). However, since Mihr is also the name of the leader of the schismatic group, that name would suggest an association with him. Sundermann, "Briefe," p. 308, n. 26.

42. It is stressed by I. Gershevitch that the four electi bearing Persian names did not necessarily interrogate the quack doctor. They may have been people she knew and to whom she reported her actions without realizing that they were making investigations. Compare Sundermann, *op. cit.,* p. 314.

43. Translation after Sundermann.
44. Apparently one of the leaders of the Syrian Manichaeans. He was a bishop.
45. Translation following Sims-Williams in Sundermann, *op. cit.,* p. 311, n. 50.
46. Translation by Sims-Williams in his "The Manichaean Commandments," pp. 576f. Cf. B. Dodge, *The Fihrist of an-Nadim* II, p. 788.
47. Sims-Williams, *op. cit.,* p. 577.
48. Cf. Sims-Williams, op. cit., p. 574.
49. Sims-Williams interprets this as "blessedly poor" and quotes Sundermann, *Texte,* p. 36, lines 335–337, translating, "Do not accept anything superfluous, [but dwell in the] blessedness (of poverty), [which] is the height of all blessedness." Sims-Williams, *op. cit.,* p. 576, n. 28.
50. Translation by Sims-Williams, *op. cit.,* pp. 577f.
51. Translation after Sims-Williams.
52. Each commandment is divided into two parts. Compare the *Book of Prayer and Confession,* ch. XII.
53. On these three seals that sum up the ten commandments by defining a "seal" of the mouth, the hands, and the bosom (i. e., the heart), compare the Introduction.
54. This word, *j'mg'n,* is restored by Sundermann on the basis of a comparable text, M 174 i R I. The significance of the three garments is obscure.
55. "'Vigilance' and 'zeal' are often mentioned in connexion with the Five Commandments." Sims-Williams, *op. cit.,* p. 574, n. 10.
56. In another text, M 14 (compare chapter VII, text 1), they are described as "the substance and the essence of the soul."
57. Cf. Sims-Williams, "The Manichaean Commandments," pp. 572f.
58. Cf. Asmussen, *Xᵘāstvānīft,* pp. 216ff. Sims-Williams thinks they "may be the converse of the Ten Commandments." Sims-Williams, *op. cit.,* p. 577, n. 39.
59. Including "false witness and the extension of truth." Sims-Williams, *op. cit.,* p. 578, n. 41, with reference to Flügel, *Mani,* pp. 301–302.
60. Translation by Sims-Williams, in his "The Manichaean Commandments," p. 578. Cf. Dodge, *Fihrist* II, p. 789.
61. Non-Manichaeans. The word *druvandān,* "sinners, infidels," is originally Zoroastrian (B).
62. For these elements contain divine particles of Light.
63. That is mixed with Darkness, or matter.
64. Boyce points out that "this probably refers to the Hearers [i. e., auditors] who in the end will attain salvation." Boyce, *Reader,* p. 56, n. 5.
65. Henning, "A Grain of Mustard," p. 31, n. 5.
66. The passage was probably formulated in East Iran or Central Asia, since there is a reference to "the Buddha and the Apostle," by which, in both cases, the divine Mani is meant. Buddhist conceptions of Hell are vividly depicted in the Uighur *Maitrisimit,* ch. 20–25; compare S. Tekin, *Maitisimit nom bitig* I, pp. 166–215.
67. Henning, "A Grain of Mustard," p. 34; Boyce, *Word-List,* s.v. *pwnw'r = punwār/punvār,* renders this word as "charitable food-offering, food given as alms."
68. Müller, "Zwei Pfahlinschriften," p. 14.
69. The last words of the previous passage, which alone are preserved, contain a reference to "the fire" of Hell.
70. The auditor.
71. The (Eastern) Manichaean Church.
72. The *elect.*
73. Or, he. "The implied subject is probably the 'Living Soul' contained in the food." Henning, "A Grain of Mustard," p. 31, n. 6.
74. Literally, "who does lies (drūγ) in/at" (H).
75. He does deeds to acquire merit (Pth. *pvn* < Skr. *punya*).
76. Cf. MacKenzie, *The Buddhist Sogdian Texts of the British Library.* Leiden, 1976, pp. 7–11 ("Sūtra of the condemnation of intoxicating drink").

CHAPTER TWENTY-TWO

Postscripts

A limited number of postscripts, or colophons, has been preserved among the Iranian Manichaean texts of Central Asia. Nevertheless they might have been as common as the colophons in the Turkish Gnostic and Buddhist texts.[1]

The oldest datable Iranian colophon we have is a fragment (IB 6371) entitled by Müller, its first editor, "The royal retinue of an Uigur King."[2] It contains a prayer for the protection of the king and his court. His name or title is "the great king who received his charisma (*qut*) from Heaven (*tängri*), who by his virtue (*ärdäm*) holds (together) the kingdom, the blessed, fortunate, wise Uighur Khan."[3] This is probably, as Zieme and Sundermann observe,[4] Bilgä Khan (*bilgä qaɣan*), or Bögü Khan, who ruled the Uighur Kingdom of the Steppes (744–840) from 759 to 779. He established Manicheism as the state religion of the Uighur empire, and hence became the "Constantine of Manichaeism." Sundermann points out, "An argument in favour of its being a colophon is the observation that in its text, passages in red and black ink follow each other, a phenomenon well known from the initial and final parts of the [Parthian] Hymn Cycles."[5] This phenomenon is also found in the colophon of the second text (M 1) to be presented here. Sundermann rightly adds, "I cannot describe here a more modest type of colophon to be found on the back of scrolls. They mention the title of a work, its writer and its owner."[6]

Such a colophon is also to be found in the Sogdian "Book of Parables." Here it says, "I was (?) taught this book of Parables. I, Tataɣur, [have] learned (?) this book. Whoever does not believe it may ask (?) Ügäbirmiš, Yamčur, Wiraɣmāx and Tataɣur. May he (also) go (?) and ask Tataɣur (himself); Nawēmax has . . . this Book of Parables. I have . . ."[7]

Our second text, long regarded as an introduction to a hymnbook, is actually a postscript, as Sundermann has convincingly shown.[8] The work is written "in late and incorrect Middle Persian."[9] It tells us that the hymnbook was begun in the year 761/762, the decisive year of Bögü Khan's conversion and proclamation of the "Religion of Light" as the state religion. We hear that it first remained

271

unfinished and was kept in the monastery of Argi, that is, Karashahr (Solmi), an important center on the northern Silk Road, west of Turfan. Finally Naxurīgrōshn, a scribe, completed it with the support of "his divinity" the Teacher Mār Aryānshāh, Bishop Mār Dōshist, Presbyter Mār Yishō Aryamān, and the Preacher Yazad-āmad, during the rule of an Uighur Khan whose name, or title, was "the valiant, wise Uighur Khan who received his charisma (*qut*) from the Moon God (Jesus the Splendor)."[10] He was the tenth ruler of the Uighur Empire of the Steppes after Bilgä Khan (Bögü Khan).[11] The historical events are quite clear. After the vast Uighur Kingdom in the Mongolian Steppes had adopted Manichaeism, various Manichaean centers along the Silk Road, though remote from that Kingdom, were overcome with a new zeal for the Manichaean faith. However, Bilgä Khan's succes-sor, whose title, Alp Qutluγ (reg. 779–789), does not include a reference to the (Manichaean) Sun or Moon God, apparently departed from the faith. There are some indications that he might have tried to make Nestorianism the state religion, or that he at least was inclined toward Christiantity. His rule must have been a set-back for Manichaeism at large in Central Asia, so that the fire of religious zeal abated for a while. Yet by the time of Bilgä Khan's tenth successor, the "Religion of Light" had so gained in strength that all the Manichaean centers on the Silk Road were inspired anew. It is interesting that our colophon mentions not only him and his retinue, but also rulers of various small kingdoms along the northern Silk Road, including the rulers of Bišbaliq, Kuča, Kashgar, Aqsu, Argi (Karashahr, Solmi) and Üč(?). Among these is also the lord of Čīnānčkand, the main city in the Turfan oasis.[12] As pointed out by Sundermann, this does not necessarily mean "that these small city states were submitted to the Uighur empire in those days. The list might enumerate as well those regions where Manichaean communities existed and enjoyed local protection."[13]

It was after the destruction of the Manichaean Uighur empire in 840 that the Uighur Turks migrated to the city states along the northern Silk Road, notably to the Turfan Basin, where they made Kocho (Chin. Kao-Ch'ang) new capital of a Turk-ish (Uighur) kingdom (ca. 850–1250). Here Manichaeism was to play a decisive role, and Manichaean art and literature were sponsored by the rulers of Kocho, as the third colophon presented here shows.

This third colophon is the end of a text illuminated by a miniature painting, showing two (of originally four) Hindu deities, or protective deities with an Indian appearance. They could be the four guardians of the world, the *lokapālas* of the Indo-Buddhist tradition, who are often referred to as "the four (divine) Mahārājas" (*catur mahārāja*). Such also appear on another miniature painting (IB 4979),[14] and these could also be such protective deities (the *lokapālas*), though in terms of Indian iconography they seem to represent Shiva, Brahma, Vishnu (with a boar's head) and Ganesha. In view of Manicheism's roots in the Jewish-Christian tradition of the Elchasites, whose traditions can in turn be traced back to Qumran, we may have here the four protective archangels—Michael, Raphael, Gabriel, and Sarael (for Uriel)—invoked both in Qumranic and Turfanic literature (e. g., in M 20), appearing in Indian, or Buddhist/Hindu garb. The *Book of Giants,* originally a Qumranic text which was known in a Manichaean form in Turfan, would suggest as much.[15]

It could very well be that some of the prayers for the ruler and his family, translated in chapter XIV, were actually colophons as well.

Manichaean culture apparently reached its apex in the kingdom of Kocho under a Khan who ruled from 1007 to 1019, and whose name, or title, was "He who received his charisma (*qut*) from the God of the Sun and the Moon, who is adorned by fortune, who holds (together) the kingdom (*il*) by virtue and valiance, who has upheld the kingdom, Alp Arslan Qutluγ Köl Bilgä Tängri."[16] His name occurs in abbreviated form in various Turkish and Iranian texts, including a text with a miniature painting depicting musicians and a floral motif into which is inscribed (in olive green) the words "the four princely gods" (*tört ilig tängrilär*),[17] probably another reference to the four Manichaean *lokapālas*. Sundermann points out, "It follows from these texts that in the beginning of the 11th century the Turkish Khan of Qočo [i. e., Kocho] was the subject of a remarkable Manichaean panegyrical poetry. In the texts accessible to us no other king of the Uygur Empire or of Qočo, not even Bilgä Khan who made Manichaeism the religion of his state, was granted praise and intercession like this ruler."[18]

The curious thing about the king in question is, however, that he was also greatly revered by the Buddhists, and that a major Manichaean sanctuary in Kocho, the so-called "ruin α" of archaeology (according to Grünwedel's plan) was exactly the site where two Buddhist inscriptions also devoted to him were found on stakes, or wedge-shaped pieces of wood. He is here called Köl Bilgä, and that he is indeed the ruler in question has been established by Zieme and Hamilton.[19] Hence Müller's early dating of these inscriptions has to be reviewed. Sundermann argues from this that "there is no need to doubt the somewhat surprising coincidence that under one and the same Uygur ruler Köl Bilgä Buddhism spread and Manichaean literature flourished."[20] This does not, however, necessarily mean that Köl Bilgä marked the end of a Manichaean and the beginning of a Buddhist period. It seems rather that with him, new syncretistic tendencies especially effecting Buddhism set in, at least in the Turfan basin.[21] The syncretistic wall paintings of the monasteries of Toyoq near Turfan, where Christian, Manichaean, and Buddhist documents were found, seem to reveal that this syncretism was to determine the ensuing period, particularly the Buddhism of this part of Central Asia with its importance for the internal development of the Indian religion in its transmission to East Asia.[22]

1. *Blessings for an Uighur Ruler* (Persian)

This is a blessing for Bilgä Khan (Bögü Khan) who established Manichaeism as the state religion of the Uighur Turks in 762/763.[23]

> . . . May [the angels], together with their own (their relatives), the (divine) friends, themselves preserve and guard[24] the whole family of auditors, and above all the great ruler, (His) Great Majesty, the benign, blessed Ruler of the East (*xvārāsān*),[25] who is worthy of both (kinds of) bliss, (of) both (kinds of) life, (of) both (kinds of) dominion, temporal (lit., of the

body) and spiritual (lit., of the soul), the Keeper (Protector) of the Faith,[26] who appoints the righteous,[27] the bright crowned auditor, the ruler bearing the praised and blessed name, "The great king who received his charisma (*qut*) from Heaven, who by his virtue holds (together) the kingdom, the blessed, fortunate, wise Uighur Khan, the Son of Mani."[28] And may (the angels) also (protect and guard)... the "grand defenders" (of the Kingdom) and the generals of the blessed ruler...[29] May they all escape harm and finally receive the reward of the pious. May it be so for ever...[30]

2. *Postscript to a hymnbook* (*Mahrnāmag*) (Persian)

The text translated here is the postscript to a hymnbook (*Mahrnāmag*), and was written on a double-sheet. The scribe started to write this book in 723. Apparently the work was finished much later. Our copy comes from the ninth century. The other pages of this double-sheet contained an index of the hymns in the book (cf. chapter XV). According to Müller, a painting of the Manichaean king and his court probably preceded our text.[31] This would indicate that the religion enjoyed royal patronage, particularly as this text contains a blessing for the ruler and the members of his court.[32] The monarch bore the title *Ay tängridä qut bulmïš alp bilgä Uiɣur qaɣan* ("The valiant, wise Uighur Khan who received his charisma from the Moon God" [i. e., Jesus]). There were two rulers with this title; they reigned from 808 to 821 and from 824 to 832 respectively. It is probably the second one who is meant here.[33] Since blessings are invoked on him and his family, as well as on personages in various cities including Kocho, his political influence in the Turfan oasis must have preceded even the establishment of the Turkish kingdom of Kocho in ca. 850.

1. (It was) in the year 546 after the birth of the Apostle of Light,[34] (that is) now in the year...[35] when He (Mani) was raised up in might, and in the year 162 after the raising (death) of the beneficent Shād Ohrmizd[36] that this hymnbook, full of living words and beautiful hymns, was begun.
2. The scribe who had started to write it at the command of the spiritual leaders was not able to finish it. As he could not devote himself to it, and because he had no time, he wrote (only) a little, (just) a few hymns, and did not complete it.
3. It remained in its incomplete form at this place for many years. It lay around and was deposited in the monastery of Argi (Karashahr). When I, Yazadāmand, the preacher, saw this hymnbook lying around, incomplete and useless, I ordered my beloved child, (my) dear son Naxurīgrōshn ("The Firstborn of the Lights"), to complete it so that it might serve to increase faith, so that (it might become) a (useful) hymnbook in the hands of the children of faith, the new pupils, so that souls should be purified and doctrine, wisdom, instruction and virtue should be taught through it.
4. Thus by the grace of his divinity Mār Āryanshāh, the new teacher and good omen, and with the blessing of Mar Dōshist, the bishop, and the fine

leadership of Mār Yisho Aryamān ("Jesus the Friend"), the presbyter, and through the diligence of the wise preacher Yazad-āmad,[37] and furthermore through the zeal and the efforts of Naxurīgrōshn, who together with other scribes worked toward that end with a warm heart and a loving mind and who transcribed them (the hymns) day and night, until everything was finished and complete, . . .

5. And I, Naxurīgrōshn, the servant and scribe, in (making) preparations and arrangements in writing for the sake of this book, . . .

3. Postscript to a religious work (Persian)

On a page preserved from a religious work, embellished by a miniature painting portraying two divinities, there is the remnant of a postscript written in red.[38] It is a prayer for blessing of the donors who provided the means to have the work copied. The translation follows Sundermann.

. . . These noble benefactors, also those whose names I have not mentioned,[39] may they all live in body and soul, may they acquire (?) from (?) this book (their) portion of well-being.[40] Amen.

Notes

1. For Turkish colophons, compare Zieme, *Buddhistische Stabreimdichtungen,* pp. 155–82; *idem; Stabreimtexte,* 282–95.
2. Müller, "Der Hofstaat eines Uiguren-Königs," pp. 207–213.
3. The Turkish title is *Uluγ ilig tängridä qut bulmïš ärdämin il tutmïs alp qutluγ külüg bilgä uyγur qaγan.* Compare Zieme, "Manichäische Kolophone und Könige," p. 326; Sundermann, "Iranian Manichaean Turfan Texts," p. 72.
4. Sundermann, *ibid.*
5. Sundermann, *op. cit., p.* 73.
6. Sundermann, *ibid.*
7. Sundermann, *Parabeltexte,* p. 34.
8. Sundermann, "Iranian Manichaean Turfan Texts," pp. 71ff.
9. Sundermann, *op. cit.,* p. 71.
10. The Turkish name is *Ay tängridä qut bulmïš alp bilgä uyγur qaγan.* Compare Sundermann, *ibid.*
11. Compare Golzio, *Kings, Khans and other Rulers of Early Central Asia,* p. 63. According to Golzio, who gives his Chinese name as *Ho-sa,* he reigned from 824 to 832.
12. Sundermann, *op. cit.,* p. 71. Sundermann identifies Čīnānčkand with Kocho.
13. Sundermann, *op. cit.,* p. 71f. As Sundermann points out, Henning had assumed that in the list of rulers "more attention is paid to ecclesiastical than to political divisions." Henning, "Argi and the 'Tocharians,'" p. 551.
14. Klimkeit, "Hindu Deities in Manichaean Art," pp. 179–99. I now revise the interpretation of the picture with the four Hindu deities in light of a discussion with Dr. Jorinde Ebert, Würzburg, who has kindly presented to me her views as a specialist in Central and East Asian art. She will be publishing her findings in due course. The interpretation of the four deities in question as *lokapālas,* guardians of the four corners or regions of the world, adapted to Manichaeism, seems convincing. Zieme had already suggested at the Second International Conference on Manichaeism in St. Augustin/Bonn (8–10 August 1989) that

these are protective powers as invoked in Manichaean and Buddhist colophons. Compare Zieme, *op. cit.*, pp. 322f.

15. Cf. Reeves, *Jewish Lore in Manichaean Cosmogony. Studies in the Book of the Giants Traditions.*

16. The Turkish title is *Kün ay tängridä qut bulmïš uluγ qut ornanmïš alpïn ärdämin il tutmïš alp arslan qutuγ köl bilgä tängri.* Sundermann, *op. cit.*, p. 66; compare Zieme, *op. cit.*, p. 324.

17. Compare Sundermann, *op. cit.*, pp. 69ff. For the picture of this miniature painting, with the text, compare Klimkeit, *Manichaean Art and Calligraphy*, ill. 25 and description p. 37.

18. cf. Sundermann, *op. cit.*, p. 69.

19. Compare Hamilton, *Manuscrits*, p. XVII, n. 30; Zieme, *op. cit.*, p. 324. The Chinese name of this ruler, *Zhi-hai* (Pinyin transcription), means "wisdom (like) the ocean." This is reminiscent of the later Mongolian title granted to the High Lama of Tibet, *Dalai Lama*, which also implies a reference to "wisdom (like) the ocean"; since the Mongolians were a landlocked people, the question arises as to whether an undercurrent of Manichaean tradition might have remained alive up to Mongol times. (Cf. Türk. *taluy;* Mong. *dalai*, "ocean.") The ocean (*taluy*) is a significant symbol in Manichaeism; in the Sogdian "Book of Parables" (ch. XIII, 1) it represents the wisdom of the religion of Mani.

20. Sundermann, *op. cit.*, p. 70.

21. Zieme kindly tells me that Japanese scholars like T. Moriyasu hold that further research on the identity of the king in question is necessary.

22. On these wall paintings, compare a forthcoming study by Huashan Chao and H.-J. Klimkeit, *Neue archäologische Funde in der Turfan-Region.*

23. Zieme, *op. cit.*, p. 326.

24. Literally, "hide" (S); but here "protect" seems more appropriate, as it also appears in similar Turkish texts.

25. Manichaean Central Asia is meant.

26. Here the Manichaean king is expressly praised as *defensor fidei.*

27. The elect.

28. This title is Turkish, the last words being MP/Pth. Compare n. 3.

29. Here follows a long list of officials with their names and titles. Among them is a "supervisor of the auditors" (*niγošakpat*).

30. A list of "renowned court officials" (*namdaran ičäki*) follows.

31. Müller, "Doppelblatt," p. 6.

32. Cf. ch. XIV, text 2.

33. A. von Gabain, "Steppe und Stadt," p. 61. Henning opted for the first of these two kings. Henning, "Argi and the Tocharians," p. 568, n. 2. Compare Zieme, *op. cit.*

34. If the year of Mani's birth is taken as 216/217, this brings us to the year 762/763. Our copy of the text, however, must be from the ninth century. B points out, "The text has some Parthian forms and also some strikingly late linguistic features . . . which accord with the 9th-century-date," Boyce, *Reader*, p. 52, n. to text s.

35. Space left open.

36. This points to 600 as the year in which Shād Ohrmizd, the founder of the Central Asian Dēnāvarīya school, died.

37. Here members of the four ranks of the Manichaean community are referred to (S).

38. Text first translated by Sundermann in Klimkeit, "Hindu Deities in Manichaean Art," p. 193. Persian (MP) text quoted there.

39. Müller had translated, "whose names I have forgotten."

40. Literally, of the good, that is, that which is good.

Turkish Texts

CHAPTER TWENTY-THREE

Hymns to Mani

In the Iranian texts Mani is honored as the "Messenger of Light" (MP *frēstag-rōšn*) and as a redeeming god (MP *bay;* Pth. *baγ*). They describe him as having been "created by the Word (of God)" (cf. chapter VIII). In Turkish texts, he is honored not only with these titles, but also Buddhist ones like "Buddha," "Buddha Maitreya," and so on. This tendency had already set in, to be sure, in Parthian texts and was followed in Sogdian texts as well. In spite of all intentions to equate him with Maitreya, the future Buddha, he is distinguished from a "false Maitreya" in one Turkish text (TM 180). This document calls the "true Maitreya" the "Son of God" (*t(ä)ngri oγli*), pointing out that the "false Maitreya" only pretends to be that, but is in reality characterized by falsehood, deceit, and black magic.[1] Whether or not this is an attempt to discredit Buddhist ideas about Maitreya is an open question.

In the Turkish texts various phrases are employed to stress Mani's Buddhahood. Quite in accordance with Buddhist parlance, he is referred to as one who has "his origin (*töz*) in good Nirvāṇa"; he has acquired the dignity of a Buddha, that is, Buddhahood (*burxan quti*); he saves living beings from the woeful cycle of rebirths (*saṃsāra*), removing from their minds psychic impurities (*kleśa*s),[2] especially greed (*lobha*), hate (*dveṣa*), and delusion (*moha*), the "three poisons" of Buddhism. He leads men to "the dignity of an *arhat*," a saint in terms of Hīnayāna Buddhism, and to "the Realm of the Gods" (*burxanlar uluši*). The latter term refers to the Manichaean Realm of Light, but is also a Buddhist term for a "Buddha Realm" (*Buddhabhūmi*), like the Western Paradise of the Buddha Amitābha. Of course he is also called "God" (*tängri*) and "Buddha" (*burxan*). Bang and von Gabain point out, "Mani was the Father, Leader, Teacher, Preacher, Physician, Awakener, Redeemer *par excellence,* yes even 'the highest God' . . . , beside whom all the other figures in 'the Land of the Gods' receded into the background."[3]

1. Great Hymn to Mani

This hymn's late linguistic features would indicate that it was probably written in the Mongol period, in the thirteenth or fourteenth century. The patently Buddhist terminology employed by the poet lends credence to this supposition. The hymn was clearly composed in Turkish and not translated from an Iranian language. Containing over 120 verses, some of which are preserved only partially or not at all, this is the longest Turkish Manichaean hymn we possess.

1. [Oh, Teacher of] the original [doctrine][4] of the noble Jesus!
   [We are prepared] to worship you with a reverent mind.
   Oh, my respected and renowned Father,
   [My] Buddha Mani!

2. We have prepared ourselves
   To worship you with a humble heart.
   Accept now, (our) hope and refuge,[5]
   [All] the worship of every one (of us).

3. We bow down before you
   With faith from deep within.
   May it be pure every time we worship,

   . . .

   [about eleven verses badly preserved][6]

14. Being in [the state of] savage, poisonous animals,
    Ceaselessly submerged in the dust
    Of forgetfulness of rebirths,
    They were perpetually mad.

15. When they were poisoned by the passion of greed,[7]
    And were dying and perishing,
    You prepared a medicament for them
    From the herb of "meditation."[8]

16. Raving in the passion of anger,
    They were without senses or thoughts.
    You ordered (lit., assembled) their thoughts,
    Causing them to comprehend their origins.[9]

17. The living beings in the five states of existence[10]
    You freed from ignorance.
    You endowed them with wisdom,
    Leading them toward Parinirvāṇa.[11]

18. Many different passions
    Such as hatred and bitterness
    Had disturbed (these) sentient beings
    And led their thoughts astray.

19. (But) when you, our holy Father,
    Descended from Heaven,
    The families of all sentient beings
    [Reached peaceful Nirvāṇa (?)]

[*a number of verses badly preserved*]

26. ...
    We miserable beings without hope
    Would have remained in the torture of Saṃsāra[12]
    Without finding the end of your path.[13]

27. You set up the ladder of Wisdom,
    You allowed us to supercede the five forms of existence
    And redeemed us,
    ...

28. We ...
    Who had been in the fetters of suffering,
    Were rescued from this Saṃsāra
    In order to see the Buddhalike Sun-God[14]
    ... similar to you.

29. To those attached to transitory pleasures
    [You] preached the [unparalleled] true Law;
    You lead them across the sea of [suffering]
    And bring them to the good Nirvāṇa.

30. To those who had been bound to the root of attachment[15]
    You showed the road to the Realm of the Buddhas.[16]
    You raised a Sumeru mountain[17] of merit,
    You allowed them to find this ... everlasting [joy (?)]

31. To those that had plunged into the water of 'pride'
    You showed the bridge of the True Law.
    You gave understanding of the good Law into their hearts;
    You entrusted them to ... the holy assembly.

32. To those that had been confused by the six organs of perception[18]
    You showed the ascending and descending states of existence.
    You imparted knowledge of the suffering in the Hell Avīci;[19]
    You allowed them to be reborn in the blessed fivefold Heaven.[20]

33. Seeking the roads and paths of salvation
    You traversed realms and lands in every direction.
    When you found the beings in need of salvation
    You rescued each of them without exception.

34. To beings like us who used to be idle,
    You preached the jewel of the Gospel-Book[21] in detail.
    We understand the roads and paths of freedom and salvation
    When we learn of them in that book.

35. If you had not preached the pure Law
    In such a thorough manner,
    Would not the world and its sentient beings
    Have come to an end by now?

36. After the [four] Buddhas,[22] you descended
    And attained truly incomparable Buddhahood.[23]
    You redeemed myriads of living beings
    And saved them from dark Hell.

37. You purged them of masterly cunning and deception
    And caused them to do works of benefit for others.
    You became a guide and leader for those who had gone astray.
    You saved them from the claws of the evil[doing] Māra.[24]

38. You rescued those who had been malevolent,
    You [healed] those who had been blind.
    You caused them to do honorable works,
    You showed them the right path to the land of the gods.

39. You were born as the hope and refuge of the world,
    You taught (the contents of) the seven precious books.[25]
    (Furthermore) you restrained those
    That would have aligned themselves with evil.
            [ten verses badly preserved]

50. Walking on foot and calling upon your name,
    Praising and lauding you with their tongues,
    They would all love you in the same way
    As children love their mothers and fathers.

51. Embracing all of them
    With your great, compassionate heart
    (You) bestowed [great] benefit and prosperity on them.[26]
    . . .

52. Without distinguishing between kin and stranger
    You made them all your own.
    You gave your own counsel
    To innumerable living beings.

53. With your . . . heart
    You do good to all.
    As a consequence of the good you have done
    All the afflicted overcame their distress.

54. You bestowed great benefits and prosperity on us
    Continuously and constantly in this manner.
    As a consequence of your merit
    You acquired complete Buddha[hood].
            [one verse badly preserved]

56. With your un[surpassed] holy tongue
    You deigned to generously bestow
    The jewel of the good Law
    To (us) miserable living beings.
            [two verses badly preserved]

59. The families of the living beings
    Had (quite) lost their minds
    Through their dark passions,
    (But) they were (then) reborn . . .
            [eighteen verses missing or badly preserved]

78. With your great, compassionate heart
    You embraced all (living beings);

You rescued them from the cycle of rebirths
And [saved] them from Saṃsāra.

79. The blessed ones with pure hearts
Ever so gradually gained insight,
Vanquished their [malevolence],
And acquired the status of Arhats.[27]

80. The [pleasures] that bind one to the world
Brought forth the mastery of cunning and deception;
To these . . .
You brought benefit and prosperity.

81. . . .
To those that had forgotten their [true] origins,
To these [you revealed yourself (?)],
Changing your form . . .[28]

82. When all of these (Living beings)
Saw that revelation of yours,
They were inspired by the desire
To escape from the suffering [of cyclical Saṃsāra].

83. To the [children] of men
You showed a benevolent form
And (turned) them back from their (evil) deeds,
And from the love of the world to which they had succumbed.

84. . . .
In the view of the blue sky of the whole realm
You were born as [Buddha]-God of Teachers.

85. Seeing you, the living beings [rejoiced?]
And gave up their doubts.
And with diligent minds,
They kept the commandments which you gave.

86. As they kept them (the commandments) . . .
The good thoughts of their minds
Increased from day to day
And shone like the Sun-God.

87. Their radiant knowledge shone forth,
Compassion increased in their hearts;
They observed the commandment to be sinless
And escaped from ever-burning Hell.

88. . . .
Exerting themselves to keep the True Law,
They observed the true commandment
Not to commit impure sins.

89. Having comprehended the transiency of the body,
They left (their) houses and homes.[29]
In practicing the good laws
They observed the commandment to be pure in body.

90. They exerted themselves to practice the pure laws
    In order to avoid the dangerous places.
    And in order to be reborn in the Palace of Immortality,
    They observed the commandment to be pure in mouth.[30]

91. They all prayed for blessing
    To walk along the blessed road . . . ;
    And to escape terrible Saṃsāra,
    They observed the commandment of blessed poverty.[31]

92. They recognized the transitory (false) doctrines,
    And in fear of the three evil ways[32]
    They observed the three seals[33]
    To be born again in the highest place.[34]
         [*more than twenty verses badly preserved or missing*]

114. You deigned to command them
     To utter praises and (sing) hymns,
     To repent of (their) evil deeds,
     To assemble and to practice meditation.

115. The living beings had been confused,
     But when they heard this command of yours,
     Their virtue flowed like streams and rivers,[35]
     And they were reborn in the Land of the Buddhas.[36]

116. Other unsophisticated men,
     Walking in pure paths,
     Practiced meditation
     And were reborn in the Palace of Immortality.[37]

117. We bow our heads and we worship
     Before you, our highest God.
     May the living beings on this earth
     Be reborn ever hereafter in Nirvāṇa!

118. We worship with a devout heart;
     May all the living beings on this earth
     Escape all perils;
     May they obtain peaceful Nirvāna.

119. As a consequence of merit of our praise and worship
     May (all) the divine powers
     Of the gods above and below
     And of the various spirits be increased.[38]
         [*last two verses fragmentarily preserved*]

2. Bilingual Hymn to Mani (Tocharian B and Turkish)

This hymn is written on the same manuscript as the previous one, a "*pothi*-book" of the Indian type. It corresponds to the "Great Hymn to Mani" in form and content. The text is written in Tocharian B, the language of the oasis of Kucha, every line being followed by a corresponding one in Turkish. We translate here the Turkish version. L. V. Clark remarks, "This hymn is modeled on the *Buddhastotras,* or praises of the Buddha, which constitute a significant portion of the Buddhist Tocharian texts. The praise is here recast and directed toward Mani rather than Buddha, but its essentially Buddhistic mold remains, especially in its praise of the Three Jewels: the Buddha = Mani . . . , the Dharma [i.e., the Law] . . . , and the Sangha [i.e., the community]."[39]

1.   Oh, bright Sun-God . . .
     Oh, bright Moon-God!
     Like the diadem of the God Ohrmizd,
     Like the garland of the God Zurvān,
     Bright in appearance is my Father, the Buddha Mani.
     Therefore I praise and worship you so.
2.   Like the *cintāmaṇi*-jewel (are you),[40]
     Worthy to be worn on the crown of the head.
     Oh, you are worthy!
     As you shone (brightly)
     With the brightness of the commandments,
     So are you shining . . .
     Radiant to behold is my Father, the Buddha Mani.
     Therefore I praise and worship you so.
3.   You who have come quite unhindered,
     Remove greed and other passions!
     As your origin is in good Nirvāṇa,
     You are worthy to be worn on the crown
     Of the heads of the former Buddhas.
     Therefore I praise and worship you so.
           [*some verses only fragmentarily preserved*]
4.   . . .
     His whole mind awakes and increases
     Great heartfelt desires.
     I, Aryaman Fristum, the Superior,
     Bow my head and worship reverently
     The holy jewel of the community.[41]
[Title]:   Buddha, Teacher, God . . .

3. *Invocation of the Buddha Mani*

This is virtually a postscript to the two hymns to Mani translated above.

Now, my God, I, Aryaman Fristum, the Superior, with a respectful and devout, pure heart, set out to honor, bow my head and worship you. Without [impurity?] in my thoughts, I bow and worship his Majesty, the holy Buddha (Mani). I worship his Majesty, the Buddha (Mani), whose highest, whole being is at peace.[42] [I worship] his Majesty, the Buddha (Mani), who bestows divine favor on all.

4. Hymn to Mani, by Prince Aprin Čor

Like the above hymns, this is an original Turkish composition, by Prince Aprin Čor, in praise of Mani. Aprin Čor is a Turkisized form of the Middle Persian title Afrin-sār, "Leader of Hymns," but here it is a name rather than a title.

1. They say the goodness [of our God] is like a jewel.
   They say the goodness [of our God] is like a jewel.
   My loving [God] is more excellent than a jewel,
   He, my hero, my royal one.
   My kind God is more excellent than a jewel,
   He, my hero, my royal one.
2. They say he is an uncut, sharp *vajra*.[43]
   They say he is an uncut, sharp *vajra*.
   You, my righteous one, my light,
   Are endowed with knowledge
   That pierces (even) the *vajra*.
   You, my wise one, my elephant,[44]
   Are (endowed) with knowledge
   That pierces (even) the *vajra*.
3. You with a (shining) breast like the radiance of the Sun God,
   You, my wise one!
   You with a (shining) breast
   Like the radiance of the Sun God,
   You, the wise one!
   My beauteous, noble God!
   My glorious one, my treasure!
   My beauteous, noble God,
   My Buddha, my insurpassable one!

Notes

1. Türk. Man. II,5. *Mitri(i)* is not to be translated as "Mithra," as von Le Coq did, but rather as Maitreya. Compare Zieme, *Schrift und Sprache,* p. 60; Zieme, *Texte,* p. 81, s.v. *mitri.*
2. *BHSD* 198a gives for *kleśa,* "impurity, depravity." This virtually amounts to sin, or sinfulness.
3. Bang and von Gabain, "Türkische Turfan-Texte III," p. 206.
4. In the sense of basic doctrine.
5. In Turkish Buddhist texts, Buddha is repeatedly addressed as "the hope and refuge" (*umuγ ïnaγ*) of all living beings, including men.
6. Some lines preserved here read, "You explained the consequences of [evil] deeds . . . You blocked the road to Hell . . . Preaching the good laws, . . . You rescued . . . eight kinds of suffering [beings] . . . mad, savage, poisonous animals."
7. The image of greed, here, is inspired by the Buddhist term (Skr. *lobha*), albeit it is also one of the cardinal vices in Manichaeism. The mention of wrath (Skr. *dveṣa*) and ignorance (Skr. *moha*) in the following verses shows that the "three poisons" (Skr. *tri-doṣa*) of Buddhism are referred to here.
8. Literally, assembling (one's thoughts).

9. In the Realm of Light.
10. These are, in the Buddhist view, the states of gods, men, hungry spirits (*pretas*), animals, and beings of Hell.
11. The Realm of Light.
12. A Buddhist phrase, the cycle of rebirths.
13. The Realm of Light.
14. Jesus the Splendor.
15. Of attachment to the world.
16. Namely, the realm of the prophets of old, the Realm of Light.
17. The Sumeru mountain is the central mountain of the universe in Buddhist cosmology.
18. The six organs of perception (Skr. *ṣaḍāyatana*) are, in Buddhism, the five sense organs and the mind (Skr. *manas*).
19. The deepest Hell in Buddhism.
20. For the conception that the Realm of Light is a fivefold space, compare Introduction, furthermore Zieme, *Texte,* p. 31.
21. Reference to Mani's *Living Gospel.*
22. The "four Buddhas," that is, Prophets or Messengers, are probably Seth, Zarathustra, Buddha, and Jesus. Compare Clark, *Pothi-Book,* pp. 196f.
23. This is a Buddhist technical term implying the highest stage of enlightenment (Skr. *anuttara-samyaksam-bodhi*).
24. The Buddhist Satan.
25. I. e., the seven books written by Mani and regarded as canonical. Compare Introduction.
26. This is a Turkish Buddhist expression.
27. I. e., the religious ideal of Hīnayāna Buddhism.
28. As in Gnosticism generally, so in Manichaeism the savior is endowed with the power to change his form and appearance. Compare Klimkeit, "Gestalt, Ungestalt, Gestaltwandel."
29. This is a standard phrase in Buddhism.
30. The purity of mouth is one of the "three seals" or basic commandments in Manichaeism.
31. Or, to be blessed (and yet) poor; "blessed poverty" is a Manichaean commandment for the elect.
32. These are the three evil "ways" or forms of existence in the Buddhist sense (Skr. *durgati*). They are the existence of animals, hungry spirits (*pretas*), and beings of Hell.
33. The three seals or basic commandments refer to the heart (bosom), the mouth, and the hands.
34. In the Realm of Light.
35. This is a Buddhist image.
36. The Realm of Light.
37. The Realm of Light.
38. This is a colophon, typical of Turkish Buddhist texts from the Silk Road.
39. L. V. Clark, *Pothi-Book,* pp. 151f.
40. The jewel granting all wishes, according to an Indian conception.
41. In this hymn, Mani, his doctrine (Turk. *nom*) and his community are invoked at the end, in a manner corresponding to the invocation of the "three jewels" (*triratna*) in Buddhism.
42. This is a Buddhist conception of the Buddha.
43. The *vajra* is a Buddhist ritual object, representing a thunderbolt or diamond.
44. In Buddhist texts, Buddha, because of his power, is referred to as an elephant.

CHAPTER TWENTY-FOUR

General Hymns and Prayers

This chapter contains sundry hymns and prayers. A hymn to the Fourfold Father (text 1) includes invocations of Jesus, the Maiden of Light, Mani, the Great Nous, and the angels; the poet prays for health for the body and salvation for the soul. This twofold concern can also be traced in other Turkish texts.

Characteristic of various Turkish texts is their elated spirit of joy, jubilation, and triumph. This can be understood against the background of the triumph of the Manichaean faith, for a certain time at least, when it was made the official religion of the Uighur Turks in 762/763, and in the Kingdom of Kocho after 850. The king himself embraced the religion, and the state supported and protected the Church. This gave rise to the feeling that sorrow and woe had been vanquished, that the Light of the world beyond had shone into this world, and that salvation was nigh, or even that it had come (text 3). The appearance of the redeeming gods had led to the suppression of demonic (i. e., anti-Manichaean) forces, a cause for gladness (texts 3 and 4). A protecting Manichaean kingship had been established (text 8). However, the supreme power of the Manichaean ruler lasted for but a limited time. Buddhism, the great rival, increasingly influenced political affairs, and it was this later period that gave rise, once again, to a great yearning for salvation, to redemption in an otherworldly Realm of Light. Hence it was a time of doubt and laxity in faith. Thus the hymnwriter could pray (text 10):

"You, my Father who enlightens my mind,
End (this) frightful state
And free me from doubt."

Here the outward oppression was paralleled by an inner challenge to the faith. In this situation, the faithful were exhorted to remain true to the faith; at the same time, they were exhorted not to cease giving alms to the elect (text 5). Such service was termed "soul-service," because it primarily served to help one's own soul. The gifts given to the elect were gifts given to the Church (*dēn*), and ultimately served to achieve a divine end.

1. Hymn to the Fourfold Father

This hymn to the Fourfold Father is a translation from an Iranian original, of which, however, only a portion has been rendered into Turkish. Hence the title, "From the hymn (*bašta*) . . ."

[Title]: From the hymn to God, Light, Power and Wisdom[1]
1. We invoke God, Light, Power and Wisdom.
   We pray to the God of the Sun and the Moon,[2]
   To the Goddess of Light,[3] the Great Nous, Mār Mani and the angels.[4]
   We make supplication (to thee), oh my God!
2. Protect our bodies,
   Redeem our souls!
   We implore thee for well-being!
   With the help of[5] the Gods of Light
   We wish to be free from distress
   And to abide in joy.

2. Hymn to the God of the Dawn

The "God of the Dawn" (*tang t(ä)ngri*) is referred to in the original of the title as "the God Vam" (Sogd. β'm βγγ, Vam vaγi). As such, he is the Great Builder, who is not invoked frequently in these hymns. In Sogdian, β'm is also the dawn. Hence the deity referred to is the God of the Dawn (not Goddess of the Dawn, as Bang had thought). He is here related to the God of the Sun and the Moon, that is, to Jesus the Splendor.

[Title]: Hymn to the God of the Dawn
1. The God of the Dawn has come,
   The God of the Dawn himself has come,
   The God of the Dawn has come,
   The God of the Dawn himself has come.
   Arise, all you masters, you brethren!
   We would praise the God of the Dawn!
2. (All)-seeing Sun God, protect us!
   Visible Moon God, redeem us!
   God of the Dawn,
   Fragrant, sweet,
   Bright, shining,
   God of the Dawn! (five times)
   God of the Dawn! (five times)
       [*the last five lines are repeated*]

3. Hymn about the descent of "our wise God"

It is not clear which deity this hymn calls the god that descended from the Realm of Light. The First Man comes to mind, but he did not bring with him the Teaching of Mani. Maybe the Living Spirit, or Jesus the Splendor is meant, if this is not a reference to a worldly ruler, as verse 8 would suggest. The God Taγay, mentioned in verses 2 and 3, also remains unidentified. Furthermore, the "Presbyter Noγdar" who accompanied the righteous king, is unknown.

The interlinking of lines is reminiscent of Semitic poetry.

1. Our pure, radiant, wise God
    Descended from the Realm of the Gods.
2. Descending from the Realm of the Gods,
    He brought (with him) [the God] Taγay.[6]
3. When the God Taγay had come,
    He redeemed our souls from Hell.[7]
       [two verses badly preserved]
6. Because he deigned to enlighten (us),
    We were saved from the place of no return.
7. Because he established the Law of the Buddha[8]
    We were freed from [distress] and misery.
8. Our king himself, clothed with Nom Qutï (the Great Nous),[9]
    Brought the Presbyter Noγdar[10] with him.
9. [When] the Presbyter Noγdar had come,
       . . .

       [remainder not preserved]

4. Hymn to Jesus as God of the Moon

This hymn is sung to a saving deity. According to Bang, it is Jesus as God of the Moon.[11]

   My God!
   [You are] the new [day],
   The bright new month (*ay*),[12]
   The newly raised year!
   You are the new, mighty, radiant God!
   When you come forth from the Land of the gods, my God,
       . . .
   [From] the sight of your appearance (*körk*)
   We have become very joyful.
   You are the wise, royal, mighty, radiant God.[13]

5. Hymn about the immortality of the soul

The verses preserved here exhort the auditors to give alms, that is, to engage in "soul service." The dire life-after-death consequences of failing to do so are vividly described. The initial verse, too fragmentary for a translation here, speaks of the immortality of the soul which never dies, in spite of being burned (i. e., in Hell).

[*beginning badly preserved*]

1. Oh, radiant soul!
    Whoever does not build a house and give it
    To the homeless *arhat*-elect[14]
    Will be put into a pit with pikes, it is said.
    The pikes will pierce him.
    They will come out from his head,
    They will scratch his skin [and his face],
    They will [cut?] his sinews.
    He will be separated from his bones;
    But the soul never dies, it is said.
2. Oh, radiant soul!
    How could you (bear it)?
    Oh, radiant soul!
    We would give alms in purity!
    Oh, radiant soul!
    We would serve with pure charity!
3. Oh, radiant soul!
    Whoever does not prepare and give
    Food to the hungry, thirsty elect

    . . .

    [*remainder missing*]

6. Description of the fate of the unrighteous soul

Here the fate of the unrighteous soul is described. After the judgment, it is subjected to manifold tortures and torments. The beginning and the end of the hymn are missing.

1. The deeds he himself has done are revealed . . .[15]
    The *nous* (*qut*)[16] of earth and water suffers . . .
    The *nous* of fire and water weeps . . .
    The *nous* of the trees and plants laments . . .
2. The Just Judge appears as in a mirror
    And seizes the impure (lit., confused) soul.
    It is placed in the scales, . . .
    When the scales dip, its deeds are pronounced,
    Its sin, the deeds it has done, is heard.
3. When the deceptive old she-demon, covered with hair, comes,
    When she seizes the impure soul,
    She will pull it into dark Hell, . . .
    Twirling around its head, she knocks it, . . .

4.   The demons in Hell seize it (the soul), . . .
     The mistending (?)[17] demons come, . . .
     They beat it with rods and want to scourge it, . . .
     It begs (her for) death, but does not receive it.

7. Hymn about the fate of the godless

This hymn first admonishes the auditors to piety. It then describes the demons in Hell that await the sinner when he dies. According to the title, this hymn was composed originally in Turkish.

[Title]:   A selected Turkish hymn
1.   We would gather together, you noble, wise men,
     We would hear God's scripture,
     We would bring honor to the four royal gods,[18]
     We would be liberated from the four great errors.[19]
2.   Those who deny the four royal gods,
     Those who despise the divine Law (doctrine),
     Those who revere the dark demons,
     (Those who) do ten thousand bad deeds,
     In the end, they, too, shall find death;
     They shall fall into dark Hell.
3.   Then ten thousand demons will come, . . .[20]
     Demons of fog will overcome them, . . .
     They (the souls) will be imprisoned, . . .
4.   She (the demoness of Darkness) sits down on his breast
     And lets him dream, . . .
     Souls that have gone astray emerge, . . .
     He (the dying one) parts from his body like *tardič* (?), . . .
     His possessions are withheld, . . .
5.   A deceptive old she-demon, covered with hair, comes, . . .
     Like clouds of hail she is *tonqï*-(?)-browed, . . .
     The black nipples of her breasts are like pegs, . . .
     A great cloud constantly billows from her nose, . . .
     Black smoke comes out of her throat, . . .
6.   Her breasts consist entirely of snakes—ten thousand of them,
     As for her limbs, they are twinelike,
     As for her fingers, they are all serpents.

8. Hymn of praise to a Manichaean ruler

In this praise of a Manichaean ruler, the poet gives expression to his loyalty to the king. Although the manuscript proves the text to be Manichaean, there is nothing specifically Manichaean about the content.

[*five lines badly preserved*]

1. Like the gray wolf,[21] I will walk [with] you.
    Like the black raven I will remain on earth.
    Like charcoal for the disease,
    Like spittle for the whetstone will I be.
    [*four lines badly preserved*]
2. You are our mighty, great ruler,
    (You are) rounded like gold,
    (You are) rounded like a ball,
    You are our wise, majestic (*qutluγ*) ruler.
3. Keeping and protecting your numerous people,
    You nurse and tend (them)
    At your wide breast,
    At the fringe of your long robe.

9. Manichaean Love Song

As Manichaeism in Central Asia encompassed all orders of life, including its secular dimensions, it also inspired worldly literature. A love song of the type we have here, with its references to the gods of Light, and to the angels (or messengers: *brištilär*) would have been quite unthinkable in the classical *gnosis* of the Mediterranean area. One can well imagine, however, that poetry of this type, like the "Song of Songs" in the Old Testament, was later given a religious meaning, referring in this case to the soul's longing for its heavenly *alter ego*.

1. [*badly preserved*]
2. Thinking of my strong one, I grieve;
    Grieving I yearn for union
    With my beautiful-browed one.
3. I think of my beloved one;
    Thinking, I turn to . . .
    I yearn to kiss my beloved one.
4. If I want to go, my beloved *bač* (?),
    I cannot go,
    Oh, you, my gracious one.
5. If I want to go to you, my dear one,
    I cannot go,
    You, my fragrant one.
6. Having been united with my gentle one
    By the grace of the radiant gods,
    We shall not be separated.
7. I will sit down joyfully
    With my dark-eyed love,
    By the power of the mighty angels.

10. *Prayer for redemption*

Here an unidentified deity is invoked.

> [*first lines badly preserved*]
> I shall dedicate myself wholly
> To the choicest songs of praise offered to you,
> And to divine faith in you,
> For I am yours!
> I have become your prisoner,
> I direct my supplication to you.
> [*a few lines badly preserved*]
> You, my king, who cleanses my soul!
> You, my God, who gives delight to my Living Self,
> You, my Father, who enlightens my mind,
> End (this) frightful state
> And free me from doubt.
> [*rest missing*]

11. *Prayer for deliverance*

This prayer is a petition for deliverance from evil, from the powers of Darkness that outwardly threaten the life of the poet, but also cloud his spiritual understanding. Thus he prays for insight and understanding. The term "master-physician" possibly refers to Zurvān, the Father of Light, as Bang surmised.

> [*beginning badly preserved*]
> Deliver me from those that do evil,
> Separate me from those that are laden with guilt,
> And deliver me from the sons of Hell
> Who are all wicked,
> And who do nothing but spread wickedness.
> My God, protect me from these devouring demons
> And from the manifold kinds of poisonous [snakes?]
> [*some lines missing*]
> My God, I direct my supplication to you,
> I pray before your countenance.
> You are the master-physician,
> You are the teacher of the well-disposed,
> Through your love you gladden those whom you accept.
> Direct my mind to knowledge *(gnosis)*;
> The evil-working Satan . . .
> [*some lines missing*]
> You are (yourself) loving, complete Wisdom,
> You deign to grant us your salvation *(qut)*,

My God! Lead me always to thoughtfulness,
(And) deign to let me understand.
   [some lines missing]
Redeem [me from] the hands of the old demoness of death,
Cleanse me from the evil of the malignant Satan's sons,
Lead me into your fragrant garden.[22]

12. *Prayer for mercy*

Only a remnant of a few verses containing a prayer for divine mercy has been preserved here. The text shows that the bestowal of insight, or understanding, is understood as divine grace.

   ... My strong God!
I pray to your majesty *(qut),* I beseech you,
Have mercy upon us in your great compassion, my God!
Our Living Self calls upon you.
   [some verses missing]
You are like one who is to be honored and truly praised.
All your great and radiant sons,
And your selected Apostles *(prištilar)*[23]

   . . .
   [rest missing]

13. *Prayer for forgiveness*

This prayer for forgiveness comes from the same manuscript as the previous text. It is not clear whether it is a continuation of that prayer or not. It is probably directed to the Fourfold Father, as the introductory words suggest.

   [beginning not preserved]
My God!
My bright, strong, beneficent, just God!
Have mercy upon me now!
From now on I shall sin no more.
Lying prostrate before you, (I profess),
I shall no more bring offerings to the demons.
   [some lines badly preserved]
You are loving, complete Wisdom.
Deign to heal me now, my God!
Forgive my sins,
Grant me dispensation from my offenses,
Wash away my misdoing,
[Grant] me good recompense now,
Through your gracious gift.
   [end missing]

Notes

1. The fourfold formula is indicated in Parthian terms: *baγ, rōšn, zāwar, zīrīft.* In the first line, it is repeated in Turkish.
2. The God of the Sun and Moon is, in this case, "Jesus the Splendor." Compare Rose, *Die manichäische Christologie*, p. 26.
3. The Goddess of Light is the Maiden of Light.
4. Or, Apostles (*frištilar*)
5. The dative used here (*tängrilärkä*) can also be translated as "through the gods."
6. This God (or Goddess?) is otherwise unknown.
7. Literally, He removed our hell-souls (*tamuluγ üzütümüz*).
8. The teaching of Mani.
9. Reference to an unnamed Manichaean king.
10. This personality with an Iranian name is otherwise unknown.
11. Bang, "Hymnen," p. 19.
12. *Ay* is also the moon.
13. The adjectives are evocative of the fourfold formula. Compare text 1 in this section.
14. The *arhat,* here equated with the elect, is, in Hīnayāna Buddhist terms, a person who has attained perfection.
15. Here and in the following parts indicated by . . . the text has "it is said/they say" (*tiyür*).
16. *Qut* is here the holy Light dispersed in the material world, that is, the "Living Self."
17. Or, misleading in the sense of making mad (*muntrumuntuz*).
18. The four royal gods are God himself, his Light, his Power, and his Wisdom.
19. Literally "afflictions," since errors entail afflictions. Those who succumb to the four great errors are referred to in the following four lines.
20. Here, and in the following parts indicated by . . . , the text has "it is said."
21. The gray wolf is said to be a totemic ancestor of the Turks.
22. The Paradise of Light is often described as a fragrant garden.
23. This word can also mean "angels."

CHAPTER TWENTY-FIVE

Confessions

The Manichaeans of Central Asia used a number of confessional prayers, both for monks (elect) and laymen (auditors). It is striking that some of them, especially confessional formulae for laymen, correspond closely to Buddhist prayers of this type. While it has often been assumed that the Manichaeans borrowed from the Buddhists, it seems just as possible that there was reciprocity in this, as in other cases. The Buddhists in India had no confessional formulae for laymen. The practice of penitence, and the emphasis on its necessity, were widespread in the early Christian Church and at its fringes, as we see from apocryphal and Gnostic literature. Fragments of the Manichaean version of the *Shepherd of Hermas*—a Christian work that emphasizes penance, from second century Rome—were found in Turfan, a fact which suggests that this practice had Christian roots. The main confessional prayer for laymen, the $X^u\bar{a}stv\bar{a}n\bar{i}ft$, uses the Parthian phrase *manāstār hirzā*, "Forgive my sins!" as a standard formula. This suggests that it probably originated in East Iran or Sogdiana. As we know from the Coptic *Homilies* (5,16ff.), the confession was also of great importance in Western Manichaeism, though no formulae like the Central Asian ones have come to light from that area. The ritualization of the confessional practice, using set prayers, is reminiscent of the ablution and baptismal rituals of the Judeo-Christian Elchasaites, among whom Mani grew up. He would have reinterpreted the necessity of repeated washings and baptisms in a spiritual sense, calling for reiterated spiritual ablution through prayer.

1. The Uighur $X^u\bar{a}stv\bar{a}n\bar{i}ft$

This confessional prayer was intended for auditors, that is, laymen.[1] It was probably recited as part of the Monday ritual, as Monday, the holy day, was the day of confession. The text was probably spoken by a *qoštar* (Sogd. *xveštar*), a "Master" or "Superior," that is, a Manichaean priest of high rank. The laymen would respond

together, reciting the same portion the Master had spoken in Turkish, or at least
the request for forgiveness, which is in Parthian, possibly the original language of
the text. This conjecture is suggested by pictorial depictions showing laymen kneel-
ing before Manichaean priests.[2] The fact that fragments of over twenty manu-
scripts of the $X^u\bar{a}stv\bar{a}n\bar{\imath}ft$ were found in Turfan and Tun-huang, and that portions
of a Sogdian version have also come to light[3] attests to the great popularity of this
text. The manuscript on which this text is based, now kept in London, was owned
by a *qoštar* by the name of Rāymast Frazend. He is also known to us from a Sogdian
colophon to a Parthian text (M 481) on "consciousness and wisdom."[4] The inser-
tion of the owner's name into the text is a feature of Buddhist confessions and other
Turkish Buddhist documents as well. Yet there are relatively few Buddhist phrases
and expressions here, although the elect are referred to as Buddhas, and the Buddhist notion of the "three Jewels" appears in Manichaean garb.

I. 1.   [Sins against Zurvān]
   2.   The God Xormuzta (the First Man) came at the command of all the gods
        and descended with the Fivefold God[5] to fight the Devil *(yäk)*. He fought
        the evildoing Šimnu (the Devil) and the five kinds of devils (escorting
        him).[6] Then God and the Devil, Light and Darkness, were mixed. The
        son of God Xormuzta, the Fivefold God, our soul, fought for some time
        against the Devil and was wounded. And, being mixed with the evil[7] of
        the leader of all devils, with the evil of the insatiable and shameless Devil
        of Greed, and the evil of the 140 myriads of devils, he lost his will and
        became weak. He completely forgot the land of the immortal gods[8] in
        which he himself had been created and born, and he was separated from
        the gods of Light.
   3.   If from that time on, my God, because the evil-working Šimnu devilishly
        seduced our intellect and our thoughts, and because we thus became will-
        less and without knowledge (of ourselves), we should have sinned and
        erred against the holy Light, God Äzrua (Zurvān, the Father of Light), the
        origin and root of all souls of Light, and should have called Him the origin
        and root of Light as well as of Darkness, and of God as well as of the Devil;
        if we should have said, "If anybody quickens, it is God that quickens; if any-
        body slays, it is God that slays"; or if we should have said, "God has created
        both the good and the evil,"[9] or if we should have said, "He (God, the
        Father of Light), has created the eternal gods";[10] or if we should have
        said, "The God Xormuzta and the Devil are brothers";[11] or if we ever, my
        God, should have thus spoken very blasphemous words involuntarily, lying
        to God, and should have committed such unpardonable sin, then, my God,
        I, Rāymast Frazend, repent now, praying to be delivered from sin. [Par-
        thian]: Forgive my sins! [Turkish]: Blessed beginning!
II. 1. Second. Sins against the God of the Sun and the Moon (Jesus the Splen-
        dor) and against the gods enthroned in the two Palaces of Light.[12]
   2.   When one goes to the Land of the gods, the origin, root and meetingplace
        of all the Buddhas (messengers of Light), (the place) of the Pure Law
        (Teaching), (the abode) of the beneficent souls,[13] and (the source of) the

Light of the world, the God of the Sun and the Moon is its front door. In order to liberate the Fivefold God and to separate Light and Darkness, they (the Sun and the Moon) revolve in a circle and light up the four quarters of the world.

3. My God, if we ever should have in any way sinned unwittingly against the God of the Sun and the Moon, and the gods who are enthroned in the two palaces of Light, and if we should have believed, "True, mighty and powerful is the God (of the Sun and the Moon)," (but) if we (at the same time) should in any way have uttered much evil, blasphemous speech, saying, "The Sun and the Moon will perish," if we should have said, "They rise and set without (their own) power; if they have power of their own, then may they try not to rise," and if we should have said with regard to our own self, "We are different from the Sun and Moon," then we pray for forgiveness for this second involuntary sin. [Parthian]: Forgive my sins!

III. 1. Third. (Sins) against the Fivefold God, God Xormuzta's Son.

2. (The five Gods are) first, the Zephyr God; second, the Wind God; third, the Light God; fourth, the Water God; fifth, the Fire God. When he (the five gods together as the Fivefold God) fought with the Devil for some time, he was wounded and mixed with Darkness. So he could not return to the Land of the gods and (that is why he) is on this earth. The ten-storied heaven above and the eight-layered earth below exist only for the sake of the Fivefold God. The Fivefold God is the blessing and happiness, the form[14] and appearance, the self and the soul, the power and the light, the origin and the root of everything on earth.

3. My God, if we should ever, involuntarily, on account of evil and wickedness, have broken or injured the Fivefold God, if we should have inflicted on Him the fourteen wounds,[15] if we should in any way have tortured and pained the Living Soul, (namely) the God (the divine element) in food and drink, with (our) ten serpentheaded fingers and (our) thirty-two teeth, and if we should in any way have sinned against the dry and wet earth, against the five kinds of living beings,[16] against the five kinds of plants,[17] then, my God, I (lit., we) now pray to be delivered from sin. [Parthian]: Forgive my sin!

IV. 1. (Sins) against the present (living) messengers of the gods, the Buddhas (the elect).

2. If we should in any way have sinned involuntarily against the holy elect who do meritorious deeds and bring salvation, and if, in spite of calling them "true messengers of God" and "Buddhas," and believing that the holy elect are characterized by good deeds, we, in our ignorance, should have opposed them when they preached God's Law, and if we should have obstructed them, by not spreading the Doctrine and the Law, then, my God, we now repent and pray to be delivered from sin. [Parthian]: Forgive my sins!

V. 1. Fifth. (Sins) against the five kinds of living beings.

2. (These are sins) first against two-legged beings; second, against four-legged living beings; third, against living beings that fly; fourth, against

living beings in the water; and fifth, against living beings creeping on the ground on their bellies.

3. If we ever, my God, should have frightened and intimidated these five kinds of living beings in any way, from the biggest to the smallest, and if we should have beaten or wounded them in any way, or in any way have pained or tortured them, or if we should have killed them in any way, then we ourselves owe life to (those) living beings to the same degree. (So) now, my God, we pray that we may be delivered from sin. [Parthian]: Forgive my sins!

VI. 1. Sixth. Likewise, my God, if we should ever have committed the ten kinds of sins in thought, word or deed,[18] (namely):

2. If we should have been false in any way or have committed perjury in any way; if we should have acted in any way as a witness for a dishonest person; if we should have prosecuted an innocent person in any way; or if we, by spreading rumors and by gossip, should have instigated a person in any way and (thus) have corrupted his heart and mind; if we should have practiced black magic in any way; if we should have killed many living beings in any way; or if we should have cheated and deceived (others) in any way; if we should in any way have used another person's goods (entrusted to our care); if we should in any way have done a deed of which the God of the Sun and the Moon would not approve; if we should have sinned and erred in any way with the "first self" and with "this self,"[19] after having been reborn as men;[20] if we should have inflicted destruction and ruin somehow on many living beings; then, my God, we now pray to be delivered from the ten kinds of sins. [Parthian]: Forgive my sins!

VII. 1. Seventh. If one should ever ask, "Who (comes) to the way leading to the beginning of the two poisonous paths[21] and the gate of Hell?" (then the answer is), "First, it is he that adheres to a wrong teaching and to a wrong law; second, likewise, it is one who worships the Devil and addresses him as God."

2. If we, my God, should ever, without recognizing and understanding the true God and the pure Law, and without believing when the Buddhas (the divine messengers), the pure elect, preached, allowing ourselves to be deceived by one who wrongly maintained, "I am a man of God and a preacher," and accepted his words; if we should have fasted falsely, should have worshipped falsely in any way, should have given alms falsely in any way, and if we should in any way, erring, have done false and evil deeds, saying, "We do meritorious deeds, such as bring salvation," and if we, when addressing the Devil and the Demon of Greed, should have worshipped them by killing living beings, and if we, saying, "(He is) a Buddha" (a messenger) should have honored a false doctrine and have worshipped and honored him (or it: the false doctrine) and (thus) have sinned against God; if we should have served the Devil, then, my God, we now repent and pray to be delivered from sin. [Parthian]: Forgive my sins!

VIII. 1. Eighth. Ever since we recognized the true God and the pure Law we know the doctrine of the "two principles and the three periods," (that is,) we know the Light principle, the Realm of the gods (or of God), and the Dark principle, the Realm of Hell. And we know what existed previously, when there was no earth or heaven; we know why God and the Devil fought, how Light and Darkness were mixed, and who created heaven and earth. And furthermore, we know why heaven and earth will cease to exist, how Light and Darkness will be separated, and what will then be (at the end of time).

2. In the God Äzrua (Zurvān), in the God of the Sun and the Moon, in the powerful God (the Fivefold God) and in the Buddhas (messengers) do we trust; we have relied on them and have become auditors (laymen). We have sealed our hearts with the four bright seals:[22] firstly, Love, the seal of the God Äzrua; secondly, Faith, the seal of the God of the Sun and the Moon; thirdly, Fear (of God), the seal of the Fivefold God; fourthly, Wisdom, the seal of the Buddhas (messengers).[23]

3. My God, if we should have let our minds and hearts stray from these four gods,[24] if we should have displaced them from their (rightful) place and if God's seal should have thus been broken, then, my God, we now pray to be delivered from sin! [Parthian]: Forgive my sins!

IX. 1. Ninth. Since we started obeying the ten commandments it was necessary to observe closely three with the mouth, three with the heart, three with the hand and one with the whole self.

2. My God, if we should voluntarily or involuntarily, while living in accordance with fleshly desires and accepting the words of a bad companion or friend, have followed their intentions, or should have disturbed our minds with cattle and property, or should have, in grief and distress, broken these ten commandments, or should in any way have had (other) shortcomings (in keeping the commandments), (then), my God, we pray to be delivered from sin. [Parthian]: Forgive my sins!

X. 1. Tenth. There is a rule to direct four prayers to the God Äzrua, the God of the Sun and the Moon, the Fivefold God and the Buddhas (the messengers) with complete attention and with an earnest heart, daily.

2. And if we, being negligent and without the fear (of God), should not have prayed correctly and wholeheartedly, or should not have directed our hearts and minds to God while praying, or if our prayers of praise and petition should not have reached God in purity, or if somewhere there should have been something that obstructed (our prayer), (then), my God, we now pray to be delivered from sin. [Parthian]: Forgive my sins!

XI. 1. Eleventh. There is also the rule that one should give sevenfold alms to the holy Church. And if the angels gathering the light of the Fivefold God and the Gods Call (Xrōshtag) and Answer (Padvāxtag) should let the light of the Fivefold God, which goes up to Heaven and is liberated, come to us, (then) there is a rule that we should prepare (the alms) carefully and bring them to the Church (?).[25]

2. If we should not have been able to give the sevenfold alms to the Church in full measure, either because of want or because we were miserly in giving alms; or if the light of the Fivefold God which goes up to Heaven and

is liberated should have been bound by us to house and property, or if we should have given it to a person of bad conduct, or to an evil being, or if we should have spilled or scattered it; or if we should have brought the light of God to an evil place, then, my God, we now pray to be delivered from sin. [Parthian]: Forgive my sins!

XII. 1. Twelfth. There is a rule that one (as an auditor) should observe the Vusanti(-Fast) for fifty days in a year, just as the holy elect do.[26] It is necessary to praise God by observing the sacred Fast.

2. If we, voluntarily or involuntarily, should have broken the Fast with a view to maintaining house and property, or because we were worried about cattle and goods, or because our need and distress mounted, or because of the insatiable and shameless Demon of Greed, or because our heart was devoid of fear (of God), or because we were lazy and indolent, or if we, in fasting, should not have fasted correctly, according to the (religious) Law and regulation, then, my God, we pray to be delivered from sin. [Parthian]: Forgive my sins!

XIII. 1. Every Monday it is necessary to request God, the Church and the holy elect to forgive our offenses and sins.[27]

2. And should we, voluntarily or involuntarily, have not gone to receive forgiveness for our sins because we were lazy and negligent, or because we used business or another undertaking as a pretext, then, my God, we now pray to be delivered from sin. [Parthian]: Forgive my sins!

XIV. 1. In the fourteenth place. There is a rule that one should celebrate the seven Yimki (festivals) in one year, and we are (furthermore) bound to the commandment concerning the month of (fasting).[28] Likewise we are obliged, after observing the Yimki (festivals) in fasting, to request the God Buddha (Mani), sincerely and with our whole hearts, to forgive our sins for the (whole) year at the Bema (festival).[29]

2. My God, if we should have not been able to celebrate the seven Yimki (festivals) adequately, or if we should have not been able to obey the commandments regarding the month's (Fast) correctly, and should not, at the Bema, have been able to celebrate the Yimki fast sincerely or correctly according to (the rules of) the religion and the doctrine, and should not have prayed (at the Bema) with all our hearts for the forgiveness of our sins in the (past) year, if we should in any way have had shortcomings (in this respect, too), then, my God, we now pray to be delivered from sin. [Parthian]: Forgive my sins!

XV. 1. In the fifteenth place. Every day we think bad thoughts, we speak sinful words which one should not speak and we do deeds which we should not do.

2. Because of (these) evil deeds and sins we incur grief upon ourselves; the Light of the Fivefold God (contained in food) which we have eaten in the course of the day goes to the evil place, because we ourselves, our souls, live in love of the insatiable and shameless Demon of Greed. Therefore, my God, we pray to be delivered from sin. [Parthian]: Forgive my sins! [Turkish]: For the sake of the divine "omen of religion"!

3. My God, we are encumbered with faults and sins, we are greatly in debt.
    We bring constant and permanent agony upon the Light of the Fivefold
    God in the dry and wet earth, in the five kinds of living beings and the five
    kinds of herbs and trees, because of the insatiable and shameless Demon
    of Greed, (acting according to him) in thought, word and deed, looking
    with his eyes, hearing with his ears, speaking with his tongue, grasping
    with his hands, and walking with his feet. Likewise we are encumbered
    with faults and sins. In view of the ten commandments, the (obligation to
    give) sevenfold alms, and the three seals, we are auditors in name, but we
    are unable to fulfill their duties.

    Likewise, if we should have in any way so sinned and erred against the
    gods of Light, the pure Law and the men of God and preachers, the holy
    elect,[30] and if we should have not lived in accordance with the doctrine
    and wisdom communicated by God, if we should have broken the hearts
    of the gods and been unable to celebrate the Yimki (festival), (and observe)
    the Fast, the prayer and commandments in accordance with (the rules of)
    the religion and the doctrine, and if we should in any way have had
    shortcomings—(for) every day, every month we sin—then we pray to the
    gods of Light, to Nom Qutï (the Great Nous) and to the holy elect so that
    we may be delivered from sin. [Parthian]: Forgive my sins!
    Eleventh month, on the twenty-fifth day.

1.1 FRAGMENTS FROM THE SOGDIAN XᵘĀSTVĀNĪFT

The Sogdian fragments of the Manichaean confessional prayer for the elect were
edited and translated by Henning and Sims-Williams.[31] They show that the text
was already extant in an East Iranian version before it was introduced in Turkish
Central Asia. We mainly follow Henning's translation here.

Fragment 1

[Title] *Xᵘāstvānīft*. [Sogdian] Confession of sins.
[Title] This is the *Saṃgha* (?) *Xᵘāstvānīft*.

Oh God, forgive my sins! Weak am I and sinful, indebted and a debtor,
moved by greed-breeding (?), shameless Greed [the Demon of Greed], in
thought, word and deed, by the looking of the eyes, the hearing of the
ears, the speaking of the tongue, the grasping of the hands, the walking
of the feet, since at every moment I hurt and injure the five Elements (of
Light), . . . the *buddha gotra*[32] (which is) in the dry and the wet ground,
the five kinds of plant beings, the five kinds of animal beings.

Again: weak am I and sin against the ten commandments, the seven
pious gifts,[33] the three seals.[34] In name I am an *auditor*, but I am unable
to perform the duties (befitting for such one). Contrary to the gods of
Light . . . I am unable to observe the [Yimki], the fasting, the prayers and
the hymns, and the commandments in full [and regularly]. If at any [time],
any moment, any day, any month, any year there was a failure or an

omission from my side, if through my [forgetfulness anything] has been omitted from this confession—for this I, N. N., say, Grant me pardon! (Grant) forgiveness for my sins! In the presence of the gods of Light, the "Glory of the Religion" (the Great Nous),[35] and the glory (*prny*) of the elect.

[Parthian]:   Forgive my sins!

Fragment 2

Tenth. Of the four prayers which it was my duty to offer in purity for the four gods every day. If because of frailty and the lack of the fear of God, or [because I thought it more important to] plant and sow [(and so) I neglected my prayers, etc.] . . . for this I say: Pardon! (I ask for) forgiveness for my sins!

Eleventh. On the daily gifts which it was my duty to offer to the Church . . .

2. Confession for the Day of the Minor Fast

The text of this confession, preserved on three different fragments, can often be reconstructed where there are lacunae, because it is a stereotypical invocation of gods of the pantheon, called upon in the sequence of the Twelve Dominions. The deities of the first and second creation are invoked, but the text breaks off before the gods of the third creation can be named. We have left out the isolated fragment T I δ recto (?) which calls upon "the living, fragrant . . . god, mighty like the wind," which could be either the Holy Spirit (although that would not fit into the general pattern) or the second son of the First Man.[36]

1.   [Invocation of the Father of Light]
2.   [Mother] Goddess! Forgive [my sins] on this blessed [Day of the Minor Fast]. My God! [Parthian]:[37] Forgive my sins!
3.   God Xormuzta (the First Man)! . . .
4.   . . . six sons [of the God Xormuzta]![38]
5.   [Friend of the Lights!]
6.   Creating God Vam (the Great Builder)! . . .
7.   God Vadzivanta (the Living Spirit)![39] . . .
8.   Celebrated bright [God of the Sun] (the Third Messenger)! . . .[40]

3. Fragment of a confession for auditors

This text[41] shows many similarities to Buddhist confessions found at Turfan. This Manichaean document, showing that the desecration of a Buddhist sanctuary was regarded as a sin, is indicative of the close contact and good relations between Manichaeans and Buddhists. The text, like corresponding Buddhist formulae,[42] speaks explicitly of a monastery (*vihāra*) of the Buddha Shākyamuni, thus making clear that "Buddha" here is not a Manichaean title for Mani, as in other texts.[43]

... or if we should have ... because of houses and possessions, ... vineyards, slaves, sheep, ... (if) we should have stolen out of (desire for) profit, ... [if we should have] ... with great whips and sticks ... , [if we should have dishonestly acquired] goods, ... , we [do penitence] and acknowledge (our sin); we wish to be delivered from sin. May there be pardon (*kšanti bolzun*)!

Third. If I should have trespassed against the pregnant woman of another man because of (my) insatiable, shameless, sinful heart, or should have destroyed the place (*yir*) of the Buddha Shākyamuni in a monastery, or if I should have sinfully harmed livestock with the help of the Devil and the demons (with black magic); if I should have thought things that should not be thought, day and night, with seeing eyes and hearing ears, or if I should have harbored many false thoughts, ... [then I pray to be delivered from sin!]

4. Confessional prayer

This confession explains sinfulness as issuing from the mixture of good and evil in man, brought about by the events in primeval times. The reference to the fact that "many bright powers (of Light)" have been saved would suggest a blossoming of Manichaeism in Central Asia at this time.

> Furthermore, [Parthian]: forgive my sins! [Turkish]: My God, we are sinful and guilty in thought, word and deed, against the order and commandment of God. This living body (of ours) bears (in it) (a part of) the evil enemy who was mixed into it at a moment in the past. It bears the (evil) substance[44] of the demonic Ahriman (Satan), the contamination (of the mind)[45] and the senses (open to evil).[46] I am beaten in the fight (of the Devil) against Xormuzta (the First Man), which took place earlier.[47] Being in the hands of the Demon of Greed since that time, (I have to) ascend, descend and be reborn (in the cycle of rebirths).[48] In the world, your God (Jesus?) has taken hold of me (to save me?). (There are) myriads of *tük* (?), so many powers of Light, that the gods (have saved).
>
> Furthermore, by the gods above, (by) the King of Light, (there are) so many powers of Light that the gods have saved. So thank the gods above, (thank) the King of Light!

5. Confession

This confession precedes a story, or parable, about a merchant named Arazan. It starts off with Arazan advising his hearers to confess their sins. The figures of speech are quite Buddhistic.

> [*first lines fragmentarily preserved*]
> ... May we unravel the net (of rebirth) and the snare of birth and death. May we break apart the bonds and the fetters of *karma* (retribution). May

we guide those who have gone astray. May we cure the chronic illness of the passions. May we open (for others) the eye of wisdom. May we give joy to those who have undergone all kinds of suffering.[49]

If I have sinned completely against living beings who [so] endure [suffering], then, in the presence of the God Nom Qutï (the Great Nous), I venture to repent of all my sins, and to ask for forgiveness. [Parthian]: Forgive my sins!

Now I, Aryaman Frištum, the Superior (*qoštar*), . . . [venture] to repent of all our (*sic*) various grievous sins, and ask for pure absolution.

Notes

1. I am indebted to Dr. Laut, Marburg, for valuable advice in the translation of this text.
2. Cf. Klimkeit, *Manichaean Art,* pl. XVII.
3. Cf. Nr. 1.1.
4. *BBB,* p. 12.
5. The five sons of the First Man. Compare Introduction.
6. These represent demonic powers opposing the five limbs of God (*membra dei*).
7. Or, wickedness.
8. Or, the eternal land of the gods.
9. The Zurvanite heresy in Iran claimed that Zurvan is the origin of good as well as of evil. The idea, which did not accord with absolute dualism, was rejected by Zoroastrians and Manichaeans.
10. According to Manichaean theology, the gods were "evoked" by the Father of Light, not created or engendered by Him.
11. Here again a Zurvanite idea is repudiated.
12. For these gods, compare Introduction.
13. In the enumeration of these three, namely, the Buddhas (Messengers, Prophets), the pure Law, and the beneficent souls, there is a correspondence to the Buddhist *triratna,* the "three jewels," Buddha, Dharma (the Teaching), and Saṃgha (the community of monks).
14. Or, color.
15. For the fourteen wounds, compare Sundermann, "Die vierzehn Wunden der Lebendigen Seele."
16. The five kinds of living beings are 1. bipeds (men), 2. quadrupeds (animals), 3. flying beings, 4. beings living in water, 5. crawling beings.
17. It is not known what the five kinds of plants are.
18. Though ten sins can be distinguished in the following, this is not really a list of ten sins, but rather an enumeration of instances of sinfulness.
19. The "first self" is the "Living Self" (or "Living Soul") unaware of its origins in the Realm of Light, whereas "this self" is the self that has received enlightening *gnosis.* Compare Asmussen, *Xᵘāstvānīft,* p. 218.
20. Literally, as sons of long-mantled ones, in this case women.
21. The two poisonous paths are probably the paths leading to rebirth, and to Hell, respectively.
22. The four bright seals (seals of Light) are enumerated in the following.
23. This divine tetrad corresponds to the Father of Light. Compare Asmussen, *Xᵘāstvānīft,* pp. 220ff.; Merkelbach, *Mani und sein Religionssystem,* pp. 39–50.
24. Or, this fourfold God.
25. Translation suggested by Laut.
26. For the Vusanti fast, compare Henning, "The Manichaean Fasts," pp. 146ff.
27. For the Monday confession, compare Asmussen, *Xᵘāstvānīft,* p. 227.

28. For the Yimki fast, compare Henning, *op. cit.*
29. For the Bema festival, compare Henning, *op. cit.*; Asmussen, *Xᵘāstvānīft*, pp. 226f.
30. Here again we have a Manichaean version of the "three jewels," corresponding to Buddha, Dharma, and Saṃgha.
31. Henning, *Sogdica*, pp. 63–67. For further fragments of this text, compare Sims-Williams, "Sogdian Fragments of Leningrad III," p. 323–28. S-W lists, edits, and translates three further fragments, namely, L 34, L 80, and L 106.
32. For the term *buddha gotra*, "the Buddha family," which is here equated to the sum of Light suffering in the world (the *Jesus patibilis* of St. Augustine), compare Asmussen, *Xᵘāstvānīft*, pp. 136f. Henning points out, "This Buddhist term *pwt'ny kwt'r* [~ Skr. *buddha gotra*] which replaces [Sogd.] *rγwšny'kh* = [Turkish] *yaruq* ["Light"], has entered the Sogdian text after the Uyghur [Turkish] translation has been made." Henning, *Sogdica*, p. 66. Compare also *BBB*, pp. 32ff.
33. The seven gifts are the seven alms. They are related to the five angels (*frištilär*) that gather in the light of the Fivefold God (the five sons of the First Man), and to the Gods Call and Answer. Compare Asmussen, *Xᵘāstvānīft*, pp. 222f.
34. The three "seals," also mentioned by St. Augustine, who speaks of the tria signacula (*De moribus Manichaeorum*, c. 10), are the commandments pertaining to the mouth, the hands, and the bosom (to speech, deed, and thought). Compare Asmussen, *Xᵘāstvānīft*, p. 230; Stroumsa, "'Seal of the Prophets.' The Nature of the Manichaean Metaphor," pp. 61–74.
35. The term βγ'yšty δyny is supplied by Henning after Turk. Nom Qutï.
36. Cf. Bang and von Gabain, "Ein uigurisches Fragment über den manichäischen Windgott."
37. As in line 2, so also in the subsequent verses.
38. The Fivefold God (the five sons of the First Man) and the God Answer.
39. This invocation has been inserted. It could be an invocation of the sons of the Living Spirit. At any rate, it does not fit in the sequence of the Light Dominions.
40. Following these, there must have been invocations of 9. the Column of Glory, 10. Jesus the Splendor, 11. the Maiden of Light, and 12. the Great Nous ("The Glory of Religion," Nom Qutï).
41. I am thankful to Dr. Laut for suggestions on the translation of this text.
42. Cf. "Uigurica II," pp. 76ff. (confession of Üträt) and "Uigurica II," pp. 84ff. (confession of Qutluγ).
43. However, in one Turkish Manichaean manuscript (T II D 173a), the title bears the word "Shākyamuni." Compare Türk. Man. I, p. 11. Since the corresponding Buddhist formulae speak of sins against the *vihāra* and *saṃghārāma*, such portions could have been borrowed from the Buddhists.
44. In the Buddhist sense of evil *kleśa*, clinging to the mind.
45. In the sense of Skr. *kleśa*. The word used in Uighur (*nizwanilar*) can also be translated as "passions."
46. In the sense of Skr. *viṣaya*, "range, sphere (of the senses)." Compare *BHSD* 502a.
47. And continues to this day.
48. This terminology is characteristic of Buddhist Turkish texts.
49. These are the characteristic wishes of a Bodhisattva, and as such, of everyone striving to be a Bodhisattva.

CHAPTER TWENTY-SIX

Parables and Narratives

Like the Iranian parable texts, those in Turkish speak of the parabolic narrative as *azand* (~ MP *āzend,* "parable, story"). There must have been a great number of Turkish parables.[1] Unfortunately, only a few of these have been preserved. They are, moreover, in a fragmentary state, and the Manichaean interpretations appended to the stories are often missing. Yet we can trace some of these stories to Islamic times, and even to modern Islamic lore, where they have been preserved in their entirety, although they were often modified. The spiritual meaning ascribed to the narrative by the Manichaeans often has not been preserved, or is no longer discernable. Some of these Turkish parables must have been translated from Sogdian or other Iranian languages. Even the Greek fables of Aesop are treated in Turkish Manichaean literature, including a story about a dying man's admonition to his sons to stay united. As Merkelbach indicates, we find this story in a Parthian text—it is probably also indicated in the fragment of a Turkish text (T II S 525)—and it found its way to the Mongols, where it was incorporated into their *Secret History.*[2]

Of course, stories, allegories, and parables from India were also known to the Manichaeans in Central Asia.[3] They could have known and used stories from the *Rāmāyaṇa,* which appear in Uighur literature.[4] The *Jātaka* and *Avadāna* stories of Buddhist India must have been a special source of inspiration for the Turkish Manichaeans. We know that they employed various Buddhist stories for their own purposes. Thus we have Manichaean fragments of the story about the good prince Kalyānamkāra and his evil brother Pāpaṃkara who both sailed across the ocean to seek the gem *cintāmaṇi,*[5] which granted every wish. Having acquired it after various adventures, Kalyāṇaṃkara lies down to sleep. Then his evil brother blinds him and takes the gem away. Finally, Kalyāṇaṃkara, whose eyesight has been restored in a miraculous manner, retrieves the jewel and returns home to govern his father's realm, while his bad brother is flung into prison. This story lent itself to a Manichaean interpretation. We can surmise that the jewel which was sought probably represented the Living Soul, and the account of its recovery the long and difficult journey of seeking salvation. It is likely that the Indian narrative cycles, the *Kathāsaritsāgara* and the *Pañcatantra,* which are represented in Uighur literature,[6] were also known to the Manichaeans. This Indian collection of stories found its way via a Middle Persian version into New Persian (cf. Rūmī, *Mathnawī* IV, 2203) and Arabic (as *Kalīla wa Dimna*) and from there into Latin.[7]

The fact that even the Sogdian Manichaeans borrowed Indian Buddhist tales is apparent from the "Book of Prayer and Confession" (cf. ch. XIII, text 9). Even the biography of the Buddha, notably the story of his leaving home in search of enlightenment,[8] seems to have been adopted and reinterpreted by the Gnostic Manichaeans in Central Asia. In a Turkish fragment published by A. von Le Coq (T II D 172a), the beginning of an apparently Buddhist narrative has been preserved: "And the divine Messenger said to Sumnaγdi, listen to this matter of which I shall speak to you. I will tell (you) a story (*az(a)nd*). A long time ago, there was a great city . . . rich in all kinds of goods. . . ."[9] Unfortunately the fragment breaks off here, but it was no doubt originally a Buddhist story, as the word for "Messenger" (lit., Messenger-Buddha: *y(a)lavačī burxan*) would suggest (even though the name Sumnaγdi is not known in Buddhist narrative literature).[10] Other Indian tales were also employed. For instance, at the end of a page from a Manichaean Turkish book these words appear: "(Here) ends this astrological Brahma parable."[11] This, too, must have been a story from India which was adapted by the Manichaeans.

Even though the texts presented here have been preserved only fragmentarily, they are an important indication of the wide range of narrative material used by the Manichaeans in Central Asia.

1. Fragments of the Fables of Aesop

The fables of Aesop were apparently very popular in the entire Hellenistic world, from Greece and Egypt to Central Asia.[12] This Turkish fragment was first published by von Le Coq in 1922.[13] Rásonyi, in his revised study of the text, shows that the fragment corresponds to a portion of the so-called "Aesop Narrative," that is, the "Life of Aesop" (*Vita Aesopi*).[14] Rásonyi comes to the conclusion that this narrative was brought to the Turkish Uighurs by way of the Sogdians.[15] A Sogdian version also existed,[16] and the Turkish text could have been translated from it. Zieme has pointed out that there are eight further Turkish Aesop fragments, all belonging to the same manuscript and written in an older type of Uighur script.[17] They are, however, too short and fragmentary to be translated here.[18]

[Title]:   The good, fine [book] of [the wise] Aesop

> . . . They all laughed at this word, and they praised Aesop. They said: "You should be happy." When Aesop asked why, (they answered): "We are all delighted. Therefore our . . . (and) his power is small. All our knowledge . . . Aesop . . ."[19]
>
> [*some lines missing*]
>
> . . . When one leads it to be killed, it howls and bellows.

Aesop said: "Therefore sheep do not bleat. Why? One by one (their) feet
are bound, they are laid down (on the ground) and their wool is shorn . . . But
the pig . . ."[20]

2. Manichaean version of the story of the Bodhisattva's three encounters

A well-known Buddhist story tells of the three encounters of the Bodhisattva, that
is, the Buddha to be, namely with an old man, a sick man, and a dead man.[21]
They make him aware of the fact that all life in the world is subject to suffering.
It is only when he encounters a monk with a serene and peaceful countenance and
composed bearing that he discovers the possibility of overcoming earthly woe and
suffering. A portion of the Buddhist story is preserved in this Manichaean fragment. The unusual spelling of the word Bodhisattva (as *bodisaw*) shows that it was
translated from a Sogdian version. The Sogdian Manichaean version must have
been the prototype of the story of *Barlaam and Joasaph,* the Buddha legend that
came to be known in Europe.[22] We have here, then, a Turkish translation of what
is probably the earliest Manichaean version of Buddha's three encounters.[23]

[Title of front page]:   The Book about Chandaka's Answer [to the Bodhisattva][24]

(*recto*)
Then the Bodhisattva prince pulled back the reins of his horse Kanthaka
and stopped. Looking (at the old man), he said to his charioteer Chandaka:[25] "This hideous (person) lying there, rolling (on the ground), what
kind of a man is he?"

Chandaka said respectfully: "Your Majesty, this man was once a
healthy, rigorous, handsome young man like you are. Now he has become
old and ill, and sickness has cast a pall upon him. That is why he is lying
there now, and has become so ugly."

Then the Bodhisattva said: "We, too, will finally turn to dust (lit., dirt)
after a long life.". . .
[*a number of lines missing*]
(*verso*)
When the Bodhisattva prince had heard these words of Chandaka, he
pulled back the reins (of his horse) and turned back in great distress and
sorrow. He entered his city and did not speak a word to anyone; he just
sat there, constantly sorrowing. When his father, the king, and his mother,
the queen, heard this, they came to him. But no matter what they said
to their son, he gave no answer. Then King Shuddhodana[26] commanded
his officers and noble ones firmly: "Follow him, and accompany him on
all the streets (?), . . . and let horns be blown[27] . . ."

3. Story of the drunken man and the corpse

This story, unfortunately preserved only fragmentarily, probably illustrates for the
Manichaean mind the reprehensible character of drunkenness and the sexual

desire to which it leads. Bang, following von Oldenburg, points out that we find the story in the work of the Islamic author Ibn Bābāye (tenth century).[28] In both the Persian and the Arabic versions of Ibn Bābāye, the drunk man of the story is a prince,[29] whereas our Manichaean version calls him "a noble man." We are reminded here of the apocryphal *Acts of John,* in which a man, "inflamed by the fiercest lust and by the influence of the many-formed Satan," enters the grave of a lady by the name of Drusiana "to perform the forbidden thing upon (her) dead body."[30] The difference in our story is that the "noble man" wants to unite with a corpse in a tomb, which he sees in a state of drunkenness, thinking it to be his wife, who has apparently just died. In the story in the *Acts of John,* the man knowingly dishonors the corpse of the dead lady.[31] The outcomes of both stories also differ considerably.[32]

> . . . He saw [the corpse] and thought, "This is my wife." He went in (into the tomb) and lay down beside the corpse. And because he was drunk and foolish, he put his arms around the corpse, behaved shamelessly and united with it. Because of his exertions the corpse burst open. Blood, pus and foul and evil things in its nauseating body oozed and flowed out. And the noble man lay in blood and pus with his whole body and all his clothes, and he was covered (thereby) from head to foot. And because of his shamelessness and having been rendered senseless in his drunken state, he thought to himself, "I am very satisfied."
>
> When morning came and the sun rose, the noble man's drunkenness passed. He awoke from his sleep. Raising his head, he saw that he was lying in a tomb, a corpse being at his bosom. Pus and blood were oozing out and spreading a terrible odor. He looked at himself and saw that he was all covered with blood and was lying in excrement. He was struck by panic and seized by fear, he screamed loudly, quickly left (the tomb) in his (defiled) mourning-dress and ran away. The more he ran the more he vomited. Then he quickly tore to bits and to shreds the gown that had (originally) been so pure, threw it away and then ran on. He reached a pond, jumped into it, and washed and cleansed himself . . .

4. Parable about the three princes

This story, preserved on three pages found in a Manichaean *stūpa* in Bäzäklik near Turfan in 1981, is still full of linguistic difficulties and puzzles regarding its sub-stance. Yet it deserves to be made known, as it belongs to the few Turkish Manichaean hagiographic texts we have. With this legendary account is connected a parable, which consists of three stories told by three princes to one King Baγtad ("Given by God," that is, Theodosius) in the presence of Mani, the divine Mes-senger (*yalavač*), and to the King's court. This is the King Bāt/Bath of other Iranian and Coptic texts.[33] This king accompanied Mani on his last journey to the court of Bahrām I, who was to imprison him.[34] In accordance with Henning, Boyce re-marks, "The king Bāt who accompanied him part of the way (a Babylonian or Armenian?) was evidently a vassal of Vahrām [Bahrām] and his adherence to

Manichaeism appears to have been one cause for the king's [i. e., Bahrām's] anger."[35]

We have here the remnants of the hagiographic account of the conversion of King Baγtad/Bāt to the Manichaean faith. As in other cases,[36] the account is introduced by a story (or, rather set of stories) which turns out to be a parable (*az(a)nt*). We have here the narrations of three princes who are brothers. They are apparently sons of King Baγtad. At least one page is missing between the second and third pages, so that only part of their narrative is preserved. At any rate, they are the princes' own stories, narrated by them in the first person. They tell of their experiences in a faraway place (on a mountain?). At the end of page 3, verso, an "interpretation" (*yörüg*) of the "parable" begins, which unfortunately has not been preserved. The distinction between the story itself and its explanation is quite in line with other parables.

The first part of our text contains the story of the first prince. It is not clear how long the beginning of this part was, as it has been lost. The prince speaks with three demons (*yäk*) who possess three "objects" or "things" (*äd*) that have "(magical) properties" or "qualities," namely, a cap that makes the one who wears it invisible; sandals that carry anyone who wears them to a desired destination; and a stick, the property of which has not been preserved in our document. Apparently the demons are fighting among themselves over these three objects, and they request the prince to distribute them. He shoots three arrows in three different directions. The demons are to get them, one from each direction, and their speed in procuring them will determine who should possess what. While the demons run off to get the arrows, the prince himself puts on the cap and the sandals, takes the stick in his hand, and is apparently transported to a remote place not named in the text preserved.

The motif of this story is well known in comparative folklore and can easily be traced in motif indexes.[37] The nearest parallels known to the translator are to be found in collections of Kashmiri, Kurdish, and Chalač folktales, which are all apparently connected with a Persian prototype.[38] The objects in these stories vary as do their properties, but the general outline remains the same. According to the Kurdish version, the characteristic feature of the stick is that, if it is hit against the sandals, they will transport one to whatever place one wishes to go.

The story of the second prince (*ortun ičisi,* "the middle brother") leaves many questions open. He talks about meeting three snakes, apparently somewhere outside the world of men, to which he subsequently wants to return with a message about the snakes' power. He brings with him a valuable vessel, or jug (*idiš*). It is unclear who the "younger sister" (*singil*) is whom he apparently wants to please by presenting this special treasure to someone.

The story of the third prince has been preserved only fragmentarily. He apparently ponders the evil consequences of his hunting wild animals, a familiar motif from Buddhist lore.

In the middle of page 3, recto, the historical or hagiographical part of the text starts. It is concerned with Mani as the divine Messenger at the court of King Baγtad. The King apparently receives religious instruction from him prior to his conversion.

(*Page 1, recto*)

[Title]:   The beautiful story

[The first prince said . . .]: "[The first (thing)] was a cap, the second (thing) a [stick], and the third (thing) a (pair of) sandals. [Then] those demons [said] to me: "You shall distribute these three things and give them (to us), without seeing . . . truly and without (?) accusing (us) of lying (?)"

Then I [said] to them: "What properties do these (three things) have?"

They said [this]: "The property of this cap is [such] that [if] someone [puts] it on his head, absolutely no one can see him. The property of the sandals [is] such that [when] someone [puts] them on his feet, [he can go] wherever he wants to go. [The property] of the stick [is such that] . . ."

[*four lines missing*]

(*Page 1, verso*)

[Title]:   The story of the King

". . . [When] . . . , I will give a reward," said I.

And then the second (lit., middle) brother [said]: "One day I was eating bread on this mountain, [when] three snakes [ap]peared. To these I [gave] three (pieces of) bread. One of the snakes quickly snapped it up and ate (all the bread). I hit it with a small [stick] and [said]: "(You) greedy one!" Then many snakes [appeared], snapped at me and drove me away. They led me into [great] danger and much distress. These furious, most [evil] snakes [came] onwards (towards) me, and when I turned around (in flight), they gave me . . . as a reward. Then [I] secretly [took] an excellent, good, new mirror. Then they turned around to me

(*Page 2, verso*)

[Title]:   The happy King Baγtad

and [wanted] to kill me. I said: "Send me, and I will go to the people (the land of men). When they see these things, they should believe that I . . . have come, and know that you have become lords and have power. At that time (then) they [dispatched] me safe and sound!

I have brought this vessel here. Of all my treasures, I now love this one (most). I shall give (this treasure) to no one. But I [will] give (this treasure) to him, so that my younger sister may be glad (?).

Then the third prince said [this]: "One day I thought this on that mountain . . . 'What will happen for my sake, as I hunt [wild animals] like suffering men (?). At night . . .'"

[*at least one page missing*]

(*Page 3, recto*)

[Title]:   The messenger

". . . died. Then I went and brought . . . And of all my [treasures], I love this one (most). I can give (it) to no one. But so that my younger sister may [be] glad, I will give a reward." Thus did he speak.

Then they said these words before the Messenger, and to all the renowned and noble people who sat up in front. Then the Messenger requested the king to stand up, and he submitted to him[39] . . . , for he knew on account of (his) [wisdom] that the king himself had the name Baγtad. (The princes?) [stood up, went?] before their father, the king, and considered . . . At this time . . . great joy arose . . . for the king, the princes

(*Page 3, verso*)

[Title]:   [The happy (King)] Baγtad

and the whole realm. Then they [went] with this King Baγtad. They fetched the daughter of the king and came (back). On this very day they celebrated a great, joyous festival. They brought these unattainable goods, which were honorable and useful for them, together with many treasures, before (King) Baγtad . . . And there were some that he took and others that he gave. And the two happy kings lived together with each other, and with all the princes, princesses and noble ones, for a long time, in great joy, without . . . , and in happiness.

And one [day] they explained the meaning of this story as [follows]: "This happy [king] . . ."

5. *Story of Mani's competition with Prince Ohrmizd*

This is apparently a legendary story rather than a parable. This text was found along with the previous one in 1981 in a star-shaped Manichaean *stupa* beneath the rubble below the well-known caves of Bäzäklik near Turfan. Early Manichaean caves with as yet unpublished paintings were found in the vicinity. Apparently Bäzäklik was originally a Manichaean site. Even so, some Buddhist elements had already left their mark on the text: for example, the founder of Manichaeism is called not only "the Messenger of God," but also "Mani (the) Buddha." The legend tells us about a contest between Mani and Prince Ohrmizd (here spelled Ohrmizt),[40] the son of the Sassanian king Šābuhr (Shāhpur) I. (He was to bear the title "the Keen," and he reigned after his father, as Ohrmizd I, from 272 to 273.) The contest to which he challenges Mani would apparently take place before he becomes king. Unfortunately, the course and outcome of the contest are not preserved. But one can be sure that in the legend Mani emerged victorious and that Ohrmizd was then converted to his religion. This surmise would be consistent with the Coptic *Homilies* (42,18), where Mani speaks favorably of King Ohrmizd, and also consistent apparently with a text in a Parthian Church history entitled, "The Speech of Ohrmizd the Keen," which, however, is very fragmentarily preserved.[41]

Sundermann points out, "This is a typical Manichaean conversion legend. The person converted is a personality of high rank; at first he is a determined opponent of Mani's . . . but then the charismatic power of Mani brings about a complete change of mind."[42]

This text throws light on the magical use of the name of the "Fourfold Father of Light," that is, "God, Light, Power, Wisdom," and it legitimizes this practice through instructions issued by Mani himself. This would concur with the magical texts used in Eastern Manichaeism, where the names of gods and angels are employed to serve magical purposes (chapter XIV).

The original language of this text is not clear. It could have been Parthian, since the fourfold designation of God is given in Parthian form. There would certainly have been a Sogdian translation, if indeed the text was not originally written in Sogdian. Our Turkish version is apparently a translation.

[Title page]:   This is the good, sweet[43] text about Ohrmizd the Bold[44]

"... Now do this: honor and praise the God of the Sun and the Moon (Jesus)[45] daily, worship the Fivefold God.[46] Wherever you go, stand, enter or go out, always say these four words: "God, Light, Power, Wisdom.""[47]

Then Ohrmizd the Bold respectfully said to the Lord,[48] Mani the Buddha: "Of what avail is it when one speaks these words?"

Then the Lord, Mani the Buddha, deigned to say: "Much distress will come (your way), (and then) nothing will be of any avail save these four words, neither your great virtue, nor your full-blooded racehorse, nor your sturdy weapon, nor your strong army, nor your heroic general. But if you will say these four words continually, you shall be saved . . . from great distress."

From this time on Ohrmizd the Bold said[49] these four words continually. He constantly uttered these four words, wherever he went, or came in, entered, or went out, sat down or stayed: [Parthian]: "God, Light, Power, Wisdom." [Turkish]: "God, Light, Power, Wisdom."

One day Ohrmizd the Bold, the prince, respectfully said to the Lord, Mani the Buddha: "My God, you are beautiful to behold; your body is very (?) lovely, and you are pleasing (in appearance). I know that you are mighty in power. Therefore I am considering this: Let us vie with one another (to see who is stronger). Which of us has more power?"

Then the Lord, Mani the Buddha, said to Ohrmizd the Bold: "Your origin (family, race) is of (the) kings that are crowned with diadems. All the people think that you are very strong and valiant. They consider you very heroic. As far as I am concerned, I am the Messenger of God. It is not necessary that we should fight with one another. For if I should throw you to the ground, if I should humiliate you, your reputation among the populace will suffer and you shall be discredited. Then everyone (will say), '(The Lord) who does not eat meat and does not drink wine has pushed Ohrmizd the Bold to the ground and has overcome him.' But if you should throw me to the ground, all the people will say, 'Mani the Buddha, the Messenger of God, is overcome and put to shame by a (mere) man.' If you can agree, then this duel will not be necessary."

Ohrmizd the Bold was not pleased in his heart at these words, for he was one who always wanted to boast. Then the Lord, Mani the Buddha, said: "If your heart is not glad, then (let us fight); there is an arena made for fighting elephants. As (the speed of) an arrow (shot) from the ground (into the air) diminishes as it reaches its highest point, we shall both go there, without arrows(?).[50] Let us have a contest there."

When Ohrmizd the Bold heard these words, his heart was (made) gladdened. The Messenger of God, Mani the Buddha, took the hand of Ohrmizd the Bold and both [went to the arena?] for fighting elephants . . .

[*remainder missing*]

6. *Story about Mār Ammō and the heathen priest*

Mār Ammō was one of Mani's most prominent disciples. He was apparently highly successful as a missionary to Parthian East Iran and the Kushan kingdom, winning kings and princes, lords and ladies for the new faith, as we read in various missionary histories. This legendary story, translated from Sogdian or some other Iranian tongue, narrates how he meets a *qam*, probably a *magus*, a priest of the indigenous (pagan) religion, who is in charge of a temple (*tängrilik*). We can surmise that he won over the temple for the new faith.

[Then] the spirit did according to the words it had said, and all the people acted in accordance with their wish. Mār Ammō the Teacher walked about within the city and begged for alms. (But) he found (only) a nut. Then Mār Ammō the Teacher went to the temple of the *magus*, because all the people honored him. The *magus* in the temple said to Mār Ammō the Teacher, "What manner of man are you and why have you come here? Stay with us and sit down."

Mār Ammō the Teacher said to the *magus*, "I am a pure elect (one), and I have come (to) . . ."

[*a number of lines missing*]

[Mār Ammō the Teacher said, "Your temple is (?)] a big and mighty building . . . I will settle here and spread God's word."

Then that *magus* said flatteringly, "This temple shall be yours; sit down." Mār Ammō the Teacher replied to the *magus*, "Say (that) three times: 'This temple shall be yours.'"

Thereupon the *magus* said three times: "This temple shall be yours." For the *magus* thought in his heart: "This man is a foreigner. Because of self-love he will meet with his death. He will be useful to me". . .

[*remainder missing*]

7. *Story of a man and his son*

This story is written on the reverse side of the sheet that bears the preceding story. Bang was of the opinion that both narratives could have belonged to the same collection.[51] However, this could be a part of a parable, not a historical legend. Unfortunately the text is in a very bad condition.

[The son said] to his father: ". . . I have seen this sign . . . ; it is a bad omen . . ."

They went a little further and saw a herd of deer, consisting of a stag and (a number of) does. The does were running lustfully after the stag.

When the son saw this sign, he became very sad and said to his father: "What curious things are these? What are these things I see?"

And again they went a little further. When they saw a pond, they descended (from their horses) and sat down to eat beside the water. They ate the flesh of the fish in the stream (running into the pond?), but they threw their skin into the water. Because of its smell, the fish in the water started to collect . . .

8. Story of the cock and the chickens

This is a story connected with the preceding one, and written immediately after it on the same manuscript. Unfortunately, its meaning remains unclear.[52]

> [A man] had put his hens into his henhouse . . . He opened the door and let the chickens out in order to feed them grain. Among these chickens there was a cock; the others were all hens. All the hens came out, but the cock did not. When the (a previously named) man saw [this], he asked the owner of the chickens: "What strange things are these? I also have many chickens in my henhouse. The cock comes out, but the hens do not. Your cock does not come out, but the hens do."
>
> The owner answered: "Up to now, my hens did not come out [either], and the cock did . . ."

9. Story of Arazan the merchant

This text, written in the Manichaean rather than the Uighur script, belongs to a *pothi*-book (a book bound in Indian fashion), containing hymns to Mani.[53] The owner of the book was a certain Aryaman Fristum, a "superior" (*qošt(a)r* = Sogd. *xvēštar*), whom we also know as the possessor of the *Xᵘāstvānīft*, the confessional prayer for laymen. The story is preceded by a confession which we translate in chapter XXV (text 5) of these Turkish texts.

> He (the merchant) advised them: ". . . Both of you, think of all your sins and trespasses, ask to be freed from your sins and for pure absolution, and make your confession."
>
> They heeded the advice of that merchant Arazan, for first, they feared death, second, they pitied all living souls possessing property, and third, they hurried to their own dwelling . . . They followed the merchant Arazan's advice and repented of their sins, let their tears flow, asked for absolution and made their confession. Because of their pure faith, they ventured to confess all their sins and trespasses . . .
>
> He said: "From . . . until today, because of the three kinds of demons, desire, shamelessness and greed, walk . . . in accordance with (?) the three kinds of pure "seals," (the commandments pertaining to thought, word and deed) and the seven jewels,[54] and reach your homes with your children." Then he abandoned his body and his soul was reborn in heaven.

Directed by the merchant Arazan, . . . (they) took precious stones and goods, as much as they could carry, and reached their own city and country . . .

10. *"Astrological Brahma parable"*

Only two short fragments of this parable, which is apparently of Indian origin, have been preserved. We can infer from the title of text B (T II D 175,2) that a homiletic type of interpretation was appended to the narrative. The other fragment, text A (T II D 175,1), must have preceded this text.[55]

Text A

The astrologer had become pious in his speech. One day he respectfully said to the king: "Your Majesty, I have seen your star and pondered it . . . I know and understand . . ."

Text B
(*recto*)

[When a person has died], this God Nom Qutï (the Great Nous) comes, along with the three gods, . . . to the soul and says many good and kind things to it.[56] Then he sends it (the soul) to the Judge (of the dead). There it finds victory (salvation) and [the prize] . . . On account of the fruit of the good deeds it has done . . .

(*verso*)

". . . I have not always done good deeds," he said. ". . . (But) on account of the alms given and the good deeds I did do, I have attained as fruit (recompense) the bright heaven of the gods;[57]. . . the beloved God (the Great Nous?) . . ."[58]

Here ends this astrological Brahma book.[59]

Notes

1. Asmussen, "Der Manichäismus als Vermittler," p. 8.
2. Merkelbach, "Manichaica (10). Eine Fabel Manis"; cf. Zieme, "Ein Turfanfragment einer türkischen Erzählung."
3. Reference was made in the introduction to the Iranian parables (ch. XV) to the Buddhist allegory of the world ocean, which is already found in the Pali Canon.
4. The Rāma story was used by the Buddhists in Turfan; compare Zieme, "Ein uigurisches Fragment der Rāma-Erzählung," in *AOH* 32 (1978), pp. 23-32.
5. For this story and its sources, compare Schlingloff, "Ein Zyklus des Buddhalebens in Ajanta," *WZKS* 27 (1983), p. 137. For the apparently Manichaean version, compare Zieme, "Ein uigurisches Turfanfragment der Erzählung vom guten und bösen Prinzen," in *AOH* 28 (1974), pp. 263-68.
6. Zieme, "Uigurische Pañcatantra-Fragmente," pp. 32-70.
7. Cf. Henning, "Die älteste persische Gedichthandschrift: eine neue Version von Barlaam und Joasaph," pp. 305-307; Asmussen, "Der Manichäismus als Vermittler," pp. 14f.; W. C. Smith, *Towards a World Theology*. Philadelphia 1981, pp. 7ff.

8. Compare text 2 in this chapter. For a painting from Kocho of this scene, which may be Manichaean, compare H.-J. Klimkeit, "Das Pferd Kaṇṭhaka," and "Indische Motive in der gnostischen Kunst."

9. Türk. Man. III, p. 14. Reedited by Bang in his "Manichäische Erzähler," p. 5.

10. At least I have not been able to trace it.

11. Türk. Man. III, p. 31. For the text preserved, compare text 10 in this chapter.

12. For the Greek version of Aesop's fables, compare B.E. Perry, *Aesopica* I. Urbana, 1925. From Egypt, we have the Greek Papyrus Golinesčev from the Fayum. Compare Rásonyi Nagy, "Das uigurische Aesop-Yosïpas-Fragment," p. 431. For the Syrian version, see C. Brockelmann, *Die syrische und die christliche arabische Litteratur.* Leipzig, 1908, p. 58. Motifs from Aesop's fables are depicted in Sogdian art, for example, the story of the goose that laid golden eggs. Compare A. M. Belenizki and D. W. Belous, *Mittelasien, Kunst der Sogden.* Leipzig, 1980, p. 207.

13. Türk. Man. III, p. 33.

14. Rásonyi, *op. cit.,* pp. 438–41. Compare *Vita Aesopi,* ch. 47–48 in the edition of Westermann, Brunswig and London, 1845, p. 25, I. 15–30.

15. Rásonyi, *op. cit.* Rásonyi thinks that Aesop's fables must have been brought to Central Asia by Nestorian Christians. Yet Asmussen calls this theory into question, pointing out that it must have been the Manichaeans who transmitted this literary material to the east. They knew the Aesopean tradition and used it in their repertoire in Central Asia. Compare Asmussen, *op. cit.,* p. 10.

16. Cf. Henning, "Sogdian Tales," pp. 474–75.

17. Zieme, "Die türkischen Yosipas-Fragmente," pp. 47–48.

18. Zieme, *op. cit.,* pp. 49–54.

19. This is apparently part of the well-known Aesopian fable about the pig and the sheep. Compare Halm, *Fabulae Aesopica collectae.* Leipzig, 1875, p. 58. In Westermann's edition, the question is raised as to why the sheep does not bleat when taken away, while the pig does make a noise. The answer is that the sheep is about to be shorn, whereas the pig is going to be killed. Compare Asmussen, *op. cit.,* p. 10.

20. For the Manichaean version of this story, compare Asmussen, *art. cit.,* pp. 9–11.

21. For this story and its sources, compare D. Schlingloff, "Ein Zyklus des Buddhalebens in Ajanta," p. 137; H.-J. Klimkeit, *Der Buddha. Leben und Lehre.* Stuttgart, 1990, pp. 70–74.

22. Asmussen, *art. cit.,* p. 8.

23. Text and German translation with notes in Bang, "Manichäische Erzähler," pp. 7–12.

24. Literally, The Sūtra of Chandaka's Answers.

25. Chandaka was the charioteer of the Buddha to be, who answered the young prince's questions about the nature of old age, illness, and death.

26. The Uighur text gives the Turkisized name Shantudan.

27. To cheer him up (?). Thus Bang, "Manichäische Erzähler," pp. 11f.

28. Bang, "Manichäische Erzähler," p. 12.

29. Compare Weisslovitz, *Prinz und Derwish,* p. 171. This is the story of a king's son who gets drunk and spends a night in a grave. See also Asmussen, "Vermittler," p. 16, who points out that the story is also known from an adaptation of the book of *Balauhar and Būdhāsaf,* translated into Persian after Ibn Bābāye. For an amazing Arabic parallel to the story of the Persian Buddha legend (Ibn Bābāye), compare S. M. Stern and S. Walzer, *Three Unknown Buddhist Stories in Arabic Version.* Oxford, 1971, pp. 32f.

30. Hennecke and Schneemelcher, *New Testament Apocrypha* II. London, 1965, p. 247 (art. by W. Schneemelcher and K. Schäferdieck).

31. *Ibid.*

32. I am indebted to Dr. Laut for making available to me his German translation of this story, which I follow.

33. For King Bāt, see Sundermann, *Texte,* p. 80, n. 2; Sims-Williams, "Baat," in *Encyclopaedia Iranica* III, 3 (1968), p. 277; Sims-Williams, "The Sogdian Texts of Leningrad II."

34. Henning, "Mani's Last Journey," pp. 942–43.

35. Boyce, *Reader,* p. 43.
36. Cf. Sundermann, "Studien zur kirchengeschichtlichen Literatur I."
37. Cf. Geng, Klimkeit and Laut, "Die Geschichte der drei Prinzen," p. 331, n. 15.
38. References were kindly given by Asmussen, Doerfer, Laut and MacKenzie. Compare J. H. Knowles, *Folk Tales of Kashmir,* London, 1893, p. 86; MacKenzie, *Kurdish Dialect Studies* II. London, 1962, pp. 59 and 127; G. Doerfer and S. Tezcan, *Chalatsch Folklore Texts* (forthcoming). I thank Professor Dörfer, Göttingen, for sending me story 103 of his forthcoming collection.
39. In the sense of told, taught, related to.
40. For this spelling (written *vrmzt*), compare Geng, Klimkeit and Laut, "Manis Wettkampf," p. 48. For Mani and Ohrmizd, compare Sims-Williams, "The Sogdian Texts of Leningrad II."
41. Sundermann, *Texte,* pp. 127f.
42. Cf. Geng, Klimkeit and Laut, *op. cit.,* p. 47.
43. Literally, of sweet taste (*talïγlïγ*).
44. By sending me his article "The Sogdian Texts of Leningrad II," Sims-Williams points out to me that behind *yaγï,* which we, in our *editio princeps* (Geng, Klimkeit and Laut, "Manis Wettkampf mit dem Prinzen") had translated as "enemy," is Sogd. *yxy,* "bold." This indeed fits very well, and is in accordance with Manichaean tradition.
45. For the God of the Sun and the Moon (*kün ay tängri*) as Jesus the Splendor, compare Rose, *Die manichäische Christologie,* pp. 26, 121ff.; Asmussen, *X^uāstvānīft,* p. 205, rightly emphasizes, "The expression *kün ay tängri,* however, in Manichaean texts, covers a widely ramified complex of thoughts and ideas concentrated on the gods of the third vocation and the work of redemption connected with them." Compare also Asmussen, *op. cit.,* p. 208.
46. The five sons of the First Man, who correspond anthropologically to the five limbs of the soul of man.
47. The words are given here in their Parthian form. They refer to the "Fourfold Father of Greatness." See Asmussen, *X^uāstvānīft,* pp. 220f. It is not clear who is speaking these sentences; it could be Mani.
48. Here the word *t(ä)ngri* is used, which can actually mean God!
49. Literally, kept in his mouth.
50. This translation is conjectural.
51. Bang, "Manichäische Erzähler," p. 19.
52. In the reading and translation I follow Bang, "Manichäischer Laienbeichtspiegel," pp. 53f.
53. I follow L. V. Clark's translation. Compare Clark, "*Pothi*-Book," pp. 189f.
54. The seven jewels are, according to S, the five sons of the First Man plus the Gods Call and Answer. Sundermann, *Parabeltexte,* p. 99, n. 1; Clark, "*Pothi*-Book," p. 207. Here virtues related to them must be meant.
55. Compare Türk. Man. III, pp. 30f. This first (?) side of the first fragment (text A) could also have belonged to the interpretation of a preceding parable. It reads, "On this earth you walk in sorrow, depressed and despised. On that earth you will walk in great (lit., wide) freedom, without encumbrance."
56. Reading and translation after Bang, "Laien-Beichtspiegel," pp. 100f. Bang points to an-Nadīm's report about the fate of the soul according to Manichaean belief (Flügel, *Mani,* pp. 100f. Compare Dodge, *The Fihrist of an-Nadīm* II, p. 795): "When death comes to one of the Elect (*Zaddīqā*), Primal Man [i. e., the First Man] sends him a light shining deity in the form of the Wise Guide. With him are three deities, with whom there are the drinking vessel, clothing, headcloth, crown and diadem of light. There a virgin accompanies them, who resembles the soul of that member of the Elect."
57. This first and the second sentence hardly seem to fit together.
58. For this reading and interpretation of the last words, compare Bang, "Hymnen," p. 25, n. 2.
59. This is apparently just a chapter from a book of parables, for the next line says, "(Here) begins the parable of . . ."

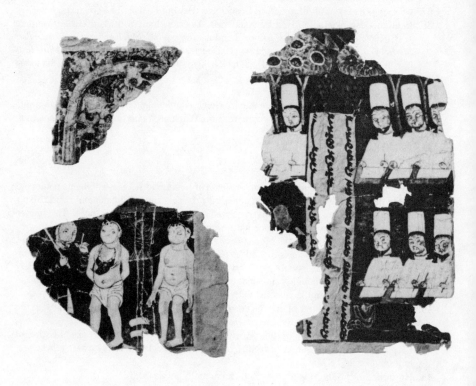

Manichaean scribes beneath the tree of life. The Uighur text is part of a confessional prayer. Staatliche Museen—Preussischer Kulturbesitz, Museum für Indische Kunst, Berlin.

CHAPTER TWENTY-SEVEN

Texts on Jesus, Mani, and the Gods

1. Texts on Jesus

The Jesus portrayed in these texts is the Manichaean Jesus who—as explained in the Introduction—is a composite of three figures:

1. First, there is the Light Messenger Jesus, "Jesus the Splendor," who brings *gnosis* to Adam, and thereafter to everyone, albeit this task is often executed by the Great Nous (Turk. *Nom Qutï*) for individuals and the Church at large. In cosmological terms "Jesus the Splendor" is called the "Moon God" (*ay tängri*), or even the "God of the Sun and Moon" (*kün ay tängri*).[1] So important is Jesus in his manifestation as Moon God that in a Turkish text (T II D 173c,1) students ask their teacher, "Why is the Moon God praised and blessed first in the Great Gospel Book (in Mani's *Living Gospel*), and only later is the great, royal King of Gods, Zurvān the God, praised?"[2] Unfortunately the answer is not preserved.

2. Second, there is the historical Jesus, "the Messiah," sometimes known as "the Messiah Buddha" (*mšixa burxan*). Though his true incarnation is called into question, and his suffering and death are depicted in a docetic manner, Nagel has pointed out that the Gnostic stance on this idea is not as pronounced and consequential as are those of other Gnostic groups.[3] Even as a forerunner of Mani, (who calls himself "the Apostle of Jesus Christ,"[4] thus expressing his own subordination), Jesus remains an important figure in his own right. Apocryphal sayings of his, many of which are not found elsewhere, are quoted. Here, too, we find a Manichaean Jesus, for his sayings lend authority to Manichaean views (cf. text 1.1). It is the historical Jesus, associated with the figure of Jesus the Splendor, that will come again to earth at the end of time. In Central Asia he is actually called Maitreya, the Buddha of the future. Even though Mani can be identified with Maitreya, it is apparently Jesus who is indicated in texts 1.2 and 1.3, as he is referred to as "the Son of God" (*tängri oγlï*), a term which is not applied to Mani.

3. Third, there is "the suffering Jesus" (the *Jesus patibilis* of St. Augustine), a term referring to the sum of Light captured by Darkness and suffering in the world. This concept of the ubiquitous savior, often found in Gnosticism,[5] is expressed clearly in the *Gospel of Thomas,* which must have been known to the Manichaeans in Central Asia.[6] In logion 77 of the Coptic version it says, "Jesus said, 'It is I who am the light which is above them all. It is I who am the all. From me did the all come forth, and unto me did the all extend. Split a piece of wood, and I am there. Lift up the stone, and you will find me there.'"[7] From this notion the Manichaeans derived the idea, well testified to in Iranian texts, that doing harm even to lifeless matter "hurts" or "injures" the divine Light contained in it. Though there are few Turkish texts which express this idea specifically, we do have Turkish Buddhist documents that show that the notion was widespread, and even influenced the Buddhists. Thus it says in the Turkish text T II D 200, "The essence (*öz*) of the Buddha Vairocana (the Sun as the primeval Buddha, from which everything issued) is everything: earth, mountains, stones, sand, the water of streams and rivers, all ponds, brooks and lakes, all plants and trees, all living beings and men. There is absolutely no place which is not filled with the essence of Vairocana. If a monk stretches out and lifts up his hand against something, he has become sinful against the essence of the Buddha Vairocana."[8] Such documents were apparently inspired by the Manichaean notion of the "suffering Jesus."

Finally we have in various texts an invocation of what are called "the twenty-two qualities of Jesus." Here Jesus is an all-encompassing divine being. The various gods and the virtues they represent stand for these qualities. We consider this text in connection with the documents on the gods (text 3).

1.1 APOCRYPHAL WORDS OF THE HISTORICAL JESUS

In this text, some apocryphal words of Jesus that serve to substantiate Manichaean teachings are quoted.[9]

> ... And the Messiah Buddha (Jesus) has called men who give alms in faith and who pray fervently "friends of his friends."[10] He deigned to say this: "Hide your hidden treasure (give alms secretly?; cf. Mt. 6:3), without being miserly against the holy Church (*arïγ nom*), with a liberal heart, in faith, without doubting." And furthermore he deigned to say the following: "Whoever strives for the sake of the body will, as requital and gain, die by the body. (But) whoever sows good seed for the sake of the soul will receive as recompense eternal life in the Realm of the Gods."[11] And furthermore he deigned to say this: "Throw away this (your) evil possession which belongs to the demons, and give it as alms to a very needy elect. (But) you (yourself) go hungry, you (yourself) endure pain and thus fill your treasure-house in eternity. And with your whole heart believe this: the reward for (a piece of) bread and a cup of water (given as alms) will never vanish, but is sure" (cf. Mt 10:42).
>
> And in the Scripture (*nom*) he deigned to say, "The auditors are not all alike. (For) there are 'perfect auditors.' Furthermore there are those of

good disposition. Then there are those who (just) accept the Law (religious teaching). The way their souls ascend to the zodiac, and the way they reach it, and the way they are transformed into another self, and the way they descend (again), is not the same. There are many differences between them, just as fetters, shackles and foot-tethers of a sinful man are either heavy or light . . ."

1.2 THE COMING JESUS AS MAITREYA

In this text the coming Jesus, who is to return to earth, is seen as the future Buddha Maitreya. In Manichaeism it is Jesus' second coming that ushers in the victory of the Good. Our text has parallels in Coptic literature. In the *Homilies* (32,14ff.), which discuss these eschatological events, it says, "The world . . . will have peace at that time. Wood will open its mouth, together with the trees, and they will (all) speak. The fruits and the fruit crop . . . will speak . . . For lo, the great King has come." In *Homilies* 39,5f. we read, ". . . And they will sweep them (the evil ones, or the demons ?) out together with everything evil that is in the world. The trees will become green (?) and will speak." And in *Homilies* 36,14ff. it says, "The angels . . . will receive power and will gather all flesh . . . All peoples (?) and all tongues will praise him . . . He (Jesus) will descend and will erect his Bēma (throne) in the midst of the great Oikumene."

> . . . Then the angels, too, will descend. They will chase these demons from this earth and will cast them into Hell. Just as the angels [vanquish?] the demons and vampires on this earth . . . , so will they end hunger, . . . illness, heat and cold on this earth completely. At [that] time all five kinds of living beings,[12] (furthermore) trees, plants, fruits and (even) stone images will acquire tongues. They will laud and praise the true Buddha Maitreya[13] in God's own language. Then the angels, at the command of the Buddha Maitreya, . . .

1.3 THE TRUE AND THE FALSE MAITREYA

This small fragment is unique in that it speaks of a true and a false Maitreya.[14] The false Maitreya is referred to as "the son of a demon" (*yäk*); the true Maitreya, called "the Son of God," refers to Jesus, not Mani. In the text we hear that the title is falsely claimed by someone who introduces himself as the coming savior to the people. It is not clear what historical events, if any, are referred to here.[15]

> (*recto*)
> ". . . Maitreya on the earth . . . ," they say. "His law and his nature are strife. The sign and the mount[16] of that son of a demon will be a bull. There are no tricks and no kinds of magic in this world which he does not know. By the power of Šimnu (the Devil) he will be able to do everything." This [he told] all the people, and to the Teacher of the Law he said: "The Buddha Maitreya, the Son of God,[17] will come . . . I am the true Son of God . . . The realm and its people . . ."

(verso)

". . . He will become an elect. He will have attained the good fortune of the mystical wisdom of the divine [Buddha?].[18] Then that son of a demon, the false Maitreya, will say this to the false elect, "For such a long time you have waited for the coming of the Son of God, the Buddha Maitreya. Now (lo), I, I am the Son of God." He assembled . . . all the [people?], (saying), "You should worship me. I am the [true] Maitreya. Believe in me . . . I am the Son [of God] . . ."

2. Texts on Mani

These texts contain praises of Mani, prayers to him, and quotations from his scriptures. The quotations from Mani's scriptures preserved in Iranian Turfan texts have been collected and assessed by H.-Ch. Puech, who, however, disregards some of the Turkish and the Chinese material.[19] In the *Traité*, there is a quotation from Mani's *Gospel* which says, "When teachers (*tien-na-wu*) are (incorporate) the good Law in their persons, then the Father and the Son of Light (Jesus) and the pure Wind of the Law (the Holy Spirit) are (present) in their persons, and they (those gods) constantly walk with them and dwell in them."[20] This is followed by a quotation from Mani's *Epistles*, which reads, "When the teachers perfectly realize (materialize) the good Law in themselves, then purity and light, great power and wisdom will be present in their persons completely. Then the merits of the New Man are perfect."[21] Various Turkish texts also contain quotations from Mani's works (cf. texts 2.3; 3.1).

2.1 PRAYER OF PRAISE TO MANI

This is a prayer of praise to Mani as God of Light. Into it is inserted an invocation of the twelve deities which comprise the "twelve hours" of the so-called "Second Bright Day" (or "Day of Light"). For that text, see 3.6.

> May the God of Light,[22] the Buddha Mani, be praised. And may the angels of Light[23] that watch over the bright and pure Law be praised. . . .[24]
> Praised be the Buddha Mani, the source of pure Light, the Water of Life, the great Tree[25] with eternal fruits . . . We ate and drank (at the sacred meal), and lo, we came to life; we partook (of the meal), and we became joyful.[26]
> You, Mani, who brings (us) faith, who gives (us) insight, who grants us eternal life, may your name be praised, my God! May you be praised, as your virtue (is praised). May this petition reach the palace of the God Might (the Column of Glory). May it be so eternally!

2.2 PRAYER TO MANI

This prayer must be from a period shortly after the victory of Manichaeism in the Uighur land.

(*recto*)

. . . We make our supplication, as though blindly, to Mani, the Apostle, the *Buddha. Because Mani, the Apostle, [gave us] vigor and fortune . . . when we came to the Uighur land, we made our supplication to the eternally praised Apostle . . . (and) the strong gods . . .

(*verso*)

. . . May you live without distress and die (?) in well-being. May your [esteemed] Law [remain valid ?] unto eternity . . .

2.3 QUOTATION FROM MANI'S SCRIPTURES

This is a quotation from one of Mani's writings, perhaps one of his letters to his community. One thinks of his "Letter of the Seal"; however, we have no proof that it is from that important Epistle.

> . . . Now consider (lit., see) with what teaching, with what precepts, with what a wide heart (and) with [what] patience I [was] with you (in areas) far and wide, since the time that I appeared in this land, up to today . . . Oh, all my dear ones, I wish that you may prosper at all times. Now act thus continually: Be calm, mild . . . and of a sweet heart. May love reign over you at all times . . .

3. *Texts on the gods*

The texts collected here are from diverse documents dealing with the gods of the Manichean pantheon. Besides texts with references to the chief gods, there are systematic lists of deities, arranged in dodecadic groups and representing the twelve "hours" of the "Days of Light" ("Bright Days") and the "Dark Nights" ("Nights of Darkness"). There are three "Bright Days" and two "Dark Nights," and the dodecadic series connected with them sum up the whole pantheon of deities and the virtues they represent.

3.1 TEXT ON THE CHIEF GODS

This text with excerpts from Mani's writings deals with the major deities of the Manichaean pantheon.[27]

> [The divine Buddha Mani deigned to say]: ". . . Having become perfect, attain eternal life joyfully on the true path, you who have been called for this purpose." And again the Father of our souls, the divine Buddha Mani, deigned to say: "My dear children! First consider the former interpretations of the words which I have preached. And be aware of (lit., know):
> 1. (a), the Maiden of Light,[28] the Mother; (b) the Holy Wind (the Great Spirit); (c) our Father, the great King, the King of gods, Zurvān the God, (and) the second Luminary[29] which is itself the Goddess Kani i Rošan (MP/Pth. Kanīg Rōšn, the Maiden of Light),

2. second the Moon God (Jesus), who raises the dead, (and)
3. third the [holy] Nom Qutï (the Great Nous), who is himself the King of the whole Law.[30]

I have announced to you the coming and the descending of these three (1–3) royal gods, their virtue, knowledge and wisdom . . . I have imparted this wisdom to you with the help of many parables, explications and testimonies, (that is,) the matters concerning the mighty ones, and also at what time these royal gods, which are Jesus, the Maiden of Light and Vahman, the God of Light, came and appeared. Thus this wisdom, which is itself that Maiden of Light . . .[31]

3.2 ANOTHER TEXT ON THE CHIEF GODS

This short text is written on the front and back of a double-page, as well as both sides of a third page with the heading *pidr zivanta,* "from the Father of Life" (or "the life-giving Father"). Page 3 contains portions of the text of page 1, as well as their continuation.

Even though it begins with a plea for liberation, our document seems to reflect the victory of Manichaeism over its foes, for it stresses that "the Light has come."[32]

(Page 1, *recto*)
. . . Protect . . . (and) save (?), . . . liberate the chosen ones, dispel the darkness, destroy the demons. May the elect be joyful! May the divine Law be spread! . . .[33]

(cont'd Page 3, *recto*)
The eternal God Zurvān is the Living Self. He is more bright and splendid than all the mighty ones and kings. For our sake he gave to (or through?) the Church[34] the remission (of sins). We have comprehended (the teaching about) the lightless earth; we have come to know and understand our bodies and our souls, that they are from above and from below, from Light and from Darkness . . . He has let . . . shine for the bright, . . . sweet Law . . . on the whole earth . . .

(Page 1, *verso* and page 3, *recto*)
. . . He has assembled the chosen ones. Because the Light has come, because Darkness has been dispelled, the evildoers have repeatedly fallen into confusion. All those who have gone astray have met with misery. Because they did not know the beneficent God they shall quiver and burn in flaming Hell. Why? Because they did not know the way to [liberation?], the ladder of ascent, and the good guide . . .

(Page 2, *recto*)
. . . The Sun [God] . . . , the bright Moon God, the Goddess Maiden of Light, the mighty God Sriin Sroshart (the Column of Glory), the two strong Lights (Gods), (that is,) the Sun and the Moon God, the seven and the twelve skipper gods,[35] the twelve good hours,[36] . . .

(Page 2, *verso*)
. . . Gods . . . of Light, the five Bright Ones that bring victory (salvation),[37] the good fruit, together with all firstborn Arhats[38] (elect) of the Church,[39]

the Calling and the Answering God, the four elder and younger brothers,[40] and the three Wheels, the Gods of Wind, Water and Fire,[41] . . .

3.3 FRAGMENTS OF A TEXT ON VARIOUS DEITIES

Here we have fragments of a significant text on various deities, probably of mythological character. The text is also of great theological importance. Unfortunately only some sentences of the *recto* and *verso* of two pages are preserved: page 1, *recto* enumerates the five sons of the First Man and tells us about their relationship to the Father of Light; page 2, *verso* is probably a text on the Third Messenger who spreads Light, by his wisdom, to all beings; page 2, *recto* gives us a glimpse of the important notion of "the first self" and "the second self," that is, unenlightened and enlightened man. Finally, page 2, *verso* appraises the Father of Light and enumerates the five limbs of the soul.

The text, or at least part of it, was written by "the Teacher Vahman" whom we know from other documents dated to the second half of the eighth century.

> (Page 1, *recto*)
> [The Fivefold God] is 1. the God of the Breeze,[42] 2. the God of Wind, 3. the God of Light, 4. the God of Water, and 5. the God of Fire. The God Äzrua (Zurvān, the Father of Light) is clothed with all of them and they are mingled with Him . . .
> (*verso*)
> . . . He (the Third Messenger?) brings forth and disperses light and brightness by his wisdom,[43] and his glory and fame (are spread) among all the gods in the Realm of the Gods; like [the God] of the Sun [and the Moon] (Jesus) [lights up] our whole earth by his brightness, [bringing light to?] the [five] kinds of living beings,[44] . . .
> (Page 2, *recto*)

[Page title]:   By the Teacher Vahman[45]

> . . . They find their "second self,"[46] the reward (consisting of) their own (spiritual) limbs,[47] which are themselves composed of those living good thoughts which spring from the God Nom Qutï (the Great Nous, when he dwells in man).
> (*verso*)

[Page title]:   I have respectfully written

> . . . the God Äzrua (Zurvān, the Father of Light), who is himself the elder brother and elder sister of all gods in the Realm of the Gods; pure reason[48] (*qut*), bright mind (*ög*), clear intelligence (**köngül*), attentive [thought] ([*saqïnč*]) (and) strong [understanding] ([*tuymaq*]) . . .

3.4 VIRTUES AND GODS OF THE FIRST DAY OF LIGHT

This text is from the Turkish version of the Parthian "Sermon on the Nous of Light," the Chinese version of which is known as the *Traité*.[49] Our document deals with the first of a series of three Days of Light, the twelve hours of which constitute the qualities of the New Man, as opposed to the Old Man, whose characteristics are exposed in the two Dark Nights or Nights of Darkness.

1. From his (spiritual) limb "reason" (*qut*) he lets *love* arise and he clothes the God of the Breeze (Ether) with it.
2. From his limb "intelligence" *(köngül)* he lets *faith* spring forth and he clothes the God of the Wind with it.
3. [From his limb "mind" (*ög*) he lets *zeal* spring forth and he clothes the God of Light with it.][50]
4. From his limb "thought" (*saqïnč*) he lets *patience* spring forth and he clothes the God of the Water with it.
5. From his limb "understanding" he lets *wisdom* spring forth and he clothes the God of Fire with it.
   And the following are to be invoked first of all: 1. the God of the Breeze, 2. the God of the Wind, 3. the God of Light, 4. the God of Water, 5. the God of Fire, 6. love, 7. faith, 8. zeal, 9. patience, 10. wisdom, 11. piety in word and speech, 12. the wisdom to teach (others skillfully), 13. the God Nom Qutï (the Great Nous).[51]
   These (forces) . . . in the body . . . are (hence) the great God of Wisdom (the Great Nous), together with the twelve gods [endowed with intellectual power],[52] as they exist in the Realm of the Gods.
   This is the First Day of Light with its twelve hours, with which He (the Nous) clothes all the elect.

3.5 VIRTUES AND GODS OF THE SECOND DAY OF LIGHT

This text also is from the Turkish version of the "Sermon."

And the "Second Day of Light" is this: the Twelve Dominions that emanate from the God Nom Qutï (the Great Nous) and that are similar to the Twelve divine virgins, (namely): 1. wielding authority and power (dominion), 2. wisdom, 3. victory (salvation), 4. joy, 5. zeal, 6. judging truthfully (truthfulness), 7. faith, 8. patience, 9. being upright and zealous, 10. doing good works (beneficence), 11. being of balanced heart (equanimity), 12. being bright and radiant (Light).
This is the "Second Day of Light" with its twelve good hours that emanate from the God Nom Qutï, just like the Sun God who has issued from that great God.

3.6 INVOCATION OF THE TWELVE GODS OF THE "SECOND DAY OF LIGHT"

This text is part of a general invocation in a document from Tun-huang.

1. [Dominion],[53] the great King, the Lord of Heaven, the God Zurvān,

2. Wisdom, the Mother Goddess,[54]
3. Valor (or Virtue), the God Xormuzta,[55]
4. Joy, the Fivefold God,[56]
5. Zeal,[57] the God Fri Rošan (Pth. Frih Rōšn, the Friend of the Lights),
6. Truthfulness, the God Vam (the Great Builder), who with the Sun God erected the New Residence (the New Paradise) for the gods,[58]
7. Faith, the God Višparkar (the Living Spirit),
8. Patience, the God "Bright Sun" (the Third Messenger),
9. Truth,[59] the God Might (or, the mighty God), who by his own power supports the strong gods (the Elements of Light) and carries them up (the Column of Glory),
10. Doing good deeds (beneficence), the bright Moon God (Jesus),
11. Equanimity, the Goddess of Lightning, the Goddess Kani Rošan (the Maiden of Light),
12. Light, the enlightened Buddhas (the enlightened Messengers who correspond to the Great Nous).

They are all complete, the twelve hours of the (Second) Bright Day.

3.7 VIRTUES AND GODS OF THE THIRD DAY OF LIGHT

These texts are again from the Turkish version of the "Sermon."

Text A (T II D 119)

And the "Third Day of Light" is itself the power of the Fivefold God (the five sons of the First Man) which are daily liberated from the bodies of the elect . . .

(In addition to these there are the five "gifts," namely, love, faith, zeal, patience and wisdom, and the Gods "Call" and "Answer." These twelve "hours" are related to the Column of Glory.[60])

Text B

Its limbs . . . are (these): 1. reason, 2. mind, 3. intelligence, 4. thought, 5. understanding, 6. love, 7. faith.[61]

Their abiding place are these your good thoughts (*biliglär*).[62]

3.8 THE EVIL POWERS THAT DISPLACE THE GODS IN THE MIND

This text, also from the Turkish version of the "Sermon," talks about the evil powers that occupy the mind if man fails to let the good powers, the gods, take possession of him. The man portrayed here is thus the Old Man, as opposed to the New Man,[63] represented by the "hours" of the First Day of Light.

. . . If he should not have destroyed the power of the Fivefold God which issues from this (spiritual) body, then the spiritual limb "mind" (*ög*) becomes mighty and strong.

But there are times when from the (evil) limb of man, (that is) "dark mind" (*ög*), demons arise and fight with the New Man. If that man loses his "mind" (*ög*) and his "intelligence" (*köngül*), then the sign thereof is this: He has no patience, he becomes contentious . . .

. . . [If the New Man wins the battle,] he (that man) joyfully lets the power of the Fivefold God ascend to the Realm of the Gods. Then the spiritual limb "thought" (*saqïnč*) becomes alert and careful.

But there are times when from the (evil) limb "dark understanding" (*tuymaq*) demons arise and fight with the New Man. When that person then loses and relinquishes his "mind" (*ög*) and his "intelligence" (*köngül*), the sign thereof is this: His wisdom vanishes, he goes about foolishly. The power of the Fivefold God which emanates from his body is injured . . .

3.9 THE TWO DARK NIGHTS

This again is from the Turkish version of the "Sermon."

The two Dark Nights are these:

The first Dark Night is the dark body itself, and its twelve hours are these: the five visible limbs of the fleshly body, (namely) 1. bones, 2. nerves (or sinews), 3. arteries (or veins), 4. flesh, 5. skin; furthermore the five invisible, intangible attributes, which are 6. hate, 7. anger, 8. shamelessness, 9. contentiousness, 10. ignorance, 11. the demon of greed and avarice, and 12. the demon of shamelessness.[64]

And the second Dark Night is this: the demon of greed, "the moribund thought."[65]

And their twelve hours are the twelve Dark Dominions.[66]

3.10 THE STRUGGLE BETWEEN THE DAYS OF LIGHT AND THE DARK NIGHTS

This again is from the Turkish version of the "Sermon."

And the Days of Light were about to oppose the Dark Nights. And the Days of Light were victorious and vanquished the Dark Nights as in the primeval battle of the God Xormuzta (the First Man).[67] And thereafter the Lords and Khans wield power and rule.[68] In their own Realm (the powers of Light in man have) 1. dominion, 2. wisdom, 3. victory, 4. joy, 5. zeal, 6. truth, 7. faith, 8. patience, 9. uprightness, 10. good deeds (beneficence), 11. harmony (?) and 12. light.

These twelve hours fill the heart and thrive in it. And they make the [qualities] in the heart visible.

And the person who sows and plants these twelve Dominions in his own heart has these signs, and his actions and deeds are like this: . . . he teaches (?) even the great ones, . . . he appears (?) in the midst of teachers and disciples. And they are the clear signs that are praised in religion.

And daily 1. their (the elects') peaceful and mild disposition is evident, (furthermore) 2. their pleasantness, 3. their mild words, 4. their wisdom, 5. their ability to differentiate (between good and evil), 6. and 7. their serene, magnanimous nature; their correct straight thought (open to) everything good increases. The seed (of good) thrives and spreads. And then those twelve kinds of good (intellectual) factors rise up in the mind of this person and they themselves give birth to many bright, divine children[69] . . .

Notes

1. Cf. Rose, *Manichäische Christologie,* pp. 26, 161.
2. Türk. Man. III, p. 12.
3. Nagel, "Wie gnostisch ist die Gnosis des Mani?"
4. E.g., *CMC* 66,5.
5. Cf. Blatz, *Studien zur gnostischen Erlösergestalt,* pp. 17–20.
6. Cf. Klimkeit, "Die Kenntnis apokrypher Evangelien in Zentral- und Ostasien."
7. Quoted after J. M. Robinson, ed., *The Nag Hammadi Library in English.* 3d ed. Leiden, 1988, p. 135.
8. New edition and translation of the whole document in Zieme, "Uigurische Steuerbefreiungsurkunden," p. 242, n. 46.
9. I am indebted to Laut for suggestions for this translation.
10. In a MP text with quotations from one of Mani's letters (M 731) it says, "May no one make you disheartened for your being in the world. For you are friends of (my) friends, . . ." *HR* II, 33.
11. This dictum sounds Gnostic, and indeed we find it expressed in Gnostic texts, for instance in the *Corpus Hermeticum.* Compare Leipoldt and Grundmann, eds., *Umwelt des Urchristentums II: Texte zum ntl. Zeitalter.* 4th ed. Berlin, 1974, p. 390. Of course reference must be made here to Gal. 6:7f.: "He that soweth unto his own flesh shall of the flesh reap corruption; but he that soweth unto his Spirit shall of the Spirit reap eternal life." Compare also 1. Peter 1:23–25.
12. The five kinds of living beings in Manichaeism are 1. bipeds, 2. quadrupeds, 3. flying beings, 4. beings living in water, 5. crawling beings.
13. As Zieme, the editor, points out, Mitri is not Mithra, but Maitreya. Zieme, *Texte,* p. 42, n. 294.
14. Here, too, Mitri is not Mithra, as von Le Coq had supposed (Türk. Man. II,5), but rather Maitreya.
15. One is reminded here of Mt. 7:15ff.: "Beware of the false prophets. . . . By their fruits ye shall know them."
16. In the sense of riding-animal (Skr. *vāhana*), the animal which a Hindu (or Buddhist) god uses as a vehicle.
17. Or, the Son of Heaven *(t(ä)ngri *oγli).*
18. Translation after Clauson, *Dictionary,* 327b.
19. H.-Ch. Puech, "Gnostic Gospels and Related Documents," in Hennecke and Schneemelcher, *New Testament Apocrypha* I., pp. 350–60. Cf. also Klimkeit, "Die Kenntnis apokrypher Evangelien in Zentral- und Ostasien."
20. Quoted after the German translation of Schmidt-Glintzer, *Chinesische Manichaica,* p. 87.
21. Schmidt-Glintzer, *ibid.*
22. Or, the bright God *(yaruq tängri).*
23. Or, the bright angels *(yaruq frištilär).*
24. Here follows the list of the twelve hours of the "[Second] Bright Day."

25. Laut points out to me that, as opposed to other instances where the term *ï ïγač* is used for "tree," only *ï* is employed here. Hence the text could be a translation from an Iranian tongue.

26. Or, After we had eaten and drunk, etc.

27. After Bang, "Hymnen," pp. 8ff., including suggestions by Laut.

28. Here the name of the Mother of the Living.

29. It is not clear whether the Second Luminary is named in apposition to Zurvān, or whether this is an individual divine being, a kind of Twin of the Father of Light. Bang suggested that what we might have here is a trinity, composed of God, Spirit, and Maiden of Light. He speaks of the second being as the "Twin Redeemer" or "Redeemer Twin," pointing to the role of such a deity in the *Pistis Sophia* (C. Schmidt, *Koptisch-gnostische Schriften* I, p. 408c). Compare Bang, "Hymnen," p. 9, n. 1.

30. This corresponds to the Skr. title *Dharmarāja*.

31. Hence the Maiden of Light represents that wisdom.

32. Translation includes suggestions by Laut.

33. Name of the scribe (?) in red: Rozbinz//.

34. The term used is Nom Qutï, which can also mean the Church (Bang, "Hymnen," p. 10).

35. The deities residing in the Sun and Moon, navigating them, as ships, across the sky.

36. The hours of the Second Bright Day ("Day of Light"). Compare texts 3.5 and 3.6.

37. The Fivefold God, the sons of the First Man? These are, however, not really victorious, redeeming gods. But there is no other pentad of saving deities, apart from the five sons of the Living Spirit.

38. A Buddhist term for holy ones.

39. Literally, of Nom Qutï, the "Majesty of Religion," otherwise the Great Nous.

40. The four brothers = ?

41. For the three wheels, refer to the Introduction.

42. The deified Ether (MP Frāhwar, Pth. Ardāw Frawardīn). According to Iranian Manichaeism, where, however, the elements are not specifically termed "gods." Compare Boyce, *Reader,* p. 9.

43. A hendiady is used for "wisdom," consisting of the Indian loanword *vidya* (< Skr. *vidyā,* "wisdom") and a Turkish derivative of *bögü,* "wise," namely, *bögülänmäk,* "being wise."

44. In Buddhist texts it is repeatedly said that the Buddha brings light to the five kinds of living beings (Skr. *pañcagati*), that is, gods, men, animals, hungry spirits (*pretas*), and beings of Hell.

45. This teacher is known from texts dated to the second half of the eighth century. Compare von Gabain, "Steppe und Stadt," pp. 55f.

46. The "second self" (*ikinti griv* or *ikinti öz*) or "this self" (*bu öz*) as opposed to "the first self" (*ilki öz*), is the self that has gained *gnosis*. Asmussen, *X^uastvānīft,* p. 218, points out, "A clear Manichaean interpretation is obtained if *ilki öz* is considered an expression of the 'unprepared' viva anima given to all people from birth, which by the acceptance and the understanding of gnosis brought to maturity becomes *bo (= bu) öz,* the conditio⁻ of final salvation. In this way *bo öz* is placed on par with *ikinti griw* in Polotsky's interpretation in *Le Muséon* 46 ["Manichäische Studien"], pp. 270f., in which the Coptic term is adduced (*tmorphē noyaine;* cf. Keph. 36,12 and 19–20, 41,11–12, and 13)." For the terms in the Uigur *X^uāstvānīft,* VI B, compare ch. III, text 1. See also Bang, "Beichtspiegel," pp. 235f.; Colpe, "Daēnā, Lichtjungfrau, zweite Gestalt," p. 70.

47. Or, provided with their own (spiritual) limbs (*öz sinliγ ögdir*).

48. Here the limbs of the soul are enumerated. We give the terms as indicated by Boyce, *Reader,* p. 10, even though the meaning of the Turkish concepts differs somewhat. For the reconstruction of this fragment, compare Zieme, *Texte,* p. 33, n. 195.

49. For the relationship between the Parthian, Sogdian, Turkish, and Chinese versions, compare Sundermann, "Der chinesische Traité Manichéen und der parthische Sermon vom Lichtnous"; Klimkeit and Schmidt-Glintzer, "Die türkischen Parallelen zum chinesisch-manichäischen Traktat."

50. This sentence has been left out inadvertently by the scribe.

51. Hence the Great Nous is the sum of the preceding categories.
52. Reconstructed after the Sogdian fragment M 9006 *recto* (?). (Reference by Sundermann and Zieme.)
53. This virtue, or quality, is not named here, but is related to the Father of Light (God Zurvān), as we know from other texts.
54. Literally, the wise (*bilgä*) Mother Goddess. We translate this in accordance with the structure of the following invocations.
55. Literally, the valiant (or virtuous: *ärdämlig*) God Xormuzta, the First Man.
56. Or, the five gods, that is, the sons of the First Man.
57. Or, assiduity (*tavranmaq*).
58. According to classical Manichaean dogma, the God Vam (the Great Builder) erects the New Paradise as a dwelling place for the redeeming gods and the Mother of Life.
59. Literally, being straight (*könin*), that is, of an ordered mind.
60. In the Chinese *Traité* it says: "These are the images that symbolize the great power of Su-la-sha-lo-i (Srōš-Ahrāy, the Column of Glory)." Compare Klimkeit and Schmidt-Glintzer, "Die Türkischen Parallelen," p. 88.
61. These two virtues are named *pars pro toto*. For the rest see text A.
62. The good thoughts (*biliglär*) are the place where these deities reside.
63. Cf. Klimkeit, "Die manichäische Lehre vom Alten und Neuen Menschen."
64. Sexual desire.
65. The "*enthymēsis* of death," the thought leading to death, that is, moribund thought. It is interesting that this is here interpreted as greed. Compare Introduction.
66. For the Dark Dominions, compare ch. VII, text 2.
67. As already pointed out, in classical Manichaeism the First Man did not originally vanquish the powers of Darkness, but was overcome by them.
68. The power of Light rules in the man from whom evil has been vanquished. This is the state of the New Man.
69. Further good thoughts.

CHAPTER TWENTY-EIGHT

Cosmological Texts

A number of Turkish texts, preserved but fragmentarily, are of a cosmological nature. They complement our Iranian texts on cosmogony and cosmology. The first text identifies a topographical pattern ascribed to the Realm of Light by relating the limbs of God (*membra dei*) (who is ultimately the essence of that Realm) to various areas in it. The second text shows us that there were various descriptions of the Realm of Light, one of which is preserved here in fragmentary form. Text 3 relates the myth about the liberation of the First Man and the creation of the cosmos by the Living Spirit and the Mother of Life. The next fragment (4) is noteworthy in that it ascribes to the First Man the power to vanquish Šimnu, the Devil: in classical mythology the former succumbed to the latter's power. A further cosmological fragment (5) apparently comes from the myth about the Living Spirit and his victory over the archons. Then follows (6) a document on the redemptive roles of Sun and Moon as ships ferrying the saved souls to the World of Light. Text 2.7 is again especially remarkable for its description of how the divine element of Wind, deified as a "son" of Xormuzta, the First Man, who is "imprisoned" in matter, is responsible for the pleasant qualities in nature. There were, for sure, similar texts on the other divine elements.

1. *Fragment on the Realm of Light*

This text is interesting because it ascribes to the limbs of God (*membra dei*) and to the soul specific topographical areas in the Realm of Light, like in a Buddhist *maṇḍala*. The pattern corresponds to Chinese cosmological symbolism, as the editor, Zieme, points out.[1]

> (*recto?*)
> . . . And fifth: From the lands and palaces of the limb "reason" (*qut*), which is further inward and higher than anything else, it (the whole Realm of Light) is praised and created (*sic*) by five hundred thousand myriads of

divine virgins and divine youths who stand by as (*sic*) the center and the place of the throne.[2] It is He, the great . . . King of the Gods, the God of Gods, Zurvān, who has seated himself on . . . God [is] in the middle of . . .[3]

(*verso?*)

. . . And furthermore, it [the Realm of Light] is the shining, bright, exalted land and abode of all the gods. And it is divided into five parts: the limb "reason" (*qut*) is in [the middle] of the whole Realm of the Gods; the limb "mind" (*ög*) is in the South; the limb "intelligence" (*köngül*) is in the East; the limb "thought" (*saqïnč*) is in the West; the limb "understanding" (*tuymaq*) is in the North . . .

2. Text on the Realm of Light

This is a fragment from a text on the Realm of Light. The editor believes it is a part of a hymn which contains sundry notions about that Realm.[4]

. . . In your great, bright Realm they (the heavenly musicians) play many joyful pieces of music. My God, each piece alone evokes countless kinds of melodies. My God, if one plays a piece of music in your Realm, (the melody) is heard (even) twenty thousand miles away in the (surrounding) land.

Furthermore I bow down, my God, before your exquisitely beautiful countenance. Completely perfect (and) merciful one, (oh) my God! You are the beneficent, true God, who has mercy on us.

. . .

3. Fragment of a cosmological text

This is a text about the redemption of the First Man after he has been vanquished by the powers of Darkness. He is lying unconscious in the deep pit of Hell, when a summons from the Realm of Light awakens him and calls for his response. Call and Answer are deified as the gods Xrōshtag and Padvāxtag; they represent, respectively, the summons that reaches everyone listening to the divine Word, and man's response to it. Here the qualities of the divine summons, the Call, are brought to mind and related to primeval events. According to the myth, the gods Call and Answer ascend to the height, and request the Living Spirit and the Mother of Life to lead the First Man, now saved, up to the Realm of Light. However, he has to leave his five sons behind in the clutches of the forces of Darkness. In order to save them, the Living Spirit, assisted by the Mother of Life, creates the world.

The page titles of two pages of this double-sheet (T II D 173b) hardly throw light on the whole text. They read, (*recto*): "May there be joy"; (*verso*): "Of all he himself (is) the blessing (*qut*)."

. . . Second: He (the god "Call") gave us the whole Realm of the Gods with its well-being. Third: He gave us the good Law.[5] Fourth: He caused us[6] to strive (for salvation) and to take heed (of the danger of evil). Fifth: On his right side he opens the door to the Realm of the Gods. As water opens the "door" of vegetation on earth (?), so does the god Xrōshtag open his door for the god Xormuzta and (his sons), the Fivefold God.

When (the god) Xrōshtag and the god Padvāxtag had left the god Xormuzta and ascended to the height from Hell, the god Vadzivanta (the Living Spirit) and the Mother Goddess (the Mother of Life) came (there) quickly. They made the god Xormuzta come out of Hell and ascend, and they sent him to the Realm of the Gods. Then the Mother Goddess and the god Vadzivanta separated[7] the Fivefold God from the God Xormuzta. And they got ready to make the earth and the heavens. First of all the two of them together[8] made and fashioned the azure tenfold sky, as one makes a new garden, or a house. And as one lets seeds grow in the newly cultivated earth, or as a son is procreated by manly power, thus it was with the creation[9] of this earth and the azure tenfold sky. And in the eleventh place (above the tenfold sky) they made the zodiac from seven kinds of virtue (*sic*). The first was to be a fetter for all the demons. The second . . .

4. *Fragment of a cosmological text*

This text is noteworthy, for it reflects a basic transformation of the Manichaean myth in Central Asia. According to classical Manichaean mythology, the god Xormuzta, the First Man, went out to fight the powers of Darkness, but succumbed to them. Only upon receiving a summons from the World of Light was he awakened from his state of unconsciousness and then led back to his heavenly home. The battle against the dark powers was then fought by the Living Spirit and his sons. Perhaps Xormuzta is mentioned too in the first sentence of our text, since it is he that descends to earth and captures the demons. Which "three demons" are meant and what his "four bright powers" represent, we do not know. However, as the story now continues with Xormuzta assuming the role of the Living Spirit as the main actor, he could be the god who is meant. At any rate, it is Xormuzta that vanquishes Šimnu, the Devil, an idea quite foreign to classical Manichaeism. The new circumstances in Central Asia, where Manichaeism, a victorious religion, had vanquished all the demonic (anti-Manichaean) forces, probably gave rise to this surprising alteration of the myth.

. . . He descended and bound those three demons to his zodiac. Together with his four bright powers he descended to this earth . . .[10] The god Xormuzta had a merciful heart. If someone should skeptically ask: "How did he kill Šimnu?" then answer: "Šimnu, changing his speech, declared to all demons: 'I will fling the poison I have taken from you against the god Xormuzta. [I will kill?] the god Xormuzta [with] this [poison].'"

But the poison he flung hit his own head; he (then) implored him (Xormuzta) ten thousand times. Šimnu (said): "I [will] . . . god Xormuzta. . . ." But he fell into the front (?) of Hell . . .

Then the god Xormuzta, making an ax from the god of Fire, split open Šimnu's head. Then, making the god of Fire into (something) like a lance seven hundred thousand miles long, he [pierced?] the head of Šimnu with the tip of the lance . . .

5. Cosmological fragment

This cosmological text[11] deals with a giant demon lying on the earth with his head to the East, weighed down by mountains and plains. It is apparently part of the myth about the Living Spirit, who, together with his sons, vanquished the demons and then fashioned the heavens and the earth. Our text is reminiscent of one on the subjugation of a monster by the Adamas of Light, the third son of the Living Spirit, who spreads out the vanquished demon from East to West and holds it down so that it can sin no more, according to M 7980–84 (MP).[12] Similarly, the MP text M 292 describes how the Adamas of Light vanquishes a monster.[13] We have a similar story about a sea monster being overcome by the King of Honor, the second son of the Living Spirit.[14]

(recto)

. . . The land in the East weighs down the head of that . . . demon. The land in the South and in the North weighs down the upper part of his two shoulders. The Sumeru mountain[15] weighs down his life-center (öz). Two by two those eight mountains weigh down his (four) limbs. The great, mighty, magical word[16] of the God Vadzivanta (the Living Spirit) (constantly) weighs down that demon. If there were no such magic, [he would] not [be held down like that?][17] . . .

(verso)

. . . Then the god Vadzivanta tucked up his tunic in the tenfold sky and put on the god of Water like armor or a garment . . .

6. Cosmological fragment

This text has to do with the rotation of the Sun and the Moon and their role in the transportation of liberated light particles, that is, souls.

(recto?)

. . . The light in the palace of the Moon goes up through (with the help of) the Sun. Every time that radiance (of the Moon) is veiled, the palace of the Moon approaches the palace[18] of the Sun. On the twenty-ninth (day of the month) the two palaces meet. From the palace of the Sun, the Sun God (the Third Messenger), the Mother Goddess (the Mother of Life) and the god Vadzivanta (the Living Spirit) . . .[19]

(verso?)

. . . The god Xormuzta (the First Man) . . . enters into the palace of the Moon.[20] On two days in every month the Moon goes about (continues in its course) without taking his (Xormuzta's) bright power. (Then) again it turns around. On the thirtieth and the fifteenth of the month, it does not take (receive) it (the Light), because the power of the Light is to remain in those strong demons like dregs[21] . . .

7. Fragment on the God of the Wind

This text talks about the qualities of the god of the Wind. The deified Wind, together with the other four divine elements, namely, Ether (Turk. *tïntura,* Breeze), Light, Water, and Fire, are the five elements that represent the divine sons of the First Man. The world was created by the Living Spirit out of the mixture of these divine elements and matter. Hence everything pleasant in the world is there on account of these good powers. There must have been similar texts on the other divine elements, as the fragments of the original Parthian text, the "Sermon on the Soul" (*Gyān Vifrās*), and its Sogdian translation show.[22]

. . .

2. The second quality and pleasant characteristic of the Wind God is this: All the different trees and plants arise out of the power of this god of the Wind. Their buds grow, gain substance and charm. (These) buds become round, swell, open up and yield fruit.
. . . And the Wind God appears in the month of . . . , and one hails him as the luminous Moon that shakes the trees and makes them grow, so that they become plump, brightly colored, oily, strong and very tall in those months. And the trees grow like a leather swimming bag is blown up by a man with the help of the wind.
3. The third quality and pleasant characteristic of the power of the Wind God is this . . . And its (the Wind's) nature, which must necessarily pass through the whole world, makes it (the earth) sweet-smelling and fragrant just as a man who takes care of the house and property of kings and mighty ones sweeps, cleans and decorates the house and makes it comfortable, and also the court and the tent; and he sets up sweet, fragrant sticks of incense which (gradually) burn down.
4. The fourth quality and pleasant characteristic of the power of the Wind God is this: It (the Wind) expels the cold, just as when hot water is added to cold water to give the beverage a pleasant quality.
5. And the fifth quality and pleasant characteristic of the Wind God is that it expels the heat, just as cold water is added to warm water to cool it. And the god is similar to . . .

Notes

1. Zieme, *Texte,* p. 31.
2. Hence these beings constitute the center and the throne.

3. There follows a fragmentarily preserved colophon type of passage which says, "I, Yanga, . . . God Zurvān . . . beautiful Law. . . ."

4. Zieme, *Texte,* p. 47, n. 387ff.

5. A Buddhist term for "religion."

6. In the sense of "awakened us (to)" (*odγur-*).

7. In the sense of "detached" (*ula-*). Compare Zieme, *Schrift und Sprache,* p. 113. This notion seems peculiar to this text.

8. Literally, with one power (*bir türkün*).

9. Literally, preparation (*yarat-*).

10. Two words here, read by von Le Coq as *abamu bu[rxan]*, are emended to *apamu bo[lgïn]ča,* "up to infinity," by Röhrborn. Compare *UigWb* 167b, s.v. *apamu.*

11. I am indebted to Laut for aid in the translation of this fragmentary text.

12. Cf. ch. XVIII, text 2.2.C.

13. Here it says, "[He chased the monster] like a gazelle on (lit., to) the hunting-ground. Then he threw it down, (its) head to the East, (its) feet to the West, (to lie) between four mountains, the middle of (its) body to the South . . . [Then he placed (his)] left foot on (its) neck (and his) right foot on [its thighs]." *Mir. Man.* I, 182, n. 2. Henning points out that a similar description is found in Theodor bar Khonai 316, 26/27 (F. Cumont, *Recherches sur le Manichéisme* I, pp. 36f.).

14. Cf. Sundermann, *Parabeltexte,* p. 48.

15. The Sumeru mountain is the central mountain of the world according to Buddhist cosmology.

16. Cf. *UigWb* 217b, s.v. *arvïš.*

17. It is interesting to note the importance ascribed to magic here.

18. In classical Manichaeism, the Sun and the Moon are referred to as ships or ferries. It is only in Turkish and Chinese texts that they appear as "palaces" (Turk. *ordular*).

19. These three gods have their thrones in the Sun. Compare Introduction.

20. The First Man, the Maiden of Light, and Jesus the Splendor have their thrones in the Moon. Compare Introduction.

21. To function as bait in order ultimately to vanquish them.

22. Sundermann kindly makes me aware of the Parthian original, the "Sermon on the Soul," and the Sogdian parallels; see Sundermann, *Der Sermon von der Seele.*

    There were similar texts in Zoroastrianism. Thus in *Dēnkard* VI, § 79, it says of the deity Ardvahisht ("The Best Truth"):

    > Ardwahišt is seven months in the material world and five months in the spiritual world. During the five months when he is in the spiritual world, he sits in the body of the plants in spiritual form, guards the roots of plants, nourishes them and causes them to grow. He creates the plants during those five months. During the seven months when he is in the material world, the body of the plants comes out, and the plants bud forth and give fruit. This is because *rapithwin* [the middle part of the day], which is the time of the god Ardwahišt, is in manifestation for seven months of the year, and for five months is not. Quoted after S. Shaked, *The Wisdom of the Sasanian Sages (Denkard VI),* p. 31.

CHAPTER TWENTY-NINE

Texts on Man and His Salvation

In this passage we have various texts on unredeemed and redeemed man. The first text vividly compares the feelings, emotions, and thoughts of unredeemed man to the tossing waves of the ocean. The second document expresses in its own dramatic imagery the fate of the suffering soul of unredeemed man. The yearning for salvation is aptly brought out in a prayer to an unnamed god, who may be Mani or Jesus (text 3). Then we have a text on the dire fate of those who fail to give alms for the cause of the faith. Finally, there is a document on the outward signs of redeemed man.

1. Excerpt from Mani's "Letter to the Presbyters"

This text, an excerpt from one of Mani's letters, compares the turbulence of man's thoughts and emotions to the waves of the ocean.[1]

> ... And in the "Letter to the Presbyters"[2] he says, "Now insofar as you are concerned, my beloved sons and my younger brothers, make every effort always to be alert for this victorious god Din Qutï (the Great Nous)[3] who has appeared for you. And consider this body that clothes you thus: It is created (only) of fraud and deception, deceit and mis- guidance. Within it there are many emotional forces (*köngüllär*), intellec- tual powers (*biliglär*) and thoughts *(saqïnčlar)* which constantly roll and stir. They are like[4] (the waves of) the great tumultuous ocean.[5] In all of this it is thus: When the wind blows seawards . . . ; and when the wind blows from the East, it drives that tumult, commotion, seething and swell- ing (of waters) to the West; and when the wind blows from the West, it brings that tumult and the commotion of waves back to the East; and when there is a north wind, it turns the commotion of water, the masses

of foam, the welter, the tumult and the surge (of waves) to the South, bringing it (all) back. Just as in that ocean . . . , (likewise) . . . in this body . . .

2. The suffering of creation

This text explains the suffering of men, and of all creatures, as the outcome of self-
inflicted anguish which is ultimately rooted in ignorance about the divine origin
of the soul. For the suffering of the soul, compare also the Turkish hymn 6 in chapter XXIV.

> . . . And . . . as the fire that springs from wood in turn ignites the wood,[6]
> and as a lamb or a calf, when they change their bodies and are reborn
> as the young of a lion or a wolf, destroy their own herd of cattle or sheep,
> and as anvil, hammer and tongs that are themselves made of iron (in turn)
> break all (kinds of) iron, and as the louse in the garment which has come
> out of the skin of a person sucks the blood of a person—and when that
> person sees it he is repelled—(thus it is with men), as he (Mani) explains:
> "Men arose in primeval time out of the Fivefold God (the divine Light in
> matter) due to the five kinds of trees[7] and from the five kinds of trees
> they have been reborn in this senseless body.[8] As they cause themselves
> distress[9] because of a former existence (öz) and as they suffer bitter tor-
> ments by illness and death everywhere these 'miserable sons of men'
> become weak on account of the suffering that they have to endure. And
> they constantly curse each other and destroy each other. This matter of
> cursing each other, devouring each other, hating each other and striking
> each other they, like ignorant people, hold to be sport and fun. Thus they
> themselves do not understand . . ."[10]

3. The yearning for salvation

This text first gives expression to a basic motif of Manichaeism, and all Gnostic
religions, namely, the profound yearning for salvation, and the notion that the way
to the Realm of Light is infinitely long in space and time. This concept has been
analyzed masterfully by Jonas.[11]

The postscript is dated to 798. This was at the time of the reign of the Turkish
Manichaean king Qutluγ Uluγ Bilgä Qaγan (reg. 795–805), also known as Tängridä
Bulmïš. He ruled in the Mongolian Steppes, the center of his state being the sacred
Ötükün mountain, which was regarded as the center of the world by the ancient
Turks. A Manichaean teacher representing the religious authority of the state and
bearing the title "Superintendent of Religion" resided there. There was another
high-ranking dignitary, also a teacher, residing at Kocho in the Turfan basin further
west. Maybe he is the teacher Aiγ mentioned in the postscript as the recipient of
some gift from the teacher in the Ötükän. Yet Turfan was threatened by the Manichaean Qaγan's power. Von Gabain explains, "The political situation of the Turfan
oasis [from which our text stems] was critical at that time. Around the year 800,

the king, after his earlier attempts had been only partially successful, succeeded in taking possession of the land of Kocho, the area of 'the Four Toxri [Tuγr]'. It seems understandable that even a Manichaean [the writer] did not dare to express allegiance to him just before that event by dating the text with reference to the threatening aggressor."[12]

The page titles of the two pages preserved here are interesting, even though they do not throw light on our text. They read, *(recto)*: "The Book about the Coming of the Buddha (Mani or Jesus)" and *(verso)*: ". . . is written by Shākyamuni."

> . . . Now, our gracious Father, our beneficent King! Countless myriads of years have passed since we have been separated from you . . . We [yearn for] that merciful, beautiful, spotless, bright image of yours. We would behold your loving, radiant, living countenance. By your power we have gone (out) in good health and have come (back) unharmed. We have fulfilled what you have commanded us (to do).
>
> Now, my gracious, royal God, be merciful! We would behold your eternally perfect, sinless nature. We would forget the affliction we have suffered for a long time. We would be filled with love and joy eternally.
>
> Furthermore many such prayers shall be said. Then the great King shall reveal his eternally merciful, beautiful image, and all the gods shall be for ever joyful and happy.
>
> [Postscript]: I, Zimtu, would share in that great (lit., good) joy. May it be so for ever and ever.
>
> Five hundred fifty-two years after the ascent of the exalted Buddha Mani to the Realm of the Gods, in the year of the pig,[13] the Superintendent of Religion,[14] residing in the Ötükän, the most virtuous, merciful Bilgä Bäg ("wise Lord"), the Teacher Tängri Mar Niv . . . Mani,[15] [gave to?] the Teacher Aiγ[16] these two . . .[17]

4. The signs of redeemed man

Various texts, especially in the Turkish version of the "Sermon on the Nous of Light," (the Chinese *Traité*), talk about the outward signs of redeemed man, or the New Man, in whom the forces of Good have gained victory over the forces of Evil.[18] This is a further text of this category which shows what happens when the gods of Light take possession of the mind of man; it is written especially for the elect.

> His acts and deeds are renowned and famous. The person who always maintains control over his own body without letting his former (evil) [nature] rule him and who upholds the Law of the King . . . (will see that) his acts and deeds become evident in five ways. This is the Law of the King:
>
> 1. (First): He does not remain in one city for long . . .
> 2. (Second): Without effort he acquires treasures. And whatever kinds of treasures and goods come into his possession, he does not keep them avariciously for himself, nor hide them.

3.   Third: He preaches being pure and chaste. He teaches others to be so, and he himself is (also) pure and chaste. He loves and esteems being constantly pure.

4.   Fourth: [He loves?] the places of the Law (where the Law is preached), the commandments (and) . . . He acquires a good disposition. And he always maintains a distance from the ignorant.

5.   Fifth: He takes his place in many religious assemblies and he loves and esteems . . . the (other) elect . . .

Notes

1. I am indebted to Laut for advice in the translation of this text.
2. In the Turkish text, it is not clear whether this is the letter of, to, or about the Presbyter(s). Bang, "Beichtspiegel," p. 192, holds it to be from the "Circular about the Presbyters" mentioned by an-Nadīm. Compare Flügel, *Mani*, p. 103; Kessler, *Mani*, p. 214; Dodge, *Fihrist* II, 799: Epistle "of the teacher." The text is also mentioned in the Iranian fragment M 2 as the "Epistle of/on the Presbyters." Compare *HR* II, 31.
3. *Din*, like *Nom*, means law, religion. The term Din Qutï, however, is rare. It suggests that the text was translated from an Iranian source.
4. Literally, they look exactly like.
5. For "ocean," a hendiady is used, consisting of a Turkish word (*taluy*) and a Turkicized Sanskrit term (*samutri* < Skr. *samudra*).
6. This is somewhat reminiscent of Buddhist imagery, though the image used there can serve to explicate quite a different teaching. Thus it says in the *Maitrisimit*, in explaining the law of conditioned causation (Skr. *pratītyasamutpāda*), "As . . . a glowing, red-hot lump of iron ignites wood and as the fire of the wood in turn heats up the iron, thus also are consciousness (Skr. *vijñāna*) (on the one hand) and name and form (Skr. *nāma-rūpa*) (on the other hand) cause and effect for one another." Ş. Tekin, *Maitrisimit nom bitig* I. Wiesbaden, 1980 (BT IX), 124.
7. This could, on the one hand, be a reference to the five trees of life, or trees of Paradise, often mentioned in apocryphal Christian literature, for example, in the *Gospel of Thomas*, logion 19: "Jesus said: 'Blessed is he who came into being before he came into being. If you become my disciples and listen to my words, these stones will minister to you. For there are five trees for you in Paradise which remain undisturbed summer and winter and whose leaves do not fall. Whoever becomes acquainted with them will not experience death.'" This can be interpreted as a reference to the preexistence of the soul in Paradise, where its five divine limbs are represented by the five trees of life. By knowing one's origin and hence becoming aware of one's trees of life one attains salvation ("life"). This interpretation agrees with the Manichaean image expounded in the Chinese *Traité* of the five trees of life (cf. Schmidt-Glintzer, *Chinesische Manichaica*, pp. 90f.). According to it, the original state was lost when the divine Light represented in the Fivefold God—the five sons of the First Man—was imprisoned in matter and bound to the five kinds of vegetation, and hence to the five kinds of living beings, as their souls. (Cf. Introduction.) According to Bang, on the other hand, the five kinds of trees refer to the five trees of death, also described in the *Traité*. (Cf. Schmidt-Glintzer, *op. cit.*, pp. 94ff., Bang, "Hymnen," p. 13.)
8. They have been born in primeval time (lit., formerly) of the substance of the Fivefold God (the divine Light) that is mixed with matter, *hylē*. See Bang, "Hymnen," p. 13.
9. Or, tortured themselves for. See Bang, "Hymnen," p. 13.
10. Translation follows a suggestion of Laut.
11. Cf. Jonas, *Gnosis und spätantiker Geist*, pp. 94ff.; Jonas, *The Gnostic Religion*, pp. 65ff.
12. Cf. von Gabain, "Steppe und Stadt," pp. 59f.

13. If we take 276 as the year of Mani's death, this leads us to 798. As G. R. Rachmati points out, there seems to be a mistake here, because 798 was a tiger year (according to the Chinese calender, at least). The year of the pig would be 795 or 807. *Türkische Turfan-Texte* VII, 82, n. 3.

14. Literally, the Great One of the Law *nom uluγï*. Von Gabain remarks that the person meant had the rank of a *praštinki,* that is, *baštinki* ("Religious Superintendent"). Von Gabain, "Steppe und Stadt," p. 60.

15. This, then, was a religious personality residing at the seat of Uighur power.

16. Or, with the help of the Teacher Aiγ. Von Gabain thus takes Aiγ-ïn to be an instrumental, rather than an accusative. Von Gabain, "Steppe und Stadt," p. 58.

17. This can hardly be a reference to the "Book of the Two Principles," as von Gabain points out (*op. cit.*).

18. Cf. Klimkeit and Schmidt-Glintzer, "Die türkischen Parallelen," pp. 92f.

A penitential scene from an illuminated manuscript. Staatliche Museen—Preussischer Kulturbesitz, Museum für Indische Kunst, Berlin.

CHAPTER THIRTY

Texts on the Manichaean Community and Manichaean Kingship

1. The Manichaean community

We do not have many documents about the life of the Manichaean community, which consisted of "the chosen ones" (*electi* and *electae,* that is, monks and nuns) and of the wider community of all believers, including the auditors (laymen). The community of the elect lived in monasteries, established along the lines of Buddhist monasteries, though the Manichaean monks had been charged to wander from place to place and to spread the divine message, living in "blessed poverty" on their peregrinations. Yet in the course of time, these monastic institutions, like those of the Buddhists, became centers not only of learning and spiritual life, but also of economic power and status, with serving staffs to care for the needs of the elect. The Chinese "Compendium"[1] throws some light on monastic life. Here we learn in the *Fifth article*[2] of the five "halls" of a monastery: 1. the "hall of the sacred scriptures and the tablets," 2. the "hall of fasting and teaching," 3. the "hall for cult and confession," 4. the "hall of teaching the Law," and 5. the "hall for ill monks," that is, the hospital ward. In the text it says (c 16), "In the five halls referred to above, the community gathers together, in order to do the good work zealously. The monks may not establish their own private quarters, kitchens or magazines. They (are to) eat vegetarian food daily. They await alms with dignity. If nobody gives them alms, they beg in order to satisfy their most pressing needs. They enlist only auditors (for help), but keep no male or female slaves, nor any of the six kinds of domestic animals, nor other things that are not in accordance with the Law."[3]

Contrary to this ideal state of affairs, the big monasteries in Central Asia had cooks and servants, craftsmen and people of various callings in their service. They possessed lands and vineyards, stables and horses, and other things of the world. We are reminded of texts on Buddhist monasteries that had specific privileges like tax exemption and also possessed material wealth in rich measure.[4]

We learn in the "Compendium" that there were three important dignitaries in the monastery: (1) the hymn and prayer-leader, who was especially concerned with "matters of the Law," (2) the head of religious instruction, who mainly dealt with "discipline and admonition," and (3) the "supervisor of the month," whose charge it was to administer tithes and alms. "All the monks," says the "Compendium," "must subject themselves to the instructions (of those three?) and may not act on their own authority."[5]

1.1 OFFICIAL DOCUMENT ON A MANICHAEAN MONASTERY

This text, the beginning of which is lost, is apparently a charter of a Manichaean monastery in Kocho in the Turfan area.[6] It was found by the Chinese archaeologist Huang Wenbi and published in his archaeological report on Turfan in 1954.[7] He had discovered it at the site of Yar Khoto (Chin. Jiaohe) a few miles west of the town of Turfan. The 2.7-meter long scroll has 125 lines of Uighur text, and there is a red Chinese seal imprinted on it at eleven different places. The seal contains four lines which read, "The precious seal of the chancellor . . . of the secretariat and the chancellery of the great, blessed, great Uighur Realm."[8] As Chinese was not an official language of the chancellery of the Uighur Realm, this document must have been officially sanctioned by Uighur as well as Chinese authorities, as in the case of newly found, but as yet unpublished Sogdian Manichaean scrolls.

The first scholar to make the Western world aware of this text was Zieme, who published excerpts from the document in 1975.[9] He states that many problems of the text remain unsolved, partly because of its content, and partly because of its state of preservation. He assumes that it was written when the Uighur Kingdom of Kocho (ca. 850–1250) was thriving.[10] Because of its linguistic features—it contains no Mongolian words—he ascribes it to the tenth or eleventh century.

The special significance of this document lies in the fact that through it we get, for the first time, an insight into the social and economic life of a Manichaean monastery in Central Asia. This information was used, along with Zieme's and Geng Shimin's Chinese study of the text, by S. N. C. Lieu in his "Study on Precept and Practice in Manichaean Monasticism,"[11] which places this text in a wider context.

Problems still abound regarding this document. Firstly, the various ranks of the people mentioned cannot be clearly discerned. In view of this fact, the Turkish rank titles have been retained. First an *ačγučï* is mentioned. A. von Gabain translates this as "supervisor." Then we hear repeatedly of the *iš ayγučï*s, which von Gabain translates as "herald." In an Uighur document from the Mongol period where men of various ranks are mentioned, the *iš ayγučï* is low ranking.[12] The *xroxan*s are often mentioned in conjunction with the *iš ayγučï*. This term can be identified with the Persian title *xrōhxvān (xrvhxv'n)*, "preacher." However, in our text the *xroxan*s do everything but preach. They are servants of a higher order, waiting on the elect, who are referred to as "lords" (lit., gods, *tängrilär*). In other texts, a preacher usually comes from the ranks of the elect. In the *Traité*, the preacher (*hu-lu-huan* for *xrōhxvān*) is mentioned as the deputy head of a monastery, his function being to exhort and admonish others. In view of the preachers in our text, Zieme assumes that they also had other functions, mainly supervision over various types of work in the monasteries.[13] We also hear of various craftsmen in our text, for whom the *iš ayɣučï*s were to keep food ready. Then there is mention of a miller serving the monastery, but also of wood-cutters, cooks, men with various supervising and serving functions, and male and female servants. Physicians belonged to the establishment as well.

The powerful economic position of the monastery is highlighted by the fact that it rented out lands and vineyards, and that it was able to take draconian measures against those that did not serve the elect properly.

According to our text there were also other, apparently smaller monasteries in the vicinity, for example, in Yar (Khoto), that is, Jiaohe,[14] and Solmï, which must here be a place other than Karashahr, with which the Solmï of other texts is identified.[15]

> ... The *ačɣučï*s may enter. And ... when they enter the first *qanïɣ*,[16] they may enter only at the behest of the rule to be observed in the monastery.[17] [If] they bring in ... , the *iš ayɣučï*s and (?) the Teacher (*Mozak*) Ilïmɣa Totoq Ïnanč may put them to work according to the forementioned rule.[18] Taš Svit Bars Tarqan and Tämir[19] should note this well.
> ...
>
> (With regard to) the store-house, ... the Ilïmɣa (a rank?) Taɣay Bars (or Taɣay Bars Ilïmɣa)[20] should do ... the work in ... well. Qumar Bars Tarqan[21] should do the work in the west of the town.[22] He should not say (excuse himself saying), "The vineyard (and) the land are dry," but should (rather) have the land cultivated well. If the vineyards in the east of the town[23] yield nothing, Taɣay Bars ... should be taken into custody.[24] [If] the work in the west of the town[25] [has been done poorly], corporal punishment should be meted out to Qumar Bars Tarqan.
>
> Ilïmɣa Tutuq should gather and store properly what has to be harvested in the east of the town.[26] If there is anything to be gathered by Qumar, the domain of Qumar [Bars] may be ...[27] That which is due to be stored [should be put] into storage; the *ayɣučï*s (?)[28] should store properly all that is due for [storage]. Both of them should have ... the work done and apply themselves to it (?) [together]. Since there is plenty of (arable) land in the east, ... Qumar Bars, who has to collect the crop and the cotton bales (*quanpo*), [should] ...[29]
>
> ... 62 cotton bales should be exchanged (for cotton?) and the cotton should be given for garments ...
>
> Every month, the two convents of the lords[30] should each be [given] 80 piculs of wheat, 7 piculs of sesame, 2 piculs of beans and 3 piculs of sorghum (millet), and they should keep these as provisions ... The two *iš ayɣučï*s should (also) give food to the craftsmen.
>
> If there is not enough food and drink for the lords (elect) left after giving food[31] to the [teacher], two *xroxan*s should ... ask for (?) provisions from the monastery at Solmï.[32] The *iš ačɣučï*s should be punished.

The rent for the . . . land in the custody of (?) the *iš aγγučï*s (amounts to) 4,125 bales of cotton. According to the law of . . . (it) should be put into the *qančïk* (store-house?) of Srošvit.

Whatever work has to be done in the monastery, two *xroxan*s and two *iš aγγučï*s together should have it done.

The miller Kädmä: of 500 cotton bales, 50 cotton bales should be given to Kädmä. The remaining 450 bales may be used for the men and the male and female attendants for winter clothes and boots. 60 cotton bales . . . may be used for [the male and] female attendants for summer clothes.

There should be [sufficient] food for the two convents of the lords. In one month, (first) one *xroxan* and (then) one *iš aγγučï* should stand and see to it that the food is prepared well. And in the next month (first) one . . . and (then) one *iš aγγučï* should stand and see to it that the food is prepared well. If the food is bad in any month, the *xroxan* and the *iš aγγučï* responsible for that month should be imprisoned. The two *xroxan*s and the two *iš aγγučï*s should be on hand (lit., stand) and organize (lit., bring together) the . . . , the cooks and the bakers.[33]

When the lords sit down for the meal, the two *xroxan*s should wait on them and bring them food in an appropriate manner, (serving everyone) right up to the *Ivrγani Zmastik*.[34] (Only) afterwards may they themselves sit down to have (their) meal.

If affairs concerning the monastery [should be laid] before the divine teacher, then, according to the forementioned rule, the *xroxan*s should not enter without the *iš aγγučï*s, and the *iš aγγučï*s should not enter [without] the *xroxan*s. The *xroxan*s should stand together with the *iš aγγučï*s, and they should put forward their request (together).

The attendants and lay members should serve the lords (the elect) that have no pages. The remaining pages should appear as servants beside (before) the *Ivrγani Zmastik,* and they should be made to serve correctly at the meal (?), in accordance with this decree (?). When the lords and the ladies (the *electi* and *electae*) take meals at the monastery, or go out when they are invited (?), they should each be brought two cups (or) bowls with water . . . , and they should be brought before the elect and the *Ivrγani Zmastik*. When the elect are invited out, . . . one should have *moin*[35] collected . . . If *qanlio*[36] is to be prepared, one may make it with . . . The divine teacher and the bishop should not be involved (in its preparation) . . . When the divine teacher orders it (*qanlio*) to be made, the *xroxan*s and the *iš aγγučï*s should go and have it prepared. The teacher and the bishop should not use[37] the two big bowls with drinks belonging to the two convents of the lords. When someone approaches the divine teacher or the bishop, he should bring (lit., give) his own drink.

200 *šiq* of wheat bran are (to be used as) fodder for one year (?). Of the 200 *šiq* of bran, the oxen that draw the carts may eat 100 *šiq*. The horses of the divine teacher and the bishop may (also) eat 100 *šiq* of the bran. Yïγmïš may store up these 100 *šiq* of bran . . .

The estates of Üč Ordu should be given to three persons.

Daily 20 melons . . . are to be brought to the monastery. (In addition?) 30 melons are to be given to the large monastery and 30 melons are to be given to the small monastery. Yïγmïš should collect the melons and bring (them). If he does [something wrong?], he should be put into custody.

One should give 1 picul of *bïsïnč sanguin* (?) to the divine teacher, to the bishop . . . , and to the two convents of elect in equal measure . . .

Two *iš ayγučï*s should cultivate the vineyards (and) fields of the eastern and western monasteries properly;[38] as far as the fallow fields are concerned, be they few or many, they should be given into tenure. Then the fields will be tilled. (The increase in value (?)) should be added to the basic rent (?). The productive fields should be tilled well (too), so that their rent may be increased.

The two *iš ayγučï*s should not quarrel; if they quarrel and do their work poorly, they should be punished. The divine teacher, the bishop and the *xroxan*s should not be involved in the affairs of the fields and the vineyards. The *iš ayγučï*s (alone) shall be responsible (for this matter).

The servant and the subordinate of the *iš ayγučï* Qumar Bars Ilïmγa Tutuq is Qutadmïš Ygän. The servant and subordinate of the *iš ayγučï* Qumar Bars Tarqan is Il Körmiš.

If the *iš ayγučï*s do their work well, they shall receive a reward; if they do it poorly, they shall receive 300 strokes of the rod . . .

The men in the monastery with Yimki Čor Baspa at their head should be put to work. The *iš ayγučï*s should give orders as to their daily work.

Every year, 20 carts of reeds should be brought to the monastery; the remaining reeds should be distributed to the vineyards.

If the *Ivryani Zmastik* or the *Sarxan Ügä*[39] fall ill, they should be looked after and medical [care] should be provided for them. One should call physicians and nurse them well. The medicine is to be taken from the *iš ayγučï*s. If any monk falls ill and Yïγmïš does not care for him, Yïγmïš should receive 300 strokes of the rod . . .

The page of Mangčor Sangun, Arslan Tonga, and his younger brother, the page of Kän-ky-ä, as well as Iγγаččï Bolmïš, these four persons from the *il* (?), should each bring one *šiq* of raw cotton. Two bushels (*küri*) of the raw cotton are to be given to the monastery at Yar, and six bushels of raw cotton are to be brought to the monastery at Kocho.

The woodcutters in the monastery are Lalan Bodtuγmïš, Lisä Šäbi Körtlä and Bäg Tur. They should deliver one load of firewood every day. Qutluγ Tonga and Qolmïš, these two, should deliver one load of firewood every other day. Yaqšï Qutluγ Arslan is to receive the firewood brought by these woodcutters.

If the food for the elect is not cooked through, (the cooks) should receive 300 strokes of the rod.

The physicians attached to the monastery are Yaqšï Ačari, together with his younger brother and his son, (namely) Sïngtay Toyïn and Taz, the son of Vapap, Qančï Yaqtsïn Toyïn, and Kädizči Oγul Bars. (These and) the *zugčï*s (?) are the persons that should work in the monastery. The physicians should be on call.

The servants and the shepherds[40] should not be involved in the affairs of the town community, or the monastic community. If there is . . . , they should do their (own) work, but they should not be involved in any other work.

2. *Texts on Manichaean Kingship*

From 762/763, when Bögü Qaghan adopted Manichaeism as state religion, to 840, when the Uighur Kingdom of the Steppes was destroyed, and in the period of ca. 850–1250 A.D., Manichaean kings ruled over Turkish subjects in the little Kingdom of Kocho. Manichaean rule had far-reaching consequences for the Gnostic religion. The Manichaeans, protected by a ruler of the faith and accepted as representatives of an official religion (which, to be sure, was increasingly being displaced by Buddhism), could feel at home in the world, at least for a certain time, unlike the adherents of classical Gnosticism. Thus it says in a fragment edited by Zieme (T I D 31 (U 197)), "Equipped with armor, they (the royal ones) stand ready to help the pure elect."[41] These words are indicative of the general situation for a considerable span of time.

It is interesting that a notion prevailed concerning the two aspects, or "orders" of life, the religious and the temporal, which were referred to by the phrase "the religion within, the realm (or kingdom) without." This formula, which is also to be found in Buddhist texts, gives the world its due significance, without neglecting the spiritual sphere, which is described as the "inner" sphere of a full life.

We refer here also to the Iranian texts on royal kingship. (cf. ch. XIV, texts 1–3).

2.1. TEXTS ON THE CONSECRATION OF A NEW MANICHAEAN KING

These texts are standardized formal accounts of the coronation of a new king, even if they present themselves as historical narratives. Yet they do include historical information. Thus we come to know (in text B) that the Manichaean king had died and that in his place another had appeared. The title shared by the old and new kings was *Iduq-qut,* "holy charisma." This was the title of the rulers of the Turkish Basmïl in early times, but the Turkish Uighurs also used it, both in the Kingdom of the Steppes and in the Kingdom of Kocho. According to A. von Gabain, the ruler referred to resided in the Ötükän mountains in the Mongolian Steppes; he ruled from 821 to 824.[42] But the text could also be of a later date.

Text A

. . . As he (the former king) descended (died), shining brightly like the sun, we all respectfully wished for (this) fortunate day (of the consecration of a new king). We were happy at heart, we who are "from within" (of the religious sphere), with . . . at the head, all (of us) . . . of the two communities (of monks and nuns), (including) all elect, as well as those "from without" (of the political sphere), living in (this) blessed land, (namely) the nobles, princesses, royal princes, administrators of the Realm, lords of the land, all dignitaries and . . . the common people that are like dogs and birds, (that is) society (as a whole) (including) subjects and servants, (and) all the souls and spirits (*qut vaxšiklar*) from the blue Heaven down to the brown Earth.[43]

As the Spirit (*qut)* of the Realm of Ötükän[44] has deigned to bestow power upon us, and as we all have found the happiness we were yearning for, we express our joy (at your coronation), oh our king, with utmost devotion and love. May our exalted king, the "*Iduq-qut,*"[45] having received from us a new exalted and blessed name (a regal name), seat himself on the golden throne, the jewel-encrusted *tau-cang,*[46] and may he be happy and blessed. May the four bright royal kings[47] and the wise Buddhas[48] of the whole world come . . .

Text B

. . . Saying "The [throne?] should not remain empty," . . . he (the new king) deigned to seat himself on that throne. All the wise Buddhas . . . , changing their names and forms,[49] appeared, in order to liberate . . . the souls . . .

As our king, the *Iduq-qut* (the former king) descended like the sun (died), all of us, the poor and common people, became sad and sorrowful. But as the bright moon (the new king) appeared in splendor in place of the sun, so did our (new) king, the *Iduq-qut* Avluč,[50] appear at (that) place. It was decided that he should ascend the golden throne. May the Spirit (*qut)* of the Realm of Ötükän, of the former wise kings, of his royal fathers and of this exalted throne come down upon our divine prince *Iduq-qut*. May power and aid come from the seven and the twelve mighty ones,[51] and may most beautiful, desired, exquisite light descend upon the majesty of our valiant, virtuous, great and mighty king. [May] his whole realm and government . . .

3.1. BLESSINGS FOR THE KING AND HIS COURT

A number of fragmentarily preserved texts contain blessings for the Uighur King of Kocho as well as high dignitaries of that court. They throw light on the institution of Manichaean kingship and thus supplement the Iranian texts on the subject.

Text A Blessing for the royal court

(*recto?*)

. . . May flaming Fortune[52] come to the heavenly King, and furthermore to . . . the noble Tarxan[53] ladies, . . . to the Bäg, the Tutuq and the Čigši,[54]

then to the distinguished spirits of [the dear] male and female auditors . . . May your spirits and your bodies find complete well-being. May
you (all) be free of suffering all your lives long, and may you become happy
and joyful. May the bright, regal gods send you the recompense for all
your pains speedily, every day . . .

(verso?)

. . . The Tarxan ladies, the distinguished spirits of the dear male and
female auditors . . . Today, on (this) holy, happy day, you have assembled
at the holy, divine monastery. The divine *Mani . . . , Jesus, Kanig (the
Maiden of Light) and the God Vahman (the Great Nous), the angels that
guard the Law (nom), the . . . Buddhas (divine Messengers) that have
descended repeatedly . . . , may they (all) bestow blessing (qut), well-being
(qiv) and strength (küč) (upon you). May the religion within and the realm
without rest upon (lit., stay with) the heavenly, royal Khan, perfect in both
kinds of excellence (ädgü) . . .

Text B Fragment on the Manichaean ruler of Kocho

On paleographical grounds this text must be assigned to the Kocho period (ca.
ninth/tenth century).

(recto)

. . . our . . . wise . . . Tängrikän[55] . . . He has subjected his jewel-like, noble
body to torture in the service of the kingdom, for the sake of the religion
within and the whole realm without . . .

(verso)

. . . All crops . . . and orchards . . . have thrived (?). Therefore the protective spirit (qut vaxsik) of the Kingdom of Kocho and of the twenty-two
cities[56] [has deigned to protect?] the great Majesty of our kind Tängrikän . . .

3.2 BLESSING FOR A MANICHAEAN KING

This text, part of a double-sheet written in Manichaean script, is reminiscent of
the preceding documents. The first page is too fragmentary to be translated. The
second page contains a prayer requesting fortune and aid for the ruler and his
nobles; the third part asks the divine powers for freedom from illness, sorrow and
pain.[57]

. . . May they (deign to) seat themselves (?) and be happy. May happiness
and increasing joy, well-being, bliss, . . . victory [and] . . . come from the
four bright [regal] gods and the wise Buddhas in the West . . .

3.3 TEXT ON THE ROYAL CEREMONY ON NEW YEAR'S DAY

New Year's Day, simply called "the New Day" (yangï kün), played a major role
in the Manichaean cycle of festivals in Central Asia, as it did for the Buddhists.

However, we are ill-informed about this festival, which must have had its roots in the Persian *Nō Rōz,* "New Day."[58] In the texts, a distinction is made between the "Great New Day" (*uluγ yangï kün*) and the "New Days" of minor importance.[59] On the "Great New Day," there was a royal ceremony attended by the king, as in Iran in former times. In the ceremony, the king was apparently likened to the Father of Light.

> . . . The ladies and the princesses, the noble princes and their blessed, golden (royal) descendents, radiant with great blessing (*qut*) and fortune *(süü),* deign to take (their) places, bright as the sun and shining like a great lake, on this blessed, fortunate (auspicious) Great New Day.

> Now, in the Realm of the Gods, the great, royal King of the gods, Zurvān, together with all (other) gods, [celebrates?] the New Day . . .

3.4 PRAYER FOR BLESSING FOR THE ROYAL HOUSE

This text shows how intimately religion and political sovereignty were connected in Central Asia.

> May happiness and joy increase, and may there come anew joy, untarnished blessing, growth, increase and new victory. Furthermore, may the valiant and mighty angels and great ones, the perfectly meritorious . . . divine beings, alight; may all the great angels grant power and help, victory and triumph. May long life and rich blessing be bestowed on our ruler, and may he always be free from danger and hardship.

> My ruler! May the sons (?) of the Law[60] . . . , beginning with the divine bishop . . . , the two convents (the communities of monks and nuns) . . . the Buddha Mani . . . "from within" (in the religious sphere) . . .

3.5 PRAYER FOR THE RULER

This is a prayer for the ruler, perhaps on the occasion of the New Year ceremony. An interesting aspect is the request for the forgiveness of the sins of the tängrilär! Probably the term *tängrilär* refers here to the elect.

> (*recto*)
> . . . On the . . . day, in the blessed month. May the victorious beginning of the year, the happy [New Year's?] Day come and may it be auspicious. May . . . blessing, fortune, happiness, benefit and victory come anew from the four bright regal gods. May (they) come [and may] the (religious) Law within and the Realm without [be preserved?] . . .
> (*verso*)
> . . . [61] May our worthy praise continue for a long time as on this (day), and may they (or we) participate in joy and blessedness. [Parthian]: Forgive the sins of the gods![62]

3.6 THE BETROTHAL OF A PRINCE

This small fragment has to do with the betrothal and marriage of a prince to a girl named Anvam. It could be a part of a betrothal or marriage song.

> . . . If he takes a liking to her, the virgin will not be suitable for anyone else. Your Majesty (*tängrim*), may she be suitable for you. It will be very lovely when you seat yourself (with her) in all joy and blessedness. You two together will be as lovely as when the sun rises over the earth, lighting up everything with its splendor. And Anvam will be like a beautiful, green tree in summer filled with various fragrant, sweet-smelling [blossoms] . . .
>
> . . . Look at Anvam; she has come for your sake. She loves you and cherishes you with her whole heart. Your Majesty, if you (so) will, become her husband, and Anvam shall be your wife . . .

Notes

1. Cf. Haloun and Henning, "The Compendium of the Doctrines and Styles of the Teaching of Mani, the Buddha of Light," pp. 184–212; H. Schmidt-Glintzer, *Chinesische Manichaica*, pp. 69–75.
2. This section was not translated by Haloun and Henning, but can be found in Schmidt-Glintzer's German translation, p. 74.
3. Schmidt-Glintzer, *op. cit.*, p. 74.
4. Compare Zieme, "Uigurische Steuerbefreiungsurkunden für buddhistische Klöster," *AoF* 7 (1981), pp. 237–63. Here we learn that Buddhist monasteries also had fields and vineyards and that they were exempt from tax and statutory labor, "for the work of the monks is directed to the mind," as one text says (p. 245). The income from the estates was to be used, according to one regal decree, to furnish and expand the monastery. The decree says, "As long as the monks are there, they should rule and be strong. . . . One should not cause work for those (lit., for the senses of those) who are at rest (lit., without change, i. e., in mind)" (p. 246).
5. Schmidt-Glintzer, *ibid.*
6. The text has been dealt with by Zieme and Geng Shimin (in Chinese). Compare Zieme, "Ein uigurischer Text über die Wirtschaft manichäischer Klöster im uigurischen Reich," pp. 331–38. Both von Gabain and Zieme were so kind as to put at my disposal their new unpublished readings and translations of this document, after Professor Geng Shimin, Peking, kindly procured new photographs of the text for us. A new, fully annotated translation is to be published by Dr. A. van Tongerloo, Leuven.
7. Cf. Zieme, "Ein uigurischer Text," p. 331.
8. Zieme, *ibid.*
9. Zieme, *art. cit.*
10. Zieme, *op. cit.*, p. 332.
11. S. N. C. Lieu, "Precept and Practice in Manichaean Monasticism," pp. 153–73.
12. L. Ligeti, "A propos d'un document ouigoure de l'epoque mongole," p. 9 and n. 34; Zieme, *art. cit.*, p. 333.
13. Zieme, *art. cit.*, p. 333.
14. A town several miles west of Turfan city.
15. We do hear of Manichaeans (albeit laymen) from Solmï (Karashahr) and Hami in a fragmentarily preserved prayer. Compare T. Handea, "A propos d'un texte fragmentaire," pp. 3–4.

16. Or, the *qaniɣ* in *ilk;* or, the *ilk* and the *qaniɣ.* The meaning of *qaniɣ* is unknown. *Ilk* is "first, previous," but it could also refer to a room or location in the monastery.

17. Literally, the commandment of the monastery.

18. Thus according to Zieme. Von Gabain translates, "When they bring in . . . , the 'herald' should make (them) work according to the custom in . . . and the custom in his *il* (place of responsibility), by (i. e., on account of) the bishop, the Ilïmqa and the Tutuq."

19. This could also be just one person, as suggested by Zieme, who reads Taš Svit Bars T(a)rqan T(ä)mir.

20. Ilïmɣa, like Tutuq, could be a title.

21. Or, the Tarqan (an official) Qumar Bars.

22. Or, in the western town (Zieme).

23. Or, in the eastern town (Zieme).

24. Thus according to von Gabain. Zieme reads and translates quite differently: "If the vine-yards in the eastern town are appropriate, Taɣay Bars may get three (?) cotton (?) . . . as reward."

25. Or, in the western town (Zieme).

26. Or, in the eastern town (Zieme).

27. "Entered," or the like.

28. Or, . . . in Kocho (they) (von Gabain).

29. Von Gabain translates, ". . . Qumar Bars should collect the normal (i. e., standardized) cotton [bales] and administer the estate."

30. It is not clear what is meant by this term; maybe it refers to a monastery and a nunnery.

31. Or, if after soup and food have been given . . . (Zieme).

32. Zieme translates, "[In . . .] the monastery of Solmï they should sit for themselves (?)." (Could this be an indication of being banished to Solmï?)

33. Von Gabain: "should have . . . the cooks and the bakers arrested."

34. This is apparently a high master of religious ceremonies. The term is Iranian. It could also be read Nyw'ɣr'y Zm'styk (Zieme).

35. Apparently a kind of soup, made with flour (Zieme).

36. Zieme translates this with "dry provision."

37. Literally, touch.

38. Von Gabain: "fields that, being in the west and the east, belong to the monasteries."

39. Apparently the title of a high-ranking celebrity.

40. Thus for *yrɣan* and *čopan* according to von Gabain.

41. Zieme, *Texte,* p. 37; cf. Klimkeit, "Manichaean Kingship."

42. Cf. von Gabain, "Steppe und Stadt," pp. 61f.; R. R. Arat, "Der Herrschertitel *Iduq qut,*" pp. 150–57.

43. The blue Heaven and the brown Earth were the two most venerable deities of the ancient Turks, and, for the Mongols four centuries later. Compare J.-P. Roux, "Les religions dans les sociétés Turco-Mongoles," *RHR* 201 (1984), pp. 393–420.

44. The "Realm of Ötükän" was the Turkish Uighur Empire of the Steppes with its capital in the Ötükän mountains in present Mongolia. It was formerly regarded as the center of the world, where the Spirit (*qut*) of the Realm resided and bestowed blessing. It is interesting to see that in this text from Turfan that Spirit is still remembered and invoked. For the significance of the Ötükän mountains for the early Turks, compare O. Pritsak, "Von den Karluken zu den Karachaniden," p. 273; T. Tekin, *A Grammar of Orkhon Turkic,* pp. 261f. (inscription of Kül Tigin).

45. For the term *Iduq-qut,* compare von Gabain, "Steppe und Stadt," p. 61.

46. *Tau-cang* < Chin. "throne."

47. God, his Power, his Light, and his Wisdom.

48. Divine Messengers.

49. For the redeeming gods' capacity to change their forms (and names), see Klimkeit, "Gestalt."

50. Written as Avlavč.

51. The gods residing in the Sun and the Moon. They are sometimes conceived of as skippers, as the two celestical bodies are sometimes referred to as "ships" or "ferries."

52. The word used for Fortune is *süü*, also meaning "Luck, Glory."

53. A title of ladies of high rank. Compare Zieme, *Texte*, p. 50, n. 436.

54. High-ranking officials.

55. Title of the king: "the Divine One."

56. These cities apparently belonged to the Kingdom of Kocho.

57. Zieme, *Texte*, pp. 52f. The editor sees in this document a blessing for the entire house of the ruler.

58. For the Persian *Nō Rōz* see Boyce, "Iranian Festivals," 792–800. In Iran there was also a "Greater *Nō Rōz*." Compare Boyce, *ibid.*, p. 800, n. 6. In Central Asia the "Great New Day" of course had another meaning for the Buddhists, for whom it apparently commemorated the day when the future Buddha Maitreya, who had an earthly existence at the time of the historical Buddha, was consecrated as his successor. It was on this day that the drama *Maitrisimit* ("Meeting Maitreya") was performed. Compare Geng Shimin and H.-J. Klimkeit, *Das Zusammentreffen mit Maitreya* I, pp. 1–9. This day was commemorated even in Tocharian Kucha following Iranian models. Compare Liu Mau-tsai, *Kutscha und seine Beziehungen zu China*, pp. 10 and 170. The Turkish Buddhist texts also speak of other "New Days," each of which had a specific religious significance, with the term "New" also being used for the first of every ten days of the month. See Tekin, *Maitrisimit nom bitig* II, p. 137, s.v. *y'nky*. For specific "New Days" see Tekin, *op. cit.,* and Zieme, *Texte*, p. 50, n. 438.

59. Regarding this document, the editor says: "It is not clear to us what the function of the 'New Day' is in this Manichaean text, especially as it is characterized as *uluγ*, 'great.'" Zieme, *Texte*, p. 50, n. 438. At any rate, the Manichaean ruler as well as high dignitaries were apparently involved in an important ceremony on this day.

60. The religion.

61. Here it says, ". . . brought wares and cut (cloth) for a garment for the . . . body." Apparently the cutting of cloth for the body has symbolic significance, for in a similar text (*recto*) we read: "He deigns to cut (cloth) for a garment for the noble, sacred body [of the king?]. As the (cloth) wares are cut, so may also the diseases and dangers in the body be cut off and be cut to pieces." Zieme, *Texte*, p. 28.

62. We read in a similar text (*verso*), ". . . in so far as we, the sons of the Law, are concerned, we ask to be liberated from sins, (we ask) for forgiveness. [Pth.]: Forgive the sins of the gods!" Zieme, *Texte*, p. 28.

CHAPTER THIRTY-ONE

Historical Texts

Only a few historical texts survive in Turkish. Text 1 shows that there must have been missionary histories or church historical works describing the "Acts" of Mani and his disciples in Turkish, as there were in Iranian languages. This is the only extant text of that category. Text 2, on the introduction of Manichaeism in the Uighur realm, is of special importance, since it supplements other sources of information on the history of Manichaeism in the Mongolian Steppes.

1. Fragment of a mission history

In a Parthian text (M 216b) we hear that Mani converted the ruler of Varučān, who bore the name Havzā. The present text, which appears to be part of an account of a miraculous healing performed by Mani or one of his disciples, also mentions the ruler of Varučān, named Havzā. The miracle was probably performed prior to his conversion. Varučān seems to have been a small kingdom near Balk, in the Kushan territory—not in Iberia, as Henning supposed for some time.[1] The account probably related how the Varučān-Shāh was won for the new religion.

> ... And the beloved son of the God Nom Qutï (the Great Nous), Havzā, the king (and?) Shad of Varučān, was in the city . . . They came (?) to the temple . . . At the gate of the temple, . . . there was . . . All lame, blind and wounded men as well as those that were maimed at the hip, (or) that had perpetic and lichenous diseases had come. When they drank that water, . . . they were healed from their diseases.
>
> Furthermore, a naked man was sitting in the temple. His feet and hands were bound securely by sharp iron shackles. . . . Within one year (?) . . .

2. Text on the introduction of Manichaeism in the Uighur Realm

The official account of the introduction of Manichaeism in the Khanate of the Uighur Turks under Bögü Khan (Tängri Qaghan, reg. 759–779) is known from the trilingual inscription of Kara Balgassun, a capital of the Uighurs in the Mongolian Steppes. The Chinese version is well preserved, but the Sogdian and Uighur versions are in a fragmentary state.[2] The Karabalgassun inscription is supplemented by a text from Turfan.

This text is written on two sheets (TM 276a and 276b) belonging to a book bound in European fashion. In spite of the philological difficulties still connected with it, the document deserves to be made known to a wider circle of readers. The editors, Bang and von Gabain, held that this was originally a letter written by Manichaean elect, who appear as the speakers and who report about the Turkish Uighur ruler Bögü Khan's conversion to Manichaeism, and his proclamation of the faith as the official state religion in 762/763. They here witnessed the occasion, and "apparently they stand in the midst of the events."[3] Of course this was not the original letter, which must have been written in Chinese or Sogdian. Anyway, it was apparently included later in a historical account whose details might have been embellished. Yet this too was written in a language other than Turkish, as various odd phrases in the text would suggest.

Besides the trilingual inscription of Kara-Balgassun, this is the only text throwing light on that decisive event of 762/763. It complements the official account in a most interesting manner in that it gives us the version of the (Sogdian) Manichaean elect who were instrumental in bringing about this change of religion. As the editors point out,

> We see that the Uighur Qaghan decided to convert only after serious inner conflicts, or rather, that he had relapsed after an initial conversion, that he committed some (anti-Manichaean?) 'deed' which the elect regarded as a great sin, and that he then humbly repented. We must assume that this 'deed' was done at the instigation of a Tarqan [a high official], who, unfortunately, remains nameless. We may probably see him as the leader of a party . . . that opposed the introduction of the new teaching, which threatened the state. Judging by the behaviour of the Qaghan vis-à-vis the clergy—they are called 'elect'—we can see that the clergy could surround itself with a bright nimbus, beside which the self-righteousness of the Qaghan vanished when the elect threatened him with heavenly judgement.[4]

After his renewed conversion, the Qaghan set up an ecclesiastical organization along the lines of the military order of his troops, which were grouped in tens, hundreds, and thousands; each group had its own leader. As Bang and von Gabain further note, "For us it is quite amusing to see how the Qaghan unhesitatingly transfers the military organisation of a bloodthirsty people to the ecclesiastical sphere, an idea that would have been worthy of the great Jinghis Khan."[5] In the Chinese version of the Kara Balgassun inscription, the people of the Uighur Realm, before the acceptance of Manichaeism, are referred to as "blood-thirsty." Here it says, "The evil custom (of drinking) hot blood was changed, and the people of the area began to cook rice. (And) a blood-thirsty state was changed to a realm where (people) exhorted (each other) in virtue."[6] Indeed, even Jinghis who made his appearance 440 years later (around 1200 A.D.), organized his troops along the lines of this old pattern which had been used by the Turks.[7] In the ecclesiastical organization established by the Constantine of Manichaeism in his realm, a *tavrat-γučï* was placed at the head of each group of ten people. It was his duty to admonish his people and exhort them to do "good works," including providing for the material needs of the elect. The idea must have been suggested to him by the Manichaean clergy itself.

The throne name of our Qaγan, referred to as "the divine king" (*Tängri Qaγan*), is given as Bögü Qaγan ("Wise Khan"). He reigned from 759 to 779, and the Chinese knew him as Mou yü.[8] His original name must have been Boγuγ ("calyx, flower-bud," or "gullet"?). The Islamic author Dzuwainī, whose account of the conversion of the Uighurs is of but limited value, calls him Buqu Khan.[9] He also seems to have been known by the name of Bilgä Qaγan ("Wise Khan"). As such, he is not to be confused with the first two rulers of the Uighur Empire, namely, Kül Bilgä Qaghan (744–747) and Bilgä Qaghan (747–759), or with the later ruler Qutluγ Bilgä Qaghan (790–795). He is also known as Tängri Qaγan (Chin. I-ti-chien).[10]

As noted in the Kara Balgassun inscription, Bögü Qaγan (759–779)[11] became acquainted with Manichean elect in China, specifically in the city of Lo-yang, and the Kara Balgassun inscription gives a "teacher" and four of them the credit for having introduced Manichaeism to the "Realm of the Steppes." Yet it is obvious that there must have already been a Manichaean presence in this area at that time. In the old Turkish inscriptions from Mongolia, especially from the Orkhon valley, we read of Sogdian settlers living amongst the Turks,[12] who must have had contact with Sogdian merchants, many of whom were Manichaeans. It is probably some Manichaean Sogdian elect who are depicted in rock carvings in the Yenissei valley.[13] There were Sogdian colonies in what is now Inner Mongolia.[14] And we have various Sogdian inscriptions from this time in the vast area between the southern Gobi Desert and northern Mongolia, not to mention the upper reaches of the Indus Valley.[15] To be sure, some of these Sogdians were Buddhists, as the inscription of Bugut would suggest,[16] and others Christians, as the Sogdian Christian manuscripts from Turfan show.[17] As Pulleyblank observes, "Pre-eminently traders,[18] but also carriers of arts and crafts and of new religions, they travelled and settled not only along the trade routes of Central Asia but also deep in the interior of China and among the nomads of the steppes. Much of this, for instance their important civilizing influence among the Uigurs, is already known. What does not seem to be known . . . is the part they played among the northern Turks who preceded the Uigurs. Later these partially Turkicized Sogdians formed a colony on the northern Chinese frontier . . ."[19]

The Chinese were uneasy about the role the Sogdians played among the Turks. In a historical text from the T'ang period it says, "The Turks are actually simple and unsophisticated, and one can easily sow discord among them. Unfortunately, many *hu* (Sogdians) . . . that are vile and shrewd and teach and lead them, live among them."[20]

Apparently Sogdian merchants introduced Manichaeism to the Uighur Turks
even before Bögü Qaγan converted to that religion. Bang, commenting on the confession for laymen, the *X^uāstvānīft,* states, "The practice of the new religion is
unthinkable without [the use of] the confession [the *X^uāstvānīft*]; it must have been
translated into Uighur quite early [i. e., after 763]. It is not certain whether there
were Manichaean Turks before the official introduction [of that religion] . . . But the
Persian elect who fled to the Turks in the wake of the persecution of Manichaeans
[in Iran] would have tried to find adherents among them."[21] Certainly we have no
clear evidence of Manichaeism in Mongolia before Bögü Khan. But the material
we do have shows that his conversion—the motives for which might have been political (or economic, considering the strong position of the Sogdians)—soon had an
effect on the Turks of the steppes. In a Turkish memorial inscription from Sudzi
in Mongolia, a certain Jaglar-Kan-Ata, a Kirghiz who had come into the land of the
Uigurs, exhorts his son to "be among the men (who live) according to (the commands) of my Teacher (*Mār*). Honor the Qaγan! Be steadfast!" As the editor, G. J.
Ramstedt, stresses, "His Teacher, or Mar, was definitely a Manichaean learned
man, and thus this grave stone tells us of the dissemination and significance of
Manichaeism [in Mongolia] at the end of the eighth century."[22]

As to the Tarqan whose name is not preserved and who opposed the official introduction of Manichaeism, may we assume that he was Ton (Inanču) Baγa Tarqan
of whom the Terkhin inscription speaks?[23] Summing up the events of 779, when
Bögü Khan was killed by rebels in his own camp, S. G. Klyashtorny says, "The
rebellion was led by Ton Baγa Tarqan, his most powerful dignitary who is mentioned in the Terkh inscription as 'the head of the inner *buyuruqs* [high officials],
Inanču Baγa Tarqan' (line 6). Ton Baγa Tarqan headed the anti-Manichaean opposition at the Uighur court and enjoyed the support of the Chinese. Among those
slaughtered by the rebels, apart from Bögü, were two of his sons, his closest
advisers, many Sogdians, and probably the Manichaean priests in the Qaγan's retinue. Ton Bilgä Tarqan himself was proclaimed Qutluγ Bilgä Qaγan (780–789)."[24]

As the inscription of Sudzi and other materials show, Manichaeism was able to
re-establish its influence at the end of this period. The kings thereafter again
assumed Manichaean titles referring to the Gods of the Moon, or the Sun, (Jesus
or the Third Messenger) as the gods who bestowed their regal charisma (*qut*) upon
them.

[The Qaγan said: ". . .] I am Tängri,[25] I will go to the Realm of the Gods
together with you."

The elect gave this answer: "We are holy, we are elect. We execute
God's commands perfectly. When we die,[26] we will go to the Realm of
the Gods, because we fulfill God's commandment to the word . . . and
because we have borne great oppression and grave [dangers?]. Therefore
we shall reach the Realm of the Gods. Your Majesty, if you yourself tres-
pass against the Law of the Eternal One,[27] your whole kingdom will fall
into confusion; all these Turkish people will sin against God (*t(ä)ngri*), and
wherever they [find] elect, they will suppress them and kill them. And [if]
these [four][28] . . . [holy] elect who are from the land of China [will have to

go?] back [with?] their four wishes (demands?),[29]. . . [then] great danger and oppression will arise for [the Law, that is, religion]. Wherever they find auditors and merchants[30] they will kill them all, leaving not even one alive.

In this your realm great, meritorious deeds are being done at your command (?), and have (already) been done in this realm of yours up to the coming of the . . . Tarqan.[31] Your Majesty, if you yourself discharge (?) (this Tarqan), then the good laws and the good works will all endure. But if the . . . Tarqan brings such great (?) difficulties [upon the land?], evil deeds will be done and your [kingdom will perish . . .]. The path on which you will have to walk from [now] on will have to be another one (lit., other than this one). And the divine Teacher[32] . . . will hear of these things (if you do not), and he will not approve of them at all.

Then the divine king and the elect discussed these things for two days and nights. On the third day the king (*tängrikän*) searched himself fully[33] . . . Then the mind of the divine king was troubled because he heard that his soul would never be liberated on account of that deed. Therefore he was afraid and trembled and his mind [was not at rest?]. Then the divine king Bögü Qaγan himself came to the assembly where the elect were; he fell down on his knees before the elect and asked for the remission of his sins, respectfully saying, "Since . . . I have caused you distress . . . I thought . . . by hunger and thirst. By such searching I have [come to a decision?]. May you have mercy upon me, support me in the faith and make me a chosen one. Up to now, my mind has not been firm. I do not like being in the world, or in my home at all. My reign (?), the joys of the body, and my . . . and my . . . have become completely worthless in my eyes. My courage is failing and I fear . . . , because you told me, 'By this kind of deed your soul will never be liberated, but rather if you (lit., it, the soul) come to the faith by way of the elect, and if you constantly do good works . . .' If you elect so desire (lit., command), I will walk in accordance with your words and your counsel. (For) you have said (to me): 'Try to regain courage, Your Majesty, and give up sin.'"

At that time, when the divine King Bögü Qaγan had spoken [thus], we elect and all the people in the realm were filled with great joy. We cannot fully express this joy of ours. Then they told each other (what had happened) over and over again and were glad. Crowds of thousands and ten thousands came together and came to . . . , (engaging) in many kinds of sports. Up to the morning they rejoiced greatly, and many were the joys in which they were glad . . . And when the new day dawned, it was (the time of) the Minor Fast. The divine King Bögü Qaγan and all the elect in his entourage mounted (their) horses, and all the great [princes] and princesses and the *taishis*[34] and the leading nobles, the great and the small, (that is,) all the people, proceeded to the gate of the city[35] in great joy and festivity. Then the divine king entered into [the city?],[36] put the crown on his head, clothed himself with his . . . red [robe] and sat down on his gilded throne. Then he issued an order to the nobility as well as for the common people, (saying): "Now you all . . . bright . . . be happy, especially (you) elect . . . ; having calmed my mind, I entrust myself to you again. I have come anew, and have seated myself on my throne. I command you: When the elect [admonish] you, and when they urge you to (partake of) the sacred meal,[37] and when they urge you to . . . and admonish you, act in accordance with their words and admonitions. And in love show . . . your respect."

When the divine (*tängrikän*) Bögü Qaɣan had issued this order, the many crowds (or, the community) (and) the common people paid homage to the divine king and rejoiced in his presence. And also to [us], the elect, they paid homage and expressed their joy. Everyone . . . was (full of) joy. For a second time, anew, they loved God . . . and believed in Him. Then they unceasingly did "soul service" (gave alms) and performed good works. And the fortunate king constantly exhorted all the people to do good works, and he urged them to do so (continually). Furthermore, the divine king [decreed] and issued (this) law: For every ten men, one man is to be appointed as their head, and shall be made (their) *tavratɣučï* (one who encourages them) with respect to good works and (the performance of) "soul [service]." And if anybody grew slack in [the religion] and fell into sin, he gave him . . . good instruction . . .

3. Note on the introduction of Manichaeism in Turfan

In a small fragment belonging to the same book as a Parthian/Turkish text on anger and greed, there is an interesting historical note.[38] It refers to a series of years termed "Great Beginning" (*uluɣ bašlaɣ*). Bang and von Gabain have pointed out that this period, which lasted from 664 to 676, is called *shan-yüan* in Chinese—if it is not an Uighur designation for a specific period of time in Turkish history.[39] If the first hypothesis, which is more probable, is true, what we have here would be a precious piece of information on the dissemination of Manichaeism *from China* to Central Asia in 665 A.D.

When his (Mani's)[40] teaching had spread in the second year of (the series of) years named "Great Beginning," from the realm of China, . . .

Notes

1. Henning, "Waručān Šāh," p. 90; Henning, "Magical Texts," pp. 39ff.; Sundermann, *Texte,* p. 24; Zieme, *Texte,* p. 51, n. 441ff.
2. Text and German translation of the Chinese version in Schlegel, "Die chinesische Inschrift auf dem uigurischen Denkmal in Kara Balgassun," i-xv; 1–141. For the Sogdian version see O. Hansen, "Zur soghdischen Inschrift auf dem dreisprachigen Denkmal von Karabalgasun," pp. 3–39; see also Y. Yoshida, "Some New Readings of the Sogdian Version of the Karabalgasun Inscription," 117–23.
3. *TT* II, p. 411.
4. *TT* II, p. 412.

5. *TT* II, p. 412.
6. Schlegel, *op. cit.*, p. 63.
7. Cf. Taube, *Die geheime Geschichte der Mongolen,* pp. 116f.
8. Cf. Golzio, *Kings, Khans and other Rulers of Early Central Asia,* p. 63.
9. *TT* II, 413. Cf. J. Marquart, "Guwainī's Bericht über die Bekehrung der Uighuren," p. 486.
10. Cf. Müller, "Hofstaat," and our translation of this blessing for the ruler in chapter XIV, text 1.
11. Cf. Golzio, *Kings, Khans and other Rulers of Early Central Asia,* p. 63.
12. Cf. Tekin, *A Grammar of Orkhon Turkic,* pp. 268–73 (Kül Tigin inscription); p. 275 (Bilgä Qaghan inscription); p. 289 (Tonyuquq inscription); Klyaštornyj, "The Terkhin Inscription," p. 345; Ramstedt, "Zwei uigurische Runeninschriften," p. 35.
13. Maenchen-Helfen, "Manichaeans in Siberia," pp. 311–26.
14. Pulleyblank, "A Sogdian Colony in Inner Mongolia," pp. 317–36.
15. Cf. Klimkeit, *Die Seidenstraße,* pp. 55–57.
16. Kljaštornyj and Livšic, "The Sogdian Inscription of Bugut Revised," 69–102. In this inscription, an unknown speaker is exhorting someone (a Turkish Khan?) to establish "a great new Saṃgha (Buddhist order)." The Sogdian inscription is accompanied by a badly preserved Skr. one in Brahmī script. It has not been deciphered yet.
17. Cf. Sims-Williams, *The Christian Sogdian Manuscript C2,* pp. 9ff. (bibliography).
18. The Chinese *New T'ang History* says that "the men of Sogdiana have gone wherever profit is found." Quoted in Pulleyblank, "A Sogdian Colony," p. 317.
19. Pulleyblank, *ibid.*
20. Liu Mau-tsai, *Chinesische Nachrichten,* p. 87. In the *Old T'ang History* it says, "The *hu* are grasping and presumptuous and by nature uncertain and changeable." Pulleyblank, *op. cit.,* p. 323.
21. Bang, "Turkologische Briefe . . . Dritter Brief," p. 392, n. 1.
22. Ramstedt, "Zwei uigurische Runeninschriften," p. 10.
23. Klyashtornyj, "The Terkhin Inscription," p. 344.
24. Compare Kljaštornyj, "The Tes Inscription," p. 147. Golzio gives the name and the date of this ruler as Alp Qutluγ (Chin. Tun-mo-ho) (779–789). Compare Golzio, *Kings,* p. 63.
25. *Tängri* is originally Heaven or God, but it is then used to designate a king. As such, it is a royal title.
26. Literally, lay down our bodies.
27. Literally, the Timeless One (*ödsüz*), that is, the Father of Light.
28. The text has *t[ört],* "*four." According to the Chinese inscription of Kara Balgassun, Bögü Qaghan brought "the *Dzui-sik*" (a Manichaean Teacher?) and four elect with him from China. Schlegel, *op. cit.,* p. 45.
29. It is not known what these four wishes, or demands (?) are.
30. These merchants were probably Iranian (Sogdian?) Manichaean merchants, doing business in the Turkish Realm of the Steppes (Mongolia).
31. Unfortunately the name of the Tarqan is preserved neither here nor at a later place.
32. This high-ranking Manichaean dignitary, residing probably at Kocho in the Turfan oasis, was head of the Eastern Patriarchate.
33. Literally, castigated himself up to the eye.
34. High officials.
35. Bang and von Gabain comment, "It cannot be determined which city is meant; perhaps it is one of the newly founded cities of the Uighurs." But it can hardly be the Chinese city of Lo-yang, near which Bögü Qaghan encamped from November 762 to March 763, as the editors think (*TT* II, p. 421, n. 65). In an Old Turkish runic inscription from Mongolia, published by Ramstedt, we read of the building of the new Uighur capital of Kara Balgassun and of the building of the city of Bay Balïq in 758 (or 759), by Sogdians and Chinese respectively, at the command of the Turkish ruler Tängridä Bolmïš Il Itmïš Bilgä Qaghan (reg. 747–759), son of the founder of the Uighur Empire, Kül Bilgä Qaghan (reg. 744–747). Compare Ramstedt, "Zwei uigurische Runeninschriften," p. 30 (cf. 60) and 35 (cf. 63).

36. Or, the temple/the palace? Compare *TT* II, p. 422, n. 67.
37. Literally, the "soul-meal" (*üzüt aši*), a meal for the sake of the soul? This is the only place in hitherto published Manichaean texts where a sacred meal for laymen is mentioned.
38. Published in *TT* II, pp. 425f.
39. Bang and von Gabain, *TT* II, *ibid.*
40. Though hypothetical, it seems that Mani's teaching is meant.

CHAPTER THIRTY-TWO

Letters and Postscripts

A number of fragmentarily preserved letters to Turkish kings and princes throw light on the understanding of Manichaean kingship, as they refer to royal titles and to related concepts of divinity. The first of these letters (1.1) is noteworthy for its recitation of the first words of something resembling a creed, in which basic religious categories are related to specific gods. The fact that only the initial sentences are quoted shows that the creed must have been widely known in Manichaean circles. These letters, sometimes referred to as "Letters of Salutation" (*äsängü bitig*), (for they ask about the recipient's well-being (*äsängü*)) include specific petitions which have not always been preserved. There are also letters to religious leaders that reflect the great respect commanded by high-ranking spiritual leaders. At the same time they show the writer's own deep sense of lowliness and sinfulness, as they refer to themselves as the addressee's "slaves." Many phrases in these letters are, however, standardized and schematic.

Of the Manichaean postscripts, the colophon of the "Book of the Two Principles" (*Iki yiltiz nom*), the Turkish version of Mani's *Šābuhragān,* is preserved relatively well. The Manichaean colophons must have been quite similar to the many Buddhist colophons which have been preserved,[1] except, of course, that the spirit and contents were Manichaean. At least a fragmentary postscript, which is not translated here, would suggest as much.[2] For purposes of comparison, reference should also be made to the postscripts in the Iranian and Chinese Manichaean texts.[3]

1. Letters to Turkish kings

1.1 LETTER TO AN UIGHUR RULER

To the Sovereign,[4] the heavenly Il Tonga Tigin, my Lord (*tängrim*), who has attained complete Fortune (*qut*) in the world through the four royal gods above[5] and has acquired the first portion (of blessing)[6] from the Buddhas (divine Messengers); who has received wisdom from the God

Nom Qutï (the Great Nous); who is valiant like the angel Jacob; whose fame has spread in the four quarters (of the world); who has a part in the two laws (the spiritual and the temporal law);[7] who is worthy of the two crowns.[8]

We, his mean and worthless[9] slaves, Xšnaki Alp Qara and Alp Qara, thinking benevolent and benign thoughts (about him) all our lives long, wishing (him) well and desiring to see him one hundred thousand times a day, do send this humble letter of petition, saying from a far and from the bottom of our hearts (the recitation): "The voice, that is the primeval Mother Goddess; speech, that is the primeval God Xormuzta; he who imparts joy, that is the God Višparkar (the Third Messenger)."[10]

One should care for one's mother well and should not cease to look after her, my Lord. How auspicious is our letter of petition! Your own wise, divine counsel was probably with the long-awaited (?) messenger . . .[11]

Our[12] own messenger Salči Tutuq will take the message to his Majesty himself,[13] auspicious as the message may be, auspicious as the letter of petition may be (?). As the messenger has offered to hurry,[14] we have sent this letter of salutation.[15] May there be no sin,[16] my Lord!

2. *Letters to religious authorities*

2.1 LETTER TO A SUPERIOR

To the Majesty of the divine superior (*xvēštar*)
From his mean and sinful slave Qutluɣ Bars.
This is my[17] simple request. Bowing down from afar, I respectfully ask that the sins I have committed be forgiven [Parthian]: Forgive my sin!
Are the noble, divine body and mind of the divine Superior well, is his body unburdened? How are you? I, (your) slave, have respectfully heard that you are healthy and well . . .

2.2 LETTER TO HIGH DIGNITARIES OF THE CHURCH

To the Majesty of Kök Sini Inal, (from) the Superior's slave, Il Bars, . . . , my letter.
Asking you respectfully (?) from afar about your health . . .
To the Majesty of . . . , (from) his slave Tängrim. [Parthian]: Forgive my sin!
To the Majesty of the Chief Auditor Ačtuq . . . furthermore (to) the divine, noble, . . .
Our divine Father, the heavenly teacher, . . . his divine, noble body . . . from afar . . .

2.3 LETTER TO A BISHOP

To the exalted Majesty of the divine bishop, (from) his slave Külüg Tonga Tigin.

This is my request. From afar we respectfully ask you about your well-being. [Parthian]: Forgive my sin!

Are the noble and sacred body and mind of the divine Bishop Yaɣnaɣ Kürlädä (?) well, is his body unburdened ? . . .

2.4 LETTER TO A MOTHER SUPERIOR

May this letter reach the Majesty of the Mother Superior (*qostiranč*).[18] We, Qutluɣ Qaraɣ Tängrim, send this letter, asking about your well-being. How are you? We are very glad to have heard that you are well . . .

2.5 LETTER TO A BISHOP AND A MOTHER SUPERIOR

To the Majesty of the Bishop and the Mother Superior, (from) their mean slave . . . We ask you about your well-being. We have heard that you are well and are glad (about that).

They have come to get the pickled cucumbers[19] . . .

3. Colophon to the "Book of the Two Principles"

This colophon (to which there are three postscripts in other hands) shows that Manichaeism must have been well established in West Turkestan, in the area of former Soviet Central Asia, since the colophon refers to cities and tribes there. As von Gabain states, the text was written at the occasion of a ruler of the Turkish Qarluqs assuming power in that area.[20] Pritsak has shown that Arslan ("Lion") and Buɣra ("Male Camel") were the totemic names of the king and the coregent of the West Turkish Karachanid kings—which also seems to be true of the Qarluqs.[21] The personal name of the king in question is Il-tirgük. He is referred to as Čigil, which was the name of the dominant tribe of the Qarluq confederation. His realm extended to the area of Talas and Arɣu, that is, the area around the cities of Talas (Tarāz) and Semiriče, the lower Ili Valley.[22] The cities mentioned—Qašu, Yigänkänt, Ordukänt, and Čigil—are related to Q(ï)z Ordu (Balaɣassun).[23] The Qarluq conquered the cities of Talas and Semiriče in 766, which is a *terminus post quem* for our text. As Il-tirgük is not called Qaɣan here, but rather Alp Tarxan Bäg, "the valiant Tarxan, the Bäg," he must have ruled before 840, when Uighur power was crushed, that is, while he was still an Uighur vassal. Hence 840 is a *terminus ante quem*. Furthermore, as von Gabain has shown,[24] the Qarluq prince in question was a contemporary of the Uighur Qaɣan Il-tutmïš (reg. 759–840), that is, Bögü Khan, who introduced Manichaeism as the state religion of the Uighurs. Hence our text was written for a Qarluq lord between 766 and 840, perhaps around 780, as the Qarluqs assumed sovereignty of parts of West Turkestan at that time. This surmise is consistent with the language of our text which is not Uighur but West Turkish (ñ-dialect).

The writer of our text was a scribe named Aɣduq. We know of him from other Turkish texts as well.[25] A. von Gabain says of his postscript, "The solemn character of this work of Aɣduq's suggests that he was writing for a special occasion. Is not the colophon to be understood as a glorification of the great hour in which the

Qarluq ruler assumed power in the territories of the former West Turkish (Türgiš) kingdom?" Yet even at this time he remained a vassal of the Uighur Qaɣan. "Therefore it is readily understandable that one and the same scribe copied the texts for the Uigur Qaɣan and the Qarluq Tarxan."[26]

In our text, five groups of religious personages corresponding to the five ranks of the Manichaean hierarchy are named, namely, 1. "the protector (or patron) of the whole Church" (*tüzü nom arqasï*), a teacher (*mozak*), 2. "the supervisors of the religion" (*nom baštanqlari*), 3. "the perfect, chosen, pure elect" (*tüzü ödrülmiš arïɣ dintarlar*), 4. the scribe (*bitgači*), writing at the command of another teacher, and 5. the auditors (*niɣošaklar*). Referring to the first teacher, von Gabain points out that "in the eyes of the scribe (writing in the Realm of Kocho), he was the head of the Manichaeans."[27]

> In the name of[28] the great royal King, Zurvān, the God. It (this book) was recited with great joy, and it was written with deep love. It was written with complete devotion[29] at the exalted place (?), . . . this . . . divine (?), holy . . . scripture which (contains) . . . many kinds of [words] that awaken the soul, that open the heart and illumine the mind, that give the correct, clear and exact understanding of (the doctrine of) the "three periods," in accordance with the (religious) Law (religion), (namely, an understanding implying) divine wisdom (*gnosis*), sweeter than the drink of immortality, which brings life[30] and leads to the bright Realm of the Gods.
>
> (Written) at a good time, on an auspicious day, in the blessed month, and in the victorious, joyous year,[31] under the patronage of the exalted, blessed, mighty Turkish Realm (*uluš*) of Arɣu Talas[32]—in the North and in the South, in the East and in the West its name has been heard and its fame has spread—and under (the care of) the Altun Arɣu Turks who are endowed with a blessed realm, in Qašu, Yägänkänt, Ordukänt and Čigil, at the abode of the god Nom Qutï (the Great Nous), at the sanitorium[33] of the Mardaspant gods,[34] at the dwelling of the pure, bright, strong angels, in the pure, undefiled (Manichaean) monasteries . . .
>
> . . . the victorious angels, . . . the venerable, sweet, famous, divine Mar Vahman Xiar Yazd Toyin, the great Tocharian teacher,[35] and the king (*xan*) of the Altun Arɣu . . . tribe, and of Qašu, the sovereign of Čigilkänt, the great Supervisor (of Religion) *(baštang)*[36] among the Turks,[37] Čigil Arslan Il-tirgüg Alp Bürgüčän Alp Tarxan Bäg, on the occasion of his assuming power and rule.[38]
>
> Now may there be well-being and blessing [1.] for "the Protector of the whole Church." And may there be joy and happiness [2.] for "the Supervisors of the Religion." Furthermore may [3.] the perfect, chosen, pure elect rejoice and be glad. And [4.] may I attain victory (salvation), I who have written (this) with great love and deep feeling (lit., wish), I, Aɣduq, the old scribe, at the command of the Teacher Mār Išoyazd ("Lord Jesus the God"). And may [5.] all the dear, conscientious[39] auditors be freed from sin. May all our bodies remain healthy and strong; we would be free from

illness and danger always. And may our hearts and minds be free from grief and affliction. We would be blessed with all good works. May our souls be liberated, (be) victorious (gain salvation) and (be) worthy of the Realm of the Gods. May it be so eternally!

[First postscript]: I, Yapγun, an auditor who believes in the two bright Palaces,[40] have respectfully recited this book[41] twice upon my return from China. May everyone who recites it after me deign to name me on account of the five (phrases?) that I have written (here) respectfully. I flee from sin. [Pth.]: Forgive my sin!

[Second postscript]: I have recited (this book) from beginning to end. [May] there be no sin!

[Third postscript]: I, Arslan Mängü, an auditor who believes firmly in the two bright Palaces of Light, have respectfully recited this "Book of the Two Principles." May the blessed one who [should] read it after me remember my meritorious deed! [Pth.]: Forgive my sin! [Turk.]: I flee from sin!

Notes

1. Cf. Klimkeit, "Der Stifter im Lande der Seidenstraßen"; Zieme, *Religion und Gesellschaft im Uigurischen Königreich von Qočo. Kolophone und Stifter des alttürkischen buddhistischen Schrifttums aus Zentralasien.*
2. T. Haneda, "A propos d'un fragmentaire de prière manichéene en ouigour provenant de Turfan," pp. 3f.
3. Cf. Tsui Chi, "Mo Ni Chiao Hsia Pu Tsan," p. 215; Schmidt-Glintzer, *Chinesische Manichaica,* pp. 67 and 102f.
4. Literally, To the Majesty (*qut*) of.
5. This is perhaps the Fourfold Father, that is, God, his Light, his Power, and his Wisdom.
6. The text has *a ülüg,* the "*a* portion," that is, "the first portion," since *a* is the first letter of the Uighur alphabet.
7. Literally, possesses, shares in, partakes of (*tükallig*) the two laws (*iki törlüg*).
8. Literally, the two diadems, as symbols of spiritual and political authority.
9. Literally, small and insignificant.
10. Only the first three invocations of a series of twenty-two are recited *pars pro toto.*
11. Perhaps a polite way of saying that they have been waiting for his answer to the last letter of petition. This is also suggested by the next sentence which is fragmentary: "Whatever favorable news there may be. . . ."
12. Literally, his, that is, his slave's.
13. Literally, with his own mouth.
14. Literally, deigns to hurry.
15. Or, letter concerning his well-being (*äsängü bitig*).
16. This formula of confession was so stereotypical that it was mechanically added to the ends of letters in later times.
17. Actually the plural is used throughout, although only one person is writing the letter.
18. This title is the Turkish form of the MP/Pth. *xvēštar,* but with a feminine Sogdian ending.
19. According to the Manichaean view, cucumbers like melons were especially rich in the substance of divine light. Thus St. Augustine, in *De moribus Manichaeorum* 39, asks, "Why do you look upon a yellow melon as part of the treasures of God . . . ?"
20. Von Gabain, "Steppe und Stadt," pp. 52f.

21. According to von Gabain, *op. cit.*; Pritsak, *Karachanidische Studien,* to which she refers (p. 63ff.), is unfortunately inaccessible to me.
22. According to Gamal al-Qaršï (who wrote around 1282), the city of Almaliq in the Ili valley belonged to the area of Arγu. It is the Argon of Marco Polo. For the Arγu tribe compare also G. Doerfer, "Mahmūd al-Kāsγarï, Arγu, Chaladsch," pp. 105–14.
23. According to von Gabain in "Steppe und Stadt," p. 53, where she refers to Pritsak's *Karachanidische Studien* V, Qašu Yägänkänt Ordukänt Čigil Balïq is the name of one city, that is, Balasaγun. However, in her "Historisches aus den Turfanfunden," p. 117, von Gabain deals with these names separately, pointing out that Ordu is near Balasaγun, Qašu (or Qasu) is a city "with relation to Balasaγun," Talas-uluš a city in the steppes of West Turkestan, and Yägän-känt a city between Talas and Mikri. Kaši (a city named after the Indian Benares) is also in West Turkestan. Here she defines Altun Arγun as an area between Talas and Balasaγun.
24. Von Gabain, "Steppe und Stadt," p. 54.
25. Von Gabain, "Steppe und Stadt," pp. 53ff.
26. Von Gabain, "Steppe und Stadt," p. 54.
27. Von Gabain, "Steppe und Stadt," p. 52.
28. *Atïnga* could also be translated "for the glory of." Compare *UigWb* 251a, s.v. *at.*
29. Literally, activity, but *itig* is also "adornment, embellishment."
30. Or, "granting (evoking) the Living Self" (*tirig öz*). We, however, follow Zieme, *Diss.,* p. 76, in understanding *tirig öz* here as "life."
31. Of the assumption of power by the ruler to be named.
32. *Uluš* can mean both "realm" and "tribe." Röhrborn translates dubiously, "the blessed tribe, the peaceful (?) tribe Gold-Arγu." *UigWb* 178, s.v. *argu.*
33. Literally, place of healing (*otačïlïqï*).
34. The gods that are the Elements of Light; in a narrower sense the sons of the First Man, *m(a)rdspant* < MP. *(a)mahrāspand.* The word is used in the plural "for the Elect, as beings of Light" (Boyce, *Word-List,* pp. 10f.).
35. The teacher residing at Kocho in the Turfan basin.
36. For *bašdang,* thus to be read instead of *pasdank* or *pr(a)šdank* (as von Gabain, "Steppe und Stadt," pp. 51f.) compare Zieme, *Texte,* p. 56, n. 14. The word also appears in the form *baštïn(kï).* It means "the Chief, Superior," literally, "the first one" (from *baš,* "head").
37. The translation "among the Turks" for *türkdün,* suggested by Zieme, *Diss.,* p. 88, seems more logical here than "of the Turks" (as von Le Coq, *Türk. Man.* I, p. 27).
38. Zieme translates, "in the wake of the ruling and assumption of power." Zieme, *Diss.,* p. 83.
39. Literally, endowed with souls (*üzütlüg*).
40. The Palace of the Sun and the Moon, with their gods. Sundermann draws my attention to the fact that they are referred to as "chariots" or "ships" in most Manichaean sources, but are called "palaces" (Turk. *ordular*) only in Turkish and Chinese sources. As the Turkish word also means "camps," this concept might be traceable to the ancient nomadic Turks.
41. As Zieme suggested to me, *namk* (book) is to be read rather than *äm(i)g* (medicament), as von Le Coq did.

Bibliography

Adam, A. *Texte zum Manichäismus*. 2d ed. Berlin, 1969 (Kleine Texte für Vorlesungen und Übungen 175).

Alfaric, P. *Les écritures manichéennes*. 2 vols. Paris, 1918.

Allberry, C. R. C. "Das manichäische Bema-Fest," *ZNW* 37 (1938), 2–10. Repr. in G. Widengren, ed., *Der Manichäismus,* 317–27.

———. *A Manichaean Psalm-Book*. Part II. Stuttgart, 1938 (Manichaean Manuscripts in the Chester Beatty Collection, Vol. II).

Andreas, F. C. and K. Barr. "Bruchstücke einer Pehlevi-Übersetzung der Psalmen," *SPAW* 1933, 91–152.

Andreas, F. C. and W. B. Henning: "Mitteliranische Manichaica aus Chinesisch-Turkestan I-III," *SPAW* 1932, 175–222; 1933, 294–362; 1934, 848–912.

Arat, R. R. [see also Rachmati, G. R.]. "Der Herrschertitel *Iduq-qut*" *UAJb* 35 (1964), 150–57.

Arnold-Döben, V. *Die Bildersprache des Manichäismus*. Cologne, 1978 (AR 3).

———. "Die Symbolik des Baumes im Manichäismus," *Symbolon. Jahrbuch für Symbolforschung* N.F. 5 (1980), 9–29.

———. *Die Bildersprache der Gnosis*. Cologne, 1986 (AR 13).

———. "Die Bildhaftigkeit der manichäischen Texte," in A. van Tongerloo and S. Giversen, eds., *Manichaica Selecta,* 1–7.

Asmussen, J. P. "Die Iranier in Zentralasien. Kultur- und religionsgeschichtliche Bemerkungen," *AcOr* 27 (1963), 119–27.

———. *X^uāstvānīft. Studies in Manichaeism*. Copenhagen, 1965 (Acta Theologica Danica 7).

———. "Der Manichäismus als Vermittler literarischen Gutes," *Temenos* 2 (1966), 5–21.

———. *Manichaean Literature*. Delmar, NY, 1975 (Persian Heritage Series 22).

———. "Der Manichäismus," in J. P. Asmussen and J. Læssøe, eds., *Handbuch der Religionsgeschichte*. Vol. 3. Göttingen, 1975, 337–50.

———. "The Sogdian and Uighur-Turkish Christian Literature in Central Asia Before the Real Rise of Islam. A Survey," in *Indological and Buddhist Studies. Volume in Honour of Professor J. W. de Jong on his Sixtieth Birthday*. Canberra, 1982, 11–29.

Bailey, H. W. *Zoroastrian Problems in the Ninth-Century Books.* 1943; Repr. Oxford, 1971 (Ratnabi Katrak Lectures).

Bang, W. "Manichäische Laien-Beichtspiegel," *Le Muséon* 36 (1923), 137–242.

———. "Manichäische Miniaturen," *Le Muséon* 37 (1924), 109–115.

———. "Manichäische Hymnen," *Le Muséon* 38 (1925), 1–55.

———. "Turkologische Briefe aus dem Berliner Ungarischen Institut. Zweiter Brief: Uzuntonluγ—die Krone der Schöpfung," *UJb* 5 (1925), 231–51.

———. "Manichäische Erzähler," *Le Muséon* 44 (1931), 1–36. Repr. in G. Widengren, ed., *Der Manichäismus,* 260–86.

Bang, W. and A. von Gabain. "Ein uigurisches Fragment über den manichäischen Wind-gott," *UJb* 8 (1928), 248–56.

———. "Türkische Turfan-Texte II: Manichaica," *SPAW* 1929, 411–30.

———. "Türkische Turfan-Texte III: Der große Hymnus auf Mani," *SPAW* 1930, 183–211.

———. "Türkische Turfan-Texte IV: Ein uigurisches Sündenbekenntnis," *SPAW* 1930, 432–50.

Bang, W. and R. Rachmati. "Uigurische Bruchstücke über verschiedene Höllen," *UJb* 15 (1935), 389–402.

Baur, F. C. *Das manichäische Religionssystem nach den Quellen neu untersucht.* 1831; Repr. Hildesheim and New York, 1973.

Beck, E. *Ephräms Polemik gegen Mani und die Manichäer im Rahmen der zeitgenössischen griechischen Polemik und der des Augustinus.* Leuven, 1984 (CSCO, Vol. 39; Sub-sidia Vol. 55).

Belenizki, A. M. and D. W. Belous. *Mittelasien. Kunst der Sogden.* Leipzig, 1980.

Benveniste, É. "Hymnes manichéens. Textes inédits traduits et annotés par É. Benve-niste avec une introduction de H. Corbin," *Yggdrasil. Bulletin Mensuel de la Poésie en France et à l'Etranger* II, No. 4–5 (1937), 54–57.

———. *Études sogdiennes.* Wiesbaden, 1979 (Beiträge zur Iranistik 19).

Bianchi, U. "Zoroastrian Elements in Manichaeism. The Question of Evil Substance," in P. Bryder, ed., *Manichaean Studies,* 13–18.

———. "Sur le dualisme de Mani," in A. van Tongerloo and S. Giversen, eds., *Mani-chaica Selecta,* 9–17.

Blatz, B. *Studien zum gnostischen Erlöser.* Phil. diss. Bonn, 1985.

Böhlig, A. *Die Bibel bei den Manichäern.* Theol. diss. Münster, 1947.

———. "Christliche Wurzeln des Manichäismus," in H. Franke, ed., *Akten des vierund-zwanzigsten Internationalen Orientalisten-Kongresses München. 28. August bis 4. September 1957.* Wiesbaden, 1959, 222–24.

———. *Mysterion und Wahrheit. Gesammelte Beiträge zur spätantiken Religions-geschichte.* Collected essays. Leiden, 1968 (Arbeiten zur Geschichte des späteren Judentums und Urchristentums 6).

———. "Jakob als Engel in Gnostizismus und Manichäismus," in G. Wiessner, ed., *Erkenntnisse und Meinungen.* Vol. 2. Wiesbaden, 1978 (Göttinger Orientforschun-gen. Veröffentlichungen des Sonderforschungsbereichs Orientalistik an der Georg-August-Universität Göttingen. I. Reihe: Syriaca 17), 1–14.

———. "Zur Vorstellung vom Lichtkreuz in Gnostizismus und Manichäismus," in B. Aland, ed., *Gnosis. Festschrift für Hans Jonas.* Göttingen, 1978, 473–91.

———. ed. *Die Gnosis.* Vol. 3: *Der Manichäismus.* Unter Mitwirkung von J. P. Asmus-sen eingeleitet, übersetzt und erläutert. Zürich and Munich, 1980 (Die Bibliothek der Alten Welt. Reihe Antike und Christentum).

———. "Der Manichäismus," in M. J. Vermaseren, ed., *Die orientalischen Religionen im Römerreich.* Leiden, 1981 (EPRO 93), 436–58.

————. "The New Testament and the Concept of the Manichaean Myth," in A. M. B. Logan and A. J. M. Wedderburn, eds., *The New Testament and Gnosis. Essays in honour of Robert McL. Wilson*. Edinburgh, 1983, 90–104.

————. "Ja und Amen in der manichäischen Dichtung," *ZPE* 58 (1985), 59–70.

————. *Gnosis und Synkretismus. Gesammelte Aufsätze zur antiken Religionsgeschichte*. 2 vols. Collected essays. Tübingen, 1989 (Wissenschaftliche Untersuchungen zum Neuen Testament 47).

Bombaci, A. "Qutluγ Bolzun! A contribution to the history of the concept of 'fortune' among the Turks. Part 1–2," *UAJb* 36 (1965), 284–91; 38 (1966), 13–43.

Bornkamm, G. *Mythos und Legende in den apokryphen Thomas-Akten*. Göttingen, 1933.

Boyce, M. "Sadwēs and Pēsūs," *BSOAS* 13 (1951), 908–15.

————. "Some Parthian abecedarian hymns," *BSOAS* 14 (1952), 435–50.

————. *The Manichaean Hymn-Cycles in Parthian*. Oxford, 1954 (London Oriental Series 3).

————. "Some remarks on the present state of the Iranian Manichaean MSS. from Turfan, together with additions and corrections to 'Manichaean Hymn-Cycles in Parthian,'" *MIO* 4 (1956), 314–22.

————. *A Catalogue of the Iranian Manuscripts in Manichaean Script in the German Turfan Collection*. Berlin, 1960 (DAWB, Inst. f. Orientforschung 45).

————. "On Mithra in the Manichaean Pantheon," in *A Locust's Leg. Studies in honour of S. H. Taqizadeh*. London, 1962, 44–54.

————. "Manichaeism," in *Encyclopaedia Britannica*. Vol. XXIII (revised). London, 1965, 783–85.

————. "Ātaš-zōhr and Āb-zōhr," *JRAS* 1966, 100–118.

————. "The Manichaean Literature in Middle Iranian," in *HO* 1, 4, 2, 1. Leiden and Cologne, 1968, 67–76.

————. "On the Calendar of Zoroastrian Feasts," *BSOAS* 33 (1970), 513–39.

————. *A Reader in Manichaean Middle Persian and Parthian*. Leiden, 1975 (Acta Iranica 9).

————. *A Word-List of Manichaean Middle Persian and Parthian*. Leiden, 1977 (Acta Iranica 9a).

————. *Zoroastrians. Their Religious Beliefs and Practices*. London, 1979 (Library of Religious Beliefs and Practices).

————. "*Āb-zōhr*," in E. Yarshater, ed., *Encyclopaedia Iranica* 1 (1982), 48–50.

————. "Iranian Festivals," in E. Yarshater, ed., *The Cambridge History of Iran*. Vol. 3, 2, 792–815.

————. "The Manichaean Middle Persian Writings," *ibid.*, 1196–1204.

————. "Parthian Writings and Literature," *ibid.*, 1151–65.

————. *Textual Sources for the Study of Zoroastrianism*. Manchester, 1984 (Textual Sources for the Study of Religions).

————. Boyce, M. and I. Gershevitch, eds. *W. B. Henning. Selected Papers*. 2 vols. Leiden, 1977 (Acta Iranica 14–15).

Brockelmann, C. *Die syrische und die christliche-arabische Literatur*. Leipzig, 1908.

Browder, M. H. *Al-Bīrūnī as a Source for Mani and Manichaeism*. Duke University, Ph.D. diss., 1982.

————. "Al-Bīrūnī's Manichaean Sources," in P. Bryder, ed., *Manichaean Studies*, 19–28.

————. "The Formulation of Manichaeism in late Umayyad Islam," in G. Wiessner and H.-J. Klimkeit, eds., *Studia Manichaica*, 328–33.

Bryder, P. *The Chinese Transformation of Manichaeism. A Study of Chinese Manichaean Terminology*. Löberöd 1985 (Ph. D. diss., Lund, 1985).

────. ed. *Manichaean Studies. Proceedings of the First International Conference on Manichaeism, August* 5-9, 1987. Lund, 1988 (Lund Studies in African and Asian Religions 1).

────. ". . . Where the faint traces of Manichaeism disappear," *AoF* 15 (1988), 201-208.

────. "Cao'an Revisited," in A. van Tongerloo and S. Giversen, eds., *Manichaica Selecta,* 35-42.

────. "Problems concerning the Spread of Manichaeism from one Culture to another," in G. Wiessner and H.-J. Klimkeit, eds., *Studia Manichaica,* 334-41.

Bultmann, R. "Die Bedeutung der neuerschlossenen mandäischen und manichäischen Quellen für das Verständnis des Johannesevangeliums," *ZNW* 24 (1925), 100-146.

────. *Das Urchristentum im Rahmen der antiken Religionen.* Hamburg, 1962.

Burkitt, F. C. *The Religion of the Manichees.* Cambridge, 1925 (Donellan Lectures for 1924).

────. "Χρōšταγ and Παδνāxταγ. *Call and Answer,*" *JThS* 36 (1935), 180-81.

Cadonna, E., ed., *Turfan and Tunhuang. The Texts. Encounter of Civilizations on the Silk Route.* Florence, 1992.

Cameron, R. and A. J. Dewey, trans. *The Cologne Mani Codex . . . "Concerning the Origin of his Body."* Missoula, 1979 (Society of Biblical Literature: Texts and Translations No. 15; Early Christian Literature Series 3).

Casadio, G. "Gender and Sexuality in Manichaean Mythmaking," in A. van Tongerloo and S. Giversen, eds., *Manichaica Selecta,* 43-47.

────. "The Manichaean Metempsychosis: Typology and Historical Roots," in G. Wiessner and H.-J. Klimkeit, eds., *Studia Manichaica,* 105-130.

Chavannes, É. and P. Pelliot. "Un traité manichéen retrouvé en Chine," *JA* 1911, 499-617; 1913, 99-392.

Cirillo, L. [in collaboration with A. Roselli], ed. *Codex Manichaicus Coloniensis. Atti del Simposio Internationale.* Cosenza, 1986.

────. "'Hermae Pastor' and 'Revelatio Manichaica'. Some Remarks," in G. Wiessner and H.-J. Klimkeit, eds., *Studia Manichaica,* 189-97.

Clark, L. V. "The Manichaean Turkic *Pothi*-Book," *AoF* 9 (1982), 145-218.

Clauson, G. *An Etymological Dictionary of Pre-Thirteenth-Century Turkish.* Oxford, 1972.

Colditz, I. "Bruchstücke manichäisch-parthischer Parabelsammlungen," *AoF* 14, (1987), 274-313.

────. "Hymnen an Šād-Ohrmezd. Ein Beitrag zur frühen Geschichte der Dīnāwarīya in Transoxanien," *AoF* 19 (1992), 322-41.

Colpe, C. *Der Manichäismus in der arabischen Überlieferung.* Phil. Diss. Göttingen, 1954 (typewritten).

────. "Anpassung des Manichäismus an den Islam (Abū 'Īsā al-Warrāq)," *ZDMG* 109 (1959), 82-91. Repr. in G. Widengren, ed., *Der Manichäismus,* 464-76.

────. "Die Formulierung der Ethik in arabischen Manichäer-Gemeinden," in *Ex orbe religionum. Studia Geo Widengren oblata.* Pars prior. Leiden, 1972 (Studies in the History of Religions 21), 401-412.

────. "Daēnā, Lichtjungfrau, zweite Gestalt. Verbindungen und Unterschiede zwischen zarathustrischer und manichäischer Selbst-Anschauung," in R. van den Broek and M. J. Vermaseren, eds., *Studies in Gnosticism and Hellenistic Religions presented to Gilles Quispel on the Occasion of his Sixty-fifth Birthday.* Leiden, 1981 (EPRO 91), 58-77.

────. "Das Siegel der Propheten," *Orientalia Suecana* 33-35 (1984-86), 71-83.

Cumont, F. *Recherches sur le Manichéisme.* 2 vols. Bruxelles, 1908.

Decret, F. *Mani et la tradition manichéenne.* Paris, 1974.

Dodge, B. *The Fihrist of al-Nadīm. A Tenth-Century Survey of Muslim Culture.* Vol. II. New York, 1970.

Doerfer, G. "Mahmūd al-Kašγarī, Arγu, Chaladsch," *UAJb* N. F. 7 (1987), 105–114.

Drijvers, H. J. W. "Conflict and Alliance in Manichaeism," in H.-G. Kippenberg, et al., eds., *Struggles of Gods.* Berlin, New York, Amsterdam, 1985 (Religion and Reason 31), 99–124.

Edgerton, F. *Buddhist Hybrid Sanskrit Grammar and Dictionary.* Vol. 2: *Dictionary.* 1953; repr. Delhi, 1985.

Emmerick, R. W. and D. Weber, eds., *Corolla Iranica. Papers in honour of Professòr Dr. David Neil MacKenzie on the occasion of his sixty-fifth birthday on April 8th, 1991.* Frankfurt, 1991.

Fauth, W. "Syzygos und Eikon. Manis himmlischer Doppelgänger vor dem Hintergrund der platonischen Urbild-Abbild-Theorie," *Perspektiven der Philosophie. Neues Jahrbuch* 12 (1986), 41–68.

Feldmann, E. *Die "Epistula Fundamenti" der nordafrikanischen Manichäer. Versuch einer Rekonstruktion.* Altenberge, 1987 (Akademische Bibliothek).

Flügel, G. *Mani, seine Lehre und seine Schriften.* Leipzig, 1862.

Frye, R. N. "Manichaean Notes," in G. Wiessner and H.-J. Klimkeit, eds., *Studia Manichaica,* 93–97.

Gabain, A. von. "Steppe und Stadt im Leben der ältesten Türken," *Der Islam* 29 (1950), 30–62.

———. *Das uigurische Königreich von Chotscho 850–1250.* Berlin, 1961 (SDAW, Klasse für Sprachen, Literatur und Kunst, 1961, no. 5).

———. "Die alttürkische Literatur," in *Philologiae Turcicae Fundamenta.* II. Wiesbaden, 1964, 211–43.

———. *Das Leben im uigurischen Königreich von Qočo (850–1250).* 2 parts. Wiesbaden, 1973 (Veröffentlichungen der Societas Uralo-Altaica 6).

———. See also Winter, W. and A. von Gabain.

Gandjeï, T. "The Prosodic Structure of an Old Turkish Poem," in M. Boyce and I. Gershevitch, eds., *W. B. Henning Memorial Volume.* London, 1970, 157–60.

Geng Shimin. "Recent Studies on Manichaeism in China," in G. Wiessner and H.-J. Klimkeit, eds., *Studia Manichaica,* 98–104.

Geng Shimin and H.-J. Klimkeit. "Zerstörung manichäischer Klöster in Turfan," *ZAS* 18 (1985), 7–11.

———. *Das Zusammentreffen mit Maitreya. Die ersten fünf Kapitel der Hami-Version der Maitrisimit.* In Verbindung mit H. Eimer und J. P. Laut herausgegeben, übersetzt und kommentiert. 2 parts. Wiesbaden, 1987 (AF 103).

Geng Shimin and H.-J. Klimkeit in collaboration with J. P. Laut. "Manis Wettkampf mit dem Prinzen. Ein neues manichäisch-türkisches Fragment aus Turfan," *ZDMG* 137 (1987), 44–58.

Geng Shimin, H.-J. Klimkeit and J.-P. Laut: "Die Geschichte der drei Prinzen. Weitere neue manichäisch-türkische Fragmente aus Turfan," *ZDMG* 139 (1989), 328–45.

Gershevitch, I. *A Grammar of Manichaean Sogdian.* Oxford, 1954 (Publications of the Philological Society 16).

———. "The Bactrian Fragment in Manichaean Script," in J. Harmatta, ed., *From Hecataeus to Al-Ḫuwārizmī,* 273–80.

———. "Beauty as the Living Soul in Iranian Manichaeism," in J. Harmatta, ed., *From Hecataeus to Al-Ḫuwārizmī,* 281–88.

Golzio, K.-H. *Rulers and Dynasties of East Asia: China, Japan, Korea.* Cologne, 1983 (AR 10).

———. *Kings, Khans and Other Rulers of Early Central Asia*. Cologne, 1984 (AR 11).

———. *Regents in Central Asia since the Mongol Empire*. Cologne, 1985 (AR 12).

Granö, J. G. "Archäologische Beobachtungen von meinen Reisen in den nördlichen Grenzgebieten Chinas in den Jahren 1906 und 1907," *JSFO* 26 (1909), 1–54 and plates.

Grözinger, K. E. "Engel III. Judentum," *TRE* 9 (1982), 586–96.

Grünwedel, A. *Alt-Kutscha*. Berlin, 1920.

Haloun, G. and W. B. Henning, "The Compendium of the Doctrines and Styles of the Teaching of Mani, the Buddha of Light," *Asia Major* (London) N.S. 3 (1952), 184–212.

Hamilton, J. *Manuscrits Ouïgours du IXe-Xe siècle de Touen-Houang*. 2 vols. Paris, 1986.

Haneda, T. "A propos d'un texte fragmentaire de prière manichéenne en ouigour provenant de Turfan," *Memoirs of the Research Department of the Toyo Bunko* (The Oriental Library) 6 (1932), 1–21.

Hansen, O. "Zur soghdischen Inschrift auf dem dreisprachigen Denkmal von Karabalgasun," *JFSO* 44, 3 (1930), 1–39.

Harmatta, J., ed. *Prolegomena to the Sources on the History of Pre-Islamic Central Asia*. Budapest, 1979 (Collection of the Sources for the History of Pre-Islamic Central Asia. Series I, Vol. I).

———. ed. *Studies in the Sources on the History of Pre-Islamic Central Asia*. Budapest, 1979 (Collection of the Sources on the History of Pre-Islamic Central Asia. Series I, Vol. II).

———. ed. *From Hecataeus to Al-Ḥuwārizmī*. Budapest, 1984 (Collection of the Sources for the History of Pre-Islamic Central Asia. Series I, Vol. III).

Heissig, W. and H.-J. Klimkeit, eds. *Synkretismus in den Religionen Zentralasiens. Ergebnisse eines Kolloquiums vom 24.5 bis 26.5.1983 in St. Augustin bei Bonn*. Wiesbaden, 1987 (StOR 13).

Heldermann, J. "Zum Doketismus und zur Inkarnation im Manichäismus," in A. van Tongerloo and S. Giversen, eds., *Manichaica Selecta*, 101–23.

Hennecke, E. and W. Schneemelcher. *New Testament Apocrypha*. Vol. I: *Gospels and Related Writings*. trans. R. McL. Wilson. London, 1963; 2d ed. (rev.), ed. W. Schneemelcher, trans. R. McL. Wilson. Cambridge (England) and Louisville, KY, 1991. Vol. II: *Writings Relating to the Apostles, Apocalypses and Related Subjects*. Trans. R. McL. Wilson. London, 1965.

Henning, W. B. "Ein manichäischer kosmogonischer Hymnus," *NGWG* 1932, 214–28.

———. "Geburt und Entsendung des manichäischen Urmenschen," *NGWG* 1933, 306–18.

———. "Neue Quellen zum Studium des Manichäismus," *Forschungen und Fortschritte* 9 (1933), 250–51.

———. "Ein manichäisches Henochbuch," *SPAW* 1934, 27–35.

———. "Zum zentralasiatischen Manichäismus," *OLZ* 37,1 (1934), 1–11.

———. "Der Traditionalismus bei Mani," *Forschungen und Fortschritte* 10 (1934), 245.

———. *Ein manichäisches Bet- und Beichtbuch*. Berlin, 1937 (APAW 1936, no. 10).

———. "Zwei Fehler in der arabisch-manichäischen Überlieferung," *Orientalia* N.S. 5 (1936), 84–87.

———. "Neue Materialien zur Geschichte des Manichäismus," *ZDMG* 90 (1936), 1–18. Repr. in G. Widengren, ed., *Der Manichäismus*, 400–417.

———. "Soghdische Miszellen," *BSOS* 8 (1936), 583–88.

———. "Argi and the 'Tokharians,'" *BSOS* 9 (1938), 545–71.

———. *Sogdica*. London, 1940 (James G. Furlong Fund 21).

————. "Mani's Last Journey," *BSOAS* 10 (1942), 941–53.

————. "The Book of the Giants," *BSOAS* 11 (1943), 52–74.

————. "Bráhman," *TPS* 1944, 108–118.

————. "The Murder of the Magi," *JRAS* 1944, 133–144.

————. "Waručān-Šāh," *Journal of the Greater India Society* 11,2 (1944), 85–90.

————. "The Manichaean Fasts," *JRAS* 1945, 146–64 (155–64: "Notes by S. H. Taqizadeh").

————. "Sogdian Tales," *BSOAS* 11 (1945), 465–87.

————. "Two Central Asian Words," *TPS* 1945 (1946), 150–62.

————. "Two Manichaean Magical Texts with an Excursus on the Parthian ending-ēndēh," *BSOAS* 12 (1947), 39–66.

————. "A Sogdian Fragment of the Manichaean Cosmogony," *BSOAS* 12 (1947–48), 306–318.

————. "The name of the 'Tokharian' language," *Asia Major* (London) N.S. 1 (1949), 158–62.

————. "A Pahlavi Poem," *BSOAS* 13 (1950), 641–48.

————. *Zoroaster, Politician or Witch-Doctor.* London, 1951 (Ratanbai Katrak Lectures, 1949).

————. "Mitteliranisch," in *HO* 1, 4,1. Leiden and Cologne, 1958, 20–129.

————. "A Fragment of the Manichaean Hymn-Cycles in Old Turkish," *Asia Major* (London) N.S.7 (1959), 122–24.

————. "Die älteste persische Gedichthandschrift: eine neue Version von Barlaam und Joasaph," in *Akten des 24. Internationalen Orientalistenkongresses München* 1957. Wiesbaden, 1959, 305–307.

————. "Persian Poetical Manuscripts from the Time of Rūdakī," in *A Locust's Leg. Studies in honour of S. H. Taqizadeh.* London, 1962, 89–104.

————. "A Grain of Mustard," *Annali. Istituto Orientale di Napoli. Sezione Linguistica* 6 (1965), 29–47.

————. *Selected Papers.* 2 vols. Ed. M. Boyce and I. Gershevitch. Leiden, 1977 (Acta Iranica 14–15).

Henrichs, A. "Mani and the Babylonian Baptists: A Historical Confrontation," *HSCP* 77 (1973), 23–59.

————. "The Cologne Mani Codex Reconsidered," *HSCP* 83 (1979), 339–67.

————. "'Thou Shalt not Kill a Tree': Greek, Manichaean and Indian Tales," *BASP* 16 (1979), 85–108.

Henrichs, A. and L. Koenen. "Ein griechischer Mani-Codex," *ZPE* 5 (1970), 97–216.

————. "Vorbericht," see A. Henrichs and L. Koenen, "Der Kölner Mani Codex."

————. "Der Kölner Mani-Codex (P. Colon. Inv.-Nr. 4780)," *ZPE* 19 (1975), 1–85; 32 (1978), 87–199; 44 (1981), 201–318; 48 (1982), 1–59.

Heuser, M. *Der manichäische Mythos nach den koptischen Quellen.* Phil. Diss. Bonn, 1992 (typewritten; English trans. by M. Franzmann in preparation).

Hoffmann, G. *Auszüge aus syrischen Akten persischer Märtyrer.* Leipzig, 1880 (Abh. für die Kunde des Morgenlandes VII,3).

Humbach, H. "Vayu, Śiva und der Spiritus Vivens im ostiranischen Synkretismus," in *Monumentum H.S. Nyberg.* Vol. I. Leiden, 1975 (Acta Iranica 4), 397–408.

————. "Die sogdischen Inschriften vom oberen Indus (Pakistan)," *Beiträge zur Allgemeinen und Vergleichenden Archäologie* 2 (1980), 201–228.

Hutter, M. *Mani und die Sasaniden. Der iranisch-gnostische Synkretismus einer Weltreligion.* Innsbruck, 1988 (Scientia 12).

————. "Das Erlösungsgeschehen im manichäisch-iranischen Mythos. Motiv- und traditionsgeschichtliche Analysen," in K. M. Woschitz, M. Hutter, and K. Penner,

Das manichäische Urdrama des Lichtes. Studien zu koptischen, mitteliranischen und arabischen Texten. Vienna, 1989, 153–236.

———. "Mani und das persische Christentum," in A. van Tongerloo and S. Giversen, eds., *Manichaica Selecta*, 125–35.

———. *Manis kosmogonische Šābuhragān-Texte*. Wiesbaden, 1992 (StOR 21).

Jackson, A. V. W. *Researches in Manichaeism with special reference to the Turfan fragments*. New York, 1932 (Columbia University Indo-Iranian Series 13).

———. "The Fourfold Aspect of the Supreme Being in Manichaeism," *Indian Linguistics* 5 (1935), 287–96.

———. "The Doctrine of the Bolos in Manichaean Eschatology," *JAOS* 58 (1938), 225–34.

———. "The Personality of Mānī, the Founder of Manichaeism," *JAOS* 58 (1938), 235–40.

Jonas, H. *The Gnostic Religion. The Message of the Alien God and the Beginnings of Christianity*. Boston, 1963.

———. *Gnosis und spätantiker Geist*. Part 1: *Die mythologische Gnosis*. 3d ed. Göttingen, 1964 (FRLANT 51).

Kephalaia see Polotsky, H. J. and A. Böhlig.

Kessler, K. *Mani. Forschungen über die manichäische Religion*. Vol. 1. Berlin, 1889.

Klengel, H. and W. Sundermann, eds. *Ägypten. Vorderasien. Turfan. Probleme der Edition und Bearbeitung altorientalischer Handschriften*. Berlin, 1991 (Schriften zur Geschichte und Kultur des Alten Orients 23).

Klima, O. *Manis Zeit und Leben*. Prague, 1963 (Edition Oriental Archives 18).

Klimkeit, H.-J. "Manichäische und buddhistische Beichtformeln aus Turfan. Beobachtungen zur Beziehung zwischen Gnosis und Mahāyāna," *ZRGG* 29 (1977), 193–228.

———. "Vairocana und das Lichtkreuz: Manichäische Elemente in der Kunst von Alchi (West-Tibet)," *ZAS* 13 (1979), 357–99.

———. "Der dreistämmige Baum: Bemerkungen zur manichäischen Kunst und Symbolik," in *Kulturwissenschaften. Festgabe für Wilhelm Perpeet zum 65. Geburtstag*. Ed. H. Lützeler, et al., Bonn, 1980, 245–62.

———. "Der Buddha Henoch: Qumran und Turfan," *ZRGG* 32 (1980), 367–77.

———. "Hindu Deities in Manichaean Art," *ZAS* 14,2 (1980), 179–99.

———. "Stūpa and Parinirvāṇa as Manichaean Motifs," in A. Dallapiccola, S. Zingel, and A. Lallemant, eds., *The Stūpa. Its religious, historical and architectural significance*. Wiesbaden, 1980 (Beiträge zur Südasienforschung 55), 229–37.

———. "Christians, Buddhists and Manichaeans in Medieval Central Asia," *Buddhist-Christian Studies* 1 (1981), 46–50.

———. *Manichaean Art and Calligraphy*. Leiden, 1982 (Iconography of Religions 20).

———. "Manichaean Kingship: Gnosis at Home in the World," *Numen* 29 (1982), 17–32.

———. "Vom Wesen manichäischer Kunst," *ZRGG* 34 (1982), 195–219.

———. "Gottes- und Selbsterfahrung in der gnostisch-buddhistischen Religionsbegegnung Zentralasiens," *ZRGG* 35 (1983), 236–47.

———. "Der Stifter im Lande der Seidenstraßen. Bemerkungen zur buddhistischen Laienfrömmigkeit," *ZRGG* 35 (1983), 289–308.

———. "The Sun and Moon as Gods in Central Asia," *South Asian Religious Art Studies Bulletin* 2 (1983), 11–23.

———. "Das Pferd Kaṇṭhaka—Symbol buddhistischer Erzähl- und Kunstelemente im zentralasiatischen Manichäismus," in J. Ozols and V. Thewalt, eds., *Aus dem Osten des Alexanderreichs. Festschrift für Klaus Fischer*. Köln, 1984, 91–97.

———. *Die Begegnung von Christentum, Gnosis und Buddhismus an der Seidenstraße.* Opladen, 1986 (RWAW, Geisteswissenschaften: Vorträge G 283).

———. "Jesus' Entry into *Parinirvāṇa.* Manichaean Identity in Buddhist Central Asia," *Numen* 33 (1986), 225–40.

———. "Der Untergang des Manichäismus in West und Ost," in H. Zinser, ed., *Der Untergang von Religionen.* Berlin, 1986, 113–24.

———. "Die Welt als Wirklichkeit und Gleichnis im Buddhismus Zentralasiens," *Eranos-Jahrbuch* 1984 (Vol. 53). Frankfurt, 1986, 83–126.

———. "Buddhistische Übernahmen im iranischen und türkischen Manichäismus," in W. Heissig and H.-J. Klimkeit, eds., *Synkretismus in den Religionen Zentralasiens,* 58–75.

———. "Gestalt, Ungestalt, Gestaltwandel. Zum Gestaltprinzip im Manichäismus," in P. Bryder, ed., *Manichaean Studies,* 45–68.

———. "Das Tor als Symbol im Manichäismus," in *A Green Leaf. Papers in Honour of Professor Jes P. Asmussen.* Leiden, 1988 (Acta Iranica 28), 365–81.

———. "Die Kenntnis apokrypher Evangelien in Zentral- und Ostasien," in A. van Tongerloo and S. Giversen, eds., *Manichaica Selecta,* 149–75.

———. "Die manichäische Lehre vom alten und neuen Menschen," in G. Wiessner and H.-J. Klimkeit, eds., *Studia Manichaica,* 131–50.

Klimkeit, H.-J. and H. Schmidt-Glintzer. "Die türkischen Parallelen zum chinesisch-manichäischen Traktat," *ZAS* 17 (1984), 82–117.

Klimkeit, H.-J. and H. Schmidt-Glintzer, eds., *Japanische Studien zum östlichen Manichäismus.* Wiesbaden, 1991 (StOR 17).

Kljaštornyj, S. G. "Sur les colonies sogdiennes de la Haute Asie," *UAJb* 33 (1961), 94–97.

———. "The Terkhin Inscription," *AOH* 36 (1983), 235–366.

Kljaštornyj, S. G. and V. A. Livšic. "Une inscription inédite turque et sogdienne: La stèle de Sevrey (Gobi Méridional)," *JA* 259 (1971), 11–20.

———. "The Sogdian Inscription of Bugut Revised," *AOH* 26 (1972), 69–102.

Koenen, L. "From Baptism to the Gnosis of Manichaeism," in B. Layton, ed. *The Rediscovery of Gnosticism. Proceedings of the International Conference on Gnosticism at Yale, New Haven, Connecticut, March 28–31, 1978.* Vol. 2: *Sethian Gnosticism.* Leiden, 1981 (Studies in the History of Religions 41), 734–56.

———. "Manichäische Mission und Klöster in Ägypten," in *Das Römisch-Byzantinische Ägypten. Akten des internationalen Symposiums 26–30 September 1978 in Trier.* Mainz, 1983 (Aegyptiaca Treverensia 2), 93–108.

———. "Manichaean Apocalypticism at the Crossroads of Iranian, Egyptian, Jewish and Christian Thought," in L. Cirillo, ed., *Codex Manichaicus Coloniensis,* 285–332.

———. "How Dualistic is Mani's Dualism?" in L. Cirillo, ed. *Codex Manichaicus Coloniensis. Atti del Secondo Simposio Internazionale (Cosenza 27–28 Maggio 1988).* Cosenza, 1990, 1–34.

Koenen, L. and C. Römer. *Der Kölner Mani-Kodex. Über das Werden seines Leibes.* Kritische Edition. Opladen, 1988. (ARWAW, Pap. Col. XIV).

Lattke, M. *Die Oden Salomos in ihrer Bedeutung für Neues Testament und Gnosis.* Vol. 1–3 (including 1a). Fribourg and Göttingen, 1979, 1980, 1986.

Laut, J. P. *Der frühe türkische Buddhismus und seine literarischen Denkmäler.* Wiesbaden, 1986 (Veröffentlichungen der Societas Uralo-Altaica 21).

Le Coq, A. von: "Ein christliches und ein manichäisches Manuskriptfragment in türkischer Sprache aus Turfan (Chinesisch-Turkistan)," *SPAW* 1909, 1202–1218.

———. *Chuastuanift, ein Sündenbekenntnis der manichäischen Auditores. Gefunden in Turfan (Chinesisch-Turkistan).* Berlin, 1910 (APAW 1910, Anhang, Abh. 4).

————. "Dr. Stein's Turkish Khuastuanift from Tun-huang. Being a Confession-Prayer of the Manichaean Auditores," *JRAS* 1911, 277–314.

————. *Türkische Manichaica aus Chotscho.* I; II; III. Berlin, 1912; 1919; 1922 (APAW 1911, no. 6; 1919, no. 3; 1922, no. 2).

————. *Die buddhistische Spätantike in Mittelasien.* Vol. 2: *Die manichäischen Miniaturen.* 1923; repr. Graz, 1973.

————. *Chotscho. Königliche Preußische Turfan-Expedition.* 1913; repr. Graz, 1979.

Legge, F. "Western Manichaeism and the Turfan Discoveries," *JRAS* 1913, 69–94.

Lentz, W. "Mani und Zarathustra," *ZDMG* 82 (1928), 179–206.

————. "What is the Manichaean Nous?" *UAJb* 33 (1961), 101–106.

————. "Note on the fragment of a Manichaean parchment. MS Kao. 0111, from Kara-Khōja," in Sir A. Stein, *Innermost Asia.* Vol. 3. 1928; repr. N. Delhi, 1981, Appendix P, 1081.

Lidzbarski, M. "Die Herkunft der manichäischen Schrift," *SPAW* 1916, 1213–22.

————. "Ein manichäisches Gedicht," *NGWG* 1918, 501–505.

Lieu, S. N. C. "A Lapsed Chinese Manichaean's Correspondence with a Confucian Official in the Late Sung Dynasty (1264): A Study of the *Ch'ung-shou-kung chi* by Huang Chen," *Bulletin of the John Rylands University Library of Manchester* 59,2 (Spring 1977), 397–425.

————. "Polemics against Manichaeism as a Subversive Cult in Sung China (A.D. c. 960–c. 1200)," *Bulletin of the John Rylands University Library of Manchester* 62,1 (Autumn 1979), 151–67.

————. *The Religion of Light. An Introduction to the History of Manichaeism in China.* Hong Kong, 1979 (Centre of Asian Studies, Occasional Papers and Monographs 38).

————. "Nestorians and Manichaeans on the South China Coast," *Vigiliae Christianae* 34 (1980), 71–88.

————. "Precept and Practice in Manichaean Monasticism," *JThS* N. S. 32 (1981), 153–73.

————. "New Light on Manichaeism in China," in *Papers in Honour of Professor Mary Boyce.* Leiden, 1985 (Acta Iranica 24), 401–419.

————. *Manichaeism in the Later Roman Empire and Medieval China. A Historical Survey.* Manchester, 1985; 2d ed. Tübingen, 1992.

Lin Wushu: "On the Joining between Two Fragments of 'The Compendium of the Teaching of Mani, the Buddha of Light,'" in P. Bryder, ed., *Manichaean Studies,* 89–93.

————. "The Origin of 'The Compendium of the Teaching of Mani, the Buddha of Light' in Chinese," in A. van Tongerloo and S. Giversen, eds., *Manichaica Selecta,* 225–32.

————. "On the Spreading of Manichaeism in Fujien, China," in G. Wiessner and H.-J. Klimkeit, eds., *Studia Manichaica,* 342–55.

Liu Mau-Tsai. *Chinesische Nachrichten zur Geschichte der Osttürken* (*T'u-küe*). Wiesbaden, 1958.

————. *Kutscha und seine Beziehungen zu China.* 2 vols. Wiesbaden, 1969 (AF 27).

————. "Traces of Zoroastrian and Manichaean Activities in Pre-T'ang China," in Liu Ts'un Yan, *Selected Papers from the Hall of Harmonious Wind.* Leiden, 1976, 3–55.

Luttikhuizen, G. P. *The Revelation of Elchasai. Investigations into the Evidence for a Mesopotamian Jewish Apocalypse of the Second Century and its Reception by Judeo-Christian Propagandists.* Tübingen, 1985 (Texte und Studien zum Antiken Judentum 8).

Machabey, A. *La Cantillation manichéenne. Notation hypothétique, métrique, analogies.* Paris, 1955 (La Revue Musicale 227).

MacKenzie, D. N. "Mani's *Šābuhragān* [I]; II," *BSOAS* 42 (1979), 500–534; 43 (1980), 288–310.

———. "Two Sogdian *HWYDGM'N* Fragments," in *Papers in Honour of Professor Mary Boyce*. Leiden, 1985 (Acta Iranica 24), 421–28.

Maenchen-Helfen, O. "Manichaeans in Siberia," in W. J. Fischel, ed., *Semitical and Oriental Studies. A Volume Presented to William Popper on the Occasion of his Seventy-fifth Birthday, October 29, 1949.* Berkeley, 1951 (University of California Publications in Semitic Philology 11), 311–26.

Maisch, E. "A propos de la notion de salut dans le manichéisme," *RHPR* 18 (1938), 332–39.

Manichäische Homilien see Polotsky, H. J.

A Manichaean Psalm-Book, see Allberry, C. R. C.

Marquart, J. "Ğuwaini's Bericht über die Bekehrung der Uiguren," *SPAW* 1912, 486–502.

Menasce, P. de. "Fragments manichéens de Paris," in M. Boyce and I. Gershevitch, eds., *W. B. Henning Memorial Volume.* London, 1970, 303–306.

Merkelbach, R. *Mani und sein Religionssystem.* Opladen, 1986 (RWAW, Geisteswissen-schaften: Vorträge G 281).

———. "Manichaica (10)—Eine Fabel Manis," *ZPE* 75 (1988), 93–94.

———. "Die Täufer, bei denen Mani aufwuchs," in P. Bryder, ed., *Manichaean Studies,* 105–133.

———. "Wann wurde die Mani-Biographie abgefaβt, und welches waren ihre Quellen?" in G. Wiessner and H.-J. Klimkeit, eds., *Studia Manichaica,* 159–66.

Michl, J. "Engel II (jüdisch); III (gnostisch); IV (christlich); V (Engelnamen); VII (Michael)," *RAC* 5 (1962), 60–97; 97–109; 109–200; 200–239; 243–51.

Milik, J. T., ed. *The Books of Enoch. Aramaic Fragments of Qumrân Cave 4.* Oxford, 1976.

———. "Turfan et Qumran. Livres des Géants juif et manichéen," in G. Jeremias, H. W. Kuhn, and H. Stegemann, eds., *Tradition und Glaube: Das frühe Christen-tum in seiner Umwelt.* Göttingen, 1971, 117–27.

Monier-Williams, Sir M. *A Sanskrit-English Dictionary.* 1899; repr. Oxford, 1964.

Morano, E. "The Sogdian Hymns of 'Stellung Jesu,'" *East and West* N. S. 32 (1982), 9–43.

Müller, F. W. K. "Handschriften-Reste in Estrangelo-Schrift aus Turfan, Chinesisch-Turkistan," *SPAW* 1904, 348–52.

———. *Handschriften-Reste in Estrangelo-Schrift aus Turfan, Chinesisch-Turkistan.* Part 2. Berlin, 1904 (APAW 1904).

———. "Eine Hermas-Stelle in manichäischer Version," *SPAW* 1905, 1077–1083.

———. "Die persischen Kalenderausdrücke im chinesischen Tripiṭaka," *SPAW* 1907, 458–65.

———. *Uigurica* [I]. Berlin, 1908 (APAW 1908, no. 2).

———. *Uigurica* II. Berlin, 1910 (APAW 1910, no. 3)

———. "Der Hofstaat eines Uiguren-Königs," in *Festschrift V. Thomsen zur Vollendung des 70. Lebensjahres.* Leipzig, 1912, 207–213.

———. *Ein Doppelblatt aus einem manichäischen Hymnenbuch (Maḥrnâmag).* Berlin, 1913 (APAW 1912).

———. *Zwei Pfahlinschriften aus den Turfanfunden.* Berlin, 1915 (APAW 1915, no. 3).

———. "Uigurische Glossen," *Ostasiatische Zeitschrift* 8 (1919–20), 310–24.

Nagel, P. (Hrsg.) *Studien zum Menschenbild in Gnosis und Manichäismus.* Halle A. D. Saale, 1979 (Martin-Luther-Universität Halle-Wittenberg. Wissenschaftliche Beiträge 1979/39 [K 5]).

————. *Die Thomaspsalmen des koptisch-manichäischen Psalmenbuches*. Berlin, 1980 (Quellen. Ausgewählte Texte aus der Geschichte der christlichen Kirche. N.F. 1).

Naveh, J. and S. Shaked. *Amulets and Magic Bowls. Aramaic Incantations of Late Antiquity*. Jerusalem and Leiden, 1985.

Nyberg, H.S. "Zum Kampf zwischen Islam und Manichäismus," *OLZ* 32 (1929), 425–41.

Oerter, W.-B. *Die Thomaspsalmen des manichäischen Psalters als genuiner Bestandteil der manichäischen Literatur*. Phil. diss. Leipzig, 1976.

————. "Das Motiv vom Garten. Betrachtungen zur manichäischen Eschatologie," in A. van Tongerloo and S. Giversen, eds., *Manichaica Selecta*, 263–72.

Olson, T. "The Manichaean Background of Eschatology in the Koran," in P. Bryder, ed., *Manichaean Studies*, 273–82.

Ort, L. J. R. *Mani. A Religio-Historical Description of His Personality*. Leiden, 1967 (Supplementa ad Numen, Altera Series 1).

Pelliot, P. "Two New Manichaean Manuscripts from Tun-huang," *JRAS* 1925, 113.

————. "[Review of] Waldschmidt, E. and W. Lentz: Die Stellung Jesu im Manichäismus," *TP* 25 (1927–28), 426–35.

Peterson, E. "Jesus bei den Manichäern," *ThLZ* 53 (1928), 241–50.

Polotsky, H. J. "Manichäische Studien," *Le Muséon* 46 (1933), 247–71.

————. *Manichäische Homilien*. Vol. I. Stuttgart, 1934 (Manichäische Handschriften der Sammlung A. Chester Beatty).

————. "Manichäismus," in *Paulys Real-Encyclopädie der Classischen Altertumswissenschaft. Neue Bearbeitung*. Suppl. Vol. VI. Stuttgart, 1935, 240–71. Repr. in G. Widengren, ed., *Der Manichäismus*, 101–144.

Polotsky, H. J. and A. Böhlig. *Kephalaia*. 1. Hälfte; 2. Hälfte. Stuttgart, 1940; 1966 (Manichäische Handschriften der Staatlichen Museen Berlin 1).

Preuschen, E., trans. *Tatians Diatessaron*. Ed. A. Pott. Heidelberg, 1926.

Pritsak, O. *Karachanidische Studien I–IV. Studien zur Geschichte der Verfassung der Türk-Völker Zentralasiens*. Phil. diss. Göttingen, 1948 (typewritten).

————. "Von den Karluk zu den Karachaniden," *ZDMG* 101 (1951), 270–300.

Puech, H.-C. "Der Begriff der Erlösung im Manichäismus," *Eranos-Jahrbuch* 1936 (1937), 183–286.

————. *Le Manichéisme. Son fondateur, sa doctrine*. Paris, 1949 (Musée Guimet. Bibliothèque de diffusion 56).

————. "Die Religion des Mani," in F. König, ed., *Christus und die Religionen der Erde. Handbuch der Religionsgeschichte*. Vol. 2. Freiburg, 1956, 499–563.

————. "Liturgie et pratiques rituelles dans le Manichéisme," *Annuaire du Collège de France* 59 (1959), 264–69.

————. "Gnostic Gospels and Related Documents," in E. Hennecke and W. Schneemelcher, eds., *New Testament Apocrypha* I. London, 1963, 231–362.

Pulleyblank, E. G. "A Sogdian Colony in Inner Mongolia," *TP* 41 (1952), 317–56.

Ramstedt, G. J. "Zwei uigurische Runeninschriften in der Nord-Mongolei," *JSFO* 1913–1918, 3–63.

Reck, C. "Ein weiterer parthischer Montagshymnus?" *AoF* 19 (1992), 342–47.

Reeves, J. C. "An Enochic Motiv in Manichaean Tradition," in A. van Tongerloo and S. Giversen, eds., *Manichaica Selecta*, 295–98.

————. *Jewish Lore in Manichaean Cosmogony. Studies in the* Book of Giants *Traditions*. Cincinatti, 1992 (Monographs of the Hebrew Union College 14).

Reitzenstein, R. *Das iranische Erlösungsmysterium*. Bonn, 1921.

Reitzenstein, R. and H. H. Schaeder. *Studien zum antiken Synkretismus aus Iran und Griechenland.* Leipzig and Berlin, 1926 (Studien der Bibliothek Warburg VII). Repr. Darmstadt, 1965.

Ries, J. "Introduction aux études manichéennes. Quatre siècles de recherches," *Ephemerides Theologicae Lovanienses* 33 (1957), 453–82; 35 (1959), 362–409.

————, ed. *La mort selon la bible, dans l'antiquité classique et selon le Manichéisme. Actes d'un Colloque de Louvain-la-Neuve.* Louvain, 1983.

————. "Le Manichéisme dans le context des grandes religions orientales," *Les civilisations orientales.* G 6. Liège n.d., 1–23.

————. "Buddhism and Manichaeism. The Stages of an Enquiry," *Buddhist Studies Review* 3,2 (1986), 108–124.

————. *Les études manichéennes. Des controverses de la Réforme aux découvertes du XXe siècle.* Louvain-la-Neuve, 1988.

Robinson, J. M., general ed. *The Nag Hammadi Library in English.* 3d rev. ed. Leiden, Cologne, and New York, 1988.

Röhrborn, K. *Uigurisches Wörterbuch. Sprachmaterial der vorislamischen türkischen Texte aus Zentralasien.* Lieferung 1–4. Wiesbaden, 1977; 1979; 1981; 1988.

Röhrborn, K. and H. W. Brands, eds. *Scholia. Beiträge zur Turkologie und Zentralasienkunde. Annemarie von Gabain zum 80. Geburtstag am 4. Juli 1981 dargebracht von Kollegen, Freunden und Schülern.* Wiesbaden, 1981 (Veröffentlichungen der Societas Uralo Altaica 14).

Römer, C. "Die manichäische Kirchenorganisation nach dem Kölner Mani-Kodex," in G. Wiessner and H.-J. Klimkeit, eds., *Studia Manichaica,* 181–88.

Rohland, J. P. *Der Erzengel Michael. Arzt und Feldherr.* Leiden, 1977 (BZRGG 19).

Rose, E. *Die manichäische Christologie.* Wiesbaden, 1979 (StOR 5).

————. "Die manichäische Christologie," *ZRGG* 32 (1980), 219–31.

Rudolph, K. *Die Gnosis. Wesen und Geschichte einer spätantiken Religion.* 3d German ed. Göttingen, 1990 (Uni-Taschenbücher 1577). English trans. of 1st German ed. (1977); *Gnosis. The Nature and History of an Ancient Religion.* Trans. and ed. by R. McL. Wilson. Edinburgh, 1983.

————. "Mani und die Gnosis," in P. Bryder, ed., *Manichaean Studies,* 191–200.

————. "Mani und der Iran," in A. van Tongerloo and S. Giversen, eds., *Manichaica Selecta,* 307–321.

Sachau, E., ed. *The Chronology of Ancient Nations.* 1879, repr. Frankfurt, 1984.

Sagaster, K. *Die Weiße Geschichte (Čaγan teüke).* Wiesbaden, 1976 (AF 41).

Salemann, C. *Ein Bruchstük* [sic] *manichäischen Schrifttums im Asiatischen Museum.* St. Pétersbourg, 1904 (MAIS, 8e série, vol. 6, no. 6).

————. "Manichaica I-IV," *BAIS,* 6e série, vol. 1 (1907), 175–84, 531–58; vol. 6 (1912), 1–32, 33–50.

————. *Manichäische Studien.* I: *Die mittelpersischen Texte.* St. Pétersbourg, 1911 (MAIS, 8e série, vol. 8, no. 10).

Schaeder, H. H. "Die islamische Lehre vom vollkommenen Menschen, ihre Herkunft und ihre dichterische Gestaltung," *ZDMG* 79 (1925), 192–268.

————. "Ein Lied von Mani," *OLZ* 29 (1926), 104–107.

————. "Urform und Fortbildung des manichäischen Systems," in F. Saxl, ed., *Vorträge der Bibliothek Warburg. Vorträge 1924-1925.* Leipzig, 1927, 65–157. Repr. in H. H. Schaeder, *Studien zur orientalischen Religionsgeschichte.* Ed. C. Colpe. Darmstadt, 1968, 15–107; also repr. in G. Widengren, ed., *Der Manichäismus,* 37–55.

————. "Studien," see R. Reitzenstein and H. H. Schaeder, *Studien zum altiranischen Synkretismus.*

————. "Manichäer und Muslime," *ZDMG* 82 (1928), LXXVI–LXXXI.

————. *Iranica.* Berlin, 1934 (AGWG, 3. Folge, no. 10).

————. "Manichäismus und spätantike Religion," *ZMR* 50 (1935), 65–86.

————. "Der Manichäismus nach neuen Funden und Forschungen," *Morgenland* 28 (1936), 80–109.

————. "Der Manichäismus und sein Weg nach Osten," in H. Runte, ed., *Glaube und Geschichte. Festschrift für Friedrich Gogarten zum 13. Januar 1947.* Giessen, 1948, 236–54.

Schaff, P., ed. *A Select Library of the Nicene and Post-Nicene Fathers of the Christian Church.* Vol. IV: *St. Augustin. The Writings against the Manichaeans and against the Donatists.* 1887; repr., Grand Rapids, 1979.

Scheftelowitz, I. *Die Entstehung der manichäischen Religion und des Erlösungsmysteriums.* Giessen, 1922.

————. "Is Manichaeism an Iranic Religion?" *Asia Major* 1 (1924), 460–90.

————. "Neues Material über die manichäische Urseele und die Entstehung des Zarvanismus," *ZII* 4 (1926), 317–44.

————. "Die manichäische Zarathustra-Hymne M 7," *Oriens Christianus* 23 (1926–27), 261–83.

————. "Der göttliche Urmensch in der manichäischen Religion," *Archiv für Religionswissenschaft* 28 (1930), 212–40.

————. "Stammt der Religionsstifter Māni aus dem iranischen Herrscherhaus der Arsakiden?" in J. D. C. Pavry, ed., *Oriental Studies in Honour of Cursetjii Erachji Pavry.* London, 1933, 403–404.

Schlegel, G. *Die chinesische Inschrift auf dem uigurischen Denkmal in Kara Balgassun.* Helsingfors, 1896 (MSFO IX).

Schmidt, C., ed. *Koptisch-Gnostische Schriften* I. 4th ed. Ed. by H.-M. Schenke. Berlin, 1981 (Die griechischen christlichen Schriftsteller).

Schmidt, C. and H. J. Polotsky. "Ein Mani-Fund in Ägypten. Originalschriften des Mani und seiner Schüler," *SPAW* 1933, 1–90. Excerpt repr. in G. Widengren, ed., *Der Manichäismus,* 37–55.

Schmidt-Glintzer, H. "Das buddhistische Gewand des Manichäismus. Zur buddhistischen Terminologie in den chinesischen Manichaica," in W. Heissig and H.-J. Klimkeit, eds., *Synkretismus in den Religionen Zentralasiens,* 76–90.

————. *Chinesische Manichaica.* Wiesbaden, 1987 (StOR 14).

Schneemelcher, W. see Hennecke, E. and W. Schneemelcher.

Shaked, S., trans. *The Wisdom of the Sasanian Sages (Dēnkard VI) by Aturpāt-i Ēmētān.* Boulder, CO, 1979 (Persian Heritage Series, no. 34).

Sieg, E. *Übersetzungen aus dem Tocharischen II.* Aus dem Nachlass hrsg. von W. Thomas. Berlin, 1952 (ADAW, Jg. 1951, no. 1).

Sims-Williams, N. "The Sogdian Fragments of the British Library," *Indo-Iranian Journal* 18 (1976), 43–74, with "Appendix" by I. Gershevitch, 75–82.

————. "[Review of] Ragoza, A.N. Sogdijskie fragmenty Central'no-aziatskogo sobranija," *BSOAS* 44 (1981), 231–40.

————. "The Sogdian Fragments of Leningrad [I]," *BSOAS* 44 (1981), 231–40.

————. "The Manichaean Commandments: A Survey of the Sources," in *Papers in Honour of Professor Mary Boyce.* Leiden, 1985 (Acta Iranica 24), 573–82.

————. *The Christian Sogdian Manuscript C2.* Berlin, 1985 (BT XII).

————. "A New Fragment from the Parthian Hymn-Cycle *Huyadagmān*," in *Études*

Irano-aryennes offertes à Gilbert Lazard. Ed. by C.-H. de Fouchécour et P. Gignoux. Paris and Leuven, 1989, 321–31.

———. "The Sogdian Fragments of Leningrad II: Mani at the court of Shahanshah, *Bulletin of the Asia Institute* 4 (1990), 281–88.

———. "The Sogdian Fragments of Leningrad III: Fragments of the *Xwāstwānīft*," in A. van Tongerloo and S. Giversen, eds., *Manichaica Selecta,* 323–28.

Soothill, W. E. and L. Hodous: *A Dictionary of Chinese Buddhist Terms.* London, 1937.

Stein, R. A. "Une mention du manichéisme dans le choix du bouddhisme comme religion d'État par le roi tibétain Khrisroñ lde-bcan," in *Indianisme et Bouddhisme. Mélanges offerts à Mgr. Étienne Lamotte.* Louvain-la-Neuve, 1980 (Publications de l'Institut Orientaliste de Louvain 23), 329–37.

Stern, S. M. and S. Walzer. *Three Unknown Buddhist Stories in an Arabic Version.* Oxford, 1971.

Strack, H. L. and P. Billerbeck. *Kommentar zum Neuen Testament aus Talmud und Midrasch.* 6 vols. 6th ed. Munich, 1974–1975.

Stroumsa, G. "'Seal of the Prophets.' The Nature of the Manichaean Metaphor," *Jerusalem Studies in Arabic and Islam* 7 (1986), 61–74.

Sundermann, W. "Christliche Evangelientexte in der Überlieferung der iranisch-manichäischen Literatur," *MIO* 14 (1968), 386–405.

———. "Zur frühen missionarischen Wirksamkeit Manis," *AOH* 24 (1971), 79–125.

———. *Mittelpersische und parthische kosmogonische und Parabeltexte der Manichäer.* Berlin, 1973 (BT IV).

———. "Iranische Lebensbeschreibungen Manis," *AcOr* 36 (1974), 125–49.

———. "Überreste manichäischer Yimki-Homilien in mittelpersischer Sprache?," in *Monumentum H.S. Nyberg.* Vol. 2. Leiden, 1975 (Acta Iranica 5), 297–312.

———. "Ein Bruchstück einer soghdischen Kirchengeschichte aus Zentralasien?" *AA* 24 (1976), 95–101. Repr. in J. Harmatta, ed., *Studies in the Sources on the History of Pre-Islamic Central Asia,* 99–106.

———. "Einige Bemerkungen zur Lehre von den Mondstationen in der altiranischen Überlieferung," *AoF* 5 (1977), 199–204.

———. "Parthisch 'bšw dg'n 'Die Täufer,'" *AA* 25 (1977 [appeared 1980]), 237–42.

———. "Some More Remarks on Mithra in the Manichaean Pantheon," in *Études Mithriaques. Actes du 2ᵉ Congrès International Téhéran, du 1ᵉʳ au 8 septembre 1975.* Leiden, 1978 (Acta Iranica 17), 485–99.

———. "Namen von Göttern, Dämonen und Menschen in iranischen Versionen des manichäischen Mythos," *AoF* 6 (1979), 95–133.

———. "The Five Sons of the Manichaean God Mithra," in U. Bianchi, ed., *Mysteria Mithrae. Proceedings of the International Seminar on the 'Religio-Historical Character of Roman Mithraism, with Particular Reference to Roman and Ostian Sources.' Rome and Ostia 28–31 March 1978.* Leiden, 1979 (EPRO 80), 777–87.

———. "Die mittelpersischen und parthischen Turfantexte als Quellen zur Geschichte des vorislamischen Zentralasien," in J. Harmatta, ed., *Prolegomena to the Sources on the History of Pre-Islamic Central Asia,* 143–51.

———. *Mitteliranische manichäische Texte kirchengeschichtlichen Inhalts.* Berlin, 1981 (BT XI).

———. "Die Bedeutung des Parthischen für die Verbreitung buddhistischer Wörter indischer Herkunft," *AoF* 9 (1982), 99–113.

———. "Il sangue nei testi Manichei," in *Atti della Settimana di Studi "Sangue e antropologia biblica nella letteratura cristiana." Roma, 29 novembre–4 dicembre 1982.* Vol. 1. Rome, 1982, 65–69.

———. "Soziale Typenbegriffe altgriechischen Ursprungs in der altiranischen Überlieferung," in E. Ch. Welskopf, ed., *Soziale Typenbegriffe im alten Griechenland.* Vol. 7. Berlin, 1982, 14–38.

———. "Probleme der Interpretation manichäisch-soghdischer Briefe," *AA* 27 (1983), 289–316. Repr. in J. Harmatta, ed., *From Hecataeus to Al-Ḫuwārizmī,* 289–316.

———. "Der chinesische Traité Manichéen und der parthische Sermon vom Lichtnous," *AoF* 10 (1983), 231–42.

———. "Die Prosaliteratur der iranischen Manichäer," in W. Skalmowski and A. van Tongerloo, eds., *Middle Iranian Studies. Proceedings of the International Symposium organized by the Katholieke Universiteit Leuven from the 17th to the 20th of May 1982.* Leuven, 1984 (Orientalia Lovaniensia Analecta 16), 227–41.

———. "Sogdisch š(')yk/qn(h) 'Palast,'" *AoF* 11 (1984), 177–79.

———. "Mani's Revelations in the Cologne Mani Codex and in Other Sources," in L. Cirillo, ed., *Codex Manichaicus Coloniensis,* 205–214.

———. "Bruchstücke einer manichäischen Zarathustralegende," in R. Schmitt and P. O. Skjaervo, eds., *Studia Grammatica Iranica. Festschrift für Helmut Humbach.* Munich, 1986, 461–82.

———. "Der Schüler fragt den Lehrer. Eine Sammlung biblischer Rätsel in soghdischer Sprache," in *A Green Leaf. Papers in Honour of Professor Jes P. Asmussen.* Leiden, 1988 (Acta Iranica 28), 173–86.

———. "Ein übersehenes Bild Manis," *AoF* 12 (1985), 172–74.

———. "Der gowišn ī grīw zīndaq-Zyklus," in *Papers in Honour of Professor Mary Boyce.* Leiden, 1985 (Acta Iranica 24), 629–50.

———. *Ein manichäisch-soghdisches Parabelbuch.* Berlin, 1985 (BT XV).

———. "Die vierzehn Wunden der Lebendigen Seele," *AoF* 12 (1985), 288–95.

———. "Mani, India and the Manichaean Religion," *South Asian Studies* 2 (1986), 11–19.

———. "Studien zur kirchengeschichtlichen Literatur der iranischen Manichäer I-III," *AoF* 13 (1986), 40–92 and 231–317; 14 (1987), 41–107.

———. "Der Paraklet in der ostmanichäischen Überlieferung," in P. Bryder, ed., *Manichaean Studies,* 201–212.

———. "La passion de Mani—Calendrier liturgique ou événement historique?" in *La Commémoration. Colloque de centenaire de la section des sciences religieuses de l'École Pratique des Hautes Études.* Sous la direction de P. Gignoux. Paris and Louvain, 1988 (Bibliothèque de l'École des Hautes Études XCI), 225–31.

———. "Ein manichäischer Bekenntnistext in neupersischer Sprache," in *Études Irano-aryennes offertes à Gilbert Lazard.* Paris and Leuven, 1989, 355–65.

———. *The Manichaean Hymn Cycles* Huyadagmān *and* Angad Rōšnān *in Parthian and Sogdian.* London, 1990 (Corpus Inscriptionum Iranicarum, Supplementary Series, Vol. II).

———. "Eine buddhistische Allegorie in manichäischer Überlieferung," in R. E. Emmerick and D. Weber, eds., *Corolla Iranica. Papers in honour of Professor Dr. David Neil MacKenzie on the occasion of his sixty-fifth birthday on April 8th, 1991.* Frankfurt, etc. 1991, 198–206.

———. "Anmerkungen zu: Th. Thilo. Einige Bemerkungen zu zwei chinesisch-manichäischen Textfragmenten der Berliner Turfansammlung," in H. Klengel and W. Sundermann, eds., *Ägypten. Vorderasien. Turfan,* 171–74.

———. "Completion and correction of archaeological work by philological means: the case of the Turfan texts," in *Histoire et cultes de l'Asie Centrale préislamique.* Paris, 1991, 283–88.

———. "Der lebendige Geist als Verführer des Dämonen," in A. van Tongerloo and S. Giversen, eds., *Manichaica Selecta,* 339–42.

———. "Probleme der Edition iranisch-manichäischer Texte," in H. Klengel and W. Sundermann, eds., *Ägypten. Vorderasien. Turfan,* 106–112.

———. *Der Sermon von der Seele.* Opladen, 1991 (RWAW, Geisteswissenschaften: Vorträge G 310).

———. "Manichaean Traditions on the Date of the Historical Buddha," in H. Bechert, ed., *The Dating of the Historical Buddha.* Part 1. Göttingen, 1991, 426–38.

———. "Iranische Kephalaiatexte?" in G. Wiessner and H.-J. Klimkeit, eds., *Studia Manichaica,* 305–318.

———. "Iranian Manichaean Turfan Texts concerning the Turfan Region," in A. Cadonna, ed., *Turfan and Tunhuang. The Texts,* 63–84.

Sundermann, W. and P. Zieme. "Soghdisch-türkische Wortlisten," in K. Röhrborn and H. W. Brands, eds., *Scholia,* 184–93.

Tardieu, M. *Le Manichéisme.* Paris, 1981.

Taube, M. *Die Geheime Geschichte der Mongolen.* Munich, 1989.

Tekin, Ş. *Maitrisimit nom bitig. Die uigurische Übersetzung eines Werkes der buddhistischen Vaibhāṣika-*Schule. 2 parts. Berlin, 1980 (BT IX).

Tekin, T. *A Grammar of Orkhon Turkic.* Bloomington and The Hague, 1968 (Indiana University Publications. Uralic and Altaic Series 69).

Thilo, Th. "Einige Bemerkungen zu zwei chinesisch-manichäischen Textfragmenten der Berliner Turfan-Sammlung," in H. Klengel and W. Sundermann, eds., *Ägypten. Vorderasien. Turfan,* 161–70.

Thomsen, V., ed., "Fragment of a Runic Turkish Manuscript. Kao. 0107, from Kara-Khōja," in Sir A. Stein, *Innermost Asia.* Vol. 3. 1928; repr. N. Delhi, 1981, 1082–83.

Tongerloo, A. van: "La structure de la communauté Manichéenne dans le Turkestan Chinois à la lumière des emprunts Moyen-Iraniens en Ouigour," *CAJ* 26 (1982), 262–88.

———. "Buddhist Indian Terminology in the Manichaean Uygur and Middle Iranian Texts," in W. Skalmowski and A. van Tongerloo, eds., *Middle Iranian Studies. Proceedings of the International Symposium organized by the Katholieke Universiteit Leuven from the 17th to the 20th of May 1982.* Leuven, 1984 (Orientalia Lovaniensia Analecta 16), 243–52.

———. "Notes on the Iranian Elements in the Old Uygur Manichaean Texts," in P. Bryder, ed., *Manichaean Studies,* 213–19.

———. "Light, More Light," in A. van Tongerloo and S. Giversen, eds., *Manichaica Selecta,* 371–78.

Tongerloo, A. van and S. Giversen, eds., *Manichaica Selecta. Studies presented to Professor Julien Ries on the occasion of his seventieth birthday.* Louvain, 1991 (Manichaean Studies 1).

Tsui Chi. "Mo Ni Chiao Hsia Pu Tsan. 'The Lower (Second?) Section of the Manichaean Hymns,'" *BSOAS* 11 (1943), 174–219, including W. B. Henning, "Annotations to Mr. Tsui's Translation," 216–19.

Uray, G. "Tibet's Connections with Nestorianism and Manicheism in the 8th–10th Centuries," in E. Steinkellner and H. Tauscher, eds., *Contributions on Tibetan Language, History and Culture. Proceedings of the Csoma de Körös Symposium held at Velm-Vienna, Austria, 13–19 September 1981.* Vol. 1. Vienna, 1983 (Wiener Studien zur Tibetologie und Buddhismuskunde 10), 399–429.

Utas, B. "Mānistān and Xānaqāh," in *Papers in Honour of Professor Mary Boyce.* Leiden, 1985 (Acta Iranica 24), 655–64.

Vajda, G. "Die zindīqs im Gebiet des Islam zu Beginn der 'Abbasidenzeit,'" in G. Widengren, ed., *Der Manichäismus*, 418–63 [first published 1938].

Vielhauer, Ph. *Geschichte der urchristlichen Literatur*. Berlin and New York, 1975.

Waldschmidt, E. "Religiöse Strömungen in Zentralasien. Zur Verbreitung der Christen und Manichäer in Ostturkistan," in E. Waldschmidt, *Von Ceylon bis Turfan. Schriften zur Geschichte, Literatur, Religion und Kunst des indischen Kulturraumes. Festgabe zum 70. Geburtstag am 15. Juli 1967*. Göttingen, 1967, 1–26 (first published 1928).

Waldschmidt, E. and W. Lentz. "A Chinese Manichaean Hymnal from Tun-Huang," *JRAS* 1926, 116–22.

——. "A Chinese Manichaean Hymnal from Tun-Huang: Additions and Corrections," *JRAS* 1926, 298–99.

——. *Die Stellung Jesu im Manichäismus*. Berlin, 1926 (APAW 1926, no. 4).

——. "Manichäische Dogmatik aus chinesischen und iranischen Texten," *SPAW* 1933, 480–607.

Weisslovits, N. *Barlaam und Joasaph. Prinz und Derwish*. Munich, 1890.

Wesendonk, O. G. von. "Jesus und der Manichäismus," *OLZ* 30 (1927), 221–27.

——. "Die Verwendung einiger iranischer Götternamen im Manichäismus," *AO* 7 (1928), 114–79.

——. "Bardesanes und Māni," *AO* 10 (1932), 336–63.

Widengren, G. *The Great Vohu Manah and the Apostle of God. Studies in Iranian and Manichean Religion*. Uppsala, 1945 (Uppsala Universtitets Årsskrift 1945, 5).

——. *Mesopotamian Elements in Manichaeism (King and Saviour II): Studies in Manichean, Mandean and Syrian-Gnostic Religion*. Uppsala, 1946 (Uppsala Universtitets Årsskrift 1946, 3).

——. *Mani und der Manichäismus*. Stuttgart, 1961 (Urban-Bücher 57).

——. *Die Religionen Irans*. Stuttgart, 1965 (RM 14).

——, ed. *Der Manichäismus*. Darmstadt, 1977 (Wege der Forschung 168).

——. "Der Manichäismus. Kurzgefaßte Geschichte der Problemforschung," in B. Aland, ed. *Gnosis. Festschrift für Hans Jonas*. Göttingen, 1978, 278–315.

Wiessner, G. "Die Offenbarung im Manichäismus," in G. Wiessner and H.-J. Klimkeit, eds., *Studia Manichaica*, 151–58.

Wiessner, G. and H.-J. Klimkeit, eds., *Studia Manichaica. II. Internationaler Kongress zum Manichäismus, 6–10. August 1989, St. Augustin and Bonn*. Wiesbaden, 1992 (StOR 23).

Winter, W. and A. von Gabain. *Türkische Turfantexte IX. Ein Hymnus an den Vater Mani auf "Tocharisch B" mit alttürkischer Übersetzung*. Berlin, 1958 (ADAW, Jh. 1956, no. 2).

Yarshater, E., ed. *The Cambridge History of Iran*. Vol. 3, 1–2: *The Seleucid, Parthian and Sasanian Periods*. Cambridge, 1983.

Yoshida, Y. "Manichaean Aramaic in the Chinese Hymnscroll," *BSOAS* 46 (1983), 326–31.

——. "On a Manichaean Middle Iranian fragment lost from the Otani collection," in O. Sakiyama and A. Sato, eds., *Asian Languages and General Linguistics*. Tokyo, 1990, 175–81.

Zaehner, R. C. *Zurvan. A Zoroastrian Dilemma*. Oxford, 1955.

Zieme, P. "Beiträge zur Erforschung des X^{u}āstvānīft," *MIO* 12 (1966), 351–60.

——. "Die türkischen Yosïpas-Fragmente," *MIO* 14 (1968), 45–67.

——. "Ein manichäisch-türkisches Gedicht," *Türk Dili Araştırmalari Yıllığı Belleten*, 1968 (1969), 39–51.

———. "Zwei Textergänzungen zu A. von Le Coq's 'Türkische Manichaica aus Chotscho III,'" *RO* 32 (1969), 7–17.

———. "Ein manichäisch-türkisches Fragment in manichäischer Schrift," *AOH* 23 (1970), 157–65.

———. *Untersuchungen zur Schrift und Sprache der manichäisch-türkischen Turfantexte.* Phil. diss. Berlin, Humboldt-Universität, Sektion Altertumswissenschaften [1970].

———. "Zu einigen Problemen des Manichäismus bei den Türken," in *Traditions religieuses et para-religieuses des peuples Altaïques. Communications présentées au XIIIᵉ Congrès de la "Permanent International Altaistic Conference," Strasbourg, 25–30 juin 1970.* Paris, 1972 (Bibliothèque des Centres d'Études Supérieures Spécialisés), 173–79.

———. "Ein uigurisches Turfanfragment der Erzählung vom guten und bösen Prinzen," *AOH* 28 (1974), 263–68.

———. "Ein Turfanfragment einer türkischen Erzählung," *AoF* 1 (1974), 374–68.

———. "Ein uigurischer Text über die Wirtschaft manichäischer Klöster im uigurischen Reich," in L. Ligeti, ed., *Researches in Altaic Languages.* Budapest, 1975, 331–38.

———. *Manichäisch-türkische Texte.* Berlin, 1975 (BT V).

———. "Ein uigurisches Fragment einer Rāma-Erzählung," *AOH* 32 (1978), 23–32.

———. "Uigurische Steuerbefreiungsurkunden für buddhistische Klöster," *AoF* 8 (1981), 237–63.

———. "Die Berliner Expeditionen nach Turfan und Zentralasienkunde heute," *Das Altertum* 29 (1983), 152–60.

———. *Buddhistische Stabreimdichtungen der Uiguren.* Berlin, 1985 (BT XIII).

———. "Ein geistiges Drogenbuch der türkischen Manichäer," in P. Bryder, ed., *Manichaean Studies,* 221–28.

———. *Die Stabreimtexte der Uiguren von Turfan und Dunhuang. Studien zur alttürkischen Dichtung.* Budapest, 1990 (Bibliotheca Orientalis Hungarica XXXIII).

———. "Manichäische Kolophone und Könige," in G. Wiessner and H.-J. Klimkeit, eds., *Studia Manichaica,* 319–27.

———. *Religion und Gesellschaft im uigurischen Königreich von Qočo. Kolophone und Stifter des alttürkischen buddhistischen Schrifttums aus Zentralasien.* Opladen, 1992 (ARWAW, Bd. 88).

Sources and Editions of Texts Translated

Iranian Texts

1. Hymns to the Father of Light

1. M 40 R (Pth.); ed. HR II, 48; Boyce, *Reader,* text af.
2. M 538 and 75 (Pth.); ed. WL II, 548 with 581f. and HR II, 70; Boyce, *Reader,* text ag.
3. M 730 R and Vii (Pth.); ed. WL II, 553f.; Boyce, *Reader,* text ah.
4. M 5262 (= T II D 66) (Pth.); ed. WL II, 549; Boyce, *Reader,* text aj.
5. M 94 V and M 173 V with two small fragments (Pth.); ed. Boyce, "Some Parthian abecedarian Hymns", 438–40; Boyce, *Reader,* text ak.
6. M 6232 R (= T II D 178) (Pth.); ed. Henning, "A Pahlavi Poem," 645; Boyce, *Reader,* text aka.

2. Hymns on Cosmogony and Eschatology

1. M 533 V (Pth.); ed. Boyce, "Some Parthian abecedarian Hymns," 443f.; Boyce, *Reader,* text al.
2. M 507 V (Pth.); ed. Boyce, "Some Parthian abecedarian Hymns," 441f.; Boyce, *Reader,* text am.
3. M 710 and M 5877 (= T II D 138c) (Pth.); ed. Boyce, "Some Parthian abecedarian Hymns," 445f.; Boyce, *Reader,* text an.
4. M 741 R (Pth.); ed. Boyce, "Sadwēs and Pēsūs," 911f.; Boyce, *Reader,* text ao.
5. M 741 V (Pth.); ed. Boyce, "Sadwēs and Pēsūs," 913f.; Boyce, *Reader,* text ap.
6. S 13 and S 9 R ii 30 (MP with Pth. words); ed. Henning, "Ein manichäischer kosmogonischer Hymnus," 214–28; Boyce, *Reader,* text aq.
7. S 9 R ii 33f. (MP with Pth. words); ed. Boyce, *Reader,* text ar.
8. M 173 R and M 94 R (Pth.); ed. Boyce, "Some Parthian abecedarian Hymns," 438–40; Boyce, *Reader,* text as.

3. *Hymns to the Living Soul*

1. M 10 R 10–V 22 (Pth.); ed. Henning, "Geburt und Entsendung des manichäischen Urmenschen," 306–318; Boyce, *Reader,* text at.
2. M 83 I R 6–V 3, M 105a, M 200, and M 234 (Pth.); ed. WL I, 116f.; Boyce, *Reader,* text au.
3. M 7 R ii–V i and M 496a R (Pth.); ed. *Mir. Man.* III, 874 (text g, 169–200); Boyce, *Reader,* text av.
4. M 7 II V i–V ii (Pth.); ed. *Mir. Man.* III, 874f. (text g, 201–234); Boyce, *Reader,* text aw.
5. M 7 I R i–V i (Pth.); ed. *Mir. Man.* III, 870f. (text g, 1–80); Boyce, *Reader,* text ax.
6. M 7 I V i–V ii (Pth.); ed. *Mir. Man.* III, 872 (text g, 82–118); Boyce, *Reader,* text ay.
7. M 7 II R i (Pth.); ed. *Mir. Man.* III, 873f. (text g, 119–68); Boyce, *Reader,* text az.
8. M 33 I V i (Pth.); ed. *Mir. Man.* III, 876 (text h, 21–53); Boyce, *Reader,* text bb.
9. M 33 I R i and M 367 V (Pth.); ed. *Mir. Man.* III, 876f. (text h, 55–66 and 912); Boyce, *Reader,* text bc.
10. M 33 II R ii with M 367 V (Pth.); ed. *Mir. Man.* III, 877f. (text h, 55–66); Boyce, *Reader,* text bd.
11. M 95 with M 1876 and M 1877 with M 564 (MP); ed. *Mir. Man.* II, 318–21; Boyce, *Reader,* text be.
12. M 6650 (= T II K) (MP); ed. WL I, 115.
13. S 8; ed. Boyce, *Reader,* text bf.
14. M 786 (MP); ed. Henning, "Persian Poetical Manuscripts," 98–104.

4. *Hymns to the Third Messenger*

1. M 67 R ii 12–end (Pth.); ed. *Mir. Man.* III, 888–90 (text o); Boyce, *Reader,* text bg.
2. M 77 R 1–15 (Pth.); ed. *Mir. Man.* III, 886f. (text n, 1–15); Boyce, *Reader,* text bh.
3. M 77 R 1–15 (Pth.); ed. *Mir. Man.* III, 887f. (text n, 16–36); Boyce, *Reader,* text bj.
4. M 39 R i–R ii (Pth.); ed. *Mir. Man.* III, 883 (text m, 1–37); Boyce, *Reader,* text bk.
5. M 39 R ii–V i (Pth.); ed. *Mir. Man.* III, 884f. (text m, 38–49); Boyce, *Reader,* text bl.
6. M 39 V i (Pth.); ed. *Mir. Man.* III, 885 (text m, 50–62); Boyce, *Reader,* text bm.
7. M 39 V ii (Pth.); ed. *Mir. Man.* III, 885f. (text m, 68–89); Boyce, *Reader,* text bn.
8. M 32 V (Pth.); ed. HR II, 63f.; Boyce, *Reader,* text bo.
9. M 737 (Pth.); ed. Boyce, "Sadwēs and Pēsūs," 915; Boyce, *Reader,* text bp.
10. M 5260 V (= T II D 66 V) (MP); ed. *Mir. Man.* I, 192, n. 6; Boyce, *Reader,* text bq.

5. *Hymns to Jesus the Splendor*

1. T II D 169 (Sogd.); ed. WL I, 94.
2. M 680 and M 189 (Pth.); ed. WL I, 95–97; Boyce, *Reader,* text br.
3. M 369 (Pth.); ed. WL I, 118; Boyce, *Reader,* text bs.
4. M 28 II R i–V i (MP); ed. *Mir. Man.* II, 312–16; Boyce, *Reader,* text bt.
5. M 28 II V i–V ii and M 612 V (MP); ed. *Mir. Man.* II, 316–18; Boyce, *Reader,* text bu.
6. M 32 R (Pth.); ed. HR II, 62f.; Boyce, *Reader,* text bv.
7. Text A: M 351 (Pth. and Sogd.); text B: TM 259 (Pth.); ed. WL I, 85–92; Morano, "The Sogdian Hymns," 10–34; Turkish parallel text: Pelliot Chinois 3049; ed. Hamilton, *Manuscrits,* 43f. (text 5).

6. Hymns and Liturgical Texts about Jesus the Messiah

1. M 18 (Pth.); ed. HR II, 34–36; Boyce, *Reader,* text bw.
2. M 104 and M 891b (Pth.); ed. *Mir. Man.* III, 881f. (text k, 1–17); Boyce, *Reader,* text bx.
3. M 104, M 734 R and M 459c (Pth.); ed. *Mir. Man.* III, 882f. (text k, 18–44); Boyce, *Reader,* text by.
4. M 734 V (Pth.); ed. Sundermann, "Evangelientexte," 397f.; Boyce, *Reader,* text bya.
5. M 4570 (Pth.); ed. partially in Boyce, *Reader,* text byb, and wholly in Sundermann, *Texte,* 76–79.
6. M 132 with M 5861 (Pth.); ed. Sundermann, "Evangelientexte," 394f.; Boyce, *Reader,* text byc.
7. M 4574 (Pth.); ed. Boyce, *Reader,* text byd; Sundermann, *Texte,* 8of. (new ed. of the whole fragment).

7. Texts on the Twelve Dominions of Light

1. M 14 R 19–28 and V 1–25 (Sogd. and Pth.); ed. WL II, 547f.; Boyce, *Reader,* text bz (Pth. text only).
2. M 34 R 6–15 (Pth.); ed. HR II, 44; Boyce, *Reader,* text ca.
3. IB 4974 (MP); ed. WL II, 558f. and 596f.; Boyce, *Reader,* text cb.
4. M 798a R ii–V ii (MP); ed. WL II, 560 and 598f; Boyce, *Reader,* text cc.
5. M 738; ed. WL II, 561–62 and 599–603; Boyce, *Reader,* text cd.

8. Hymns to Mani and Individual Church Leaders

1. Pelliot M 914, 2 (MP); ed. de Menasce, "Fragments," 304–306.
2. M 224 I (MP and Pth.); ed. *Mir. Man.* II, 322; Boyce, *Reader,* text cl.
3. M 6232 V (= T II D 178) (Pth.); ed. Reitzenstein and Schaeder, *Studien,* 291 (text b); Boyce, *Reader,* text cla.
4. M 5 (Pth.); ed. *Mir. Man.* III, 863–65 (text d); Boyce, *Reader,* text ce.
5. M 8171 R i–V i (= T III D 267) (Pth.); ed. *Mir. Man.* III, 868 (text f, 1–35); Boyce, *Reader,* text cf.
6. M 8171 V ii (= T III D 267) (Pth.); ed. *Mir. Man.* III, 868f. (text f, 37–45); Boyce, *Reader,* text cg.
7. M 6 (Pth.); ed. *Mir. Man.* III, 865–67 (text e); Boyce, *Reader,* text ch.
8. M 315 I R 9–21 (MP and Pth.), ed. WL I, 6o; Boyce, *Reader,* text cj.
9. P2 (MP); ed. H R I, 351; Boyce, *Reader,* text ck.

9. Hymns for the Church Hierarchy and Church Dignitaries

1. M 36 (MP); ed. *Mir. Man.* II, 323–26; Boyce, *Reader,* text cm.
2. M 11 (MP); ed. WL II, 556f. with 592–96; Boyce, *Reader,* text cn.
3. M 31 I R (MP); ed. *Mir. Man.* II, 327; Boyce, *Reader,* text co.
4. M 31 I V (MP); ed. *Mir. Man.* II, 328f.; Boyce, *Reader,* text cp.
5. M 31 II R and V (MP); ed. *Mir. Man.* II, 329–30; Boyce, *Reader,* text cq.
6. M 543 (MP); ed. HR II, 79; Boyce, *Reader,* text cqa.
7. M 729 (MP); ed. *Mir. Man.* II, 330–33; Boyce, *Reader,* text cr.

8. S 7 R i (MP); ed. Salemann, "Manichaica III," 4f.; Boyce, *Reader,* text cs.
9. S 7 R ii, V i and ii (MP); ed. Salemann, "Manichaica III," 4–6; Boyce, *Reader,* text ct.

10. Verses from the Parthian Hymn Cycles

1. M 93 + (a great number of fragments indicated in Boyce, *Hymn-Cycles,* 62–65:
   Sundermann, *Hymn cycles,* 33–35); eds.: Boyce, *Hymn-Cycles,* 67–111; Sundermann, *Hymn cycles,* 14–16; 19–32. Cf. also MacKenzie, "HWYDGM'N Fragments." Portions ed. in Boyce, *Reader,* texts cw and cx.
2. M 28 + (a great number of fragments indicated in Boyce, *Hymn-Cycles,* 62–65; Sundermann, *Hymn cycles,* 33–35); eds.: Boyce, *Hymn-Cycles,* 112–73, Sundermann,
   Hymn cycles, 16–18; 19–32. Portions ed. in Boyce, *Reader,* texts cy and cz.

11. Miscellaneous Verse Texts

1. M 842 R 1–4, 7–9, R 18–V 13 (MP); ed. Henning, "Mitteliranisch," 103f.; Boyce,
   Reader, text da.
2. M 42 (Pth.); ed. *Mir. Man.* III, 878–81 (text i); Boyce, *Reader,* text dc.
3. M 554 (MP with Pth. words); ed. HR II, 69; Boyce, *Reader,* text dd.
4. M 727 a V (MP); ed. Henning, "Two Central Asian Words," 152f.; Boyce, *Reader,*
   text de.
5. M 789 V (Pth.); ed. HR II, 68; Boyce, *Reader,* text df.
6. M 28 I R i 5–13; R i 33–R ii 4; R ii 24–37 (MP); ed. HR II, 94f.; Henning, *Zoroaster,*
   50, n. 1; Boyce, *Reader,* text dg.
7. M 763 (Pth.); ed. Henning, "A Pahlavi Poem," 646; Boyce, *Reader,* text dga.
8. M 83 I V, M 82 R and M 235 (MP); ed. Henning, "The Disintegration of Avestic
   Studies," 56; Boyce, *Reader,* text dgb.
9. M 90 (Pth.); ed. WL II, 955 and 586–88.
10. M 5755 (= T II D 120a) (MP); ed. Schaeder, "Beiträge," 581; Boyce, *Reader,* text dgc.

12. A Book of Prayer and Confession

1. M 801 (MP and Pth.); ed. BBB 18–32.
2. M 801 (Sogd. with MP and Pth. citations); ed. BBB 32–41.

13. Diverse Liturgical Texts

1. M 17 and M 172 I; ed. HR II, 25–27 and 100f. Boyce, *Reader,* text c.
2. M 4a (Pth.); ed. HR II, 49–52; Boyce, *Reader,* text cv.
3. M 113 (Sogd.); ed. BBB 41f.
4. M 131, M 395, and T II D 138 (Sogd.); ed. BBB 42–44.
5. M 131, M 395, and T II D 138 (Sogd.); ed. BBB 44f.
6. M 577a (= T II D 123) (MP, Pth. and Sogd.); ed. BBB 45f.
7. M 114II (Sogd. with MP and Pth. citations); ed. BBB 46f.
8. M 139 II (Sogd.); ed. BBB 50f.
9. M 131 I (Sogd.); ed. BBB 49f.
10. S (MP); ed. Salemann, "Ein Bruchstük," 2–7; Boyce, *Reader,* text dq.

14. *Prayers, Invocations, and Incantations*

1. M 43 (MP); ed. HR II, 78; Boyce, *Reader,* text cw.
2. Kao. o111; ed. W. Lentz, "Note on the Fragment of a Manichaean Parchment, MS Kao. o111, from Kara-Khoja," in A. Stein, *Innermost Asia* III, 1081 (Appendix P).
3. M 46 (MP); ed. HR II, 55–59; Boyce, *Reader,* text dt.
4. M 20 (MP); ed. HR II, 45; Boyce, *Reader,* text du.
5. M 176 (MP and Pth.); ed. HR II, 60; Boyce, *Reader,* text dv.
6. M 74 (MP with Pth. words); ed. HR II, 75f.; Boyce, *Reader,* text dx.
7. M 174 (MP); ed. WL II, 555f. and 588–91; Boyce, *Reader,* text dy.
8. M 38 V (Pth.); ed. HR II, 77; Boyce, *Reader,* text dz.
9. M 781, M 1314 and 1315 (= T I α) (MP); ed. Henning, "Magical Texts," 39–47; Boyce, *Reader,* text dr.
10. M 1202 (= T I α) (Pth.); ed. Henning, "Magical Texts," 47–57; Boyce, *Reader,* text ds.

15. *An Index of Parthian Hymns*

1. M 1, 25–445; ed. Müller, "Doppelblatt," 18–28.

16. *Parables*

1. T III T 601 (Ch/U 6914), T III 2015 (So. 15,000 (5)) and T II D 2 (Ch 5554) (Sogd.); ed. Sundermann, *Parabelbuch,* 19–28.
2. As 1; ed. Sundermann, *Parabelbuch,* 28–33.
3. M 332 and M 724 (Pth.); ed. Colditz, "Parabelsammlungen," 277–80.
4. M 499, M 706, and M 334b (Pth.); ed. Colditz, "Parabelsammlungen," 284–87.
5. M 333 (Pth.); ed. Colditz, "Parabelsammlungen," 289–91.
6. M 334a (Pth.); ed. Colditz, "Parabelsammlungen," 293–95.
7. M 44 (Pth.); ed. Colditz, "Parabelsammlungen," 300–302.
8. M 46 (MP); ed. Sundermann, *Parabeltexte,* 84–86.
9. M 625 (MP); ed. Sundermann, *Parabeltexte,* 86.
10. M 47 II (MP); ed. Sundermann, *Parabeltexte,* 87–89.
11. M 45 (MP); ed. Sundermann, *Parabeltexte,* 90.
12. M 45 (Pth.); ed. Sundermann, *Parabeltexte,* 92.
13. M 45 (Pth.); ed. Sundermann, *Parabeltexte,* 93.
14. M 221 (MP); ed. Sundermann, *Parabeltexte,* 102–104.
15. M 580 (Pth.); ed. Sundermann, *Parabeltexte,* 104–106.
16. M 6005 (Pth.); ed. Sundermann, *Parabeltexte,* 107f.
17. T M 418 (So. 18, 300) and M 135 (Sogd.); ed. Henning, "Sogdian Tales," 465–69.

17. *Historical Texts*

1.1.A M 2 I (MP); ed. *Mir. Man.* II, 301f.; Boyce, *Reader,* text h, 1–3.
1.1.B M 216c and M 1750 (Pth.); ed. Sundermann, *Texte,* 25f.
1.1.C So. 13, 941 (= T II K) and So. 14, 285 (= T II D 136) (Sogd.); ed. Sundermann, *Texte,* 34–36.
1.2.A M 2 I and II (MP); ed. *Mir. Man.* II, 302–306; Boyce, *Reader,* text h, 4–9.
1.2.B M 216c and M 1750 (Pth.); ed. Sundermann, *Texte,* 27.

1.2.C M 18, 220 (= TM 389a) (Sogd.); ed. Sundermann, *Texte,* 39–41.

1.2.D M 216b (Pth.); ed. Sundermann, *Texte,* 24f.

1.3.A M 48 (Pth.); ed. Sundermann, *Texte,* 21f.; Boyce, *Reader,* text e, 1–5.

1.3.B M 48 (Pth.); ed. Boyce, *Reader,* text e, 6–7 Cf. Sundermann, *Texte,* 21f.

2.1.A M 566 I (Pth.); ed. Sundermann, *Texte,* 23.

2.1.B So. 18, 223 (= TM 389c) and So. 18, 222 (= TM 389c) (Sogd.); ed. Sundermann, *Texte,* 42–45.

2.1.C So. 18, 224 (= TM 389d); ed. Sundermann, *Texte,* 55–57.

2.2 M 4575 (MP); ed. Sundermann, *Texte,* 46–49.

2.3 M 47 I (Pth.); ed. Sundermann, *Texte,* 102f. (Boyce, *Reader,* text f).

2.4 M 177 V (Pth.); ed. Sundermann, *Texte,* 118f. (Boyce, *Reader,* text g).

3.1.A M 6033 I R (= T II D 163) (Pth.); ed. Henning, "Mani's Last Journey," 942f.; Boyce, *Reader,* text k.

3.1.B M 6031 R ii, V ii (= T II D 163) (Pth.); ed. Henning, "Mani's Last Journey," 948f.; Boyce, *Reader,* text m.

3.2 M 3 (MP); ed. Boyce, *Reader,* text n; cf. Sundermann, *Texte,* 130f.

3.3 M 454 (MP); ed. Boyce, *Reader,* text o; cf. Sundermann, *Texte,* 135f.

3.4 M 5569 (= T II D 79) (Pth.); ed. Boyce, *Reader,* text p; cf. Sundermann, *Texte,* 30f.

4.1 M 49 II (MP); ed. Boyce, *Reader,* text b; cf. Sundermann, *Texte,* 93f.

4.2 M 5794 (= T II D 126 I) (MP); ed. Boyce, *Reader,* text a; cf. Sundermann, *Texte,* 131–33.

18. Prose Texts on Cosmogony and Cosmology

1. M 21 (Pth.); ed. *Mir. Man.* III, 89of. (text p); Boyce, *Reader,* text x.

2.1 M 98 I and M 99 I (MP); ed. Boyce, *Reader,* text y, 60–62; Hutter, Šābuhragān-*Texte,* 10–23.

2.2 M 7980–7984 (Pth.); ed. Boyce, *Reader,* text y, 63–76; Hutter, Šābuhragān-*Texte,* 36–115.

3. M 178 II (Sogd.); ed. Henning, "A Sogdian Fragment," 306–313.

19. Prose Texts on Eschatology

1. M 470 + (various fragments indicated in eds.) (MP); ed. (partially) in Boyce, *Reader,* text z; MacKenzie, "Mani's Šā*buhragān*" I, II; cf. also Hutter, Šābuhragān-*Texte,* 116–23 (German trans.).

2. M 178 I (Sogd.); ed. Henning, "A Sogdian Fragment," 306–313.

20. Texts on the Soul and Salvation

1. M 9 I (MP); ed. *Mir. Man.* II, 297–99; Boyce, *Reader,* text ad.

2. M 9 II (MP); ed. *Mir. Man.* II, 299–300; Boyce, *Reader,* text ae.

3. TM 389 α (= M 18, 220) (Sogd.); ed. Sundermann, *Texte,* 37f.

4. M 5750 (MP); ed. Sundermann, "Iranische Kephalaiatexte," 316–18.

5. M 2 II (Pth.); ed. *Mir. Man.* III, 849–53 (text a); Boyce, *Reader,* text ac.

21. Letters and Admonitions

1.1 M 733 (MP); ed. HR II, 31; Boyce, *Reader,* text do.

1.2 M 731 (MP); ed. HR II, 32f.; Boyce, *Reader,* text dp.

2. M 5815 (= T II D 134 I) (Pth.); ed. *Mir. Man.* III, 854–57 (text b); Boyce, *Reader,* text r.

3. M 5815 II (= T II D 134 II) (Pth.); ed. *Mir. Man.* III, 857–60 (text b); Boyce, *Reader,* text q.

4.1 M 112 + (various fragments enumerated in ed.); ed. Sundermann, "Probleme," 292–95 and 305–9.

4.2 M 159 + (various fragments enumerated in ed.); ed. Sundermann. "Probleme," 296–304 and 309–12.

5. So. 18, 223 (= TM 389c) and So. 18, 222 (= TM 389c) (Sogd.); ed. WL II, 548; Sundermann, *Texte,* 44. Engl. trans. in Sims-Williams, "The Manichaean Commandments," 574.

6. M 5794 II and M 6062 (MP); ed. *Mir. Man.* II, 295–97; Sundermann, *Texte,* 131–33. Engl. trans. in Sims-Williams, "The Manichaean Commandments," 578f.

7. M 49 I (MP); ed. *Mir. Man.* II, 306f.; Boyce, *Reader,* text t.

8. M 8251 (= T III D 278 II) (MP); ed. *Mir. Man.* II, 308–311; Boyce, *Reader,* text u.

9. M 6020 (= T II D 162 I) (Pth.); ed. Henning, "A Grain of Mustard," 29–35; Boyce, *Reader,* text dk.

10. M 177 R (MP); ed. HR II, 88–90; Boyce, *Reader,* text w.

22. *Postscripts*

1. IB 6371 (= T II D 135) (MP); ed. Müller, "Hofstaat," 207–213.

2. M 1, 160–227; ed. Müller; "Doppelblatt," 7–17; Boyce, *Reader,* text s.

3. IB 4959 (MP); ed. Sundermann in Klimkeit, "Hindu Deities," 193f.

Turkish Texts

23. *Hymns to Mani*

1. T II D 258, 259, 260; ed. Bang and von Gabain, "Türkische Turfan-Texte III," 183–211; Clark, "*Pothi-Book,*" 168–74; 180–87.

2. T II D 259, 260; ed. Winter and von Gabain, *Türkische Turfan-Texte* IX, 9–14; Clark, "*Pothi-Book,*" 174f., 188f.

3. T II D 260; ed. Clark, "*Pothi-Book,*" 175, 188f.

4. TM 419; ed. *Türk. Man.* II, 7f.

24. *General Hymns and Prayers*

1. T II D 169; ed. Türk. Man. II, 10; Bang, "Hymnen," 2ff.

2. T II D 169; ed. Türk. Man. II, 9f; Bang, "Hymnen," 5ff.

3. TM 296; ed. Türk. Man. III, 35f.

4. TM 166: ed. Türk. Man. III, 28.

5. TM 512; ed. Türk. Man. III, 28f.

6. T II D 178: ed. Türk. Man. II, 12.

7. T II D 169; ed. Türk. Man. II, 10f.; von Gabain, "Die alttürkische Literatur," 232f.

8. M 132; ed. Zieme, "Ein manichäisch-türkisches Gedicht," 39–51.

9. TM 419 V; ed. Türk. Man. II, 8f.

10. T II D 78a, I; ed. Türk. Man. III, 24.

11. T II D 78a, II; ed. Türk. Man. III, 24.

12. T II D 78c, I; ed. Türk. Man. III, 25.
13. T II D 78b, II; ed. Türk. Man. III, 25

25. Confessions

1. T II D 178 III and IV; London scroll. For a survey of all known texts and fragments,
   cf. Zieme, *Texte,* 19–21; ed. Asmussen, *X^uāstvānīft,* 167–93.
1.1 T I D and T I Da (Sogd.); ed. Henning, *Sogdica,* 63–67; cf. Sims-Williams, "Sogdian
    Fragments of Leningrad III."
2. T I D 615 (U 5464), T II 894 (U 5501), and T I a (Mainz 478); ed. Zieme, *Texte,* 23–25.
3. T II Y 59; ed. Asmussen, *X^uāstvānīft,* 232f.
4. Pelliot Chinois 3072; ed. Hamilton, *Manuscrits,* 6of. (text 8).
5. II D 260; ed. Clark, "*Pothi*-Book," 176f., 189.

26. Parables and Narratives

1. T I α I; ed. Türk. Man. III, 33; cf. Zieme, "Die türkischen Yosïpas-Fragmente,"
   45–67.
2. T II D 173c; ed. Bang, "Manichäische Erzähler," 7–12.
3. T II D 176; ed. Türk. Man. I, 5–7.
4. Turfan Museum, inv. no. 80.T.B I:524; ed. Geng, Klimkeit, and Laut, "Drei Prinzen."
5. Turfan Museum, inv. no. unknown; ed. Geng, Klimkeit, and Laut, "Manis Wettkampf."
6. T II D 177; ed. Türk. Man. I, 32–34; Bang, "Manichäische Erzähler," 17f.
7. T II D 177; ed. Türk. Man. I, 35f.; Bang, "Manichäische Erzähler," 19.
8. T II D 177; ed. Türk. Man. I, 36f.
9. T II D 258a (U 78) and 250 (U 77); ed. Clark, "*Pothi*-Book," 177; 18of.
10. T II D 175, 1 and 2; ed. Türk. Man. III, 3of.

27. Texts on Jesus, Mani, and the Gods

1.1 T II D 173b,2; ed. Türk. Man. III, 11f.
1.2 TM 161 (U 297), T I α (U 241a), U 241b, and T II D (U 241c); ed. Zieme, *Texte,* 39–41.
1.3 TM 180; ed. Türk. Man. II, 5f.
2.1 Pelliot Chinois 3049; ed. Hamilton, *Manuscrits,* 38ff.
2.2 T II D 62; ed. Türk. Man. III, 4of.
2.3 M 140; ed. Zieme, "Ein manichäisch-türkisches Fragment," 158f.
3.1 T II D 176; ed. Türk. Man. III, 15.
3.2 TM 140 and 147; ed. Türk. Man. III, 5f.
3.3 T II K 2a; ed. Türk. Man. I, 21f.
3.4 T II D 119; ed. Türk. Man. III, 16.
3.5 T II D 119; ed. Türk. Man. III, 16f.
3.6 Pelliot Chinois 3049; ed. Hamilton, *Manuscrits,* 38f.
3.7 Text A: T II D 119; ed. Türk. Man. III, 17; Text B: TM 423; ed. Türk. Man. III, 18.
3.8 TM 300; ed. Türk. Man. III, 17f.
3.9 TM 423c; ed. Türk. Man. III, 18f.
3.10 TM 423b and d; ed. Türk. Man. III, 19f.

28. Cosmological Texts

1. T I D 20 (U 262); ed. Zieme, *Texte,* 31–33.

2. T I D x 17 (U 219a, b); ed. Zieme, *Texte*, 46–48.

3. T II D 173b; ed. Türk. Man. I, 12–15.

4. T I x; ed. Türk. Man. I, 19f.

5. T II D 121; ed. Türk. Man. III, 8f.

6. TM 291; ed. Türk. Man. III, 7f.

7. M 748; TM 152, TM 152a, TM 158, and TM 181a; ed. Bang and von Gabain, "Windgott."

29. Texts on Man and His Salvation

1. TM 298; ed. Türk. Man. III, 9f.

2. T II D 173a; ed. Türk. Man. I, 7–10.

3. T II D 173a; ed. Türk. Man. I, 10–12.

4. TM 423e; ed. Türk. Man. III, 20f.

30. Texts on the Manichaean Community and Manichaean Kingship

1.1 Peking Museum of History, serial no. Zong 8782 T, 82. Extracts ed. and trans. in Zieme, "Ein uigurischer Text über die Wirtschaft manichäischer Klöster," 331–38; complete new ed. and trans. (with photos of the text) in Geng, "Notes on an Uighur Decree," 209–223.

2.1.A TM 417; ed. Türk. Man. III, 33f; Rahmeti Arat, "Der Herrschertitel *Iduq qut*," 151.

2.1.B TM 47; ed. Türk. Man. III, 34f.; Rahmeti Arat, *op. cit.*, 152.

3.1.A TM 164 and 174; ed. Türk. Man. III, 41f.

3.1.B TM 176; ed. Türk. III, 40.

3.2 M 525; ed. Zieme, *Texte*, 53.

3.3 T II 1457 (Ch/U 6874) V; ed. Zieme, *Texte*, 49.

3.4 T I D 3 and T II 1398 (Ch/U 6618); ed. Zieme, *Texte*, 54f.

3.5 T II D 16 (U 121) and T II D 66 (U 131); ed. Zieme, *Texte*, 28f.

3.6 T III D 172a; ed. Türk. Man. III, 14.

31. Historical Texts

1. T II K x 9 (U 237) and D (U 296); ed. Zieme, *Texte*, 50–52.

2. TM 276a and 276b; ed. Bang and von Gabain, "Türkische Turfan-Texte II," 414–22.

3. T II D 180; ed. Bang and von Gabain, "Türkische Turfan-Texte II," 425f.

32. Letters and Postscripts

1.1 Pelliot Chinois 3049; ed. Hamilton, *Manuscrits*, 40–44.

2.1 TM 107 (5281); ed. Zieme, *Texte*, 65f.

2.2 T II 897 (U 5503); ed. Zieme, *Texte*, 66–68.

2.3 T II 122 (Ch/U 6854); ed. Zieme, *Texte*, 68f.

2.4 T IV x 505 (U 5928); ed. Zieme, *Texte*, 69f.

2.5 U 6069; ed. Zieme, *Texte*, 70f.

3. T II D 171; ed. Türk. Man. I, 25–30.